THE PRACTICE OF
Research IN
Social WorK

TITLES OF RELATED INTEREST

Research, Analysis, and Evaluation

Evaluation: A Systematic Approach (2003) by Peter Rossi and Mark Lipsey

Practical Program Evaluation (2004) by Huey-Tsyh Chen

Qualitative Research and Evaluation Methods, Third Edition (2001) by Michael Quinn Patton

Designing Qualitative Research, Third Edition (1999) by Catherine Marshall and Gretchen B. Rossman

Learning in the Field: An Introduction to Qualitative Research, Second Edition (2003) by Gretchen B. Rossman and Sharon F. Rallis

Qualitative Data Analysis: An Expanded Sourcebook, Second Edition (1994) by Matthew B. Miles and A. Michael Huberman

Qualitative Inquiry and Research Design: Choosing Among Five Traditions (1998) by John Creswell

Qualitative Research Design: An Interpretive Approach, Second Edition (2004) by Joseph A. Maxwell

The SAGE Handbook of Qualitative Research, Third Edition (2005) by Norman K. Denzin and Yvonna S. Lincoln

Writing Up Qualitative Research, Second Edition (2001) by Harry F. Wolcott

The Dictionary of Statistics and Methodology, Third Edition (2005) by W. Paul Vogt

An Introductory Guide to SPSS for Windows, Second Edition (2005) by Eric L. Einspruch

Making Sense of Multivariate Data Analysis (2004) by John Spicer

Social Statistics for a Diverse Society, Fourth Edition (2005, Pine Forge Press) by Chava Frankfort-Nachmias and Anna Leon-Guerrero

Statistics: A Gentle Introduction (2000) by Frederick L. Coolidge

Statistics for People Who (Think They) Hate Statistics, Second Edition (2004) by Neil J. Salkind

Action Research, Second Edition (1999) by Ernest T. Stringer

Conducting Research Literature Reviews: From the Internet to Paper, Second Edition (2004) by Arlene Fink

Designing Surveys, Second Edition (2005, Pine Forge Press) by Ronald Czaja and Johnny Blair

Making Sense of the Social World (2003, Pine Forge Press) by Daniel Chambliss and Russell Schutt

Reading and Understanding Research, Second Edition (2004) by Lawrence F. Locke, Stephen Silverman, and Waneen Spirduso

Research Design: Qualitative, Quantitative, and Mixed Methods Approaches, Second Edition (2002) by John Creswell

Research Methods for Community Change: A Project-Based Approach (2005) by Randy Stoecker

New Sage Titles in Human Services

Effectively Managing Human Service Organizations, Third Edition by Ralph Brody

Improving the Effectiveness of the Helping Professions: An Evidence-Based Approach to Practice by Morley D. Glicken

Social Work Supervision: Contexts and Concepts by Ming-sum Tsui

Supervision as Collaboration in the Human Services: Building a Learning Culture edited by *Michael J. Austin and Karen M. Hopkins*

The Handbook of Community Practice edited by Marie Weil

Behavior Change in the Human Services: Behavioral and Cognitive Principles and Applications, Fifth Edition by Martin Sundel and Sandra S. Sundel

THE PRACTICE OF
Research IN
Social Work

RAFAEL J. ENGEL
University of Pittsburgh

RUSSELL K. SCHUTT
University of Massachusetts, Boston

SAGE Publications
Thousand Oaks ■ London ■ New Delhi

For information:

Sage Publications, Inc.
2455 Teller Road
Thousand Oaks, California 91320
E-mail: order@sagepub.com

Sage Publications Ltd.
1 Oliver's Yard
55 City Road
London EC1Y 1SP
United Kingdom

Sage Publications India Pvt. Ltd.
B-42, Panchsheel Enclave
Post Box 4109
New Delhi 110 017 India

Printed in the United States of America

Library of Congress Cataloging-in-Publication Data

Engel, Rafael J.
The practice of research in social work / Rafael J. Engel and Russell K. Schutt.
    p. cm.
Includes bibliographical references and index.
ISBN 1-4129-1385-3 (pbk.: acid-free paper)
  1. Social service—Research. I. Schutt, Russell K. II. Title.

HV11.E57 2005
361.3'072—dc22

                                2004023027

This book is printed on acid-free paper.

05 06 07 10 9 8 7 6 5 4 3 2 1

Acquiring Editor:	Jerry Westby
Associate Acquiring Editor:	Margo Beth Crouppen
Editorial Assistant:	Vonessa Vondera/Laura K. Shigemitsu
Production Editor:	Diana E. Axelsen
Copy Editor:	Jacqueline A. Tasch
Typesetter:	C&M Digitals (P) Ltd.
Indexer:	Mary Mortensen
Cover Designer:	Michelle Lee Kenny

BRIEF CONTENTS

Preface   xvii

Acknowledgments   xxi

 1. Science, Society, and Social Work Research   1

 2. The Process and Problems of Social Work Research   27

 3. Conceptualization and Measurement   63

 4. Sampling   101

 5. Causation and Research Design   133

 6. Group Experimental Designs   155

 7. Single-Subject Design   185

 8. Survey Research   221

 9. Qualitative Methods: Observing, Participating, Listening   273

10. Evaluation Research   305

11. Quantitative Data Analysis   335

12. Qualitative Data Analysis and Content Analysis   379

13. Reporting Research   409

Appendix A: Summaries of Frequently Cited Research Articles   431

Appendix B: Questions to Ask About a Research Article   441

Appendix C: How to Read a Research Article   444

Appendix D: Finding Information   463

Appendix E: Table of Random Numbers   467

Appendix F: Annotated List of Web Sites   471

Appendix G: NASW Code of Ethics   **478**

References   **499**

Glossary/Index   **517**

About the Authors   **554**

DETAILED CONTENTS

Preface   **xvii**
    Teaching and Learning Goals   xvii
    Organization of the Book   xviii
    Distinctive Features   xviii
    Ancillary Materials   xix

Acknowledgments   **xxi**

1. Science, Society, and Social Work Research   **1**
    Reasoning about the Social World   2
    Everyday Errors in Reasoning   4
        Overgeneralization   5
        Selective or Inaccurate Observation   5
        Illogical Reasoning   7
        Resistance to Change   7
    The Social Scientific Approach   8
    Social Work and the Social World   9
    The Imperative for Social Work Research   10
    Social Work Research in Practice   11
        Description: Who Are the Homeless?   13
        Exploration: What Is It Like to Live in an Emergency Shelter?   14
        Explanation: Why Do People Become Homeless?   14
        Evaluation: What Services Help the Homeless?   15
    Quantitative and Qualitative Methods   16
    Strengths and Limitations of Social Work Research   17
    Validity: The Goal of Social Work Research   18
        Measurement Validity   19
        Generalizability   19
        Causal (Internal) Validity   22
    Conclusion   22
      KEY TERMS   24
      HIGHLIGHTS   24

DISCUSSION QUESTIONS   25
PRACTICE EXERCISES   25
WEB EXERCISES   25
DEVELOPING A RESEARCH PROPOSAL   26

2. The Process and Problems of Social Work Research   **27**
Social Work Research Questions   28
  Identifying Social Work Research Questions   28
  Refining Social Work Research Questions   29
  Evaluating Social Work Research Questions   30
    Feasibility   30
    Social Importance   31
    Scientific Relevance   31
Foundations of Social Work Research   31
  Finding Information   32
    Searching the Literature   32
    Searching the Web   35
  Reviewing Research   37
Social Work Research Strategies   38
  The Role of Social Theory   38
  The Deductive/Inductive Cycle   40
    Deductive Research   40
    Domestic Violence and the Research Circle   43
    Inductive Research   45
    An Inductive Approach to Explaining Domestic Violence   45
    A Qualitative Exploration of the Response to Domestic Violence   46
  Descriptive Research   47
Philosophies Guiding Social Work Research   48
Scientific Guidelines for Social Work Research   50
Social Work Research and Ethical Guidelines   53
  Honesty and Openness   53
  The Uses of Science   54
  Research on People   54
Conclusion   58
  KEY TERMS   59
  HIGHLIGHTS   59
  DISCUSSION QUESTIONS   60
  PRACTICE EXERCISES   60
  WEB EXERCISES   60
  DEVELOPING A RESEARCH PROPOSAL   61

3. Conceptualization and Measurement   **63**
Concepts   64
  Conceptualization in Practice   65
    Defining Substance Abuse   66
    Defining Depression   66
    Defining Poverty   67
  Concepts, Constants, and Variables   68

Operationalization   69
    Indicators   70
    Scales and Indexes   71
    Treatment as a Variable   73
    Gathering Data   74
    Combining Measurement Operations   75
    Measurement in Qualitative Research   76
Levels of Measurement   76
    Nominal Level of Measurement   77
    Ordinal Level of Measurement   78
    Interval Level of Measurement   80
    Ratio Level of Measurement   80
    The Case of Dichotomies   82
    Comparison of Levels of Measurement   82
Measurement Error   83
Evaluating Measures   85
    Reliability   85
        Test-Retest Reliability   86
        Internal Consistency   86
        Alternate-Forms Reliability   87
        Interobserver Reliability   87
        Intraobserver Reliability   89
    Measurement Validity   89
        Face Validity   89
        Content Validity   89
        Criterion Validity   90
        Construct Validity   91
    Screening and Cut-Off Scores   92
    Ways to Improve Reliability and Validity of Existing Measures   94
Choosing an Instrument for Research, Evaluation, and Practice   96
Conclusion   98
    KEY TERMS   98
    HIGHLIGHTS   99
    DISCUSSION QUESTIONS   99
    PRACTICE EXERCISES   100
    WEB EXERCISES   100
    DEVELOPING A RESEARCH PROPOSAL   100

4. Sampling   **101**
Sample Planning   102
    Define Sample Components and the Population   103
    Evaluate Generalizability   105
    Assess the Homogeneity of the Population   106
    Enhance Sample Representativeness in Diverse Populations   107
Sampling Methods   110
    Probability Sampling   111
    Probability Sampling Methods   112

Simple Random Sampling   114
Systematic Random Sampling   115
Stratified Random Sampling   116
Cluster Sampling   118
Nonprobability Sampling Methods   120
Availability Sampling   120
Quota Sampling   121
Purposive Sampling   122
Snowball Sampling   123
Lessons about Sample Quality   123
Sampling Distributions   124
Estimating Sampling Error   126
Determining Sample Size   127
Conclusion   128
KEY TERMS   129
HIGHLIGHTS   129
DISCUSSION QUESTIONS   130
PRACTICE EXERCISES   131
WEB EXERCISES   131
DEVELOPING A RESEARCH PROPOSAL   132

5. Causation and Research Design   **133**
Nomothetic Causal Explanation   134
Experimental Design and the Criteria for Causal Explanation 134
Association   135
Time Order   136
Nonspuriousness   136
Mechanism   137
Context   138
Nonexperimental Designs and the Criteria for Causal Explanation 138
Cross-Sectional Designs   138
Longitudinal Designs   140
Repeated Cross-Sectional Designs   143
Fixed-Sample Panel Designs   143
Event-Based Designs   145
Units of Analysis and Errors in Causal Reasoning   146
Individual and Group Units of Analysis   147
The Ecological Fallacy and Reductionism   147
Idiographic Causal Explanation   149
Causation in Qualitative Research   149
Explanation in Qualitative Research   150
Single-Subject Design   150
Conclusion   151
KEY TERMS   152
HIGHLIGHTS   152
DISCUSSION QUESTIONS   153
PRACTICE EXERCISES   153

WEB EXERCISES   153
DEVELOPING A RESEARCH PROPOSAL   154

6. Group Experimental Designs   **155**
Threats to Validity   156
  Internal (Causal) Validity   156
    Selection Bias   157
    Endogenous Change   157
    External Events   158
    Contamination   159
    Treatment Misidentification   159
  Generalizability   160
    Sample Generalizability   160
    External Validity   160
    Reactivity   161
True Experiments   162
  Experimental and Comparison Groups   162
  Randomization   163
  Pretest and Posttest Measures   166
  Types of True Experimental Designs   166
  Difficulties in True Experiments in Agency-Based Research   170
  The Limits of True Experimental Designs   171
Quasi-Experiments   171
  Nonequivalent Control Group Designs   172
  Time Series Designs   174
  Ex Post Facto Control Group Designs   176
Common Group Designs for Program Evaluation and Research   177
  Types of Nonexperimental Designs   177
Ethical Issues in Experimental Research   179
  Deception   179
  Selective Distribution of Benefits   180
Conclusion   180
  KEY TERMS   181
  HIGHLIGHTS   182
  DISCUSSION QUESTIONS   183
  PRACTICE EXERCISES   183
  WEB EXERCISES   183
  DEVELOPING A RESEARCH PROPOSAL   184

7. Single-Subject Design   **185**
Foundations of Single-Subject Design   186
  Repeated Measurement   187
  Baseline Phase   187
    Patterns   188
    Internal Validity   189
  Treatment Phase   193
  Graphing   193
Measuring Targets of Intervention   193

Analyzing Single-Subject Designs   195
   Visual Analysis   196
     Level   196
     Trend   198
     Variability   200
   Interpreting Visual Patterns   200
   Problems of Interpretation   202
Types of Single-Subject Designs   203
   Basic Design: A-B   206
   Withdrawal Designs   207
     A-B-A Design   208
     A-B-A-B Design   209
   Multiple Baseline Designs   209
   Multiple Treatment Designs   212
   Designs for Monitoring Subjects   215
Generalizability   216
Ethical Issues in Single-Subject Design   217
Conclusion   218
   KEY TERMS   219
   HIGHLIGHTS   219
   DISCUSSION QUESTIONS   219
   PRACTICE EXERCISES   220
   WEB EXERCISES   220
   DEVELOPING A RESEARCH PROPOSAL   220

8. Survey Research   **221**
Survey Research in Social Work   222
   Attractions of Survey Research   222
     Versatility   222
     Efficiency   223
     Generalizability   223
   The Omnibus Survey   223
   Errors in Survey Research   224
Constructing Questions   226
   Writing Clear Questions   228
     Avoid Confusing Phrasing   229
     Minimize the Risk of Bias   231
     Use Specific Memory Questions   232
     Take Account of Culture   233
   Closed-Ended Questions and Response Categories   234
     Avoid Making Either Disagreement or Agreement Disagreeable   234
     Avoid Appeals to Social Desirability   234
     Minimize Fence-Sitting and Floating   235
     Use Filter Questions   236
   Sensitive Questions   236
   Single or Multiple Questions   237
Designing Questionnaires   239

Maintain Consistent Focus	239
Build on Existing Instruments	240
Refine and Test Questions	240
Add Interpretive Questions	242
Order the Questions	243
Consider Matrix Questions	244
Make the Questionnaire Attractive	246
Organizing Surveys	246
Mailed Self-Administered Surveys	248
Group-Administered Surveys	252
Telephone Surveys	252
Reaching Sample Units	252
Maximizing Response to Phone Surveys	253
In-Person Interviews	258
Balancing Rapport and Control	258
Maximizing Response to Interviews	259
Electronic Surveys	261
Mixed-Mode Surveys	264
A Comparison of Survey Designs	264
Secondary Data Surveys	266
Ethical Issues in Survey Research	268
Conclusion	268
KEY TERMS	269
HIGHLIGHTS	269
DISCUSSION QUESTIONS	271
PRACTICE EXERCISES	271
WEB EXERCISES	271
DEVELOPING A RESEARCH PROPOSAL	272
9. Qualitative Methods: Observing, Participating, Listening	**273**
Fundamentals of Qualitative Methods	274
Case Study: Making Gray Gold	276
Participant Observation	279
Choosing a Role	279
Complete Observation	279
Participation and Observation	281
Covert Participation	282
Entering the Field	283
Developing and Maintaining Relationships	285
Sampling People and Events	286
Taking Notes	289
Managing the Personal Dimensions	291
Systematic Observation	293
Intensive Interviewing	293
Establishing and Maintaining a Partnership	295
Asking Questions and Recording Answers	295
Focus Groups	297

Ethical Issues in Qualitative Research   298
Conclusion   300
   KEY TERMS   301
   HIGHLIGHTS   301
   DISCUSSION QUESTIONS   302
   PRACTICE EXERCISES   302
   WEB EXERCISES   302
   DEVELOPING A RESEARCH PROPOSAL   302

10. Evaluation Research   305

History of Evaluation Research   306
Evaluation Basics   307
   Describing the Program: The Logic Model   310
Questions for Evaluation Research   313
   Needs Assessment   313
   Process Evaluation   315
   Outcome Evaluation   318
   Efficiency Analysis   320
Design Alternatives   323
   Black Box or Program Theory?   323
   Researcher or Stakeholder Orientation?   325
   Quantitative or Qualitative Methods?   327
   Simple or Complex Outcomes?   328
Ethics in Evaluation   330
Conclusion   332
   KEY TERMS   332
   HIGHLIGHTS   333
   DISCUSSION QUESTIONS   333
   PRACTICE EXERCISES   333
   WEB EXERCISES   334
   DEVELOPING A RESEARCH PROPOSAL   334

11. Quantitative Data Analysis   335

Introducing Statistics   336
Preparing Data for Analysis   337
   Identification Numbers   337
   Reviewing the Forms   337
   Coding Open-Ended Questions   339
   Creating a Codebook   340
   Data Entry   340
   Data Cleaning   340
Displaying Univariate Distributions   342
   Graphs   343
   Frequency Distributions   347
      Ungrouped Data   348
      Grouped Data   348
      Combined and Compressed Distributions   350
Summarizing Univariate Distributions   352

Measures of Central Tendency	352
Mode	352
Median	353
Mean	354
Median or Mean?	354
Measures of Variation	357
Range	357
Interquartile Range	358
Variance	359
Standard Deviation	359
Analyzing Data Ethically: How Not to Lie with Statistics	361
Crosstabulating Variables	361
Graphing Association	364
Describing Association	364
Evaluating Association	366
Controlling for a Third Variable	369
Case Study: Perceived Health	369
Intervening Variables	370
Extraneous Variables	371
Specification	372
Analyzing Data Ethically: How Not to Lie about Relationships	374
Conclusion	375
KEY TERMS	375
HIGHLIGHTS	376
DISCUSSION QUESTIONS	376
PRACTICE EXERCISES	377
WEB EXERCISES	377
DEVELOPING A RESEARCH PROPOSAL	378
12. Qualitative Data Analysis and Content Analysis	**379**
Features of Qualitative Data Analysis	380
Qualitative Data Analysis as an Art	381
Research Questions for Qualitative Data Analysis	383
The Case Study	385
Techniques of Qualitative Data Analysis	386
Documentation	386
Conceptualization, Coding, and Categorizing	387
Examining Relationships and Displaying Data	389
Authenticating Conclusions	391
Reflexivity	393
Alternatives in Qualitative Data Analysis	394
Traditional Ethnography	394
Qualitative Comparative Analysis	395
Narrative Analysis	397
Grounded Theory	398
Computer-Assisted Qualitative Data Analysis	399
Content Analysis	402

Ethics in Qualitative Data Analysis   406
Conclusion   406
   KEY TERMS   407
   HIGHLIGHTS   407
   DISCUSSION QUESTIONS   407
   PRACTICE EXERCISES   408
   WEB EXERCISES   408
   DEVELOPING A RESEARCH PROPOSAL   408

13. Reporting Research   **409**
Social Work Research Proposals   409
   Case Study: Treating Substance Abuse   412
Comparing Research Designs   416
   Performing Meta-Analyses   419
   Case Study: Is Social Work Practice Effective? 420
Writing Research   421
Reporting Research   423
   Journal Articles   423
   Applied Research Reports   424
Ethics, Politics, and Research Reports   427
Conclusion   428
   KEY TERMS   429
   HIGHLIGHTS   429
   DISCUSSION QUESTIONS   430
   PRACTICE EXERCISES   430
   WEB EXERCISES   430
   DEVELOPING A RESEARCH PROPOSAL   430

Appendix A: Summaries of Frequently Cited Research Articles   **431**

Appendix B: Questions to Ask about a Research Article   **441**

Appendix C: How to Read a Research Article   **444**

Appendix D: Finding Information   **463**

Appendix E: Table of Random Numbers   **467**

Appendix F: Annotated List of Web Sites   **471**

Appendix G: Code of Ethics of the National Association of Social Workers   **478**

References   **499**

Glossary/Index   **517**

About the Authors   **554**

PREFACE

In a 1991 report, the Task Force on Social Work Research, chaired by David Austin, concluded that insufficient effort was given to research efforts to build the knowledge base of professional practice (Task Force on Social Work Research, 1991). In particular, the report noted a disconnect between research and practice in social work curricula.

Since that report, there has been tremendous progress in building the profession's research infrastructure, including national research centers, federal and foundation research initiatives, financial support, and dissemination efforts by professional and educational organizations. We have progressed sufficiently far in these efforts as a profession that we now integrate evidence-based practice as part of our teaching to students. It is imperative, therefore, that students understand the crucial role that research plays in developing and testing professional practice.

The purpose of this book is to introduce students to the study of research in social work and to the contributions research efforts make to our understanding of what is effective social work practice. We use examples, such as domestic violence, poverty, child welfare, and aging, that cut across the domains of social work practice. The examples include studies focused on individuals, groups, organizations, and communities.

TEACHING AND LEARNING GOALS

One goal of this book is to give students the critical skills necessary to evaluate research. It is a professional responsibility to apply effective interventions. Just reading that some conclusions are "based on a research study" is not sufficient. Students must learn to ask many questions before concluding that research-based conclusions are appropriate. What did the researchers set out to investigate? How were people selected for study? What information was collected, and how was it analyzed? Throughout this book, students will learn what questions to ask when critiquing a research study and how to evaluate the answers.

Another goal of this book is to prepare students to actually evaluate social work practice—their own and that of others. The various examples demonstrate the methods used by social work researchers to discover the efficacy of interventions, to identify needs, and to test the impact of social policies.

ORGANIZATION OF THE BOOK

The way the book is organized reflects our belief in making research methods interesting and relevant by connecting research to social work practice and by teaching students how to critique research and how to develop skills to evaluate their own practice. An underlying principle reflected throughout the text is that content on ethics and diverse populations should be infused into every research topic.

The first two chapters introduce the why and how of research in general. Chapter 1 shows how research has helped us understand domestic violence and its consequences. Chapter 2 illustrates the basic stages of research with a series of experiments on the police response to domestic violence.

The next three chapters discuss how researchers design their measures, draw their samples, and justify their statements about causal connections. Chapter 3 demonstrates how broad concepts such as substance abuse, depression, and poverty are translated into measures. Chapter 4 reviews principles of sampling and lessons about sampling quality. Chapter 5 examines issues about causality, using a series of child welfare studies about the impact of intensive, in-home, family-based services.

Chapters 6, 7, 8, and 9 present the four most important methods of data collection: experiments, single-subject design, surveys, and qualitative methods (including participant observation, intensive interviews, and focus groups). The substantive studies in these chapters show how social work researchers have used these methods to improve our understanding of the effectiveness of different treatment modalities, such as cognitive-behavioral therapy with different population subgroups, as well as our understanding of social work issues with different age groups, including youth and the elderly.

Evaluation research is the focus of Chapter 10. We illustrate how these primary methods may be used to learn about the effects of social programs and the need for others. We emphasize the importance of using a logic model to describe a program and to develop evaluation questions.

The next two chapters focus on basic techniques to analyze information and data. In Chapter 11, we describe how quantitative data are prepared for analysis. Using data from voting patterns, we describe basic statistical techniques used to analyze the results of quantitative studies. Chapter 12 then shifts our focus to qualitative data analysis techniques. In that chapter, we touch on content analysis, a quantitative technique for textual analysis. Finally, Chapter 13 finishes with an overview of the process of and techniques for reporting research results, a second examination of the development of research proposals, and an introduction to meta-analysis.

DISTINCTIVE FEATURES

This book draws from the feedback provided by faculty and students in the field of sociology to Russell Schutt's textbook, *Investigating the Social World: The Process and Practice of Research*. The content and modifications also reflect the first author's experiences when using that book to teach foundation-level social work students. It also benefits from the increasing research literature on the effectiveness of social work practice. You will find all of this reflected in innovations in approach, coverage, and organization:

Examples of research in the real-world settings of social work practice. There are interesting studies of domestic violence, child welfare, welfare reform, aging, and other pressing social concerns.

Ethical concerns and ethical decision making. Every step in the research process raises ethical concerns, so ethics should be treated in tandem with the study of specific methods. You will find ethics introduced in Chapter 2 and reviewed in the context of each method of data collection, data analysis, and reporting.

Infusion of content on diverse populations. Every step in the research process has different applications to different subgroups of the population. We attempt to address this throughout each of the chapters.

Emphasis on doing research. Many different exercises and activities are included to prepare students to conduct research and evaluation.

Thorough coverage of qualitative methods. In our chapters on qualitative research design and data analysis, you will find a thorough, engaging, and up-to-date presentation of qualitative methods appropriate to the field of social work. Many research examples in the book convey the value of using qualitative techniques, either alone or in "mixed methods" approaches, to address many research questions.

We hope that readers of this text will enjoy learning about research and apply the skills and knowledge taught in a research course to their field of practice. Social workers are in a unique position to discover what interventions work, under what circumstances, and with what populations. In so doing, we benefit our clients and broader society.

ANCILLARY MATERIALS

To enhance the use of the book, a number of high-quality, useful ancillaries have been prepared:

Student Resource CD. Bundled in the back of the text is a CD containing, among other useful items: interactive exercises (developed and class-tested by Russell Schutt); an overview on using SPSS; two datasets and links to two more available online; survey instruments; and a link to the book's study site.

Student study site. Available free on the Web at http://www.sagepub.com/prsw is a collection of high-quality materials designed to help students master the course content and gain greater insight into social work research. The study site contains interactive self-quizzes and e-flashcards, a chapter-length review of inferential statistics, articles from social work journals with guiding questions, and the Web exercises from the ends of chapters with additional online resources.

Instructor's Resource CD. For instructors who adopt the textbook, a variety of useful instructional materials are provided. For each chapter, this includes overviews and lecture outlines, PowerPoint slides, the exhibits from the chapter in reproducible form, student projects, and a complete set of test questions. There are also lists of suggested film and software resources and links to related Web sites.

To my parents, Meir and Myra Engel

—Ray Engel

To Julia

—Russ Schutt

ACKNOWLEDGMENTS

Our thanks to Jerry Westby, Executive Editor, Sage Publications/Pine Forge Press. Jerry's enthusiasm and support for this project has been crucial, and his patience extraordinary, while Rafael completed his work both on this book and on his school's self-study. The vision and matchmaking of Steve Rutter, former president of Pine Forge Press, were key to getting our project off the ground years ago. We are also deeply indebted to Vonessa Vondera, Denise Simon, Ben Penner, and the other members of the Pine Forge Press/Sage Publications staff, who made this text into something more than just words in a word processing file.

We received thoughtful comments and encouragement from a talented group of reviewers in the field of social work. Our gratitude to the following:

Leslie B. Alexander, Bryn Mawr College

Fred Brooks, Georgia State University

Jong Choi, California State Bakersfield

Julie Cooper Altman, Adelphi University

Adele Crudden, Mississippi State University

Tim Dyeson, Louisiana State University

Mark Ezell, University of Kansas

James Hanson, University of Northern Iowa

Patrick S. Bordnick, University of Georgia

Sanford Schram, Bryn Mawr College

Emily Spence-Diehl, University of Texas at Arlington

Jim Stafford, University of Mississippi

Gary Widrick, University of Vermont

Gayle Mallinger provided many new end-of-chapter exercises and identified missing reference citations; as a former and future instructor and academic, Gayle's enthusiasm about the text suggested that we were indeed headed in the right direction. Megan Reynolds of the Graduate Program in Applied Sociology at the University of Massachusetts at Boston devised many new discussion questions and updated and revised many Web exercises for social work students. Kathryn Stoeckert, MA, a stellar graduate of UMass Boston's Applied Sociology program, designed dozens of new interactive exercises based on the social work literature and culled through dozens of previously written exercises to select those most relevant to this literature. Elizabeth Schneider, MLS (University of Pittsburgh), contributed the fine appendix on Finding

Information, which provides students with the background needed to access information from a variety of media. We are grateful to all of them for sharing their talents with us.

Long before this collaboration began, Ray had used Russ's *Investigating the Social World: The Process and Practice of Research* (now in its 4th edition). He found that Russ had provided a vision and a framework for learning about research that cut across disciplines and that his writing style enabled students to easily grasp the difficult concepts and ideas associated with the language and practice of research. So Ray is grateful for the opportunity that Pine Forge Press provided to tailor this version of the text specifically to social work students. Russ is grateful to Ray for the opportunity to collaborate with such an outstanding social work researcher on a thorough revision of his core text for a field that has so often informed his own research.

Ray is very grateful to Sandra Wexler and Helen Petracchi for their tremendously supportive counsel and encouragement as he worked on the text. As program directors at the School of Social Work, they did their best to protect him from administrative distractions. Larry Davis provided quiet words of encouragement at stressful times. Ray's children, Yael and Meir, inspire him as he sees all that they accomplish. And finally, to Ray's wife, Sandy Budd, his love and gratitude for all the time they have spent together on the long, strange trip.

Russ adds his gratitude for the never-ending love and support of his wife, Elizabeth Schneider, and for their daughter, Julia.

Chapter 1

SCIENCE, SOCIETY, AND SOCIAL WORK RESEARCH

Reasoning about the Social World

Everyday Errors in Reasoning
Overgeneralization
Selective or Inaccurate Observation
Illogical Reasoning
Resistance to Change

The Social Scientific Approach

Social Work and the Social World

The Imperative for Social Work Research

Social Work Research in Practice
Description: Who Are the Homeless?
Exploration: What Is It Like to Live in an
     Emergency Shelter?

Explanation: Why Do People Become
     Homeless?
Evaluation: What Services Help the
     Homeless?

**Quantitative and Qualitative
     Methods**

**Strengths and Limitations of Social Work
     Research**

**Validity: The Goal of Social Work
     Research**
Measurement Validity
Generalizability
Causal (Internal) Validity

Conclusion

T he winter of 1997 was not a good season for people living on the street. In Boston, police found Jack Olson frozen to death on New Year's morning (Kahn, 1997). It had been 4 degrees Fahrenheit that New Year's Eve, and Mr. Olson had celebrated with an all-day vodka binge, followed by a night of drinking Listerine after the liquor stores closed. He had been panhandling and sleeping in shelters or on the streets. He had hoped to bring his two sons to Boston; he had gotten engaged to a woman two weeks earlier; he had promised his fiancée that he would get sober. But on the morning of December 31, he started drinking and didn't stop.

Jack Olson was not the only homeless person to die on the streets of Boston that winter. But his death attracted more attention than most, perhaps because he had befriended so many others: "a beautiful person," his fiancée said. "He was a fun-loving, caring person if he was sober," a homeless friend recalled. Perhaps the attention had something to do with Mr. Olson's efforts to change. He had spent many weeks in detox, and he talked about finding a restaurant job, about making a home for himself and his sons. Perhaps it was because his death seemed so senseless: If only his friends had not left him curled up on a heating grate that night. Perhaps it was just an appealing human interest story for the holidays. In any case, Jack Olson's story soon disappeared from the newspapers. He had become, so to speak, just another statistic.

Does the Jack Olson story sound familiar? Such newspaper stories proliferate when the holiday season approaches, but what do they really tell us about homelessness? Why do people live on the streets? In the rest of this chapter, you will learn how the methods of social science research go beyond stories in the popular media to help us answer questions like these. By the chapter's end, you should know what is "scientific" in **social science** and appreciate how the methods of science can help us understand the problems of society.

Social science   The use of scientific methods to investigate individuals, groups, communities, organizations, societies, and social processes; the knowledge produced by these investigations.

REASONING ABOUT THE SOCIAL WORLD

The story of just one homeless person raises many questions. Take a few minutes to read each of the following questions and jot down your answers. Don't ruminate about the questions or worry about your responses: *This is not a test;* there are no "wrong" answers.

- How would you describe Jack Olson?
- Why do you think Jack Olson died?
- Was Jack Olson typical of the homeless population?
- In general, why do people become homeless?

Now let's consider the possible answers to some of these questions. The information we have to describe Jack Olson is scant (Kahn, 1997). He had come to Boston from Arizona five years before he died, leaving a cook's job and a broken marriage. He wanted to make a new home for his two sons, but his calls back to them in Arizona often ended in disappointment. He was a heavy drinker but also was being treated for manic-depressive illness, according to friends. A staff member of the church where Mr. Olson ate his free meals noted that "Jack had a hard life out there."

Do you have enough information now to understand why Jack Olson died? His fiancée sounded bitter about the possibility that people might have stepped over his body while on their way to New Year's celebrations: "Nobody should be allowed to go out and freeze to death," she said. Should we attribute his death in part to a lack of concern by others? What about the apparent disappointments he suffered when he made calls to Arizona to talk to his sons? Was a feeling of failure in his role as a father a factor in his death? Was the cause of his death all the alcohol he imbibed? "Alcohol is killing a lot of people out there," a social service worker noted. Or is inadequate treatment for mental illness the issue?

Now can you construct an adequate description of Jack Olson? Can you explain the reason for his death? Or do you feel you need to know more about Mr. Olson, about his friends and the family he grew up in? And how about his experiences with treatment for alcoholism and an apparent manic-depressive disorder? We've attempted to investigate just one person's experiences, and already our investigation is spawning more and more questions.

We cannot avoid asking questions about the social world, which is a very complex place, and trying to make sense of our position in it, something of great personal importance. In fact, the more that you begin to think like a potential social work researcher-practitioner, the more questions will come to mind. But why does each question have so many possible answers? Surely, our perspective plays a role. One person may see a homeless individual as a victim of circumstance, another person may see the homeless as the failure of our society to care for its members, while a third person may see the same individual as a shiftless bum. When confronted with a homeless individual, one observer may stop to listen, another may recall a news story on street crime, and another may be reminded of her grandfather. Their different orientations will result in different answers to the questions prompted by the same individual or event.

When the questions concern not just one person but many people or general social processes, the number of possible questions and the difficulties in answering them multiply. For example, consider the question of why people become homeless. Responses to a 1987 survey of Nashville, Tennessee, residents, summarized in Exhibit 1.1, illustrate the diverse sentiments that people have (Lee, Jones, & Lewis, 1990).

Exhibit 1.1   Popular Beliefs about Why People Become Homeless

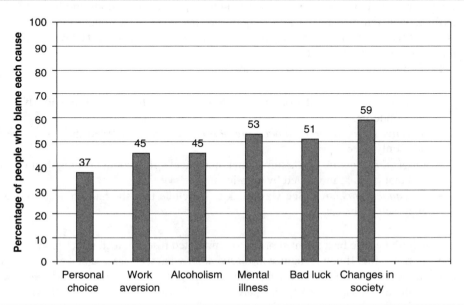

Source: Data from Lee, Jones, and Lewis, 1990, p. 257.

Compare these answers with the opinion you recorded earlier. Was your idea about the causes of homelessness one of the more popular ones? Answers to questions about the social world also vary because what people have "seen" varies. The Nashville survey—by Barrett Lee, Sue Hinze Jones, and David Lewis (1990)—gives some idea of the basis for people's opinions about homelessness: Individuals who had less education and more conservative political beliefs were more likely than others to think that homelessness is a matter of personal choice. Personal contact also made a difference: People who had been approached by a panhandling homeless person were more likely to think that homelessness is a matter of personal choice. But those who had had an informal conversation with a homeless person about something other than money were less likely to believe that homelessness is a matter of personal choice. Do these bases for opinions inspire your confidence? Is your opinion about why people become homeless based on direct experience, or is it based on what other people have said or written?

EVERYDAY ERRORS IN REASONING

People give different answers to questions about the social world for yet another reason: It's simply too easy to make errors in logic, particularly when we are analyzing the social world in which we ourselves are conscious participants. We can call some of these "everyday errors" because they occur so frequently in the nonscientific, unreflective discourse about the social world that we hear on a daily basis.

Our favorite example of everyday errors in reasoning comes from a letter to syndicated newspaper advice columnist Ann Landers. The letter was written by someone who had just moved with her two cats from the city to a house in the country. In the city, she had not let her cats outside and felt guilty about confining them. When they arrived in the country, she threw her back door open. Her two cats cautiously went to the door and looked outside for a while, then returned to the living room and lay down. Her conclusion was that people shouldn't feel guilty about keeping their cats indoors—even when cats have the chance, they don't really want to play outside.

Do you see this person's errors in reasoning?

- *Overgeneralization.* She observed only two cats, both of which previously were confined indoors.
- *Selective observation or inaccurate observation.* She observed the cats at the outside door only once.
- *Illogical reasoning.* She assumed that others feel guilty about keeping their cats indoors and that cats are motivated by emotions.
- *Resistance to change.* She was quick to conclude that she had no need to change her approach to the cats.

You don't have to be a scientist or use sophisticated research techniques to avoid these four errors in reasoning. If you recognize these errors for what they are and make a conscious effort to avoid them, you can improve your own reasoning. In the process, you will also be implementing the admonishments of your parents (or minister, teacher, or other adviser) to avoid stereotyping people, to avoid jumping to conclusions, and to look at the big picture. These are the same errors that the methods of social science research are designed to help us avoid.

Overgeneralization

Overgeneralization, an error in reasoning, occurs when we conclude that what we have observed or what we know to be true for some cases is true for all cases. We are always drawing conclusions about people and social processes from our own interactions with them but sometimes forget that our experiences are limited. The social (and natural) world is, after all, a complex place. We have the ability (and inclination) to interact with just a small fraction of the individuals who inhabit the social world, especially in a limited span of time. If we had taken what we learned about Jack Olson—his mental illness and his alcohol abuse—and concluded that these problems are typical of the homeless, we would have committed the error of overgeneralization.

Selective or Inaccurate Observation

We also have to avoid **selective observation:** choosing to look only at things that are in line with our preferences or beliefs. When we start out being inclined to criticize individuals or institutions, it is all too easy to notice their every failing. For example, if we are convinced in advance that all homeless persons are substance abusers, we can find many confirming instances. But what about homeless people like Debbie Allen, who ran away from a home she shared with an alcoholic father and psychotic mother; Charlotte Gentile, a teacher with a bachelor's degree living with two daughters in a shelter after losing her job; and Faith Brinton, who walked out of her rented home with her two daughters to escape an alcoholic and physically abusive husband and ended up in a shelter after her husband stopped paying child support? If we acknowledge only the instances that confirm our predispositions, we are victims of our own selective observation. Exhibit 1.2 depicts the difference between overgeneralization and selective observation.

Exhibit 1.2   The Difference between Overgeneralization and Selective Observation

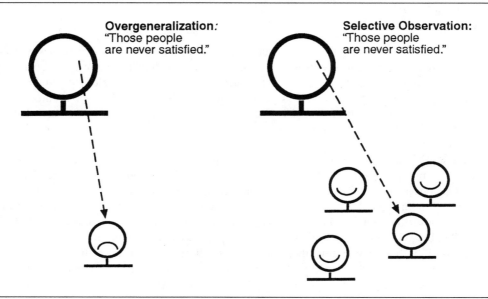

Exhibit 1.3   Anatomy of an Emotional Hijacking

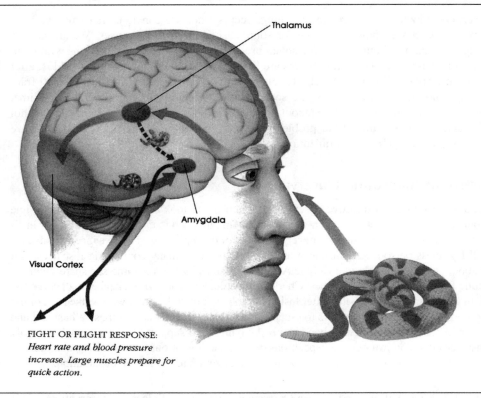

FIGHT OR FLIGHT RESPONSE:
*Heart rate and blood pressure
increase. Large muscles prepare for
quick action.*

Source: Goleman, 1995, p. 19, copyright © 1995 by Daniel Goleman. Used by permission of Bantam Books, a division of Random House, Inc.

Recent research on cognitive functioning (how the brain works) helps to explain why our feelings so readily shape our perceptions (Seidman, 1997). An external stimulus can trigger an emotional response through the brain structure called the amygdala, even before the thinking part of our brain, the neocortex, can process and make sense of the information (see Exhibit 1.3). This "emergency" response process means, according to some cognitive scientists, that "what something reminds us of can be far more important than what it 'is'" (Goleman, 1995, pp. 294–95).

Our observations can also be inaccurate. If a woman says she is *hungry* and we think she said she is *hunted,* we have made an **inaccurate observation.** If we think five people are standing on a street corner when seven actually are, we have made an inaccurate observation.

Our observations can simply be **incomplete**. For example, we may be evaluating how a teenage mother plays with her young child. There are many different dimensions to these interactions: the mother's behavior and verbal and nonverbal responses to the child and the child's behavior and verbal and nonverbal responses to the mother. We may not be able to assess all of these at one time; therefore, our overall observations about their interactions are likely to be incomplete. Sometimes, researchers will videotape an interaction so that they can watch it repeatedly in order to assess all the dimensions.

Exhibit 1.4   An Optical Illusion

Such errors occur often in casual conversation and in everyday observation of the world around us. In fact, our perceptions do not provide a direct window onto the world around us, for what we think we have sensed is not necessarily what we have seen (or heard, smelled, felt, or tasted). Even when our senses are functioning fully, our minds have to interpret what we have sensed (Humphrey, 1992). The optical illusion in Exhibit 1.4, which can be viewed as either two faces or a vase, should help you realize that perceptions involve interpretations. Different observers may perceive the same situation differently because they interpret it differently.

Illogical Reasoning

When we prematurely jump to conclusions or argue on the basis of invalid assumptions, we are using **illogical reasoning.** For example, it is not reasonable to propose that homeless individuals don't want to work if evidence indicates that the reason many are unemployed is a shortage of jobs or the difficulty of finding jobs for those unemployed because of mental or physical disabilities. On the other hand, an unquestioned assumption that everyone who can work will work is also likely to be misplaced. Logic that seems impeccable to one person can seem twisted to another—the problem usually is reasoning from different assumptions rather than just failing to "think straight."

Resistance to Change

Resistance to change, the reluctance to change our ideas in light of new information, may occur for several reasons:

Ego-based commitments. We all learn to greet with some skepticism the claims by leaders of companies, schools, agencies, and so on that people in their organizations are happy, that revenues are growing, that services are being delivered in the best possible way. We know how tempting it is to make statements about the social world that conform to our own needs rather than to the observable facts. It can also be difficult to admit that we were wrong once we have staked out a position on an issue. For instance, we may want our experiences while volunteering in a shelter for homeless people to confirm our political stance on homelessness and therefore resist changing our beliefs in response to new experiences.

Excessive devotion to tradition. Some degree of devotion to tradition is necessary for the predictable functioning of society. Social life can be richer and more meaningful if it is allowed to flow along the paths charted by those who have preceded us. But too much devotion to tradition can stifle adaptation to changing circumstances. When we distort our observations or alter our reasoning so that we can maintain beliefs that "were good enough for my grandfather, so they're good enough for me," we hinder our ability to accept new findings and develop new knowledge. In many agencies, those who want to reject an idea use those famous words: "But we've never done it that way." The consequences can be deadly, as residents of Hamburg, Germany, might have realized in 1892 (Freedman, 1991). Until the last part of the 19th century, people believed that cholera, a potentially lethal disease, was caused by minute, inanimate, airborne poison particles (miasmas). In 1850, English researcher John Snow demonstrated that cholera was, in fact, spread by contaminated water. When a cholera epidemic hit Hamburg in 1892, the authorities did what tradition deemed appropriate: They dug up and carted away animal carcasses to prevent the generation of more miasmas. Despite their efforts, thousands died. New York City adopted a new approach based on Snow's discovery, which included boiling drinking water and disinfecting sewage. As a result, the death rate in New York City dropped to a tenth of what the death rate had been in a previous epidemic.

Uncritical agreement with authority. If we do not have the courage to evaluate critically the ideas of those in positions of authority, we will have little basis for complaint if they exercise their authority over us in ways we don't like. And if we do not allow new discoveries to call our beliefs into question, our understanding of the social world will remain limited. We don't have to go so far afield to recognize that people often accept the beliefs of those in positions of authority such as supervisors or professors, and even the published word without question. Often, we automatically trust information we obtain from sources on the World Wide Web, even when we don't know if it comes from someone with any authority whatsoever.

Now take just a minute to reexamine the beliefs about homelessness that you recorded earlier. Did you grasp at a simple explanation even though reality is far more complex? Were your beliefs influenced by your own ego and feelings about your similarities to or differences from homeless persons? Are your beliefs perhaps based on stories you've heard about the "hobos" of an earlier era? Did you weigh carefully the opinions of political authorities or just accept or reject those opinions out of hand? Could knowledge of research methods help to improve your own understanding of the social world? Do you see some of the challenges faced by social science?

THE SOCIAL SCIENTIFIC APPROACH

The **social scientific approach** to answering questions about the social world is designed to reduce greatly these potential sources of error in everyday reasoning. **Science** relies on logical and systematic methods to answer questions, and it does so in a way that allows others to inspect and evaluate its methods. In the realm of social work research, these methods are not so unusual. After all, they involve asking questions, observing social groups, and counting people, which we often do in our everyday lives. However, social scientists develop, refine, apply, and report their understanding of the social world more systematically, or "scientifically," than Joanna Q. Public does:

- Social science research methods can reduce the likelihood of overgeneralization by using systematic procedures for selecting individuals or groups to study that are representative of the individuals or groups to which we wish to generalize.
- To avoid illogical reasoning, social work researchers use explicit criteria for identifying causes and for determining whether these criteria are met in a particular instance.
- Social science methods can reduce the risk of selective, inaccurate, or incomplete observation by requiring that we measure and sample phenomena systematically.
- Because they require that we base our beliefs on evidence that can be examined and critiqued by others, scientific methods lessen the tendency to develop answers about the social world from ego-based commitments, excessive devotion to tradition, and/or unquestioning respect for authority.

Science   A set of logical, systematic, documented methods for investigating nature and natural processes; the knowledge produced by these investigations.

SOCIAL WORK AND THE SOCIAL WORLD

The methods of social science are an invaluable tool for us as social work researchers and practitioners at any level of practice. The nature of our social world is the starting point for our profession, as much of what we do is in response to social, political, and economic conditions. Social work efforts, whether they are aimed at influencing or evaluating policy, working with communities, or engaging in programs to help individuals or groups, emerge in response to conditions in the social world. Our profession works with people from diverse backgrounds and promotes the social and economic participation of groups that lack access to full participation. Through systematic investigation, we begin to uncover the various dimensions of the social condition, the accuracy of our assumptions about what causes the social condition, the characteristics of people with a particular social status or social problem, and the effectiveness of our policies and programs to ameliorate the social problem.

Social policies are often designed based on assumptions about the causes of the problem. If we believe that homelessness is due to individual behavior or pathology—for example, that homeless individuals prefer separation from their friends and family, do not want to take advantage of economic opportunities, suffer from mental illness, or are alcohol and substance abusers—then policies will emerge that focus on treating these pathologies. On the other hand, if we believe that homelessness is due to structural problems—for example, the market's inability to provide enough reasonably paying jobs or problems in producing enough low-income housing—then government policies will emerge that might subsidize wages or encourage developers to build lower income housing. If we learn that the causes of homelessness are multidimensional, that there is a bit of reality to both perspectives, different government policies might emerge that both encourage housing alternatives and incorporate support services. Social work research aids us in the task of describing the characteristics of the homeless, their needs, and their prevalence, all of which can guide policy development and the distribution of resources.

The kinds of programs human service agencies develop are also based on assumptions about the causes of a social problem (Martin & Kettner, 1996). If an agency assumes that homeless adults are alienated from society and suffer from emotional or substance abuse problems, then the agency might provide transitional housing with a variety of social services integrated into the program. On the other hand, if the agency believes that homeless adults are simply in between jobs or new to a city and just need time to get started, then the agency might offer a short-term shelter. The tools of research allow social workers to examine the extent to which these assumptions are correct and to evaluate the effectiveness of these different programs.

Interventions in human service programs are related not only to assumptions about what causes the problem but also to different beliefs about what is the appropriate treatment model. Two agencies might have the same set of assumptions about what causes a problem but might use different practice models to treat the individual or group. The personal problems Jack Olson faced might have been addressed using a social systems model of treatment, or they might have been addressed using a cognitive model of treatment. The tools of research allow us to evaluate the effectiveness of different treatment models in different settings, with different problems, and with different subgroups of the population.

Finally, the tools of research allow us to challenge perceptions and popular sentiment about those who are in need. Jack Olson reflects common stereotypes about the homeless: They are male, they are substance abusers. Yet, we now know, thanks to the work of many researchers, that increasing numbers of homeless people are women with children or people diagnosed with HIV; they have different kinds of needs than Jack Olson, and they require different types of services and interventions in the kinds of housing options offered.

THE IMPERATIVE FOR SOCIAL WORK RESEARCH

As a profession, social work has faced increasing demands and pressures to demonstrate that the services delivered to clients are effective. It was not too long ago that funders and social service agencies defined *effective* in terms of process and procedure. Accountability took the nature of reporting the number of clients served and the kinds of services offered to clients. This is no longer the case; rather, effectiveness is being viewed in terms of achieving change, whether with individuals, families, or communities. The focus has shifted from indicators about the process of service delivery to the outcomes achieved by the service delivery.

This change has been shaped by different developments. Martin and Kettner (1996) attribute the changing philosophy, in part, to the passage of the Government Performance and Results Act, 1993. This law requires all federal departments to report on effectiveness, and that requirement has been passed down to states, contractors, and other providers. One manifestation of this Act can be seen in the implementation of the Personal Responsibility and Work Opportunity Reconciliation Act, which requires states to meet concrete targets for the employment of welfare recipients.

A second development has been the expansion of managed care in health and mental health. Managed care insurers demand that contractors demonstrate the effectiveness of their work. If one set of providers cannot demonstrate that they produce effective outcomes, then managed care companies will turn to other providers who can demonstrate effective outcomes.

As money has become tighter, even local funders of agencies have turned toward an outcome focus. Local United Way agencies have begun to demand that their constituent agencies demonstrate successful outcomes. In one community, the United Way asks that all agencies identify the expected outcomes, the number or percentage of clients they expect to achieve these outcomes, the methods by which the outcomes will be measured, and the data gathered. The demonstration of outcomes has become an important component of the scoring of agencies for continued funding.

Beyond these developments, social work practitioners should be accountable to their clients as they deliver services. The National Association of Social Workers Code of Ethics (http:www.naswdc.org/code/ethics.htm) states in this regard:

> 4.01(b) Social workers should strive to become and remain proficient in professional practice and the performance of professional functions. Social workers should critically examine and keep current with emerging knowledge relevant to social work. Social workers should routinely review the professional literature and participate in continuing education relevant to social work practice and social work ethics.

> 4.01 (c) Social workers should base practice on recognized knowledge, including empirically based knowledge, relevant to social work and social work ethics.

Finally, social work takes a unique perspective on the social world and the assessment and treatment of clients. Social work as a profession draws from academic disciplines such as sociology, psychology, political science, economics, anthropology, and human biology. Furthermore, it generally takes an approach that views people as operating within different systems such as the family, group, community, and organization. This integrative approach lends itself to the study of such topics as linking people to services; differentiating treatment methods for individuals, families, and groups; making efforts to enhance communities; and engaging in policy development, implementation, and evaluation.

SOCIAL WORK RESEARCH IN PRACTICE

While there are a great many studies of different phenomena and social conditions, we can classify the purposes of these studies into four categories:

Descriptive research. Defining and describing social phenomena of interest is a part of almost any research investigation, but **descriptive research** is often the primary focus of the initial research about some issue. Descriptive research typically involves the gathering of facts. Some of the central questions asked in research on homelessness have been: Who is homeless? What are the needs of homeless people? How many people are homeless? Measurement (the topic of Chapter 3) and sampling (Chapter 4) are central concerns in descriptive research. Survey research (Chapter 8) is often used for descriptive purposes.

Exploratory research. **Exploratory research** seeks to find out how people get along in the setting under question, what meanings they give to their actions, and what issues concern them. The goal is to learn "what is going on here" and to investigate social phenomena without expectations. This purpose is associated with the use of methods that capture large amounts of relatively unstructured information. For example, researchers investigating homelessness in the 1980s were encountering a phenomenon with which they had no direct experience. Thus, an early goal was to find out what it was like to be homeless and how homeless people made sense of their situation. Exploratory research like this frequently involves qualitative methods, which are the focus of Chapter 9.

Explanatory research. Many consider explanation the premier goal of any science. **Explanatory research** seeks to identify causes and effects of social phenomena and to predict how one phenomenon will change or vary in response to variation in some other phenomenon. Homelessness researchers adopted explanation as a goal when they began to ask such questions as: Why do people become homeless? and Does the unemployment rate influence the frequency of homelessness? Explanatory research depends on our ability to rule out other explanations for our findings, to demonstrate a time order between two events, and to show that the two events are related to each other. Methods with which to identify causes and effects are the focus of Chapter 5 and Chapter 6.

Evaluation research. **Evaluation research**, frequently referred to as **program evaluation** or **practice evaluation**, involves searching for practical knowledge in considering the implementation and effects of social policies and the impact of programs. Weiss (1998) defines evaluation as "the systematic assessment of the operation and/or the outcomes of a program or policy, compared to a set of explicit or implicit standards, as a means of contributing to the improvement of the program or policy" (p. 4). Evaluation research uses the tools of research to do a variety of different tasks such as describing the clients using a particular program, exploring and assessing the needs of different communities or population groups, evaluating the effectiveness of a particular program, monitoring the progress of clients, or monitoring the performance of staff. These same tools provide a standard by which we can also evaluate the evaluation. The problem of homelessness spawned many new government programs and, with them, evaluation research to assess the impact of these programs.

Because evaluation research or program evaluation uses the same tools as other research, the two often become confused in the minds of readers and even researchers. The distinctions are important, particularly as they relate to the ethical conduct of research, which we discuss in Chapter 2, and, specifically, to institutional review processes to protect human subjects, as required. Dixie E. Snider (1999), writing for the Centers for Disease Control and Prevention in *Guidelines for Defining Public Health Research and Public Health Non-Research*, provides a useful distinction between the two, based on the intent of the activity. The intent of research is to develop or contribute to generalizable knowledge, with the beneficiaries of the research usually being society and perhaps the study participants. The intent of evaluation is to assess whether a program is achieving its objectives with a specific group as a means to monitor and improve the program; therefore, it is not research. The beneficiaries of the information are the program providers and/or the clients receiving the services. Snider notes that an evaluation becomes research when it is designed to test a new, previously untested, or modified intervention or when the intent of the evaluation becomes an effort to generate generalizable knowledge.

In virtually every chapter, we will illustrate the practical use of social science tools to evaluate programs and the kinds of questions those interested in evaluation research will need to ask.

We'll now summarize one study in each of these four areas to give you a feel for the projects motivated by these different concerns.

Description: Who Are the Homeless?

In the 1980s, Dee Roth was chief of the Ohio Department of Mental Health's Office of Program Evaluation and Research. Her study of homelessness in Ohio, one of the most ambitious descriptive studies, was funded by the National Institute of Mental Health (Roth, Bean, Lust, & Saveanu, 1985). A general purpose of the study was to learn who the homeless are and how they relate to family, friends, and mental health agencies.

Because homeless people do not have regular addresses or phone numbers, Roth could not simply select individuals from a list of currently occupied residences or phone numbers in use; instead, she designed a more complex study. The study's first element was a "key informant survey." Roth asked personnel in service agencies and shelters who worked with the homeless where homeless people could be found in their local area and what the characteristics of these people were. Then, she surveyed state psychiatric hospital and community mental health agency staff and asked them to identify homeless people who had used their facilities. Finally, her staff interviewed 979 homeless people in 20 counties selected to represent urban, mixed, and rural areas throughout Ohio.

Responses in the key informant survey reinforce the importance of social scientific methods. These key informants were all employed in work with homeless people, and yet, their responses were not at all consistent. Their descriptions of the homeless population tended to focus only on the characteristics of homeless people with whom they interacted in their own work, and almost none of the informants were able to estimate accurately the size of the homeless population in their county. Direct experience alone was an insufficient basis for developing a generalizable description.

Before we tell you the results of the survey of psychiatric hospitals and community mental health centers, let's try a little experiment. You probably have heard or read statements that give you an idea about the proportion of homeless people served by such facilities. What is your guesstimate? Less than 10%, about one third, more than half, or some other proportion? The answers: 7% of new hospital patients were homeless at the time they were admitted, and 4% of the discharged hospital patients became homeless at some time after their discharge, according to reports by community mental health center staff. Are you surprised or reassured?

Roth's homeless person survey revealed a diverse population not unlike that reported in other studies of the time. About 80% of the homeless were men, 66% were White, 50% were high school graduates (just over 10% had some college experience), only 10% were married, and almost 33% were veterans. Health problems were common. Almost one third had been in a psychiatric hospital, and a similar proportion reported some psychiatric impairment; almost one third reported physical health problems; one fifth reported problem drinking.

Exploration: What Is It Like to Live in an Emergency Shelter?

One response to homelessness was that many communities created emergency shelters, despite a great deal of criticism of such facilities. Social Work Professor Alice Johnson (1999) wanted to learn about the events that led women with children to seek emergency shelter and what it was like for them to live there. To answer these questions, Johnson conducted an exploratory study using the personal narratives of women who were ex-residents of an emergency shelter in Connecticut. She interviewed 25 women with children who, when they came to the shelter, were not recipients of Aid to Families with Dependent Children. The interviews typically took place in the women's current residences and lasted between one and two hours.

One research focus was the women's perspective about entering and living in the emergency shelter. Johnson (1999) found that reactions changed over time. Initially, the women reported feeling depressed or lonely:

> I was very depressed. Especially when you have no family near you, no friends, or nobody. It's a very depressing feeling. I was depressed in the first week. I did a lot of crying. I was in my room a lot. (p. 50)

After this initial reaction to the shelter, the women developed new perceptions about their problems (Johnson, 1999). The women reported that they started to see their own lives as being better in comparison to the lives of other women in the shelter. Many reported learning that they had to be strong to take responsibility for providing for their children.

> I'm going to be honest. What helped me was my son. I would look on my son and I'd say, "I have to live for him." That's what picked me up. That's what told me to get going. For him. Find anything—whatever I can get. Go for it because of him. (p. 52)

Other women found that the shelter provided respite from their problems and an opportunity to come to grips with their problems. Finally, the women saw this respite as an opportunity to begin planning for their future.

Johnson found that the women ultimately did not see the shelter as a negative experience. Instead, they saw this as an opportunity to deal with their problems; the shelter was a place where they received emotional support and tangible help, learned how to navigate social services, and saved money.

These comments and other findings from the study suggested to Johnson that living in a shelter was part of the solution to the crises these women faced in their lives. Living in the shelter afforded them the opportunity and time to restore stability to their family life. Such information could be useful in designing emergency shelters to enable women to prepare for their future outside of the shelter.

Explanation: Why Do People Become Homeless?

Sociologist Peter H. Rossi secured funding from two private charitable foundations and the Illinois Department of Public Aid for a survey of homeless people in Chicago in the fall and winter of 1986. His comparison of these people with other extremely poor Chicagoans allowed him to address this explanatory research question: Why do people become homeless?

Rossi's (1989) book on this research, *Down and Out in America: The Origins of Homelessness*, has already become a classic.

Rossi (1989) surveyed a sample of homeless people in shelters and all those he and his assistants could find on the streets. The street sample was something of a challenge. Rossi consulted with local experts to identify which of Chicago's 19,400 blocks were the most likely resting places of homeless people at night. Then he drew samples of blocks from each of the three resulting categories: blocks with a high, medium, and low probability of having homeless people at night. Finally, Rossi's interviewers visited these blocks on several nights between 1 a.m. and 6 a.m. and briefly interviewed people who seemed to be homeless.

After extensive analysis of the data, Rossi developed a straightforward explanation of homelessness: Homeless people are extremely poor, and all extremely poor people are vulnerable to being displaced because of the high cost of housing in urban areas. Those who are most vulnerable to losing their homes are individuals with problems of substance abuse or mental illness, which leave them unable to contribute to their own support. Extremely poor individuals who have these characteristics and are priced out of cheap lodging by urban renewal and rising housing prices often end up living with relatives or friends. However, the financial and emotional burdens created by this arrangement eventually strain social ties to the breaking point, and a portion of these people therefore end up homeless.

Rossi (1989) made a series of recommendations to reduce homelessness based on his analysis of why people become homeless. Some examples: implement aggressive outreach programs to extend welfare coverage to the many eligible poor people and families who do not now receive it; subsidize housing for younger unattached people; stop the release of chronically mentally ill people from hospitals until supportive living arrangements are arranged; and furnish support to families who subsidize their destitute, unattached members.

Evaluation: What Services Help the Homeless?

What should supportive housing of the type recommended by Rossi and others consist of? Psychiatrist Stephen M. Goldfinger, psychologist Barbara Dickey, social worker Sondra Hellman, and several other investigators (Goldfinger et al., 1997)—including psychologists Walter Penk and Larry Seidman, social worker Martha O'Bryan, and Russell Schutt—designed a study of homeless mentally ill people in Boston to evaluate the effectiveness of different types of housing for this population. With funding from the National Institute of Mental Health, they recruited 118 mental health agency clients who were homeless and who were not judged to be a risk to themselves or others if they lived on their own.

They randomly assigned half of those who agreed to participate in the study to their own small efficiency apartments; the rest were assigned to one of eight group homes that were opened specifically for the study. People were assigned randomly to the two types of housing so the researchers could be more confident that any differences found between the groups at the study's end had arisen after the subjects were assigned to the housing. Case managers were assigned to all study participants in both housing types to ensure that medical and social services were provided.

The group homes were not the type of group living arrangements traditionally used by mental health authorities, with staffing around the clock and decision making firmly in the hands of the staff. Instead, the group homes were designed to assist residents to take control of their own affairs. Although the group homes began with full staffing, residents were encouraged to meet together to set rules for the household and eventually to terminate staff as they felt able to manage on their own. The authors termed this housing model *evolving consumer households.*

Most study participants—80%, in fact—were still in their housing after one year in the study, and in most respects, the two types of housing produced the same results. However, more of those living in the independent apartments left their housing at some point and returned to the streets or shelters. Paradoxically, however, those who were assigned to independent apartments were more satisfied with their housing (Schutt, Goldfinger, & Penk, 1997). Another difference, reported by the project's anthropologists, was the gradual emergence of collegial decision making in some of the group homes. Also, neuropsychological tests identified an increase in mental flexibility among group home residents.

QUANTITATIVE AND QUALITATIVE METHODS

The distinction between quantitative and qualitative methods involves more than just the type of data collected. **Quantitative methods** are most often used when the motives for research are explanation, description, or evaluation. Exploration is most often the motive for using **qualitative methods**, although researchers also use these methods for descriptive and evaluative purposes. The goals of quantitative and qualitative researchers may also differ. Whereas quantitative researchers generally accept the goal of developing an understanding that correctly reflects what is actually happening in the real world, some qualitative researchers instead emphasize the goal of developing an "authentic" understanding of a social process or social setting. An authentic understanding is one that reflects *fairly* the various perspectives of participants in that setting. We'll highlight several other differences between quantitative and qualitative methods in each of the book's chapters. Chapter 9 presents qualitative methods in much more detail.

Quantitative methods   Methods such as surveys and experiments that record variation in social life in terms of categories that vary in amount. Data that are treated as quantitative are either numbers or attributes that can be ordered in terms of magnitude.

Qualitative methods   Methods such as participant observation, intensive interviewing, and focus groups that are designed to capture social life as participants experience it, rather than in categories predetermined by the researcher. Data that are treated as qualitative are mostly written or spoken words or observations that do not have a direct numerical interpretation.

Important as it is, we don't want to place too much importance on the distinction between qualitative and quantitative methods. Often, social scientists combine these methods to enrich their research. "Qualitative knowing" about social settings can be essential for understanding patterns in quantitative data (Campbell & Russo, 1999, p. 141). Qualitative data can be converted to quantitative data, when we count the frequency of particular words or phrases in a text or measure the time elapsed between different behaviors that we have observed.

Surveys that collect primarily quantitative data may also include questions asking for written responses, and these responses may be used in a qualitative, textual analysis. Researchers using quantitative methods may engage in some exploration to find unexpected patterns in their data. Qualitative researchers may test explicit explanations of social phenomena using textual or observational data.

STRENGTHS AND LIMITATIONS OF SOCIAL WORK RESEARCH

These are only four of the dozens of large studies of homelessness done since 1980, but they illustrate some of the questions social science research can address, several different methods researchers can use, and ways research can inform public policy.

Notice how each of the four studies was designed to reduce the errors common in everyday reasoning:

- The clear definition of the population of interest in each study and the selection of a broad, representative sample of that population in two studies (Roth's and Rossi's) increased the researchers' ability to draw conclusions without overgeneralizing findings to groups to which they did not apply.
- The use of surveys in which each respondent was asked the same set of questions reduced the risk of selective or inaccurate observation, as did careful and regular note-taking by the field researchers observing homeless people on the streets of Austin, Texas, and in the evolving consumer households in Boston, Massachusetts.
- The risk of illogical reasoning was reduced by carefully describing each stage of the research, clearly presenting the findings, and carefully testing the basis for cause-and-effect conclusions.
- Resistance to change was reduced by designing an innovative type of housing and making an explicit commitment to evaluate it fairly.

Nevertheless, we would be less than honest if we implied that we enter the realm of beauty, truth, and light when we engage in social research or when we base our opinions only on the best available social research. Research always has some limitations and some flaws (as does any human endeavor), and our findings are always subject to differing interpretations. Social work research permits us to see more, to observe with fewer distortions, and to describe more clearly to others the basis for our opinions, but it will not settle all arguments. Others will always have differing opinions, and some of those others will be social scientists and social workers who have conducted their own studies and drawn different conclusions. Are people encouraged to get off welfare by requirements that they get a job? Some research suggests that they are, other research finds no effect of work incentives, and one major study found positive but short-lived effects. More convincing answers must await better research, more thoughtful analysis, or wider agreement on the value of welfare and work.

But even in areas of research that are fraught with controversy, where social scientists differ in their interpretations of the evidence, the quest for new and more sophisticated research has value. What is most important for improving understanding of the social world is not the result of any particular study but the accumulation of evidence from different studies of related issues. By designing new studies that focus on the weak points or controversial conclusions of prior research, social scientists contribute to a body of findings that gradually expands our knowledge about the social world and resolves some of the disagreements about it.

Social work researchers will always disagree somewhat because of their differing research opportunities, methodological approaches, and policy preferences. For example, much social science research indicates that low levels of social support increase the risk of psychological depression. But are these answers incorrect in some circumstances? One study of homeless people suggested that social support was not associated with less depression, perhaps because of the extremely stressful circumstances homeless people face (La Gory, Ritchey, & Mullis, 1990). But then, another study using a different indicator found social support to be as beneficial for homeless people as it is for others (Schutt, Meschede, & Rierdan, 1994). Additional studies using a variety of methods may resolve this discrepancy.

Whether you plan to conduct your own research projects, read others' research reports, or just think about and act in the social world, knowing about research methods has many benefits. This knowledge will give you greater confidence in your own opinions; improve your ability to evaluate others' opinions; and encourage you to refine your questions, answers, and methods of inquiry about the social world. Also, having the tools of research can guide you to improve the social programs in which you work, to provide better interventions with your clients, and to monitor their progress.

VALIDITY: THE GOAL OF SOCIAL WORK RESEARCH

A scientist seeks to develop an accurate understanding of empirical reality—the reality we encounter firsthand—by conducting research that leads to valid knowledge about the world. When is knowledge valid? We have reached the goal of **validity** when our statements or conclusions about empirical reality are correct. You look out your window and observe that it is raining—a valid observation, if your eyes and ears are to be trusted. You pick up the newspaper and read that the rates of violence may be climbing after several years of decline. You are less certain of the validity of this statement, based as it is on an interpretation of some trends in crime indicators obtained through some process that isn't explained.

If validity sounds desirable to you, you're a good candidate for becoming a social scientist. Social science and social work research are about validity more than anything else, about how to conduct research that leads to valid interpretations of the social world, to useful conclusions about the impact of social policy, and to valid conclusions about the effects of our practice with clients. The goal of social work research is not to come up with conclusions that people will like, to find answers that make our agencies look better or that suit our own personal preferences. The goal is to figure out how and why the social world—some aspect of it, that is—operates as it does. Throughout this book, we will be concerned with three aspects of validity: measurement validity, generalizability, and causal validity (also known as internal validity). We will learn that invalid measures, invalid generalizations, or invalid causal inferences will result in invalid conclusions.

Measurement Validity

Measurement validity is our first concern in establishing the validity of research results because if we have not measured what we think we measured, we really don't know what we're talking about. Measurement validity is the focus of Chapter 3.

Measurement validity   Exists when a measure measures what we think it measures.

To see how important measurement validity is, let's look at the case of the researchers who have found a high level of serious and persistent mental illness among homeless people, based on interviews with samples of homeless people at one point in time. The researchers have been charged with using invalid measures. Mental illness has typically been measured by individuals' responses to a series of questions that ask if they are feeling depressed, anxious, paranoid, and so on. Homeless people more commonly say yes to these questions than do other people, even other extremely poor people who have homes.

For these responses to be considered indicators of mental illness, however, the responses must indicate relatively enduring states of mind. Critics of these studies note that the living conditions of homeless people are likely to make them feel depressed, anxious, and even paranoid. Feeling depressed may be a normal reaction to homelessness, not an indication of mental illness. Thus, the argument goes, typical survey questions may not provide valid measures of mental illness among the homeless. One careful research study suggests that this criticism is not correct, that homelessness is not in itself a cause of depression. Paul Koegel and M. Audrey Burnam (1992) found that the symptoms of depression most likely to result from the living conditions of some homeless people in Los Angeles, like having trouble with sleeping or concentrating, were not particularly more common among those studied than among those with homes.

On the other hand, some measures may not be accurate measures when applied to different subgroups of the population. Returning to the example of depression, some measures of depression have been criticized as inappropriate when used with older adults (Weiss, Nagel, & Aronson, 1986), African Americans (Barbee, 1992), and women (Newmann, Engel, & Jensen, 1991). The indicators used in some measures of depression may overestimate the prevalence of depression for each of these groups because of content that may be irrelevant.

Suffice it to say at this point that we must be very careful in designing our measures and in subsequently evaluating how well they have performed. We must be careful to ensure that the measures are comparable for women and men and for different age groups, ethnic groups, and other groups of the population; we cannot just assume that measures are valid or invalid.

Generalizability

The **generalizability** of a study is the extent to which it can be used to inform us about people, places, or events that were not studied. Generalizability is the focus of Chapter 4.

Generalizability   Exists when a conclusion holds true for the population, group, setting, or event that we say it does, given the conditions that we specify.

Although most American cities have many shelters for homeless people and some homeless people sleep on the streets to avoid shelters, many studies of "the homeless" are based on surveys of individuals found in just one shelter. When these studies are reported, the authors state that their results are based on homeless people in one shelter, but then they go on to talk about "the homeless this" and "the homeless that," as if their study results represent all homeless people in the city or even in the nation.

People may be especially quick to make this mistake in discussing studies of homeless people because it's very difficult to track down homeless people outside of shelters and because some shelter directors do not allow researchers to survey individuals at their shelters. Yet, social work researchers (and most everyone else, for that matter) are eager to draw conclusions about homeless people in general. Generalizations make their work (and opinions) sound more important.

If every homeless person were like every other one, generalizations based on observations of one homeless person would be valid. But, of course, that's not the case. In fact, homeless people who avoid shelters tend to be different from those who use shelters, and different types of shelters may attract different types of homeless people. We are on solid ground if we question the generalizability of statements about homeless people based on the results of a survey in just one shelter.

Generalizability has two aspects. **Sample generalizability** refers to the ability to generalize from a sample, or subset, of a larger population to that population itself. This is the most common meaning of generalizability. **Cross-population generalizability** refers to the ability to generalize from findings about one group, population, or setting to other groups, populations, or settings (see Exhibit 1.5). In this book, we use the term **external validity** to refer only to cross-population generalizability, not to sample generalizability.

Sample generalizability   Exists when a conclusion based on a sample, or subset, of a larger population holds true for that population.

Cross-population generalizability   Exists when findings about one group, population, or setting hold true for other groups, populations, or settings (see Exhibit 1.5). Also called *external validity.*

Sample generalizability is a key concern in survey research. A community organizer may study a sample of residents living in a particular neighborhood in order to do a needs assessment, and then generalize the findings to all the residents of the neighborhood. The value of the findings is enhanced if what the community organizer learns is representative of all the residents and not just those residents who were surveyed.

Cross-population generalizability occurs to the extent that the results of a study hold true for multiple populations; these populations may not all have been sampled, or they may be represented as subgroups within the sample studied. Consider the debate over whether social support reduces psychological distress among homeless people as it does among housed people (Schutt et al., 1994). A study based on a sample of only homeless people could not in itself resolve this debate. But in a heterogeneous sample of both homeless and housed people, the effect of social support on distress among both groups could be tested.

Exhibit 1.5   Sample and Cross-Population Generalizability

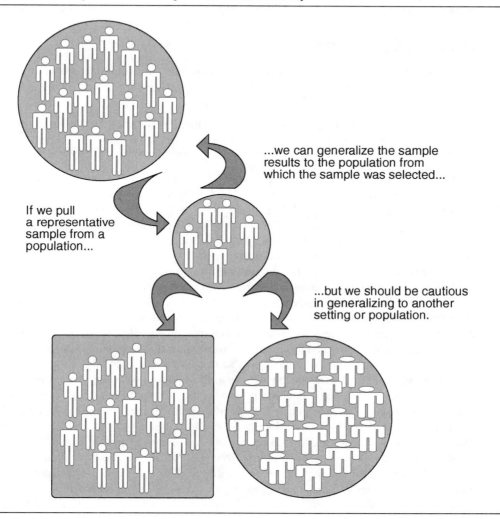

...we can generalize the sample results to the population from which the sample was selected...

If we pull a representative sample from a population...

...but we should be cautious in generalizing to another setting or population.

Or consider this when you read about an intervention to help homeless individuals obtain and maintain a permanent residence. It is likely that such a study is done in a particular agency, serving homeless individuals with particular characteristics, living in a particular community. Ideally, you would like to be able to implement that intervention with the hope of the same success in your agency, working with your particular clients, in your particular community.

Generalizability is a key concern in research design. We rarely have the resources to study the entire population that is of interest to us, so we have to select cases to study that will allow our findings to be generalized to the population of interest. We can never be sure that our propositions will hold under all conditions, so we should be cautious in generalizing to populations that we did not actually sample.

Causal (Internal) Validity

Causal validity, also known as **internal validity,** refers to the truthfulness of an assertion that A causes B. It is the focus of Chapter 5.

Causal validity (internal validity)   Exists when a conclusion that A leads to or results in B is correct.

Most research seeks to determine what causes what, so social scientists frequently must be concerned with causal validity. For example, Gary Cohen and Barbara Kerr (1998) asked whether computer-mediated counseling could be as effective as face-to-face counseling for mental health problems. They could have compared people who had experienced one of these types of treatment, but it's quite likely that individuals who sought out a live person for counseling would differ in important ways from those who were attracted to an opportunity for the less personal computer-mediated counseling. So, instead, they designed an experiment in which individuals seeking counseling were assigned randomly to either computer-mediated or face-to-face counseling. This procedure made it very unlikely that people who were less sociable, more educated, younger, and so on were disproportionately placed in the computer-mediated condition. Differences in counseling outcomes were thus more likely to be due to the differences in the types of counseling, rather than to differences in the types of people being counseled. Students in both groups benefited to the same degree, so researchers concluded that computer-mediated counseling was as effective in reducing anxiety as face-to-face counseling (see Exhibit 1.6).

On the other hand, causal conclusions also can be mistaken because of some factor that was not recognized during planning for the study, even in randomized experiments. If the computer-mediated counseling sessions were conducted in a modern building with all the latest amenities whereas face-to-face counseling was delivered in a rundown building, this might have led to different outcomes for reasons quite apart from the type of counseling.

Establishing causal validity can be quite difficult. You will learn in subsequent chapters how experimental designs and statistics can help us evaluate causal propositions, but the solutions are neither easy nor perfect: We always have to consider critically the validity of causal statements that we hear or read.

CONCLUSION

We hope this first chapter has given you an idea of what to expect in the rest of the book. Our aim is to introduce you to social work research methods by describing what social scientists have learned about the social world as well as how they learned it. The substance of social science inevitably is more interesting than its methods, but the methods also become more interesting when they're not taught as isolated techniques. We have focused attention on research on homelessness in this chapter; in subsequent chapters, we will introduce research examples from other areas.

Exhibit 1.6   Partial Evidence of Causality

Pre-counseling Anxiety Score	Type of Counseling	Post-counseling Anxiety Score
35	Computer-mediated	28
35	Face-to-face	29

| Pre-counseling anxiety score: 35 | Computer-mediated counseling | → | Post-counseling anxiety score: 28 |

| Pre-counseling anxiety score:35 | Face-to-face counseling | → | Post-counseling anxiety score: 29 |

The theme of validity ties the book's chapters together. You must learn to ask of each research technique how it helps us come to more valid conclusions. Each technique must be evaluated in terms of its ability to help us with measurement validity, generalizability, and causal validity. You must ask a critical question about each research project you examine: How valid are its conclusions?

Chapter 2 continues to build the foundation for our study of social work research by reviewing the types of problems that researchers study, the role of theory, the major steps in the research process, and other sources of information that may be used in social work research. We stress the importance of considering scientific standards in social research, and we review generally accepted ethical guidelines. Throughout the chapter, we use several studies of domestic violence to illustrate the research process.

Then, we return to the subject of validity. Chapters 3, 4, and 5 discuss the three aspects of validity and the specific techniques used to maximize the validity of our measures, our generalizations, and our causal assertions. Research about the measurement of depression, sampling of homeless people, and the causes of violence is highlighted.

Chapters 6, 7, 8, and 9 introduce the four most important methods of data collection. Group designs, including experimental studies, quasi-experimental studies, and nonexperimental studies are the subject of Chapter 6. These designs are often used for practice evaluation and policy evaluation. We turn to single-subject designs in Chapter 7; these designs are particularly effective methods to monitor and evaluate client progress. Survey research is one of the most common methods of data collection, and we devote a lot of attention to the different types of surveys in Chapter 8. Chapter 9 shows how field research techniques can uncover aspects of the social world that we are likely to miss in experiments and surveys as well as how we can gain a better understanding of the experiences of our clients. Finally, in Chapter 10, we describe evaluation research and its relationship to the four preceding data collection methods.

The following three chapters begin with an overview of the statistics that are needed to analyze most social work research data. Chapter 11 is not a substitute for an entire course in statistics, but it will give you a good idea of how to use statistics in reporting the results of studies that you conduct and in interpreting the results of research reported by others. We present an extended example that will help you learn how to use particular statistics, and we illustrate the process of analyzing secondary data, data already collected by others. Chapter 12 focuses on the different techniques used to analyze findings from qualitative studies. Finally, Chapter 13 focuses on the contents of research reports and the process of developing them. We give special attention to how to formulate research proposals and how to critique or evaluate reports of research that we encounter.

KEY TERMS

Causal validity
Cross-population generalizability
Descriptive research
Evaluation research
Explanatory research
Exploratory research
External validity
Generalizability
Illogical reasoning
Inaccurate observation
Internal validity
Measurement validity

Overgeneralization
Program (or practice) evaluation
Qualitative methods
Quantitative methods
Resistance to change
Sample generalizability
Science
Selective (or incomplete) observation
Social science
Social science approach
Validity

HIGHLIGHTS

- Social work research cannot resolve value questions or provide permanent, universally accepted answers.
- Empirical data are obtained in social work investigations from either direct experience or the statements of other people.
- Four common errors in reasoning are overgeneralization, selective or inaccurate observation, illogical reasoning, and resistance to change. These errors result from the complexity of the social world, subjective processes that affect the reasoning of researchers and the people they study, researchers' self-interest, and unquestioning acceptance of tradition or of those in positions of authority.
- Social science is the use of logical, systematic, documented methods to investigate individuals, societies, and social processes, as well as the knowledge produced by these investigations.
- Social science methods are used by social work researchers and practitioner-researchers to uncover the nature of a social condition, to test the accuracy of assumptions about the causes of

the social condition, to identify populations-at-risk, and to test and evaluate the effectiveness of interventions, programs, and policies designed to ameliorate the social condition.

- Social work research can be descriptive, exploratory, explanatory, or evaluative—or some combination of these.

- Valid knowledge is a central concern of scientific research. The three components of validity are measurement validity, generalizability (both from the sample to the population from which it was selected and from the sample to other populations), and causal (internal) validity.

- Quantitative and qualitative methods structure research in different ways and are differentially appropriate for diverse research situations.

DISCUSSION QUESTIONS

1. Select a social issue that is of interest to you. Discuss your beliefs about this social issue, for example, its causes. What is the source of these beliefs? What type of policy, program, and intervention for helping resolve this social issue would be consistent with your beliefs?

2. Social work research using different methods can yield differing results about the same topic. How might experimental, survey, and qualitative methods lead to different results in research on the impact of welfare programs?

3. Discuss three advantages of qualitative methods and three advantages of quantitative methods. What motives for research do these two methodological approaches reflect?

PRACTICE EXERCISES

1. Find a report of social work research in an article in a daily newspaper. What were the major findings? How much evidence is given about the measurement validity, generalizability, and causal validity of the findings? What additional design features might have helped to improve the study's validity?

2. Read the abstracts (initial summaries) of each article in a recent issue of a major social work journal. (Ask your instructor for some good journal titles.) On the basis of the abstract only, classify each research project represented in the articles as primarily descriptive, exploratory, explanatory, or evaluative. Note any indications that the research focused on other types of research questions.

WEB EXERCISES

1. Prepare a 5- to 10-minute class presentation on the U.S. Department of Housing and Urban Development (HUD) report, *Homelessness: Programs and the People They Serve*. Go to the National Alliance to End Homelessness's Web site at www.endhomelessness.org. From there, go to Background and Statistics, then click on the name of the report. Choose the Summary option, then Table of Contents. Access sections of the report from here or view the main points of each chapter by clicking on Highlights. Write up a brief outline for your presentation, including information on study design, questions asked, and major findings.

2. Does the HUD perspective on homelessness differ from the perspective in research reports of major social policy institutes? Check out one such report from the Urban Institute, which used data accumulated by HUD. This report, entitled *America's Homeless II*, is also available at the Background and Statistics page provided by the National Alliance to End Homelessness. Just click on the report's title and then on the link highlighted within the press release: "newest national analysis of homelessness." Write up some information regarding this survey and its goals, methods, and major findings. What

do the researchers conclude about the magnitude of homelessness and the patterns of service use among the population? How do these conclusions compare to each other and to those of HUD researchers? What aspects of the methods, questions, or findings might explain differences in their conclusions? Do you think the researchers approached their studies with different perspectives at the outset? If so, what might these perspectives have been?

To assist you in completing the Web exercises, please access the study site at http://www.sagepub.com/prsw where you will find the Web Exercises reproduced and suggested links for online resources.

DEVELOPING A RESEARCH PROPOSAL

1. Will you develop a research proposal in this course? If so, you should begin to consider your alternatives.

2. What topic would you focus on if you could design a social work-related research project without any concern for costs or time? What are your reasons for studying this topic? Develop four questions that you might investigate about the topic you just selected. Each question should reflect a different research motive: description, exploration, explanation, or evaluation. Be specific.

3. Which question most interests you? Would you prefer to attempt to answer that question with quantitative or qualitative methods? Why?

Chapter 2

THE PROCESS AND PROBLEMS OF SOCIAL WORK RESEARCH

Social Work Research Questions

Identifying Social Work Research
    Questions
Refining Social Work Research
    Questions
Evaluating Social Work Research
    Questions
    Feasibility
    Social Importance
    Scientific Relevance

Foundations of Social Work Research

Finding Information
    Searching the Literature
    Searching the Web
Reviewing Research

Social Work Research Strategies

The Role of Social Theory
The Deductive/Inductive Cycle
    Deductive Research

*Domestic Violence and the Research
    Circle*
Inductive Research
*An Inductive Approach to Explaining
    Domestic Violence*
*A Qualitative Exploration of the
    Response to Domestic Violence*
Descriptive Research

**Philosophies Guiding Social Work
Research**

**Scientific Guidelines for Social Work
Research**

**Social Work Research and Ethical
Guidelines**

Honesty and Openness
The Uses of Science
Research on People

Conclusion

Domestic violence is a major problem in our society, with police responding to between 2 million and 8 million complaints of assault by a spouse or lover yearly (Sherman, 1992, p. 6). In 1981, the Police Foundation and the Minneapolis Police Department began an experiment to determine whether arresting accused spouse abusers on the spot would deter repeat incidents. The study's results, which were widely publicized, indicated that arrest did have a deterrent effect. In part because of this, the percentage of urban police departments that made arrest the preferred response to complaints of domestic violence rose from 10% in 1984 to 90% in 1988 (Sherman, 1992, p. 14). Six other cities then hosted studies like the Minneapolis experiment, but the results were not as clear-cut as in the original study (Sherman, 1992; Sherman & Berk, 1984). The Minneapolis Domestic Violence Experiment, the studies modeled after it, and the related controversies have provided many examples for a systematic overview of the social research process.

We will examine both scientific and social aspects of the research process. We will also consider in some detail the techniques required to begin the research process: formulating research questions, finding information, reviewing prior research, and writing a research proposal. The first concern in social work research is deciding what to study. A wide variety of theoretical orientations applicable to understanding human behavior at the individual, group, community, and organizational level may help guide us to a research question, elaborate on its implications, and, later, interpret our results. The selection of a research question may be motivated by one's own personal interests or professional experiences. Next, we must decide how to go about answering the research question. We will use the Minneapolis experiment and related research to illustrate the different research strategies and some of the related techniques. The chapter also introduces ethical guidelines that should be adhered to no matter what the research strategy. By the chapter's end, you should be ready to formulate a research question, design a general strategy for answering this question, and critique previous studies that addressed this question. You can think of Chapter 1 as having introduced the "why" of social work research; Chapter 2 introduces the "how."

SOCIAL WORK RESEARCH QUESTIONS

A **social work research question** is a question that you seek to answer through the collection and analysis of firsthand, verifiable, empirical data. It is not a question about who did what to whom but a question, for example, about people in interaction with other individuals, groups, or organizations, about tendencies in community change, or about the impact of different interventions. What are the causes of child abuse? Why do some people use mental health services while others in need of such services do not? Why do some elderly participate in Supplemental Security Income while other eligible elderly do not? What is the effect of Temporary Assistance to Needy Families (TANF) on the children of recipients? Does the use of respite care reduce caregiver burden? Does reducing caregiver burden delay unnecessary institutionalization? Does cognitive behavioral therapy reduce symptoms of depression in adolescents? So many research questions are possible that it is more of a challenge to specify what does *not* qualify as a social work research question than to specify what does qualify.

But that doesn't mean it is easy to specify a research question. In fact, formulating a good research question can be surprisingly difficult. We can break the process into three stages: identifying one or more questions for study, refining the questions, and then evaluating the questions.

Identifying Social Work Research Questions

Social work research questions may emerge from your own experience—from your "personal troubles," as C. Wright Mills (1959) put it. One experience might be membership in a youth group, another could be volunteering in a woman's shelter, another could be a friend's death, and yet another might be watching your parents divorce. You may find yourself asking questions like these: In what ways do adolescents benefit from youth group membership? Does domestic violence change a person's trust in others? What are effective methods of treating bereavement or loss? What are the emotional consequences of divorce on children? Can you think of other possible research questions that flow from your own experiences?

Some research questions may emerge from your work or field practicum experiences. Working with clients, you may begin to wonder under what conditions a particular intervention will work and under what conditions it may be less successful. You may ask yourself what causes some of the problems you see, for example, what causes elder abuse or what family patterns seem related to school behavioral problems. You might also begin to think about how social policies affect the clients your agency serves or the agency itself. Has the advent of managed care changed the kinds of services provided by mental health agencies? How do TANF recipients who are going back to work manage their child care needs?

Also, other researchers may pose interesting questions for you to study. Most research articles end with some suggestions for additional research, which highlight unresolved issues. The authors may suggest repeating the research with other samples in other settings or locations. Or they may suggest that the research could have been improved by using a different design or instrument. They may suggest examining other variables to determine whether they explain a relationship. Any issue of a social work journal is likely to have articles with comments that point toward unresolved issues.

Another source of research questions for some social work researchers is social theory. Some researchers spend much of their careers conducting research intended to refine an answer to one central research question. For example, you may find rational choice theory to be a useful approach to understanding diverse forms of social behavior because you feel that people seem to make decisions on the basis of personal cost-benefit calculations. So you may ask whether rational choice theory can explain why some elderly people choose to participate in Supplemental Security Income and other eligible elderly people do not participate, or whether it can explain why some people choose to seek out and use mental health services while other people do not.

Finally, some research questions have very pragmatic sources. You may focus on a research question posed by someone else because it seems to be to your advantage to do so. Some social scientists conduct research on specific questions posed by a funding source in what is termed an RFP, a request for proposals. (Sometimes the acronym RA is used, meaning request for applications.) Or you may learn that the social workers in the homeless shelter where you volunteer need help with a survey to learn about client needs, which becomes the basis for another research question.

Refining Social Work Research Questions

The problem is not so much coming up with interesting questions for research as it is focusing on a problem of manageable size. We are often interested in much more than we can reasonably investigate with limited time and resources. Researchers may worry about staking a research project (and thereby a grant or a grade) on a particular problem, and so they address several research questions at once, often in a jumbled fashion. It might also seem risky to focus on a research question that may lead to results discrepant with your own cherished assumptions. The prospective commitment of time and effort for some research questions may seem overwhelming, resulting in a certain degree of paralysis. Or you begin to doubt the importance of what once seemed like an important question, and you prematurely discard it.

The best way to avoid these problems is to develop the research question one bit at a time. Don't keep hoping that the perfect research question will just spring forth from your pen. Instead, develop a list of possible research questions as you go along. At the appropriate time, you can look through this list for the research questions that appear more than once. Narrow your list to the most interesting, most workable candidates. Repeat this process as long as it helps to improve your research questions.

Finally, as you consider alternative research questions, it is important to remember that we live in a very diverse world. Often, we think of a family as consisting of two parents of the opposite gender, yet we know that families take on many different forms. Using a narrow definition of family, although it may reflect societal stereotypes, would certainly limit the utility of the findings. Research questions may reflect a heterosexism bias, which Gregory Herek and his colleagues (1991) defined as "conceptualizing human experience in strictly heterosexual terms and consequently ignoring, invalidating, or derogating homosexual behaviors and sexual orientation, and lesbian, gay, and bisexual relationships and lifestyles" (p. 958). K. Warner Schaie (1993, p. 49) warns that, too often, research questions about human aging reflect negative societal stereotypes of elderly people. How we conceptualize our questions and the language we use is therefore critical in the development of a research question.

Evaluating Social Work Research Questions

In the third stage of selecting a research question, we evaluate the best candidate against the criteria for good social research questions: feasibility given the time and resources available, social importance, and scientific relevance (King, Keohane, & Verba, 1994).

Feasibility

We must be able to conduct any study within the time and the resources we have available. If time is short, questions that involve long-term change may not be feasible unless we can find data that have already been collected. For example, it is difficult to study the impact of anti-drug education groups offered in middle school on subsequent adult drug use. Another issue is access to identified people or groups. It may be difficult to gain access to participants with particular characteristics. If you were interested in seeking people with a mental health diagnosis who live in your community, you might have to do an excessive amount of screening. Although you could turn to a mental health provider, the agency might not allow you access to its clients. Then we must consider whether we will have any additional resources, such as other researchers to collaborate with or research funds. Remember that there are severe limits on what one person can accomplish. On the other hand, we may be able to piggyback our research onto a larger research project. We also must take into account the constraints we face due to our schedules and other commitments as well as our skill levels.

The Minneapolis Domestic Violence Experiment shows how ambitious social research questions can be when a team of seasoned researchers secures the backing of influential groups. The project required hundreds of thousands of dollars, the collaboration of many social scientists and criminal justice personnel, and the volunteer efforts of 41 Minneapolis police officers. But many worthwhile research questions can be investigated with much more limited resources. You will read in subsequent chapters about studies that addressed important research questions with much more limited resources than the Minneapolis social scientists commanded.

Social Importance

Social work research is not a simple undertaking, so it is hard to justify the expenditures of effort and limited resources unless we focus on a substantive area that is important. There are so many substantive areas related to social work that creating an all-encompassing list is difficult. You need to feel motivated to carry out the study; there is little point in trying to answer a question that doesn't interest you.

We should also consider whether the research question is important to other people. Will an answer to the research question make a difference in improving the well-being of people? Again, the Minneapolis Domestic Violence Experiment is an exemplary case; however, social work research is not wanting for important research questions. A recent issue of *Research on Social Work Practice* included articles about reducing AIDS and substance abuse risk factors among homeless people, treating battered women, assessing the impact of short-term treatment on health promotion, examining the use of a behavioral treatment to reduce disruptive classroom behaviors, and validating a scale to predict delinquent behavior. All of these articles addressed research questions about social work interventions, and all raised new questions for additional research. Other social work journals address macro topics such as community building, organizational behavior, or policy research.

Scientific Relevance

Every research question should be grounded in both social work and social science literature. Whether we formulate a research question because we have been stimulated by an academic article or because we want to investigate a current social problem, we must turn to the literature to find out what has already been learned about this question. You can be sure that some prior study is relevant to almost any research question you can conceive.

The Minneapolis experiment was built on a substantial body of contradictory theorizing about the impact of punishment on criminality (Sherman & Berk, 1984). Deterrence theory predicted that arrest would deter individuals from repeat offenses; labeling theory predicted that arrest would make repeat offenses more likely. One prior experimental study of this issue was about juveniles; studies among adults had yielded inconsistent findings. Clearly, the Minneapolis researchers had good reason to conduct another study. Any new research question should be connected in this way to past research.

FOUNDATIONS OF SOCIAL WORK RESEARCH

How do we find prior research and theory? You may already know some of the relevant material from prior coursework or your independent reading, but that will not be enough. New research results about many questions appear continually in scholarly journals and books, in research reports from government agencies and other organizations, and on Web sites all over the world. Conducting a thorough search of these sources and reviewing critically what you have found is an essential foundation for any research project. Fortunately, most of this information can be identified online, without leaving your desk- or laptop, and an increasing fraction of published journal articles can be downloaded directly to your own computer, depending on your particular access privileges.

Finding Information

Searching the published research literature is an essential step for serious researchers, but every year the World Wide Web also offers more and more useful material (as well as inaccurate material). Everything from copies of particular rating scales to reports from research in progress to forums on related topics can be found on the Web. We will review in this section the basic procedures for finding relevant research information both in the published literature and on the Web. Appendix D provides more detailed instructions.

Searching the Literature

Literature in both social work and social science should be consulted at the beginning and end of an investigation. Even while an investigation is in progress, consultations with the literature may help to resolve methodological problems or facilitate supplementary explorations. Unlike the largely unregulated Web, research published in social work and social science journals has been subjected to a relatively rigorous review process (although standards vary by journal). No matter how tempting it is to rely on the materials more readily available on the Web, you must also search the published research literature.

Preparing the search. Formulate a research question before you begin to search, even though the question may change later. Identify the question's parts and subparts and any related issues that you think might play an important role in the research. List the authors of relevant studies you are aware of, possible keywords that might specify the subject for your search, and perhaps the most important journals that deal with your topic. For example, if your research question involves the effect of informal support on depression in the elderly, you might consider searching the literature electronically for studies that mentioned *informal support* or just *support* as well as *depression* or *elderly depression.* You might plan to check journals like the *Journal of Gerontology, Journal of Gerontological Social Work, Gerontologist, Health and Social Work,* and *Psychology and Aging.*

Conducting the search. Now you are ready to begin searching the literature. You should check for relevant books in your library and perhaps in other college libraries in your area. This usually means conducting a search of an online catalog using a list of subject terms. However, most scientific research is published in journal articles, so the primary focus of your search should be the journal literature.

Searching a computerized bibliographic database is by far the most efficient search strategy, although some libraries still carry paper indexes. The specifics of a database search will vary among libraries and according to your own computer resources. Check with your librarian for help. Most academic libraries provide access to online databases

Exhibit 2.1   A Search Result in *Social Work Abstracts* on *Informal Support*

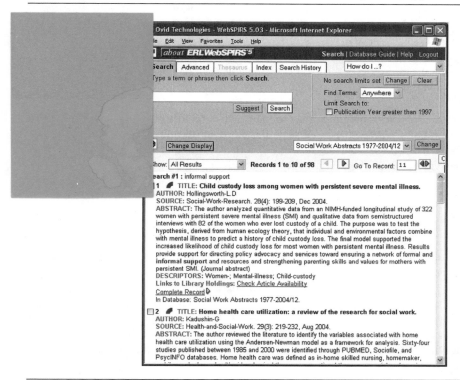

like *Social Work Abstracts, Psychological Abstracts (PsychINFO),* and the *Social Science Citation Index.*

After you have accessed the chosen index, you can locate the published articles pertaining to topics identified by your subject terms. Choose your subject terms very carefully. A good rule is to cast a net wide enough to catch most of the relevant articles with your key terms but not so wide that it identifies many useless citations. For example, a search for *informal support* would be more successful than a search for *support.* Give most attention to articles published in the leading journals in the field, but be prepared to spend a fair amount of time whittling down the list of citations if you are searching for a popular topic.

Exhibit 2.1 shows the results of a search for articles on *informal support* in *Social Work Abstracts.* The search resulted in 98 English-language documents. You should note, however, that if we had searched for *informal* and *support*, we would have found 268 abstracts. The way words are entered into the search can lead to the retrieval of a different number of documents.

The sheer number of references you find can be a problem. For example, searching for *elderly* resulted in 2,162 citations in *Social Work Abstracts.* Depending on the database you are working with and the purposes of your search, you may want to limit your search to English-language publications, to journal articles rather than conference papers or dissertations (both of which are more difficult to acquire), and to materials published in recent years.

It is often a good idea to narrow down your search by requiring that abstracts contain combinations of words or phrases. For example, searching for *elderly* and *informal support* in the same search reduced the number of documents to 38.

The choice of keywords is also crucial in searching databases. If instead of *elderly,* we had searched for *older adults,* only 319 documents would have been retrieved in *Social Work Abstracts.* And some of these 319 documents do not appear in the broader number of citations found in the search on *elderly.*

Checking the results. Check the titles, read the abstracts, and identify articles that appear to be relevant. You may even be able to click on these article titles and generate a list of their references. Now it is time to find the full text of articles of interest. If you are lucky, some of the journals you need will be available from your library in online versions, and you'll be able to link the full text of articles in those journals just by clicking on the "full text" link. However, many journals are available only in print.

You may be tempted to write up a review of the literature based on reading the abstracts or using only those articles available online, but you will be selling yourself short. Many crucial details about methods, findings, and theoretical implications will be found only in the body of the article, and many important articles will not be available online. To understand, critique, and really benefit from previous research studies, you must read the important articles, no matter how you have to retrieve them. And don't stop with the articles you identified in your initial search of the *Abstracts* or other index. Always check the bibliographies of the articles that you read for additional relevant sources and then expand your literature search by reading those articles and books. Continue this process as long as it identifies new and useful sources. You will be surprised (we always are) at how many important articles your initial search missed.

If you have done your job well, you will have more than enough literature as background for your own research, unless it is on a very obscure topic. Of course, your search will also be limited by library holdings you have access to and perhaps by the time required to order copies of conference papers and dissertations you find in your search. At this point, your main concern is to construct a coherent framework in which to develop your research problem, drawing as many lessons as you can from previous research. You may use the literature to identify a useful theory and hypotheses to be reexamined, to find inadequately studied specific research questions, to explicate the disputes about your research question, to summarize the major findings of prior research, and to suggest appropriate methods of investigation. Be sure to take notes on each article you read, organizing your notes into the standard sections: research questions, theory, methods, findings, conclusions. In any case, write the literature review so that it contributes to your study in some concrete way; don't feel compelled to discuss an article just because you have read it. Be judicious. You are conducting only one study of one issue; it will only obscure the value of that study if you try to relate it to every tangential point in related topics.

Don't think of searching the literature as a one-time-only venture—something that you leave behind as you move on to your *real* research. You may encounter new questions or unanticipated problems as you conduct your research or as you burrow deeper into the literature. Searching the literature again to determine what others have found in response to these questions or what steps they have taken to resolve these problems can yield substantial improvements in your own research. There is so much literature on so many topics that it often is not possible to figure out in advance every subject you should search the literature for or what type of search will be most beneficial.

Another reason to make searching the literature an ongoing project is that the literature is always growing. During the course of one research study, whether it takes only one semester or several years, new findings will be published and relevant questions will be debated. Staying attuned to the literature and checking it at least when you are writing up your findings may save your study from being outdated.

Searching the Web

The World Wide Web provides access to vast amounts of information of many different sorts (O'Dochartaigh, 2002). You can search the holdings of other libraries and download the complete text of government reports, some conference papers, and newspaper articles. You can find policies of local governments, descriptions of individual social scientists and particular research projects, and postings of advocacy groups. It's also hard to avoid finding a lot of information in which you have no interest, such as commercial advertisements, third-grade homework assignments, or college course syllabi. Back in 1999, there were about 800 million publicly available pages of information on the Web (Davis, 1999). Today there may be as many as 15 billion pages on the Web (Novak, 2003).

After you are connected to the Web with a browser like Microsoft Internet Explorer or Netscape Navigator, you can use three basic strategies for finding information: direct addressing, browsing, and searching. For some purposes, you will need to use only one strategy; for other purposes, you will want to use all three. Appendix D contains additional information on all three methods.

Direct addressing. Every Web information source is identified by an address (a *uniform resource locator,* or URL). If you know the URL of the information source you want to use, you can instruct your browser to go directly to that source. The end-of-chapter Web exercises, Appendix H, and the CD-ROM included with this text list many URLs relevant to social work research.

Browsing subject directories. Many Web sites maintain lists of URLs that pertain to their site and—you can hope, at least—have been selected because of their relevance and quality. When you visit one of these sites, you can browse its list of related URLs and then go directly to one of these additional sites. Many government agencies, professional organizations, academic departments, and even individuals maintain URL lists as part of their own Web sites.

Searching. Search engines are programs that index Web pages on an ongoing basis and let you search the resulting database for pages on topics of interest. A few of the popular search engines available today are Google, AltaVista, and Infoseek. When using search engines, keep in mind that not all search engines are the same.

- Search engines vary in size.
- Search engines "crawl" different sites on the Web and so will yield different results.

- Search engines use their own procedures for identifying and indexing Web resources and vary in what type of information is included. For example, some include newspapers whereas others do not.
- Search engines have their own searching syntax and relevance ranking system. You can't jump from one to another and expect each to work the same way.

When you want the words you're looking for to be next to each other, such as when looking for a concept or a person's name, you do phrase searching. Most search engines perform phrase searching by requiring the search terms to be put in quotation marks. This is a very effective way to narrow your focus and reduce the number of documents you retrieve. When searching for names, it's important to search in both normal and inverted order (i.e., "Russell K. Schutt" and "Schutt, Russell K."). Including or omitting a middle initial will also affect your search results.

The first problem that you may encounter when searching the Web is the sheer quantity of resources that are available. It is a much bigger problem when searching the Web than when searching bibliographic databases. Searching for *informal support* on Google produced 2,230,000 sites. On the Web, less is usually more. Limit your inspection of Web sites to the first few pages that turn up in your list (they're ranked by relevance). See what those first pages contain and then try to narrow your search by including some additional terms.

Remember the following warnings when you conduct searches on the Web.

- *Clarify your goals.* Before you begin the search, jot down the terms that you think you need to search for and a statement of what you want to accomplish with your search. Then you will have a sense of what to look for and what to ignore.
- *Quality is not guaranteed.* Anyone can post almost anything, so the accuracy and adequacy of the information you find may be suspect. Except for most online journals and official Web sites, many Web sites have no journal editor or librarian to evaluate quality and relevance.
- *Anticipate change.* Web sites that are not maintained by stable organizations can come and go very quickly. Any search will result in attempts to link to some URLs that no longer exist.
- *One size does not fit all.* Different search engines use different procedures for identifying and indexing Web sites. Some attempt to be all-inclusive while others aim to be selective. As a result, you can get different results from different search engines, even though you are searching for exactly the same terms.
- *Be concerned about generalizability.* You might be tempted to characterize police department policies by summarizing the documents you find at police department Web sites. But how many police departments are there? How many have posted their policies on the Web? Are these policies representative of all police departments? To answer all these questions, you would have to conduct a research project just on the Web sites alone.
- *Evaluate the sites.* There's a lot of material out there, so how do you know what's good? Some Web sites contain excellent advice and pointers on how to differentiate the good from the bad. We have included one in Appendix H.
- *Avoid Web addiction.* Another danger of the extraordinary quantity of information available on the Web is that one search will lead to another and to another and. . . . There are

always more possibilities to explore and one more interesting source to check. Establish boundaries of time and effort to avoid the risk of losing all sense of proportion.

- *Cite your sources.* Using text or images from Web sources without attribution is plagiarism. It is the same as copying someone else's work from a book or article and pretending that it is your own. Use the referencing system required in your class. Instructions for the American Psychological Association's style can be found in the 5th edition of the *Publication Manual of the American Psychological Association* (online!).

Reviewing Research

Effective review of the prior research you find is an essential step in building the foundation for new research. You must assess carefully the quality of each research study, consider the implications of each article for your own plans, and expand your thinking about your research question to take account of new perspectives and alternative arguments. Through reviewing the literature and using it to extend and sharpen your own ideas and methods, you become a part of the social work research community. Instead of being just one individual studying an issue that interests you, you are then building on an ever-growing body of knowledge that is being connected by the entire community of scholars.

The research information you find at various Web sites comes in a wide range of formats and represents a variety of sources. *Caveat emptor* (buyer beware) is the watchword when you search the Web; following review guidelines like those we have listed will minimize, but not eliminate, the risk of being led astray. By contrast, the published scholarly journal literature that you find in databases like *Social Work Abstracts* and *Psychological Abstracts* follows a standard format more closely and has been subjected to a careful review process. There is some variability—some journals publish book reviews, comments on prior articles, and even solicited reviews of the literature about particular research questions—and the major databases of research article abstracts also include references to dissertation abstracts, book reviews, conference papers, and brief reports on innovative service programs. However, most literature you will find on a research topic in these databases represents articles reporting analyses of data collected in a research project. These are the sources on which you should focus.

Reviewing the literature is really a two-stage process. In the first stage, you must assess each article separately. This assessment should follow a standard format like that represented by the "Questions to Ask about a Research Article" in Appendix B. However, you should keep in mind that you can't adequately understand a research study if you just treat it as a series of discrete steps, involving a marriage of convenience among separate techniques. Any research project is an integrated whole, so you must be concerned with how each component to the research design influenced the others—for example, how the measurement approach might have affected the causal validity of the researcher's conclusions and how the sampling strategy might have altered the quality of measures.

The second stage of the review process is to compare your separate article reviews, to assess the implications of the entire set of articles (and other materials) for the relevant aspects of your research question and procedures, and then to write an integrated review for your own article or research proposal. Although you can find literature reviews that consist simply of assessments of one published article after another—in other words, that never get beyond stage one in the review process—your understanding of the literature and the quality of your own work will be much improved if you make the effort to write an integrated review.

Exhibit 2.2   The Links between Theory and Data

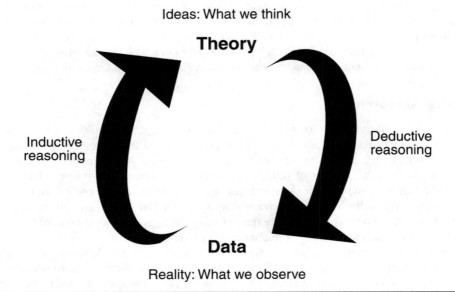

Ideas: What we think

Theory

Inductive
reasoning

Deductive
reasoning

Data

Reality: What we observe

SOCIAL WORK RESEARCH STRATEGIES

When we conduct social work research, we are attempting to connect theory with empirical data—the evidence we obtain from the social world. Researchers may make this connection by starting with a social theory and then testing some of its implications with data. This is the process of deductive research; it is most often the strategy used in quantitative methods. Alternatively, researchers may develop a connection between social theory and data by first collecting the data and then developing a theory that explains patterns in the data (see Exhibit 2.2). This inductive research process is more often the strategy used in qualitative methods. As you'll see, a research project can draw on both deductive and inductive strategies.

The Role of Social Theory

We have already pointed out that theory can be a source of research questions and that it plays an important role in literature reviews. What deserves more attention at this point is the larger role of theory in social work practice and in research. Because they work in an applied profession, social work practitioners and researchers often draw from theories developed in other academic disciplines, such as sociology, psychology, economics, or political science. A **theory** helps us make sense of many interrelated phenomena and predict behavior or attitudes that are likely to occur when certain conditions are met. Theories help us understand how social problems emerge; they guide us in the design of interventions to help individuals, families, groups, or communities; they can be used to explain relationships within organizations as well as between organizations; they are often used to design social policy. Theory helps social work researchers to know what to look for in a study and to specify the implications of their findings for other research. Building, evaluating, and testing theory is, therefore, one of the most important objectives of social work research.

Theory A logically interrelated set of propositions about empirical reality. Examples of social theories include symbolic interactionism, learning theory, conflict theory, resource dependency, and stress theory.

Many social work researchers are engaged in testing and building practice theory. There is no "one theory" of social work practice per se, as different models of social work practice draw from different broader theories often rooted in other disciplines. Social work researchers often test particular theories with individual cases or groups of cases or on different kinds of problems.

For example, William Bradshaw (1997) evaluated an intervention based on cognitive-behavioral theory that was designed to improve the psychological functioning of mentally ill individuals while at the same time reducing their symptoms and frequency of hospitalization. He noted that "cognitive-behavioral treatments had been applied to a wide range of populations and problems" (p. 419), but not to those suffering with schizophrenia. As described by Payne (1997), cognitive-behavioral therapy is based on:

- *Behavior theory,* which suggests that behavior is learned through conditioning. Behavior is something that one does in response to a stimulus such as a person or a situation. Conditioning occurs when a behavior becomes linked to a particular stimulus.
- *Cognition theory*, which "argues that behavior is affected by perception or interpretation of the environment during the process of learning" (Payne, 1997, p. 115). Therefore, if the response to a stimulus is an inappropriate behavior, the response was due to misperceptions or misinterpretations.

Based on these two theories, Bradshaw taught clients stress management skills and social skills while at the same time, clients learned techniques to replace negative thoughts.

Both of these theories have their roots in broader theories. Behavior theory reflects the assumptions of learning theory, which holds that we learn most behavior through the consequences of engaging in a particular behavior. Cognitive theory and its relation to behavior are rooted in social learning theory, which assumes that people's perceptions about what they do or experience explains behavior (Payne, 1997).

Some social work researchers use theory to examine the relationship between different phenomena. For example, stress theory suggests (among other things) that stressors in one's life can lead to poor psychological outcomes, but this depends on how the stressful event is perceived and the coping behaviors available to deal with the stressful event. This theory led Sands and Goldberg-Glen (2000) to ask whether the availability of social supports (a type of coping mechanism) was associated with different levels of distress. They thought that people with social supports would experience less distress than people without social supports. Support for such a finding would suggest practical applications when working with people who have experienced a stressful event.

The diversity of topics associated with social work research is great, and it is not limited to research that involves working directly with individuals, groups, or communities. Some researchers are interested in organizational behavior, both how organizations operate internally and how they relate to other organizations in their environment. For example, Wernet and Austin (1991) used the theory of resource dependency to explain how organizations adapt to changes in their environment.

Other researchers are interested in both the development and critique of social policies and will use different theories to test and explain policy outcomes. The Economic Opportunity Act, passed in 1965 to create the War on Poverty programs, was based on several different theories about the causes of poverty, including power theory and human capital theory. The program was based on research suggesting that poor people have less power to influence decision making (power theory) and often lack adequate education and skills to become employed, given the needs of the marketplace (human capital theory); therefore, the Act required that programs reflect "maximum community participation," leaving decision making to community members, and other War on Poverty programs included job training and early education to enhance individual skills or human capital.

Most social work research is guided by some theory, although the theory may be only partially developed in a particular study or may even be unrecognized by the researcher. When researchers are involved in conducting a research project or engrossed in writing a research report, they may easily lose sight of the larger picture. It is easy to focus on accumulating or clarifying particular findings rather than considering how the study's findings fit into a more general understanding of the social world.

Up to now, we have described the importance of theory in social work research. A competing view, expressed eloquently by Bruce Thyer (2001), suggests that social work researchers should not impose theory when engaged in studies of the effectiveness of interventions and programs in social service agencies. He does not discount the importance of theory but suggests that we can learn from evaluation research studies not driven by a theoretical perspective.

As you can see, social theories do not provide the answers to the questions we pose as topics for research. Instead, social theories suggest the areas on which we should focus and the propositions that we should consider for a test.

The Deductive/Inductive Cycle

The process of conducting research using a deductive research strategy involves moving from theory to data and then back to theory. This process can be characterized with a **research circle** (Exhibit 2.3).

Deductive Research

As Exhibit 2.3 shows, in **deductive research,** a specific expectation is deduced from a general theoretical premise and then tested with data that have been collected for this purpose. A **hypothesis** is a specific expectation deduced from the more general theory. Researchers actually test a hypothesis, not the complete theory itself. A hypothesis proposes a relationship between two or more **variables**—characteristics or properties that can vary. Variation in one variable is proposed to predict, influence, or cause variation in the other variable. The

Exhibit 2.3   The Research Circle

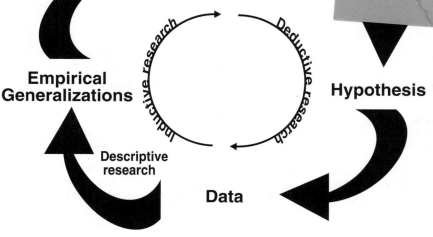

proposed influence is the **independent variable;** its effect or consequence is the **dependent variable.** After the researchers formulate one or more hypotheses and develop research procedures, they collect data with which to test the hypothesis.

Hypothesis   A tentative statement about empirical reality, involving a relationship between two or more variables.

Example of a hypothesis   The higher the poverty rate in a community, the higher the percentage of community residents who are homeless.

Variable   A characteristic or property that can vary (take on different values or attributes).

Example of a variable   The number of depressive symptoms.

Independent variable   A variable that is hypothesized to cause, or lead to, variation in another variable.

Example of an independent variable   Poverty rate.

Dependent variable   A variable that is hypothesized to vary depending on or under the influence of another variable.

Example of a dependent variable   Percentage of community residents who are homeless.

Exhibit 2.4   Examples of Hypotheses

Original Hypothesis	Independent Variable	Dependent Variable	IF-THEN Hypothesis	Direction of Association
1. As the number of stressors increases, the number of depressive symptoms increases.	Number of Stressors	Depressive symptoms	IF the number of stressor is higher, THEN the number of depressive symptoms is higher.	Positive
2. As social support increases, caregiver stress decreases.	Social support level	Caregiver stress	IF social support is higher, THEN caregiver stress is less.	Negative
3. As years of education decrease, income decreases.	Years of Education	Income	If years of education decrease, THEN income decreases.	Positive
4. Property crime is higher in urban areas than in suburban or rural areas.	Urbanization	Rate of property crimes	IF areas are urban, THEN property crime is higher compared to crime in suburban or rural areas.	NA
5. Depressive symptoms are higher for adolescents and older adults than for persons 20 to 65.	Age of person	Depressive symptoms	IF people are age 13 to 19 or 65 or older, THEN the number of depressive symptoms is higher compared to people 20 to 65.	Curvelinear

Hypotheses can be worded in several different ways, and identifying the independent and dependent variables is sometimes difficult. When in doubt, try to rephrase the hypothesis as an "if-then" statement: "*If* the independent variable increases (or decreases), *then* the dependent variable increases (or decreases)." Exhibit 2.4 presents several hypotheses with their independent and dependent variables and their "if-then" equivalents.

Exhibit 2.4 demonstrates another feature of hypotheses: **direction of association.** When researchers hypothesize that one variable increases as the other variable increases, the direction of association is positive (Hypothesis 1); when one variable decreases as the other variable decreases, the direction of association is also positive (Hypothesis 3). But when one variable increases as the other decreases, or vice versa, the direction of association is negative, or inverse (Hypothesis 2). Hypothesis 4 is a special case in which the independent variable is categorical: It cannot be said to increase or decrease. In this case, the concept of direction of association does not apply, and the hypothesis simply states that one category of the independent variable is associated with higher values on the dependent variable. Some hypotheses, such as Hypothesis 5, are not linear but rather curvilinear, meaning that the relationship does not reflect a straight line but a curve of some sort. Hypothesis 5 suggests that the percentage of people who are depressed is highest among teenagers and older adults while lower for people between the ages of 20 and 65.

Both explanation and evaluation studies are types of deductive research. The original Minneapolis Domestic Violence Experiment was an evaluation study because Sherman and Berk (1984) sought to explain what sort of response by the authorities might keep a spouse abuser from repeating the offense. The researchers deduced from deterrence theory the expectation that arrest would deter domestic violence. They then collected data to test this expectation.

In both explanatory and evaluative research, the statement of expectations for the findings and the design of the research to test these expectations strengthen the confidence we can place in the test. Deductive researchers "show their hand" or state their expectations in advance and then design a fair test of those expectations. Then "the chips fall where they may"—in other words, researchers accept the resulting data as a more or less objective picture of reality.

Domestic Violence and the Research Circle

The Sherman and Berk (1984) study of domestic violence is a good example of how the research circle works. In an attempt to determine ways to prevent the recurrence of spouse abuse, the researchers repeatedly linked theory and data, developing both hypotheses and empirical generalizations.

The first phase of Sherman and Berk's (1984) study was designed to test a hypothesis. According to deterrence theory, punishment will reduce recidivism, or the propensity to commit further crimes. From this theory, Sherman and Berk deduced a specific hypothesis: Arrest for spouse abuse reduces the risk of repeat offenses. In this hypothesis, arrest is the independent variable, and the risk of repeat offenses is the dependent variable (it is hypothesized to depend on arrest).

Of course, in another study arrest might be the dependent variable in relation to some other independent variable. For example, in the hypothesis, the greater the rate of layoffs in a community, the higher the frequency of arrest, the dependent variable is frequency of arrest. Only within the context of a hypothesis, or a relationship between variables, does it make sense to refer to one variable as dependent and the other as independent.

Sherman and Berk tested their hypothesis by setting up an experiment in which the police responded to complaints of spouse abuse in one of three ways designated by the researchers: arresting the offender, separating the spouses without making an arrest, or simply warning the offender. When the researchers examined their data (police records for the people in their experiment), they found that of those arrested for assaulting their spouse, only 13% repeated the offense, compared to a 26% recidivism rate for those who were separated from their spouse by the police without any arrest. This pattern in the data, or **empirical generalization,** was consistent with the hypothesis that the researchers deduced from deterrence theory. The theory thus received support from the experiment (see Exhibit 2.5).

Exhibit 2.5   The Research Circle: Minneapolis Domestic Violence Experiment

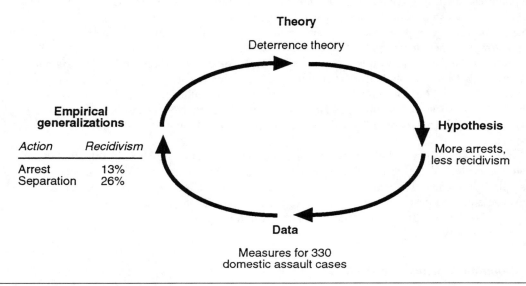

Source: Data from Sherman & Berk, 1984:267.

Because of their doubts about the generalizability of their results, Sherman, Berk, and new collaborators began to journey around the research circle again, with funding from the National Institute of Justice for **replication** (repetition) of the experiment in six more cities. These replications used the same basic research approach but with some improvements. The random assignment process was tightened up in most of the cities so that police officers would be less likely to replace the assigned treatment with a treatment of their own choice. In addition, data were collected about repeat violence against other victims as well as against the original complainant. Some of the replications also examined different aspects of the arrest process to see whether professional counseling helped and whether the length of time spent in jail after arrest mattered at all.

By the time results were reported from five of the cities in the new study, a problem was apparent. In three of the cities—Omaha, Nebraska; Charlotte, North Carolina; and Milwaukee, Wisconsin—researchers were finding long-term increases in domestic violence incidents among arrestees. But in two—Colorado Springs, Colorado, and Dade County, Florida—the predicted deterrent effects seemed to be occurring (Sherman et al., 1992).

Sherman and his colleagues had now traversed the research circle twice in an attempt to answer the original research question, first in Minneapolis and then in six other cities. But rather than leading to more confidence in deterrence theory, the research results were calling it into question. Deterrence theory now seemed inadequate to explain empirical reality, at least as the researchers had measured this reality. So the researchers began to reanalyze the follow-up data from several cities to try to explain the discrepant results, thereby starting around the research circle once again (Berk, Campbell, Klap, & Western, 1992; Pate & Hamilton, 1992; Sherman et al., 1992).

Inductive Research

In contrast to deductive research, **inductive research** begins with specific data, which are then used to develop (induce) a general explanation (a theory) to account for the data. One way to think of this process is in terms of the research circle: Rather than starting at the top of the circle with a theory, the researcher starts at the bottom of the circle with data and then develops the theory. Researchers most committed to an inductive approach even put off formulating a research question until after they begin to collect data—the idea is to let the question emerge from the situation itself (Brewer & Hunter, 1989, pp. 54–58).

Research can be designed from the start using an inductive approach, like the exploratory study about what it was like to be homeless described in Chapter 1 (Snow & Anderson, 1987). Inductive reasoning also enters into deductive research when we find unexpected patterns in the data we have collected for testing a hypothesis. We call these patterns **serendipitous findings** or **anomalous findings.** Whether we begin by doing inductive research or add an inductive element later, the result of the inductive process can be new insights and provocative questions. But the adequacy of an explanation formulated after the fact is necessarily less certain than an explanation presented prior to the collection of data. Every phenomenon can always be explained in some way. Inductive explanations are thus more trustworthy if they are tested subsequently with deductive research.

The very nature of the research circle suggests that some research studies will include strategies to do both inductive and deductive research. For example, a study (Garland, Rogers, & Yancey, 2001) of collaboration between faith-based organizations and secular organizations included two phases: an inductive research phase followed by a deductive research phase. For the inductive research, the research team conducted in-depth interviews with different stakeholders at 16 organizations to learn about the meaning and nature of the collaborative process and to identify potential relationships between and among ideas and concepts. In the second phase, the researchers developed a close-ended survey to be sent to a national sample of faith-based organizations. Using this instrument, they tested the relationships that were identified in the inductive phase of the research.

An Inductive Approach to Explaining Domestic Violence

The domestic violence research took an inductive turn when Sherman and his colleagues began trying to make sense of the differing patterns in the data collected in the different cities. Could systematic differences in the samples or in the implementation of arrest policies explain the differing outcomes? Or was the problem an inadequacy in the theoretical basis of their research? Was deterrence theory really the best way to explain the patterns in the data they were collecting?

Sherman and his colleagues found that individuals who were married and employed were deterred from repeat offenses by arrest, but individuals who were unmarried and unemployed were actually more likely to commit repeat offenses if they were arrested. What could explain this empirical pattern? The researchers turned to *control theory,* which predicts that having a "stake in conformity" (resulting from inclusion in social networks at work or in the community) decreases a person's likelihood of committing crimes (Toby, 1957). The implication is that people who are employed and married are more likely to be deterred by the threat of arrest than those without such stakes in conformity. And this is indeed what the data revealed.

Exhibit 2.6   The Research Spiral: Domestic Violence Experiment

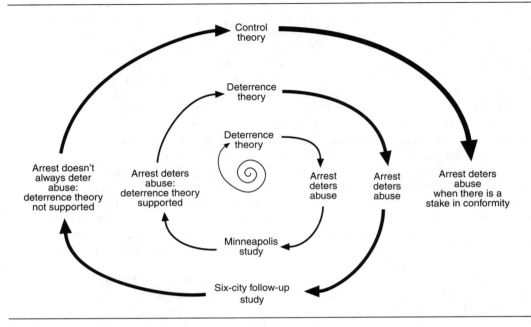

Now the researchers had traversed the research circle almost three times, a process perhaps better described as a spiral (see Exhibit 2.6). The first two times, the researchers had traversed the research circle in a deductive, hypothesis-testing way. They started with theory and then deduced and tested hypotheses. The third time, they were more inductive: They started with empirical generalizations from the data they had already obtained and then turned to a new theory to account for the unexpected patterns in the data. At this point, they believed that deterrence theory made correct predictions, given certain conditions, and that another theory, control theory, might specify what these conditions were.

This last inductive step in their research made for a more complex but also conceptually richer picture of the impact of arrest on domestic violence. The researchers seemed to have come closer to understanding how to inhibit domestic violence. But they cautioned us that their initial question—the research problem—was still not completely answered. Employment status and marital status do not solely measure the strength of social attachments; they also are related to how much people earn and the social standing of victims in court. So maybe social ties are not really what makes arrest an effective deterrent to domestic violence. The real deterrent may be cost-benefit calculations ("If I have a higher income, jail is more costly to me") or perceptions about the actions of authorities ("If I am a married woman, judges will treat my complaint more seriously"). Additional research was needed (Berk et al., 1992).

A Qualitative Exploration of the Response to Domestic Violence

Qualitative research is often exploratory and, hence, inductive: The researchers begin by observing social interaction or interviewing social actors in depth and then developing an explanation for what has been found. The researchers often ask questions like: What is going on here? How do people interpret these experiences? or Why do people do what they do? Rather than testing a hypothesis, the researchers are trying to make sense of some social phenomenon. Lauren Bennett, Lisa Goodman, and Mary Ann Dutton (1999) used this approach to investigate one of the problems that emerge when police arrest domestic batterers: The victims often decide not to press charges. Bennett et al. did not set out to test hypotheses with qualitative interviews (there was another, hypothesis-testing component in their research), but they sought, inductively, to "add the voice of the victim to the discussion" and present "themes that emerged from [the] interviews" (p. 762).

Research assistants interviewed 49 victims of domestic violence in one court; Lauren Bennett also worked in the same court as a victim advocate. The researchers were able to cull from their qualitative data four reasons why victims became reluctant to press charges. Some were confused by the court procedures, others were frustrated by the delay, some were paralyzed by fear of retribution, and others did not want to send the batterer to jail.

Explanations developed inductively from qualitative research can feel authentic because we have heard what people have to say "in their own words," and we have tried to see the social world "as they see it." One victim interviewed by Bennett (Bennett et al., 1999, pp. 768–769) felt that she "was doing time instead of the defendant"; another expressed her fear by saying that she would like "to keep him out of jail if that's what it takes to keep my kids safe." Explanations derived from qualitative research will often be richer and more finely textured than the explanations resulting from quantitative research, but they are likely to be based on fewer cases from a limited area. We cannot assume that the people studied in this setting are like others or that other researchers would develop explanations similar to ours to make sense of what was observed or heard. Because we do not initially set up a test of a hypothesis according to some specific rules, another researcher cannot come along and conduct just the same test.

Descriptive Research

You have learned in Chapter 1 that some social work research is purely descriptive. Such research does not involve connecting theory and data, but it is still part of the research circle: It begins with data and proceeds only to the stage of making empirical generalizations based on those data (refer to Exhibit 2.3).

Valid description is important in its own right—in fact, it is a necessary component of all investigations. Much important research for the government and public and private organizations is primarily descriptive: How many poor people live in this community? Is the health of the elderly improving? Where do the uninsured go to obtain medical treatment? Simply put, good description of data is the cornerstone of the scientific research process and an essential component for understanding the social world.

Good descriptive research can also stimulate more ambitious deductive and inductive research. The Minneapolis Domestic Violence Experiment was motivated in part by a growing body of descriptive research indicating that spouse abuse is very common: 572,000 cases of women victimized by a violent partner are reported each year; 1.5 million women (and 500,000 men) require medical attention each year due to a domestic assault (Buzawa & Buzawa, 1996, pp. 1–3).

PHILOSOPHIES GUIDING SOCIAL WORK RESEARCH

What influences the choice of a research strategy? The motive for conducting research is critical: An explanatory or evaluative motive implies deductive, hypothesis-testing research, whereas an exploratory motive implies an inductive research strategy. Of course, a descriptive motive means choosing a descriptive research strategy. The methods that a researcher prefers are also important: Deductive research usually relies on quantitative methods, whereas qualitative methods are used primarily in inductive research (descriptive research may be either quantitative or qualitative). One or the other of these methods may simply be most feasible for a particular investigation.

A researcher's philosophical perspective on reality and on the appropriate role of the researcher will also shape methodological preferences. Researchers who hold to a philosophy of **positivism** believe that there is an objective reality that exists apart from the perceptions of those who observe it; the goal of science is to better understand this reality.

> Whatever nature "really" is, we assume that it presents itself in precisely the same way to the same human observer standing at different points in time and space. . . . We assume that it also presents itself in precisely the same way across different human observers standing at the same point in time and space. (Wallace, 1983, p. 461)

Positivism   The belief, shared by most scientists, that there is a reality that exists quite apart from our own perception of it, although our knowledge of this reality may never be complete.

This philosophy lies behind the research circle, with its assumption that we can test theoretically based predictions with data collected from the real, objective world. It is the philosophy traditionally associated with science (Weber, 1949, p. 72), with the expectation that there are universal laws of human behavior, and with the belief that scientists must be objective and unbiased to see reality clearly. A well-designed test of a hypothesis derived from theory—like the test of the prediction that arrest will reduce domestic violence, which was derived from deterrence theory—can move us closer to understanding actual social processes.

Postpositivism is a philosophy of reality that is closely related to positivism. Postpositivists believe that there is an external, objective reality, but they are sensitive to the complexity of this reality and the limitations of the researchers who study it—in particular, for social workers, the biases they bring to the study of social beings like themselves (Guba & Lincoln, 1994, pp. 109–111). As a result, postpositivists think researchers can never be sure that their methods allow them to perceive objective reality; the goal of science can only be to achieve **intersubjective agreement** among scientists about the nature of reality (Wallace, 1983, p. 461). For example, postpositivists may worry that researchers' predispositions may bias them in favor of deterrence theory. Therefore, they will remain somewhat skeptical of results that support predictions based on deterrence until a number of researchers feel that they have found supportive evidence. The postpositivist retains much more confidence in the ability of the community of social researchers to develop an unbiased account of reality than in the ability of any individual social scientist to do so (Campbell & Russo, 1999, p. 144).

Postpositivism   The belief that there is an empirical reality, but that our understanding of it is limited by its complexity and by the biases and other limitations of researchers.

Intersubjective agreement   An agreement by different observers on what is happening in the natural or social world.

Qualitative research is often guided by a very different philosophy: **interpretivism**. Interpretive social scientists believe that social reality is socially constructed and that the goal of social scientists is to understand the meanings people give to reality, not to determine how reality works apart from these interpretations. This philosophy maintains that there is no concrete, objective reality that scientific methods help us to understand (Lynch & Bogen, 1997); instead, interpretivists believe that scientists construct an image of reality based on their own preferences and prejudices and their interactions with others. From this standpoint, the goal of validity becomes meaningless: "Truth is a matter of the best-informed and most sophisticated construction on which there is consensus at a given time" (Schwandt, 1994, p. 128).

Searching for universally applicable social laws can distract from learning what people know and how they understand their lives. The interpretive social researcher examines meanings that have been socially constructed. . . . There is not one reality out there to be measured; objects and events are understood by different people differently, and those perceptions are the reality—or realities—that social science should focus on. (Rubin & Rubin, 1995, p. 35)

Interpretivism   The belief that reality is socially constructed and that the goal of social scientists is to understand what meanings people give to that reality.

The **constructivist paradigm** extends interpretivist methodology by emphasizing the importance of exploring how different stakeholders in a social setting construct their beliefs (Guba & Lincoln, 1989, pp. 44–45). It gives particular attention to the different goals of researchers and other participants in a research setting and seeks to develop a consensus among participants about how to understand the focus of inquiry. The constructivist research report will highlight different views of the social program or other issue and explain how a consensus can be reached among participants.

Constructivist paradigm   A perspective that emphasizes how different stakeholders in social settings construct their beliefs.

Some researchers with an interpretivist or constructivist orientation reject explicitly the traditional positivist distinction between facts and values (Sjoberg & Nett, 1968). Robert Bellah and his *Habits of the Heart* coauthors (1985) have instead proposed a model of "social science as public philosophy." In this model, social work researchers focus explicit attention on achieving a more just society.

William Foote Whyte (1991) proposed a more activist approach to research called **participatory action research**. This approach encourages social work researchers to get "out of the academic rut" and bring values into the research process (Whyte, 1991, p. 285). Rosemary Sarri and Catherine Sarri (1992) suggest that participatory action research "seeks to reduce the distinction between the researcher and the researched by incorporating the latter in a collaborative effort of knowledge creation that will lead to community betterment and empowerment" (p. 100).

In participatory action research, the researcher involves as active participants members of the setting or community that is studied. Steven Hick (1997) suggests that "active involvement" often takes on different meanings and that participatory action research differs on two dimensions. One dimension is the extent to which participants are actually involved in research activities such as designing questions, gathering information, analyzing data, and writing the report. The second dimension reflects how much direct control participants have over decisions about the research process such as the overarching research goals, developing recommendations, and disseminating and using the findings.

Hidenori Yamatani, Aaron Mann, and Patricia Wright (2000) used principles of participatory action research to conduct a needs assessment focused on unemployment in a working class neighborhood in Pittsburgh. To conduct this study, the social work researchers knew they had to directly involve the community or their efforts would be unsuccessful. They chose to become research advisers assisting community members, who, in turn, defined the overall parameters of the study, designed the questionnaires, collected the data, coded the data, reviewed the findings to develop the report's recommendations, and reviewed and approved the written report. The researchers provided their advice on different steps in the research process, trained community members in various research-related tasks, analyzed the data, and wrote the report. The outcome was a report (and its recommendations) that had both community and organizational support.

Which philosophy makes the most sense to you? Do you agree with positivists and post-positivists that scientific methods can help us understand the social world as it is, not just as we would like to think it is? Does the interpretivist or constructivist focus on meanings sound like a good idea? What about participatory action research, integrating research with empowerment strategies? Whatever your answers to these questions, you would probably agree that developing a valid understanding of the social world is not an easy task. People are influenced by many other people and numerous events throughout their lives; we don't fully understand these influences until we know what meanings people attach to them; and we can't directly perceive these meanings.

There is no easy answer to which is the correct philosophy. There has been an ongoing debate among social work researchers and educators about which is the appropriate philosophical approach. There are those who believe that social work research is limited by the strict requirements of the positivist approach (Morris, 1991). Others suggest that the positivist approach is the most reliable way to gather accurate information (Thyer, 1993). We argue that there is value to both of these approaches.

SCIENTIFIC GUIDELINES FOR SOCIAL WORK RESEARCH

In Chapter 1, we described the variety of errors that can occur as people try to understand their social world. These errors included illogical reasoning, inaccurate or selective observations, overgeneralizations, and resistance to change. In this chapter, we have suggested that often social work researchers seek answers to questions they are interested in and they believe to be important. By adhering to some basic guidelines about how to conduct research, social work researchers can avoid mistakes about understanding the social world and prevent their investigations from being nothing more than a reflection of their own beliefs (although qualitative researchers interpret some of the guidelines differently from quantitative researchers):

1. *Test ideas against empirical reality without becoming too personally invested in a particular outcome.* This guideline requires a commitment to testing, as opposed to reacting to events as they happen, being swayed by the popularity or status of others, or looking for what we want to see (Kincaid, 1996, pp. 51–54). When testing ideas, researchers have to recognize that what they find from their studies may not confirm what they had predicted the studies would find. Of course, qualitative researchers who question the utility of the concept of empirical reality don't follow this guideline literally, but they do try to be sensitive to the perspectives that shape how researchers and their subjects perceive reality.

2. *Plan and carry out investigations systematically.* Social work researchers have little hope of conducting a careful test of their ideas if they do not think through in advance how they should go about the test and then proceed accordingly. But a systematic approach is not always easy. For example, Sherman and Berk (1984) needed to ensure that spouse abusers were assigned to be arrested or not on a random basis rather than on the basis of the police officers' personal preferences. They devised a systematic procedure using randomly sequenced report sheets in different colors but then found that police officers sometimes deviated from this procedure due to their feelings about particular cases. Subsequently, in some replications of the study, the researchers ensured compliance with their research procedures by requiring police officers to call in to a central number to receive the experimentally determined treatment. Qualitative researchers may not be this systematic, but they remain careful in their use of particular methods and must maintain systematic procedures for recording and analyzing data.

3. *Document all procedures and disclose them publicly.* Social work researchers who disclose the methods on which their conclusions rest allow others to evaluate for themselves the likely soundness of these conclusions. Such disclosure is a key feature of science. The community of researchers, reacting to each others' work, provides the best guarantee against purely self-interested conclusions (Kincaid, 1996). Furthermore, by documenting procedures, other researchers will know how the study was completed and can replicate the study. Again, Sherman and Berk (1984) provide a compelling example. After describing the formal research plan in their research report, they discuss the apparent "slippage" from this plan when some police officers avoided implementing the random assignment procedure. Social work researchers using qualitative methods often include in their notes some comments about how they went about interviewing or observing.

4. *Clarify assumptions.* No investigation is complete unto itself; whatever the researcher's method, the research rests on some background assumptions. Research to determine whether arrest has a deterrent effect assumes that potential law violators think rationally and that they calculate potential costs and benefits prior to committing crimes. When a researcher conducts

an election poll, the assumption is that people actually vote for the candidate they say they will vote for. By definition, research assumptions are not tested, so we do not know for sure whether they are correct. By taking the time to think about and disclose their assumptions, researchers provide important information for those who seek to evaluate the validity of research conclusions. When using qualitative methods, researchers include in their notes comments about what they are thinking and how they are reacting when they interview or observe.

5. *Specify the meaning of all terms.* Words often have multiple or unclear meanings. *Alienation, depression, strengths, information and referral, welfare,* and so on can mean different things to different people. Thus, the terms used in scientific research must be defined explicitly and used consistently. For example, Sherman and Berk (1984) identified their focus as misdemeanor domestic assault, not just "wife beating." They specified that their work concerned those cases of spouse assault in which severe injury was not involved and both partners were present when police arrived. Of course, those using qualitative methods also give special attention to the meanings of the terms people use. Rather than using predetermined definitions of terms, the meanings of terms emerge from the voices of the respondents.

6. *Maintain a skeptical stance toward current knowledge.* Scientists may feel confident about interpretations of the social or natural world that have been supported by repeated investigations, but the results of any particular investigation must be examined critically. A general skepticism about current knowledge stimulates researchers to improve the validity of current research results and expand the frontier of knowledge. For example, in response to questions raised about the Sherman and Berk study, Lawrence Sherman and Ellen Cohn (1989) discussed 13 problems in the Minneapolis Domestic Violence Experiment in a published critique, weighing carefully the extent to which these problems might have affected its validity. This critique could then stimulate additional research designed to address the problematic aspects of the research. Often, even in their own studies, researchers will conclude with a discussion of the limitations of their study designs. Interpretivist researchers see this issue somewhat differently. Different interpretations are viewed as each contributing to an overall understanding of how people view their situation.

7. *Replicate research and build social theory.* No one study is definitive by itself. We can't fully understand it apart from the larger body of knowledge to which it is related, and we can't place much confidence in it until it has been replicated. Theories organize the knowledge accumulated by numerous investigations into a coherent whole and serve as a guide to future inquiries. Different models of social work practice must be tested by repeated applications of a treatment modality with different subjects, in different settings, and with different types of concerns.

8. *Search for regularities or patterns.* Positivist and postpositivist scientists assume that the natural world has some underlying order of relationships, so that unique events and individuals can be understood at least in part in terms of general principles (Grinnell, 1992, pp. 27–29). Individuals are not unimportant to social scientists; Sherman (1992, pp. 162–164), for example, described the abuse histories of two men to provide greater insight into why arrest could have different effects for different people. But the goal of elaborating individual

cases is to understand social patterns that characterize many individuals. Interpretivists are more oriented to the particulars of situations they have studied and to providing "thick" descriptions of them.

These general guidelines are ideals for much social work research, but no particular investigation is going to follow every guideline exactly. Real investigations by social work researchers do not always include much attention to theory, specific definitions of all terms, and so forth. Researchers guided by an interpretivist philosophy may even reject some of the guidelines. But it behooves any social researcher to study these guidelines and to consider the consequences of not following any with which they do not agree.

SOCIAL WORK RESEARCH AND ETHICAL GUIDELINES

Our foundation for social work research is not complete until it includes a sensitivity to research ethics. Every scientific investigation, whether in the natural or social sciences, has an ethical dimension to it. First and foremost, the scientific concern with validity requires that scientists be honest and reveal their methods. (How can we otherwise determine if the requirement of honesty has been met?) Researchers also have to consider the uses to which their findings will be put. Often, social work research deals with topics that challenge social conditions or social policy, which places an added burden on ensuring that the research is done well. Other research may be conducted with vulnerable populations such as the elderly, children, or mentally ill, who may or may not be able to consent to research. Furthermore, some social work research includes historically oppressed populations such as people of color, women, or sexual minorities who have reasons to distrust research efforts despite the assurances of researchers. As you can see, social work researchers often confront some unique ethical challenges.

Honesty and Openness

Research distorted by political or personal pressures to find particular outcomes or to achieve the most marketable results is unlikely to be carried out in an honest and open fashion, but distinguishing between unintentional error and deliberate fraud can be very difficult. For example, a 1963 report of the U.S. Senate's Subcommittee on Problems of the Aged and Aging concluded that a study of elderly people's health needs, publicized by the American Medical Association, was a "supposedly objective, scientific, academic study" but really a "pseudo-scientific half-effort" (Cain, 1967, pp. 78–79). The researchers were accused of having an upper-class bias in the design of their sample and of using some questions that underestimated elders' health needs. Yet, the researchers were convinced they had adhered to scientific guidelines.

It is not clear in this case, nor in many others, whether the research was designed to favor particular findings or to adapt to unavoidable constraints. Error, committed without any intent to defraud, is inevitable. Social scientists who do not do their best to minimize error skirt the boundaries of fraud, but the discovery of errors in a study should not in itself be taken as an indication of dishonesty.

Openness about research procedures and results goes hand in hand with honesty in research design. Openness is also essential if researchers are to learn from the work of others.

In spite of this need for openness, some researchers may hesitate to disclose their procedures or results to prevent others from building on their ideas and taking some of the credit. You may have heard of the long legal battle between a U.S. researcher and a French researcher about how credit for discovering the AIDS virus should be allocated. Although such public disputes are unusual, concerns with priority of discovery are common. Scientists are like other people in their desire to be first. Enforcing standards of honesty and encouraging openness about research is the best solution for these problems.

The Uses of Science

Scientists must also consider the uses to which their research is put. Although many scientists believe that personal values should be left outside the laboratory, some feel that it is proper for scientists, in their role as citizens, to attempt to influence the way their research is used. Social scientists who identify with a more critical tradition question the possibility of setting our values aside and instead urge researchers to use research to achieve goals that they believe are worthy.

Sometimes it is difficult to separate research and advocacy, given the nature of many of the kinds of questions social work researchers pursue. Some social work research is conducted to monitor the impacts of social legislation: for example, research to monitor changes in health care policy or the effects of welfare reform. The findings from such studies are likely to be used to help shape changes in policy or to reinforce current policy. Whether the researchers enter into the research with an opinion, the methods they use should be objective, and their reporting of the data should be accurate and honest. This will lend credibility to the conclusions reported by the researcher.

Social work researchers who conduct research on behalf of organizations and agencies may face additional difficulties when the organization, not the researcher, controls the final report and the publicity it receives. If organizational leaders decide that particular research results are unwelcome, the researcher's desire to have findings used appropriately and reported fully can conflict with contractual obligations. Researchers can often anticipate such dilemmas in advance and resolve them when the contract for research is negotiated— or simply decline a particular research opportunity altogether. But often such problems come up only after a report has been drafted, or they are ignored by a researcher who needs to have a job or to maintain particular personal relationships. These possibilities cannot be avoided entirely, but because of them, it is always important to acknowledge the source of research funding in reports and to consider carefully the sources of funding for research reports written by others.

Research on People

In physics or chemistry, research subjects (objects and substances) may be treated to extreme conditions and then discarded when they are no longer useful. However, social work researchers must concern themselves with the way their human subjects are treated in the course of research. This treatment may involve comparisons of different interventions in social service agencies, different tests to determine effective social policy, sensitive questions in survey research, observations in field studies, or analyses of personal data. Here, we will review briefly current ethical standards for the treatment of human subjects and identify some of the issues in their application. In the later chapters on data collection, we will examine the specific ethical problems that may arise in the course of using particular research methods.

The federal government, professional associations, special university review boards, and ethics committees in other organizations all set standards for the treatment of human subjects. Federal regulations require that every institution that seeks federal funding for biomedical or behavioral research on human subjects have an **institutional review board (IRB)** that reviews research proposals. IRBs at universities and other agencies apply ethics standards that are set by federal regulations but can be expanded or specified by the IRB itself (Sieber, 1992, pp. 5, 10). To promote adequate review of ethical issues, the regulations require that IRBs include members with diverse backgrounds. The Office for Protection from Research Risks in the National Institutes of Health monitors IRBs, with the exception of research involving drugs (the responsibility of the Federal Food and Drug Administration). In addition, the National Institutes of Health began in October 2000 to require that all researchers (and key study investigators) who seek funding complete an educational or training program on the protection of human research participants.

The National Association of Social Workers (NASW), like other professional organizations, has incorporated these standards into its ethical code. **The National Association of Social Workers Code of Ethics** (1999) is reprinted in Appendix G and is posted on the NASW Web site at http://www.naswdc.org/pubs/code/code.asp. The code of ethics incorporates both practice standards and specific evaluation and research standards, some of which flow from federal regulations. Briefly, the code of ethics notes that:

- Social workers engaged in evaluation and research should follow guidelines developed for the protection of evaluation and research participants. They should consult with appropriate IRBs.
- Research should cause no harm to subjects.
- Subjects must give their informed consent to participate in the research, if capable. If not, then assent must be obtained from an appropriate proxy.
- Participation in research should be voluntary, and participants should be informed of their right to withdraw at any time without penalty.
- Researchers should fully disclose their identity. Social workers doing research should avoid conflicts of interest and reveal possible conflicts with potential participants.
- Anonymity or confidentiality must be maintained for individual research participants. Participants should be told about any limits of confidentiality and the methods to be used to ensure confidentiality.
- Findings should be reported accurately; errors later found should be corrected.
- The benefits of a research project should outweigh any foreseeable risks.
- Social workers should take steps to ensure that participants have access to appropriate supportive services. (NASW, 1999)

As simple as these guidelines may seem, they are difficult to interpret in specific cases and harder yet to define in a way agreeable to all social work researchers. For example, how should "no harm to subjects" be interpreted? Does it mean that subjects should not be harmed at all, psychologically as well as physically? That they should feel no anxiety or distress whatever during the study or only after their involvement ends? Should the possibility of any harm, no matter how remote, deter research?

Consider the question of possible harm to the subjects of a well-known prison simulation study (Haney, Banks, & Zimbardo, 1973). The study was designed to investigate the impact of social position on behavior—specifically, the impact of being either a guard or a prisoner in a prison, a "total institution." The researchers selected apparently stable and mature young male volunteers and asked them to sign a contract to work for two weeks as a guard or a prisoner in a simulated prison. Within the first two days after the prisoners were incarcerated by the "guards" in a makeshift basement prison, the prisoners began to be passive and disorganized, while the guards became verbally and physically aggressive. Five "prisoners" were soon released for depression, uncontrollable crying, fits of rage, and, in one case, a psychosomatic rash; on the sixth day, the researchers terminated the experiment. Through discussions in special postexperiment encounter sessions, feelings of stress among the participants who played the role of prisoner seemed to be relieved; follow-up during the next year indicated no lasting negative effects on the participants and some benefits in the form of greater insight.

Would you ban such experiments because of the potential for harm to subjects? Does the fact that the experiment yielded significant insights into the effect of a situation on human behavior—insights that could be used to improve prisons—make any difference (Reynolds, 1979, pp. 133–139)? Do you believe that this benefit outweighed the foreseeable risks?

The requirement of **informed consent** is also more difficult to define than it first appears. To be informed, consent must be given by people who are competent to consent, have consented voluntarily, are fully informed about the research, and have comprehended what they have been told (Reynolds, 1979). Who is competent to give consent? What does *competent* mean? Children cannot legally give consent to participate in research, but they must have the opportunity to give or withhold their *assent* to participate in research to which their legal guardians have consented (Sieber, 1992). Are people with a mental illness competent to give consent, or does the nature of their specific illness preclude their ability to comprehend the nature of the research, their rights as a research participant, and the benefits and costs of participating in the research.

Consent must be given voluntarily without coercion, that is, without forcing people to participate. Coercion need not be explicit; rather, coercion may be subtle and implicit. Where there are differences in power between the researchers and the subjects, implicit coercion may be a problem. Clients in human service agencies may feel that they may be better served by the agency if they agree to participate, or they may worry that by refusing to participate in the research, their services will be altered. To the extent possible, clients must be reassured that there is no penalty or other consequence for refusing to participate in the research. The researcher's actions and body language must help to convey the verbal assurance that consent is voluntary.

Inducements such as money may also affect the voluntary nature of participation. Even small amounts of money may be sufficient to induce people who are low income to participate in research activities that they might otherwise have refused. Inducements should be kept to a level that acknowledges the subject's participation and inconvenience but will not serve to entice people to participate. Payments, if offered, should be given even if the subject terminates participation without fully completing the research.

Fully informed consent may also reduce participation in research and, because signing consent forms prior to participation may change participants' responses, produce biased results (Larson, 1993, p. 114). Experimental researchers whose research design requires some type of subject deception try to get around this problem by withholding some information before the experiment begins but then debriefing subjects at the end. To conduct the study, the researcher must convince an IRB that the risks are minimal and the benefits of carrying out the study are substantial. In the **debriefing,** the researcher explains to the subject what happened in the experiment and why and responds to questions (Sieber, 1992, pp. 39–41). However, even though debriefing can be viewed as a substitute in some cases for securing fully informed consent prior to the experiment, if the debriefed subjects disclose the nature of the experiment to other participants, subsequent results may still be contaminated (Adair, Dushenko, & Lindsay, 1985).

To give informed consent, potential subjects must have sufficient information to weigh the benefits and risks of participation. That is why it is so important to describe as completely as possible the kinds of risks the participant will face. As part of their participation, it is also important to inform subjects that they can withdraw at any time, without penalty.

Well-intentioned researchers may also fail to foresee all the potential problems. In the prison simulation, all the participants signed consent forms, but how could they have been fully informed in advance? The researchers themselves did not realize that the study participants would experience so much stress so quickly, that some prisoners would have to be released for severe negative reactions within the first few days, or that even those who were not severely stressed would soon be begging to be released from the mock prison. If this risk was not foreseeable, was it acceptable for the researchers to presume in advance that the benefits would outweigh the risks?

Maintaining **confidentiality** is another key ethical obligation; a statement should be included in the informed consent agreement about how each subject's privacy will be protected (Sieber, 1992). Procedures such as locking records and creating special identifying codes must be created to minimize the risk of access by unauthorized people. The researcher must also be careful when reporting results to ensure that people cannot be identified from the findings. However, statements about confidentiality should be realistic: Laws allow research records to be subpoenaed and may require reporting child abuse; a researcher may feel compelled to release information if a health- or life-threatening situation arises and participants need to be alerted. The need to report such information should be included in the informed consent process. Also, the standard of confidentiality does not apply to observation in public places and information available in public records.

The potential of withholding a beneficial treatment from some subjects is also cause for ethical concern. Differential outcomes in welfare-to-work experiments mean that some individuals might well have higher earnings both in the short and long run. Experiments comparing treatment methods, such as intensive case management with traditional case management, might mean that some children have less chance of being reunified with their parents. These are not trivial consequences for the participants. The justification for such studies' design, however, is quite persuasive: The researchers don't know prior to the experiment which method would be better.

On the other hand, just because a treatment approach is new does not make it automatically a better approach. That is why it is being tested to begin with—to determine if it is beneficial. The researchers are not withholding a known, successful treatment from some subjects. You will read in many social work intervention studies that rather than withhold a treatment, one set of subjects will likely get the regular intervention rather than no intervention.

The extent to which ethical issues are a problem for researchers and their subjects varies dramatically with type of research design. Survey research, in particular, creates few ethical problems. In fact, researchers from Michigan's Institute for Survey Research interviewed a representative national sample of adults and found that 68% of those who had participated in a survey were somewhat or very interested in participating in another; the more times respondents had been interviewed, the more willing they were to participate again. Presumably, they would have felt differently if they had been treated unethically (Reynolds, 1979, pp. 56–57). On the other hand, some experimental studies in the social sciences that have put people in uncomfortable or embarrassing situations have generated vociferous complaints and years of debate about ethics (Reynolds, 1979; Sjoberg, 1967).

The evaluation of ethical issues in a research project should be based on a realistic assessment of the overall potential for harm and benefit to research subjects rather than an apparent inconsistency between any particular aspect of a research plan and a specific ethical guideline. For example, full disclosure of "what is really going on" in an experimental study is unnecessary if subjects are unlikely to be harmed. Nevertheless, researchers should make every effort to foresee all possible risks and to weigh the possible benefits of the research against these risks. They should consult with individuals with different perspectives to develop a realistic risk/benefit assessment. They should try to maximize the benefits to subjects of the research, as well as minimize the risks (Sieber, 1992, pp. 75–108).

CONCLUSION

Selecting a worthy research question does not guarantee a worthwhile research project. The simplicity of the research circle presented in this chapter belies the complexity of the social research process. In the following chapters, we will focus on particular aspects of that process.

As you encounter these specifics, don't lose sight of the basic guidelines that researchers need to follow to overcome the most common impediments to social work research. Owning a large social science toolkit is no guarantee of making the right decisions about which tools to use and how to use them in the investigation of particular research problems. More important, our answers to research questions will never be complete or entirely certain. Thus, when we complete a research project, we should point out how the research could be extended and evaluate the confidence we have in our conclusions. Recall how the elaboration of knowledge about deterrence of domestic violence required sensitivity to research difficulties, careful weighing of the evidence, and identification of unanswered questions by several research teams.

Ethical issues also should be considered when evaluating research proposals and completed research studies. As the preceding examples show, ethical issues in social work research are no less complex than the other issues that researchers confront. It is inexcusable to jump into research on people without any attention to ethical considerations.

You are now forewarned about, and thus hopefully forearmed against, the difficulties that any scientists, but social scientists in particular, face in their work. We hope that you will return often to this chapter as you read the subsequent chapters, when you criticize the research literature, and when you design your own research projects. To be conscientious, thoughtful, and responsible—this is the mandate of every researcher. If you formulate a feasible research problem, ask the right questions in advance, try to adhere to the research guidelines, and steer clear of the most common difficulties, you will be well along the road to fulfilling this mandate.

KEY TERMS

Anomalous findings
Confidentiality
Constructivist paradigm
Debriefing
Deductive research
Dependent variable
Direction of association
Empirical generalization
Hypothesis
Independent variable
Inductive research
Informed consent
Institutional Review Board (IRB)

Interpretivism
Intersubjective agreement
NASW Code of Ethics
Participatory action research
Positivism
Postpositivism
Research circle
Replication
Serendipitous findings
Social work research question
Theory
Variables

HIGHLIGHTS

- Research questions should be feasible (within the time and resources available), socially important, and scientifically relevant.
- Social work researchers often engage in testing and building practice theory. Often, practice theory is based on broader social theory from other disciplines.
- The type of reasoning in most research can be described as primarily deductive or inductive. Research based on deductive reasoning proceeds from general ideas, deduces specific expectations from these ideas, and then tests the ideas with empirical data. Research based on inductive reasoning begins with specific data and then develops general ideas or theories to explain patterns in the data.
- It may be possible to explain unanticipated research findings after the fact, but such explanations have less credibility than those that have been tested with data collected for the purpose of the study.
- The scientific process can be represented as circular, with a path from theory to hypotheses, to data, and then to empirical generalizations. Research investigations may begin at different points along the research circle and traverse different portions of it. Deductive research begins at the point of theory; inductive research begins with data but ends with theory. Descriptive research begins with data and ends with empirical generalizations.
- Positivism and postpositivism are research philosophies that emphasize the goal of understanding the real world; these philosophies guide most quantitative researchers. Interpretivism is a research philosophy that emphasizes understanding the meaning people attach to their experiences; it guides many qualitative researchers.
- Replications of a study are essential to establish its generalizability in other situations. An ongoing line of research stemming from a particular research question should include a series of studies that, collectively, traverse the research circle multiple times.
- Social work researchers, like all scientists, should structure their research so that their own ideas can be proved wrong, should disclose their methods for others to critique, and should recognize the possibility of error.
- Scientific research should be conducted and reported in an honest and open fashion. Contemporary ethical standards also require that social work research cause no harm to subjects, that participation be voluntary as expressed in informed consent, that researchers fully disclose their identity, that benefits to subjects outweigh any foreseeable risks, and that anonymity or confidentiality be maintained for participants unless it is voluntarily and explicitly waived. These standards are incorporated into the NASW Code of Ethics.

DISCUSSION QUESTIONS

1. What are the steps involved in a comprehensive literature review? What should you look for in journal articles? What cautions should you bear in mind when conducting searches on the Web?

2. Discuss the relationship of social theory to practice theory.

3. Describe the relationship between inductive and deductive research.

4. Describe the debate between positivism and interpretivism. What are the guidelines for these research philosophies and their associated goals? What do you think about each of these philosophies?

5. Discuss the relationship of social work research ethics to the NASW Code of Ethics statements on research. How are they similar? How are they different?

PRACTICE EXERCISES

1. Identify a problem related to social welfare. Develop three questions about the problem, one question that is exploratory, one that is descriptive, and one that is explanatory.

2. Evaluate the questions you developed in Exercise 1 using the criteria for a good social work question.

3. Locate three research articles on a particular social issue such as domestic violence. What is the research question in each article? Rate each question on the three criteria for a good social work research question: feasibility, social importance, and scientific relevance.

4. Evaluate one of the studies you found in Exercise 3 for its adherence to each of the ethical guidelines for research on people. How would you weigh the study's contribution to practice and social policy against its potential risks to human subjects?

WEB EXERCISES

1. Try your hand at developing a hypothesis of your own. Pick a theorist from the wide range of personality theorists at http://www.ship.edu/cgboeree/perscontents.html. Read some of what you find, and think about what behavioral phenomena this theorist focuses on. What hypotheses seem consistent with his or her theorizing? Describe a hypothetical research project to test one of these hypotheses.

2. You've been assigned to write a paper on domestic violence and the law. To start, you would like to find out what the American Bar Association's stance is on the issue. Go to the American Bar Association Commission on Domestic Violence's Web site at http://www.abanet.org/domviol/mrdv/identify.html. What is the American Bar Association's definition of domestic violence? How do they suggest one can identify a person as a victim of domestic violence? What do they identify as "basic warning signs"? Write your answers in a one- to two-page report.

> To assist you in completing the Web exercises, please access the study site at http://www.sagepub.com/prsw where you will find the Web Exercises reproduced and suggested links for online resources.

DEVELOPING A RESEARCH PROPOSAL

Now it's time to start writing the proposal. These next exercises are very critical steps.

1. What is the problem for research? Why is this an important issue for social workers to address? If you have not identified a problem for study, or if you need to evaluate whether your research problem is doable, a few suggestions should help to get the ball rolling and keep it on course:

    a.   Jot down questions that have puzzled you in some area having to do with social issues or social work practice. These may be questions that have come to mind while reading textbooks or research articles or things you might have heard about in the news. Try to identify questions that really interest you.

    b.   Now take stock of your interests, your opportunities, and the work of others. Which of your research questions no longer seem feasible or interesting? What additional research questions come to mind? Pick out a question that is of interest and seems doable.

2. What is known about the problem? Search the literature (and the Web) on the research question you identified. Try to identify recent citations to articles (with abstracts from *Social Work Abstracts* or other indexes). Get the articles and remember to inspect the article bibliographies for additional sources. Write a brief description of each article and Web site you consulted. As you read the literature, try to identify the theories used to explain the problem, the methodological approaches used to study the problem, and the results of the studies. What additions or changes to your thoughts about the research question are suggested by the various articles?

3. How does your proposed study build on the current literature? What will be the specific objective of your study?

4. Write out your research question in one sentence, and elaborate on it in one paragraph. Identify the specific aims or hypotheses that will be addressed by your study. List at least three reasons why it is a good research question for you to investigate.

5. Which standards for the protection of human subjects might pose the most difficulty for researchers on your proposed topic? Explain your answers and suggest appropriate protection procedures for human subjects.

Chapter 3

CONCEPTUALIZATION AND MEASUREMENT

Concepts

Conceptualization in Practice
  Defining Substance Abuse
  Defining Depression
  Defining Poverty
Concepts, Constants, and Variables

Operationalization

Indicators
Scales and Indexes
Treatment as a Variable
Gathering Data
Combining Measurement Operations
Measurement in Qualitative Research

Levels of Measurement

Nominal Level of Measurement
Ordinal Level of Measurement
Interval Level of Measurement
Ratio Level of Measurement
The Case of Dichotomies
Comparison of Levels of Measurement

Measurement Error

Evaluating Measures

Reliability
  Test-Retest Reliability
  Internal Consistency
  Alternate-Forms Reliability
  Interobserver Reliability
  Intraobserver Reliability
Measurement Validity
  Face Validity
  Content Validity
  Criterion Validity
  Construct Validity
Screening and Cut-Off Scores
Ways to Improve Reliability and Validity
  of Existing Measures

**Choosing an Instrument for Research,
  Evaluation, and Practice**

Conclusion

Substance abuse is a social problem of remarkable proportions. Alcohol is involved in about half of all fatal traffic crashes, and more than 1 million arrests are made annually for driving under the influence. Four in ten college students binge-drink (Wechsler, Lee, Kuo, & Lee, 2000), and 70% of college presidents consider binge drinking a problem for their school (Wechsler, Nelson, & Weitzman, 2000). Drinking is a factor in as many as two thirds of on-campus sexual assaults (National Institute of Alcohol Abuse and Alcoholism [NIAA], 1995). All told, the annual costs of prevention and treatment for alcohol and drug abuse exceed $4 billion (Gruenewald, Treno, Taff, & Klitzner, 1997).

Whether your goal is to learn how society works, to deliver useful services, or to design effective social policies, at some point, you will probably need to read the research literature on that topic. If you are reading literature about substance abuse, you will have to answer two questions: What is meant by *substance abuse* in this research? (which concerns conceptualization) and How was substance abuse measured? (which concerns measurement). If you are reading about poverty, you would ask the same two questions. No matter the topic, we cannot make sense of the results of a study until we know how the concepts were defined and measured. Nor are we ready to begin a research project until we have defined our concepts and constructed valid measures of them. Measurement validity is essential to successful research; in fact, without valid measures, it is fruitless to attempt to achieve the other two aspects of validity, causal validity and generalizability.

Measurement is our attempt to describe an object and is crucial to inform the judgments we make. Measurement means we use a set of rules to assign a value to describe a property of an object. Measurement is not essential just for research, but it is essential for carrying out social work practice at any level, whether it is macro practice or micro practice. The psychosocial assessment some of you complete with a client is a form of measurement. As you systematically or informally monitor whether a client is improving or not improving, you must have some basis to make this judgment; you must be able to make some assessment to determine whether change has occurred. The evaluation of a program's outcomes requires that the program's broadly stated goals be translated into something that can be measured. When an agency is held accountable for its activities and the director reports to funders information about the program, units of activity have to be defined and calculated.

In this chapter, we describe the process of measurement, from taking an abstract concept and translating the concept to the point that we can assign some value to represent that concept. First, we address the issue of conceptualization, using substance abuse and related concepts as examples. We then focus on the different operations necessary for operationalization. Next, we discuss the levels of measurement reflected in different measures. In the next section, we will discuss different methods to assess the quality of measures, specifically the techniques used to assess reliability and validity. Finally, we make suggestions about what to consider when choosing an already existing measurement instrument or scale for your practice or your agency. By the chapter's end, you should have a good understanding of measurement and why it is crucial for social work practice and social work research.

CONCEPTS

A May 2000 *New York Times* article (Stille, 2000) announced that the "social health" of the United States had risen a bit, after a precipitous decline in the 1970s and '80s. Should we be relieved? Concerned? What, after all, does "social health" mean? To social scientist Marc Miringoff, it has to do with social and economic inequalities. To political adviser William J. Bennett, it is more a matter of moral values. In fact, the **concept** (sometimes called a

construct) of social health means different things to different people. Most agree that it has to do with "things that are not measured in the gross national product," and it is supposed to be "a more subtle and more meaningful way of measuring what's important to [people]" (Stille, 2000, p. A19). But until we agree on a definition of social health, we can't decide whether it has to do with child poverty, trust in government, out-of-wedlock births, alcohol-related traffic deaths, or some combination of these or other phenomena.

Concept (construct)   A mental image that summarizes a set of similar observations, feelings, or ideas.

Concepts like happiness require an explicit definition before they are used in research because we cannot be certain that all readers will share the same definition. It is especially important to define concepts that are more abstract or unfamiliar. When we refer to concepts like depression or poverty, we cannot count on others knowing exactly what we mean. Even the experts may disagree about the meaning of frequently used concepts if they base their conceptualizations on different theories. That's OK. The point is not that there can be only one definition of a concept, but that we have to specify clearly what we mean when we use a concept, and we expect others to do the same.

Conceptualization in Practice

Many of the concepts we are interested in are abstract, so a beginning step in measurement is to define the concept. If we are to do an adequate job of **conceptualization,** we must do more than just think up some definition, any definition, for our concepts. We have to turn to social theory and prior research to review appropriate definitions. We may need to distinguish subconcepts, or dimensions, of the concept. We should understand how the definition we choose fits within the theoretical framework guiding the research and what assumptions underlie this framework.

Conceptualization The process of specifying what we mean by a term. In deductive research, **conceptualization** helps to translate portions of an abstract theory into testable hypotheses involving specific variables. In inductive research, conceptualization is an important part of the process used to make sense of related observations.

Researchers start with a nominal definition of the concept. In a **nominal definition,** the concept is defined in terms of other concepts, such as defining child abuse as occurring when either severe physical or emotional harm is inflicted on a child or there is contact of a sexual nature. The nominal definition of child abuse identifies the different types of abuse and specifies that the harm must be severe, but the definition does not provide the set of rules a researcher uses to identify the abuse or distinguish between severe and not severe harm. Nominal definitions are like those definitions found in dictionaries: You get an understanding of the word and its dimensions, but you still do not have a set of rules to use to measure the concept.

Defining Substance Abuse

What observations or images should we associate with the concept of substance abuse? Someone leaning against a building with a liquor bottle, barely able to speak coherently? College students drinking heavily at a party? Someone in an Alcoholics Anonymous group drinking one beer? A 10-year-old boy drinking a small glass of wine in an alley? A 10-year-old boy drinking a small glass of wine at the dinner table in France? Do all these images share something in common that we should define as substance abuse for the purposes of a particular research study? Do some of them? Should we take into account cultural differences? Gender differences? Age differences? Social situations? Physical tolerance for alcohol?

Many researchers now use the definition of substance abuse contained in the *Diagnostic and Statistical Manual, IV* (*DSM-IV*) of the American Psychiatric Association (Mueser et al., 1990): "repeated use of a substance to the extent that it interferes with adequate social, vocational, or self-care functioning" (p. 33). We cannot judge the *DSM-IV* definition of substance abuse as correct or incorrect. Each researcher has the right to conceptualize as he or she sees fit. However, we can say that the *DSM-IV* definition of substance abuse is useful, in part because it has been widely adopted. If we conceptualize substance abuse the same way that the *DSM-IV* does, many others will share our definition and understand what we are talking about. The definition is stated in clear and precise language that should minimize differences in interpretation and maximize understanding.

This clarity should not prevent us from recognizing that the definition reflects a particular theoretical orientation. *DSM-IV* applies a medical "disease model" to mental illness and substance abuse. This theoretical model emphasizes behavioral and biological criteria instead of the social expectations that are emphasized in a social model of substance abuse. How we conceptualize reflects how we theorize.

Just as we can connect concepts to theory, we can connect them to other concepts. What this means is that the definition of any one concept rests on a shared understanding of the terms used in the definition. So if our audience does not already have a shared understanding of terms like *adequate social functioning, self-care functioning, and repeated use,* we must also define these terms before we are finished with the process of defining substance abuse.

Defining Depression

Some concepts have multiple dimensions, bringing together several related concepts under a larger conceptual umbrella. One such concept is depression. Depression is unlike a normal emotional experience leading to sadness, for it includes a range of symptoms such as negative mood (sadness, loneliness, feelings of worthlessness) and somatic symptoms (loss of interest in pleasurable activities, eating and sleeping problems, loss of energy, talking less). Depression, then, is a combination of these different dimensions.

But even when there is agreement about the various dimensions that make up depression, there are still different approaches to measure the presence of depression. One approach, based on the measurement from psychology, assumes that the presence of psychological symptoms is not enough by itself, but these symptoms vary by intensity or severity (Dohrenwend & Dohrenwend, 1982). In the case of depression, it is not sufficient to look at whether the symptoms are present or not; rather, they have to be persistent, lasting for some time period. The symptoms must be so intense that they interfere with an individual's ability to function. So some researchers use scales that measure the intensity of the different items; the Center for Epidemiologic Studies Depression (CES-D) scale, for example, asks respondents to rate the intensity (or severity) of each of the items; then, the items are summed to represent a range on a continuum of intensity of depression.

The second approach to measure depression is derived from the clinical case identification model used in assessment models such as the *DSM-IV*. In the clinical diagnostic approach, researchers identify the presence of the various dimensions of depression during a specific time period, but they do not assess the intensity of the symptoms. Furthermore, researchers using this method gather additional information to assess whether the responses conform to criteria for a case of depression. Unlike the above model, this approach identifies simply whether depression is present or absent.

Do these different perspectives really matter? Joy Newmann's (1989) analysis found that the relationship between age and depression depended on the type of assessment method. Studies using scales like the CES-D scale tended to show that highest depression scores occur among the youngest and oldest age groups whereas studies using the clinical case method have found that the younger and older cohorts were less depressed than middle-aged cohorts.

Defining Poverty

Decisions about how to define a concept reflect the theoretical framework that guides the researchers. For example, the concept of poverty has always been somewhat controversial because different theoretical notions of what poverty is shape estimates of how prevalent it is and what can be done about it.

Most of the statistics that you see in the newspaper about the poverty rate reflect a conception of poverty that was formalized by Mollie Orshansky of the Social Security Administration in 1965 and subsequently adopted by the federal government and many researchers (Putnam, 1977). She defined poverty in terms of what is called an *absolute* standard, based on the amount of money required to purchase an emergency diet that is estimated to be nutritionally adequate for about two months. The idea is that people are truly poor if they can barely purchase the food they need and other essential goods. This poverty standard is adjusted for household size and composition (number of children and adults), and the minimal amount needed for food is multiplied by three because a 1955 survey indicated that poor families spend about one third of their incomes on food (Orshansky, 1977).

Other social scientists reject this way of establishing an absolute standard and suggest an alternative method, the *basic needs budget* approach (Bangs, Kerchis, & Weldon, 1997). This approach suggests that we need to establish the market cost of a basket of goods that each of us needs to meet basic needs. The cost of each category or good is estimated separately. This method also forces us to define what is an "adequate amount" of that particular good. Like the official poverty line, this definition requires adjustments for family size, but it also requires adjustments for the labor status of the parent, ages of the children, and geographic region of residence.

Some social scientists disagree with absolute standards and have instead urged adoption of a *relative* poverty standard. They identify the poor as those in the lowest 5th or 10th of the income distribution or as those having some fraction of the average income. The idea behind this relative conception is that poverty should be defined in terms of what is normal in a given society at a particular time.

Some social scientists prefer yet another conception of poverty. With the *subjective* approach, poverty is defined as what people think would be the minimal income they need to make ends meet. Of course, many have argued that this approach is influenced too much by the different standards that people use to estimate what they "need" (Ruggles, 1990, pp. 20–23).

Which do you think is a more reasonable approach to defining poverty: an absolute standard, a relative standard, or a subjective standard? Which kind of absolute standard—the multiplier approach or the basic needs approach? Our understanding of the concept of poverty is sharpened when we consider the theoretical ramifications of these alternative definitions.

Concepts, Constants, and Variables

After we define the concepts in a theory, we can identify variables (and perhaps constants) that correspond to the concepts in the setting that we will study. Consider the concept of social control, which Donald Black (1984) defines as "all of the practices by which people define and respond to deviant behavior" (p. xi). What variables can represent this conceptualization of social control? Proportion of people in a community who are arrested? Average length of sentences for crimes? Types of bystander reactions to public intoxication? Some combination of these? If we are to study variation in social control, we must identify the variables that we can measure and that are most pertinent to our theoretical concerns.

Not every concept in a particular study is represented by a variable. For example, tolerance of drinking—the presence or absence of rules against drinking—might be an important aspect of the social control of alcoholism in fraternities. However, if we study social life at only those fraternities that prohibit drinking, tolerance of drinking would not be a variable: Because all the fraternities studied have the same level of tolerance, tolerance of drinking is a **constant.** Of course, the concept of tolerance of drinking would still be important for understanding social life in the "dry" fraternities. If we studied social life in a general sample of fraternities, tolerance of drinking would then be an important variable to measure.

Concepts vary in their level of abstraction, and this in turn affects how readily we can specify the variables pertaining to the concept. We may not think twice before we move from a conceptual definition of *age* as time elapsed since birth to the variable, *years since birth.* Binge drinking is also a relatively concrete concept, but it requires a bit more thought. We may define binge drinking conceptually as episodic drinking and select for our research on binge drinking the variable, *frequency of five or more drinks in a row.* That's pretty straightforward. A very abstract concept like social status may have a clear role in social theory but a variety of meanings in different social settings. Variables that pertain to social status may include level of esteem in a group, extent of influence over others, level of income and education, or number of friends. It is very important to specify what we mean by an abstract concept like social status in a particular study and to choose appropriate variables to represent this meaning.

How do we know what concepts to consider and then which variables to select in a study? It's very tempting, and all too common, to simply try to "measure everything" by including in a study every variable we can think of that might have something to do with our research question. This haphazard approach will inevitably result in the collection of data that are useless and the failure to collect some data that are important. Instead, we must take four steps:

1. Examine the theory or theories that are relevant to our research question in order to identify those concepts that would be expected to have some bearing on the phenomena we are investigating.

2. Review the relevant research literature and assess the utility of variables used in prior research.

3. Consider the constraints and opportunities for measurement that are associated with the specific setting(s) we will study. Distinguish constants from variables in this setting.

4. Look ahead to our analysis of the data. Just what role will each variable we have measured play in our analyses?

OPERATIONALIZATION

Once we have defined our concepts in the abstract—that is, we have provided a nominal definition—and we have identified the specific variables we want to measure, we must develop measurement procedures. The goal is to devise an **operation** that actually measures the concepts we intend to measure—in other words, to achieve measurement validity. Researchers provide an **operational definition,** which includes what is measured, how the indicators are measured, and the rules used to assign a value to what is observed and to interpret the value.

Operation   A procedure for identifying the value of cases on a variable.

We will expand on each element of an operational definition, but first, it is useful to look at an example of an operational definition, in this case a possible definition for alcoholism. Previously, we have provided a nominal definition of alcoholism. An operational definition for alcoholism might include the following content.

The Michigan Alcoholism Screening Test (MAST) is a 24-item instrument that includes a variety of indicators of symptoms such as seeing drinking as a problem, seeking treatment for problem drinking, delirium tremens, severe shaking, hearing voices, complaints from others about drinking, memory loss from drinking, job loss due to drinking, social problems from drinking, arrests for drunk driving or for drunken behavior, guilt feelings about drinking, and ability to stop drinking. The scale may be administered orally or may be self-administered. Respondents respond yes or no to each item, and each item is given a weighted score ranging from 0 to 5. There are four items for which the alcoholic response is "no." The weighted item responses are summed, with a score of 0 to 3 indicating no problem with alcoholism, 4 considered to be suggestive of a problem and 5 or above an indication of alcoholism.

Exhibit 3.1   Concepts, Variables, and Indicators

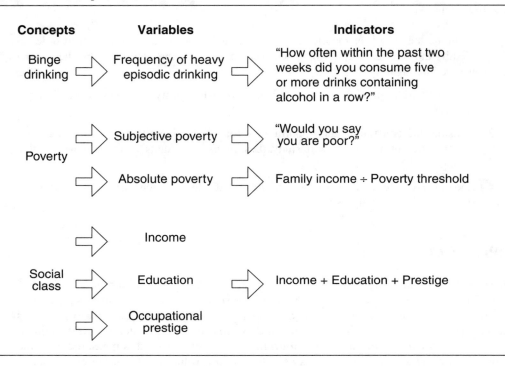

Concepts	Variables	Indicators
Binge drinking ⇨	Frequency of heavy episodic drinking ⇨	"How often within the past two weeks did you consume five or more drinks containing alcohol in a row?"
Poverty ⇨	Subjective poverty ⇨	"Would you say you are poor?"
⇨	Absolute poverty ⇨	Family income ÷ Poverty threshold
Social class ⇨	Income	
⇨	Education ⇨	Income + Education + Prestige
⇨	Occupational prestige	

As you can see from this definition, we are provided with the specific indicators included in the measure, the method(s) for data collection, specific scoring of the information, and the interpretation of scale scores. This detail is often referred to as **operationalization**.

Operationalization   The process of specifying the operations that will indicate the value of cases on a variable.

Indicators

Exhibit 3.1 represents one part of the operationalization process in three studies. The first researcher defines her concept, income, and chooses one variable, annual earnings, to represent it. This variable is then measured with responses to a single question, or an **indicator**: What was your total income from all sources in 1998? The second researcher defines her concept, poverty, as having two aspects or dimensions, subjective poverty and absolute poverty. Subjective poverty is measured with responses to a survey question: Do you consider yourself poor? Absolute poverty is measured by comparing family income to the poverty threshold. The third researcher decides that her concept is defined by a position on three measured variables: income, education, and occupational prestige.

One consideration is the precision of the information that is necessary. The first researcher in Exhibit 3.1 is seeking information that is quite precise. She is assuming that respondents will be able to accurately report the information. As an alternative, she might have asked respondents: "Please identify the income category that includes your total income from all sources in 1998." For this question, she will get less exact information. Generally, the decision about precision is based on the information that is needed for the research. It may also be based on what the researcher believes people can recall and the content people may be willing to report.

The variables and particular measurement operations chosen for a study should be consistent with the research question. If we ask an evaluative research question—for example, "Are self-help groups more effective in increasing the likelihood of abstinence among substance abusers than hospital-based treatments?"—we may operationalize *form of treatment* in terms of participation in these two types of treatment. However, if we are attempting to answer an explanatory research question—for example, "What influences the success of substance abuse treatment?"—we should probably consider what it is about these treatment alternatives that is associated with successful abstinence. Prior theory and research suggest that some of the important variables that differ between these treatment approaches are level of peer support, beliefs about the causes of alcoholism, and financial investment in the treatment.

Scales and Indexes

When several questions are used to measure one concept, the responses may be combined by taking the sum or average of responses. A composite measure based on this type of sum or average is termed an **index** or **scale.** The idea is that **idiosyncratic variation** in response to particular questions will average out, so that the main influence on the combined measure will be the concept on which all the questions focus. In addition, the scale can be considered a more complete measure of the concept than any one of the component questions.

Creating a scale is not just a matter of writing a few questions that seem to focus on a concept. Questions that seem to you to measure a common concept might seem to respondents to concern several different issues. The only way to know that a given set of questions does, in fact, form a scale is to administer the questions to people like those you plan to study. If a common concept is being measured, people's responses to the different questions should display some consistency. Special statistics called **reliability measures** help researchers decide whether responses are consistent.

Scales and indexes have already been developed to measure many concepts, and some of these scales have been demonstrated to be reliable in a range of studies. It usually is much better to use such a scale to measure a concept than it is to try to devise questions to form a new scale. Use of a preexisting scale both simplifies the work involved in designing a study and facilitates comparison of findings to those obtained in other studies.

The questions in Exhibit 3.2 are taken from the CES-D, a scale used to measure the concept of depression. The aspect of depression measured by the scale is the level (the frequency and number combined) of depressive symptoms. Many researchers in different studies have found that these questions form a reliable scale. Note that each question concerns a symptom of depression. People may have idiosyncratic reasons for having a particular symptom without being depressed; for example, people who have been suffering a physical ailment may say that they have a poor appetite. But by combining the answers to questions about several symptoms, the scale score reduces the impact of this idiosyncratic variation.

Exhibit 3.2   Example of a Scale: The Center for Epidemiologic Studies Depression Scale (CES-D)

At any time during the past week… (Circle one response on each line)	Never	Some of the time	Most of the time
a. Was your appetite so poor that you did not feel like eating?	1	2	3
b. Did you feel so tired and worn out that you could not enjoy anything?	1	2	3
c. Did you feel depressed?	1	2	3
d. Did you feel unhappy about the way your life is going?	1	2	3
e. Did you feel discouraged and worried about your future?	1	2	3
f. Did you feel lonely?	1	2	3

Source: Radloff, 1977. Copyright © 1977. Reprinted with permission of Sage Publications, Inc.

The advantages of using scales rather than single questions to measure important concepts are very clear, and so surveys and interviews often include sets of multiple-item questions. However, four cautions are in order:

Our presupposition that each component question is indeed measuring the same concept may be mistaken. Although we may include multiple questions in a survey to measure one concept, we may find that answers to the questions are not related to one another, and so the scale cannot be created. Alternatively, we may find that answers to just a few of the questions are not related to the answers given to most of the others. We may, therefore, decide to discard these particular questions before computing the average that makes up the scale.

Combining responses to specific questions can obscure important differences in meaning among the questions. Schutt et al.'s research on the impact of AIDS prevention education in shelters for the homeless (Schutt, Gunston, & O'Brien, 1992) provides an example. In this study, the researchers asked a series of questions to ascertain respondents' knowledge about HIV risk factors and about methods of preventing exposure to those risk factors. They then combined these responses into an overall knowledge index. The authors were somewhat surprised to find that the knowledge index scores were no higher in a shelter with an AIDS education program than in a shelter without such a program. However, further analysis showed that respondents in the shelter with an AIDS education program were more knowledgeable than the other respondents about the specific ways of preventing AIDS, which were in fact the primary focus of the program. Combining responses to these questions with the others about general knowledge of HIV risk factors obscured an important finding.

The questions in a scale may cluster together in subsets. All the questions may be measuring the intended concept, but we may conclude that this concept actually has several different aspects. A **multidimensional scale** has then been obtained. This conclusion can in turn help us to refine our understanding of the original concept. For example, Schutt and colleagues (Schutt, Goldfinger, & Penk, 1992) included in a survey of homeless mentally ill people a set of questions to measure their residential preferences. When the researchers designed these questions, they sought to measure the continuum of sentiment ranging from a desire to remain in a shelter, to a desire to live in a group home, to a desire to live in an independent apartment. Their questions ranged from whether people wanted to live with others or by themselves to whether they wanted to have staff in their residence. But statistical analysis indicated that the questions actually formed three subsets, corresponding to three dimensions of residential preference: desire for stable housing, desire for living in a group home with other people, and desire to have staff in the home. Identification of these three dimensions gave the researchers a better understanding of the concept of residential preference.

A scale may be designed explicitly to measure multiple conceptual dimensions, but often, the same dimensions do not reappear in a subsequent study. For example, Radloff (1977) and others have found that the CES-D scale includes four dimensions, but several studies of different population subgroups have found only three dimensions. The researcher must then try to figure out why: Does the new population studied view issues differently than prior populations surveyed with the scale? Were the dimensions found in previous research really just chance associations among the questions making up the larger scale? Have sentiments changed since the earlier studies when the multidimensional scale was developed? Only after a scale has been used in several studies can we begin to have confidence in the answers to the questions on which it is based.

Sometimes particular questions are counted, or weighted, more than others in the calculation of the index. Some questions may be more central to the concept being measured than others and so may be given greater weight in the scale score. It is difficult to justify this approach without extensive testing, but some well-established scales do involve differential weighting. For example, The MAST asks questions that are assigned different weights. The question, "Have you ever been in a hospital because of your drinking?" is given more points (weighted higher) than the question, "Do you feel you are a normal drinker?"

Treatment as a Variable

Frequently, social work researchers will examine the effectiveness of an intervention or compare two different intervention approaches. When an intervention is compared to no intervention or when two or more interventions are compared, the treatment approach is a variable and, therefore, requires both a conceptual and operational definition. The treatment or intervention becomes the independent variable that you assume will cause a change in a status or condition. Therefore, it is important for the researcher to provide a very clear nominal definition of the intervention. For example, it is not enough for the researcher to say that the study is comparing one method to another, such as "traditional" case management to "intensive" case management. Although the general meaning of such an approach may be familiar to you, the researcher must define what each approach involves. For example, case management may include full support, where the social worker working with the chronically mentally ill provides a variety of services and supports including rehabilitation, social skill building, counseling, links to resources, identification of work and social opportunities, and money management, whereas another social worker may just assess, link the client to other services, and reevaluate periodically.

Nominal definitions of an intervention only provide the characteristics or components of the intervention but fail to fully describe how the intervention was implemented. Researchers provide varying amounts of specificity regarding the actual operationalization of the intervention. For example, Christopher Mitchell (1999) operationalized his cognitive behavioral group therapy approach by designating the length of the groups (eight-week program) and the content covered in each of the weekly sessions. This amount of detail provides a much clearer sense of the nature of the intervention, but it would still not be possible to repeat the research without additional information. Without the actual description of the intervention and how the treatment model was implemented, you cannot adequately evaluate the research nor replicate what was done if you want to implement the intervention at your agency.

Gathering Data

Social work researchers and practitioners have many options for operationalizing their concepts. We will briefly mention these options here but go into much greater depth in subsequent chapters.

Measures can be based on a diverse set of activities. One method is to use a **direct measure** such as visual or recorded observation or a physical measure such as a pulse rate. Although these methods are particularly useful for gauging behavior, they are typically *intrusive.* The very act of gathering the information may change people's behavior, thereby altering the accuracy of the obtained information. If a caseworker goes to a client's home to observe the client interacting with a child, the nature of the interactions may change because the parent knows the caseworker is present. The parent is likely to behave in a manner that is more socially acceptable to the caseworker. Similarly, self-monitoring of behavior may have the same effect. If a smoker is asked to monitor the number of cigarettes smoked in a day, the act of such monitoring may reduce the number of cigarettes smoked.

Data may be gathered by interviews or self-administered scales and questionnaires. These methods appear to be direct in that we gather the information directly from the respondent or client. Yet, what we are trying to do is infer behavior, attitudes, emotions, or feelings because we cannot observe these directly. These methods may also be quite intrusive, and the quality of the responses can be affected by the nature of the questions or the characteristics of the person asking the questions, as we will discuss in Chapter 8.

There are other sources of information from which measures can be operationalized. Many large data sets have been collected by the federal government, state governments, and nongovernmental sources. Many of these data sets have social indicators that are relevant to social services such as employment, program participation, income, health, crime, mental health, and the like. A drawback to these data is that you are constrained by the way those who collected the data operationalized their measures.

Variables can be operationalized using written information in client records. The quality of these records depends on the recording accuracy of the individual staff. As with data collected by other sources, you are constrained by how variables were operationalized by the staff.

Staff may not use common definitions, and these definitions may change over time, leading to inaccuracies in the data.

When we have reason to be skeptical of potential respondents' answers to questions, when we cannot observe the phenomena of interest directly, and when there are no sources of available data, we can use **indirect** or **unobtrusive measures,** which allow us to collect data about individuals or groups without their direct knowledge or participation (Webb, Campbell, Schwartz, & Sechrest, 2000). However, the opportunities for using unobtrusive measures are few, and the information they can provide is often limited to crude counts or estimates.

The physical traces of past behavior are one type of unobtrusive measure that is most useful when the behavior of interest cannot be directly observed (perhaps because it is hidden or occurred in the past) and has not been recorded in a source of available data. To measure the prevalence of drinking in college dorms or fraternity houses, we might count the number of empty bottles of alcoholic beverages in the surrounding dumpsters. Student interest in the college courses they are taking might be measured by counting the number of times that books left on reserve as optional reading are checked out or the number of class handouts left in trash barrels outside a lecture hall.

You can probably see that care must be taken to develop trace measures that are useful for comparative purposes. For instance, comparison of the number of empty bottles in dumpsters outside different dorms could be misleading; you would need to take into account, at the least, the number of residents in the dorms, the time since the last trash collection, and the accessibility of each dumpster to passersby. Counts of usage of books on reserve will be useful only if you take into account how many copies of the books are on reserve for the course, how many students are enrolled in the course, and whether reserve reading is required.

Content analysis, another type of indirect measurement, studies representations of the research topic in such media forms as news articles, TV shows, and radio talk shows. An investigation of what motivates child abuse reporting might include a count of the amount of space devoted to newspaper articles in a sample of issues of the local newspaper. Television stories might be coded to indicate the number of times that newscasters reported on the maltreatment of children.

Combining Measurement Operations

Using available data, asking questions, making observations, and using unobtrusive indicators are interrelated measurement tools, each of which may include or be supplemented by the others. From people's answers to survey questions, the U.S. Bureau of the Census develops widely consulted census reports containing available data on people and geographic units in the United States. Data from employee surveys may be supplemented by information available in agency records. Interviewers may record observations about those whom they question. Researchers may use insights gleaned from questioning participants to make sense of the social interaction they have observed. Unobtrusive indicators could be used to evaluate the honesty of survey responses.

The choice of a particular measurement method is often determined by available resources and opportunities, but measurement is improved if this choice also takes into account the particular concept or concepts to be measured. Responses to such questions as "How socially engaged were you at the party?" or "How many days did you use sick leave last year?" are unlikely to provide information as valid, respectively, as direct observation or agency records. On the other hand, observations at social gatherings may not answer our questions about why some people do not participate; we may just have to ask people. Or if no agency is recording the frequency of job loss in a community, we may have to ask direct questions.

Triangulation—the use of two or more different measures of the same variable—can strengthen measurement considerably (Brewer & Hunter, 1989, p. 17). When we achieve similar results with different measures of the same variable, particularly when the measures are based on such different methods as survey questions and field-based observations, we can be more confident in the validity of each measure. If results diverge with different measures, it may indicate that one or more of these measures are influenced by more measurement error than we can tolerate. Divergence between measures could also indicate that they actually operationalize different concepts.

Measurement in Qualitative Research

Qualitative research projects approach measurement in a way that tends to be more inductive and holistic. Instead of deciding in advance which concepts are important for a study, what these concepts mean, and how they should be measured, qualitative researchers begin by recording verbatim what they hear in intensive interviews or what they see during observational sessions. This material is then reviewed to identify important concepts and their meaning for participants. Relevant variables may then be identified and procedures developed for indicating variation between participants and settings or variation over time. As an understanding of the participants and social processes develops, the concepts may be refined and the measures modified. Qualitative research often does not feature the sharp boundaries in quantitative research between developing measures, collecting data with those measures, and evaluating the measures. You will learn more about qualitative research in Chapter 9.

LEVELS OF MEASUREMENT

The final part of operationalization is to assign a value or symbol to represent the observation. Each variable has categories of some sort, and we need to know how to assign a symbol—typically a number—to represent what has been observed or learned. The symbol may represent a category whereby each separate category represents a different status. In this case, we have a **discrete variable.** The variable may be a **continuous variable** for which the number represents a quantity that can be described in terms of order, spread between the numbers, and/or relative amounts.

Part of operationalization then is to decide the variable's **level of measurement** that will be used in the research. When we know a variable's level of measurement, we can better understand how cases vary on that variable and so understand more fully what we have measured. Level of measurement also has important implications for the type of statistics that can be used with the variable, as you will learn in Chapter 11. There are four levels of measurement: nominal, ordinal, interval, and ratio. Exhibit 3.3 depicts the differences among these four levels.

Exhibit 3.3 Levels of Measurement

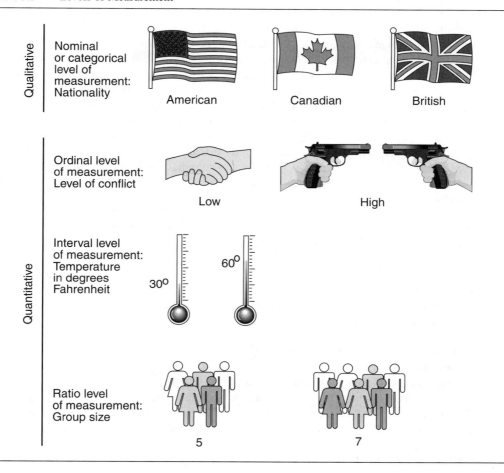

Level of measurement   The mathematical precision with which the values of a variable can be expressed. The nominal level of measurement, which is qualitative, has no mathematical interpretation; the quantitative levels of measurement—ordinal, interval, and ratio—are progressively more precise mathematically.

Nominal Level of Measurement

The **nominal level of measurement** (also called the categorical level) identifies variables whose values have no mathematical interpretation; they vary in kind or quality but not in amount. In fact, it is conventional to refer to the values of nominal variables as attributes instead of values. Discrete variables are measured at the nominal level of measurement. Gender is one example. The variable *gender* has two attributes (or categories or qualities):

male and female. We might indicate male by the value 1 and female by the value 2, but these numbers do not tell us anything about the difference between male and female except that they are different. Female is not one unit more of "gender" than male, nor is it twice as much "gender." The numbers simply represent a category.

Nominal level variables are commonplace in social work research. Such variables might include client characteristics such as ethnicity, marital status, or occupation, or they might include service-related variables such as referral source or services used and the like. A researcher might want to understand the differences between those who use respite care services for the elderly and those who do not use respite services. Another researcher might want to distinguish the characteristics of people who are poor and those people who are not poor. A third researcher might want to know if the decision to place an older parent in a nursing home (placed: yes or no) is based on economic status and use of respite care services. Respite care use, poverty status, and nursing home placement are all nominal-level variables.

Although the attributes of categorical variables do not have a mathematical meaning, they must be assigned to cases with great care. The attributes we use to measure, or categorize, cases must be mutually exclusive and exhaustive:

- A variable's attributes or values are mutually exclusive if every case can have only one attribute.
- A variable's attributes or values are exhaustive when every case can be classified into one of the categories.

When a variable's attributes are mutually exclusive and exhaustive, every case corresponds to one and only one attribute.

The only mathematical operation we can perform with nominal-level variables is a count. We can count how many clients last month were females and how many were males. From that count, we can calculate the percentage or proportion of females to males among our clients. If the agency served 150 women and 100 men, then we can say that 60% of the clients were female. But we cannot identify an average gender, nor can we add or subtract or compute any other kind of number.

Ordinal Level of Measurement

The first of the three quantitative levels is the **ordinal level of measurement**. At this level, the numbers assigned to cases specify only the order of the cases, permitting "greater than" and "less than" distinctions. The gaps between the various responses do not have any particular meaning. As with nominal variables, the different values of a variable measured at the ordinal level must be mutually exclusive and exhaustive. They must cover the range of observed values and allow each case to be assigned no more than one value.

The properties of variables measured at the ordinal level are illustrated in Exhibit 3.3 by the contrast between the levels of conflict in two groups. The first group, symbolized by two people shaking hands, has a low level of conflict. The second group, symbolized by two people pointing guns at each other, has a high level of conflict. To measure conflict, we would put the groups "in order" by assigning the number 1 to the low-conflict group and the number 2 to the high-conflict group. The numbers thus indicate only the relative position or order of the cases.

Exhibit 3.4   Example of a Goal Attainment Scale

Problem Area	Client Outcome Goal	No Achievement	Some Achievement	Major Achievement
Self-esteem	To develop increased feeling of self-esteem	Makes only negative statements Does not identify strengths No verbal expression of confidence No sense of self-worth	Some positive statements Some negative statements Can identify some strengths but overly critical about self Emerging confidence Emerging self-worth	Makes many positive statements Few to no negative statements Can identify strengths without qualifying statements Is confident Has self-worth
Mother's attitude toward child	Less of a negative attitude toward child	Constantly: Resists child's affection Shows anger verbally and nonverbally Shows frustration Shows hostility Impatient	Occasional: Affection Anger Frustration Hostility Impatience	Accepts child's affection No verbal or nonverbal signs of anger, hostility, frustration Patient

Although *low level of conflict* is represented by the number 1, it is not one unit of conflict less than *high level of conflict*, which is represented by the number 2.

A common ordinal measure used in social service agencies is client satisfaction. Often, agencies will ask a client a global question about satisfaction with the services provided by the agency, using a rating system such as 4 = *very satisfied*, 3 = *satisfied*, 2 = *dissatisfied*, and 1 = *very dissatisfied.* Someone who responds *very satisfied,* coded as 4, is clearly more satisfied than someone who responds *dissatisfied,* coded as 2, but the person responding with a 4 is not twice as satisfied as the person responding with a 2. Nor is the person responding *very satisfied* (4) two units more satisfied than the person responding *dissatisfied* (2). We do know that the first person is more satisfied than the second person, and therefore, the order has meaning. We can count the number of clients who fall into each category. We can also compute an average satisfaction, but the average is not a quantity of satisfaction; rather, the number summarizes the relative position of the group on the given scale.

Many other ordinal measures are used in social services. You might be using a goal attainment scale by which you measure the progress of a client in achieving a particular goal. These scales are usually developed by describing the worst indicators, the best indicators, and several steps in between. The gap between the steps has no meaning, but the scoring represents the progress of the client. Exhibit 3.4 provides an example of a goal attainment scale to measure self-esteem and mother's attitude toward children. The social worker evaluates the extent to which there is improvement in self-esteem based on the nature of the verbal and non-verbal responses of the client. There is an order to the levels of achievement, and we can describe how many clients fall into each category, but we cannot calculate the average level of achievement using this scale.

Interval Level of Measurement

The numbers indicating the values of a variable at the **interval level of measurement** represent fixed measurement units but have no absolute or fixed zero point. An interval level of measurement also has mutually exclusive categories, the categories are exhaustive, and there is an order to the responses. This level of measurement is represented in Exhibit 3.3 by the difference between two Fahrenheit temperatures. Although 60 degrees is 30 degrees hotter than 30 degrees, 60 in this case is not twice as hot as 30. Why not? Because "heat" does not begin at 0 degrees on the Fahrenheit scale.

An interval-level measure is created by a scale that has fixed measurement units but no absolute or fixed zero point. The numbers can, therefore, be added and subtracted, but ratios are not meaningful. Again, the values must be mutually exclusive and exhaustive.

There are few true interval-level measures in social work, but many social work researchers treat scales created by combining responses to a series of variables measured at the ordinal level as interval-level measures. Frequently, this is done because there are more mathematical operations associated with interval-level variables. For example, an index of this sort could be created with responses to Attkisson's Client Satisfaction Questionnaire (see Exhibit 3.5 for the CSQ-8). The questions in this scale have different response categories but the same response numbers. Each question can be used independently of the other questions to provide useful information: an ordinal level of measurement. Or the responses to the eight questions can be summed to reflect overall satisfaction. The scale would then range from 8 to 32, with higher scores representing greater satisfaction. A score of 24 could be treated as if it were 12 more units than a score of 12, but that does not mean that one respondent is twice as satisfied as the other person.

Ratio Level of Measurement

The numbers indicating the values of a variable at the **ratio level of measurement** represent fixed measuring units and an absolute zero point (zero means absolutely no amount of whatever the variable indicates). On a ratio scale, 10 is two points higher than 8 and is also two times greater than 5. Ratio numbers can be added and subtracted, and because the numbers begin at an absolute zero point, they can be multiplied and divided (so ratios can be formed between the numbers). For example, people's ages can be represented by values ranging from 0 years (or some fraction of a year) to 120 or more. A person who is 30 years old is 15 years older than someone who is 15 years old (30 − 15 = 15) and is twice as old as that person (30 / 15 = 2). Of course, the numbers also are mutually exclusive and exhaustive, so that every case can be assigned one and only one value.

Exhibit 3.3 displays an example of a variable measured at the ratio level. The number of people in the first group is 5, and the number in the second group is 7. The ratio of the two groups' sizes is then 1.4, a number that mirrors the relationship between the sizes of the groups.

Exhibit 3.5 Example of an Interval Level Measure: Client Satisfaction Questionnaire (CSQ-8)

Circle your answer:

1. How would you rate the quality of service you have received?

4	3	2	1
Excellent	Good	Fair	Poor

2. Did you get the kind of service you wanted?

1	2	3	4
No, definitely	No, not really	Yes, generally	Yes, definitely

3. To what extent has our program met your needs?

4	3	2	1
Almost all of my needs have been met	Most of my needs have been met	Only a few of my needs have been met	None of my needs have been met

4. If a friend were in need of similar help, would you recommend our program to him or her?

1	2	3	4
No, definitely not	No, I don't think so	Yes, I think so	Yes, definitely

5. How satisfied are you with the amount of help you have received?

1	2	3	4
Quite dissatisfied	Indifferent or mildly dissatisfied	Mostly satisfied	Very satisfied

6. Have the services you received helped you to deal more effectively with your problems?

4	3	2	1
Yes, they helped a great deal	Yes, they helped	No, they really didn't help	No, they seemed to make things worse

7. In an overall, general sense, how satisfied are you with the service you received?

4	3	2	1
Very satisfied	Mostly satisfied	Indifferent or mildly dissatisfied	Quite dissatisfied

8. If you were to seek help again, would you come back to our program?

1	2	3	4
No, definitely not	No, I don't think so	Yes, I think so	Yes, definitely

Source: Larsen, Attkisson, Hargreaves, & Nguyen, 1979.

Note that there does not actually have to be any group with a size of 0; what is important is that the numbering scheme begins at an absolute zero—in this case, the absence of any people.

As part of your practice, you might use ratio-level variables to describe characteristics of your clients such as their actual income or their actual income from Social Security. You can describe clients based on their level of depressive symptoms because zero means they have no depressive symptoms. Ratio-level variables are often used when reporting to funders or even supervisors, for example, the number of clients seen in the last month, the amount of time spent providing casework, or the number of meals delivered to homebound elderly. The information might be used to describe a community: the number of community organizations or the number of afterschool programs in a particular community. For each of these variables, the answer *zero* is meaningful, representing the complete absence of the variable.

The Case of Dichotomies

Dichotomies, variables having only two values, are a special case from the standpoint of levels of measurement. The values or attributes of a variable such as depression clearly vary in kind or quality, not in amount. Thus, the variable is categorical—measured at the nominal level. Yet, in practical terms, we can think of the variable in a slightly different way, as indicating the presence of the attribute *depressed* or *not depressed*. Viewed in this way, there is an inherent order: A depressed person has more of the attribute (it is present) than a person who is not depressed (the attribute is not present). We are likely to act given the presence or absence of that attribute. We intervene or refer to treatment a depressed client while we would not do so with a client who was not depressed. Nonetheless, although in practical terms there is an order, empirically, we treat dichotomous variables as a nominal variable.

Comparison of Levels of Measurement

Exhibit 3.6 summarizes the types of comparisons that can be made with different levels of measurement, as well as the mathematical operations that are legitimate. All four levels of measurement allow researchers to assign different values to different cases. All three quantitative measures allow researchers to rank cases in order.

Researchers choose levels of measurement in the process of operationalizing the variables; the level of measurement is not inherent in the variable itself. Many variables can be measured at different levels with different procedures. For example, the Core Alcohol and

Exhibit 3.6   Properties of Measurement Levels

Examples of comparison statements	Appropriate math operations	Relevant level of measurement			
		Nominal	Ordinal	Interval	Ratio
A is equal to (not equal to) B	= (≠)	✓	✓	✓	✓
A is greater than (less than) B	> (<)		✓	✓	✓
A is three more than (less than) B	+ (−)			✓	✓
A is twice (half) as large as B	× (÷)				✓

Drug Survey (Core Institute, 1994) identifies binge drinking by asking students, "Think back over the last two weeks. How many times have you had five or more drinks at a sitting?" You might be ready to classify this as a ratio-level measure. However, this is a closed-ended question, and students are asked to indicate their answer by checking *None, Once, Twice, 3 to 5 times, 6 to 9 times,* or *10 or more times.* Use of these categories makes the level of measurement ordinal. The distance between any two cases cannot be clearly determined. A student with a response in the *6 to 9 times* category could have binged just one more time than a student who responded *3 to 5 times.* You just can't tell.

It is a good idea to try to measure variables at the highest level of measurement possible. The more information available, the more ways we have to compare cases. We also have more possibilities for statistical analysis with quantitative than with qualitative variables. Furthermore, you can create ordinal or nominal variables from ratio-level variables, but you cannot go in the reverse direction. For example, you can measure age in years rather than in categories. If you know the actual age, you can combine the ages into categories at a later time. When asking people to respond to age by category, you cannot modify that variable to reflect their actual age. Thus, if doing so does not distort the meaning of the concept that is to be measured, measure at the highest level possible.

Be aware, however, that other considerations may preclude measurement at a high level. For example, many people are very reluctant to report their exact incomes, even in anonymous questionnaires. So asking respondents to report their income in categories (such as less than $10,000, $10,000–19,999, $20,000–29,999) will result in more responses, and thus more valid data, than asking respondents for their income in dollars.

MEASUREMENT ERROR

No matter how carefully we operationalize and design our measures, no measure is perfect, and there will be some error. It might be that the measurement instrument itself needs to be corrected or reevaluated. Sometimes people are simply inconsistent in the way that they respond to questions. For example, the U. S. Census Bureau's Survey of Income and Program Participation 1984 Panel included data collected nine times, with four months between interviews. Using this data set, Rafael Engel (1988) completed a study on poverty and aging. One of the questions dealt with marital status, seemingly an easy question to answer and one that should provide consistent responses. It turned out that a portion of the sample, primarily women, kept moving from divorced to widowed and sometimes back to divorced. On reflection, this made sense because among members of this cohort of older adults (born between 1900 and 1919), divorce was a less acceptable social status than being a widow.

In gathering data, we get a response from the participant, this response being the reported score. The reported score is not necessarily the true score or the true response because of the imperfections of measurement. The true response differs from the reported response because of measurement error, of which there are two types: systematic error and random error.

Systematic error is generally considered to be predictable error, in that we can predict the direction of the error. Think about weighing yourself on a scale each day. If you put a scale on a particular part of the floor in your house, you will always weigh less (reported score) than you actually do (true score). The direction of the error is predictable: In this case, your scale will always underreport your true weight.

There are different forms of systematic error, some of which we will detail in later chapters, but each of these forms of systematic error reflects some bias. The various forms include:

Social desirability. Social desirability bias occurs when respondents wish to appear most favorable in the eyes of the interviewer or researcher. For example, in the 1980s, polling information about elections between African American Democratic candidates and White Republican candidates typically showed larger victory margins anticipated for the Democratic candidate than actually occurred in the election. One factor was the unwillingness of White Democrats to admit they were unwilling to vote for an African American, even of the same political party.

Acquiescence bias. There is a tendency for some respondents to agree or disagree with every statement, whether they actually agree or not.

Leading questions. Leading questions have language that is designed to influence the direction of a respondent's answer. There are many different ways in which this might be done. You might encounter words that have a negative connotation in society (regardless of the reason). For example, during the 1980s, the use of the words *liberal* and *welfare* began to take on negative connotations. So a question like, Do you support the liberal position on . . . , is meant to lead people to disagree with the position. Another form of a leading question is to use the names of controversial people in the question. A third way of evoking certain responses is simply to include some responses to a question in the actual question but not all responses.

Differences in subgroup responses according to gender, ethnicity, or age. Differences in cultural beliefs or patterns, socialization processes, or cohort effects may bias findings from what otherwise might seem to be a set of neutral questions. For example, Joy Newmann (1987) has argued that gender differences in levels of depressive symptoms may reflect differences in the socialization process of males and females. She suggests that some scales ask questions about behaviors, such as crying, being lonely, and feeling sad, that are more likely to be admitted by women and not by men, because men are socialized not to express such feelings. Similarly, Debra Ortega and Cheryl Richey (1998) note that people of color may respond differently to questions used in depression scales. Some ethnic groups report feelings of sadness or hopelessness as physical complaints and, therefore, have high scores on these questions but low scores on emotion-related items. Different ethnic groups respond differently to "how do you feel" questions and "what do you think" questions. Ortega and Richey also note that some items on depression scales, such as suicidal ideation, are not meaningful to some ethnic groups.

To avoid systematic error requires careful construction of scales and questions and the testing of these questions with different population groups. We explore these methods in depth in Chapter 8.

Unlike systematic error, **random error** is unpredictable in terms of its effects. Random error may be due to the way respondents are feeling that particular day. Respondents may be fatigued, bored, or not in a very cooperative mood. On the other hand, they may be having a great day. Perhaps the lighting or the weather is making them less willing to cooperate. Respondents may also be affected by the conditions of the testing. The lighting may be bad, it may be noisy, the seating may be cramped, the lack of walls in the cubicle may mean other people can hear, there may be other people in the room, or they may not like the looks of the person gathering the information.

Another form of random error is *regression to the mean*. This is the tendency of people who score very high on some measure to score less high the next time or the reverse, for people who score very low to score higher. What might have influenced the high or low score on the first test may not operate in the second test.

Random error might occur when researchers rating a behavior are not adequately trained to do the rating. For example, two people grading an essay test might come up with different grades if they have not discussed the grading criteria beforehand. A field supervisor and a beginning student might assess a client differently, given the variation in their years of experience.

As we have already said, the effects of random error cannot be predicted: Some responses overestimate the true score while other responses underestimate the true score. Many researchers believe that if the sample size is sufficiently large, the effects of random error cancel each other out. Nonetheless, we want to use measurement scales and questions that are stable to minimize as much as possible the effects of random error.

EVALUATING MEASURES

This issue of measurement error is very important. Do the operations to measure our variables provide stable or consistent responses—are they reliable? Do the operations developed to measure our concepts actually do so—are they valid? When we test the effectiveness of two different interventions or we monitor the progress our client is making, we want the changes we observe to be due to the intervention and not the measurement instrument. We also want to know that the measure we use is really a measure of the outcome and not a measure of some other outcome. If we have weighed our measurement options, carefully constructed our questions and observational procedures, and carefully selected from the available data indicators, we should be on the right track. But we cannot have much confidence in a measure until we have empirically evaluated its reliability and validity.

Reliability

Reliability means that a measurement procedure yields consistent or equivalent scores when the phenomenon being measured is not changing (or that the measured scores change in direct correspondence to actual changes in the phenomenon). If a measure is reliable, it is affected less by random error, or chance variation, than if it is unreliable. Reliability is a prerequisite for measurement validity: We cannot really measure a phenomenon if the measure we are using gives inconsistent results. In fact, because it usually is easier to assess reliability than validity, you are more likely to see an evaluation of measurement reliability in a research report than an evaluation of measurement validity.

There are four possible indications of unreliability. For example, a test of your knowledge of research methods would be unreliable if every time you took it, you received a different score, even though your knowledge of research methods had not changed in the interim, not even as a result of taking the test more than once (test-retest reliability). Similarly, a scale composed of questions to measure knowledge of research methods would be unreliable if respondents' answers to each question were totally independent of their answers to the others (internal consistency). A measure also would be unreliable if slightly different versions of it resulted in markedly different responses (alternate forms reliability). Finally, an assessment of the level of conflict in social groups would be unreliable if ratings of the level of conflict by two observers were not related to each other (interrater reliability).

Test-Retest Reliability

When researchers measure a phenomenon that does not change between two points separated by an interval of time, the degree to which the two measurements are related to each other is the **test-retest reliability** of the measure. If you take a test of your math ability and then retake the test two months later, the test is performing reliably if you receive a similar score both times—presuming that nothing happened during the two months to change your math ability. We hope to find a correlation between the two tests of about .7 and prefer even a higher correlation, such as .8.

Of course, if events between the test and the retest have changed the variable being measured, then the difference between the test and retest scores should reflect that change. As the gap in time between the two tests increases, there is a greater likelihood that real change did occur. This also presumes you were not affected by the conditions of the testing: a **testing effect**. The circumstances of the testing, such as how you were given the test, or environmental conditions, such as lighting or room temperature, may impact test scores. The testing effect may extend to how you felt the first time you took the test; because you did not know what to expect the first time, you may have been very nervous, as opposed to the second time, when you knew what to expect.

Radloff's (1977) initial effort to evaluate the test-retest reliability of the CES-D highlights the difficulties that may emerge from the testing and that make interpreting the scores problematic. A probability sample of households was taken in one county, and then within each household, one person 18 or older was randomly chosen to participate in an interview. Each person was also asked to complete and mail back a CES-D scale either two, four, six, or eight weeks after the initial interview. Only 419 of the initial 1,089 respondents sent back mail questionnaires. The test-retest correlations were moderately high, ranging from .51 at two weeks to .59 at eight weeks. Radloff offered a variety of explanations about the moderate correlations, which included such methodological problems as the bias introduced by nonresponse (maybe those who responded differed from those who did not respond), the problem of using an interview at Time 1 and a self-administered questionnaire for the follow-up (perhaps people responded differently to the interviewer than to the questionnaire), and the effects of being tested twice. Furthermore, she noted that the CES-D was meant to capture depressive symptoms in a one-week period, and perhaps, there had been real changes. This example illustrates how test-retest reliability scores may potentially be affected by real change or by the effect of testing.

Internal Consistency

When researchers use multiple items to measure a single concept, they are concerned with **internal consistency**. This is a very common method to demonstrate reliability. For example, if we are to have confidence that a set of questions (like those in Exhibit 3.2) reliably measures depression, the answers to the questions should be highly associated with one another. The stronger the association among the individual items, and the more items that are included, the higher the reliability of the index.

One method to assess internal consistency is to divide the scale into two parts, or **split-half reliability**. We might take a 20-item scale, such as the CES-D, and sum the scores of the first 10 items, then sum the scores of the second 10 items (items 11 through 20), and then correlate the scores for each of the participants. If we have internal consistency, we should have a fairly high correlation, although this correlation typically gets higher the more items there are in the scale. So what may be considered a fairly high split-half reliability score for a 6-item scale, might not be considered a high score for a 20-item scale.

As you can imagine, there are countless ways in which you might split the scale, and in practical terms, it is nearly impossible to split the scale by hand into every possible combination. Fortunately, the speed of computers allows us to calculate a score that indeed splits the scale in every combination. A summary score, such as **Cronbach's alpha coefficient**, is calculated by the computer program. Cronbach's alpha is the average score of all the possible split-half combinations. In Radloff's study (1977), the alpha coefficients of different samples were quite high, ranging from .85 to .90.

Alternate-Forms Reliability

Researchers are testing **alternate-forms reliability** or **parallel-forms reliability** when they compare subjects' answers to slightly different versions of survey questions (Litwin, 1995, pp. 13–21). A researcher may reverse the order of the response choices in a scale, modify the question wording in minor ways, or create a set of different questions. The two forms are then administered to the subjects. If the two sets of responses are not too different, alternate-forms reliability is established.

You might remember taking the SATs or ACTs when you were in high school. When you compared notes with your friends, you found that each of you had taken different tests. The developers had evaluated these tests to ensure there they were equivalent and comparable.

Interobserver Reliability

When researchers use more than one observer to rate the same people, events, or places, **interobserver reliability** or **interrater reliability** is their goal. If observers are using the same instrument to rate the same thing, their ratings should be very similar. If they are similar, we can have much more confidence that the ratings reflect the phenomenon being assessed rather than the orientations of the observers.

Assessing interobserver reliability is most important when the rating task is complex. Consider a commonly used measure of mental health, the Global Assessment of Functioning Scale (GAF), a bit of which is shown in Exhibit 3.7. The rating task seems straightforward, with clear descriptions of the subject characteristics that are supposed to lead to high or low GAF scores. But in fact, the judgments that the rater must make while using this scale are very complex. They are affected by a wide range of subject characteristics, attitudes, and behaviors as well as by the rater's reactions. As a result, interobserver agreement is often low on the GAF unless the raters are trained carefully.

Assessments of interobserver reliability may be based on the correlation of the rating between two raters. Two raters could evaluate the quality of play between five teenage mothers and their children on a 10-point scale. The correlation would show whether the direction of the raters' scores was similar as well as how close the agreement was for the relative position for

Exhibit 3.7   The Challenge of Interobserver Reliability: Excerpt from the Global Assessment of Functioning Scale

---

Consider psychological, social, and occupational functioning on a hypothetical continuum of mental health-illness. Do not include impairment in functioning due to physical (or environmental) limitations.

Code   (**Note:** Use intermediate codes when appropriate, e.g., 45, 68, 72.)

Code	
100 – 91	**Superior functioning in a wide range of activities, life's problems never seem to get out of hand, is sought by others because of his or her many positive qualities. No symptoms.**
90 – 81	**Absent or minimal symptoms** (e.g., mild anxiety before an exam), **good functioning in all areas, interested and involved in a wide range of activities, socially effective, generally satisfied with life, no more than everyday problems or concerns** (e.g., an occasional argument with family members).
80 – 71	**If symptoms are present, they are transient and expectable reactions to psychosocial stressors** (e.g., difficulty concentrating after family argument); **no more than slight impairment in social, occupational, or school functioning** (e.g., temporarily falling behind in schoolwork).
70 – 61	**Some mild symptoms** (e.g., depressive mood and mild insomnia) **OR some difficulty in social, occupational, or school functioning** (e.g., occasional truancy or theft within the household), **but generally functioning pretty well, has some meaningful interpersonal relationships.**
60 – 51	**Moderate symptoms** (e.g., flat affect and circumstantial speech, occasional panic attacks) **OR moderate difficulty in social, occupational, or school functioning** (e.g., few friends, conflicts with peers or co-workers).
50 – 41	**Serious symptoms** (e.g., suicidal ideation, severe obsessional rituals, frequent shoplifting) **OR any serious impairment in social, occupational, or school functioning** (e.g., no friends, unable to keep a job).
40 – 31	**Some impairment in reality testing or communication** (e.g., speech is at times illogical, obscure, or irrelevant) **OR major impairment in several areas, such as work or school, family relations, judgment, thinking, or mood** (e.g., depressed man avoids friends, neglects family, and is unable to work, child frequently beats up younger children, is defiant at home, and is failing at school).
30 – 21	**Behavior is considerably influenced by delusions or hallucinations OR serious impairment in communication or judgment** (e.g., sometimes incoherent, acts grossly inappropriately, suicidal preoccupation) **OR inability to function in almost all areas** (e.g., stays in bed all day, no job, home, or friends).
20 – 11	**Some danger of hurting self or others** (e.g., suicide attempts without clear expectation of death, frequently violent, manic excitement) **OR occasionally fails to maintain minimal personal hygiene** (e.g., smears feces) **OR gross impairment in communication** (e.g., largely incoherent or mute).
10 – 1	**Persistent danger of severely hurting self or others** (e.g., recurrent violence) **OR persistent inability to maintain minimal personal hygiene OR serious suicidal act with clear expectation of death.**
0	Inadequate information.

---

each of the five scores. One rater may judge the five mothers as 1, 2, 3, 4, and 5 while the second rater scores the mothers as 6, 7, 8, 9, and 10. The correlation would be quite high, in fact, the correlation would be perfect. But as demonstrated by this example, the agreement about the quality of the interactions was quite different. So an alternative method is to estimate the percentage of exact agreement between the two raters. In this case, the rater agreement is zero.

Intraobserver Reliability

Intraobserver reliability (intrarater reliability) occurs when a single observer is assessing an individual at two or more points in time. It differs from test-retest reliability in that the ratings are done by the observer as opposed to the subjects. Intraobserver reliability is particularly important when you are evaluating a client's behavior or making judgments about the client's progress. While the GAF has been found to have low interobserver reliability, it has been found to have pretty high intraobserver reliability. It turns out that while different raters disagree, a single rater tends to provide consistent reports about an individual.

Measurement Validity

In Chapter 1, you learned that measurement validity refers to the extent to which measures indicate what they are intended to measure. More technically, a valid measure of a concept is one that is closely related to other apparently valid measures of the concept and to the known or supposed correlates of that concept, but that is not related to measures of unrelated concepts, irrespective of the methods used for the other different measures (adapted from Brewer & Hunter, 1989, p. 134). The extent to which measurement validity has been achieved can be assessed with four different approaches: face validation, content validation, criterion validation, and construct validation. The methods of criterion and construct validation also include subtypes.

Face Validity

Researchers apply the term **face validity** to the confidence gained from careful inspection of a concept to see if it is appropriate "on its face." More precisely, we can say that a measure is face valid if it obviously pertains to the meaning of the concept being measured more than to other concepts (Brewer & Hunter, 1989, p. 131). For example, a count of how many drinks people consumed in the past week would be a face-valid measure of their alcohol consumption. Political party preference is unlikely on its face to tell us about alcohol consumption, although it would be related to political beliefs and social class.

Although every measure should be inspected in this way, face validation in itself does not provide very convincing evidence of measurement validity. The question How much beer or wine did you have to drink last week? may look valid on its face as a measure of frequency of drinking, but people who drink heavily tend to underreport the amount they drink. So the question would be an invalid measure in a study that includes heavy drinkers.

Content Validity

Content validity establishes that the measure covers the full range of the concept's meaning. To determine that range of meaning, the researcher may solicit the opinions of experts and review literature that identifies the different aspects or dimensions of the concept.

An example of an alcoholism measure that covers a wide range of meaning is the MAST. The MAST includes 24 questions representing the following subscales: recognition of alcohol problems by self and others; legal, social, and work problems; help seeking; marital and family difficulties; and liver pathology (Skinner & Sheu, 1982). Many experts familiar with the direct consequences of substance abuse agree that these dimensions capture the full range of possibilities. Thus, the MAST is believed to be valid from the standpoint of content validity.

On the other hand, experts may disagree with the range of content provided in a scale. The CES-D depression scale includes various dimensions of somatic symptoms and negative feelings. Some experts (e.g. Liang, Tran, Krause, & Markides, 1989) have questioned the presence of some items such as "feeling fearful" or "people dislike me," suggesting that these items are not reflective of the dimensions of depression. Other experts have suggested that perhaps the dimensions in the scale are not appropriate for how different population subgroups, such as the elderly (Weiss, Nagel, & Aronson, 1986) or African Americans (Barbee, 1992) manifest depression.

This example illustrates one of the difficulties in relying solely on face or content validity. While face and content validity are important to establish, in the end, they are still subjective assessments of validity. The next two forms of validity, criterion validity and construct validity, provide empirical evidence about the validity of a measure.

Criterion Validity

Criterion validity is established when the scores obtained on one measure can be accurately compared to those obtained with a more direct or already validated measure of the same phenomenon (the criterion). A measure of blood-alcohol concentration or a urine test could serve as the criterion for validating a self-report measure of drinking, as long as the questions we ask about drinking refer to the same period. A measure of depression could be compared to another accepted self-administered depression scale. A scale measuring job satisfaction could be compared to staying on the job. SAT or ACT scores could be compared to academic success in college. In each of these cases, the measure is being compared to some criterion believed to measure the same construct.

The criterion that researchers select can itself be measured either at the same time as the variable to be validated or after that time. **Concurrent validity** exists when a measure yields scores that are closely related to scores on a criterion measured at the same time. A store might validate its test of sales ability by administering the test to sales personnel who are already employed and then comparing their test scores to their sales performance. Or a measure of walking speed based on mental counting might be validated concurrently with a stop watch. **Predictive validity** is the ability of a measure to predict scores on a criterion measured in the future. For example, a store might administer a test of sales ability to new sales personnel and then validate the measure by comparing these test scores with the criterion—the subsequent sales performance of the new personnel.

An attempt at criterion validation is well worth the effort because it greatly increases confidence that the measure is measuring what was intended. However, for many concepts of interest to social work researchers, no other variable might reasonably be considered a criterion. If we are measuring feelings or beliefs or other subjective states, such as feelings of loneliness, what direct indicator could serve as a criterion? Even with variables for which a reasonable criterion exists, the researcher may not be able to gain access to the criterion—as would be the case with a tax return or employer document as a criterion for self-reported income.

Construct Validity

Measurement validity can also be established by showing that a measure is related to a variety of other measures as specified in a theory. This validation approach, known as **construct validity,** is commonly used in social research when no clear criterion exists for validation purposes. Koeske (1994) suggests that this theoretical construct validation process relies on using a deductive theory with hypothesized relationships among the constructs. The measure has construct validity (or theoretical construct validity) if it "behaves" as it should relative to the other constructs in the theory. For example, Danette Hann, Kristen Winter, and Paul Jacobsen (1999) compared subject scores on the CES-D to a number of indicators that they felt from previous research and theory should be related to depression: fatigue, anxiety, and global mental health. The researchers found that individuals with higher CES-D scores tended to have more problems in each of these areas, giving us more confidence in the CES-D's validity as a measure.

A somewhat different approach to construct validation is termed **discriminant validity**. In this approach, scores on the measure to be validated are compared to scores on another measure of the same variable and to scores on variables that measure different but related concepts. Discriminant validity is achieved if the measure to be validated is related most strongly to its comparison measure and less so to the measures of other concepts. For example, if we were testing the discriminant validity of the CES-D, we might compare it to another measure of depression, such as the Beck Depression Inventory (BDI), and to related concepts such as a measure of anxiety and a measure of self-esteem. If the CES-D has good discriminant validity, it will correlate strongest with the BDI and have lower correlations with the anxiety and self-esteem measures.

Convergent validity is demonstrated when you can show a relationship between two measures of the same construct that are assessed using different methods (Koeske, 1994). For example, we might compare the CES-D scale scores to clinical judgments made by practitioners who have used a clinical protocol. The CES-D scores should correlate with the scores obtained from the clinical protocol.

Another approach to construct validity is referred to as **known-groups validity.** In this method, we might have two groups with known characteristics, and we compare our measure across these two groups. We would expect that our measure should score higher with the group that it is related to and lower with the unrelated group. For example, we might give the CES-D to a group of people who have been clinically diagnosed as depressed and to a group that does not have a clinical diagnosis of depression. We would expect the CES-D scores to be higher among those clinically depressed than those who have no clinical diagnosis.

Finally, another method that has become associated with construct validity is **factoral validity**. This approach relies on factor analysis and, in many ways, is simply an empirical extension of content analysis. This procedure is usually applied when the construct of interest has different dimensions. In the analysis, we look to see if the items thought to be measuring the same dimension are more highly related to each other than to items measuring other dimensions. The CES-D scale has been hypothesized to have four dimensions: negative affect, positive affect (lack), somatic symptoms, and interpersonal. Several items are associated with each dimension. Therefore, a factor analysis would test whether the items measuring negative affect are more highly related to each other than to items measuring somatic symptoms. Negative affect items such as *feeling blue, sad, depressed,* and the like should have stronger relationships to each other than to items measuring somatic symptoms such as *overeating, sleeping too much,* or *difficulty concentrating.* A test of factoral validity would assess the expected internal theoretical relationships of the construct.

The distinction between criterion and construct validation is not always clear. Opinions can differ about whether a particular indicator is indeed a criterion for the concept that is to be measured. For example, if you need to validate a question-based measure of sales ability for applicants to a sales position, few would object to using actual sales performance as a criterion. But what if you want to validate a question-based measure of the amount of social support that people receive from their friends? Should you just ask people about the social support they have received? Could friends' reports of the amount of support they provided serve as a criterion? Are verbal accounts of the amount of support provided adequate? What about observations of social support that people receive? Even if you could observe people in the act of counseling or otherwise supporting their friends, can an observer be sure that the interaction is indeed supportive? There isn't really a criterion here, just related concepts that could be used in a construct validation strategy. Even biochemical measures of substance abuse are questionable as criteria for validating self-reported substance use. Urine test results can be altered by ingesting certain substances, and blood tests vary in their sensitivity to the presence of drugs over a particular period. Koeske (1994) suggests that a key difference is simply that with criterion validity, "the researcher's primary concern is with the criterion in a practical context, rather than with the theoretical properties of the construct measure" (p. 50).

What both construct and criterion validation have in common is the comparison of scores on one measure to scores on other measures that are predicted to be related. It is not so important that researchers agree that a particular comparison measure is a criterion rather than a related construct. But it is very important to think critically about the quality of the comparison measure and whether it actually represents a different view of the same phenomenon. For example, it is only a weak indication of measurement validity to find that scores on a new self-report measure of alcohol use are associated with scores on a previously used self-report measure of alcohol use.

Screening and Cut-Off Scores

Many scales do not just measure the range or intensity of some phenomenon but are also used as screening methods to make educated guesses about the presence or absence of some clinical condition. The CES-D has been used not only to measure the level of depressive symptoms but also to determine whether someone might suffer from depression. Scores on the CES-D scale may range from zero to 60; people with scores above 16 may be classified as depressed while people below 16 may be classified as not depressed. Many other scales have cut-off (or clinical cut-off) scores to define the presence or absence of a clinical condition.

For a variety of reasons, we would like cut-off scores that are as accurate as possible. If not, we risk expending limited resources on what may turn out to be an inaccurate assessment, we risk missing individuals with the condition, and we risk labeling clients with a condition they might not actually have. Therefore, it is important that the validity of a cut-off score be

Exhibit 3.8   Outcomes of Screening Scale versus Clinical Assessment

	Actual Diagnosis for the Clinical Condition		
Screening Scale Result	Client does not have clinical condition	Client has clinical condition	Total
Assessed as not having condition	True negative (a)	False negative (b)	a + b
Assessed as having the condition	False positive (c)	True positive (d)	c + d
Total	a + c	b + d	

assessed. Typically, this is done by comparing the scale's classifications to an established clinical evaluation method or to an already known condition. For example, the MAST cut-off score might be evaluated against a urinalysis. The CES-D cut-off score might be compared with a clinical diagnosis using the *DSM-IV*.

A summary of the analysis of the validity of a cut-off is presented in Exhibit 3.8. Each cell provides information about the overall accuracy of the instrument. One conclusion is that the screening scale provides an accurate assessment, either a **true negative** (cell a) or a **true positive** (cell d). A true negative occurs when, based on the scale, the client is assessed as not having a problem and really does not have the problem. A true positive occurs when it is determined from the obtained scale score that the client has a problem and the client really does have the problem based on the clinical evaluation. There are also two incorrect possibilities. A **false negative** (cell b) occurs when, based on the scale score, you conclude the client does not have the problem but the client really does have the problem. A **false positive** (cell c) occurs when you conclude from the scale score that the client does have a significant problem but in reality that person does not have the problem.

You will read or hear about several calculations to determine the validity of the cut-off scores. **Sensitivity** describes the true positive cell. It is a proportion based on the number of people who are assessed as having the condition (d) relative to the number of people who actually have the condition (b + d), or d / (b + d). **Specificity** describes the true negative cell. It is a proportion based on the number of people assessed as not having a condition (cell a) relative to the number who really do not have the condition (a + c); its mathematical formula is a / (a + c). False-negative rates and false-positive rates are similarly calculated. The proportion of false negatives is calculated by comparing the number of false negatives in cell b to the total number who actually have the clinical condition, (b + d), or b / (b + d). The proportion of false positives is calculated by comparing the number of assessed as having the condition, cell c, to the total number who actually do not have the clinical condition, (a + c) or c / (a + c).

Ideally, we would like both the sensitivity and specificity of the scale's cut-off scores to be very high so that we make few mistakes. Yet there are tradeoffs. If we really wanted to capture all the true positives, we would have to ease the criteria by reducing the cut-off score. This will increase sensitivity but will also likely result in more false positives, which means a lower specificity. If we make it more difficult to test positive, for example, by setting a higher cut-off score, we will increase the specificity, but we will get more false negatives, and therefore sensitivity will decline.

Two other types of estimates you will see are the **positive predictive value** and the **negative predictive value**. The positive predictive value is the proportion of people who actually have the condition (d) to the number who were assessed by the screening tool as having the condition (c + d), that is, d / (c + d). The negative predictive value is the proportion of all those who actually do not have the condition (a) compared to all those who were assessed as having the condition (a + b); this is calculated by a / (a + b). The ability to predict accurately is useful when we decide to use a screening scale to get some sense of how prevalent a particular condition is in the community. So if we wanted to assess how common depression is in the community, we would want high predictive values.

Ways to Improve Reliability and Validity of Existing Measures

At this point, we will discuss ways to improve reliability and validity of existing measures, and in Chapter 8, we will discuss how to improve the reliability and validity of new measures. Whether we are working with a new measure or an existing measure, we must always assess the reliability of a measure if we hope to be able to establish its validity. In fact, because it usually is easier to assess reliability than validity, you will see more evaluations of measurement reliability in research reports than evaluations of measurement validity.

Remember that a reliable measure is not necessarily a valid measure, as Exhibit 3.9 illustrates. This discrepancy is a common flaw of self-report measures of substance abuse. The multiple questions in self-report indexes of substance abuse are answered by most respondents in a consistent way, so the indexes are reliable. However, a number of respondents will not admit to drinking, even though they drink a lot. Their answers to the questions are consistent, but they are consistently misleading. So the indexes based on self-report are reliable but invalid. Such indexes are not useful and should be improved or discarded. Unfortunately, many measures are judged to be worthwhile on the basis only of a reliability test.

The reliability and validity of measures in any study must be tested after the fact to assess the quality of the information obtained. But then, if it turns out that a measure cannot be considered reliable and valid, little can be done to save the study. Hence, it is supremely important to select in the first place measures that are likely to be reliable and valid. Don't just choose the first measure you find or can think of: Consider the different strengths of different measures and their appropriateness to your study. Conduct a pretest in which you use the measure with a small sample and check its reliability. Provide careful training to ensure a consistent approach if interviewers or observers will administer the measure. In most cases, however, the best strategy is to use measures that have been used before and whose reliability and validity have been established in other contexts. But the selection of "tried and true" measures still does not absolve researchers from the responsibility of testing the reliability and validity of the measure in their own studies.

When the population studied or the measurement context differs from that in previous research, instrument reliability and validity may be affected. So the researchers must take pains with the design of their study. For example, test-retest reliability has proved to be better for several standard measures used to assess substance use among homeless people when the interview was conducted in a protected setting and when the measures focused on factual information and referred to a recent time interval (Drake, McHugo, & Biesanz, 1995).

Exhibit 3.9   The Difference between Reliability and Validity: Drinking Behavior

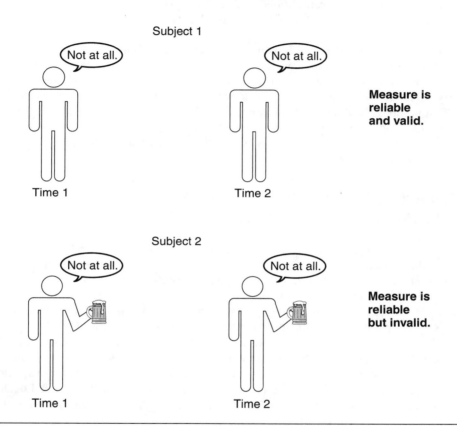

Subjects who were younger, female, recently homeless, and less severely afflicted with psychiatric problems were also more likely to give reliable answers.

It may be possible to improve the reliability and validity of measures in a study that already has been conducted if multiple measures were used. For example, in the Goldfinger et al. (1996) study of housing for homeless mentally ill people, funded by the National Institute of Mental Health, the researchers assessed substance abuse with several different sets of direct questions as well as with reports from subjects' case managers and others. They found that the observational reports were often inconsistent with self-reports and that different self-report measures were not always in agreement—hence, they were unreliable. A more reliable measure was initial reports of lifetime substance abuse problems, which identified all those who subsequently abused substances during the project. The researchers concluded that the lifetime measure was a valid way to identify people at risk for substance abuse problems. No single measure was adequate to identify substance abusers at a particular point in time during the project. Instead, the researchers constructed a composite of observer and self-report measures that seemed to be a valid indicator of substance abuse over six-month periods.

If the research focuses on previously unmeasured concepts, new measures will have to be devised. Researchers can use one of three strategies to improve the likelihood that new question-based measures will be reliable and valid (Fowler, 1995):

- *Engage potential respondents in group discussions about the questions to be included in the survey.* This strategy allows researchers to check for consistent understanding of terms and to hear the range of events or experiences that people will report.
- *Conduct cognitive interviews.* Ask people a test question, then probe with follow-up questions about how they understood the question and what their answer meant.
- *Audiotape test interviews during the pretest phase of a survey.* The researchers then review these audiotapes and systematically code them to identify problems in question wording or delivery.

CHOOSING AN INSTRUMENT FOR RESEARCH, EVALUATION, AND PRACTICE

As we have suggested throughout this chapter, measurement has relevancy beyond just research; it touches on every level of social work practice. The issues associated with measurement are crucial, both to research and practice. Hudson (1978) goes as far as stating: "If you cannot measure the client's problem, it does not exist. If you cannot measure the client's problem, you cannot treat it" (p. 65). Although these are extreme statements, they point to the importance of measurement in understanding whether clients improved.

The following, then, are suggestions for choosing an instrument when one is available. We believe these suggestions to be relevant whether you are doing research or assessing need and monitoring client progress. These suggestions come from other research and evaluation texts (see, e.g., Grinnell, 1993; Posavac & Carey, 1997; Royse, Thyer, Padgett, & Logan, 2001; Weiss, 1998) and from our own experiences in conducting research and evaluation studies.

Reliability and validity. We have already tried to convince you of the importance of reliability and validity. At a minimum, there should be evidence of measurement reliability and validity. You want to actually measure what you are trying to study. Your goal is to be able to say that the changes that occurred were due to the intervention and not the instability of the measurement instrument. When using agency-developed instruments rather than standardized scales, training staff in the use of the instrument will enhance consistency, and the measure can be evaluated by staff for face and content validity.

In evaluating the evidence of reliability and validity, focusing on the strength of the correlations or alpha coefficients is not enough. When you review the research, you need to look at the samples that were used in the studies. Too often, these studies are done without consideration of gender, race, ethnicity, or age. It may be that the samples used in the study(ies) look nothing like the population you are serving. If that is the case, the instrument may not be appropriate for your agency or setting. You cannot assume cross-population generalizability.

Cut-off scores. The same concerns regarding reliability and validity studies are true for research on the accuracy of cut-off scores. Just as with reliability and validity, we must be concerned about the cross-population generalizability of this research. Earlier, we described the CES-D as a commonly used scale with a more or less acceptable cut-off score of 16. On further inspection, researchers found that this score was too low to be useful with the elderly. Some item reports in the CES-D can be due to physical conditions that are common among the elderly. As a result, an appropriate cut-off score for elderly people with physical ailments has been determined to be 25 (Schulberg et al., 1985). The bottom line is to take nothing for granted about cut-off scores unless you believe that there is evidence of cross-population generalizability.

Feasibility of administration. As we have indicated, there are various methods to collect data, and different measures require different methods. Different methods of administration require different amounts of time to complete. If you choose a measure that requires observation, then you must be able to actually observe the behavior—you must have the time to observe the behavior, and you must be able to arrange to observe the behavior.

Different methods of administration also require skills on the part of the respondent. If you choose a scale that is self-administered, then you are assuming that the respondents can read and understand the instrument. Rafael Engel, Richard Welsh, and Laura Lewis (2000) conducted a study where the available scales are typically self-administered, but the vision level of the respondents was so poor that the scales could not be read by the respondents. These instruments had to be read to the respondent, which was an imposition on staff already busy with their primary responsibilities.

Sensitivity. If you are testing an intervention or evaluating the impact of an intervention on a group of clients or a single client, you will need a measure that is sufficiently sensitive to pick up changes in the outcome measures. The scale should have a sufficient number of items that you are able to identify changes. In addition, you want a measure that will provide a spread of responses, rather than having most or nearly all respondents provide the same response. This is a problem with client satisfaction measures because most people report that they are satisfied with services. The skewing of responses limits the analysis.

Reactivity. To the extent possible, you want measures that do not influence the responses that people provide. We have already suggested that most measures are susceptible to reactivity: The presence of an observer or self-monitoring may change behavior, or an interview may be influenced by the characteristics of the interviewer. You may need to take reactivity into account when reviewing your results.

There are times when reactivity may be useful. Shapiro and Mangelsdorf (1994) designed a parenting skills intervention for teenage moms. The researchers wanted to identify the mothers' "best" parenting skills and felt that if they videotaped the students, the latter would perform at what they considered to be the best interaction level. Reactivity in this case helped the researchers to identify what the teenagers knew, and from that, the effectiveness of the intervention could be tested.

Cost. The measure should be affordable. Many useful measures and scales can be found in the public domain, but many other scales have to be purchased, and sometimes you must also pay for their scoring.

Acceptability to staff. The measures have to be accepted by staff as measures that will provide valid information. Staff may disagree about the content of the measure, questioning the validity of the instrument in comparison to the agency's definition of the concept. If this is the case, they are less likely to use it. If the instrument provides useful information to staff as they work with clients, it is likely to be accepted.

CONCLUSION

Remember always that measurement validity is a necessary foundation for social work research. Gathering data without careful conceptualization or conscientious efforts to operationalize key concepts often is a wasted effort. The difficulties of achieving valid measurement vary with the concept being operationalized and the circumstances of the particular study.

Planning ahead is the key to achieving valid measurement in your own research; careful evaluation is the key to sound decisions about the validity of measures in others' research. Statistical tests can help to determine whether a given measure is valid after data have been collected, but if it appears after the fact that a measure is invalid, little can be done to correct the situation. If you cannot tell how key concepts were operationalized when you read a research report, don't trust the findings. If a researcher does not indicate the results of tests used to establish the reliability and validity of key measures, remain skeptical.

KEY TERMS

Alternate (or parallel) forms reliability
Concept
Conceptualization
Concurrent validity
Constant
Construct validity
Content validity
Continuous variable
Convergent validity
Criterion validity
Cronbach's alpha coefficient
Dichotomies
Direct measure
Discrete variable
Discriminant validity
Exhaustive
Face validity
Factoral validity
False positive
False negative
Idiosyncratic variation
Index
Indicator
Indirect measures
Internal consistency
Interobserver reliability
Interrater reliability
Interval level of measurement
Intraobserver reliability

Known-groups validity
Level of measurement
Multidimensional scale
Mutually exclusive
Negative predictive value
Nominal definition
Nominal level of measurement
Operation
Operational definition
Operationalization
Ordinal level of measurement
Positive predictive value
Predictive validity
Random error
Ratio level of measurement
Reliability
Reliability measures
Scale
Sensitivity
Specificity
Split-half reliability
Systematic error
Test-retest reliability
Testing effect
Triangulation
True positive
True negative
Unobtrusive measure

HIGHLIGHTS

- Conceptualization plays a critical role in research. In deductive research, conceptualization guides the operationalization of specific variables; in inductive research, it guides efforts to make sense of related observations.
- Concepts may refer to either constant or variable phenomena. Concepts that refer to variable phenomena may be very similar to the actual variables used in a study, or they may be much more abstract.
- Concepts should have a nominal definition and an operational definition. A nominal definition defines the concept in terms of other concepts whereas the operational definition provides the specific rules by which you measure the concept.
- In social work research, a treatment or intervention is often a variable. The intervention should have an operational definition, that is, a description of the intervention process.
- Indexes and scales measure a concept by combining answers to several questions and so reducing idiosyncratic variation. Several issues should be explored with every intended index: Does each question actually measure the same concept? Does combining items in an index obscure important relationships between individual questions and other variables? Is the index multidimensional?
- Measures are not perfect, and there may be two types of measurement error. Systematic error refers to predictable error and should be minimized. Random error is unpredictable in terms of effect on measurement.
- Level of measurement indicates the type of information obtained about a variable and the type of statistics that can be used to describe its variation. The four levels of measurement can be ordered by complexity of the mathematical operations they permit: nominal (least complex), ordinal, interval, ratio (most complex). The measurement level of a variable is determined by how the variable is operationalized. Dichotomies, a special case, may be treated as measured at the nominal or ordinal levels.
- The validity of measures should always be tested. There are four basic approaches: face validation, content validation, criterion validation (either predictive or concurrent), and construct validation. Criterion validation provides the strongest evidence of measurement validity, but there often is no criterion to use in validating social science measures.
- Measurement reliability is a prerequisite for measurement validity, although reliable measures are not necessarily valid. Reliability can be assessed through a test-retest procedure, in terms of interitem consistency, through a comparison of responses to alternate forms of the test, or in terms of consistency among observers and in one observer over time.
- In examining studies of measurement reliability and validity, it is important to look at the samples to ensure that there is evidence of reliability and validity for different population subgroups.
- Some scales are used to screen for the presence or absence of a clinical condition and, therefore, use cut-off scores. The accuracy of cut-off scores is assessed using measures of sensitivity and specificity.

DISCUSSION QUESTIONS

1. Describe the relationship between a nominal definition and an operational definition of a concept. How are these two types of definitions related?

2. Describe the elements of an operational definition. What information about the measurement process is provided in an operational definition? What are the various options for operationalizing concepts and gathering data? Describe the pros and cons for using direct and indirect measures for research on child abuse and neglect.

3. What are the relative merits of the different forms of measurement reliability and validity?

4. Why is it important that the reliability and validity of any scale be evaluated with different populations?

PRACTICE EXERCISES

1. Provide a nominal and operational definition for any of the following concepts: self-esteem, school stress, child abuse, alcohol abuse.

   a. Write down two observable behaviors that you believe would provide feasible measures of the concept you have chosen.

   b. Develop a scale by generating some questions that could serve as indicators for the concept you have chosen.

   c. Outline a plan to assess the validity and reliability of the behavior measures and the scale.

2. Find a research study that uses a scale to measure some concept. How does the author justify the reliability and validity of the scale? Does the author convince you that the scale can be applied to the sample in the study?

3. In the study chosen in Exercise 2, what are the variables? What is the level of measurement for each variable?

WEB EXERCISES

1. How would you define alcoholism? Write a brief definition. Based on this conceptualization, describe a method of measurement that would be valid for a study of alcoholism (as you define it). Now go to the Center of Alcohol Studies (CAS) homepage at http://www.rci.rutgers.edu/~cas2. Choose Library & Information, then Online Resources. Choose Other Related Internet Links. Choose National Council on Alcohol and Drug Dependence. Choose Facts. Choose Medical/Scientific Information, and finally click on Definition of Alcoholism.

   What is the definition of alcoholism used by the National Council on Alcohol and Drug Dependence? How is alcoholism conceptualized? Based on this conceptualization, give an example of one method that would be a valid measurement in a study of alcoholism.

   Now look at some of the other related links accessible from the CAS and NCADD Web sites. What are some of the different conceptualizations of alcoholism that you find? How does the chosen conceptualization affect one's choice of methods of measurement?

2. Compare two different measures of substance abuse. A site maintained by the University of New Mexico's Center on Alcoholism, Substance Abuse, and Addictions (http:casaa.unm.edu/inst/inst.html) provides a number of measures. Pick two of them. What concept of substance abuse is reflected in each measure? Is either measure multidimensional? What do you think the relative advantages of each measure might be? What evidence is provided about their reliability and validity, or if not available, how might you go about testing these?

> To assist you in completing the Web exercises, please access the study site at http://www.sagepub.com/prsw where you will find the Web Exercises reproduced and suggested links for online resources.

DEVELOPING A RESEARCH PROPOSAL

At this point you can begin the processes of conceptualization and operationalization.

1. Identify the concepts used in the study. Provide a nominal definition for each concept. When possible, this definition should come from the existing literature—either a book you have read for a course or a research article.

2. How will the concepts be operationalized? Identify the variables you will use to study the research question. Which of these variables are independent or dependent variables? What will be the level of measurement for each variable? How will these variables be coded?

3. Develop measurement procedures or identify existing instruments that might be used. If you are using a new measure, what procedures will you use to determine the reliability and validity of the measure? If you are using an existing instrument, what is the evidence for the instrument's reliability and validity?

Chapter 4

SAMPLING

Sample Planning

Define Sample Components and the
    Population
Evaluate Generalizability
Assess the Homogeneity of the
    Population
Enhance Sample Representativeness in
    Diverse Populations

Sampling Methods

Probability Sampling
Probability Sampling Methods
    Simple Random Sampling
    Systematic Random Sampling

    Stratified Random Sampling
    Cluster Sampling
Nonprobability Sampling Methods
    Availability Sampling
    Quota Sampling
    Purposive Sampling
    Snowball Sampling

Lessons about Sample Quality

Sampling Distributions

Estimating Sampling Error
Determining Sample Size

Conclusion

A representative of the State Department of Aging came to a social work agency's Seniors Unit as part of a service audit to determine whether the social work staff's client files were complete and included all the required information. In the unit, there were six social work staff members. The auditor walked into one social worker's office and pulled 40 client folders from the file cabinet. Unfortunately for the Seniors Unit, this staff person was notorious for not having his files completely in order. After reviewing the 40 client folders from this staffer, the auditor concluded that 50% of all the files in the Unit were out of compliance with state regulations. As a result, the agency was sanctioned, and the auditor put the unit supervisor on notice that funding would be discontinued unless all files were in compliance within five working days. The Seniors Unit staff rued their bad luck regarding how the files were chosen as they spent the next five days and nights reviewing all of their files. They knew that the auditor had reached faulty conclusions and did not get a truly representative view of the adequacy of client files.

    As you can see from this example, how we choose people from whom to gather information (or choose households, organizations, or even something as mundane as client records) has ramifications for the conclusions that can be made. Are the findings true only for those who provided the information, or can the findings from some samples be generalized to the population from which the sample was drawn? This is really the most basic question to ask about a sample, and social research methods provide many tools with which to address it.

Although we think of sampling as something limited to research, it is an important part of the overall functioning and evaluation of human service programs. When an agency is trying to demonstrate the effectiveness of services to a funding organization like the United Way, the director may choose to use a smaller group of clients to make the case. When a community organizer is trying to learn about the needs of older adults in a particular neighborhood, he or she may ask different people in the neighborhood but probably will not ask everybody; therefore, a sample of some sort is being used.

As consumers of research, we confront this question repeatedly, whether we are reading a journal article, working in an agency, or going about our everyday lives. For example, a common technique in journalism is to put a "human face" on a story. For instance, a reporter for *The New York Times* went to an emergency assistance unit near Yankee Stadium to ask homeless mothers about new welfare policies that require recipients to work. One woman with three children suggested, "If you work a minimum wage job, that's nothing. . . . Think about paying rent, with a family." In contrast, another mother with three children remarked, "It's important to do it for my kids, to set an example."

These are interesting comments, but we do not know whether they represent the opinions of most homeless people in the United States, in New York City, or even in the emergency assistance unit near Yankee Stadium. Even if the reporter had interviewed 10 homeless single mothers with children, we would not know how representative their opinions were. Because we have no idea whether these opinions are widely shared or quite unique, we cannot really judge what they tell us about the impact of welfare reform on single mothers. And we would not want to develop programs to help single mothers based on these two comments alone. In other words, we do not know whether these comments are generalizable.

In this chapter, you will learn about sampling methods, the procedures that primarily determine the generalizability of research findings. We first review the rationale for using sampling in social work research and consider two alternatives to sampling. The topic then turns to specific sampling methods and when they are most appropriate. We introduce the concept of sampling distribution and explain how it helps in estimating our degree of confidence in statistical generalizations. By the chapter's end, you should understand which questions you need to ask to evaluate the generalizability of a study as well as what choices you need to make when designing a sampling strategy.

SAMPLE PLANNING

You have encountered the problem of generalizability in each of the studies you have read about in this book. For example, Dee Roth and colleagues (1985) generalized their sample-based description of homeless people to the population of homeless people in Ohio; Peter Rossi (1989) generalized his conclusions about homelessness from a Chicago sample to the United States; and Lawrence Sherman and Richard Berk (1984) and others tried to determine the generalizability of findings from their study of domestic violence in Minneapolis. Whether we are designing a sampling strategy or evaluating the generalizability of someone else's findings, we have to understand how and why researchers decide to sample and what the consequences of these decisions are for the generalizability of the findings.

While sampling is very common in research, it is not always necessary. Often, the decision to take a sample of a population depends on the size of that population and/or the purpose of the study. If the population is very small and it is feasible to contact everyone in the population, there is no need to sample. If a program in an agency saw only 100 clients and the director wants client satisfaction data, there is no need to take a sample. The population is sufficiently small so that it would not take a great deal of time or the expenditure of a large amount of resources to try to obtain the information from all 100 clients. In addition, if there is no desire or interest in generalizing the findings to a broader population, there is no need to take a sample.

Define Sample Components and the Population

Let's say that we are designing a study of a topic that involves a lot of people (or other entities such as households, agencies, or communities). We often do not have the time or resources to study the entire **population** of elements in which we are interested, so we resolve to study a **sample**, a subset of this population of elements. The individual members of this sample are called **elements**, or elementary units.

Population   The entire set of individuals or other entities to which study findings are to be generalized.

Elements   The individual members of the population whose characteristics are to be measured.

Sample   A subset of a population that is used to study the population as a whole.

In many studies, we sample directly from the elements in the population of interest. We may survey a sample of the entire population of students at a school, based on a list obtained from the registrar's office. This list from which the elements of the population are selected is termed the **sampling frame**. The students who are selected and interviewed from that list are the elements.

Sampling frame   A list of all elements or other units containing the elements in a population.

In some studies, it is not easy to access the elements from which we want information, but we can find a group that includes those elements. For example, we may have a list of households in a town but not a list of its entire adult population, even though the adults are the elements we actually want to sample. In this situation, we could draw a sample of households and then identify the adult individuals in these households. The households are termed **enumeration units**, and the adults in the households are the elements (Levy & Lemeshow, 1999, pp. 13–14).

Enumeration units   Units that contain one or more elements and that are to be listed in a sampling frame.

Sometimes, the elements in our study are different from the individuals or other entities from which we collect information. For example, a researcher who wants to obtain information about child welfare services and programs might sample child welfare agencies for a survey and then interview a sample of staff within each of the sampled organizations. The child welfare agencies and the staff are both termed **sampling units** because we sample from both (Levy & Lemeshow, 1999, p. 22). The child welfare agencies are selected in the first stage so they are the *primary sampling units* (and in this case they are also the elements in the study). The staff are *secondary sampling units* (but they are not elements because they provide information about the entire organization). (See Exhibit 4.1)

Exhibit 4.1   Sample Components in a Two-Stage Study

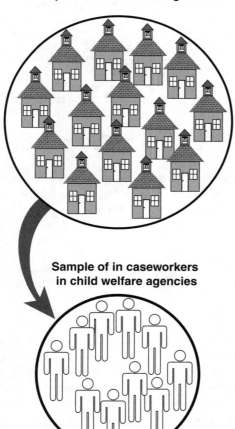

Sample of child welfare agencies

Child welfare agencies
are the elements and
the primary sampling unit.

**Sample of in caseworkers
in child welfare agencies**

Caseworkers are the
secondary sampling units;
they provide information
about the schools.

Sampling units   Units listed at each stage of a multistage sampling design.

It is important to know exactly what population a sample can represent when you select or evaluate sample components. Surveys of older adults may reasonably be construed as including individuals over the age of 65, but always be alert to ways in which the population may have been narrowed or expanded by the sample selection procedures. If a researcher used a list provided by the American Association for Retired Persons, *older* would be defined as 50 and above. In other surveys, older adults living in institutions such as skilled nursing homes or personal care homes are often excluded. Sometimes age is capped so that only people 65 to 84 are surveyed. In each survey, the sample is based on a somewhat different population. The population for a study is the aggregation of elements that we actually focus on and sample from, not some larger aggregation that we really wish we could have studied.

Some populations, such as the homeless, are not identified by a simple criterion such as a geographic boundary or an organizational membership. Clear definition of such a population is difficult but quite necessary. Anyone should be able to determine just what population was actually studied. However, studies of homeless people in the early 1980s "did not propose definitions, did not use screening questions to be sure that the people they interviewed were indeed homeless, and did not make major efforts to cover the universe of homeless people" (Burt, 1996, p. 15). (In some cases, homeless people in only one shelter were studied.) The result was "a collection of studies that could not be compared" (Burt, 1996, p. 15). Several studies of homeless people in urban areas addressed the problem by employing a more explicit definition of the population: "People are homeless if they have no home or permanent place to stay of their own (renting or owning) and no regular arrangement to stay at someone else's place" (Burt, 1996, p. 18). Even this more explicit definition still leaves some questions unanswered: What is a "regular arrangement"? How permanent does a "permanent place" have to be?

Evaluate Generalizability

Once we have defined clearly the population from which we will sample, we need to determine the scope of the generalizations we will seek to make from our sample. Do you recall from Chapter 1 two different meanings of generalizability?

- *Can the findings from a sample of the population be generalized to the population from which the sample was selected?* Did Roth's findings apply to Ohio, Rossi's to Chicago, Sherman and Berk's to Minneapolis? This type of generalizability was defined as *sample generalizability* in Chapter 1.
- *Can the findings from a study of one population be generalized to another, somewhat different population?* Are homeless people in Ohio or Chicago similar to those in other states? Were spouse abusers in Minneapolis like those in other cities or states? This type of generalizability was defined as *cross-population generalizability* in Chapter 1.

This chapter focuses attention primarily on the problem of sample generalizability: Can findings from a sample be generalized to the population from which the sample was drawn? This is really the most basic question to ask about a sample, and social research methods provide many tools with which to address it.

Sample generalizability depends on sample quality, which is determined by the amount of **sampling error**—the differences between the characteristics of a sample and the characteristics of the population from which it was selected. The larger the sampling error, the less representative the sample—and thus the less generalizable the findings. To assess sample quality when you are planning or evaluating a study, ask yourself these questions:

- From what population were the cases selected?
- What method was used to select cases from this population?
- Do the cases that were studied represent, in the aggregate, the population from which they were selected?

Sampling error   Any difference between the characteristics of a sample and the characteristics of the population from which it was drawn. The larger the sampling error, the less representative the sample.

But researchers often project their theories onto groups or populations much larger than, or simply different from, those they have actually studied. The population to which generalizations are made in this way can be termed the **target population**—a set of elements larger than or different from the population that was sampled and to which the researcher would like to generalize any study findings. When we generalize findings to target populations, we must be somewhat speculative. We must carefully consider the validity of claims that the findings can be applied to other subgroups of the population, geographic areas, cultures, or times.

Because the validity of cross-population generalizations cannot be tested empirically except by conducting more research in other settings, we will not focus much attention on this problem here. But we'll return to the problem of cross-population generalizability in Chapter 6, which addresses experimental research, and in Chapter 13, which discusses combining the results of studies that have been conducted in different settings.

Assess the Homogeneity of the Population

Sampling is unnecessary if all the units in the population are identical. Physicists don't need to select a representative sample of atomic particles to learn about basic physical processes. They can study a single atomic particle because it is identical to every other particle of its type. Similarly, biologists don't need to sample a particular type of plant to determine whether a given chemical has toxic effects on that particular type. The idea is, "If you've seen one, you've seen 'em all."

What about people? Certainly all people are not identical. The social world and the people in it are just too diverse to be considered identical units. In the past, researchers assumed that psychological and social processes were similar and generalizations could be made. There is a problem with this assumption: There is no way to know for sure if the processes being studied are identical across all people. Generalizing the results of single experiments and intervention studies is risky because such research often studies a small number of people who don't represent any particular population.

The larger point is that social work researchers as well as other social scientists rarely can skirt the problem of demonstrating the generalizability of their findings. If a small sample has been studied in a particular agency, in an experiment, or in a field research project, the study

Exhibit 4.2 Representative and Unrepresentative Samples

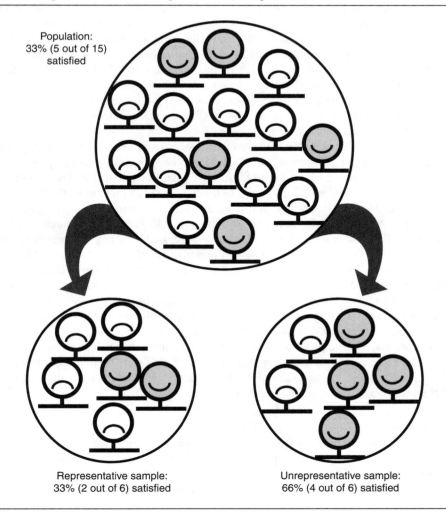

Population:
33% (5 out of 15)
satisfied

Representative sample:
33% (2 out of 6) satisfied

Unrepresentative sample:
66% (4 out of 6) satisfied

should be replicated in different settings or, preferably, with a **representative sample** of the population to which generalizations are sought (see Exhibit 4.2). Community-based and agency-based studies have produced good social work research, but they need to be replicated in other settings with other subjects to claim generalizability.

Enhance Sample Representativeness in Diverse Populations

One of the challenges for social work researchers is to ensure the representation of diverse populations in research studies. To this day, different subgroups of the population, whether categorized by gender, ethnicity, age, class, or sexual orientation, have been underrepresented in research efforts. Studies of published research in journals have found disproportionately few studies having an explicit focus on people of color or a separate analysis by race (Cauce, Ryan, & Grove, 1998; Graham, 1992). Similarly, sampling bias and gender have been discussed in critiques of various research, such as studies about the diagnostic categories of the *Diagnostic and Statistical Manual of Mental Disorders* (DSM-IV) (Hartung & Widiger, 1998) and addictions research (Brett, Graham, & Smythe, 1995).

The problems of exclusion or omission have been sufficiently problematic that Congress required the National Institutes of Health (NIH) to establish guidelines to ensure the inclusion of women and ethnic minorities in clinical research when it passed the *NIH Revitalization Act of 1993* (PL 103–43). Now NIH-supported biomedical and behavioral research projects must include women and minorities unless a "clear and compelling rationale and justification establishes to the satisfaction of the relevant Institute/Center Director that inclusion is inappropriate with respect to the health of the subjects or the purpose of the research" (NIH, 1994).

A common excuse has been that it is hard to recruit minorities to participate in research. Also, minority communities have had legitimate reasons to distrust research efforts, whether it is the exploitation of African American participants in the Tuskegee experiments on syphilis or the misuse of findings to the detriment of minority communities (Norton & Manson, 1996). Too often, research studies have not benefited the participating communities, and by couching comparative studies as evidence of "deficits," researchers have sometimes stigmatized ethnic communities. When appropriate efforts are made, people of color do participate at high rates in research activities (Milburn, Gary, Booth, & Brown, 1992; Thompson, Neighbors, Munday, & Jackson, 1996; Yamatani et al., 2000).

To encourage participation by people of color requires different strategies, and these may vary with each specific ethnic group. Yet a perusal of different research and literature suggests that there are some common strategies used to recruit and retain participants, whether it be in survey, exploratory, or experimental research.

Involve key community members and organizations. It is crucial to gain entry to the community to recruit respondents and participants. One way to obtain credibility and gain acceptance is to contact and connect to important organizations, agencies, and institutions within the community first. Norton and Manson (1996) describe the importance of first gaining the approval of the tribe before seeking individual permission of Native Americans to participate in research. When traditional methods of recruitment (advertisements in newspapers and radio) succeeded in recruiting White older adults but failed to produce African American and Hispanic older adult participants, Arean and Gallagher-Thompson (1996) knew they had to change recruitment strategies. They solicited the support of the directors of community centers and ministers of neighborhood churches. After gaining their approval, they met with potential participants with the leaders present. These efforts considerably increased the number of African American and Hispanic participants. Milburn et al. (1992) used a similar strategy as part of what ultimately led to a stratified, multistage cluster sampling of Black households. They contacted several key informants from members of the Urban League, local alumni, pastors of Black churches, and directors of local health and community centers. Through the help of two of the key informants, Milburn et al. identified city residents who were both involved in community services and respected by the community, asking them to serve on the research study's Advisory Board. These steps afforded a high rate of participation.

Demonstrate that there is a benefit to the community. Too many ethnic communities have seen research efforts that not only have not helped the community but have had adverse impacts on the community. Furthermore, we and other researchers (e.g., Milburn et al., 1992) have encountered the perception that research is done to advance the researcher's career and not for the benefit of the community. There are different avenues to benefit the community. For example, Norton and Manson (1996) suggest that two benefits to Native American tribes include employing local community members to help with the research and working with local service providers to translate the findings into action.

Understand cultural barriers. As a general rule, it is important that the research effort take into account cultural considerations. For example, Miranda, Azocar, Organista, Munoz, and Lieberman (1996) identify several different cultural norms among Latinos that may preclude or facilitate participation in treatment research including: importance of family, respect toward older adults, respect to professionals, and warmth in interactions between professionals/ researchers and clients/participants. They suggest that recruitment procedures that are too informal or cold will fail, while success comes from "treating older Latinos with respect using formal titles, while being warm and personable" (p. 870). They suggest using bilingual/ bicultural interviewers.

Another solution is to use interviewers of similar ethnicity or to train interviewers from the community. In a multistage cluster study of an African American neighborhood, Yamatani et al. (2000) achieved a high response rate in part by using local members of the community to conduct the interviews. On the other hand, using interviewers from the same tribe may impose on some Native American tribes' sense of privacy and confidentiality (Norton & Manson, 1996).

Train interviewers. It is particularly important that interviewers be well trained. Thompson et al. (1996) suggest that the interviewers practice "how to approach [participants], how to provide a general overview of the study, and the best method of presenting topics such as confidentiality and voluntary participation" (p. 863). The training should not be a one-way street; rather, input from those trained can also enhance the overall study. Yamatani and his colleagues (2000) solicited the ideas of interviewers about how to approach residents and how to improve the wording of the survey instrument.

Go to where the potential participants are. Often recruitment seems to be centered in the wrong locations. For example, African Americans and Latinos have lower rates of usage of mental health provider services, and therefore, recruitment should be at settings that they frequent, such as community hospitals or primary care providers.

Difficulties of recruitment are not limited to people of color. Other subgroups of the population have legitimate fears of being stigmatized and facing discrimination if they are identified. For example, there has been recent discussion of how to recruit gay males and lesbians to research studies. Anthony Silvestre (1994) notes that those at high risk of HIV infection are not coming forward in sufficient numbers and that those who do likely represent specific subgroups of the at-risk population.

Silvestre (1994) describes a brokering technique that was used to recruit nearly 3,000 gay and bisexual men (as of 1994) to an ongoing longitudinal epidemiological study of HIV among gay and bisexual men. The process included:

- Hiring a community organizer and having publicly known leaders in the gay community participate in the search.
- Establishing a community advisory board reflecting the diversity of interests in the community.
- Engaging in the exchange of goods and services between the researchers and the formal and informal gay leadership. Researchers provided things such as: access to the most recent information about HIV; access to university facilities for meetings and community events; public discourse and development of HIV-related public policy; protocols that both protect confidentiality and provide education to participants; participation in study decisions; a clinic with supportive and qualified staff; referrals; and the like. Gay leadership provided: statements of public support; facilities and time to present information, distribute questionnaires, and the like at their organizations or businesses; distribution of flyers, posters, and newsletters; advice; introductions to other key community members; and person–to-person communications.
- Using research to better inform the researchers about the pressing issues for the gay and bisexual community.

Roger Roffman and colleagues (1998) describe a different effort to recruit gay and bisexual males to an intervention and research project. Potential participants were given the choice of enrolling by a confidential option or anonymously. Those enrolling through the confidential option were asked for a phone number and instructions about the type of message that could be left; they were interviewed over the phone. To enroll anonymously, participants were asked to rent a postal box using a real name or a pseudonym, and they were sent a money order to pay for the postal box with no name written on the payee line. All subsequent communications about treatment, data collection, and incentive payments were conducted through the postal box. The project enrolled a large number of participants, and the researchers found differences between those who used the confidential versus anonymous approach.

Given that social work research can inform treatment effectiveness, intervention methods, and policy directions, it is important that what is learned pertains to and is useful to all segments of society (Miranda et al., 1996). To recruit and retain research participants requires an understanding of why some groups fail to participate in research as well as the cultural backgrounds of different groups. As you can see by the examples described above, recruitment and retention may require creative approaches.

SAMPLING METHODS

We can now study more systematically the features of samples that make them more or less likely to represent the population from which they are selected. The most important distinction that needs to be made is between samples that are based on a probability sampling method and those based on a nonprobability sampling method. Sampling methods that allow us to know in advance how likely it is that any element of a population will be selected for the sample are termed **probability sampling methods**. Sampling methods that do not let us know the likelihood in advance are termed **nonprobability sampling methods**.

Probability Sampling

Probability sampling methods are used particularly when we want to be able to generalize the results to the broader population, whether we are predicting the outcome of a political election, assessing community needs, or even evaluating the quality of client files. Because these methods are based on probability theory, we can estimate the extent to which the sample is actually representative of the broader population.

Probability sampling methods rely on a random, or chance, selection procedure, which is in principle the same as flipping a coin to decide which of two people "wins" and which one "loses." Heads and tails are equally likely to turn up in a coin toss, so both people have an equal chance to win. That chance, their **probability of selection**, is 1 out of 2, or .5.

Probability of selection The likelihood that an element will be selected from the population for inclusion in the sample. In a census of all the elements of a population, the probability that any particular element will be selected is 1.0. If half the elements in the population are sampled on the basis of chance (say, by tossing a coin), the probability of selection for each element is one half, or .5. As the size of the sample as a proportion of the population decreases, so does the probability of selection.

Flipping a coin is a fair way to select one of two people because the selection process harbors no **systematic bias**; nothing but chance determines which elements are included in the sample. You might win or lose the coin toss, but you know that the outcome was due simply to chance, not to bias. For the same reason, a roll of a six-sided die is a fair way to choose one of six possible outcomes (the odds of selection are 1 out of 6, or .17). Dealing out a hand after shuffling a deck of cards is a fair way to allocate sets of cards in a card game (the odds of each person getting a particular outcome, such as a full house or a flush, are the same). Similarly, state lotteries use a random process to select winning numbers. Thus, the odds of winning a lottery, the probability of selection, are known, even though they are very much smaller (perhaps 1 out of 1 million) than the odds of winning a coin toss.

There is a natural tendency to confuse the concept of **random sampling**, in which cases are selected only on the basis of chance, with a haphazard method of sampling. On first impression, "leaving things up to chance" seems to imply not exerting any control over the sampling method. But to ensure that nothing but chance influences the selection of cases, the researcher must proceed very methodically, leaving nothing to chance except the selection of the cases themselves. The researcher must follow carefully controlled procedures if a purely random process is to occur. In fact, when reading about sampling methods in research journals or papers, do not assume that a random sample was obtained just because the researcher used a random selection method at some point in the sampling process. Look for these two particular problems: selecting elements from an incomplete list of the total population and failing to obtain an adequate response rate.

If the sampling frame is incomplete, a sample selected randomly from that list will not really be a random sample of the population. You should always consider the adequacy of the sampling frame. Even for a simple population like a university's student body, the registrar's list is likely to be at least a bit out of date at any given time. For example, some students will have dropped out, but their status will not yet be officially recorded. Although you may judge the amount of error introduced in this particular situation to be negligible, the problems are greatly compounded for a larger population. The sampling frame for a city, state, or nation is always likely to be incomplete because of constant migration into and out of the area. Even unavoidable omissions from the sampling frame can bias a sample against particular groups within the population.

A very inclusive sampling frame may still yield systematic bias if many sample members cannot be contacted or refuse to participate. Nonresponse is a major hazard in survey research because nonrespondents are likely to differ systematically from those who take the time to participate. You should not assume that findings from a randomly selected sample will be generalizable to the population from which the sample was selected if the rate of nonresponse is considerable (certainly not if it is much above 30%).

Probability Sampling Methods

Probability sampling methods are those in which the probability of selection is known and is not zero so there is some chance of selecting each element. These methods randomly select elements and therefore have no **systematic bias;** nothing but chance determines which elements are included in the sample. This feature of probability samples makes them much more desirable than nonprobability samples when the goal is to generalize to a larger population.

Even though a random sample has no systematic bias, it will certainly have some sampling error due to chance. The probability of selecting a head is .5 in a single toss of a coin and in 20, 30, and however many tosses of a coin you like. But it is perfectly possible to toss a coin twice and get a head both times. The random sample of the two sides of the coin is selected in an unbiased fashion, but it still is unrepresentative. Imagine selecting randomly a sample of 10 clients from an agency program that includes 50 men and 50 women. Just by chance, can't you imagine finding that these 10 clients include 7 women and only 3 men? Fortunately, we can determine mathematically the likely degree of sampling error in an estimate based on a random sample (as we will discuss later in this chapter)—assuming that the sample's randomness has not been destroyed by a high rate of nonresponse or by poor control over the selection process.

In general, both the size of the sample and the homogeneity (sameness) of the population affect the degree of error due to chance; the proportion of the population that the sample represents does not. To elaborate:

The larger the sample, the more confidence we can have in the sample's representativeness. If we randomly pick 5 people to represent the entire population of our city, our sample is unlikely to be representative of the entire population in terms of age, gender, race, attitudes, and so on. But if we randomly pick 100 people, the odds of having a representative sample are much better; with a random sample of 1,000, the odds become very good indeed.

The more homogeneous the population, the more confidence we can have in the representativeness of a sample of any particular size. Let's say we plan to draw samples of 50 from each of two communities to estimate mean family income. One community is very diverse, with family incomes varying from $12,000 to $85,000. In the other, more homogeneous community, family incomes are concentrated in a narrow range, from $41,000 to $64,000. The estimated mean family income based on the sample from the homogeneous community is more likely to be representative than is the estimate based on the sample from the more heterogeneous community. With less variation to represent, fewer cases are needed to represent the homogeneous community.

The fraction of the total population that a sample contains does not affect the sample's representativeness, unless that fraction is large. We can regard any sampling fraction less than 2% with about the same degree of confidence (Sudman, 1976, p. 184). In fact, sample representativeness is not likely to increase much until the sampling fraction is quite a bit higher. Other things being equal, a sample of 1,000 from a population of 1 million (with a sampling fraction of 0.001, or 0.1%) is much better than a sample of 100 from a population of 10,000 (although the sampling fraction is 0.01, or 1%, which is 10 times higher). The size of the samples is what makes representativeness more likely, not the proportion of the whole that the sample represents.

Polls to predict presidential election outcomes illustrate both the value of random sampling and the problems that it cannot overcome. In most presidential elections, pollsters have predicted accurately the outcome of the actual vote by using random sampling and, these days, phone interviewing to learn for whom likely voters intend to vote. Exhibit 4.3 shows how close these sample-based predictions have been in the last 10 contests. The exceptions to accurate prediction were the 1980 and 1992 elections, when third-party candidates had an unpredicted effect. Otherwise, the small discrepancies between the votes predicted through random sampling and the actual votes can be attributed to random error.

The Gallup poll did quite well in predicting the result of the remarkable 2000 presidential election. The final Gallup prediction was that George W. Bush would win with 48% (Al Gore was predicted to receive only 46%, while Green Party nominee Ralph Nader was predicted to

Exhibit 4.3   Election Outcomes: Predicted[1] and Actual

Winner/Year	Polls	Result
Kennedy (1960)	51%	50%
Johnson (1964)	64%	61%
Nixon (1968)[2]	43%	43%
Nixon (1972)	62%	62%
Carter (1976)	48%	50%
Reagan (1980)[2]	47%	51%
Reagan (1984)	59%	59%
Bush (1988)	56%	54%
Clinton (1992)[2]	49%	43%
Clinton (1996)[2]	52%	50%
Bush, G. W. (2000)[2]	48%	50%

Source: Gallup Poll Accuracy Record, 12/13/00, www.gallup.com/poll/trends/ptaccuracy.asp.

[1]Final Gallup poll prior to the election.

[2]There was also a third-party candidate.

secure 4%). Although the race turned out much closer, with Gore actually winning the popular vote (before losing in the Electoral College), Gallup accurately noted that there appeared to have been a late-breaking trend in favor of Gore (Newport, 2000).

But election polls have produced some major errors in prediction. The reasons for these errors illustrate some of the ways in which unintentional systematic bias can influence sample results. In 1936, a *Literary Digest* poll predicted that Alfred M. Landon would defeat President Franklin Delano Roosevelt in a landslide, but instead, Roosevelt took 63% of the popular vote. The problem? The *Digest* mailed out 10 million mock ballots to people listed in telephone directories, automobile registration records, voter lists, and so on. But in 1936, the middle of the Great Depression, only relatively wealthy people had phones and cars, and they were more likely to be Republican. Furthermore, only 2,376,523 completed ballots were returned, and a response rate of only 24% leaves much room for error. Of course, this poll was not designed as a random sample, so the appearance of systematic bias is not surprising. Gallup was able to predict the 1936 election results accurately with a randomly selected sample of just 3,000 (Bainbridge, 1989, pp. 43–44).

In 1948, pollsters mistakenly predicted that Thomas E. Dewey would beat Harry S. Truman, based on the random sampling method that George Gallup had used successfully since 1934. The problem? Pollsters stopped collecting data several weeks before the election, and in those weeks, many people changed their minds (Kenney, 1987). So the sample was systematically biased by underrepresenting shifts in voter sentiment just before the election.

Because they do not disproportionately exclude or include particular groups within the population, random samples that are successfully implemented avoid systematic bias. Random error can still be considerable, however, and different types of random samples vary in their ability to minimize it. The four most common methods for drawing random samples are simple random sampling, systematic random sampling, stratified random sampling, and cluster sampling.

Simple Random Sampling

Simple random sampling requires some procedure that generates numbers or otherwise identifies cases strictly on the basis of chance. As you know, flipping a coin and rolling a die both can be used to identify cases strictly on the basis of chance, but these procedures are not very efficient tools for drawing a sample. A **random numbers table,** like the one in Appendix F, simplifies the process considerably. The researcher numbers all the elements in the sampling frame and then uses a systematic procedure for picking corresponding numbers from the random numbers table. (Exercise 2 at the end of this chapter explains the process step by step.) Alternatively, a researcher may use a lottery procedure. Each case number is written on a small card, and then the cards are mixed up and the sample selected from the cards.

When a large sample must be generated, these procedures are very cumbersome. Fortunately, a computer program can easily generate a random sample of any size. The researcher must first number all the elements to be sampled (the sampling frame) and then run the computer program to generate a **random selection** of the numbers within the desired range. The elements represented by these numbers are the sample.

The state auditor whose work was described at the beginning of this chapter could have chosen a random sample of files by having each file numbered from 1 to 600 and then using a random numbers table to pick 40 folders. Because of the small sample size, it is still possible that all 40 folders would have come from the worst caseworker, but the probability of this happening is small.

The key characteristic of a true simple random sample is that the probability of selection is equal for each element. In the case of the agency audit, if a sample of 40 files is selected from a population of 600 (that is, a sampling frame of 600), then the probability of selection for each element is 40/600, or .0667. Every element has an equal chance of being selected, just like the odds in a toss of a coin (1/2) or a roll of a die (1/6). Thus, simple random sampling is an equal probability of selection method, or EPSEM.

Simple random sampling can be done either with or without replacement sampling. In **replacement sampling**, each element is returned to the sampling frame after it is selected so that it may be sampled again. In sampling without replacement, each element selected for the sample is then excluded from the sampling frame. In practice, it makes no difference whether sampled elements are replaced after selection, as long as the population is large and the sample is to contain only a small fraction of the population. Random sampling with replacement is, in fact, rarely used.

Organizations that conduct phone surveys often draw random samples with another automated procedure, called **random digit dialing**. A machine dials random numbers within the phone prefixes corresponding to the area in which the survey is to be conducted. Random digit dialing is particularly useful when a sampling frame is not available. The researcher simply replaces any inappropriate numbers (those that are no longer in service or that are for businesses, for example) with the next randomly generated phone number.

Systematic Random Sampling

Systematic random sampling is a variant of simple random sampling. The first element is selected randomly from a list or from sequential files, and then, every nth element is selected. This is a convenient method for drawing a random sample when the population elements are arranged sequentially. It is particularly efficient when the elements are not actually printed (that is, there is no sampling frame) but instead are represented by folders in filing cabinets.

Systematic random sampling requires three steps:

1. The total number of cases in the population is divided by the number of cases required for the sample. This division yields the **sampling interval**, the number of cases between one sampled case and another. If 50 cases are to be selected out of 1,000, the sampling interval is 20; every 20th case is selected.

2. A number from 1 to 20 (or whatever the sampling interval is) is selected randomly. This number identifies the first case to be sampled, counting from the first case on the list or in the files. Alternatively, a number is selected randomly using the entire range; in this case from 1 to 1,000. In either method, a random numbers table or a computer can be used to decide on a starting number.

3. After the first case is selected, every nth case is selected for the sample, where n is the sampling interval. If the sampling interval is not a whole number, the size of the sampling interval is varied systematically to yield the proper number of cases for the sample. For example, if the sampling interval is 30.5, the sampling interval alternates between 30 and 31. Alternatively, you may round, but whatever the decimal is, you

must round up, even if the interval is 30.1. Rounding down precludes some elements from having any chance of being selected.

In almost all sampling situations, systematic random sampling yields what is essentially a simple random sample. The exception is a situation in which the sequence of elements is affected by **periodicity**—that is, the sequence varies in some regular, periodic pattern. For example, the houses in a new development that has the same number of houses on each block (eight, for example) may be listed by block, starting with the house in the northwest corner of each block and continuing clockwise. If the sampling interval is 8, the same as the periodic pattern, all the cases selected will be in the same position (see Exhibit 4.4). Some couples' research suffered from this problem when the couples were listed systematically by gender and an even number was used for the sampling interval. But in reality, periodicity and the sampling interval are rarely the same.

Stratified Random Sampling

Stratified random sampling uses information known about the total population prior to sampling to make the sampling process more efficient. First, all elements in the population

Exhibit 4.4   The Effect of Periodicity on Systematic Random Sampling

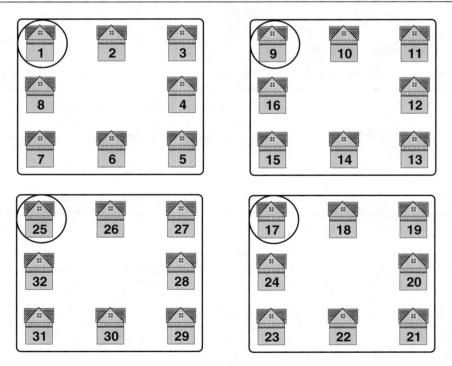

If the sampling interval is 8 for a study in this neighborhood,
every element of the sample will be a house on the northwest
corner—and thus the sample will be biased.

(that is, in the sampling frame) are distinguished according to their value on some relevant characteristic. That characteristic forms the sampling strata. Next, elements are sampled randomly from within these strata. For example, race may be the basis for distinguishing individuals in some population of interest. Within each racial category, individuals are then sampled randomly. Of course, to use this method, more information is required prior to sampling than is the case with simple random sampling. It must be possible to categorize each element in one and only one stratum and, for proportionate to size sampling, the size of each stratum in the population must be known.

This method is more efficient than drawing a simple random sample because it ensures appropriate representation of elements across strata. Imagine that you plan to draw a sample of 500 from an ethnically diverse neighborhood. The neighborhood population is 15% Black, 10% Hispanic, 5% Asian, and 70% White. If you drew a simple random sample, you might end up with disproportionate numbers of each group. But if you created sampling strata based on race and ethnicity, you could randomly select cases from each stratum: 75 Blacks (15% of the sample), 50 Hispanics (10%), 25 Asians (5%), and 350 Whites (70%). By using **proportionate stratified sampling,** you would eliminate any possibility of error in the sample's distribution of ethnicity. Each stratum would be represented exactly in proportion to its size in the population from which the sample was drawn (see Exhibit 4.5).

In **disproportionate stratified sampling**, the proportion of each stratum that is included in the sample is intentionally varied from what it is in the population. In the case of the sample stratified by ethnicity, you might select equal numbers of cases from each racial or ethnic group: 125 Blacks (25% of the sample), 125 Hispanics (25%), 125 Asians (25%), and 125 Whites (25%). In this type of sample, the probability of selection of every case is known but unequal between strata. You know what the proportions are in the population, and so you can easily adjust your combined sample statistics to reflect these true proportions. For instance, if you want to combine the ethnic groups and estimate the average income of the total population, you would have to "weight" each case in the sample. The weight is a number you multiply by the value of each case based on the stratum it is in. For example, you would multiply the incomes of all Blacks in the sample by 0.6 (75/125), the incomes of all Hispanics by 0.4 (50/125), and so on. Weighting in this way reduces the influence of the oversampled strata and increases the influence of the undersampled strata to just what they would have been if pure probability sampling had been used.

Why would anyone select a sample that is so unrepresentative in the first place? The most common reasons are to ensure that cases from smaller strata are included in the sample in sufficient numbers to allow separate statistical estimates, to have an adequate number to reflect subgroup differences or heterogeneity, and to facilitate comparisons between strata. Remember that one of the determinants of sample quality is sample size. The same is true for subgroups within samples. If a key concern in a research project is to describe and compare the incomes of people from different racial and ethnic groups, then it is important that the researchers base the mean income of each group on enough cases to be a valid representation. If few members of a particular minority group are in the population, they need to be oversampled. Such disproportionate sampling may also result in a more efficient sampling design if the costs of data collection differ markedly between strata or if the variability (heterogeneity) of the strata differs.

Stratified sampling would have helped improve the auditor's findings at the Seniors Unit. If the auditor had stratified by worker and then used a random sampling method to select from each worker's files, a more representative set of files would have been evaluated.

Exhibit 4.5   Stratified Random Sampling

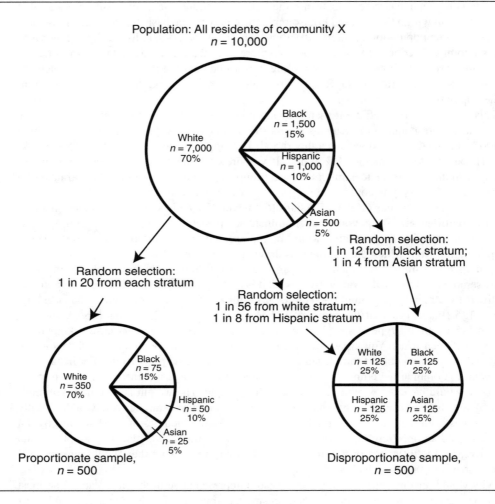

Cluster Sampling

Although all probability sampling methods use random sampling, some add additional steps to the sampling process to make sampling more efficient or easier. **Cluster sampling** is useful when a sampling frame is not available, as often is the case for large populations spread out across a wide geographic area or among many different organizations. A **cluster** is a naturally occurring, mixed aggregate of elements of the population, with each element appearing in one and only one cluster. Schools could serve as clusters for sampling students, blocks could serve as clusters for sampling city residents, counties could serve as clusters for sampling the general population, and agencies could serve as clusters for sampling social work staff.

Exhibit 4.6   Multistage Cluster Sampling

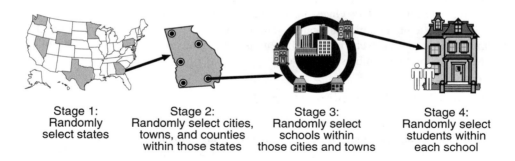

| Stage 1:
Randomly
select states | Stage 2:
Randomly select cities,
towns, and counties
within those states | Stage 3:
Randomly select
schools within
those cities and towns | Stage 4:
Randomly select
students within
each school |

Drawing a cluster sample requires at least two stages. First, the researcher draws a random sample of clusters. A list of clusters should be much easier to obtain than a list of all the individuals in each cluster in the population. Next, the researcher draws a random sample of elements within each selected cluster. Because only a fraction of the total clusters is involved, obtaining the sampling frame at this stage should be much easier.

In a cluster sample of city residents, for example, blocks could be the first-stage clusters. A research assistant could walk around each selected block and record the addresses of all occupied dwelling units (see Exhibit 4.6). Or in a cluster sample of students, a researcher could contact the schools selected in the first stage and make arrangements with the registrar to obtain lists of students at each school. Cluster samples often involve multiple stages, with clusters within clusters, as when a national sample of middle school students involves first sampling states, then counties, then schools, and finally students in each selected school.

How many clusters and how many individuals within clusters should be selected? As a general rule, cases in the sample will be closer to the true population value if the researcher maximizes the number of clusters selected and minimizes the number of individuals within each cluster. Unfortunately, this strategy also maximizes the cost of the sample. The more clusters selected, the higher the travel costs. It also is important to take into account the homogeneity of the individuals within clusters—the more homogeneous the clusters, the fewer cases needed per cluster.

Cluster sampling is a popular method among survey researchers, but it has one drawback: Sampling error is greater in a cluster sample than in a simple random sample. This error increases as the number of clusters decreases, and it decreases as the homogeneity of cases per cluster increases.

Many surveys use cluster sampling. Israel Colon and Brett Marston (1999) wanted to evaluate "not in my back yard" attitudes toward a proposed residential home for HIV-positive individuals in a community. A local agency had wanted to provide such housing but at hearings, extreme opposition was found. Although the residence was ultimately built, the authors wanted to understand the source(s) of the opposition. Was it homophobia? Fear of AIDS? Concern about property values? Proximity to the housing? Colon and Marston listed all the blocks in the community and then took a 10% random sample of the blocks. They then tried to interview a member of each household in the selected blocks.

Random digit dialing is often used for cluster sampling. When using random digit dialing to contact households in a community, the telephone exchanges (the first three numbers) are often used as the clusters. Once clusters are selected, sometimes four-digit numbers are randomly selected to complete the phone number. Sometimes a multistage random digit dialing method is used. The exchanges are chosen, then the next two numbers are chosen, and finally, the remaining two numbers are chosen.

Nonprobability Sampling Methods

Four nonprobability sampling methods are commonly used in social work research: availability sampling, quota sampling, purposive sampling, and snowball sampling. Because nonprobability sampling methods do not use a random selection procedure, we cannot expect a sample selected with any of these methods to yield a representative sample.

Nonetheless, these methods may be useful when random sampling is not possible, with a research question that does not concern a large population or require a random sample, when a random sample is not thought to be accessible, or for a preliminary, exploratory study. These four methods are often applied to experimental studies testing the effectiveness of different treatment or intervention methods. Similarly, program evaluation conducted in agencies will often employ a nonprobability sampling method.

Availability Sampling

Elements are selected for **availability sampling** because they are available or easy to find. Thus, this sampling method is also known as accidental or convenience sampling. There are many ways to select elements for an availability sample: standing on street corners and talking to whoever walks by; asking questions of employees who come to pick up their paychecks at a personnel office and who have time to talk to a researcher; surveying merchants who happen to be at work when the researcher is looking for subjects. When Philippe Bourgois, Mark Lettiere, and James Quesada (1997) studied homeless heroin addicts in San Francisco, they immersed themselves in a community of addicts living in a public park. These addicts became the availability sample.

An availability sample is often appropriate in social work research—for example, when a researcher is exploring a new setting and trying to get some sense of prevailing attitudes or when a survey researcher conducts a preliminary test of a new set of questions. Availability samples are also common techniques used in different aspects of agency-based evaluative research, such as evaluating the effectiveness of one of its programs. For example, Kinnevy, Healey, Pollio, and North (1999) studied the effectiveness of a task-centered structured group program with low-income, high-risk youth. The program, called BicycleWORKS, was based in a community agency and was designed to teach participants how to build and repair bicycles during six group sessions as well as accumulate points to earn a bicycle. Participants signed a conduct pledge and had to pass a test to graduate from the program. It was hoped that the program would impact positively on the self-esteem of the participants and their ability to work with others, while reducing problematic behaviors. The subjects were those participants who were available and people on the agency wait list.

Availability sampling often masquerades as a more rigorous form of research. Popular magazines periodically survey their readers by printing a questionnaire for readers to fill out and mail in. A follow-up article then appears in the magazine under a title such as, "What You Think about Intimacy in Marriage." If the magazine's circulation is large, a large sample can be achieved in this way. The problem is that usually only a tiny fraction of readers return the questionnaire, and these respondents are probably unlike other readers, who did not have the interest or time to participate. So the survey is based on an availability sample. Even though the follow-up article may be interesting, we have no basis for thinking that the results describe the readership as a whole—much less the population at large.

Quota Sampling

Quota sampling is intended to overcome the most obvious flaw of availability sampling— that the sample will consist of only whoever or whatever is available, without any concern for its similarity to the population of interest. The distinguishing feature of a quota sample is that quotas are set to ensure that the sample represents certain characteristics in proportion to their prevalence in the population.

Suppose that you wish to sample adult residents of a town in a study of support for a tax increase to improve the town's schools. You know from the town's annual report what the proportions of town residents are in terms of gender, employment status, age, and number of children. You think that each of these characteristics might influence support for new school taxes, so you want to be sure that the sample includes men, women, people who work, people not in the labor force, older people, younger people, big families, small families, and childless families in proportion to their numbers in the town population.

This is where quotas come in. Let's say that 48% of the town's adult residents are men and 52% are women; that 60% are employed, 5% are unemployed, and 35% are out of the labor force. These percentages and the percentages corresponding to the other characteristics become the quotas for the sample. If you plan to include a total of 500 residents in your sample, 240 must be men (48% of 500), 260 must be women, 300 must be employed, and so on. You may even set more refined quotas, such as certain numbers of employed women, employed men, unemployed women, and so on. With the quota list in hand, you (or your research staff) can now go out into the community looking for the right number of people in each quota category. You may go door to door, go bar to bar, or just stand on a street corner until you have surveyed 240 men, 260 women, and so on.

The problem is that even when we know that a quota sample is representative of the particular characteristics for which quotas have been set, we have no way of knowing if the sample is representative of any other characteristics. In Exhibit 4.7, for example, quotas have been set for gender only. Under the circumstances, it's no surprise that the sample is representative of the population only in terms of gender, not in terms of race. Interviewers are only human; they may avoid potential respondents with menacing dogs in the front yard, or they could seek out respondents who are physically attractive or who look like they'd be easy to interview. Realistically, researchers can set quotas for only a small fraction of the characteristics relevant to a study, so a quota sample is really not so much better than an availability sample (although following careful, consistent procedures for selecting cases within the quota limits always helps).

This last point leads to another limitation of quota sampling: You must know the characteristics of the entire sample to set the right quotas. In most cases, researchers know what the population looks like in terms of no more than a few of the characteristics relevant to their concerns. In some cases, they have no such information on the entire population.

Exhibit 4.7   Quota Sampling

Population
50% male, 50% female
70% white, 30% black

Quota sample
50% male, 50% female

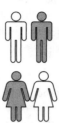

Representative of gender distribution
in population, not representative of
race distribution.

Purposive Sampling

In **purposive sampling,** each sample element is selected for a purpose, usually because of the unique position of the sample elements. Purposive sampling may involve studying the entire population of some limited group (directors of shelters for homeless adults) or a subset of a population (mid-level managers with a reputation for efficiency). Purposive sampling may be used to examine the effectiveness of some intervention with a set of subjects or clients who have particular characteristics, such as a specific diagnosis. Or a purposive sample may be a "key informant survey," which targets individuals who are particularly knowledgeable about the issues under investigation.

Herbert Rubin and Irene Rubin (1995) suggest three guidelines for selecting informants when designing any purposive sampling strategy. Informants should be

- Knowledgeable about the cultural arena or situation or experience being studied
- Willing to talk
- Represent[ative of] the range of points of view. (p. 66)

In addition, Rubin and Rubin suggest continuing to select interviewees until you can pass two tests:

- *Completeness.* "What you hear provides an overall sense of the meaning of a concept, theme, or process" (p. 72).
- *Saturation.* "You gain confidence that you are learning little that is new from subsequent interview[s]" (p. 73).

Adhering to these guidelines will help to ensure that a purposive sample adequately represents the setting or issues studied.

Leon Haley and Ralph Bangs (2000) used purposive sampling in a study of the impact of welfare reform on nonprofit organizations. They wondered whether the Personal Responsibility and Work Opportunities Act enacted in 1996 led nonprofit organizations to make changes in staffing patterns, budgets, and services provided, given new client needs. The sample consists of executive directors who were selected because their agencies provide work-related services such as employment training, literacy, education, and day care.

The executive directors were chosen with Rubin and Rubin's criteria in mind: (1) as agency directors, they should be knowledgeable about the changes that have occurred in their agencies; (2) they are willing to participate in the interviews, suggesting a willingness to talk; and (3) they represent a range of services, are located in different communities and neighborhoods, and serve different demographic groups. The findings of this study will not be generalizable to all agencies providing such services nor to all agencies providing work-related services in the communities served by the sampled agencies. Any conclusions are limited to the set of respondents.

Snowball Sampling

For **snowball sampling**, you identify one member of the population and speak to him or her, then ask that person to identify others in the population and speak to them, then ask them to identify others, and so on. The sample thus "snowballs" in size. This technique is useful for hard-to-reach or hard-to-identify, interconnected populations (at least some members of the population know each other), such as drug users, parents with small children, participants in Alcoholics Anonymous groups or other peer support groups, and informal organizational leaders. Carolyn Pryor (1992) used snowball sampling to learn about the role of social workers in school-based peer support groups because there was no known sampling frame. However, researchers using snowball sampling normally cannot be confident that their sample represents the total population of interest.

One caveat when using a snowball sampling technique is that you are asking people to identify other people with a similar status without the knowledge or consent of the people being identified. The people who are identified may not wish others to know that they have a particular status. This is particularly a concern when snowball sampling is used to identify subgroups of the population who may experience oppression or discrimination because they hold a particular status. In class, we often use a sampling exercise that requires students to identify a nonprobability sampling technique to gather information from gay and lesbian members of the community with the purpose of identifying their social service needs. Often, students will suggest snowball sampling without realizing that what they are doing is asking people to "out" their acquaintances without permission of those being identified.

LESSONS ABOUT SAMPLE QUALITY

Some lessons are implicit in the evaluations of the sampling methods in this chapter:

- We can't evaluate the quality of a sample if we don't know what population it is supposed to represent. If the population is unspecified because the researchers were never clear about just what population they were trying to sample, then we can safely conclude that the sample itself is no good.

- We can't evaluate the quality of a sample if we don't know just how cases in the sample were selected from the population. If the method was specified, we then need to know whether cases were selected in a systematic fashion and on the basis of chance. In any case, we know that a haphazard method of sampling (as in person-on-the-street interviews) undermines generalizability.

- Sample quality is determined by the sample actually obtained, not just by the sampling method itself. If many of the people selected for our sample are **nonrespondents** or people (or other entities) who do not participate in the study although they have been selected for the sample, the quality of our sample is undermined—even if we chose the sample in the best possible way.

- We need to be aware that even researchers who obtain very good samples may talk about the implications of their findings for some group that is larger than or just different from the population they actually sampled. For example, findings from a representative sample of students in one university often are discussed as if they tell us about university students in general. And maybe they do; we just don't know.

- A sample that allows for comparisons involving theoretically important variables is better than one that does not allow such comparisons. Even when we study people or processes in depth, it is best to select individuals or settings with an eye to how useful they will be for examining relationships. Limiting an investigation to just one setting or just one type of person will inevitably leave us wondering what it is that makes a difference.

SAMPLING DISTRIBUTIONS

Keep in mind that the use of probability sampling methods does not guarantee that a sample is representative of the population from which it was selected, even when we have avoided the problems of nonresponse. Random sampling (probability-based selection techniques) is an unbiased method of sample selection and so minimizes the odds that a sample is unrepresentative, but there is always some chance that the sample differs substantially from the population. Random samples are subject to sampling error due just to chance. To deal with that problem, social researchers take into account the properties of a **sampling distribution,** a hypothetical distribution of a statistic across all the random samples that could be drawn from a population. Any single random sample can be thought of as just one of an infinite number of random samples that, in theory, could have been selected from the population. Understanding sampling distributions is the foundation for understanding how statisticians can estimate sampling error.

What does a sampling distribution look like? Because a sampling distribution is based on some statistic calculated for different samples, we need to choose a statistic. Let's focus on the arithmetic average, or mean. To calculate a mean, you add up the values of all the cases and divide by the total number of cases. Let's say you draw a random sample of 500 families and find that their average (mean) family income is $36,239. Imagine that you then draw another random sample. That sample's mean family income might be $31,302. Imagine marking these two means on graph paper and then drawing more random samples and marking their means on the graph. The resulting graph would be a sampling distribution of the mean.

Exhibit 4.8 demonstrates what happened when Schutt did something very similar to what was just described—not with an infinite number of samples and not from a large population but through the same process—using the 1996 General Social Survey (GSS) sample as if it were a population. First, he drew 50 different random samples, each consisting of 30 cases, from the 1996 GSS. (The standard notation for the number of cases in each sample is $n = 30$.) Then he calculated for each random sample the approximate mean family income (approximate because the GSS does not record actual income in dollars). He then graphed the means of the 50 samples. Each column in Exhibit 4.8 shows how many samples had a particular family income. The mean for the population (the total sample) is $38,249, and you can see that the sampling distribution centers around this value. However, although many of the sample means are close to the population mean, some are quite far from it. If you had calculated the mean from only one sample, it could have been anywhere in this sampling distribution. But that one mean is unlikely to have been far from the population mean—that is, unlikely to have been close to either end (or "tail") of the distribution.

Exhibit 4.8   Partial Sampling Distribution: Mean Family Income

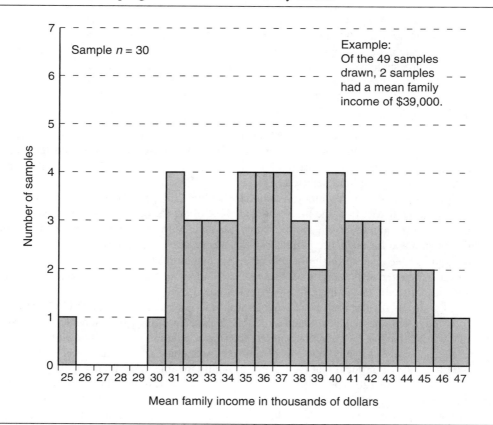

Mean family income in thousands of dollars

Source: Data from General Social Survey, 1996.

Estimating Sampling Error

We don't actually observe sampling distributions in real research; researchers just draw the best sample they can and then are stuck with the results—one sample, not a distribution of samples. A sampling distribution is a theoretical distribution. However, we can use the properties of sampling distributions to calculate the amount of sampling error that was likely with the random sample used in a study. **Inferential statistics** is a mathematical tool for estimating how likely it is that a statistical result based on data from a random sample is representative of the population from which the sample is assumed to have been selected.

Sampling distributions for many statistics, including the mean, have a "normal" shape. A graph of a **normal distribution** looks like a bell, with one hump in the middle, centered around the population mean, and the number of cases tapering off on both sides of the mean. Note that a normal distribution is symmetric: If you folded it in half at its center (at the population mean), the two halves would match perfectly. This shape is produced by **random sampling error**. The value of the statistic varies from sample to sample because of chance, so higher and lower values are equally likely. A difference between the population and the sample due to the sampling method is referred to as **systematic sampling error**.

Random sampling error (chance sampling error)   Differences between the population and the sample that are due only to chance factors (random error), not to systematic sampling error. Random sampling error may or may not result in an unrepresentative sample. The magnitude of sampling error due to chance factors can be estimated statistically.

The partial sampling distribution in Exhibit 4.8 does not have a completely normal shape because it involves only a small number of samples (50), each of which has only 30 cases. Exhibit 4.9 shows what the sampling distribution of family incomes would look like if it formed a perfectly normal distribution—if, rather than 50 random samples, thousands of random samples had been selected.

The properties of a sampling distribution facilitate the process of statistical inference. In the sampling distribution, the most frequent value of the **sample statistic** or the statistic (such as the mean) computed from sample data is identical to the **population parameter**—the statistic computed for the entire population. In other words, we can have a lot of confidence that the value at the peak of the bell curve represents the norm for the entire population. A population parameter also may be termed the true value for the statistic in that population. A sample statistic is an estimate of a population parameter.

In a normal distribution, a predictable proportion of cases also falls within certain ranges. Inferential statistics takes advantage of this feature and allow researchers to estimate how likely it is that, given a particular sample, the true population value will be within some range of the statistic. For example, a statistician might conclude from a sample of 30 families that we can be 95% confident that the true mean family income in the total population is between $23,012 and $38,120. The interval from $23,012 to $38,120 would then be called the "95% **confidence interval** for the mean." The upper ($38,120) and lower ($23,012) bounds of this interval are termed the confidence limits. Exhibit 4.9 marks such confidence limits, indicating the range that encompasses 95% of the area under the normal curve; 95% of all samples would fall within this range.

Exhibit 4.9   Normal Sampling Distribution: Mean Family Income

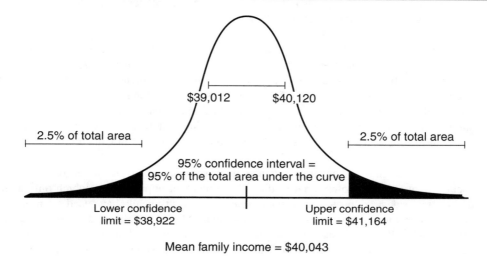

$39,012 $40,120

2.5% of total area   2.5% of total area

95% confidence interval =
95% of the total area under the curve

Lower confidence   Upper confidence
limit = $38,922   limit = $41,164

Mean family income = $40,043

If the sample size had been greater than 30 families, the sampling distribution would have been more compact. Stated another way, we can be more confident in estimates based on larger random samples because we know that a larger sample creates a more compact sampling distribution. So the confidence interval for a sample of 100 families was $25,733 and $35,399 which is narrower than the confidence level for the 30 families.

Determining Sample Size

You have learned that more confidence can be placed in the generalizability of statistics from larger samples, so you may be eager to work with random samples that are as large as possible. Unfortunately, researchers often cannot afford to sample a very large number of cases. They therefore try to determine during the design phase of their study how large a sample they must have to achieve their purposes. They have to consider the degree of confidence desired, the homogeneity of the population, the complexity of the analysis they plan, and the expected strength of the relationships they will measure:

- The less sampling error desired, the larger the sample size must be.
- Samples of more homogeneous populations can be smaller than samples of more diverse populations. Stratified sampling uses prior information on the population to create more homogeneous population strata from which the sample can be selected, so it can be smaller than if simple random sampling were used.
- If the only analysis planned for a survey sample is to describe the population in terms of a few variables, a smaller sample is required than if a more complex analysis involving sample subgroups is planned. If much of the analysis will focus on estimating the characteristics of subgroups within the sample, it is the size of the subgroups that must be considered, not the size of the total sample (Levy & Lemeshow, 1999, p. 74).

- When the researchers will be testing hypotheses and expect to find very strong relationships among the variables, they will need a smaller sample to detect these relationships than if they expect weaker relationships.

Researchers can make more precise estimates of the sample size required through a method termed *statistical power analysis* (Kraemer & Thiemann, 1987). It is increasingly used to identify the sample size necessary to identify treatment effects. Statistical power analysis requires a good advance estimate of the strength of the hypothesized relationship in the population. Statistical power analysis has become an essential component for federally submitted research proposals and is part of the Internal Review Board consideration of research propriety. Therefore, we will review these procedures in Chapter 12 on Statistical Analysis.

You can obtain some general guidance about sample sizes from the current practices of social scientists. For professional studies of the national population in which only a simple description is desired, professional social science studies typically have used a sample size of between 1,000 and 1,500, with up to 2,500 being included if detailed analyses are planned. Studies of local or regional populations often sample only a few hundred people, in part because these studies lack sufficient funding to draw larger samples. Of course, the sampling error in these smaller studies is considerably larger than in a typical national study (Sudman, 1976, p. 87).

CONCLUSION

Sampling is a powerful tool for social work research. Probability sampling methods allow researchers to use the laws of chance, or probability, to draw samples from which population parameters can be estimated with a high degree of confidence. When probability sampling methods are used, findings from a small number of cases can be generalized to a much larger population.

In many instances, a probability sampling technique is a reasonable alternative for social work researchers. Many researchers rely on these techniques when they are interested in describing population groups, understanding the impacts of different social welfare policies, or learning about community needs or attitudes.

But there are many different research questions that are not easily answered by a probability sampling technique, particularly as we seek answers about questions from vulnerable populations. The experience of Kathryn Edin and Laura Lein (1997), described in *Making Ends Meet*, offers a telling example. They wanted to know how single mothers on Aid to Families with Dependent Children or working in low-wage jobs survived economically each month. Edin started out with a survey by phone and in person of respondents who had been randomly selected for the 1983–1985 Chicago Survey of Poverty and Material Hardship. This effort failed to produce accurate information, as respondents did not trust her, "had no personal introduction to her and therefore suspected she was 'checking up' on them in some official capacity" (Edin & Lein, 1997, p. 9). She turned to a snowball technique that would facilitate personal introduction from a trustworthy individual, a technique that ultimately proved successful in gathering accurate information.

Most agency-based studies, particularly studies of the impact of a practice intervention, rely on nonprobability sampling techniques. It is rarely feasible for agencies to choose a random sample to study an intervention. As a result, replication studies at both the same and different agencies are required.

Ultimately, whether designing a study or evaluating a study, it is important to consider the type of sampling and the conclusions that might be made from the method of sampling. Can generalizations be made? To what population or population subgroups can the results be generalized? Are there characteristics about the setting that limit the generalizability of the results? Is the sample size too small? Should all elements have been studied? Is the response rate sufficiently high? Each of these questions is a consideration when thinking about applying research findings.

Social work researchers and other social scientists often seek to generalize their conclusions from the population that they studied to some larger target population. The validity of generalizations of this type is necessarily uncertain, for having a representative sample of a particular population does not at all ensure that what we find will hold true in other populations. Nonetheless, the accumulation of findings from studies based on local or otherwise unrepresentative populations can provide important information about broader populations.

KEY TERMS

Availability sampling
Cluster
Cluster sampling
Confidence interval
Disproportionate stratified sampling
Elements
Enumeration units
Nonprobability sampling methods
Nonrespondents
Normal distribution
Periodicity
Population parameter
Population
Probability of selection
Probability sampling methods
Proportionate stratified sampling
Purposive sampling
Quota sampling
Random digit dialing

Random numbers table
Random sampling
Random sampling error
Random selection
Replacement sampling
Representative sample
Sample statistic
Sample
Sampling distribution
Sampling error
Sampling frame
Sampling interval
Sampling units
Simple random sampling
Snowball sampling
Stratified random sampling
Systematic bias
Systematic random sampling
Target population

HIGHLIGHTS

- Sampling theory focuses on the generalizability of descriptive findings to the population from which the sample was drawn. It also considers whether statements can be generalized from one population to another.
- Sampling is unnecessary when the elements that would be sampled are identical, but the complexity of the social world makes it difficult to argue very often that different elements

are identical. Conducting a complete census of a population also eliminates the need for sampling, but the resources required for a complete census of a large population are usually prohibitive.

- To ensure the representation of diverse populations in research studies, a variety of different methods can and should be used to encourage participation of people of color, women, the elderly, and sexual minorities.

- Nonresponse undermines sample quality: It is the obtained sample, not the desired sample, that determines sample quality.

- Probability sampling methods rely on a random selection procedure to ensure no systematic bias in the selection of elements. In a probability sample, the odds of selecting elements are known, and the method of selection is carefully controlled.

- A sampling frame (a list of elements in the population) is required in most probability sampling methods. The adequacy of the sampling frame is an important determinant of sample quality.

- Simple random sampling and systematic random sampling are equivalent probability sampling methods in most situations. However, systematic random sampling is inappropriate for sampling from lists of elements that have a regular periodic structure.

- Stratified random sampling uses prior information about a population to make sampling more efficient. Stratified sampling may be either proportionate or disproportionate. Disproportionate stratified sampling is useful when a research question focuses on a stratum or on strata that make up a small proportion of the population.

- Cluster sampling is less efficient than simple random sampling but is useful when a sampling frame is unavailable. It is also useful for large populations spread out across a wide area or among many organizations.

- Nonprobability sampling methods can be useful when random sampling is not possible, when a research question does not concern a larger population, and when a preliminary exploratory study is appropriate. However, the representativeness of nonprobability samples cannot be determined.

- The likely degree of error in an estimate of a population characteristic based on a probability sample decreases when the size of the sample and the homogeneity of the population from which the sample was selected increase. Sampling error is not affected by the proportion of the population that is sampled, except when that proportion is large. The degree of sampling error affecting a sample statistic can be estimated from the characteristics of the sample and knowledge of the properties of sampling distributions.

DISCUSSION QUESTIONS

1. Underrepresentation of different subgroups can significantly limit the generalizability of social work research findings and their subsequent applications. Suppose you were conducting a study of barriers to health care access in urban areas. What are some of the strategies you might employ to encourage minority participation in your research project?

2. The State Department of Aging representative involved in the service audit of the Seniors Unit mentioned at the beginning of the chapter used a nonprobability sampling method. Discuss the potential weaknesses of this approach in reaching a conclusion about the entire agency's filing compliance. Identify instances in which the use of an availability sample might be more appropriate or required.

3. Although probability-based selection techniques minimize the odds of sample unrepresentativeness, there remains a chance that the sample does differ substantially from the population. What do

confidence limits tell us about the statistic we have derived from our sample and the likelihood of it being true for the population? How is the confidence interval impacted by sample size?

4. What ethical issues might you confront when using snowball sampling?

PRACTICE EXERCISES

1. Select a random sample using the table of random numbers in Appendix E. Compute a statistic based on your sample, and compare it to the corresponding figure for the entire population. Here's how to proceed:

   a. First, go to http://www.census.gov/hhes/hlthins/liuc02.html to find rates of low-income uninsured children by state.
   b. The next step is to create your sampling frame, a numbered list of all the elements in the population. When using a complete listing of all elements, as from a U.S. Census Bureau publication, the sampling frame is the same as the list. Just number the elements by writing a number next to the name of each state.
   c. Now calculate the average value of the percentage of children at or below 200% of the poverty level for the total population of states. You do this by adding up the values for each state in that column and dividing by the number of states.
   d. Decide on a method of picking numbers out of the random numbers table in Appendix E, such as taking every number in each row, row by row (or you may move down or diagonally across the columns). Use only the first (or last) digit in each number if you need to select 1 to 9 cases or only the first (or last) two digits if you want fewer than 100 cases.
   e. Pick a starting location in the random numbers table. It's important to pick a starting point in an unbiased way, perhaps by closing your eyes and then pointing to some part of the page.
   f. Record the numbers you encounter as you move from the starting location in the direction you decided on in advance, until you have recorded as many random numbers as the number of cases you need in the sample. If you are selecting states, 10 might be a good number. Ignore numbers that are too large (or small) for the range of numbers used to identify the elements in the population. Discard duplicate numbers.
   g. Calculate the average value in your sample by adding up the values of the percentage of children at or below 200% of the poverty level for each of the states (elements) in the sample you have just selected and dividing by the number of elements in the sample.
   h. How close is the sample average to the population average you calculated in step c?
   i. Guesstimate the range of sample averages that would be likely to include 90% of the possible samples of the same size.

2. Locate one or more newspaper articles reporting the results of an opinion poll. What information does the article provide on the sample that was selected? What additional information do you need to determine whether the sample was a representative one?

WEB EXERCISES

1. Research on health care concerns has increased in recent years as health care costs have risen. Search the Web for sites that include the words *medically uninsured* and see what you find. You might try limiting your search to those that also contain the word *census*. Pick a site and write a paragraph about what you learned from it.

2. Check out the people section of the U.S. Bureau of the Census Web site: www.census.gov. Based on some of the data you find there, write a brief summary of some aspect of the current characteristics of the American population.

> To assist you in completing the Web exercises, please access the study site at http://www.sagepub.com/prsw where you will find the Web Exercises reproduced and suggested links for online resources.

DEVELOPING A RESEARCH PROPOSAL

Consider the possibilities for sampling.

1. Propose a sampling design that would be appropriate for your research study. Define the population, identify the sampling frame (if any), and specify the elements. Indicate the exact procedure for selecting people to be included in the sample. Specify any specific selection criteria. How many subjects will you need?

2. Develop appropriate procedures for the recruitment of human subjects in your study. Include a recruitment form in these procedures.

Chapter 5

CAUSATION AND RESEARCH DESIGN

Nomothetic Causal Explanation

Experimental Design and the Criteria for Causal Explanation

Association
Time Order
Nonspuriousness
Mechanism
Context

Nonexperimental Designs and the Criteria for Causal Explanation

Cross-Sectional Designs
Longitudinal Designs
Repeated Cross-Sectional Designs

Fixed-Sample Panel Designs
Event-Based Designs

Units of Analysis and Errors in Causal Reasoning

Individual and Group Units of Analysis
The Ecological Fallacy and Reductionism

Idiographic Causal Explanation

Causation in Qualitative Research
Explanation in Qualitative Research
Single-Subject Design

Conclusion

Identifying causes—figuring out why things happen—is the goal of most social science research, as well as a critical interest of newspaper reporters, government officials, and ordinary citizens. Unfortunately, valid explanations of the causes of social phenomena do not come easily. Why did the poverty rate for children under age six stay relatively stable in the 1970s, increase in the 1980s and early 1990s, and then begin to decline in 1993? Changes in public policy? Variations in the economy? Changing demographic patterns? To distinguish these possibilities, we must design our research strategies carefully.

This chapter considers the meaning of nomothetic causation, the criteria for achieving causally valid explanations, and the ways in which different research designs seek to meet these criteria. We will focus attention on the differences between the experimental and nonexperimental approaches to causation. We will also contrast the nomothetic approach with idiographic causal explanation. We will focus special attention on the problem of time order—establishing whether the cause truly precedes the effect—and on the identification of units of analysis, which is a prerequisite for properly stating causal conclusions. By the end of the chapter, you should have a good grasp of the meaning of causation and be able to ask the right questions to determine whether causal inferences are likely to be valid.

NOMOTHETIC CAUSAL EXPLANATION

A cause is an explanation for some characteristic, attitude, or behavior of groups, individuals, or other entities (such as families, organizations, or communities) or for events. In social work practice, interventions are thought to explain changes in client status; frequently, social work researchers test this assumption. Other social work researchers seek to explain the causes of social conditions. For example, some researchers seek to identify the causes of poverty so that they can then recommend policy changes that would deal with the identified causes. One explanation, or cause, may be that poverty is the result of differences in human capital, that is, differences in the skills and education that people bring to the marketplace. If that is the case, then there are programs to increase human capital. You should recognize that there is a hypothesis here: Adults with less education are more likely to be poor than adults with more education. (Can you identify the dependent and independent variables?)

This is a **nomothetic causal explanation;** it means that we believe that variation in the independent variable will be followed by variation in the dependent variable, when all other things are equal (ceteris paribus). We admit that you can legitimately argue that "all" other things can't literally be equal: We will not be able to compare the same people at the same time in exactly the same circumstances except for the variation in the independent variable (King, Keohane, & Verba, 1994). However, you will see that we can design research to create conditions that are very comparable so that we can isolate the impact of the independent variable on the dependent variable.

Quantitative researchers seek nomothetic causal explanations, whether they use experimental or nonexperimental research designs. However, the way in which experimental designs attempt to identify causes differs quite a bit from the way in which nonexperimental designs attempt to identify causes. We will discuss the experimental approach first.

Causal effect (nomothetic perspective)   The finding that change in one variable leads to change in another variable, *ceteris paribus* (other things being equal).

EXPERIMENTAL DESIGN AND THE CRITERIA FOR CAUSAL EXPLANATION

Five criteria must be considered when deciding whether a causal connection exists. Research designs that allow us to establish these criteria require careful planning, implementation, and analysis. Many times, researchers have to leave one or more of the criteria unmet and therefore are left with some important doubts about the validity of their causal conclusions; or they may avoid even making any causal assertions. The first three of the criteria are generally considered the most important bases for identifying a nomothetic causal effect:

empirical association, appropriate time order, and nonspuriousness. Evidence that meets the other two criteria—identifying a causal mechanism and specifying the context in which the effect occurs—can considerably strengthen causal explanations.

Elaine Walton, Mark W. Fraser, Robert E. Lewis, Peter J. Pecora, and Wendel K. Walton's 1993 child welfare study of the impact of intensive, in-home, family-based services on rates of family reunification illustrates how an experimental approach can be used to meet the criteria for establishing causal relations. Walton and her colleagues recruited 110 families using a computer-generated list of children in substitute care. The sample included only children who had been outside the home for more than 30 days, whose return home was not imminent but still the case goal, and whose parents were not dead or incarcerated. Fifty-seven families were in the experimental group while there were 53 families in the second group. In the original study (Walton et al., 1993), information was collected at the end of the 90 days, a 6-month follow-up, and a 12-month follow-up.

Families in the experimental group received intensive services that were home-based. The intervention model was based on the idea that creating a relationship between the caseworker and the family, providing concrete services, focusing on the family and not just the child, establishing or building a supportive network, and building skills would produce better client outcomes. Families in the experimental group received these services for 90 days and were seen in the home at least three times a week. The comparison group received the traditional package of routine services that were offered; these services were provided out-of-home, caseworkers were required to see each child only once per month, and the families were helped to locate services necessary to return the child to the home, such as mental health counseling and parenting skills training.

Did the intervention make any difference? As a short-term intervention, the program was quite successful in that 53 children (93%) in the experimental group were reunited with their families during the first 90 days of intervention whereas only 15 (28%) of the control group were returned to their homes. After 15 months, of the 57 children in the experimental group, 44 (77%) had returned home without any subsequent substitute care, 5 (9%) had been briefly placed out of the home again, 12 (21%) who had returned home were back in substitute care, and one never returned home. In comparison, among those children who received traditional services, only 25 (47%) returned home without any interruption, 5 (9%) who had returned home were back in substitute care, and 23 (43%) never returned home. Although Walton and her colleagues (1993) point out various concerns, they conclude that the "results are encouraging. Intensive in-home services that have a skills focus appear to be effective in the reunification of some families with children in out-of-home care" (p. 485).

Was this causal conclusion justified? How confident can we be about its internal validity? We will answer this question by reviewing how the experiment attempted to meet each of the causal criteria and what are the key features of a **true experiment**. We will study variations on experimental designs in Chapter 6.

Association

We say that there was an **association** between the intervention and family reunification because the rate of family reunification differed according to the type of intervention a family received. An empirical (or observed) association between the independent and dependent variables is the first criterion for identifying a nomothetic causal effect.

We can determine whether an association exists between the independent and dependent variables in a true experiment because there are two or more groups that differ in terms of their value on the independent variable. One group receives some treatment, such as intensive, in-home, family-based services, that is a manipulation of the value of the independent variable. This group is termed the *experimental group.* In a simple experiment, there may be one other group that does not receive the treatment; it is termed the *control group.* Or, the other group may receive what is routinely provided so it is getting some form of treatment; this second group is termed the *comparison group.* The Walton study, as we have described it, compared two groups; other experiments may compare more groups, which represent multiple values of the independent variable or even combinations of the values of two or more independent variables. An empirical association was demonstrated by comparing the two groups using statistical techniques to show that the differences were not due to chance.

Time Order

Association is a necessary criterion for establishing a causal effect, but it is not sufficient. We must also ensure that the variation in the dependent variable occurred after the variation in the independent variable. This is the criterion of **time order.** In a true experiment, the time order is determined by the researcher. The subjects in Walton's study all started with the same status: All children had been placed out of the home with no immediate intent to reunite with their families. Walton and her colleagues (1993) then measured changes in that status, both during the 90 days of the treatment period and after the 90 days were finished. It was only during and after the interventions that children returned home.

Nonspuriousness

Another essential criterion for establishing the existence of a causal effect of an independent variable on a dependent variable is **nonspuriousness.** We say that a relationship between two variables is not spurious when it is not due to variation in a third variable. Correlation does not prove causation as an association between two variables might be caused by something else. If we measure children's shoe sizes and their academic knowledge, for example, we will find a positive association. However, the association may result from the fact that older children have larger feet as well as more academic knowledge. Shoe size does not cause knowledge or vice versa.

Do storks bring babies? If you believe that correlation proves causation, then you might think so. The more storks that appear in certain districts in Holland, the more babies are born. But the association in Holland between number of storks and number of babies is a **spurious relationship.** In fact, both the number of storks and the birth rate are higher in rural districts than in urban districts. The rural or urban character of the districts (the extraneous variable) causes variation in the other two variables.

If you think this point is obvious, consider a social science example. Do schools with better resources produce better students? Before you answer the question, consider the fact that parents with more education and higher income tend to live in neighborhoods that spend more on their schools. These parents are also more likely to have books in the home and provide other advantages for their children. Do the parents cause variation in both school resources and student performance? If so, there would be an association between school resources and student performance that was at least partially spurious.

Exhibit 5.1   Random Assignment to One of Two Groups

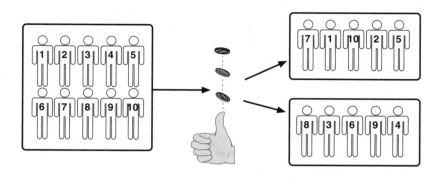

A true experiment like Walton's study of intensive in-home, family-based services uses a technique called **randomization** to reduce the risk of spuriousness. If subjects were assigned to only two groups, a coin toss could have been used (see Exhibit 5.1). The families in Walton's experiment were randomly assigned to either the experimental group or the traditional treatment group. This means that chance determined into which group a family would be placed. **Random assignment** ensures that neither the families' other characteristics or attitudes could influence which of the treatment methods they received. As a result, the different groups are likely to be equivalent in all respects at the outset of the experiment. The greater the number of cases assigned randomly to the groups, the more likely that the groups will be equivalent in all respects. Whatever the preexisting sources of variation among the families, these could not explain why the group that received intensive, in-home, family-based services had higher rates of reunification than the families receiving the traditional form of services.

These defining features of true experimental designs give us a great deal of confidence that we can meet the three basic criteria for identifying nomothetic causes: association, time order, and nonspuriousness. However, we can strengthen our understanding of causal connections and increase the likelihood of drawing causally valid conclusions by also investigating causal mechanism and causal context.

Mechanism

A **causal mechanism** is some process that creates the connection between variation in an independent variable and the variation in the dependent variable it is hypothesized to cause (Cook & Campbell, 1979, p. 35; Marini & Singer, 1988). Many social work researchers (and scientists in other fields) argue that no nomothetic causal explanation is adequate until a causal mechanism is identified.

Up to this point, we have actually described only a portion of Walton's research. In a subsequent article, Walton and her colleagues (Lewis, Walton, & Fraser, 1995) explored the process: that is, the essential actions leading to the successful outcomes. To do this, they focused only on the treatment group. They compared the kinds of activities, goals, and clinical services received by families that were reunified and those in which the child did not return to the home. They found that successful outcomes occurred when caseworkers could focus on treatment goals involving skill building, such as communication skills, parenting skills, and anger management, goals about improving school performance, and increased compliance with family rules. Service failure occurred when caseworkers had to devote their time to providing transportation or spending time on the phone with the client-family. In addition, failure to reunify was more likely when caseworkers had to focus on clarifying problems, defusing crises, and crisis or conflict management. In general, then, when caseworkers had to deal with crises, failure was more likely; when caseworkers could spend time on skill building, success was more likely.

Figuring out some aspects of the process by which the independent variable influenced the variation in the dependent variable should increase confidence in our conclusion that there was a causal effect (Costner, 1989). However, there may be many components to the causal mechanism, and we cannot hope to identify them all in one study. For example, Walton and her colleagues (Lewis et al., 1995) suggest that future research should identify the factors associated with goal achievement and success, "for goal achievement appears to be a proximal outcome measure that mediates family risk factors and more distal outcomes such as child out-of-home placement" (p. 279).

Context

No cause has its effect apart from some larger **context** involving other variables. For whom and when and in what conditions does this effect occur? A cause is really one among a set of interrelated factors required for the effect (Hage & Meeker, 1988; Papineau, 1978). Identification of the context in which a causal effect occurs is not itself a criterion for a valid causal conclusion, and it is not always attempted, but it does help us to understand the causal relationship.

Walton and colleagues (1993) noted the possibility that contextual factors influenced their findings. The state in which the study was done, Utah, has unique religious and social characteristics that might influence the findings (and that limited the generalizability of the findings). Furthermore, the researchers suggest that the decision to place a child is not just the result of the family situation but of many system-level factors as well; these factors could play a role in placement.

NONEXPERIMENTAL DESIGNS AND THE CRITERIA FOR CAUSAL EXPLANATION

The nonexperimental approach to establishing causality (sometimes called the descriptive or observational approach) involves studying naturally occurring variation in the dependent and independent variables, without any intervention by the researchers. Nonexperimental research designs can be either cross-sectional or longitudinal. In a **cross-sectional research design,** all data are collected at one point in time. Identifying the time order of effects can be an insurmountable problem with such a design. In **longitudinal research designs,** data are collected at two or more points in time, and so identification of the time order of effects can be quite straightforward.

Cross-Sectional Designs

Roberta Sands and Robin Goldberg-Glen (2000) used a cross-sectional design to study the relationship of social supports to psychological stress (or distress) with a sample of

Exhibit 5.2   Stress Theory

Relationship of Stressor to Stress

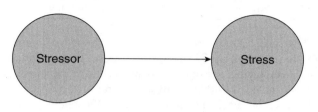

Resources as an Intervening Variable

grandparents raising grandchildren. Their theoretical framework was based on stress theory, or the idea that stressors such as individual or family changes generate stress in people's lives, but the extent or nature of that stress may be altered by the resources available to the individual or family (see Exhibit 5.2). In this study, the stressful life event was having to raise a grandchild, and the stress was psychological anxiety. One type of resource that varies among individuals or families is social support, and the researchers hypothesized that the strength of social support would explain variation in the level of psychological anxiety.

Sands and Goldberg-Glen (2000) gathered their data using face-to-face interviews. Trained female interviewers matched by race to the respondent did the interviewing. Sands and Goldberg-Glen found that a lack of social support was related to higher levels of psychological anxiety.

How well does the study meet the criteria for establishing a causal connection? Sands and Goldberg-Glen (2000) showed an association between variation in the independent variable, the level of informal social support, and the dependent variable, psychological anxiety. However, their design could not establish directly that the variation in anxiety occurred after variation in social support. Maybe people who are less anxious to begin with attract family members and use other resources. It is difficult to discount such a possibility when only cross-sectional data are available.

A nonexperimental study like Sands and Goldberg-Glen's cannot use random assignment to comparison groups to minimize the risk of spurious effects. We cannot randomly assign people to many of the social conditions they experience, such as raising a grandchild or living in a particular neighborhood. Instead, nonexperimental researchers commonly use an alternative approach to try to achieve the criterion of nonspuriousness. The technique of **statistical control** allows researchers to determine whether the relationship between the independent and dependent variables still occurs when we hold constant the values of other variables. If it does, the relationship could not be caused by variation in that other variable.

Statistical control   A technique used in nonexperimental research to reduce the risk of spuriousness. The effect of one or more variables is removed, for example, by holding them constant so that the relationship between the independent and dependent variables can be assessed without the influence of variation in the control variables.

Sands and Goldberg-Glen (2000) designed their study to control for other factors that might explain the relationship between social support and stress. They included contextual factors such as race, length of caregiving, age of the respondent, and employment status. In fact, when social support was not included in their analysis, several of these variables were associated with anxiety, specifically, race, age, and number of years of caregiving. When additional stressors were added to the analysis, they found that race of the caregiver was no longer related to anxiety, and when social support variables were added, the length of caregiving was no longer related to anxiety. We might conclude then that the relationship of race was spurious due to other stressors and the length of caregiving was spurious due to social supports.

Our confidence in causal conclusions based on nonexperimental research also increases with identification of a causal mechanism. Such mechanisms, which are termed **intervening variables** in nonexperimental research, help us to understand how variation in the independent variable results in variation in the dependent variable. In the above example, social supports served as an intervening variable for contextual variables such as race, employment status, length of caregiving, and age.

Of course, identification of one (or two or three) intervening variables does not end the possibilities for clarifying the causal mechanisms. You might ask why social supports tend to result in lower levels of psychological anxiety or whether different forms of social supports are related to anxiety. In fact, Sands and Goldberg-Glen (2000) reported that although higher social support in general was related to less anxiety, not all forms of social support were related to level of anxiety. They found that the more family cohesion, the lower the anxiety level, but other indicators of social support, such as use of community services or belonging to a support group, were unrelated to anxiety level. You could then conduct research to identify the mechanisms that link, for example, family cohesion to stress. (Perhaps the respondents who perceived the highest levels of cohesion were also receiving the most concrete support from their families so that they were less anxious.) This process could go on and on. The point is that identification of a mechanism through which the independent variable influences the dependent variable increases our confidence in the conclusion that a causal connection does indeed exist.

Specifying the context in which causal effects occur is no less important in nonexperimental than in experimental research. Nonexperimental research is, in fact, well suited to exploring the context in which causal effects occur. Administering surveys in many different settings and to different types of individuals is usually much easier than administering experiments in different ways. We will describe survey research in Chapter 8.

Longitudinal Designs

It is risky to draw conclusions about time order on the basis of cross-sectional data except in four special cases (see below). In longitudinal research, in contrast, data are collected that can be ordered in time. By measuring the value of cases on an independent variable and a dependent variable at each of these different times, the researcher can determine whether variation in the independent variable precedes variation in the dependent variable.

The four special circumstances in which cross-sectional data can reasonably be used to infer the time order of effects can actually be thought of as longitudinal designs, in the sense that the data can be ordered in time (Campbell, 1992):

The independent variable is fixed at some point prior to the variation in the dependent variable. So-called demographic variables that are determined at birth—such as sex, race, and age—are fixed in this way. So are variables like education and marital status, if we know when the value of cases on these variables was established and if we know that the value of cases on the dependent variable was set some time later. For example, say we hypothesize that education influences the type of job individuals have. If we know that respondents completed their education before taking their current jobs, we would satisfy the time order requirement, even if we were to measure education at the same time we measure type of job. However, if some respondents possibly went back to school as a benefit of their current job, the time order requirement would not be satisfied.

We believe that respondents can give us reliable reports of what happened to them or what they thought at some earlier point in time. Julie Horney, D. Wayne Osgood, and Ineke Haen Marshall (1995) provide an interesting example of the use of such retrospective data. The researchers wanted to identify how criminal activity varies in response to changes in life circumstances. They interviewed 658 newly convicted male offenders sentenced to a Nebraska state prison. In a 45- to 90-minute interview, they recorded each inmate's report of his life circumstances and of his criminal activities for the preceding two to three years. They then found that criminal involvement was related strongly to adverse changes in life circumstances, such as marital separation or drug use. Retrospective data are often inadequate for measuring variation in past psychological states or behaviors, however, because what we recall about our feelings or actions in the past is likely to be influenced by what we feel in the present. For example, retrospective reports by both adult alcoholics and their parents appear to greatly overestimate the frequency of childhood problems (Vaillant, 1995). People cannot report reliably the frequency and timing of many past events, from hospitalization to hours worked. However, retrospective data tends to be reliable when it concerns major, persistent experiences in the past, such as what type of school someone went to or how a person's family was structured (Campbell, 1992).

Our measures are based on records that contain information on cases in earlier periods. Government, agency, and organizational records are an excellent source of time-ordered data after the fact. However, sloppy record keeping and changes in data-collection policies can lead to inconsistencies, which must be taken into account. Another weakness of such archival data is that they usually contain measures of only a fraction of the variables that we think are important.

We know that cases were equivalent on the dependent variable prior to the treatment. For example, we may hypothesize that a training program (independent variable) improves the English-speaking abilities (dependent variable) of a group of recent immigrants. If we know that none of the immigrants could speak English prior to enrolling in the training program, we can be confident that any subsequent variation in their ability to speak English did not precede exposure to the training program. This is one way that traditional experiments establish time order: Two or more equivalent groups are formed prior to exposing one of them to some treatment.

When these special circumstances do not exist in nonexperimental research, we must actually collect data at two or more points in time to establish empirically the time order of effects (Campbell, 1992). In some longitudinal designs, the same sample (or panel) is followed over time; in other designs, sample members are rotated or completely replaced. The population from which the sample is selected may be defined broadly, as when a longitudinal survey of the general population is conducted. Or the population may be defined narrowly, as when members of a specific age group are sampled at multiple points in time. The frequency of follow-up measurement can vary, ranging from a before-and-after design with just one follow-up to studies in which various indicators are measured every month for many years.

Certainly, it is more difficult to collect data at two or more points in time than at one time. Quite frequently, researchers simply cannot, or are unwilling to, delay completion of a study for even one year in order to collect follow-up data. But think of the many research questions that really should involve a much longer follow-up period: What is the impact of job training on subsequent employment? How effective is a school-based program in improving parenting skills? Under what conditions do traumatic experiences in childhood result in mental illness? It is safe to say that we will never have enough longitudinal data to answer many important research questions. The value of longitudinal data is so great that every effort should be made to develop longitudinal research designs when they are appropriate for the research question asked. The following discussion of the three major types of longitudinal design will give you a sense of the possibilities (see Exhibit 5.3).

Exhibit 5.3   Three Types of Longitudinal Design

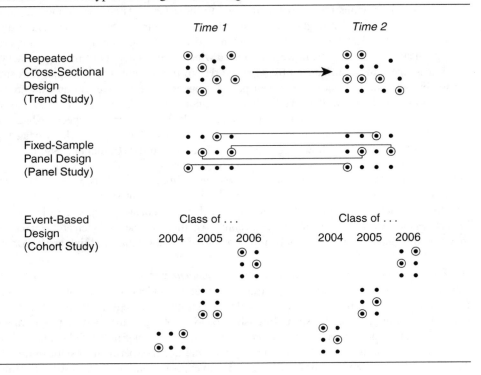

Repeated Cross-Sectional Designs

Repeated cross-sectional studies, also known as **trend studies,** have become fixtures of the political arena around election time. Particularly in presidential election years, we have all become accustomed to reading weekly, even daily, reports on the percentage of the population that supports each candidate. Similar polls are conducted to track sentiment on many other social issues. For example, a 1993 poll reported that 52% of adult Americans supported a ban on the possession of handguns, compared to 41% in a similar poll conducted in 1991. According to pollster Louis Harris, this increase indicated a "sea change" in public attitudes (Barringer, 1993). Another researcher said, "It shows that people are responding to their experience [of an increase in handgun-related killings]" (Barringer, 1993, p. 1).

A study using a **repeated cross-sectional design** is conducted as follows:

1. A sample is drawn from a population at Time 1, and data are collected from the sample.

2. As time passes, some people leave the population, and others enter it.

3. At Time 2, a different sample is drawn from this population.

These features make the repeated cross-sectional design appropriate when the goal is to determine whether a population has changed over time. Has racial tolerance increased among Americans in the past 20 years? Are employers more likely to pay maternity benefits today than they were in the 1950s? Have the characteristics of nursing home residents changed? Has client satisfaction with the services provided by a family service agency changed? Has the extent of drug and alcohol use changed in a community? These questions concern changes in the population as a whole or in defined populations, not changes in individuals within the population. We want to know whether current clients of the agency are more likely to be satisfied than clients were last year or 10 years ago, not whether this change is due to changes in the composition of clients or changes in their receptivity to help-seeking. When we need to know whether individuals in the population changed, we must turn to a panel design.

Repeated cross-sectional design   A type of longitudinal study in which data are collected at two or more points in time from different samples of the same population.

Fixed-Sample Panel Designs

Panel designs allow identification of changes in individuals, groups, or whatever we are studying. This is the process for conducting a study using a **fixed-sample panel design:**

1. A sample (called a panel) is drawn from a population at Time 1, and data are collected from the sample.

2. As time passes, some panel members become unavailable for follow-up, and the population changes.

3. At Time 2, data are collected from the same people as at Time 1 (the panel)—except for those people who cannot be located.

> ***Fixed-sample panel design***   A type of longitudinal study in which data are collected from the same individuals—the panel—at two or more points in time. In another type of panel design, panel members who leave are replaced with new members

Because a panel design follows the same individuals, it is better than a repeated cross-sectional design for testing causal hypotheses. For example, Knowlton Johnson (1997) used a fixed-sample panel design to investigate whether professional services help reduce psychological symptoms among victims of crime. He drew his sample from a larger sample of respondents to a statewide study of victimization and psychological distress. His sample included households that had experienced either a violent crime or a property crime as well as a sample of households that had not been victimized. Johnson (1997) found that the use of legal services (private lawyers, legal aid, or prosecutor's office) was associated with higher levels of distress in the short term, but 6 to 12 months later, it was associated with reduced symptoms. On the other hand, among those people using health-related services (medical, clergy, or mental health professionals), symptoms of distress increased except for those who received the services immediately and on a continuous basis. In this study, the level of psychological distress was measured before and after the use of services. If the researchers had used a cross-sectional design, it would have been impossible to establish a baseline measure of psychological distress.

If you now wonder why every longitudinal study isn't designed as a panel study, you've understood the advantages of panel designs. However, remember that this design does not in itself establish causality. Variation in both the independent variable and the dependent variables may be due to some other variable, even to earlier variation in what is considered the dependent variable. In the example in Exhibit 5.4, there is a hypothesized association between delinquency in the 11th grade and grades obtained in the 12th grade (the dependent variable).

Exhibit 5.4   Causality in Panel Studies

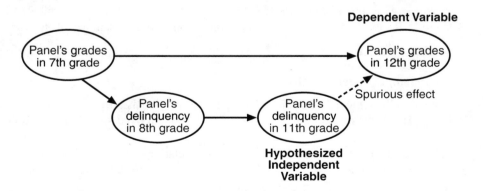

Although delinquency in the 11th grade and grades in the 12th grade are clearly associated and the time order is clear, causality cannot be assumed. In reality, grades in the 7th grade also play a role.

The time order is clear. However, both variables are consequences of grades obtained in the 7th grade. The apparent effect of 11th-grade delinquency on 12th-grade grades is spurious because of variation in the dependent variable (grades) at an earlier time.

Panel designs are also a challenge to implement successfully, and often, they are not even attempted because of two major difficulties.

Expense and attrition. It can be difficult, and very expensive, to keep track of individuals over a long period, and inevitably, the proportion of panel members who can be located for follow-up will decline over time. Panel studies often lose more than one quarter of their members through attrition (Miller, 1991, p. 170). However, subject attrition can be reduced substantially if sufficient staff can be used to keep track of panel members. In his panel study, Johnson (1997) lost only 18% of the respondents in the original wave of data collection. The consequences of a high rate of subject attrition are that the follow-up sample may no longer be representative of the population from which it was drawn and may no longer provide a sound basis for estimating change. Subjects who were lost to follow-up may have been those who changed the most, or the least, over time. It helps to compare the baseline characteristics of those who are interviewed at follow-up with characteristics of those lost to follow-up. If these two groups of panel members were not very different at baseline, it is less likely that changes had anything to do with characteristics of the missing panel members.

Subject fatigue. Panel members may grow weary of repeated interviews and drop out of the study, or they may become so used to answering the standard questions in the survey that they start giving stock answers rather than actually thinking about their current feelings or actions (Campbell, 1992). This is called the problem of **subject fatigue.** Fortunately, subjects do not often seem to become fatigued in this way, particularly if the research staff have maintained positive relations with the subjects. For example, at the end of an 18-month-long experimental study of housing alternatives for people with mental illness who had been homeless, only three or four individuals (out of 93 who could still be located) refused to participate in the fourth and final round of interviews. The interviews took a total of about five hours to complete, and participants received about $50 (Schutt, Goldfinger, & Penk, 1997).

Because panel studies are so useful, social researchers have developed increasingly effective techniques for keeping track of individuals and overcoming subject fatigue. But when resources do not permit use of these techniques to maintain an adequate panel, repeated cross-sectional designs usually can be employed at a cost that is not a great deal higher than that of a one-time-only cross-sectional study. The payoff in explanatory power should be well worth the cost.

Event-Based Designs

In an **event-based design,** often called a **cohort study,** the follow-up samples (at one or more times) are selected from the same **cohort**—people who have experienced a similar event or a common starting point. Examples include:

- Birth cohorts—those who share a common period of birth (those born in the 1940s, 1950s, 1960s, and so on)
- Seniority cohorts—those who have worked at the same place for about 5 years, about 10 years, and so on
- School cohorts—freshmen, sophomores, juniors, seniors

An event-based design can be a type of repeated cross-sectional design or a type of panel design. In an event-based repeated cross-sectional design, separate samples are drawn from the same cohort at two or more different times. In an event-based panel design, the same individuals from the same cohort are studied at two or more different times.

Event-based design   A type of longitudinal study in which data are collected at two or more points in time from individuals in a cohort.

Cohort   Individuals or groups with a common starting point. Examples include the college class of 1997, people who graduated from high school in the 1980s, General Motors employees who started work between 1990 and the year 2000, and people who were born in the late 1940s or the 1950s (the "baby boom generation").

We can see the value of event-based research in a comparison of two studies that estimated the impact of public and private schooling on high school students' achievement test scores. In a cross-sectional study, James Coleman, Thomas Hoffer, and Sally Kilgore (1982) compared standardized achievement test scores of high school sophomores and seniors in public, Catholic, and other private schools. They found that test scores were higher in the private high schools (both Catholic and other) than in the public high schools. But was this difference a causal effect of private schooling? Perhaps the parents of higher performing children were choosing to send them to private rather than to public schools. In other words, the higher achievement levels of private-sector students might have been in place before they started high school and not have developed as a consequence of their high school education.

The researchers tried to reduce the impact of this problem by statistically controlling for a range of family background variables: family income, parents' education, race, number of siblings, number of rooms in the home, number of parents present, mother working, and other indicators of a family orientation to education. But some critics pointed out that even with all these controls for family background, the cross-sectional study did not ensure that the students had been comparable in achievement when they started high school.

So James Coleman and Thomas Hoffer (1987) went back to the high schools and studied the test scores of the former sophomores two years later, when they were seniors; in other words, the researchers used an event-based panel design. This time, they found that the verbal and math achievement test scores of the Catholic school students had increased more over the two years than was the case for the public school students; it was not clear whether the scores of the other private school students had increased. Irrespective of students' initial achievement test scores, the Catholic schools seemed to "do more" for their students than did the public schools. This finding continued to be true even when dropouts were studied, too. The researchers' causal conclusion rested on much stronger ground because they used an event-based panel design.

UNITS OF ANALYSIS AND ERRORS IN CAUSAL REASONING

Regardless of the research design, we can easily come to invalid conclusions about causal influences if we do not know what **units of analysis** the measures in our study refer to—that is, the level of social life on which the research question is focused, such as individuals, families, households, groups, communities, or towns.

Individual and Group Units of Analysis

In most social work studies (and sociological and psychological studies), the units of analysis are individuals. The researcher may collect survey data from individuals, analyze the data, and then report on, say, how many individuals felt socially isolated and whether substance abuse by individuals was related to their feelings of social isolation.

The units of analysis may instead be groups of some sort, such as families, households, schools, human service organizations, neighborhoods, towns, or states. For example, a researcher may want to learn about the relationship between client satisfaction and agency auspices (public, private nonprofit, private for-profit). The researcher collects data on client satisfaction from different agencies serving similar target groups, such as the mentally ill. The researcher can then analyze the relationship between average client satisfaction and the auspices of the agency. Because the data describe the agency, agencies are the units of analysis.

We can distinguish the concept of units of analysis from the **units of observation.** In a study comparing family income, data were collected from one member of the family, the unit of observation, but the data were used to describe the family. In some studies, the units of observation and the units of analysis are the same. The important point is to know the unit of analysis because the conclusions that are made are about it. A conclusion that teen pregnancies increase with poverty rates could imply either that teenage girls who are poor are more likely to become pregnant or that a community with a high poverty rate is likely to have a high teenage pregnancy rate—or both. Whether we are drawing conclusions from data or interpreting others' conclusions, it is important to be clear about the relationship to which we refer.

We also have to know the units of analysis to interpret statistics appropriately. Measures of association tend to be stronger for group-level than for individual-level data because measurement errors at the individual level tend to cancel out at the group level (Bridges & Weis, 1989, pp. 29–31).

The Ecological Fallacy and Reductionism

Researchers should make sure that their causal conclusions reflect the units of analysis in their studies. Conclusions about processes at the individual level should be based on individual-level data; conclusions about group-level processes should be based on data collected about groups. In most cases, violation of this rule creates one more reason to suspect the validity of the causal conclusions.

A researcher who draws conclusions about individual-level processes from group-level data is making what is termed an **ecological fallacy** (see Exhibit 5.5). The conclusions may or may not be correct, but we must recognize that group-level data do not describe individual-level processes. For example, a researcher may examine factory records and find that the higher the percentage of unskilled workers in factories, the higher the rate of employee sabotage in those factories. But the researcher would commit an ecological fallacy if he or she then concluded that individual unskilled factory workers are more likely to engage in sabotage. This conclusion is about an individual-level causal process (the relationship between the occupation and criminal propensities of individuals), even though the data describe groups (factories). It could actually be that white-collar workers are the ones more likely to commit sabotage, perhaps because in factories with more unskilled workers, the white-collar workers feel they won't be suspected.

Readers of research must also beware not to confuse the unit of analysis, even when the researcher has done so correctly. The term *underclass* first referred to neighborhoods or communities with certain characteristics such as high rates of unemployment, poverty, out–of-wedlock births, and welfare recipiency and lower educational attainment. The term began to be misused when the people living in such communities were described as members of the underclass.

Bear in mind that conclusions about individual processes based on group-level data are not necessarily wrong. We just don't know for sure. Say that we find communities with higher average incomes have lower crime rates. The only thing special about these communities may be that they have more individuals with higher incomes, who tend to commit fewer crimes. Even though we collected data at the group level and analyzed them at the group level, they reflect a causal process at the individual level (Sampson & Lauritsen, 1994, pp. 80–83).

When data about individuals are used to make inferences about group-level processes, a problem occurs that can be thought of as the mirror image of the ecological fallacy: the **reductionist fallacy,** or **reductionism** (see Exhibit 5.5). For example, William Julius Wilson (1987, p. 58) notes that we can be misled into concluding from individual-level data that race

Exhibit 5.5   Errors in Causal Conclusions

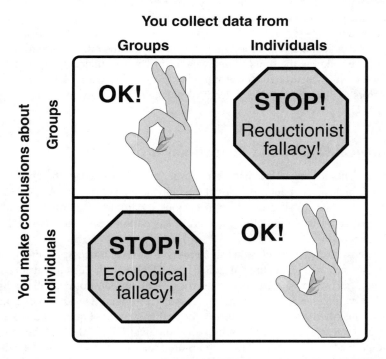

has a causal effect on violence because there is an association at the individual level between race and the likelihood of arrest for violent crime. However, community-level data reveal that almost 40% of poor Blacks lived in extremely poor areas in 1980, compared to only 7% of poor Whites. The concentration of African Americans in poverty areas, not the race or other characteristics of the individuals in these areas, may be the cause of higher rates of violence. Explaining violence in this case requires community-level data.

The fact that errors in causal reasoning can be made should not deter you from conducting research with aggregate data nor make you unduly critical of researchers who make inferences about individuals on the basis of aggregate data. When considered broadly, many research questions point to relationships that could be manifested in many ways and on many levels. Sampson's (1987) study of urban violence is a case in point. His analysis involved only aggregate data about cities, and he explained his research approach as in part a response to the failure of other researchers to examine this problem at the structural, aggregate level. Moreover, Sampson argued that the rates of joblessness and family disruption in communities influence community social processes, not just the behavior of the specific individuals who are unemployed or who grew up without two parents. Yet Sampson suggests that the experience of joblessness and poverty is what tends to reduce the propensity of individual men to marry and that the experience of growing up in a home without two parents in turn increases the propensity of individual juveniles to commit crimes. These conclusions about the behavior of individuals seem consistent with the patterns Sampson found in his aggregate, city-level data, so it seems unlikely that he is committing an ecological fallacy when he proposes them.

The solution is to know what the units of analysis and units of observation were in a study and to take these into account in weighing the credibility of the researcher's conclusions. The goal is not to reject out of hand conclusions that refer to a level of analysis different from what was actually studied. Instead, the goal is to consider the likelihood that an ecological fallacy or a reductionist fallacy has been made when estimating the causal validity of the conclusions.

IDIOGRAPHIC CAUSAL EXPLANATION

Causation in Qualitative Research

An **idiographic causal explanation** is one that identifies the concrete, individual sequence of events, thoughts, or actions that resulted in a particular outcome for a particular individual or that led to a particular event (Hage & Meeker, 1988). An idiographic explanation also may be termed a narrative, individualist, or case-oriented explanation.

A causal explanation that is idiographic includes statements of initial conditions and then relates a series of events at different times that led to the outcome, or causal effect. This narrative, or story, is the critical element in an idiographic explanation, which may therefore be classified as narrative reasoning (Richardson, 1995, pp. 200–201). Idiographic explanations focus on particular social actors, in particular social places, at particular social times (Abbott, 1992). Idiographic explanations are also holistic: They typically are concerned with context, with understanding the particular outcome as part of a larger set of interrelated circumstances.

Causal effect (idiographic perspective)   The finding that a series of events following an initial set of conditions leads in a progressive manner to a particular event or outcome.

Example of an idiographic causal explanation: An individual is neglected by her parents but has a supportive grandparent. She comes to distrust others, has trouble in school, is unable to keep a job, and eventually becomes homeless. She subsequently develops a supportive relationship with a shelter case manager, who helps her find a job and regain her housing (based on K. Hirsch, 1989).

Explanation in Qualitative Research

When qualitative researchers seek to develop causal explanations, they often take an idiographic approach. The rich detail about events and processes that field research generates (see Chapter 9) can be the basis for a convincing idiographic, narrative account of why things happened as they did. Elijah Anderson's (1990) field research in a poor urban community produced a narrative account of how drug addiction often resulted in a downward slide into residential instability and crime:

> When addicts deplete their resources, they may go to those closest to them, drawing them into their schemes. . . . [T]he family may put up with the person for a while. They provide money if they can. . . . They come to realize that the person is on drugs. . . . Slowly the reality sets in more and more completely, and the family becomes drained of both financial and emotional resources. . . . Close relatives lose faith and begin to see the person as untrustworthy and weak. Eventually the addict begins to "mess up" in a variety of ways, taking furniture from the house [and] anything of value. . . . Relatives and friends begin to see the person . . . as "out there" in the streets. . . . One deviant act leads to another. (pp. 86–87)

An idiographic explanation like Anderson's (1990) pays close attention to time order and causal mechanisms. Nonetheless, it is difficult to make a convincing case that one particular causal narrative should be chosen over an alternative narrative (Abbott, 1992). Does low self-esteem result in vulnerability to the appeals of drug dealers, or does a chance drug encounter precipitate a slide in self-esteem? The prudent causal analyst remains open to alternative explanations.

Single-Subject Design

An alternative to group designs available to social work researchers is to use a single-subject design. The name aptly describes the sample size of these designs, for typically they involve a single case, whether an individual, an agency, or a community. Single-subject designs involve closely monitoring the impact of an intervention on a particular client. For example, a researcher may examine the impact of cognitive behavioral therapy with a depressed, 50-year-old male. The close monitoring allows the researcher to identify the point at which improvement or change occurs and to examine the factors that are associated with the change. You can see how this is a form of idiographic research; the researcher starts with a particular client having a particular condition, and data are collected to see if an event (the intervention or other life changes) results in a new or changed condition.

Single-subject designs may be used to better specify findings from experimental group designs. Researchers using experimental group designs typically report aggregate findings, so we do not know what happened with each of the individuals. Single-subject designs examine individual changes rather than group changes. Single-subject designs can be used to test findings produced from such a nomothetic method with specific clients in specific contexts.

Making a case for causality using single-subject designs is much more difficult. While often an association and a time-order can be demonstrated, it is much more difficult to establish nonspuriousness. And the nature of the design—a sample size of one, the specific context, the specific provider—makes it very difficult to establish generalizability. We will describe in detail single-subject designs in Chapter 7.

CONCLUSION

Causation and the means for achieving causally valid conclusions in research is the last of the three legs on which the validity of research rests. In this chapter, you have learned about the two main meanings of causation (nomothetic and idiographic) and about the five criteria used to evaluate the extent to which particular research designs may achieve causally valid findings. You have been exposed to the problem of spuriousness and the ways that randomization and statistical control deal with it. You also have learned how to establish the time order of effects in nonexperimental research and how to come to causal conclusions that are appropriate to the research design.

We should reemphasize that the results of any particular study are part of an always changing body of empirical knowledge about social reality. Thus, our understandings of causal relationships are always partial. Researchers always wonder whether they have omitted some relevant variables from their controls or whether their experimental results would differ if the experiment were conducted in another setting or whether they have overlooked a critical historical event. But by using consistent definitions of terms and maintaining clear standards for establishing the validity of research results—and by expecting the same of others who do research—social researchers can contribute to a growing body of knowledge that can reliably guide social policy and social understanding.

When you read the results of a social scientific study, you should now be able to evaluate critically the validity of the study's findings. If you plan to engage in social research, you should now be able to plan an approach that will lead to valid findings. With a good understanding of the three dimensions of validity (measurement validity, generalizability, and causal validity) under your belt, you are ready to focus on the four major methods of data collection used by social scientists. Each of these methods tends to use a somewhat different approach to achieving validity.

KEY TERMS

Association
Causal effect (nomothetic perspective)
Causal effect (idiographic perspective)
Causal mechanism
Ceteris paribus
Cohort
Cohort study
Context
Cross-sectional research design
Ecological fallacy
Event-based design
Fixed-sample panel design
Idiographic causal explanation
Intervening variables
Longitudinal research design

Nomothetic causal explanation
Nonspuriousness
Random assignment
Randomization
Reductionism
Reductionist fallacy
Repeated cross-sectional design
Spurious relationship
Statistical control
Subject fatigue
Time order
Trend studies
True experiment
Units of analysis
Units of observation

HIGHLIGHTS

- Causation can be defined in either nomothetic or idiographic terms. Nomothetic causal explanations deal with effects on average. Idiographic causal explanations deal with the sequence of events that led to a particular outcome.
- The concept of nomothetic causal explanation relies on a comparison. The value of cases on the dependent variable is measured after they have been exposed to variation in an independent variable. This measurement is compared to what the value of cases on the dependent variable would have been if they had not been exposed to the variation in the independent variable. The validity of nomothetic causal conclusions rests on how closely the comparison group comes to the ideal counterfactual.
- From a nomothetic perspective, three criteria are generally viewed as necessary for identifying a causal relationship: association between the variables, proper time order, and nonspuriousness of the association. In addition, the basis for concluding that a causal relationship exists is strengthened by identification of a causal mechanism and the context.
- Association between two variables is in itself insufficient evidence of a causal relationship. This point is commonly made with the expression, "Correlation does not prove causation."
- Experiments use random assignment to make comparison groups as similar as possible at the outset of an experiment to reduce the risk of spurious effects due to extraneous variables.
- Ethical and practical constraints often preclude the use of experimental designs.
- Nonexperimental designs use statistical controls to reduce the risk of spuriousness. A variable is controlled when it is held constant so that the association between the independent and dependent variables can be assessed without being influenced by the control variable.
- Longitudinal designs are usually preferable to cross-sectional designs for establishing the time order of effects. Longitudinal designs vary in terms of whether the same people are measured at different times, how the population of interest is defined, and how frequently follow-up measurements are taken. Fixed-sample panel designs provide the strongest test for the time order of effects, but they can be difficult to carry out successfully because of their expense and subject attrition and fatigue.
- Units of analysis refer to the level of social life about which we can generalize our findings and include such levels as individuals, groups, families, communities, or organizations.
- Invalid conclusions about causality may occur when relationships between variables measured at the group level are assumed to apply at the individual level (the ecological fallacy) and when

relationships between variables measured at the level of individuals are assumed to apply at the group level (the reductionist fallacy). Nonetheless, many research questions point to relationships at multiple levels and may profitably be answered by studying different units of analysis.

- Idiographic causal explanations can be difficult to identify because the starting and ending points of particular events and the determination of which events act as causes in particular sequences may be ambiguous.

DISCUSSION QUESTIONS

1. In cross-sectional research designs, satisfying the time order criterion for causal explanations can be very challenging. There are, however, four special circumstances in which cross-sectional data can provide adequate information to infer time order of effects. Review these special circumstances, and discuss the potential difficulties present in each of these situations.

2. Compare and contrast the nomothetic and idiographic explanations of causation. How do the approaches or goals of each vary? Review the Walton et al. (1993) study of the effects of intensive family-based services on family reunification described at the beginning of the chapter. What were the advantages of using a nomothetic perspective? What advantages might have been gained using an idiographic perspective? If you were to conduct the study, which approach would you choose?

3. Develop an explanation of the relationship between juvenile delinquency and the poverty rate by specifying intervening variables that might link the two. Is your proposed causal mechanism more compatible with a "culture of poverty" explanation of this relationship or with a conflict theory explanation? Explain your answer.

PRACTICE EXERCISES

1. Review articles in several newspapers, copying down all causal assertions. These might range from assertions that the increasing divorce rate is due to women's liberation from traditional gender roles to explanations about why welfare rates are decreasing or child abuse reports are increasing. Inspect the articles carefully, noting all evidence used to support the causal assertions. Are the explanations nomothetic, idiographic, or a combination of both? Which criteria for establishing causality in a nomothetic framework are met? How satisfactory are the idiographic explanations? What other potentially important influences on the reported outcome have been overlooked?

2. Search *Social Work Abstracts* for several articles on studies using any type of longitudinal design. You will be searching for article titles that use words like *longitudinal, panel, trend,* or *over time.* How successful were the researchers in carrying out the design? What steps did the researchers who used a panel design take to minimize panel attrition? How convinced are you by those using repeated cross-sectional designs that they have identified a process of change in individuals? Did any researchers use retrospective questions? How did they defend the validity of these measures?

WEB EXERCISES

1. Go to Crime Stoppers International's (CSI) Web site at http://www.c-s-i.org. Check out About Us and Crime Stoppers. How is CSI fighting crime? What does CSI's approach assume about the cause of crime? Do you think CSI's approach to fighting crime is based on valid conclusions about causality? Explain.

2. What are the latest trends in crime? Write a short statement after inspecting the FBI's Uniform Crime Reports at www.fbi.gov (go to the Library and References section). You will need to use the Adobe Acrobat Reader to access some of these reports (those in PDF format). Follow the instructions on the site if you're not familiar with this.

> To assist you in completing the Web exercises, please access the study site at http://www.sagepub.com/prsw where you will find the Web Exercises reproduced and suggested links for online resources.

DEVELOPING A RESEARCH PROPOSAL

How will you try to establish the causal effects you hypothesize?

1. Identify at least one hypothesis involving what you expect is a causal relationship.

2. Identify key variables that should be controlled to increase your ability to avoid arriving at a spurious conclusion about the hypothesized causal effect. Draw on relevant research literature and social theory to identify these variables.

3. Review the criteria for establishing a nomothetic causal effect, and discuss your ability to satisfy each one. Include in your discussion some consideration of how well your design will avoid each of the threats to experimental validity.

Chapter 6

GROUP EXPERIMENTAL DESIGNS

Threats to Validity

Internal (Causal) Validity
Selection Bias
Endogenous Change
External Events
Contamination
Treatment Misidentification
Generalizability
Sample Generalizability
External Validity
Reactivity

True Experiments

Experimental and Comparison
Groups
Randomization
Pretest and Posttest Measures
Types of True Experimental Designs

Difficulties in True Experiments in
Agency-based Research
The Limits of True Experimental Designs

Quasi-Experiments

Nonequivalent Control Group Designs
Time Series Designs
Ex Post Facto Control Group Designs

**Common Group Designs for Program
Evaluation and Research**

Types of Nonexperimental Designs

**Ethical Issues in Experimental
Research**

Deception
Selective Distribution of Benefits

Conclusion

A continuing challenge for social work researchers is to demonstrate that different treatment modalities and interventions are effective and to examine accurately the impact of social policy changes. All too often in the past, evidence demonstrating the effectiveness of interventions and policy changes, was based on research designs that did not meet the criteria for causality described in Chapter 5. More recently, there has been a trend among funders of programs, such as the United Way, to require evidence that a funded program is producing the kinds of outcomes that were promised. The level of evidence may not be so stringent that causality must be demonstrated, but minimal evidence of an association is required.

We begin this chapter by discussing in greater detail validity and experimental research designs. The ability to demonstrate internal validity provides the framework by which we will then discuss three different types of group designs that social work researchers and agencies use to test or demonstrate treatment effectiveness and to show the impact of policy changes. Although the examples we use in this chapter relate specifically to research and evaluation in social work practice and social policy, the same principles apply to research in other disciplines. The independent variable in many of the examples is an intervention or social policy change, but the independent variable could just as easily be "the amount of exposure to violence in television" or "presence of seat belt laws."

THREATS TO VALIDITY

Researchers face challenges in establishing causal relationships. As we described in Chapter 5, to establish causality, researchers must be able to demonstrate that three criteria have been achieved: time order, evidence of an association, and nonspuriousness. These criteria need to be considered when you look at any research design, whether it is a research design you read about in a journal article or a research design you are considering for your own study. In this section, we expand on the issue of nonspuriousness; you may remember from Chapter 5 that this means the relationship between two variables is not due to a third variable. We describe alternative explanations—third variables—that may limit the researcher's ability to attribute causality to the effects of the independent variable on the dependent variable in experimental research. We refer to these alternative explanations as "threats to the internal validity" of the design.

Internal (Causal) Validity

An experiment's ability to yield valid conclusions about causal effects is determined by the comparability of its experimental and comparison groups. First, of course, a comparison group must be created. Second, this comparison group must be so similar to the experimental group or groups that it shows what the experimental group would be like if it had not received the experimental treatment—if the independent variable had not varied.

There are four basic sources of noncomparability (other than the treatment) between a comparison group and an experimental group. They produce four of the five sources of internal invalidity:

- *Selection bias.* When characteristics of the experimental and comparison group subjects differ.
- *Endogenous change.* When the subjects develop or change during the experiment as part of an ongoing process independent of the experimental treatment.
- *External events.* When something occurs during the experiment, other than the treatment, that influences outcome scores.
- *Contamination.* When either the experimental group or the comparison group is aware of the other group and is influenced in the posttest as a result (Mohr, 1992).

The fifth source of internal invalidity can be termed **treatment misidentification:** Variation in the independent variable (the treatment) is associated with variation in the observed outcome, but the change occurs through a process that the researcher has not identified.

Selection Bias

One of the problems frequently encountered in experimental research is **selection bias,** which affects the comparability of the groups used to compare the effects of the independent variable. How participants are assigned to the groups may affect the comparability of the two groups. As we noted in Chapter 5, randomization should result in similar group characteristics, although with some possibility for error due to chance. The likelihood of difference due to chance can be identified with appropriate statistics. When subjects are not assigned randomly to treatment and comparison groups, the threat of selection bias is very great.

In some experiments what had been planned as a random assignment process may deteriorate when it is delegated to the front-line program staff. Front-line staff may ignore the procedures established to randomly assign participants. For example, Sherman and Berk (1984) described a domestic violence experiment in which police officers were to randomly assign suspects to either a treatment or comparison group. Sometimes the officers violated the random assignment plan because they thought the circumstances warranted arresting a suspect who had been randomly assigned to receive just a warning.

Even when random assignment works as planned, the groups can become different over time because of **differential attrition,** or what can be thought of as "deselection." That is, the groups become different because subjects are more likely to drop out of one of the groups for various reasons. This is not a likely problem in a laboratory experiment that occurs in one session. But most intervention studies typically involve more than one interaction or session, as do field experiments that evaluate the impact of social programs, and so differential attrition can become a problem. Subjects who experience the experimental condition may become more motivated than comparison subjects to continue in the experiment. Subjects who receive some advantageous program benefit are more likely to stay in the experiment (making themselves available for measurement in the posttest); subjects who are not receiving program benefits are more likely to drop out.

In research that involves monitoring program impact over an extended period, the possibility of differential attrition can be very high. When the treatment group is receiving some service or benefit that the control group is not, individuals in the control group will be more likely to drop out of the study altogether. A study of the benefits of a health insurance program actually had to abandon tracking its control group because subjects weren't cooperating (Hunt, 1985, pp. 274–275).

Endogenous Change

The type of problem subsumed under the label **endogenous change** occurs when natural developments in the subjects, independent of the experimental treatment itself, account for some or all of the observed change between a pretest and posttest. Endogenous change includes these three specific threats to internal validity:

- *Testing.* Taking the pretest can in itself influence posttest scores. Subjects may learn something or be sensitized to an issue by the pretest and, as a result, respond differently the next time they are asked the same questions on the posttest. Subjects may not behave the same when they are under observation. Just having taken a test the first time often reduces anxiety provoked by the unknown, and subjects will be more comfortable with subsequent **testing.**

- *Maturation.* Changes in outcome scores during experiments that involve a lengthy treatment period may be due to maturation. Subjects may age or gain experience in school or grow in knowledge, all as part of a natural maturational experience and thus respond differently on the posttest than on the pretest. For example, after the death of family member or friend, feelings of depression and sadness become less intense with the passing of time.
- *Regression.* People experience cyclical or episodic changes that result in different posttest scores, a phenomenon known as a **regression effect**. Subjects who are chosen for a study because they received very low scores on a test may show improvement in the posttest simply because some of the low scorers were having a bad day. On the other hand, individuals selected for an experiment because they are suffering from tooth decay will not show improvement in the posttest because a decaying tooth is not likely to improve in the natural course of things. It is hard in many cases to know whether a phenomenon is subject to naturally occurring fluctuations, so the possibility of regression effects should be considered whenever subjects are selected because of their extremely high or low values on the outcome variable (Mohr, 1992, pp. 56, 71–79).

External Events

External events during the experiment (things that happen outside the experiment) could change subjects' outcome scores. One type of problem is an event that subjects are exposed to during the course of the experiment or evaluation. For example, a new cook is hired at a nursing home, and the food improves at the same time a researcher is evaluating a group intervention to improve the morale of residents. This problem is often referred to as a **history effect**—history during the experiment, that is.

Causal conclusions can be invalid in true experiments because of the influence of external events, but not every experiment is affected by them. For example, in an experiment in which subjects go to a particular location for the treatment and the control group subjects do not, something in that location unrelated to the treatment could influence the experimental subjects. In this way, external events are a major concern in evaluation studies that compare programs in different cities or states (Hunt, 1985, pp. 276–277).

Broader social or economic trends may also impact on the findings of a study, creating a problem called **secular drift.** For example, trends in the economy may impact on the findings of the efficacy of a job training program. You might have a comparison group and an experimental group and end up with no group differences if the economy is in a severe recession (members of both groups have difficulty finding jobs) or no group differences if the economy is in a period of growth (members of both groups find jobs). The impact of the changes in welfare legislation in 1996 has been deemed successful in reducing the number of people on welfare, but this trend had already started prior to 1996. Was the reduction in the number of people on welfare due to the policy, or did the reduction reflect a trend that had already begun as the economy improved?

A third possibility is **instrumentation**. When the same method of measurement is used for the pretest and posttest, the measures must be stable (demonstrate measurement reliability), otherwise the findings may reflect the instability of the measurement and not the effect of the treatment. When different methods of measurement are used, such as a paper measure for the pretest and behavioral observations for the posttest, the two methods must be equivalent (again measurement reliability), otherwise any changes might be due to the lack of equivalency.

Contamination

Contamination occurs in an experiment when the comparison group is in some way affected by, or affects, the treatment group. This problem arises from failure to control adequately the conditions of the experiment. When comparison group members are aware that they are being denied some advantage, they may increase their efforts to compensate, creating a problem termed **compensatory rivalry**, or the **John Henry effect** (Cook & Campbell, 1979, p. 55). On the other hand, comparison group members may become demoralized (called **resentful demoralization**) if they feel that they have been left out of some valuable treatment and, hence, perform worse than they would have outside the experiment. The treatment may seem, in comparison, to have had a more beneficial effect than it actually did. Both compensatory rivalry and demoralization may distort the impact of the experimental treatment. Another form of contamination may occur when treatment and control (comparison) groups interact, and the nature of the treatment becomes known to the control group. This problem, called **diffusion of treatment**, may result in the control group sharing in the benefits of the treatment.

Treatment Misidentification

Treatment misidentification occurs when some process that the researcher is not aware of is responsible for the apparent effect of treatment. The subjects experience something other than, or in addition to, what the researchers believe they have experienced. Treatment misidentification has at least two sources:

Expectancies of experimental staff. Change among experimental subjects may be due to the positive **expectancies of the experimental staff** who are delivering the treatment rather than the treatment itself. Even well-trained staff may convey their enthusiasm for an experimental program to the subjects in subtle ways. Such positive staff expectations create a **self-fulfilling prophecy.** Because social programs are delivered by human beings, such expectancy effects can be very difficult to control in field experiments. On the other hand, staff providing services to the comparison group may feel that it is unfair and, therefore, work harder or do more than they might have if there had been no experiment. This effect is called **compensatory equalization of treatment.** However, in experiments on the effects of treatments like medical drugs, **double-blind procedures** can be used: Staff delivering the treatments do not know which subjects are getting the treatment and which are receiving a placebo, something that looks like the treatment but has no effect.

Placebo effect. Treatment misidentification may occur when subjects receive a treatment that they consider likely to be beneficial and improve because of that expectation rather than because of the treatment itself. In medical research, where the placebo is often a chemically inert substance that looks like the experimental drug but actually has no effect, research indicates that the **placebo effect** itself produces positive health effects in two thirds of patients suffering from relatively mild medical problems (Goleman, 1993a, p. C3). Placebo effects can also occur in social science research. The only way to reduce this threat to internal validity is to treat the comparison group with something similar.

Process analysis is a technique to avoid treatment misidentification. Periodic measures are taken throughout an experiment to assess whether the treatment is being delivered as planned. In the Goldfinger et al. (1996) housing study (introduced in Chapter 1), treatment group subjects actually resided in eight different group homes. The researchers monitored the operation of these homes to determine that each was being run according to the principles underlying the "evolving consumer household" model being tested.

Generalizability

The need for generalizable findings can be thought of as the Achilles heel of group experimental design. The design components that are essential to minimize the threats to internal validity make it more difficult to achieve sample generalizability, that is, being able to apply the findings to some clearly defined larger population. Thus, it becomes even more difficult to achieve cross-population generalizability across subgroups and to other populations and settings.

Sample Generalizability

Subjects who can be recruited for a laboratory experiment, randomly assigned to a group, and kept under carefully controlled conditions for the study's duration are unlikely to be a representative sample of any large population of interest to social work researchers. Can they be expected to react to the experimental treatment in the same way as members of the larger population? The generalizability of the treatment and of the setting for the experiment also must be considered (Cook & Campbell, 1979, pp. 73–74).

A researcher can take steps both before and after an experiment to increase a study's generalizability. In a few field experiments, participants can be selected randomly from the population of interest, and thus, the researchers can achieve results generalizable to that population. For example, some studies of the effects of income supports on the work behavior of poor people have randomly sampled people within particular states before randomly assigning participants to experimental and comparison groups.

But in most experiments, neither random selection from the population nor selection of the entire population is possible. Potential subjects must make a conscious decision to participate—thus probably resulting in an unrepresentative pool of volunteers. Or the experiment must be conducted in a limited setting, perhaps a particular organization, and thus, the results may not apply to other settings.

When random selection is not feasible, the researchers may be able to increase generalizability by selecting several sites for conducting the experiment that offer marked contrasts in key variables of the population. As a result, although the findings are not statistically generalizable to a larger population, they do give some indication of the study's general applicability (Cook & Campbell, 1979, pp. 76–77). Ultimately, generalizability is enhanced through replication of the study with different groups, in different settings, and in different communities.

External Validity

Researchers are often interested in determining whether treatment effects identified in an experiment hold true for subgroups of subjects and across different populations, times, or settings. Of course, determining that a relationship between the treatment and the outcome variable holds true for certain subgroups does not establish that the relationship also holds true for these subgroups in the larger population, but it suggests that the relationship might be externally valid.

On the other hand, evidence of an overall sample effect does not mean that the effect holds true for subgroups within the study. For example, Roger Roffman, Lois Downey, Blair Beadnell, Judith Gordon, Jay Craver, and Robert Stephens (1997) examined the effectiveness of a 17-session HIV prevention group with gay and bisexual males. The researchers found that those in the treatment group had better outcomes than those in the control group. But within the treatment group, outcomes were better for exclusively gay males than for bisexual males. This study shows how an interaction effect limits the generalizability of the findings.

Reactivity

A variant on the problem of external validity, called **reactivity** occurs when the experimental treatment has an effect only when the particular conditions created by the experiment occur. Without the experimental conditions, there would be no effect. This is a problem as social work providers try to translate research findings into practice. The agency does not want to have to re-create the experimental conditions in order to provide an effective treatment. Reactivity takes several different forms:

Interaction of testing and treatment. One such problem occurs when the treatment has an effect only if subjects have had the pretest. The pretest sensitizes the subjects to some issue, so that when they are exposed to the treatment, they react in a way they would not have reacted if they had not taken the pretest. In other words, **testing** and **treatment** interact to produce the outcome. For example, answering questions in a pretest about anti-Semitism may sensitize subjects so that when they are exposed to the experimental treatment, seeing a film about prejudice, their attitudes are different than they would have been. In this situation, the treatment truly had an effect, but it would not have had an effect if it were repeated without the sensitizing pretest.

Reactive effects of experimental arrangement. Members of the treatment group change in terms of the dependent variable because their participation in the study makes them feel special. Experimental group members could feel special simply because they are in the experiment. This is called a **Hawthorne effect**, named after a famous productivity experiment at the Hawthorne electric plant outside Chicago. No matter what conditions researchers changed, and whether the goal was to improve or diminish productivity, the workers seemed to work harder simply because they were part of a special experiment.

Interaction of selection and treatment. This effect occurs when the results are related to selection biases in who receives the treatment and who serves in the comparison group. For example, voluntary clients often do better than involuntary clients. If the treatment group consists of voluntary clients and the comparison group consists of involuntary clients, the findings of the study are likely to be influenced by the biased assignment.

Multiple treatment interference. This refers to clients or subjects who have been exposed to other interventions prior to the experiment. The question of multiple treatment interference is:

Was the intervention successful on its own, or was it successful because of the subject's cumulative experience with other treatments or interventions? For example, chronically mentally ill individuals are likely to have had past treatment experiences, both in the community and perhaps in an institutional setting. If multiple treatment interference is a problem, the generalizability of the findings may be limited to a population having experienced a similar treatment pattern.

We have described in detail the problems of internal validity and generalization because they provide a framework by which group designs can be compared. Group designs fall into three categories, **true experimental designs, quasi-experimental designs,** and **nonexperimental designs,** which are distinguished by the extent to which threats to internal validity are controlled.

TRUE EXPERIMENTS

True experimental research designs are used when a social work researcher wants to show that an intervention (independent variable) caused a change in an outcome (the dependent variable). This type of design achieves the three criteria for causality by having at least three things:

- Two comparison groups (in the simplest case, an experimental and a control group)
- Random assignment to the two (or more) comparison groups
- Variation in the independent variable before assessment of change in the dependent variable

The combination of these features permits researchers and consumers of research to have much greater confidence in the validity of causal conclusions than is possible in other research designs. Confidence in the validity of an experiment's findings is further enhanced by

- Identification of the causal mechanism
- Control over the context of an experiment

Experimental and Comparison Groups

True experiments must have at least one **experimental group**—subjects who receive some treatment—and at least one second group—subjects to whom the experimental group can be compared. The second group differs from the experimental group in terms of one or more independent variables, whose effects are being tested. In other words, the difference between the experimental and second groups is determined by variation in the independent variable.

In many social work research experiments, the independent variable indicates that the subject is receiving a particular type of intervention or not receiving the intervention. In experiments consisting of subjects who do not receive the intervention, the second group is termed a **control group.** In other experiments, the second group receives what is considered to be the traditional intervention or can be exposed to an alternative intervention. In these experiments, the second group is referred to as a **comparison group.**

Comparison groups as opposed to control groups are often used in social work research. Many times, providers have concerns about delaying treatment for their clients. Using a comparison group ensures that a treatment is provided. Second, providing the intervention to the comparison group helps recruit subjects, as they do receive something for their participation. Finally, because they receive treatment, subjects in the comparison group are less likely to drop out.

An experiment can have more than one experimental group if the goal is to test several versions of the treatment (the independent variable) or several combinations of different treatments. For example, a researcher testing different interventions for depression might include a control group, a group receiving medication, a group receiving counseling, and a group receiving both medication and counseling. An experiment may have more than one comparison group, as when outcome scores for the treatment group need to be compared to more than one comparison group.

Experimental group In an experiment, the group of subjects that receives the treatment or experimental manipulation.

Control group A comparison group that receives no treatment instead of a different treatment.

Comparison group The group of subjects that is exposed to the traditional treatment rather than the experimental treatment.

Randomization

Randomization, or random assignment, is what makes the comparison group in a true experiment such a powerful tool for identifying the effects of the treatment. A randomized control group can provide a good estimate of the counterfactual—the outcome that would have occurred if the subjects who were exposed to the treatment actually had not been exposed but otherwise had the same experiences (Mohr, 1992, p. 3; Rossi & Freeman, 1989, p. 229). If the comparison group differed from the experimental group in any way besides not receiving the treatment (or receiving a different treatment), a researcher would not be able to determine for sure what were the unique effects of the treatment.

Assigning subjects randomly to the experimental and control or comparison groups ensures that systematic bias does not affect the assignment of subjects to groups. Of course, random assignment cannot guarantee that the groups are perfectly identical at the start of the experiment. Randomization removes bias from the assignment process—but only by relying on chance, which itself can result in some intergroup differences. Fortunately, researchers can use statistical methods to determine the odds of ending up with groups that differ very much on the basis of chance, and these odds are low even for groups of moderate size. The larger the group, the less likely it is that even modest differences will occur on the basis of chance and the more possible it becomes to draw conclusions about causal effects from relatively small differences in the outcome.

Note that the random assignment of subjects to experimental and comparison groups is not the same as random sampling of individuals from some larger population (see Exhibit 6.1).

Exhibit 6.1   Random Sampling Versus Random Assignment

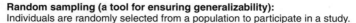

Random sampling (a tool for ensuring generalizability):
Individuals are randomly selected from a population to participate in a study.

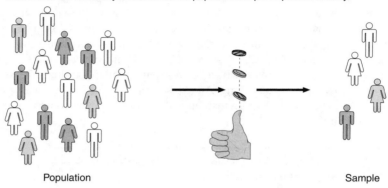

Random assignment, or randomization (a tool for ensuring internal validity):
Individuals who are to participate in a study are randomly divided into an
experimental group and a comparison group.

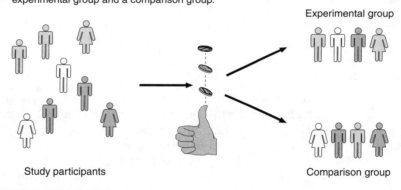

In fact, random assignment (randomization) does not help at all to ensure that the research
subjects are representative of some larger population; instead, representativeness is the goal
of random sampling. What random assignment does—create two (or more) equivalent
groups—is useful for ensuring internal validity, not generalizability.

Why is random assignment useful for ensuring internal validity? The underlying assumption of random assignment is that if chance is used to determine who goes into a particular
group, equivalent groups are created. The groups are believed not only to be more or
less equal in demographic make-up and to have similar scores on the dependent variable
(something we can check), but also to be more or less equal with regard to the impact of
different threats to internal validity. For example, some people in a bereavement group might
be susceptible to a maturation effect. Through the use of random assignment, such people are
believed to be more or less equally distributed between the experimental group and the control

group; therefore, the effects of maturation will cancel each other out. Similarly, some people are highly motivated, others less motivated; random assignment distributes these individuals into the two groups so that motivation for change does not explain away the treatment's effects. It is very difficult to control conditions when research about treatment is occurring in community-based settings. When subjects are randomly assigned to groups, the home and community environments during the treatment period should be the same on average.

There are different ways random assignment into groups can be done. Because assignment to a group is by chance, you can toss a coin, use a table of random numbers, or generate random numbers with a computer. While these methods should result in similar groups, **matching** is sometimes used to better equate the experimental and comparison groups.

One form of matching is to match pairs of individuals (see Exhibit 6.2). You start by identifying important characteristics that might impact on the study, and then you match pairs of individuals with similar or identical characteristics. For example, a study of older adults might match subjects by gender and age. These two characteristics are important for the elderly, given that gender and increasing age are associated with a wide variety of differences among the elderly such as health, marital status, and economic well-being. In this study, you might match a 75-year-old female with a 76-year-old female. Once the pairs have been identified, you would then use a random assignment procedure to determine which one of the pair would go into the experimental group and which one would go into the control group. This method eliminates the possibility of differences due to chance in the gender and age composition of the groups.

Exhibit 6.2   Experimental Design Combining Matching and Random Assignment

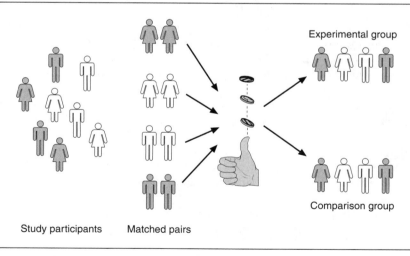

The basic problem is that, as a practical matter, individuals can be matched on only a few characteristics; unmatched differences between the experimental and comparison groups may still influence outcomes. However, matching combined with randomization can reduce the possibility of differences due to chance. A second problem occurs when one of the matched pair drops out of the study, unbalancing the groups. In this case, researchers will often exclude the findings of the individual who remained in the study.

A second form of matching involves the grouping of individuals by their characteristics. A gerontologist might group older adults by age and gender, creating a group of men between the ages of 65 and 74, a second group between 75 and 84, and a third group 85 and older. The same grouping by age would be done with female participants. Within each group, the members are randomly assigned into the experimental and treatment group. This kind of matching is typically referred to as **block matching**.

Finally, matching might take place by group, or **aggregate matching**. This type of matching has often been done in education where the group might be a classroom. The researcher is assuming that the mix of students in each class is alike. To compare two teaching methods, such as lecture versus problem focused, a researcher might choose two MSW research classes. The classes are then randomly assigned to one of the two teaching conditions.

Pretest and Posttest Measures

All true experiments have a **posttest**—that is, measurement of the outcome in both groups after the experimental group has received the treatment. Many true experiments also have **pretests,** which measure the dependent variable prior to the experimental intervention. Usually, the pretest measurement of the dependent variable is exactly the same as the posttest measurement of the dependent variable. We say *usually* because sometimes the measurement methods used for the pretest and posttest differ, although both methods must be equivalent measures of the same construct. One researcher might use the same children's behavior checklist scale for the pretest and posttest. Another researcher might use the checklist scale for the pretest but observe actual behavior for the posttest. This is appropriate as long as the two methods have measurement equivalence.

Strictly speaking, a true experiment does not require a pretest. When researchers use random assignment, the groups' initial scores on the dependent variable and on all other variables are very likely to be similar. Any difference in outcome between the experimental and comparison groups should be due to the intervention (or to other processes occurring during the experiment), and the likelihood of a difference just on the basis of chance can be calculated.

But, in fact, having pretest scores can be advantageous. They provide a direct measure of how much the experimental and comparison groups changed over time. They allow the researcher to verify that randomization was successful (that chance factors did not lead to an initial difference between the groups). In addition, by identifying subjects' initial scores on the dependent variable, a pretest provides a more complete picture of the conditions in which the intervention had (or didn't have) an effect (Mohr, 1992, pp. 46–48).

An experiment may have multiple posttests and perhaps even multiple pretests. Multiple posttests can identify just when the treatment has its effect and for how long. They are particularly important for treatments delivered over time (Rossi & Freeman, 1989, pp. 289–290).

Types of True Experimental Designs

In this section, we focus on three particular true experimental designs as well as several variations of these designs. Other designs, such as using placebos, are common in other disciplines like medical or pharmaceutical research but are quite rare in social work research. Furthermore, there are additional variations that we will not describe in detail, such as incorporating multiple measures or taking measures during the course of treatment. To describe the designs, we will use abbreviations and symbols. The symbols and abbreviations are displayed in Exhibit 6.3.

Exhibit 6.3   Design Abbreviations

R	Random assignment
O	Observation taken for dependent or outcome variable
X	Intervention or treatment
X_e	Experimental or new intervention
X_t	Traditional intervention
A, B, etc.	Group A, Group B, etc.

One of the most common true experimental designs is the Pretest-Posttest Control Group Design (Classical Experimental Design; Randomized Before/After Control Group Design).

$$RA \qquad O_{1a} \qquad X \qquad O_{2a}$$
$$RB \qquad O_{1b} \qquad\qquad O_{2b}$$

As you can see from the design above, the steps involved include (1) random assignment into two groups (A and B); (2) taking an observation of the dependent/outcome variable prior to the intervention; (3) implementing the intervention in Group A; and (4) taking a second observation after the intervention.

A variation on this design is to use a comparison group, so that Group A receives the new intervention while Group B receives the traditional or alternative intervention.

$$RA \qquad O_{1a} \qquad X_e \qquad O_{2a}$$
$$RB \qquad O_{1b} \qquad X_t \qquad O_{2b}$$

What kinds of comparisons might you make with this design? If you want to assume that the Time 1 observations are more or less equal, you only need to compare O_{2a} with O_{2b}. But in this case, you are making an assumption that really is not necessary; instead, it is common to compare the change between observations in Group A (ΔO_A) with the change in Group B (ΔO_B).

What can we say about causality with these two designs? First, we can establish *time order,* given that the treatment precedes the second observation. Second, we can statistically evaluate whether there is a relationship between the treatment variable and change so we can establish an *association.* And, because there is random assignment, different *threats to internal validity* may be ruled out. History, maturation, instrumentation, and statistical regression can be ruled out because we would expect those threats to apply equally to both groups, and therefore, they would cancel each other out. In principle, we should be able to rule out selection bias, but if you are at all nervous about selection bias, the design allows you to compare Time 1 observations on the dependent variable to determine if they are more or less equal. Testing may be ruled out, although it is possible that a test effect might explain a finding of no differences between the two groups. The threat to internal validity that is most difficult to rule out is attrition (differential mortality). The results need to be considered in light of possible attrition, particularly in situations in which there is a control group as opposed to a comparison group.

Catherine Alter (1996) used a Pretest-Posttest Control Group Design to evaluate the impact of a family support intervention, Family Development and Self-Sufficiency program (FaDSS), on female, long-term recipients of Aid to Families With Dependent Children (see Exhibit 6.4).

Exhibit 6.4   Examples of Pretest-Posttest Group Designs

Pretest-Posttest Control Group Design:
Family support as an intervention with female long-term AFDC recipients (Alter, 1996)

Subjects:	Random Assignment	O_1	X	O_2
Actual or at-risk of long-term AFDC recipiency	Group A	Self-efficacy Competency Confidence	FaDSS	Self-efficacy Competency Confidence Employment
	Group B	Self-efficacy Competency Confidence		Self-efficacy Competency Confidence Employment

Pretest-Posttest Comparison Group Design with repeated measurements:
A comparison of two welfare-to-work case management models (Brock and Harknett, 1998)

Subjects:	Random Assignment	O_1 (Pretest)	X	O_2 O_3 O_4 ... O_{22} O_{23} O_{24} (Posttests Monthly for 2 Years)
Single parents, AFDC recipients, youngest child 3 years or older	Group A	AFDC income and employment-related data	Traditional: Income maintenance worker JOBS case manager	AFDC income and employment related data JOBS participation data
	Group B	AFDC income and employment related data	Integrated: Single case manager Sanctions	AFDC income and employment related data JOBS participation data
	Group C	AFDC income and employment related data	Control: On their own	AFDC income and employment related data

The intervention was based on the idea that if clients' personal self-sufficiency could be improved—if they learned how to plan for the future, obtain services, and be more assertive—the clients would then be more likely to achieve economic self-sufficiency. The intervention involved ongoing home visits by a family development specialist who provided training and linkages to other resources. Beginning in 1989, recipients were randomly assigned into the FaDSS group or the control group. Time 1 interviews were conducted at the time of assignment, with follow-up interviews taking place in late 1993. Alter found that the FaDSS group achieved higher levels of competence and self-efficacy. FaDSS group members also became better off economically more quickly than control group members.

Variations on the Pretest-Posttest Control Group Design can be quite complex. The following example, which is also summarized in Exhibit 6.4, illustrates one variation as well as a model that allowed for the examination of the causal mechanisms leading to differences. Thomas Brock and Kristen Harknett (1998) used this design with multiple measures to compare the effectiveness of two welfare-to-work case management models in helping recipients get off the Temporary Assistance to Needy Families program. In the traditional case-management model, income maintenance and employment services were separated into two different jobs performed by two different staff members. The researchers compared the traditional model to an integrated model in which both income-maintenance and employment services were provided by the same person. The researchers believed that this would result in speedier job placement and lower payments of cash assistance. They randomly assigned 6,912 single parents in which the youngest child was 3 or older into three groups: a group receiving the traditional services, a group receiving integrated services, and a control group in which members received cash assistance but no employment service assistance by a case manager. Baseline measures were taken, assignment was made, and then repeated measures were taken for two years. Brock and Harknett then took a random sample of each group and did a series of comparisons. They found that subjects in the integrated model group participated in more job-related activities, were less likely to be referred for sanctioning for nonparticipation, and received less cash assistance from welfare benefits. On the other hand, the researchers found no differences in employment earnings between the integrated and traditional model subjects. Both treatment groups did better than the control group on all of these measures.

Brock and Harknett were intrigued by the finding that despite differences in cash benefits, there were no differences in employment and earnings between the two case-management model groups. This finding was contrary to what they had expected. To understand the cause or explanation for this unexpected finding, they interviewed welfare department staff. They found that when the income maintenance and JOBS search staff positions were combined (integrated model), the case manager was able to detect unreported income. On the other hand, when the functions were separate (traditional model), the income maintenance workers did not pursue unreported income and JOBS compliance. From this example, you can see why it is important to try to understand the underlying causal mechanism for different findings.

The weakness of the Pretest-Posttest Control Group Design is that a testing-treatment interaction effect may occur, posing a threat to external validity. It is possible that the test can sensitize respondents to the treatment and therefore make the treatment effective or more effective than it would have been without the test.

To safeguard the reactive effects of testing and treatment, a second research design, the Posttest-Only Control Group Design (Randomized Control Group After-Only Design) can be used. Like the preceding design, this one may use a comparison group as opposed to a control group.

$$RA \quad X_e \quad\quad\quad O_{2a} \quad\quad RA \quad X_e \quad\quad\quad O_{2a}$$
$$RB \quad\quad\quad\quad\quad O_{2b} \quad \text{or} \quad RB \quad X_t \quad\quad\quad O_{2b}$$

As you can see, the process is the same except that no baseline measurement is taken. The only comparison made is between O_{2a} and O_{2b}. In this case, the researcher assumes that the baseline measures would be more or less equal because random assignment is used. But because random assignment is based on probability, there is the possibility that unequal groups were formed. Because of the structure of this design, it is impossible to check whether the groups are equivalent initially, and therefore, the internal validity threat of selection is a possibility.

Sometimes researchers want to test whether there is a test-treatment interaction and do so by combining both designs, conducting a Solomon Four Group Design.

$$
\begin{array}{llll}
\text{RA} & O_{1a} & X_e & O_{2a} \\
\text{RB} & O_{1b} & & O_{2b} \\
\text{RC} & & X_e & O_{2c} \\
\text{RD} & & & O_{2d}
\end{array}
$$

If testing and treatment do interact, the difference in outcome scores between the experimental and comparisons groups will be different for subjects who took the pretest compared to those who did not.

Remember why this interaction is problematic. As human service providers apply research findings, they do not want to have to re-create the research conditions. The interaction of testing and treatment might be an exception to this concern. It is common for clients to receive an initial test, one that we typically might refer to as an initial assessment or even a follow-up assessment. The testing effect may be beneficial if it adds to the effectiveness of the intervention. It depends on the test and an agency's ability to adapt the test as part of the assessment process.

Difficulties in True Experiments in Agency-Based Research

If true experimental designs are powerful tools to demonstrate causality, why are they typically the province of social work researchers and used less often by agencies to evaluate their programs? Implementing true experimental designs requires expertise, sufficient numbers of clients, and plenty of time. In addition, there are real and imagined criticisms, such as:

- The program cannot change during the course of the experiment or evaluation (Weiss, 1998). This poses a problem because managers want continual improvement. Weiss (1998) recommends that if a program does change, it is important to note the timing of the change and to keep accurate records of outcomes at different points in time as the program changes.
- Even if the program or treatment does not change, implementation depends on staff who have different skill levels such as ability to engage clients or provide services. Weiss (1998) notes that this is less likely to be a problem if the sample is large, as variations should cancel out. On the other hand, with small numbers of clients, differences may be magnified.
- The more controlled the conditions under which the treatment or program is provided, the less generalizable it will be to other times or locations. This is certainly a concern and points to the importance of being able to describe the context and the conditions under which the evaluation is taken. One solution is to replicate the intervention in different sites and with different samples.
- Threats to professional judgment may arise. Posavac and Carey (1997) refer to these problems as "I know what is best for my client" (p. 184). This concern manifests itself in two ways. One concern is about random assignment. Typically, social workers choose clients for treatment based on need or when someone comes to seek help. Many social

workers (including our students) object to letting chance (randomization) dictate who gets help and who has to wait; rather, they want to base their decisions on their professional judgment. The second concern is that an experiment defines the intervention that is provided to clients and how the intervention is provided. Some social workers believe this threatens their ability to make decisions about how to best meet their clients' needs.

- Some staffers might feel that "if the experimental approach is believed to be so good, I want all my clients to get it." The reason for trying a new method is based on some belief—whether anecdotal or theoretical—that suggests that the model is indeed better. Staff want their clients to receive the best service so they argue "why delay implementing what we know should work?" Yet social workers have an ethical responsibility to have evidence that the new intervention is better before it is widely implemented.

- Others may say, "Don't experiment on me" (Posavac & Carey, 1997, p. 183). People are suspicious of experimentation, and clients, who are particularly vulnerable, may be even more suspicious of experimentation. This makes recruitment and retention more difficult. With proper human subject protections, such as the use of informed consent, these fears can be mitigated.

The Limits of True Experimental Designs

The distinguishing features of true experiments–experimental and comparison groups, pretests and posttests, and randomization–do not help researchers identify the mechanisms by which treatments have their effects. In fact, this question of causal mechanism often is not addressed in experimental research. The hypothesis test itself does not require any analysis of mechanism, and if the experiment is conducted under carefully controlled conditions during a limited span of time, the causal effect (if any) may seem to be quite direct. But attention to causal mechanisms can augment experimental findings. For example, researchers often focus attention on the mechanism by which a social program has its effect (Mohr, 1992, pp. 25–27; Scriven, 1972). The goal is to measure the intermediate steps that lead to the change that is the program's primary focus. This is also the place where theory can inform or provide an explanation for the findings.

True experimental designs also do not guarantee that the researcher has been able to maintain control over the conditions to which subjects are exposed after they are assigned to the experimental and comparison groups. If these conditions begin to differ, the variation between the experimental and comparison groups will not be that which was intended. Such unintended variation is often not much of a problem in laboratory experiments, where the researcher has almost complete control over the conditions (and can ensure that these conditions are nearly identical for both groups). But control over conditions can become a very big concern for field- or agency-based experiments in real world settings.

QUASI-EXPERIMENTS

Although some social work research does use true experimental designs, such designs are often not feasible when testing hypotheses about the impact of service delivery, the effectiveness of a treatment modality, or the manner in which services are provided. Such a test may be too costly or take too long to carry out; it may be inappropriate for the particular research problem; it may not be ethical to assign subjects randomly to different conditions; or it may presume ability to manipulate an intervention that already has occurred. Furthermore, as practitioners respond to the demands for outcome accountability and monitoring of practice, true experimental designs are often unnecessary. A variety of designs can be used by researchers to overcome these problems, yet still benefit from the logic of the experimental method; agency directors and program evaluators may also use these designs for outcome evaluation.

A **quasi-experimental design** is one in which we may be able to rule out at least some threats to internal validity. A quasi-experimental design is one in which there is no random assignment when there is a comparison group. Instead, the comparison group is predetermined to be comparable to the treatment group in critical ways, like being eligible for the same services or being in the same school cohort (Rossi & Freeman, 1989, p. 313). As a result, we cannot be as confident about the comparability of the groups as in true experimental designs.

We will discuss here the two major types of quasi-experimental designs (others can be found in Cook & Campbell, 1979; Mohr, 1992):

- *Nonequivalent control group designs.* In nonequivalent control group designs, experimental and comparison groups are designated before the treatment occurs and are not created by random assignment.
- *Time series design.* A time series design typically has no comparison group (although it may) and has repeated pretest and posttest measures. The repeated measurement at pretest allows the subjects to serve as their own controls.

Nonequivalent Control Group Designs

The **nonequivalent control group design** is exactly like the Pretest-Posttest Control Group Design except that there is no random assignment into the groups.

$$
\begin{array}{cccc}
A & O_{1a} & X & O_{2a} \\
B & O_{1b} & & O_{2b}
\end{array}
\quad \text{or} \quad
\begin{array}{cccc}
A & O_{1a} & X_e & O_{2a} \\
B & O_{1b} & X_t & O_{2b}
\end{array}
$$

As you can see, there are two groups, one of which is exposed to the independent variable while the other group is not exposed to the independent variable. Furthermore, researchers may use this design to compare two (or more) interventions rather than compare one group to a control group.

In this type of quasi-experimental design, a comparison group is selected to be as comparable as possible to the treatment group. Two selection methods can be used:

Individual matching. Individual cases in the treatment group are matched with similar individuals in the comparison group. In some situations, this can create a comparison group that is very similar to the experimental group, as when Head Start participants were matched with their siblings to estimate the effect of participation in Head Start. However, one problem with this method is determining in advance which variables should be used for matching. Furthermore, in many studies, it may not be possible to match on the most important variables. It is also unlikely that a match can actually be found for all cases.

Aggregate matching. In most situations when random assignment is not possible, the second method of matching makes more sense: identifying a comparison group that matches the treatment group in the aggregate rather than trying to match individual cases. Matching in the aggregate means finding a group that has similar distributions on key variables: the same average age, the same percentage female, and so on. For this design to be considered even quasi-experimental, however, individuals may not choose which group to join or where to seek services; in other words, they themselves cannot opt for or against the experimental treatment.

Where are "matches" to be found? One potential source for finding matches is an agency waiting list. People on the waiting list are, as yet, not receiving services from the agency and, therefore, are a comparison group that is likely to be similar to the treatment group. Another alternative is locating similar individuals in the community who are willing to serve as a control group. A third option is to compare client outcomes in one agency with client outcomes in another agency, assuming of course that the second agency is serving a similar population group.

Gary Goldapple and Dianne Montgomery (1993) used a clever strategy to construct a comparison group for their study (see Exhibit 6.5). They were concerned with the high rates

Exhibit 6.5   Nonequivalent Group Designs

Nonequivalent control group design:
Evaluating a behaviorally based intervention to improve client retention in therapeutic community treatment for drug dependency (Goldapple and Montgomery, 1993)

	O_1 *(weeks 1-2)*		O_2 *(weeks 5-6)*
Group A: admits Weeks 1 and 2	Beck Depression Inventory Problem Solving Inventory		Beck Depression Inventory Problem Solving Inventory

	O_1 *(weeks 7-8)*	*X (weeks 8-11)*	O_2 *(weeks 11-12)*
Group B: admits Weeks 7 and 8	Beck Depression Inventory Problem Solving Inventory	Cognitive behavioral therapy groups	Beck Depression Inventory Problem Solving Inventory

Nonequivalent comparison group design:
Treatment of anxiety in a managed care setting (Mitchell, 1999)

	O_1	*X*	O_2
Group A: willing to be treated	Anxiety measures	Medication Eight weeks cognitive behavioral therapy	Anxiety measures
Group B: unwilling to be treated	Anxiety measures	Medication only	Anxiety measures

of attrition in therapeutic community treatment for drug abusers. Attrition, based on other research, was linked to depression and client confidence in the ability to solve problems. To reduce depression and increase confidence, Goldapple and Montgomery designed a three-week, eight-session group intervention based on cognitive behavioral therapy. They used new admissions to form their two groups. New admissions during Weeks 1 and 2 of the study were administered the pretest and then during Weeks 4 to 6 were given the posttest. This group formed the control group. New admissions during Weeks 7 and 8 were given the pretest, received the intervention during Weeks 9 through 11, and then were given the posttest in Weeks 11 and 12. The authors compared changes in the scores of the dependent variables.

Christopher Mitchell's (1999) study of the impact of an eight-week cognitive behavioral group treatment on treating panic disorders illustrates the use of a waiting list to create a matched group. Mitchell wanted to examine whether medication and the cognitive behavioral therapy group would reduce anxiety to a lower level than medication only. The sample included 56 people seeking treatment at an HMO. Comparisons were made for the 30 participants who received medications and participated in therapy groups with 26 people who were on the waiting list for the group therapy or who had declined therapy but were receiving medication.

Nonequivalent control or comparison group designs are particularly useful for researchers and evaluators. Because of the pretest and posttest, both time order and a statistical association can be demonstrated, suggesting that if not causal, there is a correlational relationship between the treatment and outcome. Furthermore, if the selection process appears sound, the effects of history, maturation, testing, and instrumentation can be ruled out. The key is whether you are convinced that the matched comparison group has been chosen and evaluated in such a way that you are willing to accept the comparability between the two groups despite the lack of random assignment. In the studies described above, the researchers tried to find as close a comparison group as possible. Furthermore, the researchers demonstrated to the reader the comparability of the demographic composition of the groups as well as the similarity of scores on the dependent variables in their efforts to rule out selection bias.

Time Series Designs

A different type of quasi-experimental research design is a time series design. A **time series design** stands in contrast to the other research designs we have described up until now in that no control or comparison group is needed. Rather, a time series design typically involves only one group for which multiple observations of data have been gathered both prior to and after the intervention. Although many methodologists distinguish between **repeated measures panel designs,** which include several pretest and posttest observations, and time series designs, which include many (preferably 30 or more) such observations in both pretest and posttest periods, we will not make that distinction here.

A common design is the Interrupted Time-Series Design, where three or more observations are taken before and after the intervention.

$$O_1 \qquad O_2 \qquad O_3 \qquad X \qquad O_4 \qquad O_5 \qquad O_6$$

Like other designs, there are variations on this basic design including time series designs with comparison or control groups and time series designs in which observations are also gathered during the course of the intervention.

A time series design is a particularly useful design both for researchers and for practitioners in agencies to evaluate whether changes have occurred. One advantage of a time series design is that there is only one group, so a second group need not be created. A second advantage is that, depending on the question, both the pretest and posttest observations need not occur prospectively; rather, the impacts of programmatic or policy changes can be based on data already collected. For example, Sandy Wexler and Rafael Engel (1999) wanted to know whether returning cash assistance policy to the states as mandated under the 1996 Federal Personal Responsibility and Work Opportunities Act would lead to what many scholars thought would be a "rush to the bottom" in the level of cash assistance given by the states. To examine this question, they used data published in the 1940 to 1990 *Social Security Bulletins* and comparable data for 1995 obtained from the Office of Family Assistance, Administration on Children and Families, U.S. Department of Health and Human Services.

Another advantage is that time series designs can be used to assess a variety of issues ranging from changes in policy to changes in agency administrative practices to changes in agency programs. For example, time series designs can answer questions like the following: (1) Did the number of families receiving cash assistance change after the implementation of welfare reform? (2) Did community employment increase after the creation of empowerment zones? (3) Did the number of phone calls to an information and referral line increase after a period of extensive outreach? (4) Did absenteeism rates decline after a stress reduction program was put into place? We will draw from these principles when we discuss designs to evaluate the effectiveness of treatment with a single client in Chapter 7.

A time series design is based on the idea that by taking repeated measures prior to an intervention or programmatic change, you have the opportunity to identify a pattern. A pattern may show a trend reflecting an ongoing increase or decline, or it may simply stay flat at either too high or too low a level. The pattern may be seasonal, with differences based on time of year; use of a homeless shelter may decline in the summer while peaking in the winter.

Having identified the preintervention pattern, the question then is whether an intervention or program altered the nature of the pattern to what is considered to be a more favorable state. Furthermore, by taking repeated measures after the intervention, you can determine whether the impact of the intervention persisted.

The analysis of time series data can become quite complex statistically, but to start, it is best to graph the observations. A key question is what to graph. There are times when graphing the actual number of what is being measured is sufficient. Sometimes numbers need to be converted into percentages so that differences in the length of time or the number of cases in a particular time period are standardized. Because the value of money changes over time, Wexler and Engel (1999) reported AFDC benefit levels between 1940 and 1995 in 1995 dollars. Dattalo (1998) describes methods that might be used when it is difficult to identify a pattern, such as graphing three-month moving averages, as well as statistical techniques that can be used to analyze the patterns.

What can we say about causality when using a time series design? We can establish a time order and an association. If we are looking at a treatment's impact, we should be able to rule out several threats to internal validity such as maturation, regression, testing, and instrumentation. Any changes due to these threats would have been observed during the course of the pretest observations. The major threat to internal validity is history; it is possible that shifts may be due to some extraneous event happening during the period of treatment, that is, an event happening between the last observation of the pretest period and the first observation of the posttest period.

Ex Post Facto Control Group Designs

The **ex post facto control group design** appears to be very similar to the nonequivalent control group design, and the two are often confused. The ex post facto design meets fewer of the criteria to demonstrate causality than other quasi-experimental designs. Like non-equivalent control group designs, this design has experimental and comparison groups that are not created by random assignment. But unlike the groups in nonequivalent control group designs, the groups in ex post facto (after the fact) designs are designated after the treatment has occurred. The problem with this is that if the treatment takes any time at all, people with particular characteristics may select themselves for the treatment or avoid it. However, the particulars will vary from study to study; in some circumstances, we may conclude that the treatment and control groups are so similar that causal effects can be tested (Rossi & Freeman, 1989, pp. 343–344).

Joseph Walsh's (1994) study of social support outcomes for participants in assertiveness community treatment used an ex post facto design (see Exhibit 6.6). He compared clients at two agencies that provide assertiveness community treatment programs. In one agency, clients received a variety of on-site group interventions and individualized case management services, while at the second agency, clients received just the individualized case management. Both agencies were located in the same county, and the staff had a common philosophy of care.

Exhibit 6.6   Ex Post Facto Control Group Designs

Social Support Resource Outcomes (Walsh, 1994)

	Pretest	Intervention	Posttest
Experimental group	Measures of social support	Group interventions and individualized case management	Measures of social support
Comparison group	Measures of social support	Individualized case management only	Measures of social support

Walsh found the self-reported size of personal social support networks was higher for the clients receiving the group intervention than for clients receiving just individualized case management. On the other hand, there were no differences in the number of social support clusters (such as family, recreation, friends), perceived support from friends, or perceived support from family. Nonetheless, the finding that the size of the social support network is larger is important, as network size is a predictor of overall social integration.

What distinguishes this study design from a quasi-experimental design is the fact that the programs were already operating. These two teams were chosen from 23 county teams because they represented treatment approaches while serving demographically similar mental health clients. Walsh (1994) was aware that he could not rule out other explanations, noting that "it is also difficult to rule out individual case manager effects unrelated to the basic intervention format" (p. 461).

COMMON GROUP DESIGNS FOR PROGRAM EVALUATION AND RESEARCH

A third set of designs, described as nonexperimental or pre-experimental research designs, are classified as such because they provide little to no control over internal threats to validity. To the extent that social work researchers are trying to demonstrate that different treatment modalities cause a change, the lack of control over internal threats to validity is a glaring weakness. This weakness often leads researchers, evaluators, and consumers of research to discount the utility of these designs and the findings from studies using these designs. Yet, these designs have utility for research, and we will point out how the designs might be used. The simplicity of these designs makes them extraordinarily useful for the evaluation of programs within agencies. As a result, they are commonly used for program evaluation.

Types of Nonexperimental Designs

The One-Group Pretest-Posttest Design (Before-After One-Group Design) is characterized by the absence of a comparison group, and unlike the time series design, it lacks repeated pretest measures. All cases are exposed to the experimental treatment. The basis for comparison is provided by the pretreatment measures in the group.

$$A \qquad O_{1a} \qquad X \qquad O_{2a}$$

This is a popular form of design for program evaluation. It is far simpler to implement than group designs because no comparison group is needed. The design flows from a typical practice model of assessment, intervention, and evaluation of the impact of the intervention (follow-up assessment). This conformity to a practice model is more easily understood by and more comfortable for agency directors and practitioners.

This design answers a variety of questions that interest social service agency staff and the funders of social services. For example, this design demonstrates whether improvement occurred, how much change occurred, and how many individuals improved. The design can be used to determine how well clients are functioning and the number of clients who have achieved some minimum standard of functioning at the end of the program.

Because there are a pretest and a posttest, demonstrating a time order is possible. Similarly, having pretest and posttest scores means statistical analyses can be used to determine whether there is an association between the independent and dependent variables. The great weakness of this design is that there are many different threats to the internal validity of the design. History, maturation, testing, instrumentation, statistical regression, and selection bias as well as the interactions of selection and history or testing cannot be ruled out.

R. Steven Harrison, Scott Boyle, and O. William Farley (1999) used a pretest-posttest design to study the effectiveness of a 12-week family-based intervention for children. The intervention was a course for parents and children that emphasized learning and practicing new skills such as parenting behaviors, communication skills, and anger and stress management. In addition, there were three weekend outdoor recreational activities to practice the skills. Harrison and colleagues selected one particular agency because it had a comprehensive program and available subjects. Several positive changes were identified between pretest and posttest scores.

A less rigorous one-group design is the After-only Design (Posttest-only; A Cross-Sectional Group; One-shot Only):

$$A \qquad X \qquad O_2$$

This design is characterized by only one group, without a control or comparison group, and it includes no pretest observations so that there are no benchmarks to which the posttest scores can be compared.

This design may be used to provide factual information for the agency. For example, the design has been used to describe participant functioning at the end of the program. How many clients are no longer depressed? How many are no longer abusing alcohol? How many are employed after a job training program? But as we have said, changes in depression, alcohol abuse, or employment cannot be attributed solely to the program. This is also the typical design used to assess client satisfaction. Although it may be argued that client satisfaction should be monitored during the program, most agencies still examine satisfaction only after completion of the program.

For research examining causal impacts, this design is particularly useless. Unlike the previous design, because there is no pretest, both time order and association cannot be determined. The researcher does not know if the final outcomes are higher, lower, or equal to the preintervention level. Furthermore, it is impossible to rule out other explanations.

This design does offer some benefit to social work researchers. It is useful for piloting and developing measures and for developing hypotheses about relationships that then require more rigorous designs, and it may provide some sense of attrition related to the treatment.

Sometimes, when it has been impossible to do a pretest, evaluators and researchers may try to construct a baseline so that the design looks more like the One Group Pretest-Posttest Design. There are different ways that a baseline might be constructed. One way is to look at initial intakes or initial assessments. Another way is to ask clients to recall what their status was prior to the intervention. Both of these mechanisms suffer from the reliability of the data collected. Another method to improve this design is to create a comparison group by comparing people at different stages of the intervention. In this case, the scores of people who have completed the intervention might be compared to the scores of those currently receiving the intervention.

A third nonexperimental design is the *Static-group Design*. It includes two groups, without random assignment: One group gets the treatment while the other does not receive the treatment, and there is no pretest or baseline. This design is frequently used when a program has already begun and baseline information cannot be obtained.

$$A \qquad X \qquad O_{2a}$$
$$B \qquad\qquad O_{2b}$$

The central issue of this design is finding a comparable group. If an agency waiting list is used, perhaps an argument might be made about the comparability of Group B. Or one might find nonparticipants who are eligible for the program to use as a comparison group. The problem persists that without a pretest, the comparability of the groups cannot be tested. Without such a test, it is a leap of faith to say that comparing posttest scores provides evidence of a time order and an association, let alone controls for internal threats to validity.

One alternative to modify this design is to compare program methods or intensity. The Comparative Intensity Design compares two groups receiving intervention. The two groups may be receiving different services within the same agency or across two agencies. While the selection problem persists, a potential argument (although a weak argument) is that clients having the same difficulty probably are alike.

$$A \qquad X_{t1} \qquad O_{2a}$$
$$B \qquad X_{t2} \qquad O_{2b}$$

One way that the usefulness of nonexperimental designs can be enhanced is replication. Conducting a single after-only design provides limited information. But repeating this design systematically and following similar procedures provides additional support for suggesting the program may be related to the outcome, if consistently positive results are found.

ETHICAL ISSUES IN EXPERIMENTAL RESEARCH

Social science experiments often involve subject deception. Primarily because of this feature, some experiments have prompted contentious debates about research ethics. Experimental evaluations of social programs also pose ethical dilemmas because they require researchers to withhold possibly beneficial treatment from some of the subjects just on the basis of chance. In this section, we will give special attention to the problems of deception and the distribution of benefits in experimental research.

Deception

Deception occurs when subjects are misled about research procedures because researchers want to determine how they would react to the treatment if they were not research subjects. Deception is a critical component of many social experiments, although it occurs less frequently in social work research. One reason deception is used is because of the difficulty of simulating real-world stresses and dilemmas in a laboratory setting. Elliot Aronson and Judson Mills (1959), for example, wanted to learn how severity of initiation to real social groups influences liking for those groups. But they could not practically design a field experiment on initiation. Their alternative, which relied on a tape-recorded discussion staged by the researcher, was of course deceptive. In many experiments, if subjects understood what was really happening to them, the results would be worthless.

The ethical dilemma posed by deceptive research is whether it precludes potential subjects from offering informed consent, given that they will not have full information about the experiment. In other words, if subjects do not have full information about the experiment, it limits their ability to weigh the risks of participation.

Aronson and Mills's (1959) study of severity of initiation (at an all-women's college in the 1950s) is a good example of experimental research that does not pose greater-than-everyday risks to subjects. The students who were randomly assigned to the *severe initiation* experimental condition had to read a list of embarrassing words. We think it's fair to say that even in the 1950s, reading a list of potentially embarrassing words in a laboratory setting and listening to a taped discussion are unlikely to increase the risks to which students are exposed in their everyday lives. Moreover, the researchers informed subjects that they would be expected to talk about sex and could decline to participate in the experiment if this require-ment would bother them. None dropped out.

To further ensure that no psychological harm was caused, Aronson and Mills (1959) explained the true nature of the experiment to subjects after the experiment. The subjects' reactions were typical:

> None of the Ss expressed any resentment or annoyance at having been misled. In fact, the majority were intrigued by the experiment, and several returned at the end of the academic quarter to ascertain the result. (p. 179)

This procedure is called **debriefing,** and it is usually a good idea. Except for those who are opposed to any degree of deception whatsoever in research (and there are some), the minimal deception in the Aronson and Mills (1959) experiment, coupled with the lack of any ascer-tainable risk to subjects and a debriefing, would meet most standards of ethical research.

Selective Distribution of Benefits

Field experiments conducted to evaluate social programs also can involve issues of informed consent (Hunt, 1985, pp. 275–276). One ethical issue that is somewhat unique to field experi-ments is the **distribution of benefits:** How much are subjects harmed by the way treatments are distributed in the experiment? For example, participation in the Brock and Harknett (1998) study of different models of case management for TANF recipients had serious implications. The requirements of TANF impose a lifetime limit on participation so people receiving a poten-tially less adequate method of case management could lose valuable time. Furthermore, it was thought that one method would help people find work faster and that those people would earn more from employment than would participants receiving the other method.

Is it ethical to give some potentially advantageous or disadvantageous treatment to people on a random basis? Random distribution of benefits is justified when the researchers do not know whether some treatment actually is beneficial or not—and, of course, it is the goal of the experiment to find out. Chance is as reasonable a basis for distributing the treatment as any other. Also, if insufficient resources are available to fully fund a benefit for every eligible person, distribution of the benefit on the basis of chance to equally needy people is ethically defensible (Boruch, 1997, pp. 66–67).

CONCLUSION

True experiments play two critical roles in social work research. First, they are the best research designs for testing nomothetic causal hypotheses. Even when conditions preclude use of a true experimental design, many research designs can be improved by adding some experimental components. Second, true experiments also provide a comparison point for eval-uating the ability of other research designs to achieve causally valid results.

In spite of their obvious strengths, true experiments are used infrequently to study many of the research problems that interest social work researchers. There are three basic reasons:

The experiments required to test many important hypotheses require far more resources than most social scientists have at their disposal; most of the research problems of interest to social work researchers simply are not amenable to experimental designs, for reasons ranging from ethical considerations to the limited possibilities for randomly assigning people to different conditions in the real world; and finally, the requirements of experimental design usually preclude large-scale studies and so limit generalizability to a degree that is unacceptable to many social scientists.

Just because it is possible to test a hypothesis with an experiment does not mean it will always be desirable to do so. When a social program is first being developed and its elements are in flux, it is not a good idea to begin a large evaluation study that cannot possibly succeed unless the program design remains constant. Researchers should wait until the program design stabilizes somewhat. It also does not make sense for researchers engaged in program evaluation to test the impact of programs that cannot actually be implemented or to test programs that are unlikely to be implemented in the real world because of financial or political problems (Rossi & Freeman, 1989, pp. 304–307).

Many forms of social work research, particularly research and evaluation done in agencies, will require design decisions about what is feasible. As you can see from the contents of this chapter, there are many components and factors to consider in choosing a group design, but regardless of the design used, it is important to understand the limits of the conclusions that can be made, both in terms of the internal validity of the design and the generalizability of the findings.

KEY TERMS

Aggregate matching
Block matching
Comparison group
Compensatory equalization of treatment
Compensatory rivalry
Contamination
Control group
Debriefing
Deception
Differential attrition
Diffusion of treatment
Distribution of benefits
Double-blind procedure
Endogenous change
Ex post facto control group design
Expectancies of the experimental staff
Experimental group
External events
Hawthorne effect
History effect
Instrumentation
John Henry effect

Matching
Nonequivalent control group designs
Nonexperimental or preexperimental designs
Placebo effect
Posttest
Pretest
Pretest-posttest control group design
Process analysis
Quasi-experimental designs
Randomization
Reactivity
Regression effect
Repeated measures panel designs
Resentful demoralization
Secular drift
Selection bias
Self-fulfilling prophecy
Testing
Time series design
Treatment
Treatment misidentification
True experimental designs

HIGHLIGHTS

- The independent variable in an experiment is represented by a treatment or other intervention. Some subjects receive one type of treatment; others may receive a different treatment or no treatment. In true experiments, subjects are assigned randomly to comparison groups.

- Experimental research designs have three essential components: use of at least two groups of subjects for comparison, measurement of the change that occurs as a result of the experimental treatment, and use of random assignment. In addition, experiments may include identification of a causal mechanism and control over experimental conditions.

- Random assignment of subjects to experimental and comparison groups eliminates systematic bias in group assignment. The odds of a difference between the experimental and comparison groups on the basis of chance can be calculated. Those odds become very small for experiments with at least 30 subjects per group.

- Random assignment and random sampling both rely on a chance selection procedure, but their purposes differ. Random assignment involves placing predesignated subjects into two or more groups on the basis of chance; random sampling involves selecting subjects out of a larger population on the basis of chance. Matching of cases in the experimental and comparison groups is a poor substitute for randomization because identifying in advance all important variables on which to make the match is not possible. However, matching can improve the comparability of groups when it is used to supplement randomization.

- Causal conclusions derived from experiments can be invalid because of selection bias, endogenous change, the effects of external events, cross-group contamination, or treatment misidentification. In true experiments, randomization should eliminate selection bias and bias due to endogenous change. External events, cross-group contamination, and treatment misidentification can threaten the validity of causal conclusions in both true experiments and quasi-experiments.

- Process analysis can be used in experiments to identify how the treatment had (or didn't have) its effect—a matter of particular concern in field experiments. Treatment misidentification is less likely when process analysis is used.

- The generalizability of experimental results declines if the study conditions are artificial and the experimental subjects are unique. Field experiments are likely to produce more generalizable results than experiments conducted in the laboratory.

- The external validity of causal conclusions is determined by the extent to which they apply to different types of individuals and settings. When causal conclusions do not apply to all the subgroups in a study, they are not generalizable to corresponding subgroups in the population—and so they are not externally valid with respect to those subgroups. Causal conclusions can also be considered externally invalid when they occur only under the experimental conditions.

- Quasi-experimental group designs control for some threats to internal validity while nonexperimental group designs tend to control for few or no threats to internal validity. It is common to find both types of designs in agency settings.

- Using any type of experimental design in an agency setting requires expertise and a sufficient number of clients. To carry out the design, it is important to gain the trust and cooperation of the staff.

- Subject deception is common in laboratory experiments and poses unique ethical issues. Researchers must weigh the potential harm to subjects and debrief subjects who have been deceived. In field experiments, a common ethical problem is selective distribution of benefits. Random assignment may be the fairest way of allocating treatment when treatment openings are insufficient for all eligible individuals and when the efficacy of the treatment is unknown.

DISCUSSION QUESTIONS

1. Critique the ethics of one of the experiments presented in this chapter. What specific rules do you think should guide researchers' decisions about subject deception and the selective distribution of benefits?

2. Discuss how controls are created in nonequivalent control group and time series designs. What are the key threats to causal validity present with the use of either? How do these compare with the threats associated with nonexperimental designs?

3. Three types of true experimental design are covered in the chapter: pretest/posttest control group design, posttest only control group design and the Solomon Four Group Design. Imagine you were investigating the effects of vocational skills training for people recently released from prison. Given the various potential threats to validity, which of these designs would you choose? Explain why.

PRACTICE EXERCISES

1. A program has recently been funded to provide casework intensive services to the homeless. The mission of the program is to provide skills that will lead to self-sufficiency and employment. Develop a research study using:

> Experimental design
> Quasi-experimental design
> Pre-experimental design

Be specific in describing the procedures you would have to do to implement your design. This may mean specifying how you will assign clients to groups (if you have more than one group) or where you would find clients for your control/comparison groups (if you have such groups).

2. Identify the benefits and weaknesses of each of the specific designs you chose for Exercise 1.

3. Search for a research study using a true experimental design to examine the effects of hospice care. Diagram the experiment using the exhibits in this chapter as a model. How generalizable do you think the study's results are to the population from which cases were selected? To other populations? To specific subgroups in the study? To other settings? How thoroughly do the researchers discuss these issues?

WEB EXERCISES

1. Try out the process of randomization. Go to the Web site www.randomizer.org. Type numbers into the randomizer for an experiment with two groups and 20 individuals per group. Repeat the process for an experiment with four groups and 10 individuals per group. Plot the numbers corresponding to each individual in each group. Does the distribution of numbers within each group truly seem to be random?

2. Participate in a social psychology experiment on the Web. Go to http://www.socialpsychology. org/expts.htm. Pick an experiment in which to participate and follow the instructions. After you finish, write up a description of the experiment and evaluate it using the criteria discussed in the chapter.

> To assist you in completing the Web exercises, please access the study site at http://www.sagepub.com/prsw where you will find the Web Exercises reproduced and suggested links for online resources.

DEVELOPING A RESEARCH PROPOSAL

If you are planning to use a group design:

1. What specific design will you use? How long will the study last? At what time points will data be collected? How will the data be collected?

2. If you are using a design with more than one group, describe how participants are assigned to each group.

3. Discuss the extent to which each source of internal validity is a problem in the study.

4. How generalizable would you expect the study's findings to be? What can be done to improve generalizability?

5. Develop appropriate procedures for the protection of human subjects in your study. Include in these procedures a consent form.

Chapter 7

SINGLE-SUBJECT DESIGN

Foundations of Single-Subject Design
Repeated Measurement
Baseline Phase
  Patterns
  Internal Validity
Treatment Phase
Graphing

Measuring Targets of Intervention

Analyzing Single-Subject Designs
Visual Analysis
  Level
  Trend
  Variability
Interpreting Visual Patterns
Problems of Interpretation

Types of Single-Subject Designs
Basic Design: A-B
Withdrawal Designs
  A-B-A Design
  A-B-A-B Design
Multiple Baseline Designs
Multiple Treatment Designs
Designs for Monitoring Subjects

Generalizability

Ethical Issues in Single-Subject Design

Conclusion

Jody was a 26-year-old Caucasian female employed as a hairdresser. . . She lived with her two children, ages 7 and 3 in a substandard basement apartment in the house of her mother-in-law, a woman who was emotionally and sometimes physically abusive to Jody. Jody came from a divorced family where she had been physically abused by both parents. . . . In the second session she expressed feeling severely depressed because her estranged husband had abducted the children and refused to return them. . . . She and her husband had lived together for five years, split for 7 years, and until the recent separation, had lived together for 3 years. . . . Jody said she felt helpless, immobilized and unable to protect her children. She reported difficulty in sleeping and eating and had frequent crying episodes. She reported a 25-pound weight loss in the past 3 months. She had been unable to work for 1 week because of a high level of anxiety and fatigue. Jody also said she had recurring suicidal thoughts.

(Jensen, 1994, p. 273)

It is not unusual for social work practitioners to have clients such as Jody who have a mental health condition such as depression. As practitioners, we often think we "know" when a client is improving. Yet, when we use our own subjective conclusions, we are prone to human error. In this chapter, you will learn how single-subject designs can be used to systematically test the effectiveness of a particular intervention as well as to monitor client progress.

Single-subject (sometimes referred to as single-case or single-system) designs offer an alternative to group designs. The very name suggests that the focus is on an $N = 1$, a single subject, in which the "1" can be an individual, an agency, or a community. The structure of these designs, which are easily adapted to social work practice, makes them useful for research on interventions in direct and community practice. In particular, the process of assessment, establishing intervention goals and specific outcomes, providing the intervention, and evaluating progress have direct parallels to the structure of single-subject design, which depends on identifying target problems, taking preintervention measures, providing the intervention, taking additional measures, and making decisions about the efficacy of the intervention. Because of these parallels, social work educators have increasingly described how single-subject design can be used to evaluate practice and to improve client outcomes through monitoring a client's progress.

Contrast this design with group designs. In Chapter 6, we noted that group designs do not naturally conform to practice, particularly when the practice involves interventions with individuals. The analysis of group designs typically refers to the "group's average change score" or "the number of subjects altering their status." By describing the group, we miss each individual's experience with the intervention. Once a group design is implemented, it is difficult to change the nature of the treatment, yet individual participants within the group may not respond to the particular type of treatment offered.

In this chapter, we first take you through the components of single-subject designs, including their basic features, measurement of the target problem, and interpretation of the findings. We then describe different designs and connect them to their different roles for social work research, practice evaluation, and client monitoring. Finally, we end the chapter with a discussion about establishing the generalizability of findings from single-subject designs and the ethical issues associated with single-subject designs.

FOUNDATIONS OF SINGLE-SUBJECT DESIGN

The underlying principle of a single-subject design as a social work research tool is that if an intervention with a client, agency, or community is effective, it should be possible to see a change in status from the period prior to intervention to the period during and after the intervention. As a social work research tool, this type of design minimally has three components:

1. Repeated measurement

2. Baseline phase

3. Treatment phase

Furthermore, the baseline and treatment phase measurements are usually displayed using graphs.

Repeated Measurement

Single-subject designs require the repeated measurement of a dependent variable or, in other words, the target problem. So, both prior to starting an intervention and during the intervention itself, you must be able to measure the subject's status on the target problem at regular time intervals, whether the intervals are hours, days, weeks, months or the like. In the ideal research situation, measures of the target problem are taken with the client prior to actually implementing the intervention, for example, during the assessment process, and then continued during the course of the intervention. Gathering information may mean withholding the intervention until the repeated measures can be taken. Alternatively, repeated measures of the dependent variable can begin when the client is receiving an intervention for other problems. For example, a child may be seen for behavioral problems, but eventually, communication issues will be a concern. The repeated measurement of the communication issues could begin prior to that specific intervention focus.

There are times when it is not possible to delay the intervention, either because there is a crisis or because to delay intervention would not be ethically appropriate. Yet, you may still be able to construct a set of preintervention measures using data already collected or asking about past experiences. Client records may have information from which a baseline can be produced. Some client records, such as report cards, may have very complete information, but other client records, such as case files, may or may not. When using client records, you are limited to the information that is available, and even that information may be incomplete. Another option is to ask clients about past behavior, such as how many drinks they had each week in the last several weeks. Similarly, if permission is granted, significant members of the client's network could be asked questions about the client's behaviors. Trying to construct measures by asking clients or family members depends on the client's or family member's memories or opinions and assumes that the information is both remembered and reported accurately. Generally, behaviors and events are easier to recall than moods or feelings. Even the recall of behaviors or events becomes more difficult with the passage of time and probably should be limited to the preceding month. Although recognizing the limits of these retrospective data collection methods is important, the limitations should not preclude using the information if that is all that is available, particularly for evaluating practice.

There are other times when using retrospective data is quite feasible and realistic. Agencies often collect quite a bit of data about their operations, and these data can be used to obtain repeated measurements. For example, if an agency director was trying to find an outreach method that would increase the number of referrals, previous monthly referral information could be used and the intervention begun immediately. Or if an organizer was interested in the impact of an empowerment zone on levels of employment in a community, the preintervention employment data are likely to exist.

Baseline Phase

The **baseline phase**, typically abbreviated by using the letter **A**, represents the period in which the intervention to be evaluated is not offered to the subject. During the baseline phase, repeated measurements of the dependent variable are taken or reconstructed. These measures reflect the status of the client (agency or community) on the dependent variable prior to the implementation of the intervention. The baseline phase measurements provide two aspects of control analogous to a control group in a group design. First, in a group design, we expect the treatment group to have different scores than the control group after the intervention. In a single-subject design, the subject serves as the control as the repeated baseline measurements establish the pattern of scores that we expect the intervention to change. Without the intervention, researchers assume that the baseline pattern of scores would continue its course. Second, in a control group design, random assignment controls for threats to internal validity. In a single-subject design, the repeated baseline measurements allow the researcher to discount some of the threats to the internal validity of the design.

Patterns

In the baseline phase, measurements are taken until a pattern emerges. Different types of patterns are summarized on Exhibit 7.1 on pages 190 and 191. One type of pattern is a **stable line**. A stable line, as displayed in Exhibit 7.1a, is a line that is relatively flat, with little variability in the scores so that the scores fall in a narrow band. This kind of line is desirable because changes can easily be detected, and it is likely that there are few problems of testing, instrumentation, statistical regression, and maturation in the data. More problematic is the pattern displayed in Exhibit 7.1b, where there appears to be a horizontal line but the scores fall within a wide band or range. As we will discuss later, this type of pattern makes interpreting the data more difficult than a stable line with little variation.

Stable line   A stable line is a line that is relatively flat with little variability in the scores so that the scores fall in a narrow band.

A second pattern is a **trend,** in which the scores may be either increasing or decreasing during the baseline period. Some trends may be linear, as reflected in the trend observed in Exhibit 7.1c. As you can see in this trend, the scores seem to be increasing at a more or less constant rate over time. Although that example is not displayed, a trend may also be declining at a more or less constant rate. Alternatively, the trends may be curvilinear (see Exhibit 7.1d) so that the rate of change is accelerating over time, rather than increasing or decreasing at a constant rate.

Trend   An ascending or descending line.

A third type of pattern is a **cycle** as displayed in Exhibit 7.1e. Some issues or problems may be cyclical in nature depending on the time of month or time of year. For example, use of a homeless shelter may be cyclical depending on the time of year.

Cycle   A pattern reflecting ups and downs depending on time of measurement.

Finally, there are situations, such as the display in Exhibit 7.1f, in which no pattern is evident. With such baseline patterns, it is important to consider the reasons for the variability in scores. Is it due to the lack of reliability of the measurement process? If so, then an alternative measure might be sought. On the other hand, the client may be using a good measure but not reporting information consistently, for example, completing a depression scale at different times of day. Also, the variability in scores may be due to some changing circumstance in the life of the client.

You know you have a pattern when you can predict with some certainty what might be the next score. To be able to predict the next score requires a minimum of three observations in the baseline stage. When there are only two measures, as shown in Exhibit 7.2a on page 192, can you predict the next score with any certainty? The next data point could be higher, lower, or the same as the previous data points (see Exhibit 7.2b). With three measures, your certainty increases about the nature of the pattern. But even three measures might not be enough, depending on the pattern that is emerging. In Exhibit 7.2c, is the pattern predictable? You probably should take at least two more baseline measures, but three or four additional measures may be necessary to see a pattern emerge. As a general rule, the more data points, the more certain you will be about the pattern; it takes at least three consecutive measures that fall in some pattern for you to have confidence in the shape of the baseline pattern.

Internal Validity

As you may remember from Chapter 5, findings of causality depend on the internal validity of the research design. When repeated measurements are taken during the baseline phase, several threats to internal validity are controlled. Specifically, problems of maturation, instrumentation, statistical regression, and testing may be controlled by the repeated measurement because patterns illustrative of these threats to internal validity should appear in the baseline. On the other hand, when the measurement in the baseline phase is reconstructed from existing data or memory, these threats to internal validity are problematic.

When baseline measures are stable lines, these threats may be ruled out, but it is more difficult to rule out some threats if the pattern is a trend, particularly if the trend is in the desired direction. For example, if maturation is a problem, you would expect that the line would be linear or curvilinear and not horizontal. Perhaps you have a client who has suffered a loss and you are measuring sadness. If there is a maturation effect, the level of sadness should decline from time point to time point. This does not mean that an intervention would not be effective, but it may be more difficult to demonstrate its effectiveness.

If statistical regression and testing effects occur, the impact is likely to appear initially in the baseline measures. A high score obtained from a measurement may be lower in a second measurement because of statistical regression or because of the respondent's acclimation to the measurement process. If there were only one baseline measure, then the first intervention measure might reflect these effects. But with multiple measures, the effect of statistical regression, if present, should occur in the beginning of measurement, and continued measurement should produce a stable baseline pattern. The testing effect should be observable early in the baseline measurement process, as the subject adjusts to the testing requirements.

Repeated measurement in a baseline will not control for an extraneous event (history) that occurs between the last baseline measurement and the first intervention measurement. The longer the time period between the two measurement points, the greater the possibility that an event might influence the subject's scores. Later, we will describe single-subject designs that will control for the potential threat of history.

Exhibit 7.1   Different Baseline Patterns

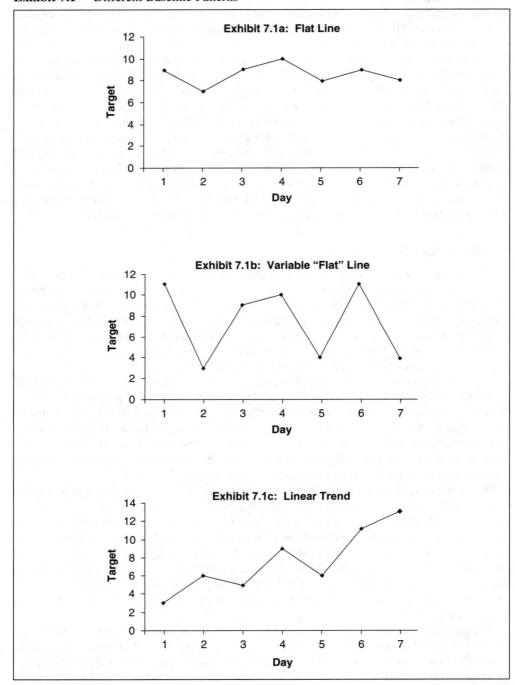

(Continued)

Exhibit 7.1 (Continued)

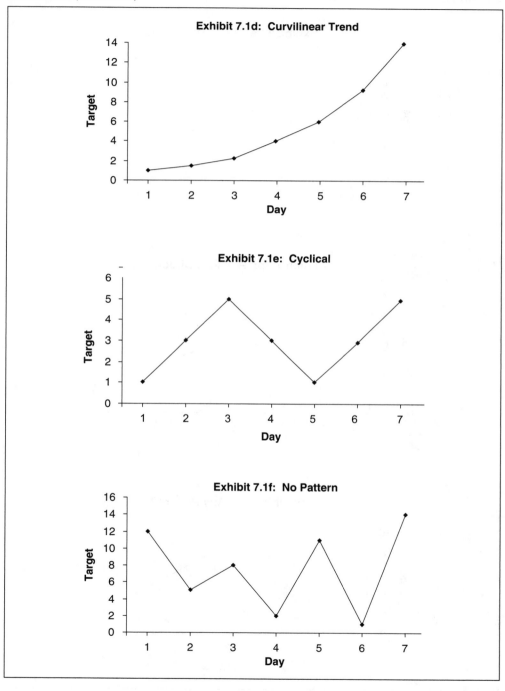

Exhibit 7.2   Predicting a Pattern

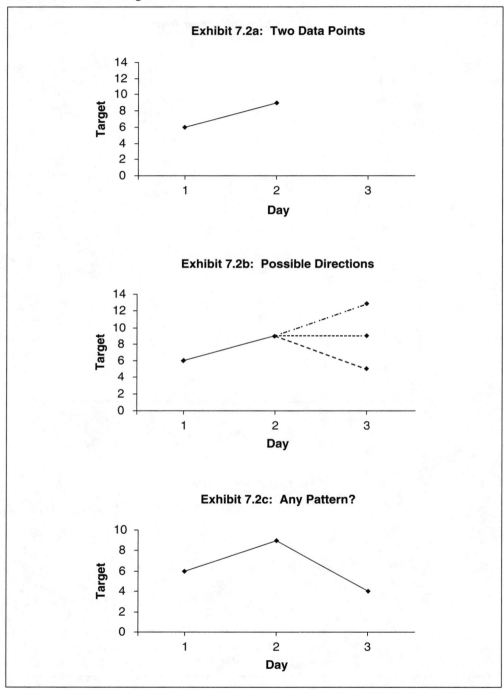

Treatment Phase

The **treatment phase**, signified by a **B**, represents the time period during which the intervention is implemented. As during the baseline phase, repeated measurements of the same dependent variable using the same measures are obtained. Ultimately, the patterns and magnitude of the data points will be compared to the data points in the baseline phase to determine whether a change has occurred. Tony Tripodi (1994) and David Barlow and Michel Hersen (1984) recommend that the length of the treatment phase be as long as the baseline phase.

Graphing

The phases of a single-subject design are virtually always summarized on a graph. Graphing the data facilitates monitoring and evaluating the impact of the intervention. The y-axis is used to represent the scores of the dependent variable, while the x-axis represents a unit of time, such as an hour, a day, a week, or a month. Although you may make your graph by hand, both statistical software and spreadsheet software offer the tools to present data in graphs. For example, James Carr and Eric Burkholder (1998) provide simple, step–by-step instructions for using Microsoft Excel to create graphs for different types of single-subject designs.

MEASURING TARGETS OF INTERVENTION

Measurement, as we described in Chapter 3, requires answers to a set of questions. These questions include deciding what to measure, how to measure the target of the intervention, and who will do the measuring. With each decision, there are important issues to consider. For social work research as well as for other uses of single-subject design, there should be some certainty based on theoretical literature, empirical support, or practice experience to suggest that the chosen intervention is an appropriate method to address the target problem.

The dependent variable in a single-subject design is the concern or issue that is the focus of the intervention. For research purposes, the target and intervention are usually established as part of the research project. On the other hand, social work practitioners using single-subject design methods to evaluate practice or monitor their work typically arrive at the target problem through their interaction with clients or client systems. So clients may start with some general problem or need that, through the process of assessment and discussion, becomes narrowed to a specific set of treatment goals. Similarly, a community organizer may identify the general needs of a community, and through discussion and meetings, specific outcomes are identified.

The target may focus on one specific problem or different aspects of that problem. For example, with an adolescent who is having behavioral problems in school, you may decide to measure the frequency of the behavioral problems. Or you may hypothesize that the adolescent's behavioral problems are caused by poor family communication and low self-esteem. Therefore, you would measure family communication and self-esteem in addition to school behavior. The target problems can be measured simultaneously or sequentially.

But we want you to remember that single-subject design is applicable to other systems, such as agencies and communities. Therefore, an agency director may decide to evaluate the efficacy of different methods to improve agency functioning or examine the extent to which a community-based program produces changes in the community. The choice of the target then becomes a question of determining the information that is important to the agency or community.

Once the target of the intervention has been identified, you must determine how you will operationalize the outcome. Generally, in a research study, operationalization occurs prior to the beginning of the study. When evaluating practice or monitoring clients, operationalization may occur through client-practitioner interactions. For example, if you are evaluating the impact of positive parenting techniques on altering a child's behavior, you would identify jointly with the parents a behavior such as tantrums. You would then guide the parents to be able to distinguish a tantrum from other behaviors or verbal expressions. Judith Nelson (1994) suggests that such engagement is particularly important because there may be gender and ethnic differences in how a general problem may manifest itself.

Measures of behaviors, status, or functioning are often characterized in four ways: frequency, duration, interval, and magnitude.

- **Frequency** refers to counting the number of times a behavior occurs or the number of times people experience different feelings within a particular time period. Based on the above example, you could ask the parents to count the number of tantrums their child had each week. Frequency counts are useful for measuring targets that happen regularly, but counting can be burdensome if the behavior occurs too often. On the other hand, if the behavior happens only periodically, the counts will not be meaningful.

- **Duration** refers to the length of time an event or some symptom lasts and usually is measured for each occurrence of the event or symptom. Rather than counting the number of tantrums in a week, the parents could be asked to time the length of each tantrum. The parents would need a clear operational definition that specifies what constitutes the beginning of a tantrum and what constitutes the end of a tantrum. A measure of duration requires fewer episodes than do frequency counts of the target problem.

- Rather than look at the length of an event, we can examine the **interval,** or the length of time between events. Using a measure of interval, the parents in our example would calculate the length of time between tantrums. Just as a clear operational definition was necessary for the duration measure, the parents would need a clear definition when measuring the interval between tantrums. This kind of measure may not be appropriate for events or symptoms that happen frequently unless the intent of the intervention is to delay their onset.

- Finally, the magnitude or intensity of a particular behavior or psychological state can be measured. A scale might be developed by which the parents rate or score the intensity of the tantrum—how loud the screaming is, whether there is rolling around on the floor or hitting, and the like. Often, magnitude or intensity measures are applied to psychological symptoms or attitudes such as measures of depressive symptoms, quality of peer interactions, or self-esteem.

Social work researchers and practitioners have a variety of alternative methods available to measure the target problem. Standardized instruments and rapid assessment tools cover a wide range of psychological dimensions, family functioning, individual functioning, and the like. Another option is to collect data based on clinical observations. Observations are particularly useful when the target problem involves a behavior. A third option is to develop measures within the agency such as a goal attainment scale. Regardless of how the data are collected, the principles about measurement reliability and validity described in Chapter 3 apply to measurement in single-subject designs. In particular, the reliability and validity of the instruments should have been tested on subjects of the same age, gender, and ethnicity as the client who is the focus of the single-subject design (Nelson, 1994).

It is important to consider who will gather the data and to understand the potential consequence of each choice. Participants or clients can be asked to keep logs and to record information in the logs. Participants can complete instruments at specified time points, either through self-administration or by an interview; or the social work researcher may choose to observe the participant's behavior.

A particular problem in gathering the data is the issue of reactivity. In Chapter 3, we suggested that it is important to have measures that are nonreactive; that is, you want measures that do not influence the responses that people provide. The very process of measurement might change a subject's behavior. If you ask a subject to keep a log and to record each time a behavior occurred, the act of keeping the log may reduce the behavior. Observing a father interacting with his children might change the way the father behaves with the children. Staff, knowing that supervisors are looking for certain activities, may increase the number of those activities. Tony Tripodi (1994) suggests that changes due to reactivity may be short in duration and observable in the baseline, so repeated measurements in the baseline might mitigate this problem. Nonetheless, it is important to recognize that there might be reactivity and to choose methods that limit reactivity.

Yet, reactivity is not always a problem, either for research or practice. If you were testing an intervention to improve a father's interaction skills with his children and you decided to observe the interactions, reactivity is likely to occur. The father, knowing that he is under observation, is likely to perform at his best. But, in this case, reactivity is useful, for the researcher wants to see what the father thinks is the best way of interacting. It could be that the "best" is not very good, and the intervention could work on improving those skills. Moreover, reactivity may have clinical utility for practice interventions. For example, observing oneself, for example, by keeping a log, may enhance the impact of the intervention. This finding could then be integrated into the actual intervention. But we would still have to test whether different methods of gathering data produce different outcomes.

An additional concern about measurement is the feasibility of the measurement process. Repeatedly taking measures can be cumbersome, inconvenient, and difficult. Is it going to be possible to use the method time and time again? Is the method too time-consuming for the subject and/or the researcher or practitioner? Will continuous measurements reduce the incentive of the subject to participate in the research or treatment?

Finally, the choice of measurement must be sensitive enough to detect changes. If the measuring device is too global, it may be impossible to detect incremental or small changes, particularly in such target problems as psychological status, feelings, emotions, and attitudes. In addition, whatever is measured must occur frequently enough or on a regular basis so that repeated measurements can be taken. If an event is a fairly rare occurrence, unless the research is designed to last a long time, it will be impractical to take repeated measures.

ANALYZING SINGLE-SUBJECT DESIGNS

When you are engaged with a client, you are typically most concerned about the client's status and whether the intervention is making a difference for that client. If the intervention seems to be making a difference, then you continue with the intervention as it is needed; if the intervention is not leading to meaningful change, then you will likely abandon the intervention and try another intervention or vary the intensity of the intervention you are already providing. Because the methods described in this chapter help you to *systematically* describe the changes that have or have not occurred with your clients, how then can we use single-subject designs to decide whether the intervention has been effective? One way is to visually examine the graphed data. Visual inspection is the most common method of evaluating the data, and in the following sections, we describe the presentation and possible interpretations of the data. A second option is to use a statistical technique such as the two-standard deviation-band, chi-square analysis, or time series to analyze the data (see Barlow & Hersen, 1984; Bloom, Fischer, & Orme, 2003; Franklin, Allison, & Gorman, 1997).

Regardless of whether you use visual inspection or one of these statistical approaches, the overriding issue is the **practical (or clinical) significance** of the findings. Has the intervention made a meaningful difference in the well-being of the subject? Although practical significance at times is subjective, there are several principles you might apply to reduce the uncertainty. These include:

- *Setting criteria.* One simple method is to establish with the client or community the criteria for success. If the intervention reaches that point, then the change is meaningful.
- *Cut-off scores.* A second method, particularly useful for psychological symptoms, is whether the intervention has reduced the problem to a level below a clinical cut-off score. For example, if you are using the Center for Epidemiologic Depression Scale (described in Chapter 3), you would determine if the depressive symptom scores fall below the cut-off score for depression for that particular scale. Visual inspection or a statistical test may lead you to conclude that the intervention did reduce the number of reported symptoms of depression, but the number did not fall below a cut-off score for depression. Is it a clinically meaningful change if the client is still depressed?
- *Costs and benefits.* A third way to view practical significance is to weigh the costs and benefits to produce the change (see Chapter 10). Do efforts to increase employment in a community result in sufficient change to be worth the cost and effort to produce the improvement in employment?

Visual Analysis

Visual analysis is the process of looking at a graph of the data points to determine whether the intervention has altered the subject's preintervention pattern of scores. Three concepts that help guide visual inspection are level, trend, and variability.

Level

One option is to examine the **level** or the amount or magnitude of the target variable. A question that you might ask is whether the amount of the target variable has changed from the baseline to the intervention period. One option to describe the level is simply to inspect the actual data points, as illustrated in Exhibit 7.3a. It appears that the actual amount of the target variable, anxiety, has decreased.

Alternatively, the level of the phase scores may be summarized by drawing a line at the typical score for each phase separately. For example, the level may be summarized into a single observation using the mean (the average of the observations in the phase), or the median

Exhibit 7.3   Level

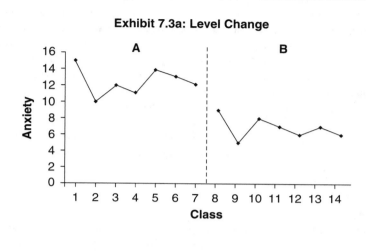

Exhibit 7.3a: Level Change

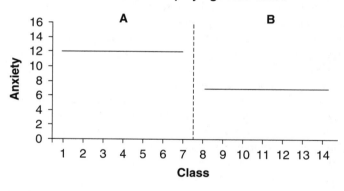

Exhibit 7.3b: Displaying Mean Lines

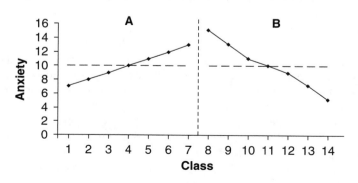

Exhibit 7.3c: Mean Lines with Trends

(the value at which 50% of the scores in the phase are higher and 50% are lower). The median is typically used in place of the mean when there are outliers or one or two extreme scores that greatly alter the mean. The mean of the baseline scores is calculated, and a horizontal line is drawn across the baseline phase at the mean. Then the mean of the intervention scores is calculated, and a horizontal line is drawn at the mean score across the intervention phase. How these lines appear is displayed in Exhibit 7.3b. The summary line for the baseline phase can then be compared to the summary line for the intervention phase. You can see how this method simplifies the interpretation of the level.

Changes in level are typically used when the observations fall along relatively stable lines. Imagine the case, displayed in Exhibit 7.3c where there is an ascending trend in the baseline phase and a descending trend in the intervention phase. As you can see, the direction has changed but the mean for each phase may not have changed or changed only insignificantly.

Trend

Another way to view the data is to compare trends in the baseline and intervention stages. As we have suggested earlier, a trend refers to the direction in the pattern of the data points and can be increasing, decreasing, cyclical, or curvilinear. When there is a trend in the baseline, you might ask whether the intervention altered the direction of the trend. When the direction does not change, you may be interested in whether the **rate** of increase or decrease in the trend has changed. Does it alter the slope of the line?

Trends can also be represented by summary lines. Different methods may be used to represent the best line to describe the trend, as displayed in Exhibit 7.4. In Exhibit 7.4a, ordinary least squares (OLS) regression is used to calculate a regression line that summarizes the scores in the baseline and another regression line to summarize the scores in the intervention phase. The baseline OLS regression line is extended into the intervention phase, and the two lines are visually examined to determine whether the trend has changed. In the example in Exhibit 7.4a, the increasing level of anxiety reflected in the baseline has stopped and the level of anxiety has dropped. A computer is usually required to do this, as the actual computation is quite complicated. Spreadsheet software such as Microsoft Excel and statistical software such as SPSS can produce OLS regression lines.

William Nugent (2000) has suggested a simpler approach to represent the trend in a phase, an approach that does not require a computer. When the trend is linear (as opposed to curvilinear), he suggests drawing a straight line connecting the first and last data points in the baseline phase with an arrow at the end to summarize the direction. A similar line would then be drawn for the points in the intervention phase. These two lines could then be compared. In the case of an outlier, Nugent recommends that the line be drawn either from the second point, if the first point is the outlier, to the last point or from the first point to the second to last point if the last point is the outlier. Nugent suggests the same methods can be used to summarize nonlinear trends except that two lines are drawn, one representing the segment of the first point to the lowest (or highest) point and the second line from the lowest (or highest point) to the last data point.

Exhibit 7.4b illustrates the use of Nugent's method. A line was drawn through the first and last time points in the baseline; this line was extended into the intervention phase. A similar line was drawn through the first and last time points in the intervention phase. A comparison of the lines suggests that the level of anxiety was no longer increasing but had stabilized at a much lower score.

Exhibit 7.4   Displaying Trend Lines

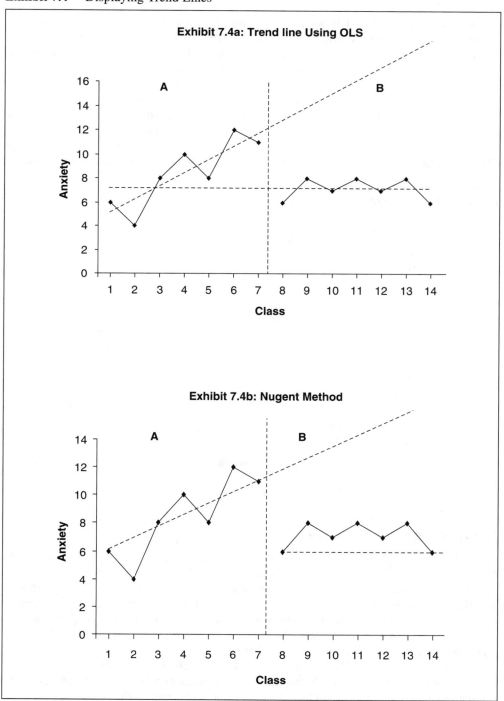

Variability

The interpretation of visually inspecting scores may depend on the stability or variability of the data points. By **variability** we mean how different or divergent the scores are within a baseline or intervention phase. Widely divergent scores in the baseline make the assessment of the intervention more difficult, as do widely different scores in the intervention phase. One way to summarize variability with a visual analysis is to draw range lines, as was done in Exhibit 7.5. Whether the intervention had an effect depends on what goal was established with the client. As you can see in this graph, the only change has been a reduction in the spread of the points. But this does not mean that the intervention has not been effective, as it depends on the goal of the intervention. There are some conditions and concerns for which the lack of stability is the problem, and so creating stability may represent a positive change.

Exhibit 7.5   Variability and Range Bars

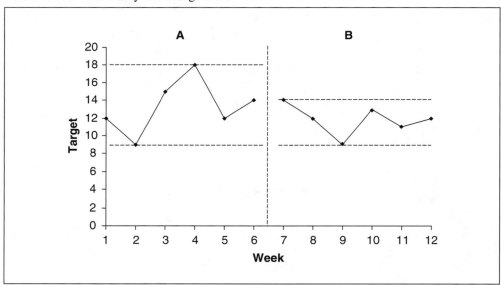

Interpreting Visual Patterns

We next turn to patterns of level and trend that you are likely to encounter, although the patterns we present are a bit neater or more ideal than what actual data might look like. Exhibit 7.6a displays a situation in which there is a stable line (or a close approximation of a stable line), and so the level of the target problem is of interest. The target in this exhibit is the amount of anxiety, with lower scores being desired. For Outcome A, the intervention has only made the problem worse, for Outcome B the intervention has had no effect, and Outcome C suggests that there has been an improvement.

In addition to the level-level comparisons, two other common patterns are displayed on Exhibit 7.6b, labeled Outcomes D and E. In both cases, there have been trend changes from no trend to a deteriorating trend, Outcome D, and an improving trend, Outcome E.

Exhibit 7.6   Typical Baseline-Intervention Patterns

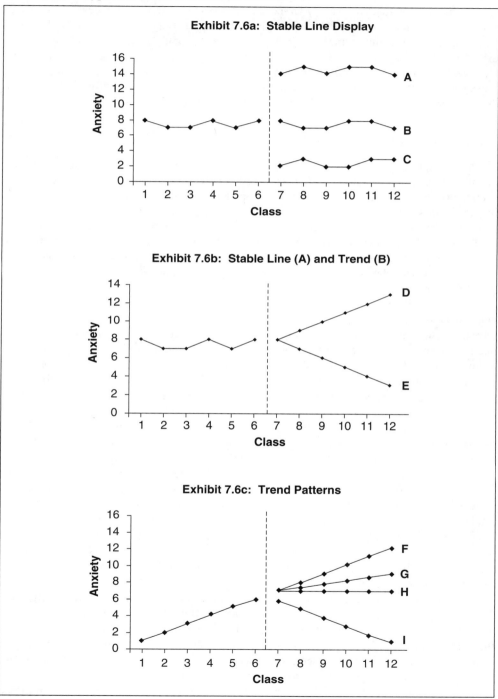

Exhibit 7.6c displays common patterns when there is a trend in the baseline. As you can see, the baseline phase is marked by an increase in anxiety from week to week. In the case of Outcome F, the intervention had no effect on the level of anxiety. For Outcome G, there was no change in the direction of the trend, but the rate of deterioration has slowed suggesting that the intervention has been effective at least in slowing the increase of the problem but has not alleviated the problem. Outcome H represents the situation in which the intervention has improved the situation only to the extent that it is not getting worse. Finally, for Outcome I, the intervention has resulted in an improvement in the subject's status.

Problems of Interpretation

The examples presented up to now have been quite neat, but when you are engaged in real practice research or evaluation, you are less likely to obtain such clear patterns. It is possible, even likely, that you will encounter far messier patterns, which make conclusions from visual inspection less certain.

One problem occurs when there are widely discrepant scores in the baseline, as was the case in Exhibit 7.1f on page 191. When scores in the baseline differ, it becomes difficult to determine if there is any pattern at the baseline, and measures of level or a typical score may not be at all representative of the data points. Therefore, judging whether the intervention has made a difference is more difficult.

A second problem is how to interpret changes in the intervention phase that are not immediately apparent. For example, the changes in anxiety displayed in Exhibit 7.7a and Exhibit 7.7b took place several weeks into the intervention. Is the change due to the intervention or is it due to some extraneous event or factor unrelated to the intervention? There is no easy answer to this question. It may depend on the nature of the intervention and when it is hypothesized that change will occur. Not all treatment modalities will produce instantaneous improvement. On the other hand, the alternative interpretation that "something happened" (i.e., history) is equally plausible.

Another problem occurs when there is improvement in the target problem scores during the baseline phase, even prior to the onset of the intervention. This improvement may occur for a variety of reasons, including the impact of an event or the passage of time (i.e., maturation). The effectiveness of the intervention may then depend on whether there is a shift in level or in the rate of the improvement. In Exhibit 7.8a on page 204, you see a pattern in which the intervention had no impact, as the improvement continues unchanged after the intervention has begun. Based on the pattern of scores in Exhibits 7.8b and 7.8c, there may have been an intervention effect on the target problem. In Exhibit 7.8b, there was a shift in level while in Exhibit 7.8c, the rate of improvement has accelerated. Of course, these changes may still be due to an event occurring between the last baseline measure and the first intervention measure.

The act of graphing can create visual distortions that can lead to different conclusions. As you can see in Exhibit 7.9 on page 205, three different pictures of the baseline data appear, with the lines becoming increasingly flat, depending on the scale that is used on the vertical axis. Furthermore, the nature of the graph may prevent small but meaningful changes from being visually evident. So a small change in the unemployment rate may not be visible, yet the change includes the employment of many individuals. Therefore, when making a graph, it is important to make the axes as proportionate as possible to minimize distortions.

Exhibit 7.7   Delayed Change

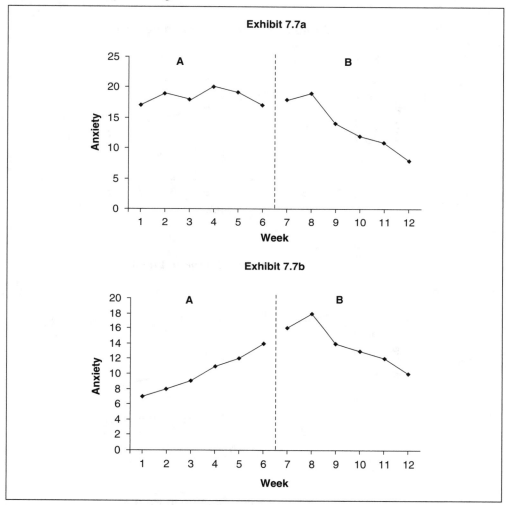

TYPES OF SINGLE-SUBJECT DESIGNS

You now have the different tools and components necessary to use a single-subject design. As we set out to describe single-subject designs, we need to distinguish single-subject design as a research tool from single-subject design as a method to assess practice outcomes or as a tool to monitor client progress. There are more constraints when using single-subject design for research purposes than when using single-subject designs for practice evaluation; monitoring client progress has even fewer constraints.

The purpose of a research experiment within a single-subject design is to test the efficacy of an intervention on a particular target problem and, therefore, to enhance social work knowledge about what works. The intervention has already been specified, as has the target problem(s) that will be evaluated. The measures should be reliable and valid indicators of the

Exhibit 7.8   Improvement in the Baseline

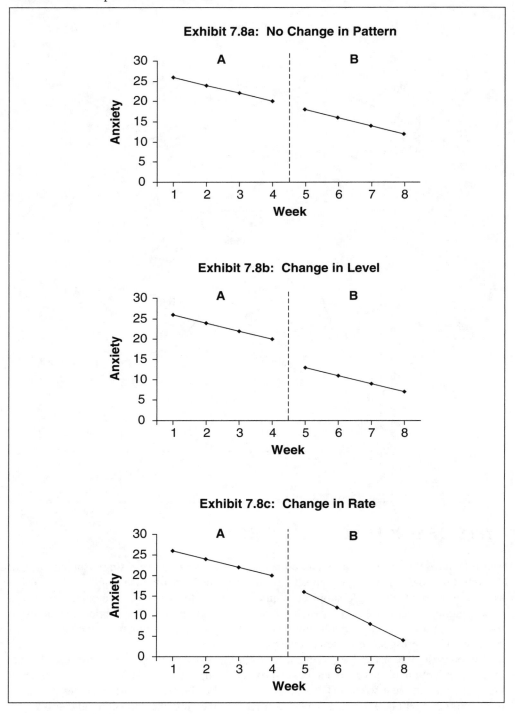

Exhibit 7.9   Distorted Pictures

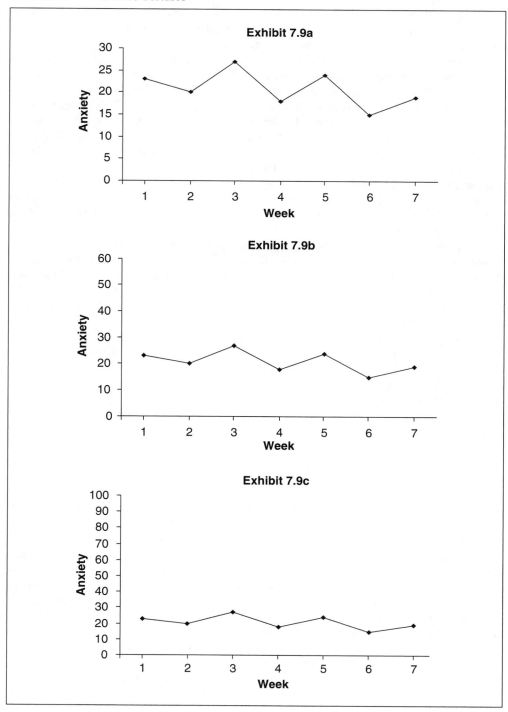

target problem(s). Typically, the baseline should include at least three data points, and there should be a pattern. The baseline measures should also be collected during the course of the experiment. Finally, the design should control for all internal validity threats, including history, because the goal of the research is to demonstrate causality.

The focus of practice evaluation is to describe the effectiveness of the program or particular intervention approach. Increasing knowledge about a particular treatment approach may be a goal, but that is secondary to the overall purpose of evaluation. Practice or program evaluation is conducted to provide feedback about the program to agency staff and funders so that demonstrating a causal relationship is less important. The specific target and the appropriate intervention emerge from the interaction of the social worker with the client, rather than being established before the interaction. As in a research study, the measures should be reliable and valid indicators of the target problem. Ideally, the baseline should include at least three measures and be characterized by a stable pattern, but this may not be possible; only one or two measures may be available. Furthermore, unlike the case in a research design, the baseline measures may be produced through the recollection of the client, significant others, or client records. Finally, controlling for causality is less important.

The purpose of monitoring is to systematically keep track of the client's progress. Monitoring using single-subject design provides ongoing feedback that may be more objective than just relying on the practitioner's impressions. Monitoring helps to determine if the intervention should continue without change or be modified. As with practice evaluation, the target problem and intervention are not specified in advance; rather, they emerge through the client-social worker interaction. Ideally, the measures are reliable and valid indicators. There may not be any baseline, or the baseline may be limited to a single assessment. When the techniques are used to monitor a client's progress, threats to internal validity are not a concern.

As we describe different designs, it is important to keep these distinctions clear. Some designs can be used for both research and practice evaluation. Other designs are more limited and relevant only for monitoring.

Basic Design (A-B)

The *A-B design* is the basic single-subject design. It includes a baseline phase with repeated measurements and an intervention phase continuing the same measures. Take, for example, two parents who are having problems with one of their children. Meeting with their social worker, they complain that over the last month, the child has been squabbling constantly with her brother and being rude and sarcastic with her parents. The social worker suggests that they use a point system, with points being accrued for poor behavior. Once a certain number of points are attained, the child will begin to lose certain privileges. To test the intervention, the parents are instructed to count and record every three days over a fifteen-day period the number of instances of sibling arguments begun by the child and the number of rude and sarcastic comments. The intervention begins on the 16th day, with the parents explaining how the child might get negative points and face the consequences of accumulating points. The results of the intervention are displayed in Exhibit 7.10.

As you can see, there is a very significant improvement. The question is whether the improvement is due to the intervention alone. The parents thought so, but in a debriefing with the social worker, it appears that other factors might have been involved. For example, each day during the first week, the child asked her parents if they were proud of her behavior. The

Exhibit 7.10 A-B Design of Behavior

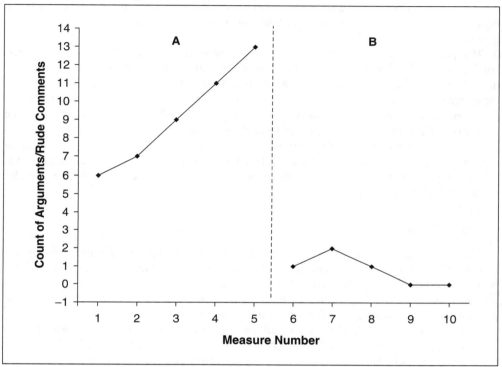

parents lavished praise on the child. The threat associated with the negative consequences may have been confounded by the positive reinforcement provided by the parents. It also turned out that about the same time the intervention began, the child stopped hanging out with two peers who had begun to tease her. So the changes could be attributable to the child's removing herself from a negative peer group.

The example points to the limits of the A-B design as a tool for research. The design cannot rule out other extraneous events, so it is impossible to conclude that the treatment *caused* the change. The repeated measurement in the baseline does permit ruling out other threats to internal validity. Therefore, the A-B design provides evidence of an association between the intervention and the change, and given that some threats to internal validity are controlled, it is analogous to a quasi-experimental design.

Withdrawal Designs

There are two withdrawal designs: the *A-B-A design* and the *A-B-A-B design.* By withdrawal, we mean that the intervention is concluded (A-B-A design) or is stopped for some period of time before it is begun again (A-B-A-B design). In other fields, such as medicine, it has been suggested that these designs serve a research purpose that improves on the A-B design. The premise is that if the intervention is effective, the target problem should be improved only during the course of intervention, and the target scores should worsen when the intervention is removed. If this assumption is correct, then the impact of an extraneous event (history) between the baseline and intervention phase would not explain the change.

This premise, however, is problematic for social work research. Ideally, the point of intervention is to reduce or eliminate the target problem without the need for ongoing intervention. We would like the impact of the intervention to be felt long after the client has stopped the intervention itself. Practice theories, such as behavioral or cognitive behavioral treatment, are based on the idea that the therapeutic effects will persist. This concern, referred to as the **carryover effect,** may inhibit the use of these designs for research. To be used for research, the implementation of each of the withdrawal designs may necessitate limiting the length of the intervention and ending it prematurely. If the designs are being used for evaluation, it is unnecessary to prematurely withdraw the intervention; rather, the second baseline provides important follow-up information.

A-B-A Design

The A-B-A design builds on the A-B design by integrating a posttreatment follow-up that would typically include repeated measures. This design answers the question left unanswered by the A-B design: Does the effect of the intervention persist beyond the period in which treatment is provided? Depending on the length of the follow-up period, it may also be possible to learn how long the effect of the intervention persists.

The follow-up period should include multiple measures until a follow-up pattern emerges. This arrangement is built into the research study. For practice evaluation, the practicality of this depends on whether the relationship with the client extends beyond the period of the actual intervention. For example, the effect of an intervention designed to reduce problem behaviors in school might be amenable to repeated measurement after the end of the intervention, given that the client is likely still to be in school. Some involuntary clients are monitored after the end of the intervention period. The effects of community practice interventions or organizational changes are more amenable to follow-up repeated measurements.

On the other hand, a voluntary client who has come to a family service agency for treatment of depression might be more difficult to locate or might be unwilling to go through repeated follow-up measurements. Nevertheless, do not be dissuaded from trying to obtain follow-up measures. Some clients may not find the continued monitoring cumbersome, particularly if they understand that they may benefit as well. The methods of collecting data may be simplified and adapted to further reduce the burden on ex-clients, such as using phone interviews rather than face-to-face interviews.

Through replication and the aggregation of findings, the A-B-A design provides additional support for the effectiveness of an intervention. For example, Kirsten Ferguson and Margaret Rodway (1994) explored the effectiveness of cognitive-behavioral treatment on perfectionism by applying an *A-B-A design* to nine clients. They used two standardized scales to measure perfectionist thoughts and a nonstandardized client rating of perfectionist behaviors. In the baseline stage, clients completed the measurement twice a week (once a week at the beginning of an assessment with the practitioner and once a week at home three days after the session). Data were collected over four weeks. The intervention stage lasted eight weeks, with assessment prior to each counseling session, but only one follow-up measure was obtained, three weeks after the last counseling session.

A-B-A-B Design

The A-B-A-B design builds in a second intervention phase. The intervention in this phase is identical to the intervention used in the first B phase. The second intervention phase makes this design useful for social work practice research. The design replicates the intervention. For example, if during the follow-up phase, the effects of the intervention began to reverse (see Exhibit 7.11a), then the effects of the intervention can be established by doing it again. If there is a second improvement, the replication reduces the possibility that an event or history explains the change.

Just as with the A-B-A design, there is no guarantee that the effects will be reversed by withdrawing the intervention. If the practice theory holds, then it is unlikely that the effects will actually be reversed. So it may be that this first intervention period has to be short and ended just as evidence of improvement appears. Even if the effect is not reversed during the follow-up, reintroducing the intervention may demonstrate a second period of additional improvement, as displayed in Exhibit 7.11b. This pattern suggests that the changes between the no-treatment and treatment phases are due to the intervention and not the result of history.

Kam-fong Monit Cheung (1999) used an A-B-A-B design to evaluate the effectiveness of a combination of massage therapy and social work treatment on six residents in three nursing homes. Measurements included an assessment of activities of daily living and the amount of assistance received. Each phase took seven weeks, with the massage therapy applied in Weeks 8 through 14 and Weeks 22 through 28 In the first seven weeks (the A phase), residents received their usual social work services, and in the second seven weeks (the B phase), residents received massage therapy and social work services. In the third seven-week period (the second A phase), residents received just social work services, and in the fourth seven-week period (the second B phase) massage therapy resumed. The measurements at the baseline were retrospectively constructed from client, nursing aide, and social work assessments. Subsequent measurements were taken from logs and reported behavior by the clients.

Multiple Baseline Designs

In the withdrawal designs, the individual serves as the control for the impact of the intervention. Yet, the withdrawal designs suffer from the problem that often the target behavior cannot be reversed, and it may not be ethical to withdraw treatment early. A solution to these problems is to add additional subjects, target problems, or settings to the study. This method provides social work researchers with a feasible method of controlling for the effects of history.

The basic format is a **concurrent multiple baseline design** in which a series of A-B designs (although A-B-A or A-B-A-B designs could also be used) are implemented at the same time for at least three cases (clients, target problems, or settings). Therefore, the data will be collected at the same time. The unique feature of this design is that the length of the baseline phase is staggered (see Exhibit 7.12) to control for external events (i.e., history) across the three cases. The baseline phase for the second case extends until the intervention data points for the first case become more or less stable. Similarly, the intervention for the third case does not begin until the data points in the intervention phase for the second case become stable. The second and third cases act as a control for external events in the first case, and the third case acts as a control for the second case.

One problem with a design requiring that all subjects start at the same time is having enough available subjects. An alternative that has been used is a **nonconcurrent multiple baseline design**. In this case, the researcher decides on different lengths of time for the baseline period. Then as clients or subjects meeting the selection criteria become available,

Exhibit 7.11   A-B-A-B Designs

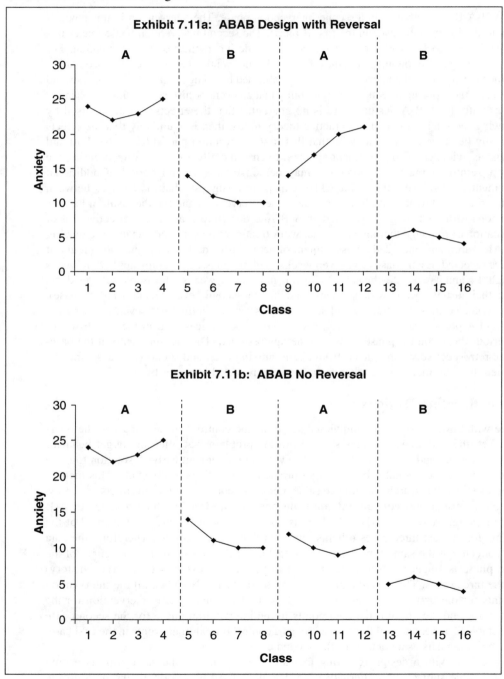

Exhibit 7.12 Multiple Baseline Design

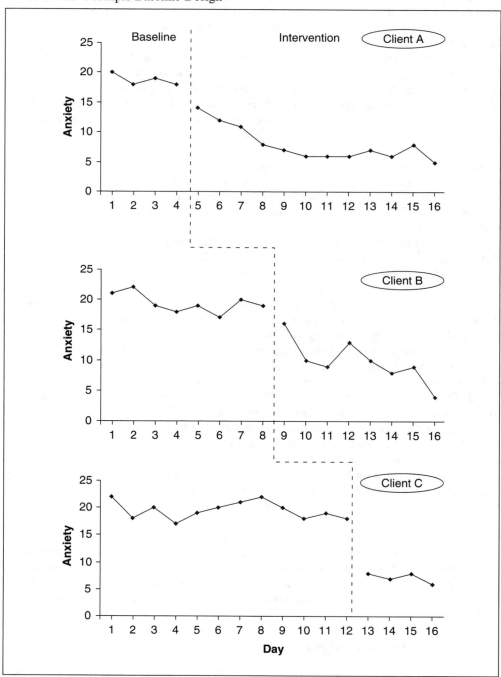

they are randomly assigned into one of the baseline phases. For example, Carla Jensen (1994) used this approach to test the effectiveness of an integrated short-term model of cognitive behavioral therapy and interpersonal psychotherapy. Jensen randomly assigned clients to a baseline phase of three, four, or five weeks.

As a research tool, multiple baseline designs are particularly useful. They introduce two replications, so that if consistent results are found, the likelihood that some external event is causing the change is reduced. If some extraneous event might impact all three cases, the effect of the event may be picked up by the control cases. The pattern of change in Exhibit 7.13 suggests that something occurred that affected not only Client A but also simultaneously Clients B and C, as they reported changes and improvement even before they received the intervention.

Across subjects. When a multiple baseline is used across subjects, each subject receives the same intervention sequentially to address the same target problem. For example, David Besa (1994) used a multiple baseline design to assess the effectiveness of narrative family therapy to reduce parent-child conflict in six families. Besa used a nonconcurrent approach because he could not find six family pairs to start at the same time. Families were started sequentially and essentially paired together based on the similarity of the problem. Each family identified a child's behavior that produced conflict. The length of the baseline varied: Family 1, seven weeks; Family 2,10 weeks; Family 3, 10 days; Family 4, 15 days; Family 5, three weeks; and Family 6, four weeks.

Across target problems. In this case, there is one client, and the same intervention is applied to different but related problems or behaviors. The application of the intervention as it relates to the target problems or behaviors is staggered. For example, Christina Johnson and Jeannie Golden (1997) used a multiple baseline design to examine whether an intervention using both prompting and reinforcement would have a positive impact on different aspects of peer interactions for a child with language delays. The three behaviors measured were *social response,* verbal or non-verbal efforts to join in play with another child; *approach behavior,* approaching another child using vocal expressions or gestures; and *play organizer,* the child organizing play by specifying an activity, its rules, or inviting another child to play. The baseline period for social response lasted three sessions, the baseline for approach behavior overlapped these three sessions and continued for seven more sessions, and the baseline for play organizer overlapped the above two baselines and continued for four more sessions, lasting a total of fourteen sessions. Measuring these different behaviors for different periods allowed Johnson and Golden to determine which behaviors were influenced by the intervention while controlling for external events.

Across different settings. Multiple baseline designs can be applied to test the effect of an intervention as it is applied to one client, dealing with one behavior but sequentially applied as the client moves to different settings. You might imagine a client with behavioral problems in school, at home, and at play with friends. A behavioral intervention might be used, with the application of rewards introduced sequentially across the three settings, starting with home, then school, then play.

Multiple Treatment Designs

In a multiple treatment design, the nature of the intervention changes over time and each change represents a new phase of the design. One type of change that might occur is the *intensity* of the intervention. For example, you might be working with a family that is having

Exhibit 7.13   Multiple Baseline Designs with History?

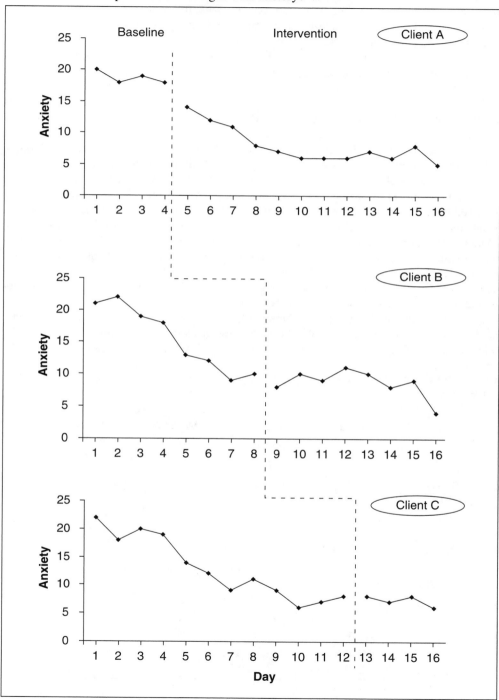

communication problems. The actual amount of contact you have with the family may change over time, starting with counseling sessions twice a week, followed by a period of weekly sessions, and concluding with monthly interactions. In this case, the amount of contact declines over time. Changing intensity designs are characterized by $A\text{-}B_1\text{-}B_2\text{-}B_3$.

Another type of changing intensity design is when during the course of the intervention you add additional tasks to be accomplished. For example, older adults who lose their vision in later life need to relearn how to do different independent activities of daily living taking into account their vision loss. The intervention is learning independent self-care. The B_1 may involve walking safely within the house, the B_2 may add methods for using a checkbook, the B_3 adds a component on cooking, and the like.

Alternatively, the actual intervention may change over time, and therefore, the multiple treatment design phase reflects these changes. These designs are characterized by A-B-C-D with the C and D phases representing different interventions. We once had a student who evaluated the impact of different methods of agency outreach on the number of phone calls received by a help line (information and referral). The baseline period represented a time in which there was no outreach; rather, knowledge about the help line seemed to spread by word of mouth. The B phase represented the number of calls after the agency had sent notices about its availability to agencies serving older adults and families. During the C phase, the agency ran advertisements using radio, television, and print media. Finally, during the last phase, agency staff went to a variety of different gatherings, such as community meetings or programs run by different agencies, and described the help line.

As you can see by the graph in Exhibit 7.14, the number of phone calls did not increase appreciably after notices were sent to other professionals or after media efforts, but it did increase dramatically in the final phase of the study. This graph demonstrates how tricky

Exhibit 7.14   Multiple Treatment Design

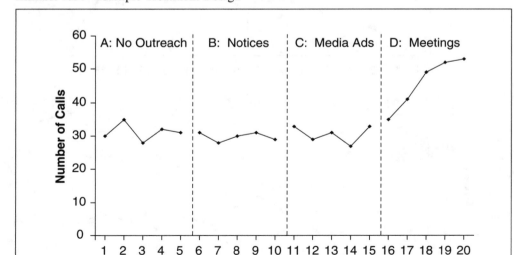

interpretation of single-subject data can be. A difficulty in coming to a conclusion with such data is that only adjacent phases can be compared so that the effect for nonadjacent phases cannot be determined. One plausible explanation for the findings is that sending notices to professionals and media efforts at outreach were a waste of resources in that the notices produced no increase in the number of calls relative to doing nothing, and advertising produced no increase relative to the notices. Only the meetings with community groups and agency-based presentations were effective, at least relative to the advertising. An alternative interpretation of the findings is that the order of the activities was essential. There might have been a carryover effect from the first two efforts that added legitimacy to the third effort. In other words, the final phase was effective only because it had been preceded by the first two efforts. If the order had been reversed, the impact of the outreach efforts would have been negligible. A third alternative is that history or some other event occurred that might have increased the number of phone calls.

Multiple treatment designs might also include interactions where two treatments are combined. An interaction design often parallels experiences with clients or agency activities, in which interventions are combined or done simultaneously. In the previous example, the agency outreach effort might have included its baseline, A, notices to agencies (B), media efforts (C), and then a combination of the two (BC phase).

Designs for Monitoring Subjects

When you are engaged in research or program evaluation, the previously discussed designs are the preferable design options. Even when monitoring a client's progress, the A-B design is recommended for the baseline information it provides. But there are times when establishing a baseline is not possible, other than to have a single point based on an initial assessment. Nonetheless, to ascertain whether a client is making progress, a form of monitoring should be done. Therefore, a social worker might use a B or a B-A design.

By its designation, a B design (see Exhibit 7.15a) has only an intervention phase. During the course of the intervention, the social worker takes repeated measurements. This design can be used to determine if the client is making progress in the desired direction. If the client is not making progress, the social worker may decide to change the type of intervention or the intensity of the intervention. For example, if you were working with a client who had symptoms of depression, but after four weeks, there was no reduction in these symptoms, you would change the intensity or type of intervention. Or it might be that the symptoms reduced somewhat but then leveled off at a level still above a cut-off score; as a result, you might again alter the nature of the intervention.

With a B design, the actual improvement cannot be attributed to the intervention. There is no baseline, and therefore, changes might be due to different threats to internal validity, reactivity to the measurement process, or reactivity to the situation.

If a period of follow-up measurements can be introduced, then a B-A design might be used (see Exhibit 7.15b). The intervention period is followed by a period of no intervention for the specific problem. Although it is harder to get repeated measurements of a client after the intervention has concluded, if treatment about other problems continues, then follow-up measures are possible. Having reduced depressive symptoms to an acceptable level, the social worker may address social support network building with the client. Measurement of the depressive symptoms might still continue.

Exhibit 7.15 Two B Designs

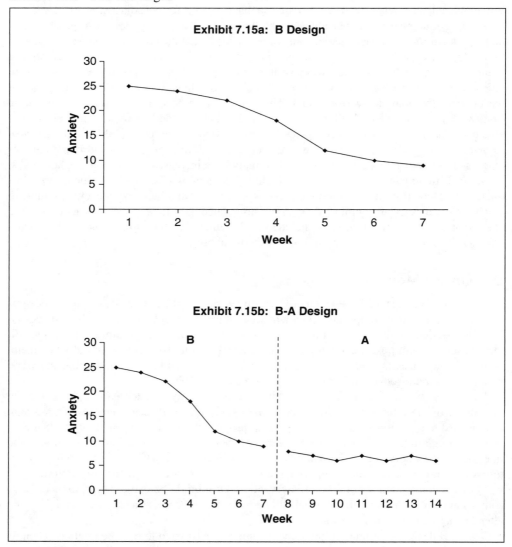

GENERALIZABILITY

Generalizability in the context of single-subject design—or group design, for that matter—is not an issue of representativeness or drawing generalizations to broader populations; rather, it is an issue of external validity. Therefore, the ideal is to take what has been tested in one research context and apply the findings to different settings, clients, or communities, to other providers, and even to other problems related to the target concern of the research. To do so when the sample consists of a single subject engaged in a particular intervention provided by a particular individual is challenging. To demonstrate the external validity of single-subject design requires replication both of the research conditions and beyond the research conditions.

David Barlow and Michel Hersen (1984) suggest that three sequential replication strategies be used to enhance the external validity of single-subject design. These are: direct replication, systematic replication, and clinical replication.

Direct replication. **Direct replication** involves repeating the same procedures, by the same researchers, including the same providers of the treatment, in the same setting, and in the same situation, with different clients. Barlow and Hersen (1984) would add that even the clients should have similar characteristics. The strength of the findings is enhanced by having successful outcomes with these other clients. When the results are inconsistent, differences in the clients can be examined to identify characteristics that may be related to success or failure.

Systematic replication. From direct replication, the next step is **systematic replication,** which involves repeating the experiment in different settings, using different providers, and other related behaviors (Barlow & Hersen, 1984). Systematic replication also increases the number and type of clients exposed to the intervention. Through systematic replication, the applicability of the intervention to different conditions is evaluated. Like direct replication, systematic replication helps to clarify conditions in which the intervention may be successful and conditions in which the intervention may not be successful.

Clinical replication. The last stage is **clinical replication,** which Barlow and Hersen (1984) define as combining different interventions into a clinical package to treat multiple problems. The actual replication takes place in the same setting and with clients who have the same types of problems. In many ways, findings from practice evaluation can enhance clinical replications.

For any replication effort to be successful, the treatment procedures must be clearly articulated, identified, and followed. Failing to adhere to the treatment procedures changes the intervention, and therefore, there is not a true replication of the experiment.

ETHICAL ISSUES IN SINGLE-SUBJECT DESIGN

Like any form of research, single-subject designs require the informed consent of the participant. The structure of single-subject designs for research involves particularly unique conditions that must be discussed with potential participants. As we discussed in Chapter 2, all aspects of the research, such as the purpose, measurement, confidentiality, and data collection, are a part of the information needed for informed consent. In particular, the need for repeated baseline measurements and the possibility of premature withdrawal of treatment are particularly unique to single-subject design research.

Participants must understand that the onset of the intervention is likely to be delayed until either a baseline pattern emerges or some assigned time period elapses. Until this condition is met, a needed intervention may be withheld. Furthermore, the length of the baseline also depends on the type of design. In a multiple baseline design, the delay in the intervention may be substantial. The implications of this delay must be discussed as part of obtaining informed consent.

When a withdrawal or reversal design is used, there are additional considerations. The structure of such designs means that the intervention may be withdrawn just as the research subject is beginning to improve. The risks associated with prematurely ending treatment may be hard to predict. If there is a carryover effect, the subject's condition may not worsen, but it is possible that the subject's condition or status may indeed worsen. Given this possibility, the use of an A-B-A-B design as opposed to the A-B-A design is preferable for the purpose of research.

Obtaining informed consent may not be limited to the use of single-subject design for research purposes. As we have noted in Chapter 2, the National Association of Social Workers Code of Ethics does not distinguish between the need for informed consent in research and the need for informed consent for practice evaluation. Specifically:

> 5.02(e) Social workers engaged in evaluation or research should obtain voluntary and written informed consent from participants, when appropriate, without any implied or actual deprivation or penalty for refusal to participate; without undue inducement to participate; and with due regard for participants' well-being, privacy, and dignity. Informed consent should include information about the nature, extent, and duration of the participation requested and disclosure of the risks and benefits of participation in research.

Others suggest that informed consent may not be necessary. For example, Royse et al. (2001) suggest that written informed consent is not necessarily required for practice evaluation because the intent is not to provide generalized knowledge or to publish the results.

Even if written informed consent is not required when using these tools for practice evaluation and monitoring, social workers using these tools should be guided by practice ethics. According to the NASW Code of Ethics, social work practitioners should as a part of their everyday practice with clients

> provide services to clients only in the context of a professional relationship based, when appropriate, on valid informed consent. Social workers should use clear and understandable language to inform clients of the purpose of the services, risks related to the services, limits to services because of the requirements of a third-party payer, relevant costs, reasonable alternatives, clients' right to refuse or withdraw consent, and the time frame covered by the consent. (NASW, 1999, 1.03[a])

Therefore, if such techniques are going to be used as part of the overall intervention, clients should be aware of the procedures.

CONCLUSION

Single-subject designs are useful for doing research, evaluating practice, and monitoring client progress. Single-subject designs have been underutilized as a research tool by social work researchers. Yet, researchers using these designs can make a unique contribution to social work practice knowledge because so much of practice is with individuals. Done systematically, the success or failure of different interventions can be evaluated with distinct clients and under differing conditions. Furthermore, single-subject designs may be useful for understanding the process of change and how change occurs with particular clients.

KEY TERMS

Baseline phase (A)
Carry over effect
Clinical replication
Concurrent multiple baseline design
Cycle
Direct replication
Duration
Frequency
Interval

Level
Nonconcurrent multiple baseline design
Practical (or clinical) significance
Rate
Stable line
Systematic replication
Treatment phase (B)
Trend
Variability

HIGHLIGHTS

- Single-subject designs are tools for researchers and practitioners to evaluate the impact of an intervention on a single system such as an individual, community, or organization.
- Single-subject designs have three essential components: the taking of repeated measurements, a baseline phase (A), and a treatment phase (B).
- Repeated measurement control for many of the potential threats to internal validity. The period between the last baseline measure and the first treatment measure is susceptible to the effect of history.
- The baseline phase typically continues, if practical, until there is a predictable pattern. To establish a pattern requires at least three measurements. The pattern may include a stable line, an increasing or decreasing trend line, or a cycle of ups and downs dependent on time of measurement.
- Researchers often measure behaviors, status, or level of functioning. These measures are typically characterized by frequency (counts), duration (length of time), interval (time between events), or magnitude (intensity).
- Reactivity to the process of measurement may impact the outcomes, and efforts to limit reactivity are important.
- Data analysis typically involves visually inspecting graphs of the measurements. A researcher may look for changes in level (magnitude), rate or directional changes in the trend line, or reductions in variability. The most important criterion is whether the treatment has made a practical (or clinical) difference in the subject's well-being.
- Generalizability from single-subject designs requires direct replication, systematic replication, and clinical replication.

DISCUSSION QUESTIONS

1. Visual analysis is used to communicate the impact of an intervention in visual form. What are the three primary ways that the pattern of scores established during a baseline or intervention stage may be viewed? When is each of them best used? What information is conveyed and what information may be omitted by choosing each one of them over the others?

2. Single-subject designs lack the inclusion of additional subjects serving as controls to demonstrate internal validity. How do the measurements during the baseline phase provide another form of control?

3. Social work research seeks to confirm an intervention's effectiveness by observing scores when clients no longer receive the intervention. Yet, the carryover effect may necessitate using a withdrawal design—ending a treatment prematurely—to do this successfully. Debate the merits of the withdrawal design in social work research. What are the advantages and disadvantages? Do the benefits outweigh the risks or vice versa?

4. How can a researcher enhance the external validity of a single-subject design?

PRACTICE EXERCISES

1. Stress is a common occurrence in many students' lives. Measure the frequency, duration, interval, and magnitude of school-related stress in your life in a one-week period of time. Take care to provide a clear operational definition of stress and construct a meaningful scale to rate magnitude. Did you notice any issues of reactivity? Which of the measurement processes did you find most feasible? Finally, do you believe that your operational definition was sufficient to capture your target problem and to detect changes?

2. Search *Social Work Abstracts* for articles describing single-subject designs. Try to identify the type of design used. Read over the article. How well did this design satisfy the need for internal validity?

3. Patterns detected in the baseline phase of single-subject designs also emerge in the larger population. Obtain a copy of a national newspaper and locate stories describing contemporary issues that can be described as having the pattern of a stable line, a trend, and a cycle. Is information provided about the number of observations made? If so, does this number seem sufficient to warrant the conclusion about what type of pattern it is?

WEB EXERCISES

1. Visit the Northwest Regional Education Laboratory's site at www.nwrel.org and click on Programs and Projects, then School Improvement Program. Next, choose School Improvement Research Series Materials and then Series V. Finally, select Classroom Management and Discipline. Select three of the techniques that educators use to minimize disruption in educational settings and then suggest a single-subject design that could be used to evaluate the effectiveness of each technique. Bear in mind the nature of the misbehavior and the treatment. Which of the designs seems most appropriate? How would you go about conducting your research? Think about things such as operationalizing the target behavior, determining how it will be measured (frequency, duration, magnitude, etc.), deciding on the length of the baseline and treatment periods, and accounting for threats to internal validity.

2. Access the Psychinfo database through your university library's Web site. Perform a search using the words *comparative single subject research*. Click on the link to the full text version of the article by Holcombe, Wolery, and Gast (1994). Review the description of the designs used and then the discussion of the problems faced in each of these. Can you think of any other issues the authors may have neglected? Which of these methods would you employ? Why?

> To assist you in completing the Web exercises, please access the study site at http://www.sagepub.com/prsw where you will find the Web Exercises reproduced and suggested links for online resources.

DEVELOPING A RESEARCH PROPOSAL

If you are planning to use a single-subject design:

1. What specific design will you use? How long will the study last? How will the data be collected? How often?

2. Discuss the extent to which each source of internal validity is a problem in the study.

3. Discuss the extent to which reactivity is a problem. How will you minimize the effects of reactivity?

4. How generalizable would you expect the study's findings to be? What can be done to improve generalizability?

5. Develop appropriate procedures for the protection of human subjects in your study. Include in these procedures a consent form.

Chapter 8

SURVEY RESEARCH

Survey Research in Social Work
Attractions of Survey Research
   Versatility
   Efficiency
   Generalizability
The Omnibus Survey
Errors in Survey Research

Constructing Questions

Writing Clear Questions
   Avoid Confusing Phrasing
   Minimize the Risk of Bias
   Use Specific Memory Questions
   Take Account of Culture
Closed-ended Questions and Response
   Categories
   Avoid Making Either Disagreement or
     Agreement Disagreeable
   Avoid Appeals to Social Desirability
   Minimize Fence-Sitting and Floating
   Use Filter Questions
Sensitive Questions
Single or Multiple Questions

Designing Questionnaires

Maintain Consistent Focus
Build on Existing Instruments

Refine and Test Questions
Add Interpretive Questions
Order the Questions
Consider Matrix Questions
Make the Questionnaire Attractive

Organizing Surveys

Mailed Self-Administered Surveys
Group-Administered Surveys
Telephone Surveys
   Reaching Sample Units
   Maximizing Response to Phone
     Surveys
In-Person Interviews
   Balancing Rapport and Control
   Maximizing Response to
     Interviews
Electronic Surveys
Mixed-Mode Surveys
A Comparison of Survey Designs

Secondary Data Surveys

Ethical Issues in
   Survey Research

Conclusion

The intersection between work and family life has changed considerably during the 20th century. For much of the industrial period, separation of work and family activities and a gender-based division of responsibilities were the norm. But we have seen in recent decades a dramatic increase in the proportion of two-income families, many more single-parent/single-earner families, more telecommuting and other work-at-home arrangements, and some changes in the household division of labor. Social scientists who seek to understand these changes in the social structure have had plenty to keep themselves busy.

Ohio State sociology professor Catherine Ross (1990) wanted to know how these changes shape people's sense of control and, in turn, how their sense of control affects feelings of depression, anxiety, and distress. To answer these questions, she proposed to the National Science Foundation a survey of adult Americans. In this chapter, we will use her successful project to illustrate some key features of survey research. After an initial review of the reasons for using survey methods, we explain the major steps in questionnaire design and then consider the features of four types of surveys, highlighting the unique problems attending each one and suggesting some possible solutions. We discuss ethics issues in the final section. By the chapter's end, you should be well on your way to becoming an informed consumer of survey reports and a knowledgeable developer of survey designs—as well as a more informed student of the relationships among work, family, and well-being.

SURVEY RESEARCH IN SOCIAL WORK

Survey research involves the collection of information from a sample of individuals through their responses to questions. As you probably have observed, a great many researchers—as well as newspaper editors, political pundits, and marketing gurus—make the same methodological choice. In fact, surveys have become such a vital part of our social fabric that we cannot assess much of what we read in the newspaper or see on TV without having some understanding of this method of data collection (Converse, 1984).

Attractions of Survey Research

Regardless of its scope, survey research owes its continuing popularity to three features: versatility, efficiency, and generalizability.

Versatility

First and foremost is the versatility of survey methods. Although a survey is not the ideal method for testing all hypotheses or learning about every social process, a well-designed survey can enhance our understanding of just about any social issue. Social work researchers have used survey methods to investigate every field of social work practice including (but not limited to) child welfare, gerontology, health, mental health, income maintenance, community building, and community development. If you have worked in an agency or you are in field practicum, you have probably noticed that the methods of survey research have been adapted by the agency for program evaluation and practice. Surveys are used in agencies to assess the impact of policy changes, identify community needs, track changes in community characteristics, monitor and evaluate program effectiveness, and assess client satisfaction with programs. Your supervisor or the agency executive director has probably responded to surveys sent by the state, accrediting boards, or funding agencies such as the United Way.

Efficiency

Surveys also are popular because data can be collected from many people at relatively low cost and, depending on the survey design, relatively quickly. Catherine Ross contracted with the University of Illinois Survey Research Laboratory (SRL) for her 1990 telephone survey of 2,000 adult Americans. SRL estimated that the survey would incur direct costs of $60,823—only $30.41 per respondent—and take five to six months to complete. Large mailed surveys cost even less, about $10 to $15 per potential respondent, although the costs can increase greatly when intensive follow-up efforts are made. Surveys of the general population using personal interviews are much more expensive, with costs ranging from about $100 per potential respondent for studies in a limited geographical area to $300 or more when lengthy travel or repeat visits are needed to connect with respondents (Fowler, personal communication, January 7, 1998; see also Dillman, 1982; Groves & Kahn, 1979). As you would expect, phone surveys are the quickest survey method, followed by mail surveys and then interviews.

Surveys also are efficient because many variables can be measured without substantially increasing the time or cost. Mailed questionnaires can include up to 10 pages of questions before respondents begin to balk. In-person interviews can be much longer, taking more than an hour; for example, the 1991 General Social Survey included 196 questions, many with multiple parts, and was 75 pages long. The upper limit for phone surveys seems to be about 45 minutes.

Of course, these efficiencies can be attained only in a place with a reliable communications infrastructure (Labaw, 1980, pp. xiii–xiv). A reliable postal service, which is required for mail surveys, has generally been available in the United States—although residents of the Bronx, New York, have complained that delivery of local first-class mail often takes two weeks or more, almost ruling out mail surveys (Purdy, 1994). Phone surveys can be effective in the United States because 95% of households have phones (Czaja & Blair, 1995), and only 4% of people live in households without a phone (Levy & Lemeshow, 1999, p. 456).

Generalizability

Survey methods lend themselves to probability sampling from large populations. Thus, survey research is very appealing when sample generalizability is a central research goal. In fact, survey research is often the only means available for developing a representative picture of the attitudes and characteristics of a large population.

Surveys also are the method of choice when cross-population generalizability is a key concern, because they allow a range of social contexts and subgroups to be sampled. The consistency of relationships can then be examined across the various subgroups.

The Omnibus Survey

An omnibus survey shows just how versatile, efficient, and generalizable a survey can be. An **omnibus survey** covers a range of topics of interest to different researchers, in contrast to the typical survey, which is directed at a specific research question. The omnibus survey has multiple sponsors or is designed to generate data useful to a broad segment of the social science community rather than to answer a particular research question. It is usually directed to a sample of some general population, so the questions about a range of different issues are appropriate to at least some sample members. Communities across the country are developing their own omnibus surveys, designed to document a variety of different economic, political, social, health, and demographic trends in the particular communities.

One of the most successful omnibus surveys is the General Social Survey (GSS) of the National Opinion Research Center at the University of Chicago. It is a 90-minute interview administered biennially to a probability sample of almost 3,000 Americans, with a wide range of questions and topic areas chosen by a board of overseers. Some questions are asked of only a randomly selected subset of respondents. This **split-ballot design** allows more questions without increasing the survey's cost. It also facilitates experiments on the effect of question wording: Different forms of the same question are included in the split-ballot subsets. The GSS is widely available to universities, instructors, and students (Davis & Smith, 1992; National Opinion Research Center, 1992), as are many other survey data sets archived by the Inter-University Consortium for Political and Social Research (ICPSR) (more details about the ICPSR appear later in this chapter.

Errors in Survey Research

It might be said that surveys are too easy to conduct. Organizations and individuals often decide that a survey would help to solve some important problem because it seems so easy to prepare a form with some questions and send it out. But without careful attention to sampling, measurement, and overall survey design, the effort is likely to be a flop. Such flops are too common for comfort, and the responsible survey researcher must take the time to design surveys properly and to convince sponsoring organizations that this time is worth the effort (Turner & Martin, 1984, p. 68).

For a survey to succeed, it must minimize the risk of two types of error: poor measurement of cases that are surveyed (**errors of observation**) and omission of cases that should be surveyed (**errors of nonobservation**) (Groves, 1989). Measurement error was a key concern in Chapter 3, but there is much more to be learned about how to minimize these errors of observation in the survey process. We will consider in this chapter potential problems with the questions we write, the characteristics of the respondents who answer the questions, the way we present these questions in our questionnaires, and the interviewers we may use to ask the questions. The potential measurement errors that survey researchers confront in designing questions and questionnaires are summarized in Exhibit 8.1; we will discuss each of these sources of error throughout this chapter.

There are three sources of errors of nonobservation:

- Coverage of the population can be inadequate due to a poor sampling frame.
- The process of random sampling can result in sampling error—differences between the characteristics of the sample members and the population, which arise due to chance.
- Nonresponse can distort the sample when individuals refuse to respond or cannot be contacted. Nonresponse to specific questions can distort the generalizability of the responses to those questions.

We considered the importance of a good sampling frame and the procedures for estimating and reducing sampling error in Chapter 4; we will add only a few more points here. We

Exhibit 8.1   Measurement Errors Associated With Surveys

Question Wording	Does the question have a consistent meaning to respondents? Problems can occur with:
• *Lengthy wording*	Words that are unnecessary, long, and complicated
• *Length of question*	The question is unnecessarily long
• *Lack of specificity*	It is not clear from the question what information is desired
• *Lack of frame of reference*	The question does not specify to what reference comparisons should be made
• *Vague language*	Words and phrases can have different meanings to respondents
• *Double negatives*	Use of two or more negative phrases in the question
• *Double–barreled question*	Question actually asks two or more questions
• *Using jargon and initials*	Professional or academic discipline specific terms are used
• *Leading questions*	Question phrasing meant to bias the response
• *Cultural differences in meaning*	Phrases or words that have different meanings to different population subgroups
Respondent Characteristics	Characteristics of respondents may produce inaccurate answers. These include:
• *Memory recall*	Problems of remembering events or details about events
• *Telescoping*	Remembering events as happening more recently than when they really occurred
• *Agreement or acquiescence bias*	Tendency for respondents to "agree"
• *Social desirability*	Tendency to want to appear in a positive light and therefore provide the desirable response
• *Floaters*	Respondents who choose a substantive answer when they really don't know
• *Fence-sitters*	People who see themselves as being neutral so as not to give the wrong answer
• *Sensitive questions*	Questions deemed too personal
Presentation of Questions	The structure of questions and the survey instrument may produce error including:
• *Open-ended questions*	Response categories are not provided, left to respondent to provide
• *Closed-ended questions*	Possible response categories are provided
• *Agree-disagree*	Tendency to agree when only two choices are offered
• *Question order*	The context or order of questions can effect subsequent responses as respondents try to remain consistent
• *Response set*	Giving the same response to a series of questions
• *Filter questions*	Questions used to determine if other questions are relevant
Interviewer	The use of an interviewer may produce these errors.

• *Mismatch of interviewer-interviewee demographic characteristics*
• *Unconscious judgmental actions to responses*

will give much more attention in this chapter to procedures for reducing nonresponse in surveys. Unfortunately, nonresponse is becoming an increasing concern for survey researchers. For reasons that are not entirely understood, but that may include growing popular cynicism and distrust of government, nonresponse rates have been growing in the United States and Western Europe since the early 1950s (Groves, 1989, pp. 145–155; Groves & Couper, 1998, pp. 155–189).

We can begin to anticipate problems that lead to survey errors and identify possible solutions if we take enough time to think about the issue theoretically. Survey expert Don Dillman (2000, pp. 14–15) suggests using the framework of social exchange theory, which asserts that behavior is motivated by the return the individual expects for the behavior (Blau, 1964). Expected returns include the social rewards that the individual thinks will be received for the behavior, the costs that will be incurred, and the trust that in the long run, the rewards will exceed the costs. A well-designed survey will maximize the social rewards, minimize the costs for participating in the survey, and establish trust that the rewards will outweigh the costs.

Using clear and interesting questions and presenting them in a well-organized questionnaire go a long way to reducing the cost of responding carefully to a survey. Question writing will be the focus of the next section, and questionnaire design will be discussed in the section that follows. Other steps for increasing rewards, reducing costs, and maximizing trust in order to reduce nonresponse in each type of survey will be the focus of the last section.

CONSTRUCTING QUESTIONS

Questions are the centerpiece of survey research. In the social sciences, asking people questions is the most common method for measuring variables, and social work research (or practice for that matter) is no different. Some questions may focus on knowledge or what people know or do not know. Some questions focus on attitudes, or what people say they want or how they feel about something. Some questions focus on feelings or symptoms or how they feel about themselves. Some questions focus on behavior, or what people do. And some questions focus on attributes, or what people are like or have experienced (Dillman, 1978, pp. 79–118; Gordon, 1992). Rarely can a single question effectively address more than one of these dimensions at a time. Nor should we try to focus on more than one dimension, lest the question become too complex.

In principle, survey questions can be a straightforward and efficient means to measure different variables, but in practice, survey questions can result in misleading or inappropriate answers. All questions proposed for a survey must be screened carefully for their adherence to basic guidelines and then tested and revised until the researcher feels some confidence that they will be clear to the intended respondents (Fowler, 1995). Some variables may prove to be inappropriate for measurement with any type of question. We have to recognize the limits of memories and perceptions of the events about which we might like to ask.

Questions can be designed with or without explicit response choices. When explicit response categories are offered, the type of question is a **closed-ended question,** or **fixed-choice question**. For example, the following question asked in a survey of clients receiving vision-related services is closed-ended because the desired response categories are provided.

```
Overall, how would you rate your health? Would you say your health
is excellent, very good, good, fair, or poor?
```

    _ Excellent

    _ Very good

    _ Good

    _ Fair

    _ Poor

Most surveys of a large number of people contain primarily closed-ended questions, which are easy to process with computers and analyze with statistics. With closed-ended questions, respondents are also more likely to answer the question that the researcher really wants them to answer. Including the response choices reduces ambiguity. However, fixed-response choices can obscure what people really think unless the choices are designed carefully to match the range of possible responses to the question. Respondents can become frustrated when they are not able to find a category to fit their desired answer. And finally, closed-ended questions do not create rapport when conducting an interview.

Most important, response choices should be mutually exclusive and exhaustive, so that every respondent can find one and only one choice that applies to him or her (unless the question is of the "Check all that apply" format). To make response choices exhaustive, researchers may need to offer at least one option with room for ambiguity. For example, older adults were asked to check all social services they had used in the past month. The list included 15 different services but concluded with a category,

```
Other (please specify _____)
```

because the researchers were not sure they had all the possible services on their list. If respondents do not find a response option that corresponds to their answer to the question, they may skip the question entirely or choose a response option that does not indicate what they are really thinking.

Open-ended questions are questions without explicit response choices, so that respondents provide their own answers in their own words. This question is an open-ended version of the earlier closed-ended question asked of the older adults.

```
Please identify the kinds of social services you have used in the
past month.
```

An open-ended format is preferable with questions for which the range of responses cannot adequately be anticipated—namely, questions that have not previously been used in surveys and questions that are asked of new groups.

Open-ended questions provide additional information that may not be available from a closed-ended question. For example, in a questionnaire dealing with psychiatric conditions, respondents were asked a "Yes-No" question, "In the last 2 weeks, have you had thoughts that you would be better off dead or of hurting yourself in some way?" They were then asked, "Can you tell me about it?" The purpose of the second question was to expand on the first question and help the analyst to determine whether there was a threat of suicide.

Open-ended questions can be used to explain what a concept means to the respondent. For example, mental illness is a complex concept that tends to have different meanings for different people. In a survey that Schutt (1992) conducted in homeless shelters, staff were asked whether they believed that people at the shelter had become homeless due to mental illness. About 47% chose *Agree* or *Strongly agree* when given fixed-response choices. However, when these same staff members were interviewed in depth using open-ended questions, it became clear that the meaning of these responses varied among staff. Some believed that mental illness caused homelessness by making people vulnerable in the face of bad luck and insufficient resources:

> Mental illness [is the cause]. Just watching them, my heart goes out to them. Whatever the circumstances were that were in their lives that led them to the streets and being homeless I see it as very sad. . . . Maybe the resources weren't there for them, or maybe they didn't have the capabilities to know when the resources were there. It is misfortune. (Schutt, 1992, p. 7)

Other staff believed that mental illness caused people to reject housing opportunities:

> I believe because of their mental illness that's why they are homeless. So for them to say I would rather live on the street than live in a house and have to pay rent, I mean that to me indicates that they are mentally ill. (Schutt, 1992, p. 7)

Although open-ended questions provide a wealth of information, they are not always easy to use. Administering, analyzing, and summarizing open-ended questions can be time consuming and difficult. Some respondents do not like to write a lot and may find open-ended questions taxing. Interviewing is not necessarily the solution: The amount of information provided by a respondent may depend on the respondent's personality—some respondents may provide short or cursory answers while other respondents may provide extensive answers with a great deal of relevant (and irrelevant) information.

Writing Clear Questions

Because the way questions are worded can have a great effect on the way they are answered, selecting good questions is the single most important concern for survey researchers. All hope of achieving measurement validity is lost unless the questions in a survey are clear and convey the intended meaning to respondents. You may be thinking that you ask people questions all the time and have no trouble understanding the answers you receive, but can't you also think of times when you've been confused in casual conversation by misleading or misunderstood questions? Now consider just a few of the differences between everyday conversations and standardized surveys that make writing survey questions much more difficult:

- Survey questions must be asked of many people, not just one.
- The same survey question must be used with each person, not tailored to the specifics of a given conversation.
- Survey questions must be understood in the same way by people who differ in many ways.
- You will not be able to rephrase a survey question if someone doesn't understand it because that would result in a different question for that person.
- Survey respondents don't know you and so can't be expected to share the nuances of expression that help you and your friends and family to communicate.

Question writing for a particular survey might begin with a brainstorming session or a review of previous surveys. Then, whatever questions are being considered must be systematically evaluated and refined. Although most professionally prepared surveys contain previously used questions as well as some new ones, every question that is considered for inclusion must be reviewed carefully for its clarity and ability to convey the intended meaning. Questions that were clear and meaningful to one population may not be so to another. Nor can you simply assume that a question used in a previously published study was carefully evaluated.

Adherence to a few basic principles will go a long way toward ensuring clear and meaningful questions. Each of these principles summarizes a great deal of the wisdom of experienced survey researchers, although none of them should be viewed as an inflexible mandate. As you will learn in the next section, every question must be considered in terms of its relationship to the other questions in a survey. Moreover, every survey has its own unique requirements and constraints; sometimes, violating one principle is necessary to achieve others.

Avoid Confusing Phrasing

What's a confusing question? Try this question sent by The Planetary Society in their National Priorities Survey, United States Space Program:

```
The Moon may be a place for an eventual scientific base, and even
for engineering resources. Setting up a base or mining experiment
will cost tens of billions of dollars in the next century. Should
the United States pursue further manned and unmanned scientific
research projects on the surface of the Moon?

 _ Yes                  _ No                  _ No opinion
```

Does a *yes* response mean that you favor spending tens of billions of dollars for a base or mining experiment? In the 20th or 21st centuries (the survey was distributed in the 1980s)? Could you favor further research projects on the Moon but oppose funding a scientific base or engineering resources? Are engineering resources supposed to have something to do with a mining experiment? Does a mining experiment occur "on the surface of the Moon"? How do you answer if you favor unmanned scientific research projects but not manned projects?

There are several ways to avoid such confusing phrasing. In most cases, a simple direct approach to asking a question minimizes confusion. Use shorter rather than longer words: *brave* rather than *courageous*, *job concerns* rather than *work-related employment issues* (Dillman, 2000, p. 52). Use shorter sentences when you can. The longer the question, the more confusing it will be to the respondent. A lengthy question often forces the respondent to have to "work hard," that is, to have to read and reread the entire question. Lengthy questions may go unanswered or may be given only a cursory reading without much thought to the answer.

On the other hand, questions shouldn't be abbreviated in a way that results in confusion: To ask, "In what city or town do you live?" is to focus attention clearly on a specific geographic unit, a specific time, and a specific person (you). The simple statement

```
Residential location: _____
```

does not provide sufficient focus. It is a general question when a specific kind of answer is intended. There are many different reasonable answers to this question such as: Squirrel Hill (a neighborhood), rural, or a busy street. Researchers cannot assume that we have all been trained by past surveys to know what is being asked in this particular question, and the phrasing should provide sufficient specificity to clarify for the respondent the intent of the question.

Researchers can also be confused by the answers respondents give when the question lacks a frame of reference. A frame of reference provides specificity about how respondents should answer a question. Take the question:

```
Overall, the performance of this caseworker is:

   _____   Excellent

   _____   Good

   _____   Average

   _____   Poor
```

The problem with this question is that the researcher does not know the basis of comparison the respondent is using. In formulating an answer, some respondents may compare the caseworker to other caseworkers. On the other hand, some respondents may use their personal "absolute scale" about a caseworker's performance, so that no one may be excellent. To avoid this kind of confusion, the basis of comparison should be specifically stated: "Compared to other caseworkers you have had, the performance of this caseworker is . . . ."

In addition to questions lacking specificity, another issue arises from the fact that many words have different meanings. It is important to avoid vague language. For example, the question

```
How many times in the last year have you talked with a doctor?"
```

has at least two words, *doctor* and *talk,* that create ambiguity. Any kind of doctor (dentist, medical doctor, chiropractor)? What does talk mean—a conversation about a physical problem or social problem, or a casual conversation? A conversation over the phone, in the doctor's office, at a hospital?

Some words are vague, and their meaning may differ from respondent to respondent. The question

```
Do you usually or occasionally attend programs at the community
center?
```

will not provide useful information because the meaning of *usually* or *occasionally* can differ for each respondent. A better alternative is to define the two terms, such as *usually (2–3 times a week)* and *occasionally (2–3 times a month).* A second option is to ask the respondent how often they attend programs at the community center; the researcher can then classify the responses into categories.

A sure way to muddy the meaning of a question is to use **double negatives:** "Do you *disagree* that there should *not* be a tax increase?" Respondents have a hard time figuring out which response matches their sentiments. Such errors can easily be avoided with minor wording changes, but even experienced survey researchers can make this mistake unintentionally, perhaps while trying to avoid some other wording problem. For instance, in a survey commissioned by the American Jewish Committee, the Roper polling organization wrote a question about the Holocaust that was carefully worded to be neutral and value-free: "Does it seem possible or does it seem impossible to you that the Nazi extermination of the Jews never happened?" Among a representative sample of adult Americans, 22% answered that it was possible the extermination never happened (Kifner, 1994, p. A12). Many Jewish leaders and politicians were stunned, wondering how one in five Americans could be so misinformed. But a careful reading of the question reveals how confusing it is: Choosing *possible,* the seemingly positive response, means that you don't believe the Holocaust happened. In fact, the question was then rephrased to avoid the double negative; it gave a brief definition of the Holocaust and then asked, "Do you doubt that the Holocaust actually happened or not?" Only 9% responded that they doubted it happened. When a wider range of response choices was given, only 2.9% said that the Holocaust *definitely* or *probably* did not happen.

So-called **double-barreled questions** are also guaranteed to produce uninterpretable results because they actually ask two questions but allow only one answer. For example, during the Watergate scandal, Gallup poll results indicated that, when the question was "Do you think President Nixon should be impeached and compelled to leave the presidency, or not?" only about a third of Americans supported impeaching President Richard M. Nixon. But when the Gallup organization changed the question to ask respondents if they "think there is enough evidence of possible wrongdoing in the case of President Nixon to bring him to trial before the Senate, or not," over half answered yes. Apparently the first, double-barreled version of the question confused support for impeaching Nixon—putting him on trial before the Senate—with concluding that he was guilty before he had had a chance to defend himself (Kagay & Elder, 1992, p. E5).

You should also avoid the use of jargon or technical language related to a profession or academic discipline. It is easy for each of us to write questions in language that is specific to our profession. Words like *social justice, empowering,* and *strengths* may appear in social work literature, but they do not necessarily have a shared meaning in the profession, let alone the broader community. Using initials to abbreviate phrases is also a form of professional jargon. For example, to some social work students (particularly those students specializing in gerontology), AAA refers to the Area Agency on Aging, but to other social work students and the general population, the initials are just as likely to refer to the Automobile Association of America.

Minimize the Risk of Bias

Specific words in survey questions should not trigger biases, unless that is the researcher's conscious intent. Such questions are referred to as leading questions as they lead the respondent to particular answer. Biased or loaded words and phrases tend to produce misleading answers. For example, a 1974 survey found that 18% of respondents supported sending U.S. troops "if a situation like Vietnam were to develop in another part of the world." But when the question was reworded to mention sending troops to "stop a communist takeover"—*communist takeover* being a loaded phrase—favorable responses rose to 33% (Schuman & Presser, 1981, p. 285).

Answers can also be biased by more subtle problems in phrasing that make certain responses more or less attractive to particular groups. There are words, such as *welfare* or *liberal,* that over time have taken on meanings that stir reactions, at least in some people.

To minimize biased responses, researchers have to test reactions to the phrasing of a question. When Catherine Ross (1990) was seeking to determine respondents' interests in household work rather than formal employment, she took special care to phrase her questions in a balanced, unbiased way. For example, she asked, "If you could choose, would you rather do the kind of work people do on jobs or the kind of work that is done around the house?" Her response options were *Jobs, House, Both, Neither, Don't care,* and *Don't know.* She could easily have biased the distribution of responses to this question by referring to housework as "the kind of work that women traditionally have done around the house." The explicit gender-typing would probably have made men less likely to choose housework as their preference. Note that if Ross's purpose had been to find out how men respond to explicitly gender-linked roles, this wording would have been appropriate. Bias can only be defined in terms of the concept that the question is designed to measure.

Responses can also be biased when response alternatives do not reflect the full range of possible sentiment on an issue. When people pick a response choice, they seem to be influenced by where they are placing themselves relative to the other response choices. For example, the Detroit Area Study (Turner & Martin, 1984, p. 252) asked the following question: "People feel differently about making changes in the way our country is run. In order to keep America great, which of these statements do you think is best?" When the only response choices were "We should be very cautious of making changes" and "We should be free to make changes," only 37% said that we should be free to make changes. However, when a response choice was added that suggested we should "constantly" make changes, 24% picked that response and another 32% chose the "free to make changes" response, for a total of 56% who seemed open to making changes in the way our country is run (Turner & Martin, 1984, p. 252). Including the more extreme positive alternative ("constantly" make changes) made the less extreme positive alternative more attractive.

A similar bias occurs when some but not all possible responses are included in the question. "What do you like about your community, such as the parks and schools?" focuses respondents on those categories, and other answers may be ignored. It is best left to the respondent to answer the question without such response cues.

When the response alternatives fall on a continuum from positive to negative sentiment of some type, it is important that the number of positive and negative categories be balanced so that one end of the continuum doesn't seem more attractive (Dillman, 2000, pp. 57–58). If you ask respondents, "How satisfied are you with the child care program here?" and include *completely satisfied* as the most positive possible response, then *completely dissatisfied* should be included as the most negative possible response.

Use Specific Memory Questions

Often we ask respondents to try to remember an event. We are assuming that the respondent can actually remember when something happened or that it happened at all. Yet, memory of an event will be affected by the length of time since the event occurred and how important the event was to the respondent. Events important to the respondent are likely to be remembered, even if they happened long ago, whereas events unimportant to the respondent, even if they happened recently, are likely to be forgotten. Even when the event is important, the length of time from the event can affect memory. The actual event may become distorted as we may remember only aspects of what actually happened.

Researchers confront problems with recall loss when a respondent does not remember an event or behavior or can remember only aspects of the event. They also face a second issue, called a telescoping effect, which occurs when an event is thought to have happened during a particular time period when it actually happened before that time period. Some things we remember, "just like it happened yesterday" because they are so meaningful or important. Unfortunately, they can be reported that way, too.

Adding questions may improve memory about specific past events. This is the approach taken in cognitive interviewing, in which a series of questions help to improve memories about the event of real interest (Dillman, 2000, pp. 66–67). Imagine the problem you might have identifying the correct response to the question "How often did you receive help from classmates while preparing for exams or completing assignments during the last month? (*very often, somewhat often, occasionally, rarely,* or *never*)." Now imagine a series of questions that asks you to identify the exams and assignments you had in the past month and, for each one, inquires whether you received each of several types of help from classmates: study suggestions, study sessions, related examples, general encouragement, and so on. The more specific focus on particular exams and assignments should result in more complete recall.

Questions about thoughts and feelings will be more reliable if they refer to specific times or events (Turner & Martin, 1984, p. 300). Usually, a question like "On how many days did you read the newspaper in the last week?" produces more reliable answers than one like "How often do you read the newspaper? (*frequently, sometimes, never*)." In her survey, Ross (1990) sensibly asked the question "Do you currently smoke 7 or more cigarettes a week?" rather than the vaguer question "Do you smoke?" Of course, being specific doesn't help if you end up making unreasonable demands of your respondents' memories. One survey asked, "During the past 12 months, about how many times did you see or talk to a medical doctor?" According to their written health records, respondents forgot 60% of their doctor visits (Goleman, 1993b, p. C11). Another method used to improve memory about life events is to use a life history calendar (Axinn, Pearce, & Ghimire, 1999). Life history calendars are used to help sequence the timing of personal events by using standardized visual cues including years (or months) and other cues related to individual responses such as births, job changes, or moves. Using such cues, the respondent is then asked about the events related to the study. In this way, respondents can focus on less important events using the important events as cues (Axinn et al., 1999). Life history calendars have been used in studies of subjects such as the transition from adolescence to adulthood (Caspi et al., 1996), the effect of stressors on psychological distress over a 15-year period (Ensel, Peek, Lin, & Lai, 1996), and the relationship of the use of child care with behavior and hospitalization of young children (Youngblut & Brooten, 1999).

Take Account of Culture

Although the term *culture* is often linked to ethnicity, shared belief systems may develop among members of different social groups (Stewart & Napoles-Springer, 2000), and therefore, when we speak of culture, we are including different subgroups of the population such as gender, ethnicity, age cohort, or socioeconomic class. When developing individual questions, we need to be careful about our choice of language. The goal is to have all survey respondents attach the same meaning to a question; therefore, it is necessary to ensure that the question has the same meaning across different population subgroups. Although it is important that the wording be appropriate for different groups, it is also necessary to show that the concept being examined is equivalent across groups—that questions adequately reflect group values, traditions, and beliefs (Marin & Marin, 1991). Ideally, we want measures that capture not only universal definitions of the concept but also group-specific concerns and issues (Stewart & Napoles-Springer, 2000).

Even when there is evidence that a measure is reliable and valid across groups, the concept may still not be equivalent in meaning. For example, the meaning of a concept such as *family* can differ across subgroups. Various groups may have different concepts about the boundaries of who is included in family or the obligations expected of family (Luna et al., 1996). Therefore, the wording and response categories would need to account for these differences.

Closed-Ended Questions and Response Categories

When writing response categories for closed-ended questions, there are several guidelines which might help improve the questions. We have already mentioned that it is important to ensure that the responses are mutually exclusive and that the list is exhaustive. We offer these additional guidelines to consider when designing questions.

Avoid Making Either Disagreement or Agreement Disagreeable

People often tend to agree with a statement just to avoid seeming disagreeable. This tendency is referred to as **acquiescence** or **agreement bias**. You can see the impact of this human tendency in a 1974 Michigan Survey Research Center survey that asked who was to blame for crime and lawlessness in the United States. When one question stated that individuals were more to blame than social conditions, 60% of the respondents agreed. But when the question was rephrased so respondents were asked, in a balanced fashion, whether individuals or social conditions were more to blame, only 46% chose individuals.

You can take several steps to reduce the likelihood of agreement bias. As a general rule, you should present both sides of attitude scales in the question itself (Dillman, 2000, pp. 61–62): "In general, do you believe that *individuals* or *social conditions* are more to blame for poverty in the United States?" The response choices themselves should be phrased to make each one seem as socially approved, as "agreeable," as the others. You should also consider replacing a range of response alternatives that focus on the word *agree* with others. For example, "To what extent do you support or oppose the new health care plan?" (response choices range from *strongly support* to *strongly oppose*) is probably a better approach than the question "To what extent do you agree or disagree with the statement: 'The new health care plan is worthy of support'?" (response choices range from *strongly agree* to *strongly disagree*).

Avoid Appeals to Social Desirability

A related problem that often occurs in interviews is **social desirability** or the tendency for individuals to respond in ways that make them appear in the best light to the interviewer. The error, in this case, is that respondents are not providing their true opinions or answers. Social desirability effects are likely to occur when discussing issues that are controversial or when expressing a view that is not popular. Some surveys include scales to determine if a respondent is providing socially desirable responses.

Minimize Fence-Sitting and Floating

Two related problems in question writing also stem from people's desire to choose an acceptable answer. There is no uniformly correct solution to these problems; researchers have to weigh the alternatives in light of the concept to be measured and whatever they know about the respondents.

Fence-sitters, people who see themselves as being neutral, may skew the results if you force them to choose between opposites. In most cases, 10% to 20% of such respondents—those who do not have strong feelings on an issue—will choose an explicit middle, neutral alternative (Schuman & Presser, 1981, pp. 161–178). Adding an explicit neutral response option is appropriate when you want to find out who is a fence-sitter. But adding a neutral response may provide an easy escape for respondents who do not want to reveal their true feelings. Some respondents will choose the neutral response to avoid thinking about the question.

Even more people can be termed **floaters:** respondents who choose a substantive answer when they really don't know. A third of the public will provide an opinion on a proposed law that they know nothing about if they are asked for their opinion in a closed-ended survey question that does not include *Don't know* as an explicit response choice. However, 90% of these people will select the *Don't know* response if they are explicitly given that option. On average, offering an explicit response option increases the *Don't know* responses by about a fifth (Schuman & Presser, 1981, pp. 113–160).

Exhibit 8.2 depicts the results of one study that tested the effect of giving respondents an explicit *No opinion* option to the question "Are government leaders smart?" Notice how many more people chose *No opinion* when they were given that choice than when their only explicit options were *Smart* and *Not smart*.

Exhibit 8.2   The Effect of Floaters on Public Opinion Polls

Responses to "Are government leaders smart?"

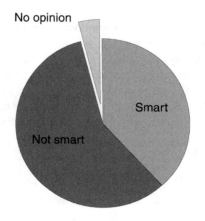

No explicit "No opinion" option given

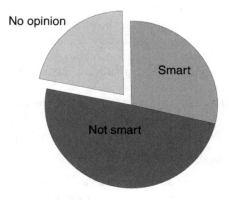

Explicit "No opinion" option given

Source: Data from Schuman & Presser, 1981, p. 121.

Because there are so many floaters in the typical survey sample, the decision to include an explicit *Don't know* option for a question is important. This decision is particularly important with surveys of less-educated populations because *Don't know* responses are offered more often by those with less education—except for questions that are really impossible to decipher, to which more educated people are likely to say they don't know (Schuman & Presser, 1981, pp. 113–146). Unfortunately, the inclusion of an explicit *Don't know* response choice leads some people who do have a preference to take the easy way out and choose *Don't know.*

There are several ways to phrase questions and response choices to reduce the risk of completely missing fence-sitters and floaters. One good idea is to include an explicit *no opinion* category after all the substantive responses; if neutral sentiment is a possibility, also include a neutral category in the middle of the substantive responses (such as *neither agree nor disagree*) (Dillman, 2000, pp. 58–60). Adding an open-ended question in which respondents are asked to discuss their opinions (or reasons for having no opinion) can help by shedding some light on why some choose *Don't know* in response to a particular question (Smith, 1984). Researchers who use in-person or telephone interviews (rather than self-administered questionnaires) may get around the dilemma somewhat by reading the response choices without a middle or *Don't know* alternative but recording a noncommittal response if it is offered.

Use Filter Questions

Often, there are questions that will not apply to all survey respondents. To avoid asking irrelevant questions, researchers use a type of closed-ended question called a **filter question**. Based on the response to a filter question, respondents will be asked either to skip one or more questions or to answer those questions. The questions asked of the more limited group of people are referred to as **contingency questions.** For example, if you were interested in the current employment experiences of women who had participated in a job training program, you would want to ask those questions of women who were currently working and not of women who were no longer working. As you can see in Exhibit 8.3, the women who answer *yes,* go on to answer the next question whereas those women not currently working skip to a subsequent question.

One concern in surveys, particularly lengthy surveys, is that respondents learn during the course of the survey how to answer filter questions so that they can avoid a set of additional questions. While a student, Engel conducted very lengthy interviews during a study of adult children with aging parents. There were many subsections that were asked of people who responded *yes* to particular filter questions. At least some respondents began to answer *no* as a way to avoid increasing the length of the interview. Although this was a problem of the length of the survey, filter questions enabled respondents to skip questions that were nonetheless relevant to them.

Sensitive Questions

There are topics, such as drug use, sexual activity, or the use of mental health services, that respondents may consider too sensitive or embarrassing to discuss. Some respondents will be reluctant to agree that they have ever done or thought such a thing. In this situation, the goal is to write a question and response choices that will reduce the anxiety or threat of providing an answer. To do so may violate some of the guidelines we have mentioned.

Exhibit 8.3   Filter Questions and Skip Patterns

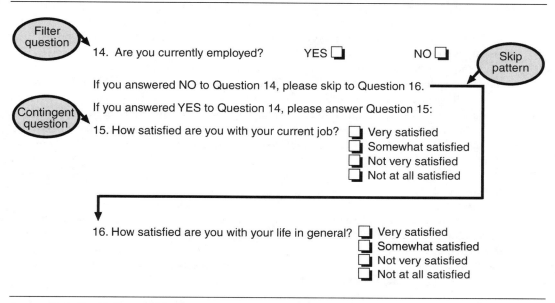

Source: Catherine E. Ross, 1990.

One way is to make agreement seem more acceptable. For example, Dillman (2000, p. 75) suggests that we ask, "Have you ever taken anything from a store without paying for it?" rather than "Have you ever shoplifted something from a store?" Asking about a variety of behaviors or attitudes that range from socially acceptable to socially unacceptable will also soften the impact of agreeing with those that are socially unacceptable. The behavior will also be softened by asking "How often have you . . ." rather than using a filter and asking "Have you ever . . ." and having *never* as one of the response categories.

Single or Multiple Questions

Writing single questions that yield usable answers is always a challenge, whether the response format is fixed-choice or open-ended. Simple though they may seem, single questions are prone to problems due to **idiosyncratic variation,** which occurs when individuals' responses vary because of their reactions to particular words or ideas in the question. Differences in respondents' backgrounds, knowledge, and beliefs almost guarantee that they will understand the same question differently. If some respondents do not recognize some of the words in a question, we will not know what their answers mean—if they answer at all. If a question is too complex, respondents may focus on different parts of the question. If prior experiences or culturally based orientations lead different groups to interpret questions differently, answers will not have a consistent meaning.

If just one question is used to measure a variable, the researcher may not realize that respondents had trouble with a particular word or phrase in the question. One solution is to phrase questions more carefully; the guidelines for writing clear questions should help to reduce idiosyncratic variation due to different interpretations of questions. But the best option is to devise multiple rather than single questions to measure concepts, as we discussed in Chapter 3. Therefore, you might choose to use a scale or index that includes multiple questions to measure the concept.

Because of the popularity of survey research, scales already have been developed to measure many concepts, and some of these scales have been demonstrated to be reliable in a range of studies. It usually is much better to use such a scale to measure a concept than to try to devise questions to form a new scale. Use of a preexisting scale both simplifies the work involved in designing a study and facilitates comparison of findings to those obtained in other studies. But it is also important to remember that the scale should be appropriate for the population you want to study and there should be evidence of its reliability and validity for your study population.

You will come across different kinds of scales, but several of the most popular types include the following:

Likert-scale. Likert-scale responses reflect the extent to which a respondent holds a particular attitude or feeling. Typically, respondents are given a set of alternatives to select the level at which they hold a feeling. For instance, if you were collecting information about client satisfaction with services, you might offer the respondent a list of alternatives reflecting degrees of satisfaction. A statement might look like:

```
Overall, how satisfied are you with the service you have
received?

    _   Very Satisfied

    _   Somewhat satisfied

    _   Neither satisfied nor dissatisfied

    _   Somewhat dissatisfied

    _   Very dissatisfied
```

Similar kinds of responses could be applied to attitudes such as agreement (*strongly agree* to *strongly disagree*), opinions (*strongly support* to *strongly oppose*), or behaviors (*very frequently* to *not at all* or *almost always* to *almost never*). Likert scales provide both the sense of what the respondent feels about the question (for example, satisfied or not satisfied) and how strongly that feeling is held. When the response categories are the same, Likert-scale items can be added to create a summate scale. As with any scale, the reliability and the validity of the measure can be evaluated using the techniques described in Chapter 3.

Semantic differential. In a semantic differential scale, the concept of interest is described by a number of opposite pairs of words, with each pair being an adjective that captures some aspect of the concept. If you were interested in measuring mood, one pair might be *happy-sad*. Respondents then rate themselves on a five- or seven-point scale for each of the paired opposite words. The scores are then summed to obtain a measure of the attitude. The challenge is to identify a set of adjectives that captures all the dimensions of the concept. Judith Lee and James Twaite (1997) assessed the impact of contact between birth mothers and adoptive mothers on attitudes toward the birth mother and attitudes toward parenting. To measure the adoptive mother's attitude toward the birth mother, they developed a semantic differential scale. They used 30 adjective pairs, such as *grateful-ungrateful, honest-dishonest,* and *successful-unsuccessful,* with respondents using a seven-point rating scale to rate each adjective pair.

Guttman scale. Another variation of a scale is a Guttman scale. Guttman scales are meant to be unidimensional so that the scale measures only one concept. They are designed to try to capture different levels of the concept, where the different levels might be differences in the strength of an attitude, different intensity of services, or difficulty in answering the question. The assumption is that if you can answer the difficult question, then you are likely to answer the easier question. In a Guttman scale, there is a hierarchy from the easiest to the hardest or the most general to the most specific. Michael Zakour (1994) developed a Guttman scale to describe the use of volunteering as a career development method. The scale appeared to have a hierarchy of five steps, with most respondents endorsing that their experience led them to "develop new interests"; a smaller number agreed with the statement "accept other volunteer jobs," and the fewest endorsed "return to school." Respondents who agreed with the last response typically also agreed with the previous responses.

DESIGNING QUESTIONNAIRES

Survey questions are answered as part of a **questionnaire** (or **interview schedule,** as it's often called in interview-based studies), not in isolation from other questions. The context created by the questionnaire has a major impact on how individual questions are interpreted and whether they are even answered. As a result, survey researchers must give very careful attention to the design of the questionnaire as well as to the individual questions that it includes.

Questionnaire The survey instrument containing the questions in a self-administered survey.

Interview schedule The survey instrument containing the questions asked by the interviewer in an in-person or phone survey.

The way a questionnaire should be designed varies with the specific survey method used and with other particulars of a survey project. There can be no precise formula for identifying questionnaire features that reduce error. Nonetheless, some key principles should guide the design of any questionnaire, and some systematic procedures should be considered for refining it. We will use Ross's (1990) questionnaire for studying the psychological effects of changes in household structure to illustrate some of these principles and procedures.

Maintain Consistent Focus

A survey (with the exception of an omnibus survey) should be guided by a clear conception of the research problem under investigation and the population to be sampled. Does the study seek to describe some phenomenon in detail, to explain some behavior, or to explore some type of social relationship? Until the research objective is formulated clearly, survey design cannot begin. Throughout the process of questionnaire design, this objective should be the primary basis for making decisions about what to include and exclude, what to emphasize or treat in a cursory fashion. Moreover, the questionnaire should be viewed as an integrated whole, in which each section and every question serves a clear purpose related to the study's objective and is a complement to other sections or questions.

Surveys often include too many irrelevant questions and fail to include questions that, the researchers realize later, are crucial. One way to ensure that possibly relevant questions are asked is to use questions suggested by prior research, theory, or experience or by experts (including participants) who are knowledgeable about the setting under investigation. Of course, not even the best researcher can anticipate the relevance of every question. Researchers tend to try to avoid "missing something" by erring on the side of extraneous questions (Labaw, 1980, p. 40).

Build on Existing Instruments

If another researcher already has designed a set of questions to measure a key concept and evidence from previous surveys indicates that this measure is reliable and valid, then by all means use that instrument. Resources like Delbert Miller's (1991) *Handbook of Research Design and Social Measurement* can give you many ideas about existing instruments; your literature review at the start of a research project should be an even better source. Catherine Ross drew many of her measures from an extensive body of prior research (including her own). She measured feelings of distress with the well-established Center for Epidemiological Studies Depression scale (see Chapter 3), self-esteem with a measure developed by Morris Rosenberg (1965), and "learned helplessness" with Martin Seligman's (1975) scale.

But there is a trade-off here. Questions used previously may not concern quite the right concept or may not be appropriate in some ways to your population. For example, scales developed much earlier may no longer be appropriate for your population—times change. Ross (1990) used the need to develop new measures for the study of work and family issues as a selling point in her research proposal: "Part of the proposed project will be to refine, modify, and develop measures, in addition to reviewing literature on already developed measures" (p. 8). Together with John Mirowsky (Mirowsky & Ross, 1991), she developed a new measure of the sense of control, the central concept in her 1990 survey. So even though using a previously designed and well-regarded instrument may reassure other social scientists, it may not be appropriate for your own specific survey. A good rule of thumb is to use a previously designed instrument if it measures the concept of concern to you and if you have no clear reason for thinking it is inappropriate with your survey population. You can always solicit the opinions of other researchers before making a final decision.

Refine and Test Questions

Adhering to the preceding question-writing guidelines will go a long way toward producing a useful questionnaire. However, simply asking what appear to you to be clear questions does not ensure that people have a consistent understanding of what you are asking. You need some external feedback—the more of it the better. This feedback is obtained from some type of pretest (Dillman, 2000, pp. 140–147).

One important form of feedback results from simply discussing the questionnaire content with others. People who should be consulted include expert researchers, key figures in the locale or organization to be surveyed (such as elected representatives, company presidents, and community leaders), and some individuals from the population to be sampled. Run your list of variables and specific questions by such people whenever you have a chance. Reviewing the relevant literature to find results obtained with similar surveys and comparable questions is also an important step to take, if you haven't already conducted such a review before writing your questions.

Another increasingly popular form of feedback comes from guided discussions among potential respondents, called focus groups, to check for consistent understanding of terms and to identify the range of events or experiences about which people will be asked to report. By listening to and observing the focus group discussions, researchers can validate their assumptions about what level of vocabulary is appropriate and what people are going to be reporting (Fowler, 1995). Focus group techniques are particularly useful for developing questionnaires with different economic and ethnic groups because participants will answer in their own terms and language. Kerth O'Brien (1993) described using focus groups to develop a survey of social relationships and health behavior among gay and bisexual men at risk for AIDS. In part, the groups were conducted to "learn the language the men used to discuss their private emotional and sexual experiences" (p. 106). (To learn more about focus groups, see Chapter 9.)

Professional survey researchers have also developed a technique for evaluating questions called the **cognitive interview** (Fowler, 1995). Although the specifics vary, the basic approach is to ask people to "think aloud" as they answer questions. The researcher asks a test question, then probes with follow-up questions to learn how the question was understood and whether its meaning varied for different respondents. This method can identify many potential problems, particularly if the individuals interviewed reflect much of the diversity of the population to be surveyed. A different approach to identifying problems is **behavior coding**: A researcher observes several interviews or listens to taped interviews and codes according to strict rules the number of times that difficulties occur with questions. Such difficulties include respondents asking for clarification and interviewers rephrasing questions rather than reading them verbatim (Presser & Blair, 1994, pp. 74–75).

Conducting a pilot study is the final stage of questionnaire preparation. Prepare for the pilot study by completing the questionnaire yourself and then revising it. Next, try it out on some colleagues or other friends, and then revise it. For the actual pilot study, draw a small sample of individuals from the population you are studying or one very similar to it, and carry out the survey procedures with them. This should include as many mailings as you plan for a mailed questionnaire and actual interviews if you are preparing to conduct in-person interviews. You may include in the pretest version of a written questionnaire some space for individuals to add comments on each key question or, with in-person interviews, audiotape the test interviews for later review (a good idea particularly if you have not conducted cognitive interviews).

Review the distribution of responses to each question, listen to the audiotapes, or read all the comments, and then code what you heard or read to identify problems in question wording or delivery. Revise any questions that respondents do not seem to interpret as you had intended or that are not working well for other reasons. If the response rate is relatively low, consider whether it can be improved by some modifications in procedures.

Ross's (1990) survey of U.S. households included limited pretesting, as Johnny Blair noted in a letter to Ross summarizing the procedure to be used:

Before being used for data collection, the survey questionnaire will be given a pretest consisting of 30 interviews conducted in Illinois. The pretest will be used to evaluate the adequacy of the questionnaire, to try out systematically all the various procedures in the main survey, to establish and evaluate codes for questionnaire responses, and to gauge the length of the interview. Only upon the basis of the diagnostic information obtained in the pretest interviews will the fully refined version of the survey questionnaire be prepared, ready for administration in the full-scale survey. (Personal communication, April 10, 1989)

Which pretesting method is best? They each have some unique advantages and disadvantages. Behavior coding, with its clearly specified rules, is the most reliable method across interviewers and repetitions, whereas pilot studies are the least reliable. However, behavior coding provides no information about the cause of problems with questions; the other methods are better at this. Review of questions by an expert panel is the least expensive method and identifies the greatest number of problems with questions (Presser & Blair, 1994).

Add Interpretive Questions

A survey researcher can also try to understand what respondents mean by their responses after the fact—that is, by including additional questions in the survey itself. Adding such **interpretive questions** after key survey questions is always a good idea, but it is of utmost importance when the questions in a survey have not been thoroughly pretested.

An example from a study of people with motor vehicle driving violations illustrates the importance of interpretive questions:

When asked whether their emotional state affected their driving at all, respondents would reply that their emotions had very little effect on their driving habits. Then, when asked to describe the circumstances surrounding their last traffic violation, respondents typically replied, "I was mad at my girlfriend," or "I had a quarrel with my wife," or "We had a family quarrel," or "I was angry with my boss." (Labaw, 1980, p. 71)

Were these respondents lying in response to the first question? Probably not. More likely, they simply didn't interpret their own behavior in terms of general concepts like *emotional state*. But their responses to the first question were likely to be misinterpreted without the further detail provided by answers to the second.

Consider five issues when you develop interpretive questions—or when you review survey results and need to consider what the answers tell you:

- *What do the respondents know?* Answers to many questions about current events and government policies are almost uninterpretable without also learning what the respondents know. Surveys about service utilization often find that respondents are aware that a particular social service or a service provider exists, but the respondents do not know that the service applies to their needs or that they are eligible for the service (Krout, 1985).

- *What relevant experiences do the respondents have?* Such experiences undoubtedly color the responses. For example, the meaning of opinions about crime and punishment may be quite different for those who have been crime victims themselves and those who have not been. Ross (1990) had to begin her survey with a question about the respondent's current employment status, which determined whether many of the work-related questions would be relevant. Similarly, her questions about child care were preceded by questions to determine whether the respondent had children.

- *How consistent are the respondents' attitudes, and do they express some larger perspective or ideology?* An employee who seeks more wages because she believes that all employer profits result from exploitation is expressing a different sentiment from one who seeks more wages because she really wants a more expensive car with which to impress her neighbors.

- *Are respondents' actions consistent with their expressed attitudes?* We probably should interpret differently the meaning of expressed support for gender equality from married men who help with household chores and from those who do not. Questions about behavior may also provide a better way to assess orientations than questions about attitudes. Labaw (1980) points out that "the respondent's actual purchase of life insurance is a more accurate representation of what he believes about his life insurance needs than anything he might say in response to a direct question [about whether it is important to carry life insurance]" (p. 100). In her study, Ross eschewed attitudinal questions about household roles altogether, instead focusing on behaviors in such questions as "What percentage [of the housework] do you do?" and "Who makes decisions in your household?"

- *How strongly are the attitudes held?* The attitudes of those with stronger beliefs are more likely to be translated into action than attitudes that are held less strongly. Just knowing the level of popular support for, say, abortion rights or gun control thus fails to capture the likelihood that people will march or petition their representatives on behalf of the cause; we also need to know what proportion of supporters feel strongly (Schuman & Presser, 1981, Chapter 9). Thus, rather than just asking if respondents favored or opposed their spouse having a job, Ross (1990) used the following question and response choices to measure attitude strength in her telephone survey:

```
How do you feel about your (spouse/partner) having a job? (Are
you/Would you be) . . .

    strongly in favor            1
    somewhat in favor            2
    somewhat opposed or          3
    strongly opposed?            4
    mixed                        5
    does not care/up to him/her  6
```

Order the Questions

The order in which questions are presented will influence how respondents react to the questionnaire as a whole and how they may answer some questions. As a first step, the individual questions should be sorted into broad thematic categories, which then become separate sections in the questionnaire. Ross's (1990) questionnaire contained the following four sections: sociodemographics, social-psychological attitudes, health and well-being, and work and employment. Both the sections and the questions within the sections must then be organized in a logical order that would make sense in a conversation. Throughout the design process, the grouping of variables in sections and the ordering of questions within sections should be adjusted to maximize the questionnaire's overall coherence.

The first question deserves special attention, particularly if the questionnaire is to be self-administered. This question signals to the respondent what the survey is about, whether it will be interesting, and how easy it will be to complete it. For these reasons, the first question should be connected to the primary purpose of the survey, it should be interesting, it should be easy, and it should apply to everyone in the sample (Dillman, 2000, pp. 92–94).

Question order can lead to **context effects** when one or more questions influence how subsequent questions are interpreted (Schober, 1999, pp. 89–88). For example, when a sample of the general public was asked, "Do you think it should be possible for a pregnant woman to obtain a legal abortion if she is married and does not want any more children?" 58% said yes. However, when this question was preceded by a less permissive question that asked whether the respondent would allow abortion of a defective fetus, only 40% said yes. Asking the question about a defective fetus altered respondents' frame of reference, perhaps by making abortion simply to avoid having more children seem frivolous by comparison (Turner & Martin, 1984, p. 135). Context effects have also have been identified in the measurement of general happiness. Married people tend to report that they are happier "in general" if the general happiness question is preceded by a question about their happiness with their marriage (Schuman & Presser, 1981, pp. 23–77).

Prior questions can influence how questions are comprehended, what beliefs shape responses, and whether comparative judgments are made (Tourangeau, 1999). The potential for context effects is greatest when two or more questions concern the same issue or closely related issues, as in the example of the two questions about abortion. The impact of question order also tends to be greater for general, summary-type questions, as with the example about general happiness.

Context effects can be identified empirically if the question order is reversed on a subset of the questionnaires (the so-called split-ballot design) and the results compared. However, knowing that a context effect occurs does not tell us which order is best. Reviewing the overall survey goals and any other surveys with which comparisons should be made can help to decide on question order. What is most important is to be aware of the potential for problems due to question order and to evaluate carefully the likelihood of context effects in any particular questionnaire. Those who report survey results should mention, at least in a footnote, the order in which key questions were asked when more than one question about a topic was used (Labaw, 1980).

Consider Matrix Questions

Some questions may be presented in a matrix format. **Matrix questions** are actually a series of questions that concern a common theme and that have the same response choices. The questions are written so that a common initial phrase applies to each one (Question 49 in Exhibit 8.4). This format shortens the questionnaire by reducing the number of words that must be used for each question. It also emphasizes the common theme among the questions and so invites answering each question in relation to other questions in the matrix. It is very

Exhibit 8.4   A Page From Ross's Interview Schedule

---

45. In the past 12 months about how many times have you gone on a diet to
     lose weight?   v94

     Never 0

     Once 1

     Twice 2

     Three times or more 3

     Always on a diet 4

46. What is your height without shoes on?   v95

     _____ ft.   _____ in.

47. What is your weight without clothing?   v96

     _____ lbs.

48a. Do you currently smoke 7 or more cigarettes a week?   v97

     Yes . . . . 1 --> (SKIP TO Q.49)

     No 2

48b. Have you ever smoked 7 or more cigarettes a week?   v98

     Yes 1

     No 2

49. How much difficulty do you have . . .

		No diffi- culty,	Some diffi- culty, or	A great deal of diffi- culty?	
a.	Going up and down stairs? Would you say	1	2	3	v99
b.	Kneeling or stooping?	1	2	3	v100
c.	Lifting or carrying objects less than 10 pounds, like a bag of groceries?	1	2	3	v101
d.	Using your hands or fingers?	1	2	3	v102
e.	Seeing, even with glasses?	1	2	3	v103
f.	Hearing?	1	2	3	v104
g.	Walking?	1	2	3	v105

Source: Ross, 1990, pp. 11–12.

important to provide an explicit instruction to "Check one response on each line" in a matrix question because some respondents will think that they have completed the entire matrix after they have responded to just a few of the specific questions.

Matrix questions are susceptible to another form of error called a **response set**. When scales are used (or a set of single questions, for that matter) with the same set of response categories, there is the possibility that rather than reading and answering each question, the respondent simply circles the same response down the entire set of questions. If a respondent was to answer each question in Question 49 of Exhibit 8.4 with *1 (no difficulty)*, the respondent may truly have no difficulty or may have tired and just circled *1* for all the questions without bothering to read them.

To avoid this problem, researchers often phrase some questions in the opposite direction. For example, the developers of the Center for Epidemiological Studies Depression Scale (see Chapter 3 to see the questions) wrote 16 questions reflecting negative feelings and 4 questions reflecting positive feelings. The developers assumed that if you answered that you were rarely sad, then you were unlikely to answer that you were rarely happy unless you were just answering the questions in the same way across all the items without reading them, that is, a response set.

Make the Questionnaire Attractive

An attractive questionnaire is more likely to be completed and less likely to confuse either the respondent or, in an interview, the interviewer. An attractive questionnaire also should increase the likelihood that different respondents interpret the same questions in the same way.

Printing a multipage questionnaire in booklet form usually results in the most attractive and simplest-to-use questionnaire. Printing on both sides of folded over legal size paper (8½ by 14) is a good approach, although pages can be printed on one side only and stapled in the corner if finances are very tight (Dillman, 2000, pp. 80–86). An attractive questionnaire does not look cramped; plenty of white space—more between questions than within question components—makes the questionnaire appear easy to complete. Response choices are distinguished clearly and consistently, perhaps by formatting them with light print (while questions are formatted with dark print) and keeping them in the middle of the pages. Response choices are listed vertically rather than horizontally across the page.

The proper path through the questionnaire for each respondent is identified with arrows or other graphics and judicious use of spacing and other aspects of layout. Respondents should not be confused about "where to go next" after they are told to skip a question. Instructions should help to route respondents through **skip patterns**, and such skip patterns should be used infrequently. Instructions should also explain how each type of question is to be answered (such as by circling a number or writing a response)—in a neutral way that isn't likely to influence responses. Some distinctive type of formatting should be used to identify instructions.

Exhibit 8.4 contains portions of the questionnaire Ross (1990) used in her phone survey of contemporary families. This page illustrates three of the features that we have just reviewed: numeric designation of response choices, clear instructions, and an attractive open layout. Because this questionnaire was read over the phone rather than self-administered, there was no need for more explicit instructions about the matrix question (Question 49) or for a more distinctive format for the response choices (Questions 45 and 48).

ORGANIZING SURVEYS

There are five basic social science survey designs: mailed, group-administered, phone, in-person, and electronic. Exhibit 8.5 summarizes the typical features of the five different survey designs. Each design differs from the others in one or more important features.

Exhibit 8.5   Typical Features of the Five Survey Designs

Design	Manner of Administration	Setting	Questionnaire Structure	Cost
Mailed survey	Self	Individual	Mostly structured	Low
Group survey	Self	Group	Mostly structured	Very low
Phone survey	Professional	Individual	Structured	Moderate
In-person interview	Professional	Individual	Structured or unstructured	High
Electronic survey	Self	Individual	Mostly structured	Very low

Manner of administration. The five survey designs differ in the manner in which the questionnaire is administered. Mailed, group, and electronic surveys are completed by the respondents themselves. During phone and in-person interviews, however, the researcher or a staff person asks the questions and records the respondent's answers.

Questionnaire structure. Survey designs also differ in the extent to which the content and order of questions are structured in advance by the researcher. Most mailed, group, phone, and electronic surveys are highly structured, fixing in advance the content and order of questions and response choices. Some of these types of surveys, particularly mailed surveys, may include some open-ended questions (respondents write in their answers rather than checking off one of several response choices). In-person interviews are often highly structured, but they may include many questions without fixed response choices. Moreover, some interviews may proceed from an interview guide rather than a fixed set of questions. In these relatively unstructured interviews, the interviewer covers the same topics with respondents but varies questions according to the respondent's answers to previous questions. Extra questions are added as needed to clarify or explore answers to the most important questions.

Setting. Most surveys are conducted in settings where only one respondent completes the survey at a time; most mail and electronic questionnaires and phone interviews are intended for completion by only one respondent. The same is usually true of in-person interviews, although sometimes researchers interview several family members at once. On the other hand, a variant of the standard survey is a questionnaire distributed simultaneously to a group of respondents, who complete the survey while the researcher (or assistant) waits. Students in classrooms are typically the group involved, although this type of group distribution also occurs in surveys of employees and members of voluntary groups.

Cost. As mentioned earlier, in-person interviews are the most expensive type of survey. Phone interviews are much less expensive, but surveying by mail is even cheaper. Electronic surveys are now the least expensive method because there are no interviewer costs, no mailing costs, and, for many designs, almost no costs for data entry. Of course, extra staff time and expertise is required to prepare an electronic questionnaire.

Because of their different features, the five designs vary in the types of error to which they are most prone and the situations in which they are most appropriate. The rest of this section focuses on their unique advantages and disadvantages and identifies techniques for reducing error with each design.

Mailed Self-Administered Surveys

A **mailed survey** is conducted by mailing a questionnaire to respondents, who then administer the survey themselves. The central concern in a mailed survey is maximizing the response rate. Even an attractive questionnaire full of clear questions will probably be returned by no more than 30% of a sample unless extra steps are taken to increase the rate of response. It's just too much bother for most potential recipients; in the language of social exchange theory, the costs of responding are perceived to be much higher than any anticipated rewards for doing so. Of course, a response rate of 30% is a disaster; even a response rate of 60% represents so much nonresponse error that it is hard to justify using the resulting data. Fortunately, the conscientious use of a systematic survey design method can be expected to lead to an acceptable 70% or higher rate of response to most mailed surveys (Dillman, 2000).

Sending follow-up mailings to nonrespondents is the single most important requirement for obtaining an adequate response rate to a mailed survey. The follow-up mailings explicitly encourage initial nonrespondents to return a completed questionnaire; implicitly, they convey the importance of the effort. Don Dillman (2000, pp. 155–158, 177–188) has demonstrated the effectiveness of a standard procedure for the mailing process:

1. A few days before the questionnaire is to be mailed, send a brief letter to respondents that notifies them of the importance of the survey they are to receive.

2. Send the questionnaire with a well-designed, personalized cover letter (see the next section), a self-addressed stamped return envelope, and, if possible, a token monetary reward. The materials should be inserted in the mailout envelope so that they will all be pulled out together when the envelope is opened (Dillman, 2000, pp. 174–175). There should be no chance that the respondent will miss something.

3. Send a reminder postcard, thanking respondents and reminding nonrespondents, to all sample members two weeks after the initial mailing. The postcard should be friendly in tone and must include a phone number for those people who may not have received the questionnaire. It is important that this postcard be sent before most nonrespondents have discarded their questionnaires even though this means the postcard will arrive before all those who might have responded to the first mailing have done so.

4. Send a replacement questionnaire with a new cover letter only to nonrespondents two to four weeks after the initial questionnaire mailing. This cover letter should be a bit shorter and more insistent than the original cover letter. It should note that the recipient has not yet responded and stress the survey's importance. Of course, a self-addressed stamped return envelope must be included.

5. The final step is taken six to eight weeks after the initial survey mailing. This step uses a different mode of delivery—either priority or special delivery—or a different survey design—usually an attempt to administer the questionnaire over the phone. These special procedures emphasize the importance of the survey and encourage people to respond.

The **cover letter** for a mailed questionnaire is critical to the success of a mailed survey. This statement to respondents sets the tone for the entire questionnaire. A carefully prepared cover letter should increase the response rate and result in more honest and complete answers to the survey questions; a poorly prepared cover letter can have the reverse effects.

The cover letter or introductory statement must be:

- *Credible.* The letter should establish that the research is being conducted by a researcher or organization that the respondent is likely to accept as a credible, unbiased authority. Research conducted by government agencies, university personnel, and recognized research organizations (like Gallup or RAND) is usually credible in this sense, with government surveys getting the most attention. On the other hand, a questionnaire from an animal rights group on the topic of animal rights will probably be viewed as biased.
- *Personalized.* The cover letter should include a personalized salutation (using the respondent's name, not just "Dear Student," for example), close with the researcher's signature (blue ballpoint pen is best because it makes it clear that the researcher has personally signed), and refer to the respondent in the second person ("Your participation . . .").
- *Interesting.* The statement should interest the respondent in the contents of the questionnaire. Never make the mistake of assuming that what is of interest to you will also interest your respondents. Try to put yourself in their shoes before composing the statement, and then test your appeal with a variety of potential respondents.
- *Responsible.* Reassure the respondent that the information you obtain will be treated confidentially, and include a phone number to call if the respondent has any questions or would like a summary of the final report. Point out that the respondent's participation is completely voluntary (Dillman, 1978, pp. 165–172).

Exhibit 8.6 is an example of a cover letter for a questionnaire.

Other steps are necessary to maximize the response rate (Fowler, 1988, pp. 99–106; Mangione, 1995, pp. 79–82; Miller, 1991, p. 144):

- It is particularly important in self-administered surveys that the individual questions are clear and understandable to all the respondents because no interviewers will be on hand to clarify the meaning of the questions or to probe for additional details.
- Use no more than a few open-ended questions because respondents are likely to be put off by the idea of having to write out answers.
- Have a credible research sponsor. According to one investigation, a sponsor known to respondents may increase their rate of response by as much as 17%. Government sponsors also tend to elicit high rates of response. The next most credible sponsors are state headquarters of an organization and then other people in a similar field. Publishing firms, college professors or students, and private associations elicit the lowest response rates.
- Write an identifying number on the questionnaire so you can determine who nonrespondents are. This is essential for follow-up efforts. Of course, the identification must be explained in the cover letter.
- Enclosing a token incentive with the survey can help. Even a coupon or ticket worth $1 can increase the response rate, but a $2 or $5 bill seems to be the best incentive. Such an incentive is both a reward for respondents and an indication of your trust that they will carry out their end of the bargain. Offering a large monetary reward or some type of lottery ticket only for those who return their questionnaire is actually less effective, apparently because it does not indicate trust in the respondent (Dillman, 2000, pp. 167–170).

Exhibit 8.6   Sample Questionnaire Cover Letter

University of Massachusetts at Boston
Department of Sociology
May 24, 2003

Jane Doe
AIDS Coordinator
Shattuck Shelter

Dear Jane:

   AIDS is an increasing concern for homeless people and for homeless shelters. The enclosed survey is about the AIDS problem and related issues confronting shelters. It is sponsored by the Life Lines AIDS Prevention Project for the Homeless—a program of the Massachusetts Department of Public Health.

   As an AIDS coordinator/shelter director, you have learned about homeless persons' problems and about implementing programs in response to those problems. The Life Lines Project needs to learn from your experience. Your answers to the questions in the enclosed survey will improve substantially the base of information for improving AIDS prevention programs.

   Questions in the survey focus on AIDS prevention activities and on related aspects of shelter operations. It should take about 30 minutes to answer all the questions.

   Every shelter AIDS coordinator (or shelter director) in Massachusetts is being asked to complete the survey. And every response is vital to the success of the survey: The survey report must represent the full range of experiences.

   You may be assured of complete confidentiality. No one outside of the university will have access to the questionnaire you return. (The ID number on the survey will permit us to check with nonrespondents to see if they need a replacement survey or other information.) All information presented in the report to Life Lines will be in aggregate form, with the exception of a list of the number, gender, and family status of each shelter's guests.

   Please mail the survey back to us by Monday, June 4, and feel free to call if you have any questions.

   Thank you for your assistance.

   Yours sincerely,

   Russell K. Schutt   *Stephanie Howard*

   Russell K. Schutt, Ph.D.   Stephanie Howard
   Project Director   Project Assistant

Source: Russell Schutt.

- Include a stamped, self-addressed return envelope with each copy of the questionnaire. This reduces the cost of responding. The stamp helps to personalize the exchange and is another indication of trust in the respondent (who could use the stamp for something else). Using a stamp rather than metered postage on the mail-out envelope does not seem to influence the response rate, but it is very important to use first class rather than bulk rate postage (Dillman, 2000, pp. 171–174).
- Consider presurvey publicity efforts. A vigorous advertising campaign increased considerably the response to the 2000 Census mailed questionnaire; the results were particularly successful among members of minority groups, who had been targeted due to low response rates in the 2000 Census (Holmes, 2000).

If Dillman's procedures are followed, and the guidelines for cover letters and questionnaire design also are adopted, the response rate is almost certain to approach 70%. One review of studies using Dillman's method to survey the general population indicates that the average response to a first mailing will be about 24%; the response rate will rise to 42% after the postcard follow-up, to 50% after the first replacement questionnaire, and to 72% after a second replacement questionnaire is sent by certified mail (Dillman, Christenson, Carpenter, & Brooks, 1974).

The response rate may be higher with particular populations surveyed on topics of interest to them, and it may be lower with surveys of populations that do not have much interest in the topic. When a survey has many nonrespondents, getting some ideas about their characteristics by comparing late respondents to early respondents can help to determine the likelihood of bias due to the low rate of response. If those who returned their questionnaires at an early stage are more educated or more interested in the topic of the questionnaire, the sample may be biased; if the respondents are not more educated or more interested than nonrespondents, the sample will be more credible.

If resources did not permit phone calls to all nonrespondents, a random sample of nonrespondents can be selected and contacted by phone or interviewed in person. It should be possible to secure responses from a substantial majority of these nonrespondents in this way. With appropriate weighting, these new respondents can then be added to the sample of respondents to the initial mailed questionnaire, resulting in a more representative total sample (for more details, see Levy and Lemeshow, 1999, pp. 398–402).

Related to the threat of nonresponse in mailed surveys is the hazard of incomplete response. Some respondents may skip some questions or just stop answering questions at some point in the questionnaire. Fortunately, this problem does not occur often with well-designed questionnaires. Potential respondents who have decided to participate in the survey usually complete it. But there are many exceptions to this observation because questions that are poorly written, too complex, or about sensitive personal issues simply turn off some respondents. The revision or elimination of such questions during the design phase should minimize the problem. When it does not, it may make sense to impute values for the missing data. One imputation procedure would be to substitute the mean (arithmetic average) value of a variable for those cases that have a missing value on the variable (Levy & Lemeshow, 1999, pp. 404–416).

Finally, with a mailed questionnaire, there is no control over the manner in which the respondent answers the questions. Despite efforts to create a meaningful order to the questions, the respondent can choose in what order the questions will be answered. Furthermore, the respondent can choose to answer all the questions at once or answer them over several days. The respondent may even discuss the questions with significant others, family, friends, and coworkers.

Group-Administered Surveys

A **group-administered survey** is completed by individual respondents assembled in a group. The response rate is not usually a major concern in surveys that are distributed and collected in a group setting because most group members will participate. The real difficulty with this method is that it is seldom feasible, for it requires what might be called a captive audience. With the exception of students, employees, members of the armed forces, and some institutionalized populations, most populations cannot be sampled in such a setting.

Whoever is responsible for administering the survey to the group must be careful to minimize comments that might bias answers or that could vary between different groups in the same survey (Dillman, 2000, pp. 253–256). A standard introductory statement should be read to the group that expresses appreciation for their participation, describes the steps of the survey, and emphasizes (in classroom surveys) that the survey is not the same as a test. A cover letter like the one used in mailed surveys also should be distributed with the questionnaires. To emphasize confidentiality, respondents should be given an envelope in which to seal their questionnaire after it is completed.

Another issue of special concern with group-administered surveys is the possibility that respondents will feel coerced to participate and as a result will be less likely to answer questions honestly. Also, because administering a survey in this way requires approval of the powers that be—and this sponsorship is made quite obvious by the fact that the survey is conducted on the organization's premises—respondents may infer that the researcher is not at all independent of the sponsor. No complete solution to this problem exists, but it helps to make an introductory statement emphasizing the researcher's independence and giving participants a chance to ask questions about the survey. The sponsor should also understand the need to keep a low profile and to allow the researcher both control over the data and autonomy in report writing.

Telephone Surveys

In a **phone survey,** interviewers question respondents over the phone and then record respondents' answers. Phone interviewing has become a very popular method of conducting surveys in the United States because almost all families have phones. But two matters may undermine the validity of a phone survey: not reaching the proper sampling units and not getting enough complete responses to make the results generalizable.

Reaching Sample Units

There are three different ways of obtaining a sampling frame of telephone exchanges or numbers: Phone directories provide a useful frame for local studies, a nationwide list of area code-exchange numbers can be obtained from a commercial firm (random digit dialing is used to fill in the last four digits), and commercial firms prepare files based on local directories from around the nation. There are coverage errors with each of these frames: 10–15% of directory listings will turn out to be no longer valid residential numbers; more than 35% of U.S. households with phones have numbers that are unlisted in directories—and the percentage is as high as 60% in some communities; less than 25% of the area codes and exchanges in the one national comprehensive list (available from Bell Core Research, Inc.) refer to residential units (Levy & Lemeshow, 1999, pp. 455–460). Survey planning must consider the advantages and disadvantages of these methods for a particular study and develop means for compensating for the weaknesses of the specific method chosen.

Most telephone surveys use random digit dialing at some point in the sampling process (Lavrakas, 1987). A machine calls random phone numbers within the designated exchanges, whether or not the numbers are published. When the machine reaches an inappropriate household (such as a business in a survey that is directed to the general population), the phone number is simply replaced with another. The University of Illinois Survey Research Laboratory used the following procedures to draw a sample for Ross's (1990) study of social structure and well-being:

> The universe for this study will be all persons 18–65 years of age, in the coterminous United States. A national probability sample designed to yield 2,000 interviews will be generated by the random-digit-dialing technique developed by J. Waksberg. The Waksberg method involves a two-stage sample design in which primary sampling units (PSUs) are selected with probabilities proportionate to size at the first stage and a specified cluster size at the second stage. To achieve 2,000 interviews, approximately 8,400 telephone numbers will be sampled. In order to avoid any potential bias in the sex or age distributions of the sample that might result from simply interviewing the persons who answer the telephone, a further sampling stage is required. For each selected household, one person will be chosen from all adults 18–65 years of age in that household in such a way that each adult has an equal probability of being selected for an interview. (J. E. Blair, personal communication to C. E. Ross, April 10, 1989)

However households are contacted, the interviewers must ask a series of questions at the start of the survey to ensure that they are speaking to the appropriate member of the household. Exhibit 8.7 displays a phone interview schedule, the instrument containing the questions asked by the interviewer. This example shows how appropriate and inappropriate households can be distinguished in a phone survey, so that the interviewer is guided to the correct respondent.

Maximizing Response to Phone Surveys

Four issues require special attention in phone surveys. First, because people often are not home, multiple callbacks will be needed for many sample members. The failure to call people back was one of the reasons for the discrepancy between poll predictions and actual votes in the 1988 presidential race between George Bush and Michael Dukakis. Andrew Kohut (1988) found that if pollsters in one Gallup poll had stopped attempting to contact unavailable respondents after one call, a 6-percentage-point margin for Bush would have been replaced by a 2-point margin for Dukakis. Those with more money and education are more likely to be away from home, and such people are also more likely to vote Republican.

Exhibit 8.7   Phone Interview Procedures for Respondent Designation

---

PATH COMMUNITY SURVEY
CALL RECORD (CR)

Metro Social Services
Nashville-Davidson County, TN
October 1987

Respondent Household (RH)

_____

Case No. [SEE TOP OF
_____ INTERVIEW FORM]

Date Precontact Letter
Mailed

_____

[TRY REACHING RH ON FIVE
DIFFERENT DAYS BEFORE
CLOSING OUT CR]

Call Outcome Codes

CI = Completed interview
PC = Partially completed
RI = Refused interview
II   = Impossible: language
         etc.
BN = Business number
OC = Number outside county
NA = No answer
BS = Busy signal
LD = Line disconnected
WN= Wrong number
UL = Unlisted number
ML = Message left on machine
NC = Number changed
CB = Call back [WRITE DATE]
        Date:
        Time:
        R's First Name:

Call Record:	Day/Date	Call No.	Time	Call Outcome

_____ Case No.

Introduction

A. **Hello, is this the (_R's last name_) residence?**

 * [IF NOT, SAY: The number I was calling is (_R's phone no._) and
   it was for the (_R's first and last name_) residence. IF WRONG
   NUMBER, CODE OUTCOME IN CR AND TERMINATE WITH: I'm sorry to
   have bothered you. Goodbye.]

(Continued)

Exhibit 8.7 (Continued)

B. **My name is** _____ . **I'm calling for Metro Social Services
and the Tennessee Department of Human Services. We're
conducting a study to find out how local residents feel about
the issue of homelessness in our community. Your household
has been randomly selected to help us with this important
task.**

C. **I don't know if you've seen it yet, but a letter about the
study was mailed to your home several days ago. Just to
verify our records, your home is located in Davidson County,
isn't it?**

*[IF NOT, ASK: What county are you in? WRITE COUNTY ON RH
LABEL, CODE OUTCOME IN CR, AND TERMINATE WITH: I'm sorry but
only Davidson County residents are eligible for the study.
Thanks anyway. Goodbye.]

D. **We need to interview men in some households and women in
others so that our results will represent all adults in the
county. According to our selection method, I need to
interview the . . .**

DESIGNATED R: youngest / oldest / man / woman

**presently living in your household who is at least 18 years
of age. May I please speak with him/her?**

*[IF PERSON ON PHONE, GO TO E.]

*[IF NO SUCH PERSON, ASK: As a substitute, then, may I please
speak with the . . . SUBSTITUTE R: youngest / oldest / man /
woman in your household who is at least 18? IF PERSON ON
PHONE, GO TO E. IF NOT AVAILABLE, MAKE ARRANGEMENTS TO CALL
BACK AND WRITE DATE, TIME, AND R'S FIRST NAME IN CR. CLOSE
WITH: Please tell (R's first name) that I will be calling back on
(date and time). Thank you.]

*[IF DIFFERENT PERSON COMES TO PHONE, REPEAT B AND ADD: You
are the adult who's been randomly chosen in your household.
GO TO E.]

*[IF NOT AVAILABLE, MAKE ARRANGEMENTS . . . (see above).]

E. **The questions I'd like to ask you are easy to answer and
should take only about 15 minutes. Everything you tell me
will be kept strictly confidential. If you have any questions
about the study, I'll be happy to answer them now or later.
Okay?**

Time interview started:

Person actually interviewed:

    1 Designated R
    2 Substitute R

(Continued)

Exhibit 8.7 (Continued)

I'll be using the word "homeless" to mean not having a permanent address or place to live. Please think about all types of people who fit that description as we go through the interview.

Here's the first question.

1. Right now, how important is homelessness as a public issue in Nashville? Would you say it's . . . [READ 0–2]

0	Not too important	8	DK
1	Somewhat important, or	9	NR
2	Very important?		

Source: Metro Social Services, Nashville-Davidson County, TN, 1987. Path Community Survey.

The number of callbacks needed to reach respondents by telephone has increased greatly in the last 20 years, with increasing numbers of single-person households, dual-earner families, and out-of-home activities. Survey research organizations have increased the usual number of phone contact attempts from just 4–8 to 20. The growth of telemarketing has created another problem for telephone survey researchers: Individuals have become more accustomed to "just say no" to calls from unknown individuals and organizations or to simply use their answering machines to screen out unwanted calls (Dillman, 2000, pp. 8, 28).

Phone surveys also must cope with difficulties due to the impersonal nature of phone contact. Visual aids cannot be used, so the interviewer must be able to convey verbally all information about response choices and skip patterns. With phone surveys, then, instructions to the interviewer must clarify how to ask each question, and response choices must be short. The Survey Research Laboratory developed the instructions shown in Exhibit 8.8 to clarify procedures for asking and coding a series of questions that Ross (1990) used to measure symptoms of stress within households.

In addition, interviewers must be prepared for distractions as the respondent is interrupted by other household members. Sprinkling interesting questions throughout the questionnaire may help to maintain respondent interest. In general, rapport between the interviewer and the respondent is likely to be lower with phone surveys than with in-person interviews, and so respondents may tire and refuse to answer all the questions (Miller, 1991, p. 166).

Careful interviewer training is essential for phone surveys. This is how one polling organization describes its training:

In preparation for data collection, survey interviewers are required to attend a two-part training session. The first part covers general interviewing procedures and techniques as related to the proposed survey. The second entails in-depth training and practice for the survey. This training includes instructions on relevant subject matter, a question-by-question review of the survey instrument, and various forms of role-playing and practice interviewing with supervisors and other interviewers. (J. E. Blair, personal communication to C. E. Ross, April 10, 1989)

Exhibit 8.8   Sample Interviewer Instructions

Question:
41. On how many of the past 7 days have you...

Number of days

a.   Worried a lot about little things? .... _____

b.   Felt tense or anxious? .... _____

Instructions for interviewers:
Q41 For the series of "On how many of the past 7 days," make sure the respondent gives the numerical answer. If he/she responds with a vague answer like "not too often" or "just a few times," ask again "On how many of the past 7 days would you say?" Do NOT lead the respondent with a number (e.g., "would that be 2 or 3?"). If R says "all of them," verify that the answer is "7."

Question:
45. In the past 12 months about how many times have you gone on a diet to lose weight?

Never 0

Once 1

Twice 2

Three times or more 3

Always on a diet 4

Instructions for interviewers:
Q45 Notice that this question ends with a question mark. That means that you are not to read the answer categories. Rather, wait for R to respond and circle the appropriate number.

Source: Ross, 1990.

Procedures can be standardized more effectively, quality control maintained, and processing speed maximized when phone interviewers are assisted by computers using **computer-assisted telephone interviews (CATI)**:

> The interviewing will be conducted using "CATI" (Computer-Assisted Telephone Interviewing). . . . The questionnaire is "programmed" into the computer, along with relevant skip patterns throughout the instrument. Only legal entries are allowed. The system incorporates the tasks of interviewing, data entry, and some data cleaning. (J. E. Blair, personal communication to C. E. Ross, April 10, 1989)

Phone surveying is the method of choice for relatively short surveys of the general population. Response rates in phone surveys traditionally have tended to be very high—often above 80%—because few individuals would hang up on a polite caller or refuse to stop answering questions (at least within the first 30 minutes or so). Ross (1990) achieved a response rate of 82% over a three-month period at the end of 1990, resulting in a final sample of 2,031 Americans. However, as we have noted, the refusal rate in phone interviews is rising with the prevalence of telemarketing and answering machines.

In-Person Interviews

What is unique to the **in-person interview,** compared to the other survey designs, is the face-to-face social interaction between interviewer and respondent. If money is no object, in-person interviewing is often the best survey design.

In-person interviewing has several advantages: Response rates are higher than with any other survey design; questionnaires can be much longer than with mailed or phone surveys; the questionnaire can be complex, with both open-ended and closed-ended questions and frequent branching patterns; the order in which questions are read and answered can be controlled by the interviewer; the physical and social circumstances of the interview can be monitored; and respondents' interpretations of questions can be probed and clarified.

But researchers must be alert to some special hazards due to the presence of an interviewer. Respondents should experience the interview process as a personalized interaction with an interviewer who is very interested in the respondent's experiences and opinions. At the same time, however, every respondent should have the same interview experience—asked the same questions in the same way by the same type of person, who reacts similarly to the answers. Therein lies the researcher's challenge—to plan an interview process that will be personal and engaging and yet consistent and nonreactive (and to hire interviewers who can carry out this plan). Careful training and supervision are essential (Groves, 1989, pp. 404–406). Without a personalized approach, the rate of response will be lower and answers will be less thoughtful—and potentially less valid. Without a consistent approach, information obtained from different respondents will not be comparable—and thus, less reliable and less valid.

Balancing Rapport and Control

Adherence to some basic guidelines for interacting with respondents can help interviewers to maintain an appropriate balance between personalization and standardization:

- Project a professional image in the interview, that of someone who is sympathetic to the respondent but nonetheless has a job to do.
- Establish rapport at the outset by explaining what the interview is about and how it will work and by reading the consent form. Ask the respondent if he or she has any questions or concerns, and respond to these honestly and fully. Emphasize that everything the respondent says is confidential.
- During the interview, ask questions from a distance that is close but not intimate. Stay focused on the respondent and make sure that your posture conveys interest. Maintain eye contact, respond with appropriate facial expressions, and speak in a conversational tone of voice.
- Be sure to maintain a consistent approach; deliver each question as written and in the same tone of voice. Listen empathetically, but avoid self-expression or loaded reactions.
- Repeat questions if the respondent is confused. Use nondirective probes—such as "Can you tell me more about that?"—for open-ended questions.

As with phone interviewing, computers can be used to increase control of the in-person interview. In a **computer-assisted personal interviewing (CAPI)** project, interviewers carry a laptop computer that is programmed to display the interview questions and to process the responses that the interviewer types in, as well as to check that these responses fall within allowed ranges. Interviewers seem to like CAPI, and the quality of data obtained this way is at least as good as data from a noncomputerized interview (Shepherd, Hill, Bristor, & Montalvan, 1996). A CAPI approach also makes it easier for the researcher to develop skip patterns and experiment with different types of questions for different respondents without increasing the risk of interviewer mistakes (Couper et al., 1998).

The presence of an interviewer may make it more difficult for respondents to give honest answers to questions about sensitive personal matters. For this reason, interviewers may hand respondents a separate self-administered questionnaire containing the more sensitive questions. After answering these questions, the respondent then seals the separate questionnaire in an envelope so that the interviewer does not know the answers. When this approach was used for the GSS questions about sexual activity, about 21% of men and 13% of women who were married or had been married admitted to having cheated on a spouse ("Survey on Adultery," 1993, p. A20). You may have heard reports of much higher rates of marital infidelity, but these were from studies using unrepresentative samples.

The degree of rapport becomes a special challenge when survey questions concern issues related to such demographic characteristics as race or gender (Groves, 1989). If the interviewer and respondent are similar on the characteristics at issue, the responses to these questions may differ from those that would be given if the interviewer and respondent differ on these characteristics. For example, a White respondent may not disclose feelings of racial prejudice to an African American interviewer that he or she would admit to a White interviewer.

Although in-person interview procedures are typically designed with the expectation that the interview will involve only the interviewer and the respondent, one or more other household members are often within earshot. In a mental health survey in Los Angeles, for example, almost half the interviews were conducted in the presence of another person (Pollner & Adams, 1994). It is reasonable to worry that this third-party presence will influence responses about sensitive subjects—even more so because the likelihood of a third party being present may correspond with other subject characteristics. For example, in the Los Angeles survey, another person was present in 36% of the interviews with Anglos, in 47% of the interviews with African Americans, and in 59% of the interviews with Hispanics. However, there is no consistent evidence that respondents change their answers because of the presence of another person. Analysis of this problem with the Los Angeles study found very little difference in reports of mental illness symptoms between respondents who were alone and those who were in the presence of others.

Maximizing Response to Interviews

Even if the right balance has been struck between maintaining control over interviews and achieving good rapport with respondents, in-person interviews can still have a problem. Because of the difficulty of catching all the members of a sample, response rates may suffer. Exhibit 8.9 displays the breakdown of nonrespondents to the 1990 GSS. Of the total original sample of 2,165, only 86% (1,857) were determined to be valid selections of dwelling units with potentially eligible respondents. Among these potentially eligible respondents, the

Exhibit 8.9   Reasons for Nonresponse in Personal Interviews (1990 General Social Survey)

Of 1,857 units in the sample . . .

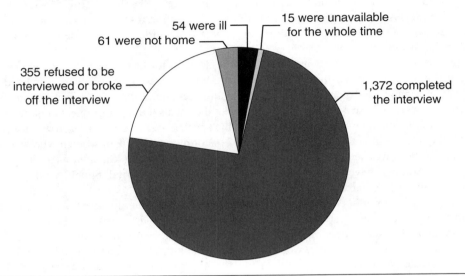

54 were ill
61 were not home
355 refused to be interviewed or broke off the interview
15 were unavailable for the whole time
1,372 completed the interview

Source: Data from Davis & Smith, 1992, p. 54

response rate was 74%. The GSS is a well-designed survey using carefully trained and supervised interviewers, so this response rate indicates the difficulty of securing respondents from a sample of the general population even when everything is done "by the book."

Several factors affect the response rate in interview studies. Contact rates tend to be lower in central cities, in part because of difficulties in finding people at home and gaining access to high-rise apartments and in part because of interviewer reluctance to visit some areas at night, when people are more likely to be home (Fowler, 1988, pp. 45–60). On the other hand, households with young children or elderly adults tend to be easier to contact, whereas single-person households are more difficult to reach (Groves & Couper, 1998, pp. 119–154).

Refusal rates vary with some respondent characteristics. People with less education participate somewhat less in surveys of political issues. Less education is also associated with higher rates of *don't know* responses (Groves, 1989). High-income people tend to participate less in surveys about income and economic behavior (perhaps because they are suspicious about why others want to know about their situation). Unusual strains and disillusionment in a society can also undermine the general credibility of research efforts and the ability of interviewers to achieve an acceptable response rate. These problems can be lessened with an advance letter introducing the survey project and by multiple contact attempts throughout the day and evening, but they cannot entirely be avoided (Fowler, 1988, pp. 52–53; Groves & Couper, 1998).

Electronic Surveys

The widespread use of personal computers and the growth of the Internet have created new possibilities for survey research. In 1999, 43% of American households were connected to the Internet, and another 22% had personal computers without Internet connections (Nie & Erbring, 2000). These percentages are growing rapidly; it is not unreasonable to think that use of the Internet will soon become comparable to the use of telephones. Already, some credible surveys have been conducted with the Internet (National Geographic Society, 2000; Nie & Erbring, 2000). As the proportion of the population that is connected increases, the Internet will become the preferred medium for survey research on many topics.

Electronic surveys can be prepared in two ways (Dillman, 2000, pp. 352–354). **E-mail surveys** can be sent as messages to respondent e-mail addresses. Respondents then mark their answers in the message and send them back to the researcher. This approach is easy for researchers to develop and for respondents to use. However, this approach is cumbersome for surveys that are more than four or five pages in length. By contrast, **Web surveys** are designed on a server controlled by the researcher; respondents are then asked to visit the Web site and respond to the Web questionnaire by checking answers. This approach requires more programming by the researcher and in many cases requires more skill on the part of the respondent. However, Web surveys can be quite long, with questions that are inapplicable to a given respondent hidden from them so that the survey may actually seem much shorter than it is.

Web surveys are becoming the more popular form of Internet survey because they are so flexible (see Exhibit 8.10). The design of the questionnaire can use many types of graphic and typographic features. Respondents can view definitions of words or instructions for answering questions by clicking on linked terms. Lengthy sets of response choices can be presented with pull-down menus. Pictures and audio segments can be added when they are useful. Because answers are recorded directly in the researcher's database, data entry errors are almost eliminated, and results can be reported quickly.

The most important drawback to either Internet survey approach is the large fraction of households that are not yet connected to the Internet. For special populations with high rates of Internet use, however, the technology makes possible fast and effective surveys. Another problem researchers must try their best to avoid is creating survey formats that are so complicated that some computers cannot read them or would display them in a way that differs from what the researcher intended. Access to a Web survey must be limited to sample members, perhaps by requiring use of a personal identification number (PIN) (Dillman, 2000, pp. 353–401).

Computerized **interactive voice response** (IVR) systems already allow the ease of Internet surveys to be achieved with a telephone-based system. In IVR surveys, respondents receive automated calls and answer questions by pressing numbers on their touch-tone phones or speaking numbers that are interpreted by computerized voice recognition software. These surveys can also record verbal responses to open-ended questions for later transcription. Although they present some difficulties when many answer choices must be used or skip patterns must be followed, IVR surveys have been used successfully with short questionnaires and when respondents are highly motivated to participate (Dillman, 2000, pp. 402–411). When these conditions are not met, potential respondents may be put off by the impersonal nature of this computer-driven approach.

Exhibit 8.10   SURVEY.NET–Year 2000 Presidential Election Survey

Your source for information, opinions & demographics from the Net Community!

SURVEY.NET ™

Year 2000 Presidential Election Survey

Take the year 2000 presidential election survey!

1. **What is your age?**
   No Answer ⇕

2. **Your Sex:**
   No Answer ⇕

3. **Your highest level of education completed:**
   No Answer ⇕

4. **Your political affiliation:**
   No Answer ⇕

5. **Who did you vote for in 1996?**
   No Answer ⇕

6. **Even though not all of these candidates are necessarily running, if the presidential election were held today, who would you vote for?**
   No Answer ⇕

7. **Of the following TWO potential presidential candidates, who would you vote for?**
   No Answer ⇕

8. **Of the following presidential candidates, who would you vote for?**
   No Answer ⇕

9. **Do you consider yourself...**
   No Answer ⇕

(Continued)

Exhibit 8.10 (Continued)

10. What political concepts do you agree with? *(check all that apply)*

☐ - We need less government regulation in general
☐ - We need more responsible government regulation
☐ - States should have more responsibility than the Federal Gov.

☐ - The government should NOT mandate moral standards
☐ - The government SHOULD mandate moral standards

☐ - Tax breaks are more important than reducing the deficit
☐ - Reducing the deficit is more important than tax breaks

☐ - Unions are destroying American productivity
☐ - Unions protect the worker

☐ - The economy is more important than the environment
☐ - The environment is more important than the economy

11. In your opinion, what is the worst problem with our society?
    `No Answer ⬍`

12. Of those items listed, what should be our next President's highest priority?
    `No Answer ⬍`

13. Without turning this into a partisan/rhetorical argument, who do you want to see for president in 2000 and why? (*Limit this to one or two sentences*)

Thanks very much for participating in the survey!

To submit your survey choices, select:
`SUBMIT SURVEY`

or `Reset survey settings`

You can view the latest survey results after you submit your answers.

We hope you will also participate in other surveys online as well. Please note that you should only complete each survey <u>once</u>.

Source: www.survey.net.

Mixed-Mode Surveys

Survey researchers increasingly are combining different survey designs. **Mixed-mode surveys** allow the strengths of one survey design to compensate for the weaknesses of another and can maximize the likelihood of securing data from different types of respondents. For example, a survey may be sent electronically to sample members who have e-mail addresses and mailed to those who don't. Alternatively, nonrespondents in a mailed survey may be interviewed in person or over the phone. As noted previously, an interviewer may use a self-administered questionnaire to present sensitive questions to a respondent.

Mixing survey designs in this way makes it possible that respondents will give different answers to different questions because of the mode in which they are asked, rather than because they actually have different opinions. However, use of what Dillman (2000, pp. 232–240) calls *unimode design* reduces this possibility substantially. A unimode design uses questions and response choices that are least likely to yield different answers according to the survey mode that is used. Unimode design principles include use of the same question structures, response choices, and skip instructions across modes, as well as using a small number of response choices for each question.

A Comparison of Survey Designs

Which survey design should be used when? Group-administered surveys are similar in most respects to mailed surveys, except that they require the unusual circumstance of having access to the sample in a group setting. We therefore don't need to consider this survey design by itself; what applies to mailed surveys applies to group-administered survey designs, with the exception of sampling issues. The features of mixed-mode surveys depend on the survey types that are being combined. Thus, we can focus our comparison on the four survey designs that involve the use of a questionnaire with individuals sampled from a larger population: mailed surveys, phone surveys, in-person surveys, and electronic surveys. Exhibit 8.11 summarizes the strong and weak points of each design.

The most important consideration in comparing the advantages and disadvantages of the four methods is the likely response rate they will generate. Because of the great weakness of mailed surveys in this respect, they must be considered the least preferred survey design from a sampling standpoint. However, researchers may still prefer a mailed survey when they have to reach a widely dispersed population and don't have enough financial resources to hire and train an interview staff or to contract with a survey organization that already has an interview staff available in many locations.

Contracting with an established survey research organization for a phone survey is often the best alternative to a mailed survey. The persistent follow-up attempts that are necessary to secure an adequate response rate are much easier over the phone than in person. But the process is not simple:

> Working phone numbers in the sample are called up to 10 times at different times of the day and on different days of the week before the number is recorded as a noncontact. To facilitate contact with households and individuals, telephoning is done in the evening during the week, and during the day over weekends. A final disposition is obtained and recorded for each sample telephone number, i.e., whether an interview, refusal,

Exhibit 8.11   Advantages and Disadvantages of the Four Survey Designs

Characteristics of Design	Mail Survey	Phone Survey	In-person Survey	Electronic Survey
Representative sample				
Opportunity for inclusion is known				
For completely listed populations	High	High	High	Medium
For incompletely listed populations	Medium	Medium	High	Low
Selection within sampling units is controlled	Medium	High	High	Low
(e.g., specific family members must respond)				
Respondents are likely to be located				
If samples are heterogeneous	Medium	High	High	Low
If samples are homogeneous and	High	High	High	High
specialized				
Questionnaire construction and question design				
Allowable length of questionnaire	Medium	Medium	High	Medium
Ability to include				
Complex questions	Medium	Low	High	High
Open questions	Low	High	High	Medium
Screening questions	Low	High	High	High
Tedious, boring questions	Low	High	High	Low
Ability to control question sequence	Low	High	High	High
Ability to ensure questionnaire	Medium	High	High	Low
completion				
Distortion of answers				
Odds of avoiding social desirability bias	High	Medium	Low	High
Odds of avoiding interviewer distortion	High	Medium	Low	High
Odds of avoiding contamination by others	Medium	High	Medium	Medium
Administrative goals				
Odds of meeting personnel requirements	High	High	Low	Medium
Odds of implementing quickly	Low	High	Low	High
Odds of keeping costs low	High	Medium	Low	High

Source: Adapted from Dillman, 1978, pp. 74–75. Copyright © 1978. Reprinted with permission of John Wiley and Sons, Inc.

noncontact, nonworking number, or other disposition. "Control" reports are issued weekly showing progress of the work through various stages of data collection. (J. E. Blair, personal communication to C. E. Ross, April 10, 1989)

In-person surveys are clearly preferable in terms of the possible length and complexity of the questionnaire itself, as well as the researcher's ability to monitor conditions while the questionnaire is being completed. Mailed surveys often are preferable for asking sensitive questions, although this problem can be lessened in an interview by giving respondents a separate sheet to fill out on their own. Although interviewers may themselves distort results, either by changing the wording of questions or failing to record answers properly, this problem can be lessened by careful training, monitoring, and tape-recording the answers.

A phone survey limits the length and complexity of the questionnaire but offers the possibility of very carefully monitoring interviewers (Dillman, 1978; Fowler, 1988, pp. 61–73):

> Supervisors in [one organization's] Telephone Centers work closely with the interviewers, monitor their work, and maintain records of their performance in relation to the time schedule, the quality of their work, and help detect and correct any mistakes in completed interviews prior to data reduction and processing. (J. E. Blair, personal communication to C. E. Ross, April 10, 1989)

The advantages and disadvantages of electronic surveys must be weighed in light of the capabilities at the time that the survey is to be conducted. At this time, too many people lack Internet connections for general use of Internet surveying, and too many people who have computers lack adequate computer capacity for displaying complex Web pages.

These various points about the different survey designs lead to two general conclusions. First, in-person interviews are the strongest design and generally preferable when sufficient resources and a trained interview staff are available; telephone surveys have many of the advantages of in-person interviews at much less cost, but response rates are an increasing problem. Second, a decision about the best survey design for any particular study must take into account the unique features and goals of the study.

SECONDARY DATA SURVEYS

Secondary data (most often the term is used in reference to quantitative data) are data that the researcher did not collect to answer the research question of interest. Instead, secondary data are obtained from publicly available data archives, from another researcher, or even from one's own previous projects, which were designed to address some other research question.

Analysis of secondary data presents several challenges, ranging from uncertainty about the methods of data collection to the lack of maximum fit between the concepts that the primary study measured and each of the concepts that are the focus of the current investigation. Responsible use of secondary data requires a good understanding of the primary data source. The researcher should be able to answer the following questions (most adapted from Riedel, 2000, pp. 55–69, and Stewart, 1984, pp. 23–30):

1. What were the agency's goals in collecting the data? If the primary data were obtained in a research project, what were the project's purposes?

2. Who was responsible for data collection, and what were their qualifications? Are they available to answer questions about the data? Each step in the data collection process should be charted and the personnel involved identified.

3. What data were collected, and what were they intended to measure?

4. When was the information collected?

5. What methods were used for data collection? Copies of the forms used for data collection should be obtained and the way in which these data are processed by the agency/agencies should be reviewed.

6. How is the information organized (by date, event, etc.)? Are identifiers used to distinguish the different types of data available on the same case? In what form are the data available (computer tapes, disks, paper files)? Answers to these questions can have a major bearing on the work that will be needed to carry out the study.

7. How consistent are the data with data available from other sources?

8. What is known about the success of the data collection effort? How are missing data treated and indicated? What kind of documentation is available?

Answering these questions helps to ensure that the researcher is familiar with the data he or she will analyze and can help to identify any problems with it.

Data quality is always a concern with secondary data, even when the data are collected by an official government agency. Census counts can be distorted by incorrect answers to census questions as well as by inadequate coverage of the entire population. For example, the percentage of the U. S. population not counted in the U. S. Census appears to have declined since 1880 from 7% to 1%, but undercounting continues to be more common among poorer urban dwellers and recent immigrants (King & Magnuson, 1995). The relatively successful 2000 U. S. Census reduced undercounting (Forero, 2000b) but still suffered from accusations of shoddy data-collection procedures in some areas (Forero, 2000a).

Researchers who rely on secondary data analysis inevitably make trade-offs between their ability to use a particular data set and the specific hypotheses they can test. If a concept that is critical to a hypothesis was not measured adequately in a secondary data source, the study may have to be abandoned until a more adequate source of data can be found. Alternatively, hypotheses or even the research question itself may be modified to match the analytic possibilities presented by the available data (Riedel, 2000, p. 53).

Many sources of data and surveys relevant to social work are available on the Internet. The U. S. Bureau of the Census Web site (www.census.gov) provides access to a wide variety of surveys in addition to the decennial Census. Some of these data sets include: *Current Population Survey* (monthly survey of 72,000 households looking at employment and economic status), *National Health Interview Survey* (which looks at acute and chronic illness and health-related services), *National Long Term-Care Survey* (data on elderly individuals including demographic characteristics and their ability to perform activities of daily living), and the *Survey of Income and Program Participation* (a series of panel studies of households providing data about source and amount of income, labor force participation, program participation, and program eligibility data) (U. S. Bureau of the Census, 2003). The ICPSR at the University of Michigan (www.icpsr.umich.edu) provides access to a large number of survey data sets that are of interest to social work researchers and students. In addition to the many surveys on economics, business, politics, and social relations, there are special archives related to health, mental health, aging, criminal justice, substance abuse, and child care. These and other Web sites of interest are described in Appendix F.

ETHICAL ISSUES IN SURVEY RESEARCH

Survey research usually poses fewer ethical dilemmas than do experimental or field research designs. Potential respondents to a survey can easily decline to participate, and a cover letter or introductory statement that identifies the sponsors of and motivations for the survey gives them the information required to make this decision. The methods of data collection are quite obvious in a survey, so little is concealed from the respondents. Only in group-administered survey designs might the respondents be, in effect, a captive audience (probably of students or employees), and so special attention is required to ensure that participation is truly voluntary. (Those who do not wish to participate may be told they can just hand in a blank form.)

Confidentiality is most often the primary focus of ethical concern in survey research. Many surveys include some essential questions that might in some way prove damaging to the subjects if their answers were disclosed. To prevent any possibility of harm to subjects due to disclosure of such information, it is critical to preserve subject confidentiality. Nobody but research personnel should have access to information that could be used to link respondents to their responses, and even that access should be limited to what is necessary for specific research purposes. Only numbers should be used to identify respondents on their questionnaires, and the researcher should keep the names that correspond to these numbers in a safe, private location, unavailable to staff and others who might otherwise come across them. Follow-up mailings or contact attempts that require linking the ID numbers with names and addresses should be carried out by trustworthy assistants under close supervision. If an electronic survey is used, encryption technology should be used to make information provided over the Internet secure from unauthorized people.

Not many surveys can provide true **anonymity,** so that no identifying information is ever recorded to link respondents with their responses. The main problem with anonymous surveys is that they preclude follow-up attempts to encourage participation by initial nonrespondents, and they prevent panel designs, which measure change through repeated surveys of the same individuals. In-person surveys rarely can be anonymous because an interviewer must in almost all cases know the name and address of the interviewee. However, phone surveys that are meant only to sample opinion at one point in time, as in political polls, can safely be completely anonymous. When no future follow-up is desired, group-administered surveys also can be anonymous. To provide anonymity in a mail survey, the researcher should omit identifying codes from the questionnaire but could include a self-addressed, stamped postcard so the respondent can notify the researcher that the questionnaire has been returned without creating any linkage to the questionnaire itself (Mangione, 1995, p. 69).

CONCLUSION

Survey research is an exceptionally efficient and productive method for investigating a wide array of social research questions. In six months, Catherine Ross's (1990) survey produced a unique, comprehensive data set on work, family, and health issues. These data allowed Ross and her coauthors to investigate the relations among sex stratification, health lifestyle, and perceived health (Ross & Bird, 1994); between education and health (Ross & Wu, 1995); between physical impairment and income (Mirowsky & Hu, 1996); among gender, parenthood, and anger (Ross & Van Willigen, 1996); and among age, the sense of control, and health

(Mirowsky, 1995; Mirowsky & Ross, 1992, 1999; Ross & Wu, 1996). As a result, we know much more about how social structure influences health, what might be done to mitigate the negative health consequences of aging and low income, and where social theories of health need to be improved.

In addition to the potential benefits for social science, considerations of time and expense frequently make a survey the preferred data collection method. One or more of the six survey designs reviewed in this chapter (including mixed-mode) can be applied to almost any research question. It is no wonder that surveys have become the most popular research method in sociology and that they frequently inform discussion and planning about important social and political questions. As use of the Internet increases, survey research should become even more efficient and popular.

The relative ease of conducting at least some types of survey research leads many people to imagine that no particular training or systematic procedures are required. Nothing could be further from the truth. But as a result of this widespread misconception, you will encounter a great many nearly worthless survey results. You must be prepared to examine carefully the procedures used in any survey before accepting its findings as credible. If you decide to conduct a survey, you must be prepared to invest the time and effort required by proper procedures.

KEY TERMS

Acquiescence (agreement) bias
Anonymity
Behavior coding
Closed-ended question
Cognitive interview
Computer-assisted personal interviewing
Computer-assisted telephone interview
Confidentiality
Context effect
Contingency question
Cover letter
Double negatives
Double-barreled question
Electronic surveys
E-mail surveys
Errors of nonobservation
Errors of observation
Fence-sitter
Filter question
Fixed-choice question
Floater

Group-administered survey
Idiosyncratic variation
In-person interview
Interactive voice response (IVR)
Interpretative question
Interview schedule
Mailed survey
Matrix questions
Mixed-mode surveys
Omnibus survey
Open-ended question
Phone survey
Questionnaire
Response set
Secondary data
Skip pattern
Social desirability
Split-ballot design
Survey research
Web survey

HIGHLIGHTS

- Surveys are the most popular form of social research because of their versatility, efficiency, and generalizability. Many survey data sets, like the National Longitudinal Survey of Youth, Survey of Income and Program Participation, or the General Social Survey, are available for social work researchers and students.

- Survey designs must minimize the risk of errors of observation (measurement error) and errors of nonobservation (errors due to inadequate coverage, sampling error, and nonresponse). The likelihood of both types of error varies with the survey goals.
- Social exchange theory asserts that behavior is motivated by the return the individual expects for the behavior. Survey designs must maximize the social rewards, minimize the costs for participating, and establish trust that the rewards will outweigh the costs.
- A survey questionnaire or interview schedule should be designed as an integrated whole, with each question and section serving some clear purpose and complementing the others.
- Questions must be worded carefully to avoid confusing respondents, encouraging a less-than-honest response, or triggering biases. Question wording should have the same meaning to all respondents regardless of race, ethnicity, gender, age, or class.
- Inclusion of *Don't know* choices and neutral responses may help, but the presence of such options also affects the distribution of answers. Open-ended questions can be used to determine the meaning that respondents attach to their answers. Answers to any survey question may be affected by the questions that precede it in a questionnaire or interview schedule.
- Questions can be tested and improved through review by experts, focus group discussions, cognitive interviews, behavior coding, and pilot testing. Every questionnaire and interview schedule should be pretested on a small sample that is like the sample to be surveyed.
- Interpretive questions should be used in questionnaires to help clarify the meaning of responses to critical questions.
- The cover letter for a mailed questionnaire should be credible, personalized, interesting, and responsible.
- Response rates in mailed surveys are typically well below 70% unless multiple mailings are made to nonrespondents and the questionnaire and cover letter are attractive, interesting, and carefully planned. Response rates for group-administered surveys are usually much higher.
- Phone interviews using random digit dialing allow fast turnaround and efficient sampling. Multiple callbacks are often required, and the rate of nonresponse to phone interviews is rising. Phone interviews should be limited in length to about 30 to 45 minutes.
- In-person interviews have several advantages over other types of surveys: They allow longer and more complex interview schedules, monitoring of the conditions when the questions are answered, probing for respondents' understanding of the questions, and high response rates. However, the interviewer must balance the need to establish rapport with the respondent with the importance of maintaining control over the delivery of the interview questions.
- Electronic surveys may be e-mailed or posted on the Web. Interactive voice-response systems using the telephone are another option. At this time, use of the Internet is not sufficiently widespread to allow e-mail or Web surveys of the general population, but these approaches can be fast and efficient for populations with high rates of computer use.
- Mixed-mode surveys allow the strengths of one survey design to compensate for the weaknesses of another. However, questions and procedures must be designed carefully using unimode design principles to reduce the possibility that responses to the same question will vary as a result of the mode of delivery.
- The decision to use a particular survey design must take into account the unique features and goals of the study. In general, in-person interviews are the strongest but most expensive survey design.
- Most survey research poses few ethical problems because respondents are able to decline to participate—an option that should be stated clearly in the cover letter or introductory statement. Special care must be taken when questionnaires are administered in group settings (to captive audiences) and when sensitive personal questions are to be asked; subject confidentiality should always be preserved.

DISCUSSION QUESTIONS

1. Why is survey research popular among social work researchers and social service agencies? Even though popular, survey research is at risk for error. What are the two potential errors common in survey research? How can the researcher minimize the risk of error?

2. What does the researcher need to consider when constructing a survey instrument? What are the advantages of fixed-choice questions? What are the disadvantages? How can the researcher achieve clarity in constructing questions?

3. Discuss the relative advantages and disadvantages of using a preexisting instrument in your survey. What are the merits of pretesting your survey instrument? What are the merits of using interpretive questions?

4. Consider how you could design a split-ballot experiment to determine the effect of phrasing a question or its response choices in different ways. Check recent issues of the local newspaper for a question used in a survey of attitudes about some social policy. Propose some hypothesis about how the wording of the question or its response choices might have influenced the answers people gave and devise an alternative that differs only in this respect. Distribute these questionnaires to a large class (after your instructor makes the necessary arrangements) to test your hypothesis.

5. Thinking about the primary benefits and disadvantages of each of the five basic survey designs, which would you choose if you were interested in learning more about the caregiver burden experienced by parents raising young children below the age of six? How would you try to ensure sample representativeness? What steps would you take to maximize the rate of response?

PRACTICE EXERCISES

1. Develop 10 survey questions about beliefs of social work students about the causes of urban violence. Did you use open or closed-ended questions or both? What demographic information did you query? Did you attend to attractiveness? Is the instrument user friendly?

2. After putting the survey you have developed for Question 1 away for several days, review the questions for the following: confusing phrasing, vague language, double negatives, double-barreled questions, jargon, and leading questions. Once you have revised your survey instrument, pilot it with your classmates. Ask for their critical feedback.

3. Examine an existing instrument measuring beliefs about the causes of urban violence. Would you consider using this instrument for your own research? Why or why not? How does the published instrument compare to yours? Is it measuring the same concept?

4. In Chapter 6, review the description of the experiment by Catherine Alter (1996). Propose a survey design that would test the same hypothesis but with a sample from a larger population. Your survey design can be longitudinal but should remain experimental, not quasi-experimental. Compare your survey design to the original experimental design. What are the advantages and disadvantages of your survey design in terms of causal validity? Generalizability? Measurement validity? What about versatility and efficiency?

WEB EXERCISES

1. Go to the Research Triangle Institute site at http://www.rti.org and then click on Tools and Methods, then Surveys, and then Survey Design and Development. Read about their methods for

computer-assisted interviewing (under Survey Methods) and their cognitive laboratory methods for refining questions (under Usability Testing). What does this add to the treatment of these topics in this chapter?

2. Go to the CyClone Project home page by William Sims Bainbridge at http://mysite.verizon.net/ william.bainbridge/system/cyindex.htm. Now examine the Emotions section and try converting the items into survey questions, as suggested. How well do the questions capture your own emotion? What would you add, omit, or change? Why? Now, using some of the examples listed under the heading Pride, take a shot at creating questions to measure sense of control, emulating the work of Catherine Ross. Do you think these questions could accurately measure one's sense of control? Why?

> To assist you in completing the Web exercises, please access the study site at http://www.sagepub.com/prsw where you will find the Web Exercises reproduced and suggested links for online resources.

DEVELOPING A RESEARCH PROPOSAL

These questions apply both to survey research and to data collection in group and single-subject designs.

1. How will you gather the data? What specific data collection method will you use (e.g., mail, telephone interview, self-administered)?

2. Write questions for a one-page questionnaire that relates to your proposed research question. The questions should operationalize the variables on which you are focused.

3. Conduct a pretest of the questionnaire by conducting cognitive interviews with several respondents. For example, if you have closed-ended questions, ask the respondents what they meant by each response or what came to mind when they were asked each question.

4. Polish up the organization and layout of the questionnaire, following the guidelines in the chapter.

5. List the relative advantages and disadvantages to the way you will collect the data.

6. Develop appropriate procedures for the protection of human subjects in your study. Include a cover letter directed to the appropriate population that contains relevant statements about research ethics.

Chapter 9

QUALITATIVE METHODS: OBSERVING, PARTICIPATING, LISTENING

Fundamentals of Qualitative Methods
Case Study: Making Gray Gold

Participant Observation
Choosing a Role
    Complete Observation
    Participation and Observation
    Covert Participation
Entering the Field
Developing and Maintaining
    Relationships
Sampling People and Events
Taking Notes

Managing the Personal Dimensions
Systematic Observation

Intensive Interviewing
Establishing and Maintaining a
    Partnership
Asking Questions and Recording
    Answers

Focus Groups

Ethical Issues in Qualitative Research

Conclusion

"**Y**ou have to look into a patient's eyes as much as you can, and learn to get the signals from there." This suggestion was made by a nurse explaining to future nursing home assistants how they were to deal with a dying patient. One of those future assistants, Timothy Diamond (1992, p. 17), was also a researcher intent on studying work in nursing homes. For us, the statement he recorded has a dual purpose: It exemplifies qualitative methods, in which we learn by observing as they participate in a natural setting; it also reminds us that some features of the social world are ill-suited to investigation with experiments or surveys.

In this chapter, you will learn how Tim Diamond (1992) used qualitative methods to illuminate the inside of a nursing home and the attitudes and actions of its staff. You will also see how gerontologists have used qualitative methods to make sense of other institutional settings and to understand seniors who have made recreational vehicles (RVs) their chosen way of life. Throughout the chapter, you will learn from a variety of examples that some of our greatest insights into the social processes that influence social work can result from what appear to be very ordinary activities: observing, participating, listening, and talking.

But you will also learn that qualitative research is much more than just doing what comes naturally in social situations. Qualitative researchers must observe keenly, take notes systematically, question respondents strategically, and prepare to spend more time and invest more of their whole selves than is usually necessary when doing experiments or surveys. Moreover, if we are to have any confidence in the validity of a qualitative study's conclusions, each element of its design must be reviewed as carefully as we would review the elements of an experiment, single-subject design, or survey.

The chapter begins with an overview of the major features of qualitative research, as reflected in Diamond's (1992) study of nursing homes. The next section discusses the various approaches to participant observation research, which is the most distinctive qualitative method, and it reviews the stages of research using participant observation. In the next section, we review in some detail the issues involved in intensive interviewing before briefly explaining focus groups, an increasingly popular qualitative method. The last section covers ethical issues that are of concern in any type of qualitative research project. By the chapter's end, you should appreciate the hard work required to translate "doing what comes naturally" into systematic research, be able to recognize strong and weak points in qualitative studies, and be ready to do some of it yourself.

FUNDAMENTALS OF QUALITATIVE METHODS

Qualitative methods refer to several distinctive research designs: **participant observation**, **intensive interviewing**, and **focus groups**. Participant observation and intensive interviewing are often used in the same project; focus groups combine some elements of these two approaches into a unique data-collection strategy.

Participant observation   A qualitative method for gathering data that involves developing a sustained relationship with people while they go about their normal activities.

Intensive interviewing   A qualitative method that involves open-ended, relatively unstructured questioning in which the interviewer seeks in-depth information on the interviewee's feelings, experiences, and perceptions (Lofland & Lofland, 1984, p. 12).

Focus groups   A qualitative method that involves unstructured group interviews in which the focus group leader actively encourages discussion among participants on the topics of interest.

Although these three qualitative designs differ in many respects, they share several features that distinguish them from experimental and survey research designs (Denzin & Lincoln, 1994; Maxwell, 1996; Wolcott, 1995).

Collection primarily of qualitative rather than quantitative data. Any research design may collect both qualitative and quantitative data, but qualitative methods emphasize observations about natural behavior and artifacts that capture social life as it is experienced by the participants rather than in categories predetermined by the researcher.

Exploratory research questions, with a commitment to inductive reasoning. Qualitative researchers typically begin their projects seeking not to test preformulated hypotheses but to discover what people think and how they act, and why, in some social setting. Only after many observations do qualitative researchers try to develop general principles to account for their observations.

A focus on previously unstudied processes and unanticipated phenomena. Previously unstudied attitudes and actions can't adequately be understood with a structured set of questions or within a highly controlled experiment. So qualitative methods have their greatest appeal when we need to explore new issues, investigate hard-to-study groups, or determine the meaning people give to their lives and actions. Diamond (1992, p. 4) asked, "What was life like inside, day in and day out? Who lived in nursing homes, and what did they do there?"

An orientation to social context, to the interconnections between social phenomena rather than to their discrete features. The context of concern may be a program or organization, a case, or a broader social context. For example, in a study of institutionalized elderly people, Eva Kahana, Boaz Kahana, and Kathryn P. Riley (1988), reported several ways in which the institutional context influenced responses to interview questions:

> Many contextual issues affect the responses residents living in institutions give to research questions. . . . When staff members coax or pressure residents to participate, biased responses may be evoked. Similarly, staff members who participate in research only to please their superiors or to take a break from unpleasant chores are not very likely to invest themselves in research tasks such as rating residents or environments. (p. 206)

A focus on human subjectivity, on the meanings that participants attach to events and that people give to their lives. "Through life stories, people 'account for their lives.'. . . The themes people create are the means by which they interpret and evaluate their life experiences and attempt to integrate these experiences to form a self-concept" (Kaufman, 1986, pp. 24–25).

Use of idiographic rather than nomothetic causal explanation. With its focus on particular actors and situations and the processes that connect them, qualitative research tends to identify causes as particular events embedded within an unfolding, interconnected action sequence (Maxwell, 1996, pp. 20–21). The language of variables and hypotheses appears only rarely in the qualitative literature.

Reflexive research design, in which the design develops as the research progresses:

> Each component of the design may need to be reconsidered or modified in response to new developments or to changes in some other component. . . . The activities of collecting and analyzing data, developing and modifying theory, elaborating or refocusing the research

questions, and identifying and eliminating validity threats are usually all going on more or less simultaneously, each influencing all of the others. (Maxwell, 1996, pp. 2–3)

J. Neil Henderson (1994, pp. 41–42) explains how a qualitative research design changed in a study of the involvement of ethnic minority elders in support groups. In the original plan, support group meetings were to be held at one African American church, after publicity in other churches. After this approach failed to generate any participation, the researchers learned that the plan violated very strong implicit "congregational loyalty boundaries." When the meetings were instead held in a neutral setting unaffiliated with any of the churches (a local public library), many community members attended.

Sensitivity to the subjective role of the researcher. Little pretense is made of achieving an objective perspective on social phenomena:

> I was embarrassed and I did not know what to say. I had not bargained for this kind of experience when my research started. As I sat by his bed, my mind would be a confusing welter of thoughts and emotions. Sometimes I experienced anger. "Damn it. You can't die now. I haven't finished my research." Immediately I would be overtaken by feelings of self revulsion. Did our friendship mean only this? . . . Thus would I engage in the conflict between my human sensibilities and my scholarly purpose. (Rowles, 1978, p. 19)

William Miller and Benjamin Crabtree (1999, p. 16) capture the entire process of qualitative research in a simple diagram (Exhibit 9.1). In this diagram, qualitative research begins with the qualitative researcher reflecting on the setting and the researcher's relation to it and interpretations of it. The researcher then describes the goals and means for the research. This description is followed by *sampling* and *collecting* data, *describing* the data and *organizing* that data. Thus, the *gathering process* and the *analysis process* proceed together, with repeated description and analysis of data as it is collected. As the data are organized, *connections* are identified between different data segments and efforts are made to *corroborate* the credibility of these connections. This *interpretive process* begins to emerge in a written account that represents what has been done and how the data have been interpreted. Each of these steps in the research process informs the others and is repeated throughout the research process.

Case Study: *Making Gray Gold*

You can get a better feel for qualitative methods by reading the following excerpts from Timothy Diamond's (1992) book about nursing homes, *Making Gray Gold*, and reasoning inductively from his observations. See if you can induce from these particulars some of the general features of field research. Ask yourself: What was the research question? How were the issues of generalizability, measurement, and causation approached? How did social factors influence the research?

Let's begin near the beginning of Diamond's (1992) account:

> First I went to school for six months in 1982, two evenings a week and all day Saturdays, to obtain the certificate the state required [to work in a nursing home]. Then, after weeks

Exhibit 9.1   Qualitative Research Process

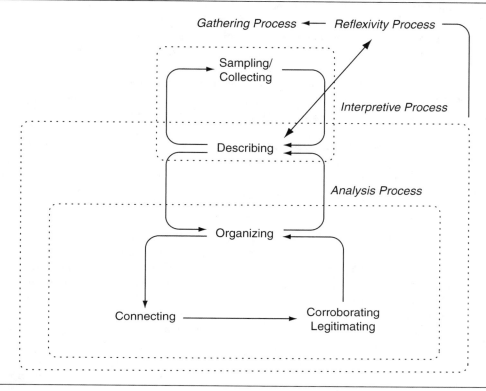

Source: Adapted from Miller & Crabtree, 1999, p. 16. Copyright © 1999. Reprinted with permission from Sage Publications, Inc.

of searching for jobs, I worked in three different nursing homes in Chicago for periods of three to four months each. (p. 5)

As this excerpt indicates, Diamond's research involved becoming a participant in the social setting that was the object of his study. Note how long Diamond spent gathering data: more than a year of full-time work.

Diamond (1992) also describes for us the development of his research questions. A medical sociologist, his curiosity about health care for older people was piqued when he happened to become acquainted with Ina Williams and Aileen Crawford in a coffee shop across the street from the nursing home where they worked as assistants. He began to wonder,

How does the work of caretaking become defined and get reproduced day in and day out as a business? . . . How, in other words, does the everyday world of Ina and Aileen and their co-workers, and that of the people they tend, get turned into a system in which gray can be written about in financial journals as producing gold, a classic metaphor for money? What is the process of making gray gold? (p. 5)

With these exploratory research questions in mind, Diamond (1992) explains why he chose participant observation as his research method:

> I wanted to collect stories and to experience situations like those Ina and Aileen had begun to describe. I decided that . . . I would go inside to experience the work myself. (p. 5)

The choice of participant observation precluded random sampling of cases, but Diamond did not ignore the need to generalize his findings. He went to considerable lengths to include three nursing homes that would represent a range of caregiving arrangements:

> These [nursing] homes were situated in widely different neighborhoods of the city. In one of them residents paid for their own care, often with initial help from Medicare. In the other two, most of the residents were supported by Medicaid . . . In the course of writing, I visited many homes across the United States to validate my observations and to update them in instances where regulatory changes had been instituted. (p. 6)

The data in Diamond's (1992) study were notes on the activities of the people as he observed and interacted with them. He did not use structured questionnaires and other formal data collection instruments, so his data are primarily qualitative rather than quantitative.

As for his method, it was inductive. First, he gathered data. Then, as data collection continued, Diamond (1992) figured out how to interpret the data—how to make sense of the social situations he was studying. His analytic categories ultimately came not from social theory but from the categories by which people themselves described one another and made sense of their social world. These categories seem to have broad applicability, suggesting the generalizability of the researcher's findings. For instance, one of the teachers Diamond encountered while earning his certificate passed along a unique way of making sense of the caregiver's role in a nursing home:

> The tensions generated by the introductory lecture and . . . ideas of career professionalism were reflected in our conversations as we waited for the second class to get under way. Yet within the next half hour they seemed to dissolve. Mrs. Bonderoid, our teacher, saw to that. A registered nurse and nurse practitioner, an African American woman of about fifty, she must have understood a lot about classroom jitters and about who was sitting in front of her as well. "What this is going to take," she instructed, "is a lot of mother's wit." "Mother's wit," she said, not "mother wit," which connotes native intelligence irrespective of gender. She was talking about maternal feelings and skills. (p. 17)

Diamond (1992) did develop general conclusions about social life from his research. In the nursing home, he argues,

> There were two kinds of narratives on caregiving: one formal, written, and shared by the professionals and administrators; another submerged, unwritten, and shared by the people who lived and worked on the floors. (p. 215)

To summarize, Diamond's (1992) research began with an exploratory question (to find out what was going on) and proceeded inductively throughout, developing general concepts to make sense of specific observations. Although Diamond, a white man, was something of an outsider in a setting dominated by women of color, he was able to share many participants' experiences and perspectives. His in-depth descriptions and idiographic connections of sequences of events enabled him to construct plausible explanations about what seemed to be a typical group. He thus successfully used field research to explore human experiences in depth, carefully analyzing the social contexts in which they occur.

PARTICIPANT OBSERVATION

Diamond (1992) carried out his study through participant observation, termed *fieldwork* in anthropology. It is a method in which natural social processes are studied as they happen (in the field, rather than in the laboratory) and left relatively undisturbed. It is the seminal field research method—a means of seeing the social world as the research subjects see it, in its totality, and of understanding subjects' interpretations of that world (Wolcott, 1995, p. 66). By observing people and interacting with them in the course of their normal activities, participant observers seek to avoid the artificiality of experimental designs and the unnatural structured questioning of survey research (Koegel, 1987, p. 8). This method encourages consideration of the context in which social interaction occurs, of the complex and interconnected nature of social relations, and of the sequencing of events (Bogdewic, 1999, p. 49).

The term *participant observer* actually represents a continuum of roles (see Exhibit 9.2), ranging from being a complete observer, who does not participate in group activities and is publicly defined as a researcher, to being a covert participant, who acts just like other group members and does not disclose his or her research role. Many field researchers develop a role between these extremes, publicly acknowledging being a researcher but nonetheless participating in group activities. In some settings, it also is possible to observe covertly, without acknowledging being a researcher or participating.

Choosing a Role

The first concern of all participant observers is to decide what balance to strike between observing and participating and whether to reveal their role as a researcher. These decisions must take into account the specifics of the social situation being studied, the researcher's own background and personality, the larger sociopolitical context, and ethical concerns. Which balance of participating and observing is most appropriate also changes during most projects, often many times. Also, the researcher's ability to maintain either a covert or an overt role will many times be challenged.

Complete Observation

In **complete observation,** researchers try to see things as they happen, without actively participating in these events. Although there is no fixed formula to guide the observational process, observers try to identify the who, what, when, where, why, and how of activities in the setting. Their observations will usually become more focused over time, as the observer develops a sense of the important categories of people and activities and gradually develops a theory that accounts for what is observed (Bogdewic, 1999, pp. 54–56).

Exhibit 9.2   The Observational Continuum

To study a political activist group...

You could take the role of complete observer:

You could take the role of participant and observer:

You could take the role of covert participant:

Of course, the researcher's very presence as an observer alters the social situation being observed. This is the problem of **reactive effects**. It is not "natural" in most social situations for an observer—someone who will record her or his observations for research and publication purposes—to be present, so individuals may alter their behavior. In social settings involving many people, in which observing while standing or sitting does not attract attention, the complete observer is unlikely to have much effect on social processes. On the other hand, when the social setting involves few people and observing is unlike the usual activities in the setting, or when the observer differs in obvious respects from the participants, the complete observer is more likely to have an impact. For example, some Alzheimer's day care staff members who were aware of Karen Lyman's (1994) note-taking staged interactions or monitored their speech "for the record":

> Some workers displayed frustration over the heads of clients (eyes rolling, sighs) or made humorous comments to clients about their personal quirks, clearly intended for me as the observer. . . . At one site a program aide caught himself midsentence: "They're all cra— . . ." (p. 166)

Participation and Observation

Most field researchers adopt a role that involves some active participation in the setting. Usually, they inform at least some group members of their research interests, but then they participate in enough group activities to develop rapport with members and to gain a direct sense of what group members experience. This is not an easy balancing act, but

> the key to participant observation as a fieldwork strategy is to take seriously the challenge it poses to participate more, and to play the role of the aloof observer less. Do not think of yourself as someone who needs to wear a white lab coat and carry a clipboard to learn about how humans go about their everyday lives. (Wolcott, 1995, p. 100)

Karen Lyman (1994) provides a good example of the rapport-building function of participation in her study of staff and patients in Alzheimer's day care centers:

> My role was to become a part of these social worlds as much as possible, to overcome the status of outsider. I helped with the work of day care: serving and cleaning up after meals, walking with "agitated" people, directing confused people to a destination. I worked "on the floor" to assist one short-staffed center during a flu epidemic in which several clients died, including a man with whom I had danced the previous week. (p. 165)

As a result of her involvement, all eight program directors and their staff were very cooperative during Lyman's research, even offering unsolicited and candid interviews (p. 168).

Participating and observing have two clear ethical advantages as well. Because group members know the researcher's real role in the group, they can choose to keep some information or attitudes hidden. By the same token, the researcher can decline to participate in unethical or dangerous activities without fear of exposing his or her identity.

Most field researchers who opt for disclosure get the feeling that after they have become known and at least somewhat trusted figures in the group, their presence does not have any palpable effect on members' actions. The major influences on individual actions and attitudes are past experiences, personality, group structure, and so on, so the argument goes, and these continue to exert their influence even when an outside observer is present. The participant observer can presumably be ethical about identity disclosure and still observe the natural social world. Of course, the argument is less persuasive when the behavior to be observed is illegal or stigmatized, so that participants have reason to fear the consequences of disclosure to any outsider.

In practice, it can be difficult to maintain a fully open research role, even in a setting without these special characteristics:

> During and after the fieldwork the first question many people asked was "Did you tell them?" . . . I had initially hoped to disclose at every phase of the project my dual objective of working as a nursing assistant and writing about these experiences. In some instances it was possible to disclose this dual purpose, in others it was not. I told many nursing assistants and people who lived in the homes that I was both working and investigating. I told some of my nursing supervisors and some administrators. . . . The short answer is that as the study proceeded it was forced increasingly to become a piece of undercover research. (Diamond, 1992, pp. 7–8)

Even when researchers maintain a public identity as researchers, ethical dilemmas arising from participation in the lives of their research subjects do not go away. In fact, social workers conducting qualitative research may obtain information that suggests some clinical intervention may be warranted to improve the life or health of a research subject, and then, they must decide whether taking action would be consistent with research guidelines. When Jeanie Kayser-Jones and Barbara A. Koenig (1994, pp. 21–23) found that one of their elderly demented nursing home patients seemed to be dying from an untreated illness, they encouraged a nurse to override the wishes of the family to avoid any "heroic" measures and convinced the doctor on call to begin intravenous fluids. Kathleen MacPherson (1988) found that she had to side with the majority of leaders of a menopause collective she was studying in their decision to ask another leader to leave:

> There was no neutral third side. . . . Because I had assumed a researcher role while fully participating in the group under study, I was compelled to take sides in disagreements as they arose. (p. 192)

Such actions, whether taken to improve the health of some research subjects or to remedy problems in group process, inherently create ethical dilemmas and heighten the potential for strains with other participants in the setting.

Experienced participant observers try to lessen some of the problems of identity disclosure by evaluating both their effect on others in the setting and the effect of others on the observers, writing about these effects throughout the time they are in the field and while they analyze their data. While in the field, they nevertheless preserve some physical space and regular time when they can concentrate on their research, and they schedule occasional meetings with other researchers to review the fieldwork. Participant observers modify their role as circumstances seem to require, perhaps not always disclosing their research role at casual social gatherings or group outings but being sure to inform new members of it.

Covert Participation

To lessen the potential for reactive effects and to gain entry to otherwise inaccessible settings, some field researchers have adopted the role of covert participant, keeping their research secret and trying their best to act like other participants in a social setting or group. **Covert participation** is also known as **complete participation.** Laud Humphreys (1970) served as a "watch queen" so that he could learn about men engaging in homosexual acts in a public restroom. Randall Alfred (1976) joined a group of Satanists to investigate group members and their interaction. Erving Goffman (1961) worked as a state hospital assistant while studying the treatment of psychiatric patients.

Although the role of covert participant lessens some of the reactive effects encountered by the complete observer, covert participants confront other problems:

Covert participants cannot take notes openly or use any obvious recording devices. They must write up notes based solely on memory and must do so at times when it is natural for them to be away from group members.

Covert participants cannot ask questions that will arouse suspicion. Thus, they often have trouble clarifying the meaning of other participants' attitudes or actions.

The role of covert participant is difficult to play successfully. Covert participants will not know how regular participants would act in every situation in which the researchers find themselves. Regular participants have entered the situation from different social backgrounds and with different goals from the researchers. Researchers' spontaneous reactions to every event are unlikely to be consistent with those of the regular participants (Mitchell, 1993). Suspicion that researchers are not "one of us" may then have reactive effects, obviating the value of complete participation (Erikson, 1967). In his study of the Satanists, for example, Alfred pretended to be a regular group participant until he completed his research, at which time he informed the group leader of his covert role. Rather than act surprised, the leader told Alfred that he had long considered Alfred to be "strange," not like the others—and we will never know for sure how Alfred's observations were affected. Even Diamond (1992), although an acknowledged researcher in the nursing home, found that simply disclosing the fact that he did not work another job to make ends meet set him apart from other nursing assistants:

> "There's one thing I learned when I came to the States," [said a Haitian nursing assistant]. "Here you can't make it on just one job." She tilted her head, looked at me curiously, then asked, "You know, Tim, there's just one thing I don't understand about you. How do you make it on just one job?" (pp. 47–48)

Covert participants need to keep up the act at all times while in the setting under study. Researchers may experience enormous psychological strain, particularly in situations where they are expected to choose sides in intragroup conflict or to participate in criminal or other acts. Of course, some covert observers may become so wrapped up in the role they are playing that they adopt not just the mannerisms but also the perspectives and goals of the regular participants—they "go native." At this point, they abandon research goals and cease to evaluate critically what they are observing.

Ethical issues have been at the forefront of debate over the strategy of covert participation. Kai Erikson (1967) argues that covert participation is by its very nature unethical and should not be allowed except in public settings. Covert researchers cannot anticipate the unintended consequences of their actions for research subjects, Erikson points out. If others suspect the researcher's identity or if the researcher contributes to, or impedes, group action, these consequences can be adverse. In addition, other social scientists are harmed when covert research is disclosed—either during the research or on its publication—because distrust of social scientists increases and access to research opportunities may decrease.

But a total ban on covert participation would "kill many a project stone dead" (Punch, 1994, p. 90). Studies of unusual religious or sexual practices and of institutional malpractice would rarely be possible. "The crux of the matter is that some deception, passive or active, enables you to get at data not obtainable by other means" (Punch, 1994, p. 91). Therefore, some field researchers argue that covert participation is legitimate in some settings. If the researcher maintains the confidentiality of others, keeps commitments to others, and does not directly lie to others, some degree of deception may be justified in exchange for the knowledge gained (Punch, 1994, p. 90).

Entering the Field

Entering the field, the setting under investigation, is a critical stage in a participant observation project because it can shape many subsequent experiences. Some background work is necessary before entering the field—at least enough to develop a clear understanding of what the research questions are likely to be and to review one's personal stance toward the people and problems likely to be encountered. With participant observation, researchers must also learn in advance how participants dress and what their typical activities are, so as to avoid being caught completely unprepared. Finding a participant who can make introductions is often critical (Rossman & Rallis, 1998, pp. 102–103), and formal permission may be needed in an organizational setting (Bogdewic, 1999, pp. 51–53). It can take weeks or even months until entry is possible.

For his study, Diamond (1992) tried to enter a nursing home twice, first without finding out about necessary qualifications:

> My first job interview. . . . The administrator of the home had agreed to see me on [the recommendation of two current assistants]. The administrator . . . probed suspiciously, "Now why would a white guy want to work for these kinds of wages?" . . . He continued without pause, "Besides, I couldn't hire you if I wanted to. You're not certified." That, he quickly concluded, was the end of our interview, and he showed me to the door. (pp. 8–9)

After taking a course and receiving his certificate, Diamond was able to enter the role of nursing assistant as others did.

Many field researchers avoid systematic study and extensive reading about a setting for fear that it will bias their first impressions, but entering without any sense of the social norms can lead to disaster. Whyte (1955) came close to such disaster when he despaired of making any social contacts in Cornerville and decided to try an unconventional entry approach (unconventional for a field researcher, that is). In *Street Corner Society,* the account of his study, Whyte describes what happened when he went to a hotel bar in search of women to talk with:

> I looked around me again and now noticed a threesome: one man and two women. It occurred to me that here was a maldistribution of females which I might be able to rectify. I approached the group and opened with something like this: "Pardon me. Would you mind if I joined you?" There was a moment of silence while the man stared at me. He then offered to throw me downstairs. I assured him that this would not be necessary and demonstrated as much by walking right out of there without any assistance. (p. 289)

Whyte (1955) needed a **gatekeeper** who could grant him access to the setting; he finally found one in "Doc" (Rossman & Rallis, 1998, pp. 108–111). A helpful social worker at the local settlement house introduced Whyte to this respected leader, who agreed to help:

> Well, any nights you want to see anything, I'll take you around. I can take you to the joints—gambling joints—I can take you around to the street corners. Just remember that you're my friend. That's all they need to know [so they won't bother you]. (p. 291)

When participant observing involves public figures or organizations that are used to or are seeking publicity, a more direct approach may secure entry into the field. Dorothy and David Counts (1996, pp. 7–8) simply wrote a letter to the married couple who led the Escapees RV Club describing their project and asking for permission to work with members. After a warm welcome from the leaders, the Counts were able to meet with Escapees at regular park gatherings and distribute questionnaires. They received few refusals, attributing this high rate of subject cooperation to members' desires to increase understanding of and appreciation for their lifestyle. Other groups have other motivations, but in every case, some consideration of these potential motives in advance should help smooth entry into the field.

In short, field researchers must be very sensitive to the impression they make and the ties they establish when entering the field. This stage lays the groundwork for collecting data from people who have different perspectives and for developing relationships that researchers can use to surmount the problems in data collection that inevitably arise in the field. Researchers should be ready with a rationale for their participation and some sense of the potential benefits to participants. Discussion about these issues with key participants or gatekeepers should be honest and should identify what the participants can expect from the research, without necessarily going into detail about the researcher's hypotheses or research questions (Rossman & Rallis, 1998, pp. 51–53, 105–108).

Developing and Maintaining Relationships

Researchers must be careful to manage their relationships in the research setting so they can continue to observe and interview diverse members of the social setting throughout the long period typical of participant observation (Maxwell, 1996, p. 66). Every action the researcher takes can develop or undermine this relationship. Interaction early in the research process is particularly sensitive because participants don't know the researcher and the researcher doesn't know the routines. Dorothy and David Counts (1996, p. 8) laid the foundation for their participant observation study of RVing seniors by joining the group they were to study and gaining trust from others as sympathetic observers. Eve Kahana, Boaz Kahana, and Kathryn Riley (1988) give some specific advice for those studying institutional settings for the aged:

> Prior to implementation of the project, it is useful for the research team to spend some time in the facility, familiarizing themselves with the staff and with the physical and social environment and becoming acceptable additions to the institutional setting. (p. 200)

Whyte (1955) used what in retrospect was a sophisticated two-part strategy to develop and maintain relationships with the Cornerville street-corner men. The first part of Whyte's strategy was to maintain good relations with Doc and, through Doc, to stay on good terms with the others. Doc became a **key informant** in the research setting—a knowledgeable insider who knew the group's culture and was willing to share access and insights with the researcher (Gilchrist & Williams, 1999). The less obvious part of Whyte's strategy was a consequence of his decision to move into Cornerville, a move he decided was necessary to really understand and be accepted in the community. The room he rented in a local family's home became his base of operations. In some respects, this family became an important dimension of Whyte's immersion in the community: He tried to learn Italian by speaking with family members, and they conversed late at night as if Whyte were a real family member. But Whyte recognized that he needed a place to unwind after his days of constant alertness in the field, so he made a conscious decision not to include the family as an object of study. Living in this family's home became a means for Whyte to maintain standing as a community insider without becoming totally immersed in the demands of research (Whyte, 1955, pp. 294–297).

Experienced participant observers have developed some sound advice for others seeking to maintain relationships in the field (Bogdewic, 1999, pp. 53–54; Rossman & Rallis, 1998, pp. 105–108; Whyte, 1955, pp. 300–306; Wolcott, 1995, pp. 91–95):

- Develop a plausible (and honest) explanation for yourself and your study.
- Maintain the support of key individuals in groups or organizations under study.
- Be unobtrusive and unassuming. Don't "show off" your expertise.
- Don't be too aggressive in questioning others (for example, don't violate implicit norms that preclude discussion of illegal activity with outsiders). Being a researcher requires that you not simultaneously try to be the guardian of law and order. Instead, be a reflective listener.
- Ask very sensitive questions only of informants with whom your relationship is good.
- Be self-revealing, but only up to a point. Let participants learn about you as a person, but without making too much of yourself.
- Don't fake your social similarity with your subjects. Taking a friendly interest in them should be an adequate basis for developing trust.
- Avoid giving or receiving monetary or other tangible gifts but without violating norms of reciprocity. Living with other people, taking others' time for conversations, going out for a social evening all create expectations and incur social obligations, and you can't be an active participant without occasionally helping others. But you will lose your ability to function as a researcher if you come to be seen as someone who gives away money or other favors. Such small forms of assistance as an occasional ride to the store or advice on applying to college may strike the right balance.
- Be prepared for special difficulties and tensions if multiple groups are involved. It is hard to avoid taking sides or being used in situations of intergroup conflict.

Nonetheless, even the most careful strategies for maintaining relations can founder on unforeseen resentments, as when Kahana and Kahana (1970) found that an order from administrators to cooperate in their research was resented as just another example of the administrators' insensitivity. Being adaptable and self-critical is essential.

Sampling People and Events

Sampling decisions in qualitative research are guided by the need to study intensively the people, places, or phenomena of interest. In fact, most qualitative researchers limit their focus to just one or a few sites, programs, or specific types of people, so that they can focus all their attention on the social dynamics of those settings or the activities and attitudes of these people. This focus on a limited number of cases does not mean that sampling is unimportant. Researchers must be reasonably confident that they can gain access and that the site can provide relevant information. The sample must be appropriate and adequate for the study, even if it is not representative. Qualitative researchers may select one or more "critical cases" that are unusually rich in information pertaining to the research question, "typical cases" precisely because they are judged to be typical, and/or deviant cases that provide a useful contrast (Kuzel, 1999). Within a research site, plans may be made to sample different settings, people, events, and artifacts (see Exhibit 9.3).

Exhibit 9.3   Sampling Plan for a Participant Observation Project in Schools

Information Source*	Collegiality	Goals and Community	Action Expectations	Knowledge Orientation	Base
Settings:					
Public places (halls, main offices)	X	X	X	X	X
Teachers' lounge	X	X		X	X
Classrooms		X	X	X	X
Meeting rooms			X	X	
Gymnasium or locker room		X			
Events:					
Faculty meetings	X		X		X
Lunch hour	X				X
Teaching		X	X	X	X
People:					
Principal		X	X	X	X
Teachers	X	X	X	X	X
Students		X	X	X	
Artifacts:					
Newspapers		X	X		X
Decorations		X			

Source: Adapted from Marshall & Rossman, 1999, pp. 75–76. Copyright © 1999. Reprinted with permission from Sage Publications, Inc.

Studying more than one case or setting almost always strengthens the causal conclusions and makes the findings more generalizable (King et al., 1994). To make his conclusions more generalizable, Diamond (1992) worked in three different Chicago nursing homes "in widely different neighborhoods" and with different fractions of residents supported by Medicaid; he then "visited many homes across the United States to validate my observations" (p. 5). J. Brandon Wallace (1994, pp. 143–144) encourages "efforts to include all kinds of people— African-Americans, Hispanics, males, females, rich and poor" to provide a more complete experience of aging in life history interview research.

Other approaches to sampling in field research are more systematic. You already learned in Chapter 4 about some of the nonprobability sampling methods that are used in field research. For instance, purposive sampling can be used to identify opinion leaders and representatives of different roles. With snowball sampling, field researchers learn from participants about who represents different subgroups in a setting. Quota sampling also may be employed to ensure the representation of particular categories of participants. Using some type of intentional sampling strategy within a particular setting can allow tests of some hypotheses that would otherwise have to wait until comparative data could be collected from several settings (King et al., 1994).

Theoretical sampling is a systematic approach to sampling in participant observation studies (Glaser & Strauss, 1967). When field researchers discover in an investigation that particular processes seem to be important, implying that certain comparisons should be made or that similar instances should be checked, the researchers then choose new settings or individuals that permit these comparisons or checks (Ragin, 1994, pp. 98–101) (see Exhibit 9.4). However, sampling in qualitative studies, for example, of elderly people in institutional settings, can be biased by staff motivation to suggest residents who will present the institution in a particular light or simply by staff lack of reliable knowledge about residents' diagnoses,

Exhibit 9.4   Theoretical Sampling

Original cases interviewed in a study of cocaine users:

Realization: Some cocaine users are businesspeople.
Add businesspeople to sample:

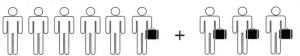

Realization: Sample is low on women.
Add women to sample:

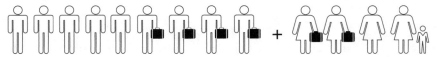

Realization: Some female cocaine users are mothers of young children.
Add mothers to sample:

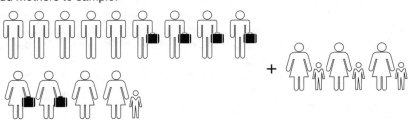

tenure, or other characteristics that are important in the researcher's sampling strategy (Kahana et al., 1988, p. 205). Carrying out a theoretical sampling plan thus may require selecting cases systematically from a sampling list that contains information on potential sample members.

Taking Notes

Written notes are the primary means of recording participant observation data (Emerson, Fretz, & Shaw, 1995). Of course, *written* no longer means handwritten; many field researchers jot down partial notes while observing and then retreat to their computer to write up more complete notes on a daily basis. The computerized text can then be inspected and organized after it is printed out, or it can be marked up and organized for analysis using one of several computer programs designed especially for the task.

It is almost always a mistake to try to take comprehensive notes while engaged in the field—the process of writing extensively is just too disruptive. The usual procedure is to jot down brief notes about highlights of the observation period. These brief notes (called **jottings**) can then serve as memory joggers when writing the actual **field notes** at a later session. It will also help to maintain a daily log in which each day's activities are recorded (Bogdewic, 1999, pp. 58–67). With the aid of the jottings and some practice, researchers usually remember a great deal of what happened—as long as the comprehensive field notes are written immediately afterward, or at least within the next 24 hours, and before they have been discussed with anyone else.

The following excerpts shed light on the note-taking processes that Diamond and Lyman used while in the field. Taking notes was more of a challenge for Diamond (1992), because many people in the setting did not know that he was a researcher:

> While I was getting to know nursing assistants and residents and experiencing aspects of their daily routines, I would surreptitiously take notes on scraps of paper, in the bathroom or otherwise out of sight, jotting down what someone had said or done. (pp. 6–7)

Karen Lyman (1994) was able to take notes openly:

> I took care to overcome the artificial barriers of note-taking through reassurances, humor, volunteered labor, food sharing, and casual conversations with the notepad conspicuously left on the table. . . . Note-taking was a daily reminder to all that I was an outsider, which at times created barriers to be overcome, but which also allowed me to extricate myself from what could have become all-consuming volunteer tasks when I felt the need to record something. One clear advantage of visible note-taking was that some people volunteered information they felt should be recorded. A social worker took me aside and . . . recounted an important incident on a particularly difficult day. (p. 167)

Usually, writing up notes takes much longer—at least three times longer—than the observing did. Field notes must be as complete, detailed, and true to what was observed and heard as possible. Direct quotes should be distinguished clearly from paraphrased quotes, and both should be set off from the researcher's observations and reflections. Pauses and interruptions should be indicated. The surrounding context should receive as much attention as possible, and a map of the setting always should be included, with indications of where individuals were at different times.

Careful note-taking yields a big payoff. On page after page, field notes will suggest new concepts, causal connections, and theoretical propositions. Social processes and settings can be described in rich detail, with ample illustrations. Exhibit 9.5, for example, contains field notes recorded by Norma Ware, an anthropologist studying living arrangements for homeless mentally ill people (Goldfinger et al., 1997). The notes contain observations of the setting, the questions the anthropologist asked, the answers she received, and her analytic thoughts about one of the residents. What can be learned from just this one page of field notes? The mood of

Exhibit 9.5   Field Notes from the Evolving Consumer Household (ECH)

I arrive around 4:30 P.M. and walk into a conversation between Jim and somebody else as to what color jeans he should buy. There is quite a lot of joking going on between Jim and Susan. I go out to the kitchen and find Dick about to take his dinner out to the picnic table to eat (his idea?) so I go ask if I can join him. He says yes. In the course of the conversation, I find out that he works 3 days a week in the "prevoc" program at the local day program, Food Services branch, for which he gets $10 per week. Does he think the living situation will work out? Yes. All they need is a plan for things like when somebody buys something and then everybody else uses it. Like he bought a gallon of milk and it was gone in two days, because everyone was using it for their coffee. I ask if he's gone back to the shelter to visit and he says "No. I was glad to get out of there." He came to the [ECH] from [a shelter] through homeless outreach [a Department of Mental Health Program]. Had been at [the shelter] since January. Affirms that [the ECH] is a better place to live than the shelter. Why? Because you have your own room and privacy and stuff. How have people been getting along with each other? He says, "Fine."

I return to the living room and sit down on the couch with Jim and Susan. Susan teases Jim and he jokes back. Susan is eating a T.V. dinner with M and M's for dessert. There is joking about working off the calories from the M and M's by doing sit-up's, which she proceeds to demonstrate. This leads to a conversation about exercise during which Jim declares his intention to get back into exercise by doing sports, like basketball.

Jim seems to have his mind on pulling himself together, which he characterizes as "getting my old self back." When I ask him what he's been doing since I saw him last, he says, "Working on my appearance." And in fact, he has had a haircut, a shave, and washed his clothes. When I ask him what his old self was like, he says, "you mean before I lost everything?" I learn that he used to work two jobs, had "a family" and was into religion." This seems to have been when he was quite young, around eighteen. He tells me he was on the street for 7-8 years, from 1978-1985, drinking the whole time. I ask him whether he thinks living at [the ECH] will help him to get his "old self back" and he says that it will "help motivate me." I observe that he seems pretty motivated already. He says yes, "but this will motivate me more."

Jim has a warm personality, likes to joke and laugh. He also speaks up—in meetings he is among the first to say what he thinks and he talks among the most. His "team" relationship with Bill is also important to him—" me and Bill, we work together."

Source: Norma Ware, Ph.D., Department of Psychiatry, Harvard Medical School, unpublished ethnographic notes, 1991.

the house at this time is evident, with joking, casual conversation, and close friendships. "Dick" remarks on problems with household financial management, and at the same time, we learn a bit about his own activities and personality (a regular worker who appears to like systematic plans). We see how a few questions and a private conversation elicit information about the transition from the shelter to the house, as well as about household operations. The field notes also provide the foundation for a more complete picture of one resident, describing "Jim's" relationships with others, his personal history, his interests and personality, and his orientation to the future. We can see analytic concepts emerge in the notes, such as the concept of "pulling himself together" and of some house members working as a "team." You can imagine how researchers can go on to develop a theoretical framework for understanding the setting and a set of concepts and questions to inform subsequent observations.

Complete field notes must provide even more than a record of what was observed or heard. Notes also should include descriptions of the methodology: where researchers were standing or sitting while they observed, how they chose people for conversation or observation, what counts of people or events they made and why. Sprinkled throughout the notes also should be a record of the researchers' feelings and thoughts while observing: when they were disgusted by some statement or act, when they felt threatened or intimidated, why their attention shifted from one group to another, and what ethical concerns arose. Notes like these provide a foundation for later review of the likelihood of bias or of inattention to some salient features of the situation.

Notes may in some situations be supplemented by still pictures, videotapes, and printed material circulated or posted in the research setting. Such visual material can bring an entirely different qualitative dimension into the analysis and call attention to some features of the social situation and actors within it that were missed in the notes (Grady, 1996). Commentary on this material can be integrated with the written notes (Bogdewic, 1999, pp. 67–68).

Managing the Personal Dimensions

Our overview of participant observation would not be complete without considering its personal dimensions. Because field researchers become a part of the social situation they are studying, they cannot help but be affected on a personal, emotional level. At the same time, those being studied react to researchers not just as researchers but as personal acquaintances—often as friends, sometimes as personal rivals. Managing and learning from this personal side of field research is an important part of any project.

The impact of personal issues varies with the depth of researchers' involvement in the setting. The more involved researchers are in multiple aspects of the ongoing social situation, the more important personal issues become and the greater the risk of "going native." Even when researchers acknowledge their role, "increased contact brings sympathy, and sympathy in its turn dulls the edge of criticism" (Fenno, 1978, p. 277). To study the social life of "corner boys," however, Whyte (1955) could not stay so disengaged. He moved into an apartment with a Cornerville family and lived for about four years in the community he was investigating:

> The researcher, like his informants, is a social animal. He has a role to play, and he has his own personality needs that must be met in some degree if he is to function successfully. Where the researcher operates out of a university, just going into the field for a few hours at a time, he can keep his personal social life separate from field activity. His problem of role is not quite so complicated. If, on the other hand, the researcher is living for an

extended period in the community he is studying, his personal life is inextricably mixed with his research. (p. 279)

The correspondence between researchers' social attributes—age, sex, race, and so on—and those of their subjects also shapes personal relationships, as Diamond (1992) noted:

The staff were mostly people of color, residents mostly white. . . . Never before, or since, have I been so acutely aware of being a white American man. At first the people who lived in the homes stared at me, then some approached to get a closer look, saying that I reminded them of a nephew, a son, a grandson, a brother, a doctor. This behavior made more sense as time went on: except for the few male residents and occasional visitors, I was the only white man many would see from one end of the month to the next. (p. 39)

Barrie Thorne (1993), observing school girls at recess, wondered whether "the times when I felt like a ten-year-old girl, [were] a source of distortion or insight?" She concluded they were both: "Memory, like observing, is a way of knowing and can be a rich resource." But "When my own responses . . . were driven by emotions like envy or aversion, they clearly obscured my ability to grasp the full social situation" (p. 26).

There is no formula for successfully managing the personal dimension of field research. It is much more art than science and flows more from the researcher's own personality and natural approach to other people than from formal training. But novice field researchers often neglect to consider how they will manage personal relationships when they plan and carry out their projects. Then suddenly, they find themselves doing something they don't believe they should, just to stay in the good graces of research subjects, or juggling the emotions resulting from conflict within the group. As Whyte (1955) noted:

The field worker cannot afford to think only of learning to live with others in the field. He has to continue living with himself. If the participant observer finds himself engaging in behavior that he has learned to think of as immoral, then he is likely to begin to wonder what sort of a person he is after all. Unless the field worker can carry with him a reasonably consistent picture of himself, he is likely to run into difficulties. (p. 317)

If you plan a field research project, follow these guidelines (Whyte, 1955, pp. 300–317):

• Take the time to consider how you want to relate to your potential subjects as people.
• Speculate about what personal problems might arise and how you will respond to them.
• Keep in touch with other researchers and personal friends outside the research setting.
• Maintain standards of conduct that make you comfortable as a person and that respect the integrity of your subjects.

When you evaluate participant observers' reports, pay attention to how they defined their role in the setting and dealt with personal problems. Don't place too much confidence in such research unless the report provides this information.

Systematic Observation

We would be remiss if we failed to note that observations can be made in a more systematic, quantitative design that allows systematic comparisons and more confident generalizations. A research study using **systematic observation** develops a standard form on which to record variation within the observed setting in terms of the variables of interest. Such variables might include the frequency of some behavior(s), the particular people observed, and environmental conditions.

Janet Shapiro and Sarah Mangelsdorf (1994) used systematic observation and surveys to look for factors related to the parenting abilities of adolescent mothers. Participants first completed the survey, which consisted of a variety of measures such as self-efficacy, life events, self-concept, life stress, and demographic information. The participants were then videotaped engaging in three parenting activities: feeding, unstructured play, and structured play. Coders viewed the videotapes and, using standardized scales, rated the adolescent mothers on their parental sensitivity, expressiveness with the child, positive regard, negative regard, caretaking ability, and the extent to which the adolescents permitted their child autonomy, as well as child responsiveness to the interaction (Shapiro & Mangelsdorf, 1994, p. 627).

INTENSIVE INTERVIEWING

Asking questions is part of almost all participant observation (Wolcott, 1995, pp. 102–105). However, many qualitative researchers employ intensive or depth interviewing exclusively, without systematic observation of respondents in their natural setting.

Unlike the more structured interviewing that may be used in survey research (discussed in Chapter 8), intensive or depth interviewing relies on open-ended questions. Qualitative researchers do not presume to know the range of answers that respondents might give and seek to hear these answers in the respondents' own words. Rather than asking standard questions in a fixed order, intensive interviewers may allow the specific content and order of questions to vary from one interviewee to another.

What distinguishes intensive interviewing from less structured forms of questioning is consistency and thoroughness. The goal is to develop a comprehensive picture of the interviewee's background, attitudes, and actions, in his or her own terms; to "listen to people as they describe how they understand the worlds in which they live and work" (Rubin & Rubin, 1995, p. 3). For example, Sharon Kaufman (1986) sought through intensive interviewing to learn how old people cope with change. She wanted to hear the words of the elderly themselves, for "the voices of individual old people can tell us much about the experience of being old" (p. 6).

Intensive interview studies do not reveal as directly as does participant observation the social context in which action is taken and opinions are formed. But like participant observation studies, intensive interviewing engages researchers more actively with subjects than does standard survey research. The researchers must listen to lengthy explanations, ask follow-up questions tailored to the preceding answers, and seek to learn about interrelated belief systems or personal approaches to things, rather than measure a limited set of variables. As a result, intensive interviews are often much longer than standardized interviews, sometimes as long as 15 hours, conducted in several different sessions. The intensive interview becomes more like a conversation between partners than between a researcher and a subject (Kaufman, 1986, pp. 22–23). Some call it "a conversation with a purpose" (Rossman & Rallis, 1998, p. 126).

Intensive interviewers actively try to probe understandings and engage interviewees in a dialogue about what they mean by their comments. To prepare for this active interviewing, the interviewer should learn in advance about the setting and people to be studied. Preliminary discussion with key informants, inspection of written documents, and even a review of your own feelings about the setting can all help (Miller & Crabtree, 1999, pp. 94–96). Robert Bellah, Richard Madsen, William Sullivan, Ann Swidler, and Steven Tipton (1985) elaborate on this aspect of intensive interviewing in a methodological appendix to their national best-seller about American individualism, *Habits of the Heart:*

> We did not, as in some scientific version of "Candid Camera," seek to capture their beliefs and actions without our subjects being aware of us. Rather, we sought to bring our preconceptions and questions into the conversation and to understand the answers we were receiving not only in terms of the language but also, so far as we could discover, in the lives of those we were talking with. Though we did not seek to impose our ideas on those with whom we talked, . . . we did attempt to uncover assumptions, to make explicit what the person we were talking to might rather have left implicit. The interview as we employed it was active, Socratic. (p. 304)

The intensive interview follows a preplanned outline of topics. It may begin with a few simple questions that gather background information while building rapport. These are often followed by a few general **"grand tour" questions** that are meant to elicit lengthy narratives (Miller & Crabtree, 1999, pp. 96–99). For example, Sharon R. Kaufman (1994, p. 129) asked an 18-year-old woman who had been crippled by osteoarthritis after a series of falls, "Could you start off by telling me how and when your health changed?" She received a lengthy reply about "the beginning of the complete change in my whole life" and what it meant to her respondent.

Some projects may use relatively structured interviews, particularly when the focus is on developing knowledge about prior events or some narrowly defined topic. But more exploratory projects, particularly those aiming to learn about interviewees' interpretations of the world, may let each interview flow in a unique direction in response to the interviewee's experiences and interests (Kvale, 1996, pp. 3–5; Rubin & Rubin, 1995, p. 6; Wolcott, 1995, pp. 113–114). In either case, qualitative interviewers must adapt nimbly throughout the interview, paying attention to nonverbal cues, expressions with symbolic value, and the ebb and flow of the interviewee's feelings and interests. "You have to be free to follow your data where they lead" (Rubin & Rubin, 1995, p. 64). The interview guide becomes a tool for ensuring that key topics are covered, rather than a guide to the ordering or language of specific questions.

Random selection is rarely used to select respondents for intensive interviews, but the selection method still must carefully be considered. If interviewees are selected in a haphazard manner, for example, by speaking to those who happen to be available at the time that the researcher is on site, the interviews are likely to be of less value than when a more purposive selection strategy is used. Researchers should try to select interviewees who are knowledgeable about the subject of the interview, who are open to talking, and who represent the range of perspectives (Rubin & Rubin, 1995, pp. 65–92). Selection of new interviewees should continue, if possible, at least until the **saturation point** is reached, the point when new interviews seem to yield little additional information (see Exhibit 9.6). As new issues are uncovered, additional interviewees may be selected to represent different opinions about these issues.

Exhibit 9.6   The Saturation Point in Intensive Interviewing

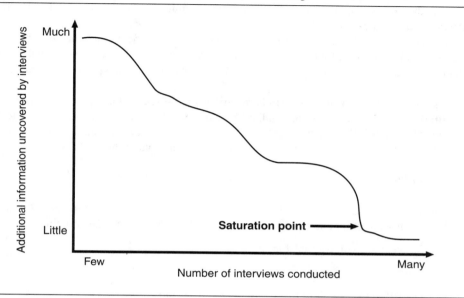

Establishing and Maintaining a Partnership

Because intensive interviewing does not engage researchers as participants in subjects' daily affairs, the problems of entering the field are much reduced. However, the logistics of arranging long periods for personal interviews can still be pretty complicated. It also is important to establish rapport with subjects by considering in advance how they will react to the interview arrangements and by developing an approach that does not violate their standards for social behavior. Interviewees should be treated with respect, as knowledgeable partners whose time is valued (among other things, that means you should avoid coming late for appointments). A commitment to confidentiality should be stated and honored (Rubin & Rubin, 1995).

But the intensive interviewer's relationship with the interviewee is not an equal partnership because the researcher seeks to gain certain types of information and strategizes throughout to maintain an appropriate relationship (Kvale, 1996, p. 6). In the first few minutes of the interview, the goal is to show interest in the interviewee and to explain clearly the purpose of the interview (Kvale, 1996, p. 128). During the interview, the interviewer should maintain an appropriate distance from the interviewee, one that doesn't violate cultural norms, and the interviewer should maintain eye contact and not engage in distracting behavior. An appropriate pace is also important; pause to allow the interviewee to reflect, elaborate, and generally not feel rushed (Gordon, 1992). When an interview covers emotional or otherwise stressful topics, the interviewer should give the interviewee an opportunity to unwind at the interview's end (Rubin & Rubin, 1995, p. 138).

Asking Questions and Recording Answers

Intensive interviewers must plan their main questions around an outline of the interview topic. The questions should generally be short and to the point. More details can then be elicited through nondirective probes (such as "Can you tell me more about that?" or "uh-huh," echoing the respondent's comment, or just maintaining a moment of silence). Follow-up questions can then be tailored to answers to the main questions.

Interviewers should strategize throughout an interview about how best to achieve their objectives while taking into account interviewees' answers. They must also be sensitive to the ways in which they shape the answers by their words, style of questioning, and personal characteristics:

> It is the combination of personal characteristics and expectations of the interviewer, the attitudes toward aging he or she indicates, and the conceptual grounding of the questions themselves that influence the topics informants choose to express and expand on as well as the topics they omit from discussion entirely." (Kaufman, 1994, p. 128)

Habits of the Heart (Bellah et al., 1985) provides a useful illustration:

> [Coinvestigator Steven] Tipton, in interviewing Margaret Oldham [a pseudonym], tried to discover at what point she would take responsibility for another human being:
>
> Q: So what are you responsible for?
>
> A: I'm responsible for my acts and for what I do.
>
> Q: Does that mean you're responsible for others, too?
>
> A: No.
>
> Q: Are you your sister's keeper?
>
> A: No.
>
> Q: Your brother's keeper?
>
> A: No.
>
> Q: Are you responsible for your husband?
>
> A: I'm not. He makes his own decisions. He is his own person. He acts his own acts. I can agree with them, or I can disagree with them. If I ever find them nauseous enough, I have a responsibility to leave and not deal with it any more.
>
> Q: What about children?
>
> A: I . . . I would say I have a legal responsibility for them, but in a sense I think they in turn are responsible for their own acts. (p. 304)

Do you see how the interviewer actively encouraged the subject to explain what she meant by *responsibility*? This sort of active questioning undoubtedly did a better job of clarifying her concept of responsibility than a fixed set of questions would have.

Tape recorders commonly are used to record intensive and focus group interviews. Most researchers who have tape-recorded interviews (including the authors) feel that they do not inhibit most interviewees and, in fact, are routinely ignored. The occasional respondent is very concerned with his or her public image and may therefore speak "for the tape recorder," but such individuals are unlikely to speak frankly in any research interview. In any case, constant note-taking during an interview prevents adequate displays of interest and appreciation by the interviewer and hinders the degree of concentration that results in the best interviews.

FOCUS GROUPS

Focus groups are groups of unrelated individuals that are formed by a researcher and then led in group discussion of a topic for one to two hours. The researcher asks specific questions and guides the discussion to ensure that group members address these questions, but the resulting information is qualitative and relatively unstructured. Focus groups do not involve representative samples; instead, a few individuals are recruited for the group who have the time to participate, have some knowledge pertinent to the focus group topic, and share key characteristics with the target population.

Focus groups have their roots in the interviewing techniques developed in the 1930s by sociologists and psychologists who were dissatisfied with traditional surveys. Traditionally, in a questionnaire survey, subjects are directed to consider certain issues and particular response options in a predetermined order. The spontaneous exchange and development of ideas that characterize social life outside the survey situation is lost—and with it, some social scientists feared, the prospects for validity. The ability of focus group research to stimulate spontaneity in expression and social interaction has prompted social scientists to use them to evaluate social programs and to assess social needs (Krueger, 1988, pp. 18–22).

Most focus groups involve 7 to 10 people, a number that facilitates discussion by all in attendance. Participants usually do not know one another, although some studies in organized settings may include friends or coworkers. Opinions differ on the value of using homogeneous versus heterogeneous participants. Homogeneous groups may be more convivial and willing to share feelings, but heterogeneous groups may stimulate more ideas (Brown, 1999, pp. 115–117). Of course, the characteristics of individuals that determine their inclusion are based on the researcher's conception of the target population for the study. Focus group leaders must begin the discussion by creating the expectation that all will participate and that the researcher will not favor any particular perspective or participant.

Focus groups are used to collect qualitative data, with open-ended questions posed by the researcher (or group leader). Thus, a focused discussion mimics the natural process of forming and expressing opinions—and may give some sense of validity. The researcher, or group moderator, uses an interview guide, but the dynamics of group discussion often require changes in the order and manner in which different topics are addressed (Brown, 1999, p. 120). No formal procedure exists for determining the generalizability of focus group answers, but the careful researcher should conduct at least several focus groups on the same topic and check for consistency in the findings. Some focus group experts advise conducting enough focus groups to reach the point of saturation, when an additional focus group adds little new information to that which already has been generated (Brown, 1999, p. 118).

Berit Ingersoll-Dayton, Margaret Neal, Jung-hwa Ha, and Leslie Hammer (2003) provide a good example of how focus groups can offer unexpected responses that produce new knowledge. They had organized 17 focus groups comprising adult children caring for parents or in-laws for at least three hours a week. The groups focused on caregiving and work, as well as caregiving and family responsibilities. "Although no specific questions about caregiving relationships among siblings were posed, participants initiated discussion of this topic in

16 of the 17 focus groups" (Ingersoll-Dayton et al., 2003, p. 55). Focusing on these responses, the researchers concluded:

> By examining caregiving from a collaborative perspective, this study revealed caregiving as a dynamic process. In fact, we found that sibling caregivers consciously switched from primary to secondary roles on a regular basis. As illustrated by the two sisters who planned to take turns caring for their dying father, siblings may purposefully vary their caregiving responsibilities. . . . Another important discovery is that aging parents can facilitate collaboration among adult siblings. . . . Our study shows how older parents can help their children cooperate by providing the same information or instructions to all of them. In so doing, siblings can concentrate their efforts on a similar goal rather than feeling confused and conflicted when parents provide contradictory instructions to different children. (p. 62)

Focus groups are now used extensively to identify social service needs and utilization patterns. For example, Caroline Rosenthal Gelman (2002) describes findings of a focus group with older Latinos. Service providers in a Massachusetts community asked for a needs assessment of elderly Latinos due to their low service utilization. A focus group with 10 elderly Latinos was used to discuss topics such as the needs of older Latinos, formal services, how they became aware of these services, and informal supports.

Focus group methods share with other field research techniques an emphasis on discovering unanticipated findings and exploring hidden meanings. Although they do not provide a means for developing reliable, generalizable results (the traditional strong suits of survey research), focus groups can be an indispensable aid for developing hypotheses and survey questions, for investigating the meaning of survey results, and for quickly assessing the range of opinion about an issue.

ETHICAL ISSUES IN QUALITATIVE RESEARCH

Qualitative research can raise some complex ethical issues. No matter how hard the field researcher strives to study the social world naturally, leaving no traces, the very act of research itself imposes something unnatural on the situation. It is up to researchers to identify and take responsibility for the consequences of their involvement. Five main ethical issues arise:

Voluntary participation. Ensuring that subjects are participating in a study voluntarily is not often a problem with intensive interviewing and focus group research, but it is often a point of contention in participant observation studies. Few researchers or institutional review boards are willing to condone covert participation because it offers no way to ensure that participation by the subjects is voluntary. Even when the researcher's role is more open, interpreting the standard of voluntary participation still can be difficult. Practically, much field research would be impossible if the participant observer were required to request permission of everyone having some contact, no matter how minimal, with a group or setting being observed. Should the requirement of voluntary participation apply equally to every member of an organization being observed? What if the manager consents, the workers are ambivalent, and the union says no? Requiring everyone's consent would limit participant observation research to settings without serious conflicts of interest.

Subject well-being. Every field researcher should consider carefully before beginning a project how to avoid harm to subjects. It is not possible to avoid every theoretical possibility of harm nor to be sure that any project will cause no adverse consequences whatsoever to any individual. Some of the Cornerville men read Whyte's (1955) book and felt discomfited by it (others found it enlightening). But such consequences could follow from any research, even from any public discourse. Direct harm to the reputations or feelings of particular individuals is what researchers must carefully avoid. They can do so in part by maintaining the confidentiality of research subjects. They must also avoid adversely affecting the course of events while engaged in a setting. Whyte (1955, pp. 335–337) found himself regretting having recommended that a particular politician be allowed to speak to a social club he was observing because the speech led to serious dissension in the club and strains between Whyte and some club members. These problems are rare in intensive interviewing and focus groups, but even there, researchers should try to identify negative feelings and help distressed subjects cope with their feelings through debriefing or referrals for professional help.

Identity disclosure. We already have considered the problems of identity disclosure, particularly in the case of covert participation. Current ethical standards require informed consent of research subjects, and most would argue that this standard cannot be met in any meaningful way if researchers do not disclose fully their identity. But how much disclosure about the study is necessary, and how hard should researchers try to make sure that their research purposes are understood? In field research on Codependents Anonymous, Leslie Irvine (1998) found that the emphasis on anonymity and the expectations for group discussion made it difficult to disclose her identity. Less educated subjects may not readily comprehend what a researcher is or be able to weigh the possible consequences of the research for themselves. Should researchers inform subjects if the study's interests and foci change while it is in progress? Can a balance be struck between the disclosure of critical facts and a coherent research strategy?

Confidentiality. Field researchers normally use fictitious names for the characters in their reports, but doing so does not always guarantee confidentiality to their research subjects. Individuals in the setting studied may be able to identify those whose actions are described and may thus become privy to some knowledge about their colleagues or neighbors that had formerly been kept from them. Researchers should thus make every effort to expunge possible identifying material from published information and to alter unimportant aspects of a description when necessary to prevent identity disclosure. In any case, no field research project should begin if some participants clearly will suffer serious harm by being identified in project publications.

Online research. The large number of discussion groups and bulletin boards on the Internet has stimulated much research. Such research can violate the principles of voluntary participation and identity disclosure when researchers participate in discussions and record and analyze text but do not identify themselves as researchers (Kleinman, 2002).

These ethical issues cannot be evaluated independently. The final decision to proceed must be made after weighing the relative benefits and risks to participants. Few qualitative research projects will be barred by consideration of these ethical issues, however, except for those involving covert participation. The more important concern for researchers is to identify the ethically troublesome aspects of their proposed research and resolve them before the project begins and to act on new ethical issues as they come up during the project. Combining methods is often the best strategy.

CONCLUSION

Qualitative research allows the careful investigator to obtain a richer and more intimate view of the social world than more structured methods. It is not hard to understand why so many qualitative studies have become classics in the sociological literature. The emphases in qualitative research on inductive reasoning and incremental understanding help to stimulate and inform other research approaches, too. Exploratory research to chart the dimensions of previously unstudied social settings and intensive investigations of the subjective meanings that motivate individual action are particularly well served by the techniques of participant observation, intensive interviewing, and focus groups.

The very characteristics that make qualitative research techniques so appealing restrict their use to a limited set of research problems. It is not possible to draw representative samples for study using participant observation, and for this reason, the generalizability of any particular field study's results cannot really be known. Only the accumulation of findings from numerous qualitative studies permits confident generalization, but here again, the time and effort required to collect and analyze the data make it unlikely that many field research studies will be replicated.

Even if qualitative researchers made more of an effort to replicate key studies, their notion of developing and grounding explanations inductively in the observations made in a particular setting would hamper comparison of findings. Measurement reliability is thereby hindered, as are systematic tests for the validity of key indicators and formal tests for causal connections.

In the final analysis, qualitative research involves a mode of thinking and investigating different from that used in experimental and survey research. Qualitative research is inductive and idiographic; experiments and surveys tend to be conducted in a deductive, quantitative, and nomothetic framework. Both approaches can help social scientists learn about the social world; the proficient researcher must be ready to use either. Qualitative data are often supplemented with counts of characteristics or activities. As you have already seen, quantitative data are often enriched with written comments and observations, and focus groups have become a common tool of survey researchers seeking to develop their questionnaires. Thus, the distinction between qualitative and quantitative research techniques is not always clear-cut, and combining methods is often a good idea.

KEY TERMS

Complete observation
Complete participation
Covert participation
Field notes
Focus groups
Gatekeeper
Grand tour questions
Intensive interviewing

Jottings
Key informant
Participant observation
Qualitative methods
Reactive effects
Saturation point
Systematic observation
Theoretical sampling

HIGHLIGHTS

- Qualitative methods are most useful in exploring new issues, investigating hard-to-study groups, and determining the meaning people give to their lives and actions. In addition, most social research projects can be improved in some respects by taking advantage of qualitative techniques.
- Qualitative researchers tend to develop ideas inductively, try to understand the social context and sequential nature of attitudes and actions, and explore the subjective meanings that participants attach to events. They rely primarily on participant observation, intensive interviewing, and focus groups.
- Participant observers may adopt one of several roles for a particular research project. Each role represents a different balance between observing and participating. Many field researchers prefer a moderate role, participating as well as observing in a group but acknowledging publicly the researcher role. Such a role avoids ethical issues posed by covert participating while still allowing the insights into the social world derived from participating directly in it. The role that the participant observer chooses should be based on an evaluation of the problems likely to arise from reactive effects and the ethical dilemmas of covert participating.
- Systematic observation techniques quantify the observational process to allow more systematic comparison between cases and greater generalizability.
- Field researchers must develop strategies for entering the field, developing and maintaining relations in the field, sampling, and recording and analyzing data. Selection of sites or other units to study may reflect an emphasis on typical cases, deviant cases, and/or critical cases that can provide more information than others. Sampling techniques commonly used within sites or in selecting interviewees in field research include theoretical sampling, purposive sampling, snowball sampling, quota sampling, and in special circumstances, random selection.
- Recording and analyzing notes is a crucial step in field research. Jottings are used as brief reminders about events in the field, while daily logs are useful to chronicle the researcher's activities. Detailed field notes should be recorded and analyzed daily. Analysis of the notes can guide refinement of methods used in the field and of the concepts, indicators, and models developed to explain what has been observed.
- Intensive interviews involve open-ended questions and follow-up probes, with specific question content and order varying from one interview to another. Intensive interviews can supplement participant observation data.
- Focus groups use elements of participant observation and intensive interviewing. They can increase the validity of attitude measurement by revealing what people say when presenting their opinions in a group context, instead of the artificial one-on-one interview setting.
- Four main ethical issues in field research that should be given particular attention concern voluntary participation, subject well-being, identity disclosure, and confidentiality.

DISCUSSION QUESTIONS

1. Define and describe participant observation, intensive interviewing, and focus groups. What features do these research designs share? How are they different?

2. Discuss the relative merits of complete observation, participant observation, and covert participation. What are the ethical considerations inherent in each?

3. Compare and contrast intensive interviewing with interviews used in survey research. Under what circumstances might you choose intensive interviewing techniques? What are the potential difficulties of using this type of research?

PRACTICE EXERCISES

1. Take a seat at a restaurant near campus. For exactly 10 minutes, be a complete observer, taking copious notes on everything you watch. Review your notes. How would you have perceived things from a different vantage point? How would you have perceived things if you had engaged some of the patrons and staff in conversation? How would things have looked to you if you had covertly participated as a server? How would you have perceived things as a patron?

2. With the permission of your field placement supervisor, establish a focus group of staff in the agency in which you are placed. What research question do you want to address? How would you recruit staff for the group? What types of staff would you try to include? How would you introduce the topic and the method to the group? What questions would you ask? What problems would you anticipate, such as discord between focus group members or digressions from the chosen topic? How would you respond to these problems?

WEB EXERCISES

1. Go to the Social Science Information Gateway (SOSIG) at http://sosig.esrc.bris.ac.uk. Choose Research Tools and Methods and then Qualitative. Now choose three or four interesting sites to find out more about field research. Explore the sites to find out what information they provide regarding field research, what kinds of projects are being done that involve field research, and the purposes for which specific field research methods are being used.

2. You have been asked to do field research on the World Wide Web's impact on the socialization of children in today's world. The first part of the project involves your writing a compare and contrast report on the differences between how you and your generation were socialized as children and the way children today are being socialized. Collect your data by surfing the Web "as if you were a kid." Using any of the major search engines, explore the Web within the Kids or Children subject heading, keeping field notes on what you observe. Write a brief report based on the data you have collected. How has the Web affected child socialization in comparison to when you were a child?

> To assist you in completing the Web exercises, please access the study site at http://www.sagepub.com/prsw where you will find the Web Exercises reproduced and suggested links for online resources.

DEVELOPING A RESEARCH PROPOSAL

If you choose either to conduct a qualitative study or to add a qualitative component to your proposed study:

1. Pick the method that seems most likely to help answer the research question for the overall project.

For a participant observation component, propose an observational plan that would answer your research question. Present in your proposal the following information about your plan:

    a. Choose a site and justify its selection in terms of its likely value for the research.

    b. Choose a role along the participant-observation continuum and justify your choice.

    c. Describe access procedures and note any likely problems.

    d. Discuss how you will develop and maintain relations in the site.

    e. Review any sampling issues.

    f. Present an overview of the way in which you will analyze the data you collect.

2. For an intensive interview component, propose a focus for the intensive interviews that you believe will add the most to your research question. Present in your proposal the following information about your plan:

    a. Present and justify a method for selecting individuals to interview.

    b. Write out several introductory biographical questions and five "grand tour" questions for your interview schedule.

    c. List different probes you may use.

    d. Present and justify at least two follow-up questions for one of your grand tour questions.

Chapter 10

EVALUATION RESEARCH

History of Evaluation Research

Evaluation Basics
Describing the Program:
   The Logic Model

Questions for Evaluation Research
Needs Assessment
Process Evaluation
Outcome Evaluation
Efficiency Analysis

Design Alternatives
Black Box or Program Theory?
Researcher or Stakeholder
   Orientation?
Quantitative or
   Qualitative Methods?
Simple or Complex Outcomes?

Ethics in Evaluation

Conclusion

D.A.R.E.: Drug Abuse Resistance Education. As you probably know, this program is offered in elementary schools across America. For parents worried about drug abuse among youth, for any concerned citizens, the program has immediate appeal. It brings a special police officer into the schools once a week to speak with classes about the hazards of drug abuse and to establish a direct link between local law enforcement and young people. You only have to check out bumper stickers or attend a few PTA meetings to learn that it's a popular program.

And it is appealing. D.A.R.E. seems to improve relations between the schools and law enforcement and to create a positive image of the police in the eyes of students. One principal said,

> It's a very positive program for kids . . . a way for law enforcement to interact with children in a nonthreatening fashion . . . D.A.R.E. sponsored a basketball game. . . . The middle school jazz band played. . . . We had families there. (Taylor, 1999, p. 11)

Yet when all is said and done, D.A.R.E. hasn't worked. It doesn't do what it was designed to do—lessen the use of illicit drugs among D.A.R.E. students, either while they are enrolled in the program or, more important, after they enter middle or high school. Research designed to evaluate D.A.R.E. using social science methods has repeatedly come to the same conclusion:

Students who have participated in D.A.R.E. are no less likely to use illicit drugs than comparable students who have not participated in D.A.R.E. (Ringwalt et al., 1994).

If you have children who enjoyed D.A.R.E., or were yourself a D.A.R.E. student, this may
seem like a depressing way to begin a chapter on **evaluation research**. Nonetheless, it drives
home an important point: To know whether social programs work, or how they work, we have
to evaluate them systematically and fairly, whether we personally like the program or not. And
there's actually an optimistic conclusion to this introductory story: Evaluation research can make a
difference. A new D.A.R.E. program has been designed to remedy the deficiencies identified by
evaluation researchers (Toppo, 2002). This new program brings D.A.R.E. into a wider range of
classes and integrates the program with regular instruction. Of course, it's now being evaluated, too.

In this chapter, you will read about a variety of social program evaluations as we introduce
the evaluation research process, illustrate the different types of evaluation research, highlight
alternative approaches, and review ethical concerns.

HISTORY OF EVALUATION RESEARCH

Evaluation research is not a method of data collection, like survey research or experiments,
nor is it a unique component of research designs, like sampling or measurement. Instead,
evaluation research is social work research that is conducted for a distinctive purpose: to
investigate social programs (such as substance abuse treatment programs, welfare programs,
mental health programs, or employment and training programs). For each project, an evaluation researcher must select a research design and method of data collection that are useful for
answering the particular research questions posed and appropriate for the particular program
investigated. So you can see why this chapter comes after those on experiments, single-
subject designs, surveys, and qualitative methods: When you review or plan evaluation
research, you have to think about the research process as a whole and how different parts of
that process can best be combined.

The development of evaluation research as a major enterprise followed on the heels of the
expansion of the federal government during the Great Depression and World War II. Large
Depression-era government outlays for social programs stimulated interest in monitoring program output, and the military effort in World War II led to some of the necessary review and
contracting procedures for sponsoring evaluation research. In the 1960s, criminal justice
researchers began to use experiments to test the value of different policies (Orr, 1999, p. 24).
New government social programs of the 1960s often came with evaluation requirements
attached, and more than 100 contract research and development firms began operation in the
United States between 1965 and 1975 (Dentler, 2002; Rossi & Freeman, 1989, p. 34). The
RAND Corporation expanded from its role as a U.S. Air Force planning unit into a major
social research firm, SRI International spun off from Stanford University as a private firm,
and Abt Associates in Cambridge, Massachusetts, begun in a garage in 1965, grew to employ
more than 1,000 staff in five offices in the United States, Canada, and Europe. The World
Bank and International Monetary Fund (IMF) also began to require evaluation of the programs they funded in other countries (Dentler, 2002, p. 147).

The New Jersey Income Maintenance Experiment was the first large-scale, randomized
experiment to test social policy in action. Designed in 1967, the New Jersey Experiment
randomly assigned 1,300 families to different income support levels to test the impact of

cash transfers to the working poor on their work effort. It was soon followed by even larger experiments to test other income maintenance questions, most notably the Seattle-Denver Income Maintenance Experiment (Orr, 1999, pp. 24–26).

In the early 1980s, after this period of rapid growth, many evaluation research firms closed in tandem with the decline of many Great Society programs. However, the demand for evaluation research continues, due in part to government requirements. The Community Mental Health Act Amendments of 1975 (Public Law 94–63) requires quality assurance (QA) reviews, which often involve evaluation-like activities (Patton, 2002, pp. 147–151), and the Government Performance and Results Act of 1993 requires some type of evaluation of all government programs (U.S. Office of Management and the Budget Executive Office of the President, 2002). At century's end, the federal government was spending about $200 million annually on evaluating $400 billion in domestic programs, and the 30 major federal agencies had between them 200 distinct evaluation units (Boruch, 1997). In 1999, the new Governmental Accounting Standards Board urged that more attention be given to "service efforts and accomplishments" in standard government fiscal reports (Campbell, 2002).

The growth of evaluation research is also reflected in the social science community. The American Evaluation Association was founded in 1986 as a professional organization for evaluation researchers (merging two previous associations) and publisher of an evaluation research journal. In 1999, evaluation researchers founded the Campbell Collaboration to publicize and encourage systematic review of evaluation research studies. Their online archive contained 10,449 reports on randomized evaluation studies (Davies, Petrosino, & Chalmers, 1999).

EVALUATION BASICS

Exhibit 10.1 illustrates the process of evaluation research as a simple systems model. First, clients, customers, students, or some other people or units—cases—enter the program as **inputs**. (You'll notice that this model treats programs like machines, with people functioning as raw materials to be processed.) Students may begin a new school program, welfare recipients may enroll in a new job training program, or crime victims may be sent to a victim advocate. Clients or consumers should reflect the **target population**, that is, the population for whom the program was intended. Besides clients, social programs require other inputs, such as staff with certain types of expertise or knowledge and resources such as money, supplies, equipment, and the like.

Inputs Resources, raw materials, clients, and staff that go into a program.

Target population The population the program is designed to serve.

Next, some service or treatment is provided to the clients or consumers. This may be a research class, assistance with independent living, counseling about family issues, housing, or special cash benefits. The **program process** may be simple or complicated, short or long, but it is designed to have some impact on the clients.

Program process The complete treatment or service delivered by the program.

Exhibit 10.1   A Model of Evaluation

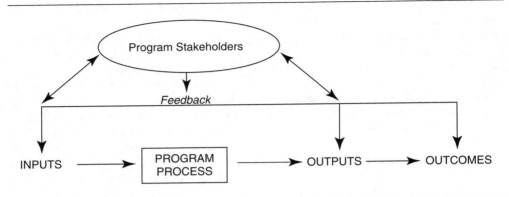

Source: From Martin, L., & Kettner, P., *Measuring the Performance of Human Service Programs.* Copyright © 1996. Reprinted with permission from Sage Publications, Inc.

The direct product of the program's service delivery process is its **output.** Program outputs may include clients served, case managers trained, food parcels delivered, or child abuse reports investigated. The program outputs may be desirable in themselves, but they primarily serve to indicate that the program is operating. Notice that with each of these outputs, there is no mention as to whether the clients improved or not, whether the case managers actually acquired the skills, whether the food enhanced the health of the recipients, or whether the child was placed in a safe environment.

Program **outcomes** indicate the impact of the program on the recipients of the activities. Outcomes can range from improved social functioning or improved job-seeking skills to fewer substantiated child abuse reports, and lower rates of poverty. Any social program is likely to have multiple outcomes, some intended and some unintended, some positive and others that are viewed as negative.

Outputs   The services delivered or new products produced by the program process.

Outcomes   The impact of the program process on the cases processed.

Variation in both outputs and outcomes in turn influence the inputs to the program through a **feedback** process. If too few clients are being served, resources may be devoted to the recruitment of new clients. If staff members lack the skills to implement the program, they may need to attend training workshops, or new staff may be hired. If the program fails to achieve its outcomes, the program may be modified or terminated. If a program does not appear to lead to improved outcomes, clients may go elsewhere.

Feedback   Information about service delivery system outputs, outcomes, or operations that is available to any program inputs.

Evaluation research is a systematic approach to feedback; it strengthens the feedback loop through credible analyses of program operations and outcomes. Evaluation research also broadens this loop to include connections to parties outside of the program itself. A funding agency or political authority may mandate the evaluation, outside experts may be brought in to conduct the evaluation, and the evaluation findings may be released to the public, or at least funders, in a formal report.

The evaluation process as a whole, and feedback in particular, can be understood only in relation to the interests and perspectives of program stakeholders. **Stakeholders** are those individuals and groups who have some interest in the program. They might be clients, staff, managers, funders, or the public. The board of a program or agency, the parents or spouses of clients, the foundations that award program grants, the auditors who monitor program spending, the members of Congress—each is a potential stakeholder, and each has an interest in the outcome of any program evaluation. Some may fund the evaluation, some may provide research data, and some may review, or even approve, the research report (Martin & Kettner, 1996, p. 3). Who the program stakeholders are and what role they play in the program evaluation will have tremendous consequences for the research.

Stakeholders Individuals and groups who have some basis of concern with the program

---

Can you see the difference between evaluation research and traditional social science research (Posavac & Carey, 1997)? Evaluation research is not designed to test the implications of a social theory; the basic issue is often the program's impact. Process evaluation, for instance, often uses qualitative methods in the same way traditional social science does. Unlike exploratory research, the goal is not to induce a broad theoretical explanation for what is discovered; instead, the question is how the program does what it does. Unlike social science research, evaluation studies are not designed in accord only with the highest scientific standards and the most important research questions; instead, program stakeholders set the agenda. But there is no sharp boundary between social science research and evaluation studies. In their attempt to explain how and why the program has an impact, and whether the program is needed, evaluation researchers often bring theories into their projects, but for immediately practical aims.

This does not mean that practice theories are not important. Many social work interventions are designed to apply a particular treatment model to a particular problem. These models may have their roots in particular social theories. For example, some treatment programs for depression are based on cognitive-behavioral therapy, which, as we described in Chapter 2, is based on learning and social learning theories.

Furthermore, we do not mean to suggest that the principles associated with the highest scientific standards are not important. For a variety of reasons, researchers and evaluators may not be able to use the best methods, given time, feasibility, and other practical concerns. Nonetheless, to the extent possible, evaluators try to achieve the highest standard possible. The types of practices we have described in the preceding chapters provide a framework that can be compared to the method used in a particular evaluation; evaluators use these comparisons to describe the limitations to their findings and conclusions.

Describing the Program: The Logic Model

Program assumptions. Target populations. Inputs. Outputs. Outcomes. Program activities. How can we put all these pieces of a program together and summarize it in an easy fashion? One method increasingly being used is a **logic model**—a schematic representation of the various components that make up a social service program. The popularity of logic models as a tool for program planning, program implementation, and program evaluation has grown throughout the 1990s, and funders such as the United Way and the W. K. Kellogg Foundation often use them.

A logic model is nothing more than a picture or chart of the different components that go into a program. There is no single logic model design; the categories you choose to include often depend on the purpose for the logic model. Logic models may describe: (1) theory and its link to change (theory approach model), where attention is on how and why a program works; (2) outcomes (outcome approach model), where the focus of the logic model is to connect resources and activities to expected changes; or (3) activities (activities approach model), which describes what the program actually does (W. K. Kellogg Foundation, 2001).

The basic components of a logic model include the following:

Social problem. Programs are designed to address a social condition deemed undesirable or to enhance desirable conditions. The range of social conditions is vast and might include the social isolation among the elderly, child abuse, lack of income, drug use, homelessness, or employee productivity. The specific program is likely to address only a small component of the broader social problem.

Target population. In the "For Whom" section, the evaluator identifies the criteria, if any, used to define an appropriate recipient of the service. Potential recipients may need to be in a particular age group, to reside in a particular geographical area, or to have a particular psychiatric symptom. A wide range of possible criteria can be used to describe the target population.

Program assumptions. Evaluators consider two different types of program assumptions. First, the evaluator identifies the particular program's assumptions about the causes of the social condition. A program designed to delay or prevent adolescent use of alcohol and other drugs may assume that the reason adolescents use drugs is that they lack knowledge about the consequences of drug use. Another program designed to address the same social problem may assume that adolescents who use drugs lack self-esteem and need strategies to cope with peer pressure. The second program assumption deals with the treatment model employed by the program. The type of intervention used by the agency is often derived from a particular practice orientation.

Inputs. We have already defined inputs as clients, staff, and resources. For the logic model, the description of inputs is more specific, identifying each type of staff, their number, and their expertise.

Activities. With the program staff, the evaluator identifies the specific activities that make up the program. Some activities, such as a psychosocial assessment or a group counseling session, may directly involve the client whereas other activities necessary for the program, such as a psychiatric consult, do not directly include the client in the interaction. Activities often include intake, assessment, treatment planning, specific interventions, evaluation, and termination.

Outputs. In the preceding section, we suggested that outputs are what the program produces. Martin and Kettner (1996) suggest that programs produce two types of outputs: (1) intermediate outputs, referred to as units of service, and (2) final outputs, referred to as service completions. Units of service are activities undertaken by the program staff; such units of service are often described in terms of frequency or number, time or duration, or tangible good. For example, the output of a counseling session might be described as the number of counseling sessions, the amount of time spent in providing counseling, or the number of counseling sessions lasting a certain amount of time. What is unique about units of service is that we count not what is provided to one client but what is provided to all clients.

Service completions refer to the agency's definition of a client who has received the "full package of services" as opposed to someone who began the program but dropped out prematurely (Martin & Kettner, 1996). Often, service completions are defined as encompassing a mix of services; for example, clients in a drug treatment program would be deemed to have completed the full range of services if they attended 80% of their assigned groups and participated in 80% of their scheduled individual counseling sessions. Another way of defining a service completion is by using some measure of time. A nursing home resident is likely to live in the institution for an extended time period. Because in some states nursing homes must complete an evaluation of the resident every 90 days, a service completion for a particular person might be defined by that time period: residence for 90 days. In a given year, a resident may "complete service" four times.

Defining a service completion is particularly important for evaluations that examine program impact on the clients. The logic model's assumption is that a client should have the "full dose" of activities, if improvements are to occur, or else, why provide the various activities. The reasoning is analogous to when the doctor prescribes an antibiotic and warns that if you do not take the antibiotic for the full 12 days, you won't get better. When evaluators do studies of client change, they want to do it with those people who have received the right mix of program activities.

Outcomes. In the last category of the logic model, the evaluator defines the kinds of changes expected to occur as the result of the program. There are intermediate outcomes and final or ultimate outcomes. Intermediate outcomes are the changes in the client that are necessary before the final or ultimate outcome might occur. To prevent or delay adolescent use of alcohol and other drugs, certain intermediate outcomes must be achieved, such as increased knowledge about the consequences of drug use or enhanced self-esteem or improved coping strategies. If the assumptions are correct about the use of alcohol and other drugs, and if the intermediate outcomes are achieved, the ultimate outcome of delayed use or abstinence should be more likely.

Exhibit 10.2 illustrates a logic model of a partial hospitalization program to treat children with psychiatric problems. Partial hospitalization programs are an alternative to complete hospitalization in that the child is not completely removed from the community and the program provides for a transition to outpatient services (Whitelaw & Perez, 1987). Partial hospitalization programs typically provide both therapeutic services and educational classes to their clients (Kotsopoulos, Walker, Beggs, & Jones, 1996).

The social problem in this case is that children with moderate or severe psychiatric disorders have difficulty functioning in the community and, therefore, may need to be placed in a full-time hospital environment. The target population has been defined by age, residence, and the presence of a psychiatric disorder (see Exhibit 10.2, *For Whom*). The program providers

Exhibit 10.2   Program Logic Model: Partial Hospitalization Program

Social Problem: Inability to function independently in the community

For Whom	Assumptions	Inputs	Activities	Outputs	Outcomes
Children age 6 to 12, living in the county who display moderate to severe psychiatric disorders and are at risk of inpatient hospitalizations.	The inability to function independently in the community is due to: a. increased psychiatric symptoms b. lack of anger management skills c. behavioral problems d. lack of problem solving skills e. lack of communication skills f. poor coping skills g. low self-esteem h. parental lack of knowledge	3 MSW level therapists 1 child psychiatrist 1 nurse M.Ed. in special education space chairs, desks educational materials computers money	Assessment Treatment planning Individual counseling Group therapy Family meetings Team meetings Discharge planning Discharge Educational classes	Intermediate: # of assessments completed/ month # of hours of individual counseling provided/ month # of group therapy sessions held/month # of hours of family meetings # of team meetings # of hours of discharge planning # of discharges	Intermediate: 1. Reduction in psychiatric symptoms 2. Increased anger management skills 3. Fewer behavioral problems 4. Improved problem solving skills 5. Improved communication skills 6. Improved coping skills 7. Increased self-esteem 8. Parents have more knowledge about diagnosis and symptoms
	Treatment Model: Multiple interventions including cognitive behavioral therapy and medication management			Service Completion: Child attends 80% of individual and group counseling sessions and Family attends all family meetings	Final: Child can function independently in school, home, and community.

believe that this social problem is the outcome of several different problems including the failure to control psychiatric symptoms, deficiencies in anger management, behavioral issues, inadequate coping and communication skills, poor self-esteem, and the lack of parental knowledge (see *Assumptions*). The range of program activities is deemed sufficient to resolve these various problems. Program activities include group therapy and individual counseling (see *Activities*) and are based on cognitive behavioral therapy (see *Assumptions*).

The assumptions about the factors are related to the social problem and the intermediate and final outcomes. The activities in the program are intended to improve on each of the areas identified in the assumptions, so the intermediate outcomes reflect the desired changes in each of these areas. One problem is increased psychiatric symptoms; therefore, the intermediate outcome is a reduction in psychiatric symptoms. Each of the factors listed in the assumptions has a parallel intermediate outcome (see *Outcomes*). The same is true with the overall social problem; if the problem is the inability of children to function independently in the community, then the ultimate outcome is that this is no longer a problem, rather, the child can function independently.

This symmetry occurs with activities and intermediate outputs as well. As you can see in Exhibit 10.2, there is a measure of service for each activity. In this example, the evaluator chose to measure service activity using a count or frequency of activity. If it was important, the evaluator might have used a measure of time—for example, the number of hours spent completing assessments each month. Remember, this count (or length of time) is how many times the staff person conducted the activity with all clients in that month (or how much time staff spent), and not how much time the *client* spent on each activity.

As you can see, a logic model provides a great deal of information about the program in a succinct manner. After completing the logic model, the evaluator, and often stakeholders, should have a better understanding about the logic underlying the program. Also, the logic model may help clarify the specific interests or questions for the evaluation.

QUESTIONS FOR EVALUATION RESEARCH

Evaluation projects can focus on a variety of questions related to the operation of social programs and the impact they have:

- Is the program needed?
- How does the program operate?
- What is the program's impact?
- How efficient is the program?

You can see how a logic model is helpful because it provides detailed answers for these questions. If you want to measure program activities, the outputs column provides measures. If you are interested in the program's impact, then the intermediate and final outcomes can serve as a guide. The specific methods used in an evaluation research project depend in part on the particular question of interest.

Needs Assessment

Is a new program needed or an old one still required? Is there a need at all? A **needs assessment** attempts to answer this question with systematic, credible evidence. Need may be identified and enumerated by social indicators such as the poverty rate or school dropout rate, by interviews of such local experts such as mental health providers, by surveys of populations in need or service providers, by structured groups such as focus groups with community residents, or by taking a resource inventory of available services and service capacity, as is often done by a local United Way (McKillip, 1987). The evaluation will enumerate need, while the assessment of need and subsequent priorities will depend ultimately on the final judgment of key stakeholders.

It is not as easy as it sounds (Posavac & Carey, 1997). Whose definitions or perceptions should be used to shape our description of the level of need? How will we deal with ignorance of need? How can we understand the level of need without understanding the social context from which that level of need emerges? (Short answer to that one: We can't!) What, after all, does *need* mean in the abstract? We won't really understand what the level of need is until we develop plans for implementing a program in response to identified needs.

The results of the Boston McKinney Project reveal the importance of taking a multidimensional approach to the investigation of need. The Boston McKinney Project evaluated the merits of providing formerly homeless mentally ill people with staffed group housing as compared to individual housing (Goldfinger et al., 1997). In a sense, you can think of the whole experiment as involving an attempt to answer the question: What type of housing do these people need? Goldfinger and colleagues examined this question at the start of the project by asking two clinicians to estimate which of the two housing alternatives would be best for each project participant (Goldfinger & Schutt, 1996) and by asking each participant which type of housing he or she wanted (Schutt & Goldfinger, 1996).

Clinicians recommended staffed group housing for 69% of the participants, whereas most of the participants (51%) sought individual housing. In fact, the housing recommendations of the clinicians did not correspond to the housing preferences of the participants (who did not know what the clinicians had recommended for them). So, which perspective reveals the level of need for staffed group housing as opposed to individual housing?

Yet another perspective on housing needs is introduced by the project's outcomes. Individuals assigned to the group housing were somewhat more successful in retaining their housing than those who were assigned to individual housing (Goldfinger et al., 1999). Does this reveal that these homeless mentally ill people needed group housing more than they needed individual housing, in spite of their preferences? What should we make of the fact that participants with the stronger preference for individual housing were more likely to lose their housing during the project, whereas the participants whom the clinicians had rated as ready for independent living were less likely to lose their housing? What should we make of the fact that whether or not participants received the type of housing the clinicians recommended or that they themselves preferred made no difference in the likelihood of their losing their housing during the project? Does this mean that neither initial preferences nor clinician recommendations tell us about need for one or the other type of housing, only about the risk of losing whatever housing they were assigned?

The methodological lesson here is that in needs assessment, as in other forms of evaluation research, it is a good idea to use multiple indicators. You can also see that there is no absolute definition of *need* in this situation, nor is there likely to be in any but the most simplistic evaluation projects. Good evaluation researchers will do their best to capture different perspectives on need and help others make sense of the results.

A wonderful little tale, popular with evaluation researchers, reveals the importance of thinking creatively about what people need:

The manager of a 20-story office building had received many complaints about the slowness of the elevators. He hired an engineering consultant to propose a solution. The consultant measured traffic flow and elevator features and proposed replacing the old elevators with new ones, which could shave 20 seconds off the average waiting time. The only problem: it cost $100,000. A second consultant proposed adding 2 additional elevators, for a total wait time reduction of 35 seconds and a cost of $150,000. Neither alternative was affordable. A third consultant was brought in. He looked around for a few days and announced that the problem was not really the waiting times, but boredom. For a cost of less than $1000, the manager had large mirrors installed next to the elevators so people could primp and observe themselves while waiting for an elevator. The result: no more complaints. Problem solved. (Witkin & Altschuld, 1995, p. 38)

Process Evaluation

What actually happens in a social program? In the New Jersey Income Maintenance Experiment, some welfare recipients received higher payments than others (Kershaw & Fair, 1976). The design was simple enough, and it was not too difficult to verify that the right people received the intended treatment. In the Minneapolis experiment on the police response to domestic violence (Sherman & Berk, 1984), some individuals accused of assaulting their spouses were arrested, whereas others were just warned. This is a little bit more complicated because the severity of the warning might have varied between police officers; also, to minimize the risk of repeat harm, police officers were allowed to override the experimental assignment. To identify the extent of variation from the intended experimental design, the researchers would have had to keep track of the treatments delivered to each accused spouse and collect some information on what officers actually did when they warned an accused spouse. This would be **process evaluation**—research to investigate how the program is operating.

Process evaluation　Evaluation research that investigates the process of service delivery.

Process evaluations are completed to answer a variety of different questions related to the operation of a particular program: Is the program serving its target population? Has the program been implemented as designed? What are the outputs of various program activities? In the past, process evaluations were the primary response to funders who wanted to know whether the agency had actually carried out its planned activities. Increasingly, process evaluation is conducted to identify specific activities that lead to program outcomes as well as to determine client satisfaction with the program activities.

Process evaluation is even more important when more complex programs are evaluated. Many social programs involve multiple elements and are delivered over an extended period of time, often by different providers in different areas. Due to this complexity, it is quite possible that the program as delivered is not the same for all program recipients, nor consistent with the formal program design.

The evaluation of D.A.R.E. by Research Triangle Institute researchers Christopher Ringwalt and colleagues (1994, p. 7) included a process evaluation with three objectives:

Exhibit 10.3   Components of D.A.R.E. and Other Alcohol and Drug Prevention Programs
Rated as Very Satisfactory (%)

Components	D.A.R.E. Program (N = 222)	Other AOD Programs (N = 406)
Curriculum	67.5	34.2
Teaching	69.7	29.8
Administrative Requirements	55.7	23.1
Receptivity of Students	76.5	34.6
Effects on Students	63.2	22.8

Source: Ringwalt et al., 1994:58.

- Assess the organizational structure and operation of representative D.A.R.E. programs nationwide
- Review and assess factors that contribute to the effective implementation of D.A.R.E. programs nationwide
- Assess how D.A.R.E. and other school-based drug prevention programs are tailored to meet the needs of specific populations

The process evaluation (they called it an *implementation assessment*) was an ambitious research project in itself, with site visits, informal interviews, discussions, and surveys of D.A.R.E. program coordinators and advisers. These data indicated that D.A.R.E. was operating as designed and was running relatively smoothly. As shown in Exhibit 10.3, drug prevention coordinators in D.A.R.E. school districts rated the program components as much more satisfactory than did coordinators in school districts with other types of alcohol and drug prevention programs.

Process evaluation can be used to identify the specific aspects of the service delivery process that have an impact. This, in turn, will help to explain why the program has an effect and which conditions are required for these effects. (In Chapter 5, we described this as identifying the causal mechanism.) Implementation problems identified in site visits included insufficient numbers of officers to carry out the program as planned and a lack of Spanish-language D.A.R.E. books in a largely Hispanic school. Classroom observations indicated engaging presentations and active student participation (Ringwalt et al., 1994, p. 58).

Process evaluation of this sort can also help to show how apparently unambiguous findings may be incorrect. The apparently disappointing results of the Transitional Aid Research Project (TARP) provide an instructive lesson of this sort. TARP was a social experiment designed to determine whether financial aid during the transition from prison to the community would help released prisoners to find employment and avoid returning to crime. Two thousand participants in Georgia and Texas were randomized to receive a particular level of benefits over a particular period of time or no benefits (the control group). Initially, it seemed that the payments had no effect: The rate of subsequent arrests for both property and non-property crimes weren't affected by TARP treatment condition.

But this wasn't all there was to it. Peter Rossi tested a more elaborate causal model of TARP effects, which is summarized in Exhibit 10.4 (Chen, 1990, p. 210). Participants who received TARP payments had more income to begin with and so had more to lose if they were

Exhibit 10.4   Model of Effects of Transitional Aid Research Project (TARP)

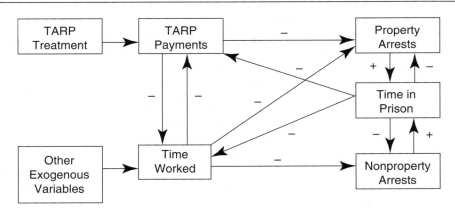

Source: Chen, H., Theory-Driven Evaluations. Copyright © 1990. Reprinted with permission from Sage Publications, Inc.

arrested; therefore, they were less likely to commit crimes. However, TARP payments also created a disincentive to work and therefore increased the time available in which to commit crimes. Thus, the positive direct effect of TARP (more to lose) was cancelled out by its negative indirect effect (more free time).

The term **formative evaluation** may be used instead of process evaluation when the evaluation findings are used to help shape and refine the program (Rossi & Freeman, 1989). Formative evaluation procedures that are incorporated into the initial development of the service program can specify the treatment process and lead to changes in recruitment procedures, program delivery, or measurement tools (Patton, 2002, p. 220).

> ***Formative evaluation***   Process evaluation that is used to shape and refine program operations.

You can see the formative element in the following government report on the performance of the Health Care Finance Administration (HCFA):

> While HCFA's performance report and plan indicate that it is making some progress toward achieving its Medicare program integrity outcome, progress is difficult to measure because of continual goal changes that are sometimes hard to track or that are made with insufficient explanation. Of the five fiscal year 2000 program integrity goals it discussed, HCFA reported that three were met, a fourth unmet goal was revised to reflect a new focus, and performance data for the fifth will not be available until mid-2001. HCFA plans to discontinue three of these goals. Although the federal share of Medicaid is projected to be $124 billion in fiscal year 2001, HCFA had no program integrity goal for Medicaid for fiscal year 2000. CFA has since added a developmental goal concerning Medicaid payment accuracy. (U.S. Government Accounting Office, 2001, p. 7)

Process evaluation can employ a wide range of indicators. Program coverage can be monitored through program records, participant surveys, and community surveys or by comparing program users with dropouts and ineligibles. Service delivery can be monitored through service records completed by program staff, a management information system maintained by program administrators, or reports by program recipients (Rossi & Freeman, 1989).

Service delivery can also be reviewed through the use of a flowchart to describe program activities. The flowchart typically includes program activities, decision points at which a client may receive a different set of activities, and points at which documentation is necessary. Flowcharts are used to answer questions such as: Are all necessary activities present in the program, or are there missing activities? Is there duplication of service effort? How long does it take for a client to go through the entire process? How long does it take for a client to go from initial intake to assessment to intervention?

Increasingly, both program providers and those funding programs are interested in client satisfaction with program processes. A well-designed client satisfaction survey focused on the specific operation of the program can provide useful information about how to improve the program. Martin and Kettner (1996) suggest that rather than using global measures of satisfaction, providers should include questions that focus on particular dimensions of interest to the agency such as the accessibility of services, courtesy of staff, timeliness of services, competency of practitioners, staff attitudes toward the client, or the appearance of the facilities, staff, and program materials.

Qualitative methods are often a key component of process evaluation studies because they can be used to elucidate and understand internal program dynamics—even those that were not anticipated (Patton, 2002, p. 159; Posavac & Carey, 1997). Qualitative researchers may develop detailed descriptions of how program participants engage with each other, how the program experience varies for different people, and how the program changes and evolves over time.

Outcome Evaluation

The core questions of evaluation research are: Did the program work? Did the intervention have the intended result? This part of the research is called **outcome evaluation,** or in some cases impact evaluation or summative evaluation. Formally speaking, outcome evaluation compares what happened after a program with what would have happened had there been no program.

Outcome evaluation   The extent to which a treatment or other service has an effect. Also known as *impact evaluation* or *summative evaluation*.

Think of the program—a new strategy for combating domestic violence, an income supplement, whatever—as an independent variable, and the result it seeks as a dependent variable. The DARE program (independent variable), for instance, tries to reduce drug use (dependent variable). When the program is present, we expect less drug use. In a more elaborate study, we might have multiple values of the independent variable; for instance, we might look at *no program, DARE program,* and *other drug/alcohol education* conditions and compare the results of each.

As in other areas of research, an experimental design is the preferred method for maximizing internal validity—that is, for making sure your causal claims about program impact are justified. Cases are assigned randomly to one or more experimental treatment groups and to a control group so that there is no systematic difference between the groups at the outset (see Chapter 6). The goal is to achieve a fair, unbiased test of the program itself so that the judgment about the program's impact is not influenced by differences between the types of people who are in the different groups. This can be a difficult goal to achieve because the usual practice in social programs is to let people decide for themselves whether they want to enter a program or not; also, it can be difficult to establish eligibility criteria that ensure that people who enter the program are different from those who do not (Boruch, 1997). In either case, a selection bias is introduced.

Sometimes, researchers are able to use true experimental designs in which individuals are assigned randomly either to the program or to some other condition. Robert Drake, Gregory McHugo, Deborah Becker, William Anthony, and Robin Clark (1996) evaluated the impact of two different approaches to providing employment services for people diagnosed with severe mental disorders, using a randomized experimental design. One approach, group skills training (GST), emphasizes preemployment skills training and uses separate agencies to provide vocational and mental health services. The other approach, individual placement and support (IPS), provides vocational and mental health services in a single program and places people directly into jobs without preemployment skills training. The researchers hypothesized that GST participants would be more likely than IPS participants to obtain jobs during the 18-month study period.

Their experimental design is depicted in Exhibit 10.5. Cases were assigned randomly to the two groups, and then:

1. Both groups received a pretest.

2. One group received the experimental intervention (GST), and the other received the IPS approach.

3. Both groups received three posttests, at 6, 12, and 18 months.

Contrary to the researchers' hypothesis, the IPS participants were twice as likely to obtain a competitive job as the GST participants. The IPS participants also worked more hours and earned more total wages. Although this was not the outcome Drake and his colleagues had anticipated, it was valuable information for policymakers and program planners—and the study was rigorously experimental.

Outcome evaluations that do not use an experimental design still provide useful information and may be all that is feasible or ethically permissible. Therefore, program outcomes are often evaluated with quasi-experimental designs, particularly *nonequivalent control group designs;* nonexperimental designs such as the *one group pretest-posttest design; and* survey, single-subject, or field research methods. When we use such designs, causal conclusions about program outcomes will be on much shakier ground. If current participants who are already in a program are compared to nonparticipants, it is unlikely that the treatment group will be comparable to the control group. Participants will probably be a selected group, different at the outset from nonparticipants. For instance, when a study at New York's maximum-security prison for women found that "Income Education [i.e., classes] Is Found to Lower Risk of New Arrest," the conclusions were immediately suspect: The research design did not ensure that the women who enrolled in the prison classes had the same characteristics as those

Exhibit 10.5   Randomized Comparative Change Design: Employment Services for People with Severe Mental Disorders

Key: R = Random assignment
       O = Observation (employment status at pretest or posttest)
       X = Experimental treatment

	O_1	X	O_2	O_3	O_4
Experimental Group	Pretest	Preemployment skills training	Posttest at 6 months	Posttest at 12 months	Posttest at 18 months
Comparison Group	Pretest		Posttest at 6 months	Posttest at 12 months	Posttest at 18 months

R (with arrows to Experimental Group and Comparison Group)

Source: Drake, McHugo, Becker, Anthony, & Clark, 1996, pp. 391–399. Copyright © 1996. Reprinted with permission of the American Psychological Association.

Key: R = Random assignment; O = Observation (employment status at pretest or posttest); X = Experimental treatment.

who were not, "leaving open the possibility that the results were due, at least in part, to self-selection, with the women most motivated to avoid reincarceration being the ones who took the college classes" (Lewin, 2001a, p. A18; see also Lewin, 2001b).

Outcome evaluation is an important undertaking that fully deserves the attention it has been given in the program funding requirements of local United Ways, foundations, and the government. It is important to establish the most rigorous designs feasible and to acknowledge the limitations of the design. However, you should realize that more rigorous evaluation designs are less likely to conclude that a program has the desired effect; as the standard of proof goes up, success is harder to demonstrate.

Efficiency Analysis

Whatever the program's benefits, are they sufficient to offset the program's costs? Are the funders getting their money's worth? These efficiency questions can be the primary reason that funders require evaluation of the programs they fund. As a result, **efficiency analysis**, which compares program effects to costs, is often a necessary component of an evaluation research project.

Efficiency analysis   A type of evaluation research that compares program costs to program effects. Can be either cost-benefit analysis or cost-effectiveness analysis.

A **cost-benefit analysis** must identify the specific costs and benefits that will be studied, which requires in turn that the analyst identify whose perspective will be used to determine what can be considered a benefit rather than a cost. Program clients will have a different perspective on these issues than do taxpayers or program staff. Consider, for example, the

Exhibit 10.6   Conceptual Framework for Cost-Benefit Analysis of an Employment and Training Program

Costs/Benefits	Perspective of Program Participants	Perspective of Rest of Society	Perspective of Entire Society*
Costs			
Operational costs of the program	0	–	–
Forgone leisure and home production	–	0	–
Benefits			
Earnings gains	+	0	+
Reduced costs of nonexperimental services	0	+	+
Transfers			
Reduced welfare benefits	–	+	0
Wage subsidies	+	–	0
Net benefits	+/–	+/–	+/–

Source: Orr, L., 1999. Reprinted with permission from Sage Publications, Inc.

Key: – = program costs; + = program benefits; +/– = program costs and benefits' O = no program costs or benefits. * Entire society = program participants + rest of society

costs and benefits you might list as a student versus the costs and benefits that the university might include. Tuition and fees, which are costs to you, are benefits for the university.

> ***Cost-benefit analysis*** A type of evaluation research that compares program costs to the economic value of program benefits.

Exhibit 10.6 lists factors that can be considered costs or benefits in an employment and training program from the standpoint of program participants, the rest of society, and the society as a whole (the combination of program participants and the rest of society) (Orr, 1999, p. 224). Note that some anticipated impacts of the program—for example, on welfare benefits and wage subsidies—are considered a cost to one group and a benefit to the other, whereas some are not relevant to one of the groups.

Once potential costs and benefits have been identified, they must be measured. This is a need highlighted in recent government programs:

> The Governmental Accounting Standards Board's (GASB) mission is to establish and improve standards of accounting and financial reporting for state and local governments in the United States. In June 1999, the GASB issued a major revision to current reporting requirements ("Statement 34"). The new reporting will provide information that citizens

and other users can utilize to gain an understanding of the financial position and cost of programs for a government and a descriptive management's discussion and analysis to assist in understanding a government's financial results. (Campbell, 2002, p. 1)

In addition to measuring services and their associated costs, a cost-benefit analysis must be able to make some type of estimation of how clients benefit from the program. Normally, this will involve a comparison of some indicators of client status before and after clients received program services, or between clients who received program services and a comparable group who did not. In a cost-benefit analysis, these benefits are assigned a cash value.

A recent study of therapeutic communities provides a clear illustration. A *therapeutic community* is a method for treating substance abuse in which abusers participate in an intensive, structured living experience with other addicts who are attempting to stay sober. Because the treatment involves residential support as well as other types of services, it can be quite costly. Are those costs worth it?

Sacks, McKendrick, DeLeon, French, and McCollister (2002) conducted a cost-benefit analysis of a modified therapeutic community (TC). Three hundred and forty-two homeless mentally ill chemical abusers were randomly assigned to either a TC or a "treatment-as-usual" comparison group. Employment status, criminal activity, and utilization of health care services were each measured for the three months prior to entering treatment and the three months after treatment. Earnings from employment in each period were adjusted for costs incurred by criminal activity and utilization of health care services.

Was it worth it? The average cost of TC treatment for a client was $20,361. In comparison, the economic benefit (based on earnings) to the average TC client was $305,273, which declined to $273,698 after comparing post- to pre-program earnings, but it was still $253,337 even after adjustment for costs. The resulting benefit-cost ratio was 13:1, although this ratio declined to only 5.2:1 after further adjustments (for cases with extreme values). Nonetheless, the TC program studied seems to have had a substantial benefit relative to its costs.

It is often difficult to assign a dollar value to outcomes produced in social work programs. **Cost-effectiveness analysis** is a common alternative to cost-benefit analysis; this analysis compares the costs of different programs (or interventions) to the actual program outcomes in lieu of assigning a dollar value to the outcomes. In these comparisons, the program costs are calculated while the benefits are listed and not assigned a cash value.

Cost-effectiveness analysis A type of evaluation research that compares program costs to actual program outcomes.

A study by Susan Essock, Linda Frisman, and Nina Kontos (1998) illustrates the use of cost-effectiveness analysis. They compared the costs and benefits of assertive community treatment (ACT) to standard case management (SCM) to treat people with serious mental disorders. Each method of treatment is designed to help clients function in the community. ACT used a multidisciplinary team and provided 24-hour coverage, whereas the SCM model offered only a case manager. The ACT team members offered and provided treatment services, whereas in SCM, the case manager either provided the service or arranged for an independent provider to offer the service. The study included 262 participants with serious mental disorders who had difficulty functioning in the community. Participants were randomly assigned to ACT or SCM. Data were collected at baseline and 6, 12, and 18 months after baseline. Essock and colleagues examined the number of days hospitalized, quality of life, psychiatric symptoms, and family burden.

Over the 18 month period, ACT clients reported higher quality of life, including personal safety, leisure activities, living situation, and frequency of contact with friends, and they spent more days in the community. Although there were no overall differences in family burden as reported by family members, ACT client family members with high objective burden reported lower subjective burden than did SCM family members. The actual cost of the program to the state department of mental health, the state overall, or society did not differ significantly for ACT and SCM, although in each category the ACT program was slightly cheaper. Therefore, at about the same cost, the ACT program produced more desirable outcomes.

DESIGN ALTERNATIVES

Once we have decided on, or identified, the goal or focus for a program evaluation, important decisions must be made about how to design the specific evaluation project. The most important decisions are the following:

- *Black box or program theory:* Do we care how the program gets results?
- *Researcher or stakeholder orientation:* Whose goals matter most?
- *Quantitative or qualitative methods:* Which methods provide the best answers?
- *Simple or complex outcomes:* How complicated should the findings be?

Black Box or Program Theory?

The "meat and potatoes" of most evaluation research involves determining whether a program has the intended effect. If the effect occurred, the program "worked"; if the effect didn't occur, then, some would say, the program should be abandoned or redesigned. In this approach, the process by which a program has an effect on outcomes is often treated as a **black box**, that is, the focus of the evaluation researcher is on whether cases seem to have changed as a result of their exposure to the program, between the time they entered the program as inputs and when they exited the program as outputs (Chen, 1990). The assumption is that program evaluation requires only the test of a simple input/output model, like the one shown in Exhibit 10.1. There may be no attempt to open the black box of the program process.

But there is good reason to open the black box and investigate how the process works (or doesn't work). Consider recent research on welfare-to-work programs. The Manpower Demonstration Research Corporation reviewed findings from research on these programs in Florida, Minnesota, and Canada. In each location, adolescents with parents in a welfare-to-work program were compared to a control group of teenagers whose parents were on welfare but were not enrolled in welfare-to-work. In all three locations, teenagers in the welfare-to-work families actually did worse in school than those in the control group— troubling findings.

But why? Why did requiring welfare mothers to work hurt their children's schoolwork? Unfortunately, because the researchers had not investigated program process—had not "opened the black box"—we can't know for sure. Martha Zaslow, an author of the resulting research report, speculated that

> parents in the programs might have less time and energy to monitor their adolescents' behavior once they were employed. . . . under the stress of working, they might adopt harsher parenting styles . . . the adolescents' assuming more responsibilities at home when parents got jobs was creating too great a burden. (Lewin, 2001b, p. A16)

But as Ms. Zaslow admitted, "We don't know exactly what's causing these effects, so it's really hard to say, at this point, what will be the long-term effects on these kids" (p. A16).

Now look at the flip side: when evaluators investigate what happens in the program. Wynne Korr and Antoine Joseph (1996) had found that a demonstration case management program for homeless mentally ill people implemented at two different sites resulted in vastly different outcomes. At each site, clients were randomly assigned to a control group receiving the traditional case management program and to an experimental group receiving assertive case management. The goals of the program were to identify and place clients in independent living situations and then help the clients maintain their independence. After six months, two thirds of clients in the experimental group at Site 1 were housed compared to 34% of the control group, while at Site 2, 53% of the experimental group and 66% of the control group were housed.

Why the contradictory findings? The investigators reviewed the client, organizational, and community context in which the program is located, using a model described by Chen (1990). After interviewing program staff, they found differences in client characteristics and reasons for homelessness, some differences in managerial style, and a difference in the way the program was delivered.

Some of the differences they found turned out to be quite important in explaining the contradictory outcomes. Prior to the intervention, most clients at Site 1 had been evicted from single-resident occupancy rooms and apartments, whereas most clients at Site 2 had lived with family or in board and care homes and were homeless because of family disputes. By itself, this finding, while interesting, did not fully explain the differences. It turns out that the available housing also differed by site. Site 1 was located in a neighborhood with most of the city's single-room occupancy housing whereas Site 2 had very few to no single-room occupancy alternatives but many board and care facilities. Because the ACT staff at Site 2 were trying to follow the intervention's guidelines, their efforts to place clients in single-room housing may have been contrary to the participants' wishes.

If an investigation of program process is conducted, a **program theory** may be developed. A program theory describes what has been learned about how the program has its effect. When a researcher has sufficient knowledge before the investigation begins, outlining a program theory can help to guide the investigation of program process in the most productive directions. This is termed a **theory-driven evaluation**.

Program theory   A descriptive or prescriptive model of how a program operates and produces effects.

A program theory specifies how the program is expected to operate and identifies which program elements are operational (Chen, 1990, p. 32). In addition, a program theory specifies how a program is to produce its effects and so improves understanding of the relationship

Exhibit 10.7   Program Theory Model

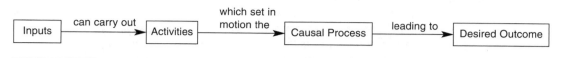

Source: Carol Weiss, 1978: 38.

between the independent variable (the program) and the dependent variable (the outcome or outcomes). Exhibit 10.7, based on the work of Carol Weiss (1972, 1998), shows the logical sequence for a successful program: The inputs (resources) are sufficient and appropriate to carry out the specific activities of the program, which set into motion a causal process (based on some practice theory) that results in the desired outcome. Programs may fail to achieve their desired outcomes for different reasons. The inputs may not be sufficient to carry out the program activities (input failure); the inputs may be sufficient, but the actual activities may be incomplete, insufficient, or poorly designed so that they do not set into motion the causal process (program failure); or the inputs may be sufficient and the program activities appropriate, but the causal process does not produce the desired outcomes (theory failure or wrong theory).

Program theory can be either descriptive or prescriptive (Chen, 1990). Descriptive theory specifies what impacts are generated and how they occur. It suggests a causal mechanism, including intervening factors, and the necessary context for the effects. Descriptive theories are generally empirically based. On the other hand, prescriptive theory specifies what ought to be done by the program and is not actually tested. Prescriptive theory specifies how to design or implement the treatment, what outcomes should be expected, and how performance should be judged. Comparison of the descriptive and prescriptive theories of the program can help to identify implementation difficulties and incorrect understandings that can be corrected (Patton, 2002, pp. 162–164).

Researcher or Stakeholder Orientation?

Whose prescriptions specify how the program should operate, what outcomes it should try to achieve, or who it should serve? Most social work research assumes that the researcher specifies the research questions, the applicable theory or theories, and the outcomes to be investigated. Social work research results are most often reported in a professional journal or at professional conferences, where scientific standards determine how the research is received. In program evaluation, however, the research question is often set by the program sponsors or the government agency that is responsible for reviewing the program. It is to these authorities that research findings are reported. Most often, this authority also specifies the outcomes to be investigated. The first evaluator of the evaluation research is the specific agency or the funder and not the professional social science community. Evaluation research is research for a client, and its results may directly affect the services or treatments that program users receive.

Should evaluation researchers insist on designing the evaluation project and specifying its goals, or should they accept the suggestions and adopt the goals of the funding agency? What role should the preferences of program staff or clients play? What responsibility do evaluation researchers have to politicians and taxpayers when evaluating government-funded programs? The different answers that various evaluation researchers have given to these questions are reflected in different approaches to evaluation (Chen, 1990, pp. 66–68).

Stakeholder approaches encourage researchers to be responsive to program stakeholders. Issues for study are to be based on the views of people involved with the program, and reports are to be made to program participants (Shadish, Cook, & Levitan, 1991, pp. 275–276). The researcher creates a program theory to clarify and develop the key stakeholders' theory of the program (Shadish et al., 1991, pp. 254–255). In one stakeholder approach, termed *utilization-focused evaluation*, the evaluator forms a task force of program stakeholders who help to shape the evaluation project so that they are most likely to use its results (Patton, 2002, pp. 171–175). One research approach that has been termed *appreciative inquiry* eliminates the professional researcher altogether in favor of a structured dialogue about needed changes among program participants themselves (Patton, 2002, pp. 177–185). In *stakeholder participatory research*, stakeholders are engaged with the researchers as co-researchers and help to design, conduct, and report the research (Rossi & Freeman, 1989).

Shantha Balaswamy and Holly Dabelko (2002) used the stakeholder participatory research approach to conduct a community-wide needs assessment of elderly residents. The agency initiating the project identified stakeholders, who were defined as "people with a vested interest in improving, protecting, and developing services for the community elders" (p. 60). An oversight committee was formed and included "aging service providers, funders, the city administrator, agency board members, research sponsors, administrator and faculty from local educational institution, seniors, community residents, administrators from private corporations, private non-profit funding organizations, and administrators from other social service agencies" (p. 60). This committee provided input and feedback on every phase of the needs assessment: establishing goals and objectives, developing the needs assessment tool, determining sampling issues and data collection methods, and implementing the actual data collection, data analysis, and dissemination. Because the stakeholders had been a part of the entire evaluation, the findings were used even when they were unexpected and negative. The oversight committee even created subcommittees to follow up on the community's use of the information.

Social science approaches emphasize the importance of researcher expertise and maintenance of some autonomy to develop the most trustworthy, unbiased program evaluation. It is assumed that "evaluators cannot passively accept the values and views of the other stakeholders" (Chen, 1990, p. 78). Evaluators who adopt this approach derive a program theory from information they obtain on how the program operates and from extant social science theory and knowledge, not from the views of stakeholders. In one somewhat extreme form of this approach, *goal-free evaluation*, researchers do not even permit themselves to learn what goals the program stakeholders have for the program. Instead, the researcher assesses and then compares the needs of participants to a wide array of program outcomes (Scriven, 1972). The goal-free evaluator wants to see the unanticipated outcomes and to remove any biases caused by knowing the program goals in advance.

Of course, there are disadvantages to both stakeholder and social science approaches to program evaluation. If stakeholders are ignored, researchers may find that participants are uncooperative, that their reports are unused, and that the next project remains unfunded. On the other hand, if social science procedures are neglected, standards of evidence will be compromised, conclusions about program effects will likely be invalid, and results are unlikely to be generalizable to other settings. These equally undesirable possibilities have led to several attempts to develop more integrated approaches to evaluation research.

Integrative approaches attempt to cover issues of concern to both stakeholders and evaluators and to include stakeholders in the group from which guidance is routinely sought (Chen & Rossi, 1987, pp. 101–102). The emphasis given to either stakeholder or social science concerns is expected to vary with the specific project circumstances. Integrative approaches seek to balance the goal of carrying out a project that is responsive to stakeholder concerns with the goal of objective, scientifically trustworthy and generalizable results. When the research is planned, evaluators are expected to communicate and negotiate regularly with key stakeholders and to take stakeholder concerns into account. Findings from preliminary inquiries are reported back to program decision makers so that they can make improvements in the program before it is formally evaluated. When the actual evaluation is conducted, the evaluation research team is expected to operate more or less autonomously, minimizing intrusions from program stakeholders.

Many evaluation researchers now recognize that they must take account of multiple values in their research and be sensitive to the perspectives of different stakeholders, in addition to maintaining a commitment to the goals of measurement validity, internal validity, and generalizability (Chen, 1990).

Quantitative or Qualitative Methods?

Evaluation research that attempts to identify the effects of a social program typically is quantitative: Did the response times of emergency personnel tend to decrease? Did the students' test scores increase? Did housing retention improve? Did substance abuse decline? It's fair to say that when there is an interest in comparing outcomes between an experimental and a control group, or tracking change over time in a systematic manner, quantitative methods are favored.

But qualitative methods can add much to quantitative evaluation research studies, including more depth, detail, nuance, and exemplary case studies (Patton, 2002). Perhaps the greatest contribution qualitative methods can make in many evaluation studies is investigating program process—finding out what is "inside the black box." Although it is possible to track service delivery with quantitative measures such as staff contact hours and frequency of complaints, finding out what is happening to clients and how clients experience the program can often best be accomplished by observing program activities and interviewing staff and clients intensively. For example, Patton (2002, p. 160) describes a study in which process analysis in an evaluation of a prenatal clinic's outreach program led to program changes. The process analysis revealed that the outreach workers were spending much time responding to immediate problems, such as needs for rat control, protection from violence, and access to English classes. As a result, the outreach workers were recruiting fewer community residents for the prenatal clinic. New training and recruitment strategies were adopted to lessen this deviation from program goals.

Another good reason for using qualitative methods in evaluation research is the importance of learning how different individuals react to the treatment. For example, a quantitative evaluation of student reactions to an adult basic skills program for new immigrants relied heavily on the students' initial statements of their goals. However, qualitative interviews revealed that most new immigrants lacked sufficient experience in America to set meaningful goals; their initial goal statements simply reflected their eagerness to agree with their counselors' suggestions (Patton, 2002, pp. 177–181).

Qualitative methods can also help in understanding how social programs actually operate. Complex social programs have many different features, and it is not always clear whether some particular feature or a combination of features is responsible for the program's effect— or for the absence of an effect. Lisbeth B. Schorr, director of the Harvard Project on Effective Interventions, and Daniel Yankelovich, president of Public Agenda, put it this way (Schorr & Yankelovich, 2000): "Social programs are sprawling efforts with multiple components requiring constant mid-course corrections, the involvement of committed human beings, and flexible adaptation to local circumstances" (p. A19).

The more complex the social program, the more value that qualitative methods can add to the evaluation process. Schorr and Yankelovich (2000) point to the Ten Point Coalition, an alliance of black ministers that helped to reduce gang warfare in Boston through multiple initiatives, "ranging from neighborhood probation patrols to safe havens for recreation" (p. A19). Qualitative methods would help to describe a complex, multifaceted program like this.

Simple or Complex Outcomes?

Does the program have only one outcome? Unlikely. How many outcomes are anticipated? How many might be unintended? Which are direct consequences of program action, and which are indirect effects that occur as a result of the direct effects (Mohr, 1992)? Do the longer term outcomes follow directly from the immediate program outputs? Does the output (the increase in test scores at the end of the preparation course) result surely in the desired outcomes (increased rates of college admission)? Due to these and other possibilities, the selection of outcome measures is a critical step in evaluation research.

The decision to focus on one outcome rather than another, on a single outcome or on several, can have enormous implications. When Sherman and Berk (1984) evaluated the impact of an immediate-arrest policy in cases of domestic violence in Minneapolis, they focused on recidivism as the key outcome. Similarly, the reduction of recidivism was the single desired outcome of prison boot-camps opened in the 1990s. Boot-camps are military-style programs for prison inmates that provided tough, highly regimented activities and harsh punishment for disciplinary infractions, with the goal of scaring inmates "straight." They were quite the rage in the 1990s, and the researchers who evaluated their impact understandably focused on criminal recidivism.

But these single-purpose programs turned out not to be quite so simple to evaluate. The Minneapolis researchers found that there was no adequate single source for records of recidivism in domestic violence cases, so they had to hunt for evidence from court and police records, follow-up interviews with victims, and family member reports. More easily measured variables, such as partners' ratings of the accused's subsequent behavior, eventually received more attention. Boot-camp research soon concluded that the experience did not reduce recidivism, although some participants felt the study had missed something:

> [A staff member] saw things unfold that he had never witnessed among inmates and their caretakers. . . . [This] profoundly affected the drill instructors and their charges . . . graduation ceremonies routinely reduced inmates . . . sometimes even supervisors to tears. . . . Here, it was a totally different experience. (Latour, 2002, p. B7)

Some now argue that the failure of boot-camps to reduce recidivism was due to the lack of post-prison support, rather than to failure of the camps to promote positive change in inmates. Looking only at recidivism rates would ignore some important positive results.

Exhibit 10.8   Outcomes in Project New Hope

Income and Employment (2nd Program year)	New Hope	Control group
Earnings	$6,602	$6,129
Wage subsidies	1,477	862
Welfare income	1,716	1,690
Food stamp income	1,418	1,242
Total income:	11,213	9,915
% above poverty level:	27%	19%
% continuously unemployed for 2 years	6%	13%
Hardships and Stress	New Hope	Control group
% reporting:		
Unmet medical needs	17%	23%
Unmet dental needs	27%	34%
Periods without health insurance	49%	61%
Living in overcrowded conditions	14%	15%
Stressed much or all of the time	45%	50%
Satisfied or very satisfied with standard of living	65%	67%

So in spite of the additional difficulties they can introduce, most evaluation researchers attempt to measure multiple outcomes (Mohr, 1992). The result usually is a much more realistic and richer understanding of program impact.

Some of the multiple outcomes measured in the evaluation of Project New Hope appear in Exhibit 10.8. Project New Hope was an ambitious experimental evaluation of the impact of guaranteeing jobs to poor people (DeParle, 1999). It was designed to answer the question: If low-income adults are given a job at a sufficient wage, above the poverty level, with child care and health care assured, how many would ultimately prosper?

Six hundred and seventy-seven low-income adults in Milwaukee were offered a job involving work for 30 hours a week as well as child care and health care benefits. The outcome? Only 27% stuck with the job long enough to lift themselves out of poverty, and their earnings as a whole were only slightly higher than those of a control group that did not receive guaranteed jobs. Levels of depression were not decreased, nor was self-esteem increased by the job guarantee. But there were some positive effects: The number of people who never worked at all declined, and rates of health insurance and use of formal child care increased. Perhaps most important, the classroom performance and educational hopes of participants' male children increased, with the boys' test scores rising by the equivalent of 100 points on the SAT, and their teachers ranked them as better behaved.

So did the New Hope program "work"? Clearly, it didn't live up to initial expectations, but it certainly showed that social interventions can have some benefits. Would the boys' gains continue through adolescence? Longer term outcomes would be needed. Why didn't girls (who were already performing better than the boys) benefit from their parents' enrollment in New Hope just as the boys did? A process analysis would add a great deal to the evaluation design. The long and short of it is that collection of multiple outcomes gave a better picture of program impact.

Of course, there is a potential downside to the collection of multiple outcomes. Policymakers may choose to publicize those outcomes that support their own policy preferences and ignore the rest. Often, evaluation researchers themselves have little ability to publicize a more complete story.

In a sense, all of these choices (black box or program theory, researcher or stakeholder interests, and so on) hinge on (1) what your real goals are in doing the project and (2) how able you will be, in a "research for hire" setting, to achieve those goals. Not every agency really wants to know if its programs work, especially if the answer is no. Dealing with such issues and the choices they require is part of what makes evaluation research both scientifically and politically fascinating.

ETHICS IN EVALUATION

Evaluation research can make a difference in people's lives while it is in progress, as well as after the results are reported. Job opportunities, welfare requirements, housing options, treatment for substance abuse, training programs—each is a potentially important benefit, and an evaluation research project can change both their type and availability. This direct impact on research participants and, potentially, their families heightens the attention that evaluation researchers have to give to human-subjects concerns. Although the particular criteria that are at issue and the decisions that are most ethical vary with the type of evaluation research conducted and the specifics of a particular project, there are always serious ethical as well as political concerns for the evaluation researcher (Boruch, 1997, p. 13; Dentler, 2002, p. 166).

Assessing needs and examining the process of treatment delivery have few special ethical dimensions. Cost-benefit analyses in themselves also raise few ethical concerns. It is when program impact is the focus that human-subjects considerations multiply. What about assigning people randomly to receive some social program or benefit? One justification given by evaluation researchers has to do with the scarcity of these resources. If not everyone in the population who is eligible for a program can receive it due to resource limitations, what could be a fairer way to distribute the program benefits than through a lottery? Random assignment also seems like a reasonable way to allocate potential program benefits when a new program is being tested with only some members of the target recipient population. However, when an ongoing entitlement program is being evaluated and experimental subjects would normally be eligible for program participation, it may not be ethical simply to bar some potential participants from the program. Instead, evaluation researchers may test alternative treatments or provide some alternative benefit while the treatment is being denied.

There are many other ethical challenges in evaluation research:

- How can confidentiality be preserved when the data are owned by a government agency or are subject to discovery in a legal proceeding?
- Who decides what level of burden an evaluation project may tolerably impose on participants?
- Is it legitimate for a research decision to be shaped by political considerations?
- Must evaluation findings be shared with stakeholders, rather than only with policymakers?
- Is the effectiveness of the proposed program improvements really uncertain?
- Will a randomized experiment yield more defensible evidence than the alternatives?
- Will the results actually be used?

The Health Research Extension Act of 1985 (Public Law 99–158) mandated that the U.S. Department of Health and Human Services require all research organizations receiving federal funds to have an Institutional Review Board (IRB) to assess all research for adherence to ethical practice guidelines. We have already reviewed the federally mandated criteria (Boruch, 1997, pp. 29–33):

- Are risks minimized?
- Are risks reasonable in relation to benefits?
- Is the selection of individuals equitable? (Randomization implies this.)
- Is informed consent given?
- Are the data monitored?
- Are privacy and confidentiality assured?

Evaluation researchers must consider whether it will be possible to meet each of these criteria long before they even design a study.

The problem of maintaining subject confidentiality is particularly thorny because researchers, in general, are not legally protected from the requirement that they provide evidence requested in legal proceedings, particularly through the process known as discovery. However, it is important to be aware that several federal statutes have been passed specifically to protect research data about vulnerable populations from legal disclosure requirements. For example, the Crime Control and Safe Streets Act (28 CFR Part 11) includes the following stipulation:

Copies of [research] information [about people receiving services under the act or the subjects of inquiries into criminal behavior] shall be immune from legal process and shall not, without the consent of the persons furnishing such information, be admitted as evidence or used for any purpose in any action, suit, or other judicial or administrative proceedings. (Boruch, 1997, p. 60)

When it appears that it will be difficult to meet the ethical standards in an evaluation project, at least from the perspective of some of the relevant stakeholders, modifications should be considered in the study design. Several steps can be taken to lessen any possibly detrimental program impact (Boruch, 1997, pp. 67–68):

- Alter the group allocation ratios to minimize the number in the untreated control group.
- Use the minimum sample size required to be able to adequately test the results.
- Test just parts of new programs, rather than the entire program.
- Compare treatments that vary in intensity (rather than presence or absence).
- Vary treatments between settings, rather than among individuals within a setting.

Essentially, each of these approaches limits the program's impact during the experiment and so lessens any potential adverse effects on human subjects. It is also important to realize that it is costly to society and potentially harmful to participants to maintain ineffective programs. In the long run, at least, it may be more ethical to conduct an evaluation study than to let the status quo remain in place.

CONCLUSION

Hopes for evaluation research are high: Society could benefit from the development of programs that work well, accomplish their goals, and serve people who genuinely need them. At least that is the hope. Unfortunately, there are many obstacles to realizing this hope (Posavac & Carey, 1997):

- Because social programs and the people who use them are complex, evaluation research designs can easily miss important outcomes or aspects of the program process.
- Because the many program stakeholders all have an interest in particular results from the evaluation, researchers can be subjected to an unusual level of cross-pressures and demands.
- Because the need to include program stakeholders in research decisions may undermine adherence to scientific standards, research designs can be weakened.
- Because some program administrators want to believe their programs really work well, researchers may be pressured to avoid null findings, or if they are not responsive, they may find their research report ignored. Plenty of well-done evaluation research studies wind up in a recycling bin or hidden away in a file cabinet.
- Because the primary audience for evaluation research reports is program administrators, politicians, or members of the public, evaluation findings may need to be overly simplified, distorting the findings.

The rewards of evaluation research are often worth the risks, however. Evaluation research can provide social scientists with rare opportunities to study complex social processes with real consequences and to contribute to the public good. Although evaluation researchers may face unusual constraints on their designs, most evaluation projects can result in high-quality analyses and publications in reputable social science journals. In many respects, evaluation research is an idea whose time has come. We may never achieve Donald Campbell's (Campbell & Russo, 1999) vision of an "experimenting society," in which research is consistently used to evaluate new programs and to suggest constructive changes, but we are close enough to continue trying.

KEY TERMS

Black box evaluation
Cost-benefit analysis
Cost-effectiveness analysis
Efficiency analysis
Evaluation research
Feedback
Formative evaluation
Inputs
Integrative approach
Logic model
Needs assessment

Outcome evaluation
Outcomes
Output
Process evaluation
Program process
Program theory
Social science approach
Stakeholder approach
Stakeholders
Target population
Theory-driven evaluation

HIGHLIGHTS

- Evaluation research is social work research that is conducted to investigate social problems.
- The development of evaluation research as a major enterprise followed on the heels of the expansion of the federal government during the Great Depression and World War II.
- The evaluation process can be modeled as a feedback system with inputs entering the program, which generates outputs and then outcomes, which feed back to program stakeholders and affect program inputs.
- The evaluation process as a whole, and the feedback process in particular, can be understood only in relation to the interests and perspectives of program stakeholders.
- A logic model provides a schematic representation of the various components that make up a social service program.
- There are four primary types of program evaluation: needs assessment, process evaluation, outcome evaluation, and efficiency analysis.
- The process by which a program has an effect on outcomes is often treated as a black box, but there is good reason to open the black box and investigate the process by which the program operates and produces, or fails to produce, an effect.
- A program theory may be developed before or after an investigation of program process is completed. It may be either descriptive or prescriptive.
- Qualitative methods are useful in describing the process of program delivery.
- Multiple outcomes are often necessary to understand program effects.
- Evaluation research raises complex ethical issues because it may involve withholding desired social benefits.

DISCUSSION QUESTIONS

1. Would you prefer that evaluation researchers use a stakeholder or a social science approach? Compare and contrast these perspectives and list at least four arguments for the one you favor.

2. Is it ethical to assign people to receive some social benefit on a random basis? Form two teams and debate the ethics of the TARP randomized evaluation of welfare payments described in this chapter.

3. Discuss the advantages of using a black box or program theory approach to evaluation research. What might be some disadvantages or limitations of this approach?

PRACTICE EXERCISES

1. Choose a social program with which you are familiar and construct a logic model.

2. Select a social program with which you are familiar and list its intended outcomes. What other outcomes might result from the program, both direct and indirect? Try to identify outcomes that would be deemed desirable as well as some that might not be desirable.

3. Review a social work agency's description of one of its primary programs and the objectives it aims to meet. Create a flowchart illustrating the service delivery process. Do you believe that the program design reflects the stated goals? Are necessary activities absent or activities present that do not appear to contribute to the desired outcomes?

4. Propose an evaluation of a social program you have heard about. Identify a research question you would like to answer about this program, and select a method of investigation. Discuss the strengths and weaknesses of your proposed method.

5. Read and summarize a quantitative research article published in the journal, *Evaluation and Program Planning*. Read the article and suggest how qualitative methods might have been added to the research and what benefits these methods might have had for it.

WEB EXERCISES

1. Describe the resources available for evaluation researchers at one of the following three Web sites: http://www.wmich.edu/evalctr/; http://www.stanford.edu/~davidf/empowermentevaluation.html; or http://www.worldbank.org/oed/.

2. You can check out the latest information regarding the D.A.R.E. program at www.dare.com. What is the current approach? Can you find information on the Web about current research on D.A.R.E.?

> To assist you in completing the Web exercises, please access the study site at http://www.sagepub.com/prsw where you will find the Web Exercises reproduced and suggested links for online resources.

DEVELOPING A RESEARCH PROPOSAL

1. Develop a logic model for a program that might influence the type of attitude or behavior in which you are interested. List the key components of this model.

2. Design a program evaluation to test the efficacy of your program model, using an impact analysis approach.

3. Add to your plan a discussion of a program theory for your model. In your methodological plan, indicate whether you will use qualitative or quantitative techniques and simple or complex outcomes.

4. Who are the potential stakeholders for your program? How will you relate to them before, during, and after your evaluation?

Chapter 11

QUANTITATIVE DATA ANALYSIS

Introducing Statistics

Preparing Data for Analysis
Identification Numbers
Reviewing the Forms
Coding Open-ended Questions
Creating a Codebook
Data Entry
Data Cleaning

Displaying Univariate Distributions
Graphs
Frequency Distributions
  Ungrouped Data
  Grouped Data
  Combined and Compressed
    Distributions

Summarizing Univariate Distributions
Measures of Central Tendency
  Mode
  Median
  Mean
  Median or Mean?

Measures of Variation
  Range
  Interquartile Range
  Variance
  Standard Deviation

Analyzing Data Ethically: How Not to Lie with Statistics

Crosstabulating Variables
Graphing Association
Describing Association
Evaluating Association
Controlling for a Third Variable
Case Study: Perceived Health
  Intervening Variables
  Extraneous Variables
  Specification

Analyzing Data Ethically: How Not to Lie about Relationships

Conclusion

$\mathbf{T}$his chapter will introduce several common statistics in social work research and evaluation and highlight the factors that must be considered in using and interpreting statistics. Think of it as a review of fundamental social statistics, if you have already studied them, or as an introductory overview, if you have not. Two preliminary sections lay the foundation for studying statistics. In the first, we will discuss the role of statistics in the research process, returning to themes and techniques with which you are already familiar. In the second preliminary section, we will outline the process of preparing data for statistical analysis. In the rest of the chapter, we will explain how to describe the distribution of single variables and the relationship between variables. Along the way, we will address ethical issues related to data analysis, and you will learn about some of the findings from an innovative study about social influence on health by James Jackson and David Williams (2004). This chapter will have been successful if it encourages you to use statistics responsibly, to evaluate statistics critically, and to seek opportunities for extending your statistical knowledge.

Although many colleges and universities offer social statistics in a separate course, and for good reason (there's a *lot* to learn), we do not want you to think of this chapter as somehow on a different topic than the rest of this book. Data analysis is an integral component of research methods, and it's important that any proposal for quantitative research or an evaluation plan include a section on data analysis that will follow data collection. You have to anticipate your data analysis needs if you expect your research or evaluation to secure the requisite data.

INTRODUCING STATISTICS

Statistics is often the word social work students love to hate. Do not fear statistics—they are simply a tool to summarize and analyze data. Statistics provide us with a means to report what we do as social workers: to document what we do for agency administrators or funding agencies, to monitor our practice, to determine whether interventions are achieving the desired outcome, or to assess community needs. We need a sufficient understanding of basic statistical techniques to produce the kinds of reports stakeholders and the general population demand. At the same time, a basic knowledge of statistics permits us to be informed consumers of research and to critically evaluate findings reported in the popular media or in the professional literature.

Statistics play a key role in achieving valid research results, in terms of measurement, causal validity, and generalizability. Some statistics are useful primarily to describe the results of measuring single variables and to construct and evaluate multi-item scales. These statistics include frequency distributions, graphs, measures of central tendency and variation, and reliability tests. Other statistics are useful primarily in achieving causal validity by helping us to describe the association among variables and to control for or otherwise take account of other variables. Crosstabulation, the technique for measuring association and controlling other variables, is introduced in this chapter. All of these statistics are termed **descriptive statistics** because they are used to describe the distribution of and relationship among variables.

You already learned in Chapter 4 that it is possible to estimate the degree of confidence that can be placed in generalizations from a sample to the population from which the sample was selected. The statistics used in making these estimates are termed **inferential statistics**. In this chapter, we will refer briefly to inferential statistics, but we will emphasize later their importance for testing hypotheses involving sample data and as a tool for program evaluation.

Social theory and the results of prior research should guide our statistical choices, as they guide the choice of other research methods. There are so many particular statistics and so many ways for them to be used in data analysis that even the best statisticians can become lost in a sea of numbers if they do not use prior research and theorizing to develop a coherent analysis plan.

It is also important to choose for analysis statistics that are appropriate to the level of measurement of the variables to be analyzed. As you learned in Chapter 3, numbers used to represent the values of variables may not actually signify different quantities, meaning that many statistical techniques will not be applicable.

PREPARING DATA FOR ANALYSIS

If you have conducted your own survey or experiment, the information that you may have on assorted questionnaires, survey instruments, observational checklists, or tape transcripts needs to be prepared in a format suitable for analyzing data. Generally, this will involve a process of assigning a number to a particular response to a question, observation, case record response, and the like. For the most part, this is a straightforward process, but there are pitfalls and decisions you will have to make. You will have to make decisions to ensure the consistency of how you transform these responses, and you will need to take steps to ensure the accuracy of the data you enter in the computer. Throughout this section, we discuss these issues and offer suggestions as you prepare your data for analysis.

Identification Numbers

Although it may seem obvious, it is worth noting that a **unique identifier** such as a number should be assigned to each respondent and that this identifier should appear on the form, questionnaire, survey, or transcript. This identifier should be included as a variable in the data you enter. Several of the activities done to prepare data for analysis, particularly checking the accuracy of the data, will mean going back from data already entered into the computer to the original forms. And, if you are using data about the same people collected at different points in time, the unique identifier helps you link their responses.

Reviewing the Forms

As an initial step you will need to review the instruments or questionnaires used to record responses. As you review the instruments, there are four different questions you will need to consider.

Are responses clearly indicated? In reviewing the forms, it is not unusual to see mistakes like the one in Exhibit 11.1, where a circle crosses more than one category, or an X or a check that falls between responses. This presents a dilemma because the respondent has given a response but because of the ambiguity of what was circled or checked, you may not be sure what the actual response was. You have to make a decision about how you are going to treat such cases. One possibility is to simply take the first response or to take the second response. Although such decisions may ultimately lead you to overestimate certain responses while underestimating other responses, by being consistent, you can identify the source of the bias. Or, you may decide to treat the response as a missing response, accepting that you will lose information. The important point is that you establish a rule of thumb that you are going to follow and acknowledge the shortcomings of the decision you make.

Exhibit 11.1   Unclear Responses

Thanks. This set of questions deals with different feelings and emotions. For each of these questions, please answer for how you felt over the past week by responding yes or no.

In the last week . . .

Yes   No   1. Are you basically satisfied with your life?

Now I am going to ask you a couple of questions about your vision and health.

2. Overall, how would you rate your health? Would you say your health is excellent, very good, good, fair, or poor?

   1   Excellent

   2   Very good

   3   Good

   4   Fair

   5   Poor

3. In which category does your annual earned income fall? (please check)

   _____   less than $10,000

   _____   10,000 - 14,999

   _____   15,000 - 19,999

   _____   20,000 - 24,999

   _____   25,000 - 29,999

   _____   30,000 or more

Did respondents misread instructions? Another form of this problem occurs occasionally when respondents do not follow instructions about how to respond correctly. For example, we encountered this problem in a housing needs assessment survey. Respondents were asked to choose from a list of 25 different social services the five most important services by indicating with a *1* the most important, *2* the second most important, and so on. Instead, some respondents simply checked all (often more than five) that they thought were important. When this happened, we decided to treat the responses as missing information. In a large sample, this decision might have made little difference, but in a small sample, losing information might dramatically alter the findings.

Are questionnaires complete? Some respondents may decide not to complete the entire instrument or may end the interview before it is completed. You have to decide whether to include the responses you have obtained and treat the rest as missing or to consider the entire instrument as missing. There are no hard rules. Your decision is likely to be influenced by the sample size; when you have a large sample, there is less cost to treating the entire questionnaire as missing. In the case of the housing needs survey mentioned above, because there were only 20 respondents, the responses of the two people who completed only half the questionnaire were included. Your decision might be influenced by how many questions were answered or whether the questions crucial to your study were answered.

Are any responses unexpected? It is also not unusual to get unexpected responses. For example, you might ask *age* and get responses like *30½*. Again, you must decide how you will treat such responses and then be consistent throughout.

Coding Open-Ended Questions

It is relatively simply to assign values to closed-ended questions, given that the responses are already defined. With open-ended questions, the process is more difficult as you need to create the attributes or categories of the variable. There are two types of open-ended questions for which you will have to create these categories: (1) when the entire question is left open-ended and 2) where you have *Other (specify)* _____ as a potential response in a list of responses. The process for developing categories is similar in each case, although it is far easier in the case of *other* as the responses are likely to be far fewer in number and the most common responses—or at least most anticipated responses—already appear in the questionnaire.

With open-ended questions, it is not unusual to get multiple responses to the question. For example, in a study assessing the potential roles of settlement houses in the community (Engel, 1994), respondents were asked to comment on a proposed definition. Many respondents gave lengthy responses that involved different ideas, such as:

> I would revise activities to give stronger emphasis on the necessities of life. To feed the soul is an important task of course, but to feed the physical body and to keep people safe, warm, and dry is imperative. A neighborhood center, just as the neighborhood itself, should be open to all including those who may be attracted from without. It must also be a part of the larger community and not strive to protect itself or discourage its members from moving throughout this larger community. It must be democratic to a fault and find a meaningful role for all. (p. 6)

As you can see, different ideas are mentioned in this response. Therefore, you will need to decide how many different responses you will code; in this case, the researcher decided to code all responses.

To begin to identify possible response categories, you can rely on your own knowledge of the area and what might emerge as likely response categories. This list, however, is still likely to be insufficient, for if the options had been known, a closed-ended question probably would have been used. Therefore, the next step is to list the responses; multiple responses by a respondent should be separated, with each treated as a single response. Next, you look to see if patterns begin to emerge, representing potential response categories for the variable. This should be followed by additional reviews until you are convinced that you have interpreted the responses correctly and the categories are sufficient. Finally, a second opinion should be obtained with at least a subset of responses to establish consistency and accuracy for your conclusions. When you have a small number of respondents, all responses should be used to create the categories; when the number of respondents is large, it is easier to use a sample of the responses to create the categories.

Creating a Codebook

A **codebook** is nothing more than a set of instructions used to link a number to a category for a particular variable. The codebook page shown in Exhibit 11.2 includes the question, the variable name, the value labels, the values for each variable category including values for missing respondents or responses that are not applicable to the respondent, and the columns in which the response will be coded on the sheet (if using an optical scan sheet). It is important that the codebook be kept up-to-date. Often, once the data are entered into the computer, new variables are created or older variables are recoded or transformed. By updating the codebook, you will remember exactly how you created or modified the variable rather than depending on your memory.

Data Entry

There are several common methods of data entry. Research studies using computer assisted telephone interviews (CATI, described in Chapter 8) are designed so that as responses are given, the data are immediately entered into a computer program. A more common method is to use optical scan sheets. These are the familiar sheets many of us have used to take standardized tests or to do class evaluations. Data are coded on the sheet, and then the sheets are read by an optical scanner.

Another method is simply inputting the data by hand into a spreadsheet such as Excel or Lotus or into a statistical package such as SPSS or SAS. If the data are typed into a text file or entered directly through the data sheet of a statistics program, a computer program must be written to "define the data." A data definition program identifies the variables that are coded in each column or range of columns, attaches meaningful labels to the variables and the codes, distinguishes values representing missing data, and establishes the variable's level of measurement. The procedures for doing so vary with the specific statistical or spreadsheet package. A useful feature of a statistical package such as SPSS is that you can produce the entire data definition file, which, in turn, is a reflection of your codebook.

Data Cleaning

Of course, numbers stored in a computer file are not yet numbers that can be analyzed with statistics. After the data are entered, they must be checked carefully for errors—a process called **data cleaning**. If a data entry program has been used and programmed to flag invalid values, the cleaning process is much easier. If you do not have a programmed method to flag mistakes, there are other techniques that should be used.

One method to check for mistakes is **check coding**. Using check coding, it is possible to estimate the extent to which there may be coding mistakes. The researcher defines the degree of desired accuracy for the coding. Ideally, you hope for 100% accuracy, but this is probably unrealistic to expect, particularly with large samples. A second person then recodes a sample of the forms. The percentage of agreement on all the items on the forms is computed, and if the percentage falls below the desired criterion, then all forms should be recoded and reevaluated a second time.

Once the data are entered, it is important to compute frequencies for every variable. By computing frequencies, it is possible to see if there are cases with **invalid codes**. Invalid codes are values that fall outside the range of allowable values for a given variable. For example, if

Exhibit 11.2 Pages from a Codebook

Variable Number	Column Number		
001	1	Q1.	Are you infected with HIV?

		1	Yes
		2	No (code 8 in VAR 002)
		9	No response

| 002 | 2 | Q2. | What is your current HIV status? |

		1	Asymptomatic
		2	Symptomatic
		3	Aids Diagnosis
		8	Not applicable (coded 2 in VAR 001)
		9	No Response

| 003 | 3-6 | Q3 | What year did you learn that you were HIV positive? |

Code actual year (e.g. 1993)
9998   Not applicable (coded 2 in VAR 001)
9999   No response

| 004 | 7-9 | Q4 | What county did you live in when you learned about your HIV positive status? |

		101	Allegheny
		102	Armstrong
		103	Beaver
		104	Blair
		105	Butler
		106	Cambria
		998	Not appropriate (coded 2 in VAR 001)
		999	No response

| 005 | 10 | Q5 | What state did you live in when you learned about your HIV positive status? |

		1	Pennsylvania
		2	Other (specify on card)
		8	Not appropriate (coded 2 in VAR 001)
		9	No response

| 006 | 11 | Q6 | Are you a parent or caregiver to a child under the age of 18? |

		1	Yes
		2	No
		9	No response

you were coding gender as *1 = female* and *2 = male,* finding *3* would mean that at least one or more cases had been miscoded or the data entered incorrectly. The cases for which this happened can be identified and corrections made.

At times, contingency questions may lead the interviewer or respondent to skip some questions. For example, a positive response to the question, "Are you currently employed" might lead to additional questions about work whereas a negative response would mean that those additional work-related questions should be skipped. To check that there were no errors in the coding, crosstabulations are computed. A crosstabulation (explained in far greater detail later) compares responses to two variables. Looking at the crosstabulation, it is possible to identify instances where a person should have skipped a question, but a response was actually coded.

When you find mistakes, you can easily correct them because you have established unique identifying numbers for each respondent. You can go back to the original questionnaire with the corresponding identification number, find the actual response, and make the correction in the computer file in which the data are stored. Unfortunately, what appears as a mistake may not always be a mistake, or it may not be easily corrected. In a panel study conducted by the U.S. Census Bureau, several elderly women in their first interview reported that they were widowed but four months later, they reported that they were divorced (Engel, 1988). In this case, it was impossible to determine what the correct marital status was.

DISPLAYING UNIVARIATE DISTRIBUTIONS

The first step in data analysis is usually to display the variation in each variable of interest. For many descriptive purposes, the analysis may go no further. Graphs and frequency distributions are the two most popular approaches; both allow the analyst to display the distribution of cases across the categories of a variable. Graphs have the advantage of providing a picture that is easier to comprehend, although frequency distributions are preferable when exact numbers of cases having particular values must be reported and when many distributions must be displayed in a compact form.

Whichever type of display is used, the primary concern of the data analyst is to display accurately the distribution's shape, that is, to show how cases are distributed across the values of the variable. The analyst may describe the shape in terms of: the common or typical response, or **central tendency**; the spread or variability of the responses, or **variability**; and the shape of the responses, or **skewness**. All three features can be represented in a graph or in a frequency distribution.

Central tendency The most common value (for variables measured at the nominal level) or the value around which cases tend to center (for a quantitative variable).

Variability The extent to which cases are spread out through the distribution or clustered in just one location.

Skewness The extent to which cases are clustered more at one or the other end of the distribution of a quantitative variable, rather than in a symmetric pattern around its center. Skew can be positive (a "right skew"), with the number of cases tapering off in the positive direction, or negative (a "left skew"), with the number of cases tapering off in the negative direction.

These features of a distribution's shape can be interpreted in several different ways, and they are not all appropriate for describing every variable. In fact, all three features of a distribution can be distorted if graphs, frequency distributions, or summary statistics are used inappropriately.

A variable's level of measurement is the most important determinant of the appropriateness of particular statistics. For example, we cannot talk about the skewness (lack of symmetry) of a qualitative variable (those measured at the nominal level). If the values of a variable cannot be ordered from lowest to highest—if the ordering of the values is arbitrary—we cannot say that the distribution is not symmetric because we could just reorder the values to make the distribution more (or less) symmetric. Some measures of central tendency and variability are also inappropriate for qualitative variables.

The distinction between variables measured at the ordinal level and those measured at the interval or ratio level should also be considered when selecting statistics to use, but social work researchers differ in just how much importance they attach to this distinction. Many social work researchers think of ordinal variables as imperfectly measured interval level variables and believe that in most circumstances, statistics developed for interval level variables also provide useful summaries for ordinal variables. Other social work researchers believe that variation in ordinal variables will often be distorted by statistics that assume an interval level of measurement. We will touch on some of the details in the following sections on particular statistical techniques.

We will now examine graphs and frequency distributions that illustrate these three features of shape. Summary statistics used to measure specific aspects of central tendency and variability will be presented in a separate section. There is a summary statistic for the measurement of skewness, but it is used only rarely in published research reports and will not be presented here. Many of our examples in the next two sections come from the General Social Survey (GSS), a nationwide attitudinal survey conducted every two years by the National Opinion Research Center (Davis & Smith, 1992).

Graphs

A picture often is worth some immeasurable quantity of words. Even for the uninitiated, graphs can be easy to read, and they highlight a distribution's shape. They are useful particularly for exploring data because they show the full range of variation and identify data anomalies that might be in need of further study. Also, good professional-looking graphs can now be produced relatively easily with software available for personal computers. In Chapter 7, we used line graphs to display single-subject data. There are many types of graphs, but the most common and most useful are bar charts, histograms, and frequency polygons. Each has two axes, the vertical axis (the y-axis) and the horizontal axis (the x-axis), and labels to identify the variables and the values, with tick marks showing where each indicated value falls along the axis.

A **bar chart** contains solid bars separated by spaces. It is a good tool for displaying the distribution of variables measured at the nominal level and other discrete categorical variables because there is, in effect, a gap between each of the categories. The bar chart of marital status in Exhibit 11.3 indicates that almost half of adult Americans were married at the time of the survey. Smaller percentages were divorced, separated, widowed, or never married. The most common value in the distribution is married, so this would be the distribution's central tendency. There is a moderate amount of variability in the distribution, as the half who are not married are spread across the categories of widowed, divorced, separated, and never married.

Exhibit 11.3   Bar Chart of Marital Status

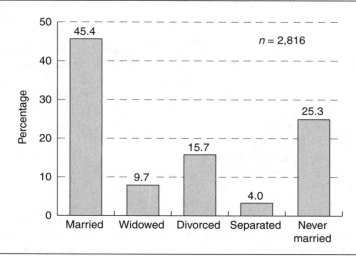

Note: Percentages do not add up to 100 due to rounding error.
Source: General Social Survey, 2000.

Because marital status is not a quantitative variable, the order in which the categories are presented is arbitrary, and skewness is not defined.

Histograms, in which the bars are adjacent, are used to display the distribution of quantitative variables that vary along a continuum that has no necessary gaps. Exhibit 11.4 shows a histogram of years of education from the 2000 GSS data. The distribution has a clump of cases centered at 12 years, with the most common value of 12. The distribution is not symmetric because there are more cases just above the central point than below it.

In a **frequency polygon,** a continuous line connects the points representing the number or percentage of cases with each value. The frequency polygon is an alternative to the histogram when the distribution of a quantitative continuous variable must be displayed; this alternative is particularly useful when the variable has a wide range of values. It is easy to see in the frequency polygon of years of education in Exhibit 11.5 that the most common value is 12 years, high school completion, and that this value also seems to be the center of the distribution. There is moderate variability in the distribution, with many cases having more than 12 years of education and about one quarter having completed at least 4 years of college (16 years). The distribution is highly skewed in the negative direction, with few respondents reporting less than 10 years of education. This same type of graph can use percentages rather than frequencies.

If graphs are misused, they can distort, rather than display, the shape of a distribution. Compare, for example, the two graphs in Exhibit 11.6. The first graph shows that high school seniors reported relatively stable rates of lifetime use of cocaine between 1980 and 1985. The second graph, using exactly the same numbers, appeared in a 1986 *Newsweek* article on the coke plague (Orcutt & Turner, 1993). To look at this graph, you would think that the rate of cocaine usage among high school seniors increased dramatically during this period. But, in fact, the difference between the two graphs is due simply to changes in how the graphs are drawn. In the plague graph, the percentage scale on the vertical axis begins at 15 rather than at 0, making what was about a 1 percentage point increase look very big indeed. In addition, omission from the

Exhibit 11.4   Histogram of Years of Education

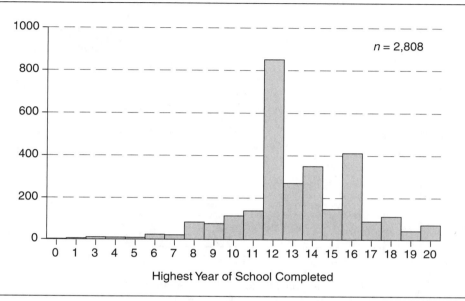

Source: General Social Survey, 2000.

Exhibit 11.5   Frequency Polygon of Years of Education

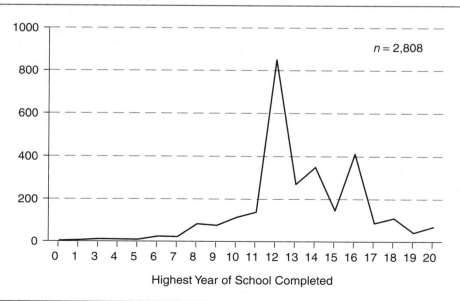

Source: General Social Survey, 2000.

Exhibit 11.6   Two Graphs of Cocaine Usage

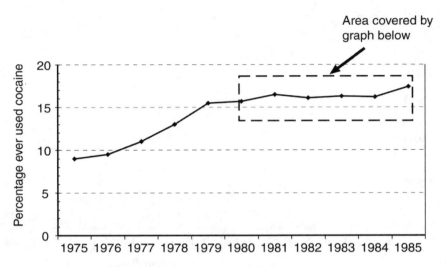

A. University of Michigan Institute for Social Research,
Time Series for Lifetime Prevalence of Cocaine Use

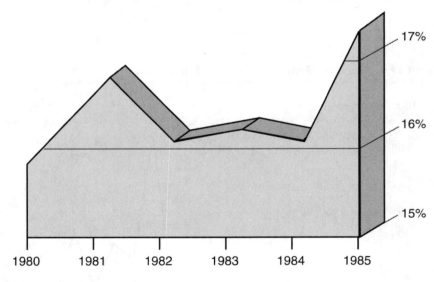

B. Final Stages of Construction

Source: Orcutt, J. D., & Turner, J. B., "Shocking numbers and graphic accounts: Quantified images of drug problems in the print media," in Social Problems, 49(May), pp. 190–206. Copyright © 1993. Reprinted with permission.

plague graph of the more rapid increase in reported usage between 1975 and 1980 makes it look as if the tiny increase in 1985 were a new, and thus more newsworthy, crisis.

Adherence to several guidelines (Tufte, 1983; Wallgren, Wallgren, Persson, Jorner, & Haaland, 1996) will help you to spot these problems and to avoid them in your own work:

- The difference between bars can be exaggerated by cutting off the bottom of the vertical axis and displaying less than the full height of the bars. Instead, begin the graph of a quantitative variable at 0 on both axes. It may at times be reasonable to violate this guideline, as when an age distribution is presented for a sample of adults, but in this case be sure to mark the break clearly on the axis.
- Bars of unequal width, including pictures instead of bars, can make particular values look as if they carry more weight than their frequency warrants. Always use bars of equal width.
- Either shortening or lengthening the vertical axis will obscure or accentuate the differences in the number of cases between values. The two axes usually should be of approximately equal length.
- Avoid chart junk that can confuse the reader and obscure the distribution's shape (a lot of verbiage or umpteen marks, lines, lots of crosshatching, and the like).

Frequency Distributions

A **frequency distribution** displays the number or percentage (the relative frequencies), or both, of cases corresponding to each of a variable's values or group of values. For continuous variables, a frequency distribution provides information about the spread of a variable, providing the lowest and highest categories with valid responses and some sense of the shape of the responses. The components of the frequency distribution should be clearly labeled, with a title, a stub (labels for the values of the variable), a caption (identifying whether the distribution includes frequencies, percentages, or both), and perhaps the number of missing cases. If percentages are presented rather than frequencies (sometimes both are included), the total number of cases in the distribution (the **base number** *N*) should be indicated (see Exhibit 11.7).

Exhibit 11.7   Frequency Distribution of Voting in the 1996 Presidential Election

Value	Frequency	Valid Percentage
Voted	1,737	68.5%
Did not vote	799	31.5
Not eligible	201	–
Refused	9	–
Don't know	64	–
No answer	7	–
Total	2,817	100.0%
		(2,536)

Source: General Social Survey, 2000.

Ungrouped Data

Constructing and reading frequency distributions for variables with few values is not difficult. The frequency distribution of voting in Exhibit 11.7, for example, shows that 68.5% of the respondents eligible to vote said they voted and that 31.5 reported they did not vote. The total number of respondents to this question was 2,536, although 2,817 actually were interviewed. The rest were ineligible to vote, just refused to answer the question, said they did not know whether they had voted or not, or gave no answer.

Political ideology was measured with a question having seven response choices, resulting in a longer but still relatively simple frequency distribution (see Exhibit 11.8). The most common response was moderate, with 39.9% of the sample choosing this label to represent their political ideology. The distribution has a symmetric shape, with about equal percentages of respondents identifying themselves as liberal and conservative. About 3% of the respondents identified themselves as extremely conservative and about 4% as extremely liberal. This table also reports the cumulative percentage, which gives the total percentage below or above a category. In Exhibit 11.8, 26.4% of the respondents lean to the liberal political identification while 33.7% lean to the conservative political identification.

If you compare Exhibits 11.8 and 11.5, you can see that a frequency distribution (Exhibit 11.8) can provide more precise information than a graph (Exhibit 11.5) about the number and percentage of cases in a variable's categories. Often, however, it is easier to see the shape of a distribution when it is graphed. When the goal of a presentation is to convey a general sense of a variable's distribution, particularly when the presentation is to an audience that is not trained in statistics, the advantages of a graph outweigh those of a frequency distribution.

Exhibit 11.8 Frequency Distribution of Political Views

Value	Frequency	Valid Percentage
Extremely liberal	107	4.0%
Liberal	308	11.6
Slightly liberal	285	10.8
Moderate	1054	39.9
Slightly conservative	390	14.8
Conservative	411	15.5
Extremely conservative	89	3.4
Total	2,644	100.0%

Source: General Social Survey, 2000.

Grouped Data

Many frequency distributions (and graphs) require grouping of some values after the data are collected. A frequency of group data is made by first combining scores into unique score intervals so that there is no overlap. All of the ungrouped scores are included in an interval. There are three reasons for grouping:

- There are more than 15–20 values to begin with, a number too large to be displayed in an easily readable table.

Exhibit 11.9   Ungrouped and Grouped Age Distributions

Ungrouped		Grouped	
Age	Percentage	Age	Percentage
18	0.2%	18–19	1.8%
19	1.6	20–29	16.9
20	1.4	30–39	21.7
21	1.3	40–49	22.6
22	1.4	50–59	14.5
23	1.7	60–69	9.7
24	1.8	70–79	7.9
25	1.9	80–89	4.8
26	2.1		
27	1.7		99.9%
28	1.6		(2,809)
29	2.0		
30	2.2		
31	2.2		
32	2.7		
33	1.6		
34	2.0		
35	2.0		
36	2.2		
37	2.2		
38	2.7		
39	1.9		
40	2.6		
41	2.1		
42	2.6		
43	2.5		
44	2.5		
45	2.5		
46	2.0		
. . .	. . .		

Source: General Social Survey, 2000.

Note: Percentages do not add to 100% due to rounding error.

- There are few cases with the same exact scores, resulting in many categories with a frequency of 1.
- The distribution of the variable will be clearer or more meaningful if some of the values are combined.

On the other hand, when you group data, you lose some information. Nonetheless, given that the data are easier to interpret and understand, it is often worth the loss of the information.

Inspection of Exhibit 11.9 should clarify these reasons. In the first distribution, which is only a portion of the entire ungrouped GSS age distribution, it is very difficult to discern any shape, much less the central tendency. In the second distribution, age is grouped in the

Exhibit 11.10   Years of Education Completed

Years of Education	Percentage
Less than 8	2.4%
8–11	15.1
12	29.3
13–15	28.2
16	14.0
17 or more	11.1
	100.1%
	(2,808)

Source: General Social Survey, 2000.

Note: Percentages do not add to 100% due to rounding error.

familiar 10-year intervals (except for the first, abbreviated category), and the distribution's shape is immediately clear.

Once we decide to group values, or categories, we have to be sure that in doing so, we do not distort the distribution. Adhering to the following guidelines for combining values in a frequency distribution will prevent many problems:

- Categories should be logically defensible and preserve the distribution's shape.
- Categories should be mutually exclusive and exhaustive, so that every case should be classifiable in one and only one category.

Violating these two guidelines is easier than you might think. If you were to group all the ages above 59 together, as 60 or higher, it would create the appearance of a bulge at the high end of the age distribution, with 22% of the cases. The same type of misleading impression could be created by combining other categories so that they include a wide range of values. In some cases, however, the most logically defensible categories will vary in size. A good example would be grouping years of education as less than 8 (did not finish grade school), 8 to 11 (finished grade school), 12 (graduated high school), 13 to 15 (some college), 16 (graduated college), and 17 or more (some postgraduate education). Such a grouping captures the most meaningful distinctions in the educational distribution and preserves the information that would be important for many analyses (see Exhibit 11.10).

It is also easy to imagine how the requirement that categories be mutually exclusive can be violated. You sometimes see frequency distributions or categories in questionnaires that use such overlapping age categories as 20 to 30, 30 to 40, and so on, instead of mutually exclusive categories like those in Exhibit 11.9. The problem is that we then can't tell which category to place someone in who is age 30, age 40, and so on.

Combined and Compressed Distributions

In a **combined frequency display,** the distributions for a set of conceptually similar variables having the same response categories are presented together. Exhibit 11.11 is a

Exhibit 11.11   Government Responsibilities

Government's Responsibility	Definitely Should Be (%)	Probably Should Be (%)	Probably Should Not Be (%)	Definitely Should Not Be (%)	Total (%)	n
Provide for the elderly	39.8	47.2	10.2	2.8	100	432
Provide jobs for all	0.0	42.8	57.2	0.0	100	423
Assist low income college students	34.4	51.9	10.4	3.3	100	422
Provide housing to the poor	19.3	46.9	23.9	9.9	100	414
Assist industrial growth	17.1	49.8	24.4	8.8	100	410
Provide for the unemployed	13.5	32.5	33.4	20.7	100	416
Reduce income differences	16.1	29.4	27.7	26.8	100	411
Keep prices under control	24.5	45.3	19.8	10.4	100	424

Source: General Social Survey 1996 Data File.

combined display reporting the frequency distributions in percentage form for eight variables that indicate the degree to which government should be responsible for a variety of activities. The different variables are identified in the leftmost column, and their values are labeled along the top. By looking at the table, you can see quickly that providing for the elderly and assisting low-income college students receive the most support as government responsibilities. A much smaller portion of the American public thinks the government should be responsible for reducing income differences or providing for the unemployed.

Compressed frequency displays can also be used to present crosstabular data and summary statistics more efficiently by eliminating unnecessary percentages (such as those corresponding to the second value of a dichotomous variable) and by reducing the need for repetitive labels. Exhibit 11.12 presents a compressed display of agreement with different roles for women. Note that this display presents the number of cases on which the percentages are based in parentheses.

Combined and compressed statistical displays facilitate the presentation of a large amount of data in a relatively small space. They should be used with caution, however, because people who are not used to them may be baffled.

Exhibit 11.12   Appropriate Roles for Women

Statement	% Agree	n
Women should take care of home not country.	15.4	1,814
Women should work.	82.2	1,837
I would vote for a woman for president.	93.6	1,803
Women are not suited for politics.	23.2	1,747

Source: General Social Survey, 1998.

SUMMARIZING UNIVARIATE DISTRIBUTIONS

Summary statistics focus attention on particular aspects of a distribution and facilitate comparison among distributions. For example, if your purpose is to report variation in income by state in a form that is easy for most audiences to understand, you would usually be better off presenting average incomes; many people would find it difficult to make sense of a display containing 50 frequency distributions, although they could readily comprehend a long list of average incomes. A display of average incomes would also be preferable to multiple frequency distributions if your only purpose was to provide a general idea of income differences among states.

Of course, representing a distribution in one number loses information about other aspects of the distribution's shape and so creates the possibility of obscuring important information. If you need to inform a discussion about differences in income inequality among states, for example, measures of central tendency and variability would miss the point entirely. You would either have to present the 50 frequency distributions or use some special statistics that represent the unevenness of a distribution. For this reason, analysts who report summary measures of central tendency usually also report a summary measure of variability, and sometimes several measures of central tendency, variability, or both.

Measures of Central Tendency

Central tendency is usually summarized with one of three statistics: the mode, the median, or the mean. For any particular application, one of these statistics may be preferable, but each has a role to play in data analysis. To choose an appropriate measure of central tendency, the analyst must consider a variable's level of measurement, the skewness of a quantitative variable's distribution, and the purpose for which the statistic is used.

Mode

The **mode** is the most frequent value in a distribution. It is also termed the **probability average** because being the most frequent value, it is the most probable. For example, if you were to pick a case at random from the distribution of political views (refer back to Exhibit 11.8), the probability of the case being a moderate would be .40 out of 1, or 40%—the most probable value in the distribution.

The mode is used much less often than the other two measures of central tendency because it can so easily give a misleading impression of a distribution's central tendency. One problem with the mode occurs when a distribution is bimodal, in contrast to being **unimodal.** A **bimodal** (or trimodal, and so on) distribution has two or more categories with an equal number of cases and with more cases than any of the other categories. There is no single mode. Imagine that a particular distribution has two categories, each having just about the same number of cases (and these are the two most frequent categories). Strictly speaking, the mode would be the one with more cases, even though the other frequent category had only slightly fewer cases. When the categories are close to each other, this is not really a problem; it becomes more of a problem when the categories are far apart. For example, the modal age of students at one school of social work is 24 (22%). The percentage at each age drops until 29 and then rises again until reaching the second most common age, 33 (20%). It is useful in this situation to report that the actual age distribution is bimodal.

Another potential problem with the mode is that it might happen to fall far from the main clustering of cases in a distribution. It would be misleading in most circumstances to say simply that the variable's central tendency was whatever the modal value was. In a study of caregivers, the modal response for monthly hours of respite care use was zero, as a sizable proportion of caregivers did not use respite care (Cotrell & Engel, 1998). But to say the typical score was zero distorts the typical number of hours reported by those who did use respite care.

Nevertheless, on occasion, the mode is very appropriate. Most important, the mode is the only measure of central tendency that can be used to characterize the central tendency of variables measured at the nominal level. We can't say much more about the central tendency of the distribution of marital status in Exhibit 11.3 than that the most common value is married. The mode also is often referred to in descriptions of the shape of a distribution. The terms *unimodal* and *bimodal* appear frequently, as do descriptive statements like "The typical [most probable] respondent was in her 30s." Of course, when you want to show the most probable value, the mode is the appropriate statistic. Which diagnostic category is most common in a community mental health center? The mode provides the answer.

Median

The **median** is the position average, or the point that divides the distribution in half (the 50th percentile). The median is inappropriate for variables measured at the nominal level because their values cannot be put in order, and so there is no meaningful middle position. To determine the median, we simply array a distribution's values in numerical order and find the value of the case that has an equal number of cases above and below it. If the median point falls between two cases (which happens if the distribution has an even number of cases), the median is defined as the average of the two middle values and is computed by adding the values of the two middle cases and dividing by 2.

The median in a frequency distribution is determined by identifying the value corresponding to a cumulative percentage of 50. Starting at the top of the years of education distribution in Exhibit 11.10, for example, and adding up the percentages, we find that we have reached 46.8% in the 12 years category and then 75% in the 13 to 15 years category. The median is therefore 13 to 15.

With most variables, it is preferable to compute the median from ungrouped data because that method results in an exact value for the median, rather than an interval. In the grouped age distribution in Exhibit 11.9, for example, the median is in the 40 to 49 interval. But if we determine the median from the ungrouped data, we can state the exact value of the median as 42.

Mean

The **mean,** or arithmetic average, takes into account the values of each case in a distribution— it is a weighted average. The mean is computed by adding up the value of all the cases and dividing by the total number of cases, thereby taking into account the value of each case in the distribution:

Mean = Sum of value of cases/Number of cases

In algebraic notation, the equation is

$$\bar{X} = \sum X_i / N$$

For example, to calculate the mean value of eight cases, we add the value of all cases ($\sum X_i$) and divided by the number of cases (N):

$$(28 + 117 + 42 + 10 + 77 + 51 + 64 + 55) / 8 = 444 / 8 = 55.5$$

Since computing the mean requires adding up the values of the cases, it makes sense to compute a mean only if the values of the cases can be treated as actual quantities—that is, if they reflect an interval or ratio level of measurement, or if they are ordinal and we assume that ordinal measures can be treated as interval. It would make no sense to calculate the mean religion, for example. Imagine a group of four people in which there were two Protestants, one Catholic, and one Jew. To calculate the mean you would need to solve the equation (Protestant + Protestant + Catholic + Jew)/ 4 = ?. Even if you decide that Protestant = 1, Catholic = 2, and Jewish = 3, for data entry purposes, it still doesn't make sense to add these numbers because they don't represent quantities of religion.

Median or Mean?

Both the median and the mean are used to summarize the central tendency of quantitative variables, but their suitability for a particular application must be carefully assessed. The key issues to be considered in this assessment are the variable's level of measurement, the shape of its distribution, and the purpose of the statistical summary. Consideration of these issues will sometimes result in a decision to use both the median and the mean, and sometimes, neither measure is seen as preferable. But in many other situations, the choice between the mean and median will be clear-cut as soon as the researcher takes the time to consider these three issues.

Level of measurement is a key concern because to calculate the mean, we must add up the values of all the cases—a procedure that assumes the variable is measured at the interval or ratio level. So even though we know that coding *satisfied* with a 2 and *dissatisfied* with a 3 does not really mean that *dissatisfied* is 1 unit more satisfaction, the calculation of the mean assumes this difference to be true. Because calculation of the median requires only that we order the values of cases, we do not have to make this assumption. Technically speaking, then, the mean is an inappropriate statistic for variables measured at the ordinal level (and you already know that it is completely meaningless for qualitative variables). In practice, however, many social work researchers use the mean to describe the central tendency of variables measured at the ordinal level, for the reasons outlined earlier. So it is not unusual to see, for example, agencies report the mean (or average) satisfaction with services.

The shape of a variable's distribution should also be taken into account when deciding whether to use the median or mean. When a distribution is perfectly symmetric, so that the distribution of values below the median is a mirror image of the distribution of values above the median, the mean and median will be the same. But the values of the mean and median are affected differently by skewness, or the presence of cases with extreme values on one side of the distribution but not the other side. Because the median takes into account only the number of cases above and below the median point, not the value of these cases, it is not affected in any way by extreme values. Because the mean is based on adding the value of all the cases, it will be pulled in the direction of exceptionally high (or low) values. When the value of the mean is larger than the median, we know that the distribution is skewed in a positive direction, with proportionately more cases with higher than lower values. When the mean is smaller than the median, the distribution is skewed in a negative direction.

This differential impact of skewness on the median and mean is illustrated in Exhibit 11.13. On the first balance beam, the cases (bags) are spread out equally, and the median and mean are in the same location. On the second and third balance beams, the median corresponds to the value of the middle case, but the mean is pulled toward the value of the one case with an extremely low value. For this reason, the mean age (44.78) for the 2,898 cases represented partially in the detailed age distribution in Exhibit 11.9 is higher than the median age (42). Although in this instance the difference is small, in some distributions, the two measures will have markedly different values, and in such instances, the median may be preferred.

The single most important influence on the choice of the median or the mean should be the purpose of the statistical summary. If the purpose is to report the middle position in one or more distributions, then the median is the appropriate statistic, whether or not the distribution is skewed. For example, with respect to the age distribution from the GSS, you could report that half the American population is younger than 41 years old and half the population is older than that. But if the purpose is to show how likely different groups are to have age-related health problems, the measure of central tendency for these groups should take into account people's ages, not just the number who are older and younger than a particular age. For this purpose, the median would be inappropriate because it would not distinguish the two distributions, as shown in Exhibit 11.14. In the top distribution, everyone is between the ages of 35 and 45, with a median of 41. In the bottom distribution, the median is still 41 but half of the cases have ages above 60. The higher mean in the second distribution reflects the fact that it has more older people.

Keep in mind that it is not appropriate to use either the median or the mean as a measure of central tendency for variables measured at the nominal level because at this level, the different attributes of a variable cannot be ordered as higher or lower. Technically speaking, the mode should be used to measure the central tendency of variables measured at the nominal level (and it can also be used to measure the central tendency of variables measured at the ordinal, interval, and ratio levels). The median is most suited to measure the central tendency of variables measured at the ordinal level (and it can also be used to measure the central tendency of variables measured at the interval and ratio levels). Finally, the mean is only suited to measure central tendency for variables measured at the interval and ratio levels.

Exhibit 11.13   The Mean as a Balance Point

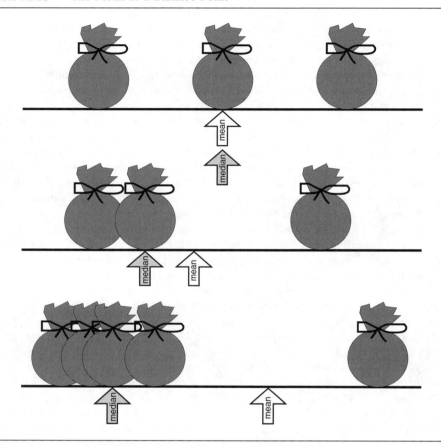

It is not entirely legitimate to represent the central tendency of a variable measured at the ordinal level with the mean: Calculation of the mean requires summing the values of all cases, and at the ordinal level, these values indicate only order, not actual numbers. Nonetheless, as we have already said, many social work researchers use the mean with ordinal-level variables and find that this is potentially useful for comparison among variables and as a first step in more complex statistical analyses. The median and the mode can also be useful as measures of central tendency for variables measured at the interval and ratio levels, when the goal is to indicate middle position (the median) or the most frequent value (the mode). In summary:

Level of Measurement	Most Appropriate Measure of Central Tendency	Other Potentially Useful Measure of Central Tendency	Definitely Inappropriate Measure of Central Tendency
Nominal	Mode	None	Median, Mean
Ordinal	Median	Mean	None
Interval, Ratio	Mean	Median, Mode	None

Exhibit 11.14   Insensitivity of Median to Variation at End of Distribution

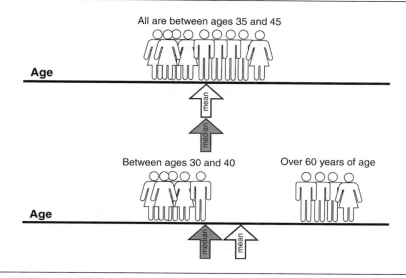

In general, the mean is the most commonly used measure of central tendency for quantitative variables, both because it takes into account the value of all cases in the distribution and because it is the foundation for many other more advanced statistics. However, the mean's very popularity results in its use in situations for which it is inappropriate. Keep an eye out for this problem.

Measures of Variation

You already have learned that central tendency is only one aspect of the shape of a distribution—the most important aspect for many purposes, but still just a piece of the total picture. A summary of distributions based only on their central tendency can be very incomplete, even misleading. For example, three towns might have the same mean and median income but still be very different in their social character due to the shape of their income distributions. As illustrated in Exhibit 11.15, Town A is a homogeneous middle-class community; Town B is very heterogeneous; and Town C has a polarized, bimodal income distribution, with mostly very poor and very rich people and few in between.

The way to capture these differences is with statistical measures of variation. Four popular measures of variation are the range, the interquartile range, the variance, and the standard deviation (which is the most popular measure of variability). To calculate each of these measures, the variable must be at the interval or ratio level. Statistical measures of variation are used infrequently with qualitative variables, so these measures will not be presented here.

Range

The **range** is a simple measure of variation, calculated as the highest value in a distribution minus the lowest value:

$$\text{Range} = \text{Highest value} - \text{Lowest value}$$

Exhibit 11.15   Distributions Differing in Variability but Not Central Tendency

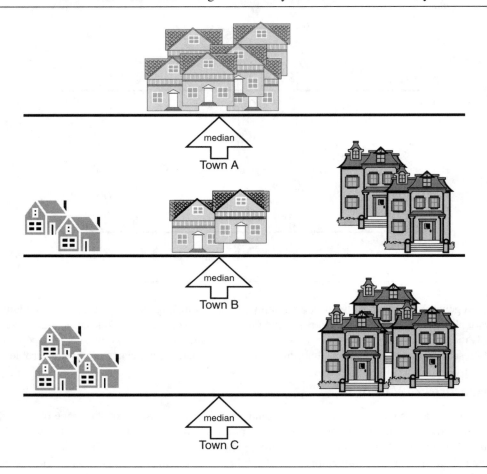

It often is important to report the range of a distribution, to identify the whole range of actual values that might be encountered. However, because the range can be drastically altered by just one exceptionally high or low value (termed an **outlier**), it does not do an adequate job of summarizing the extent of variability in a distribution.

Interquartile Range

A version of the range statistic, the **interquartile range,** avoids the problem created by outliers. **Quartiles** are the points in a distribution corresponding to the first 25% of the cases, the first 50% of the cases, and the first 75% of the cases. You already know how to determine the second quartile, corresponding to the point in the distribution covering half of the cases—it is another name for the median. The first and third quartiles are determined in the same way, but by finding the points corresponding to 25% and 75% of the cases, respectively. The interquartile range is the difference between the first quartile and the third quartile.

Exhibit 11.16   Calculation of the Variance

Case #	Score (X_i)	$X_i - \bar{X}$	$(X_i - \bar{X})^2$
1	21	−3.27	10.69
2	30	5.73	32.83
3	15	−9.27	85.93
4	18	−6.27	39.31
5	25	0.73	0.53
6	32	7.73	59.75
7	19	−5.27	27.77
8	21	−3.27	10.69
9	23	−1.27	1.61
10	37	12.73	162.05
11	26	1.73	2.99
	267		434.15

Mean: $\bar{X} = 267/11 = 24.27$

Sum of squared deviations $= 434.15$

Variance; $\sigma^2 = 434.15/11 = 39.47$

Variance

A problem with using the range and interquartile range statistics to describe variation is that they do not take into account all of the reported scores. For example, the range is based only on the upper and lower extreme scores. We do not learn from these statistics the extent to which observed scores are clustered close together or spread far apart. The **variance** provides a statistic that does account for all the scores to determine the spread. The variance is the average squared deviation of each case from the mean, so it takes into account the amount by which each case differs from the mean. Exhibit 11.16 shows an example of how to calculate the *sample variance*, using the formula

$$s^2 = \frac{\sum(X_i - \bar{X})^2}{n - 1}$$

where $\bar{X}$ is the sample mean, n is the sample size, $\sum$, is the total for all cases, and Xi is the value of each case i on variable X. The population variance only differs by dividing by the total number of cases rather than the total minus 1.

The variance is used in many other statistics, although it is more conventional to measure variability with the closely related standard deviation than with the variance.

Standard Deviation

Because the variance provides a measure of the square of the deviations, it does not express the spread in the original units of the measure, and it is hard to interpret the variance. For example, what does a variance of 43.415 mean in relation to the actual reported scores in Exhibit 11.16? To correct this, variation is often expressed by the **standard deviation,** which is simply the square root of the variance. By taking the square root, the sample standard deviation is expressed in the original units of the measure. It is the square root of the average squared deviation of each case from the mean:

$$s = \sqrt{\frac{\sum (X_i - \bar{X})^2}{n - 1}}$$

where $\sqrt{\ }$ is the square root. When the standard deviation is calculated from population data, the denominator is N, rather than $n - 1$, an adjustment that has no discernible effect when the number of cases is reasonably large. You also should note that the use of *squared* deviations in the formula accentuates the impact of relatively large deviations because squaring a large number makes that number count much more.

The standard deviation has mathematical properties that make it the preferred measure of variability in many cases, particularly when a variable is normally distributed. A graph of a **normal distribution** looks like a bell, with one "hump" in the middle, centered around the population mean, and the number of cases tapering off on both sides of the mean (see Exhibit 11.17). A normal distribution is symmetric: If you folded it in half at its center (at the population mean), the two halves would match perfectly. If a variable is normally distributed, 68% of the cases will lie between plus and minus 1 standard deviation from the distribution's mean, and 95% of the cases will lie between 1.96 standard deviations above and below the mean.

The correspondence of the standard deviation to the normal distribution enables us to infer how confident we can be that the mean (or some other statistic) of a population sampled randomly is within a certain range of the sample mean. This is the logic behind calculating confidence intervals around the mean, as we did in Chapter 4. Confidence intervals indicate how confident we can be, given our particular random sample, that the value of some statistic in the population falls within a particular range.

Exhibit 11.17   The Normal Distribution

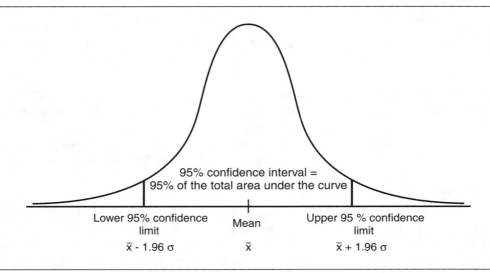

ANALYZING DATA ETHICALLY: HOW NOT TO LIE WITH STATISTICS

Using statistics ethically means first and foremost being honest and open. Findings should be reported honestly, and researchers should be open about the thinking that guided their decision to use particular statistics. Although this section has a humorous title (after Darrell Huff's 1954 little classic, *How to Lie with Statistics*), make no mistake about the intent. It is possible to distort social reality with statistics, and it is unethical to do so knowingly, even when the error is due more to carelessness than deceptive intent.

Summary statistics can easily be used unethically, knowingly or not. When we summarize a distribution in a single number, even in two numbers, we are losing much information. Neither central tendency nor variation describes a distribution's overall shape. Taken separately, neither measure tells us about the other characteristic of the distribution (central tendency or variation). So reports using measures of central tendency should normally also include measures of variation. Also, we should inspect the shape of any distribution for which we report summary statistics to ensure that the summary statistic does not mislead us (or anyone else) because of an unusual degree of skewness.

It is possible to mislead those who read statistical reports by choosing summary statistics that accentuate a particular feature of a distribution. For example, imagine an unscrupulous realtor trying to convince a prospective home buyer in Community B that it is a community with very high property values when it actually has a positively skewed distribution of property values (see Exhibit 11.18). The realtor compares the mean price of homes in Community B to that for Community A (one with a homogeneous mid-priced set of homes) and therefore makes Community B look much better. In truth, the higher mean in Community B reflects a very skewed, lopsided distribution of property values; most residents own small, cheap homes. A median would provide a better basis for comparison.

You have already seen that it is possible to distort the shape of a distribution by ignoring some of the guidelines for constructing graphs and frequency distributions. Whenever you need to group data in a frequency distribution or graph, you can reduce the potential for problems by inspecting the ungrouped distributions and then using a grouping procedure that does not distort the distribution's basic shape. When you create graphs, be sure to consider how the axes you choose may change the distribution's apparent shape.

CROSSTABULATING VARIABLES

Most data analyses focus on relationships among variables in order to test hypotheses or just to describe or explore relationships. For each of these purposes, we must examine the association among two or more variables. **Crosstabulation** (**crosstab**) is one of the simplest methods for doing so. A crosstabulation displays the distribution of one variable for each category of another variable; it can also be termed a *bivariate distribution.* You can also display the association between two variables in a graph; we will see an example in this section. Crosstabs also provide a simple tool for statistically controlling one or more variables while examining the associations among others. In the next section, you will learn how crosstabs used in this way can help to test for spurious relationships and to evaluate causal models. Examples in both of these sections come from the 1995 Detroit Area Study by Jackson and

Exhibit 11.18   Using the Mean to Create a More Favorable Impression

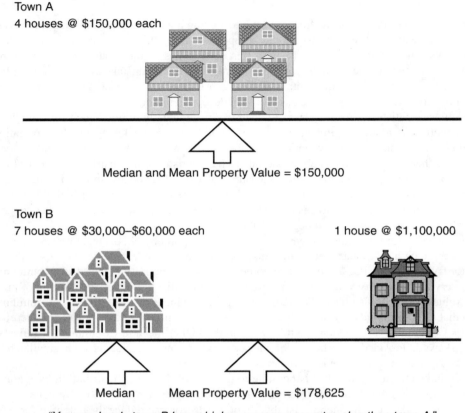

Town A
4 houses @ $150,000 each

Median and Mean Property Value = $150,000

Town B
7 houses @ $30,000–$60,000 each   1 house @ $1,100,000

Median   Mean Property Value = $178,625

"Yes, our lovely town B has a higher average property value than town A."

Williams (2004), entitled "Social Influence on Health: Stress, Racism, and Health Protective Resources." Through these examples, we will learn a bit about social influences on health as well as about the logic of data analysis.

Exhibit 11.19 displays the crosstabulation of self-reported health by education, so that we can test the hypothesis that perceived health increases with education (Franks, Gold, & Fiscella, 2003). The table is first presented with frequencies and then again with percentages. In both tables, the *body* of the table is the part between the row and column labels and the row and column totals. The *cells* of the table are defined by combinations of row and column values. Each cell represents cases with a unique combination of values of the two variables, corresponding to that particular row and column. The **marginal distributions** of the table are on the right (the *row marginals*) and underneath (the *column marginals*). These are just the frequency distributions for the two variables (in number of cases, percentages, or both), considered separately (the column marginals in Exhibit 11.19 are for the categories of education; the row marginals are for the distribution of health). The independent variable is usually the column variable; the dependent variable, then, is the row variable.

Exhibit 11.19   Crosstabulation of Health by Education

HIGHEST GRADE COMPLETED: CELL COUNTS				
HEALTH	*<High School*	*High School*	*College*	*Total*
Excellent	18	109	65	192
Very Good	37	233	115	385
Good	53	222	50	325
Fair or Poor	79	127	26	232
Total (n)	187	691	256	1134

HIGHEST GRADE COMPLETED: PERCENTAGES				
HEALTH	*<High School*	*High School*	*College*	*Total*
Excellent	9.6%	15.8%	25.4%	16.9%
Very Good	19.8	33.7	44.9	34.0
Good	28.3	32.1	19.5	28.7
Fair or Poor	42.2	18.4	10.2	20.5
Total	99.9%	100.0%	100.0%	100.1%

Source: Jackson & Williams, 2004.

Note: Percentages do not add to 100% due to rounding error.

The first table in Exhibit 11.19 shows the number of cases with each combination of values of health and education. It is hard to look at the table in this form and determine whether there is a relationship between the two variables. We need to convert the cell frequencies into percentages, as in the second table in Exhibit 11.19. This table presents the data as **percentages** within the categories of the independent variable (the column variable, in this case). In other words, the cell frequencies have been converted into percentages of the column totals (the *n* in each column). For example, in Exhibit 11.19, the number of people with less than a high school degree who felt in *excellent* health is 18 out of 187, or 9.6% (which rounds off to 10%). Because the cell frequencies have been converted to percentages of the column totals, the numbers add up to 100 in each column but not across the rows.

To read the percentage table, compare the percentage distribution of health across the columns, starting with the lowest educational category (in the left column). There is a strong association. As education increases, the percentage in *excellent* and *very good* health also rises, from about 30% of those with less than a high school degree (adding rounded values 10 + 20, in the first two cells in the first column) up to 70% of those with a college degree (adding rounded values 25 + 45, in the first two cells in the last column). This result is consistent with the hypothesis.

When the data in a table are percentages, usually just the percentages in each cell should be presented, not the number of cases in each cell. Include 100% at the bottom of each column (if the independent variable is the column variable) to indicate that the percentages add up to 100, as well as the ***base number (n)*** for each column (in parentheses). If the percentages add up to 99 or 101 due to rounding error, just indicate so in a footnote.

There is no requirement that the independent variable always be the column variable, although consistency within a report or paper is a must. If the independent variable is the row variable, we compute percentages based on the table's row totals (the *n* in each row), and so the percentages add up to 100 across the rows (see Exhibit 11.20). When you read the table

Exhibit 11.20 Crosstabulation of Health by Marital Status (Row Percentages)

Marital Status	HEALTH					
	Excellent	Very Good	Good	Fair or Poor	Total	(n)
Married	18.9%	34.6	28.7	17.8	100.0%	(471)
Live w/ Partner	6.7%	42.2	40.0	11.1	100.0%	(45)
Sep or Divorc'd	14.4%	29.4	28.9	27.4	100.0%	(201)
Widowed	9.2%	21.1	33.8	35.9	100.0%	(142)
Never married	21.4%	41.3	24.3	13.0	100.0%	(276)

Source: Jackson and Williams, 2004.

in Exhibit 11.20, you find that 18.9% of married respondents were in *excellent* health, compared to 6.7% of those who were living with a partner, 14.4% of those who were separated or divorced, 9.2% of those who were widowed, and 21.5% of those who had never been married (the cell frequencies were omitted from this table). What explanations can you suggest for these patterns?

Graphing Association

Graphs provide an efficient tool for summarizing relationships among variables. Exhibit 11.21 displays the relationship between race and region in graphic form. It shows that the percentage of the population that is Black is highest in the South, whereas people of "other" races are most common on the coasts.

Another good example of the use of graphs to show relationships is provided by a Bureau of Justice Statistics report on criminal victimization (Rand, Lynch, & Cantor, 1997, p. 1). Exhibit 11.22, taken from that report, shows how the rates of different violent crimes have varied over time, with most rates falling in the late 1980s, rising in the early 1990s, and then falling again by 1995.

Describing Association

A crosstabulation table reveals four aspects of the association between two variables:

- *Existence.* Do the percentage distributions vary at all between categories of the independent variable?
- *Strength.* How much do the percentage distributions vary between categories of the independent variable?
- *Direction.* For quantitative variables, do values on the dependent variable tend to increase or decrease with an increase in value on the independent variable?
- *Pattern.* For quantitative variables, are changes in the percentage distribution of the dependent variable fairly regular (simply increasing or decreasing), or do they vary (perhaps increasing, then decreasing, or perhaps gradually increasing, then rapidly increasing)?

In Exhibit 11.19, an association exists; it is moderately strong (the difference in percentages between the first and last column is about 15 percentage points), and the direction of association between perceived health and education is positive. The pattern in this table is close to what is termed monotonic. In a **monotonic** relationship, the value of cases consistently

Exhibit 11.21   Race by Region of the United States

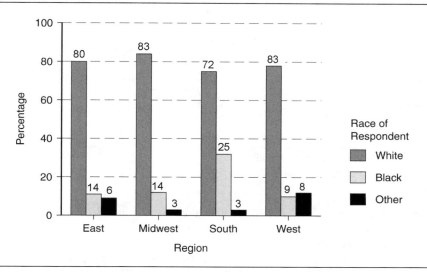

Source: Orcutt and Turner, 1993. Copyright © 1993. Reprinted with permission.

Exhibit 11.22   Violent Crime Rates, 1973–1995*

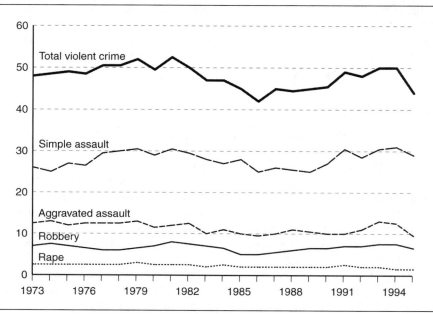

*Victimization rate per 1,000 people age 12 or older.

Source: Rand, Lynch, & Carter, 1997, p. 1.

Exhibit 11.23   Health by Race/Ethnicity

	RACIAL/ETHNIC GROUP	
Health	White	Minority
Excellent	19%	15%
Very Good	39	29
Good	27	30
Fair or Poor	14	25
Total	99%*	99%*
(n)	(520)	(619)

* Percents do not add to 100 due to rounding.

Source: Jackson and Williams, 2004.

increases (or decreases) on one variable as the value of cases increases on the other variable. Monotonic is often defined a bit less strictly, with the idea being that as the value of cases on one variable increases (or decreases), the value of cases on the other variable tends to increase (or decrease), and at least does not change direction. This describes the relationship between health and education: Self-reported health increases as education increases, with shifts in the direction of better health in the columns after the first.

The relationship between race, another potential correlate (Franks et al., 2003), and health appears in Exhibit 11.23. There is a moderate association: 19% of Whites rate their health as *excellent,* compared to 15% of those who are members of a minority racial or ethnic group. Between the minority and White columns, the entire distribution of health shifts in the direction of better health. Note that we rounded off the percents, and as a result, they no longer total 100 in each column. A table footnote makes this clear to the reader.

Exhibit 11.24, by contrast, gives almost no evidence of an association between gender and health. There is no more than five percentage points separating the self-rated health of men and women in each health category.

Evaluating Association

When you read research reports and journal articles, you will find that social work researchers usually make decisions about the existence and strength of association on the basis of more statistics than just a single crosstabulation.

A **measure of association** is a type of descriptive statistic used to summarize the strength of an association. There are many measures of association, some of which are appropriate for variables measured at particular levels. One popular measure of association in crosstabular analyses with variables measured at the ordinal level is **gamma.** As with many measures of association, the possible values of gamma vary from −1, meaning the variables are perfectly associated in an inverse direction; to 0, meaning there is no association of the type that gamma measures; to +1, meaning there is a perfect positive association of the type that gamma measures.

Inferential statistics are used in deciding whether it is likely that an association exists in the larger population from which the sample was drawn. Even when the association between two variables is consistent with the researcher's hypothesis, it is possible that the association was just due to chance—the vagaries of sampling on a random basis. (The problem is much

Exhibit 11.24   Health by Gender

Health	GENDER	
	Male	Female
Excellent	20%	15%
Very Good	37	32
Good	26	30
Fair or Poor	18	22
Total	101%*	99%*
(n)	(429)	(710)

* Percents do not add to 100 due to rounding.

Source: Jackson and Williams, 2004.

worse if the sample is not random because we cannot use inferential statistics to estimate the likelihood that the association is just due to chance). When the analyst feels reasonably confident that an association was not due to chance, based on a calculation using inferential statistics, it is said that the association is statistically significant. **Statistical significance** means that an association is not likely to be due to chance, according to some criterion set by the analyst. The criterion is referred to as the *alpha* level (α)—the probability level that will be used to evaluate statistical significance. It is conventional in statistics to use an alpha level of .05—that is, to avoid concluding that an association exists in the population from which the sample was drawn unless the probability that the association was due to chance is less than 5%. In other words, a statistician normally will not conclude that an association exists between two variables unless he or she can be at least 95% confident that the association was not due to chance. This is the same type of logic that you learned about earlier this chapter, when we introduced the concept of 95% confidence limits for the mean.

Many inferential statistics are used to estimate the probability that a particular association is due to chance, but **chi square** is the inferential statistic that is used in most crosstabular analyses. There is a customary form for reporting the probability that a relationship is due to chance, whether that probability is calculated using chi square or another inferential statistic: $p < .05$, which can be translated as: "The probability that the association was due to chance is less than 5 out of 100 [5%]." The alpha level was set at .05 in this example; other common alpha levels used in inferential statistics are .01 (less than 1 chance out of 100) and .001 (less than 1/10 of a chance out of 100).

Note that we have emphasized that the analyst "feels reasonably confident" that the association is "not likely to be due to chance" when there is a statistically significant relationship. There is still a degree of doubt because statistical testing is based on probability, which means that whatever we conclude, it is possible we could be wrong. As we described in Chapter 4, when we draw a random sample from a population, we have no guarantee that the sample is truly representative; rather, we are confident it is representative within some degree of error. Because the conclusion made from statistical testing is based on probability, it is possible to make the wrong conclusion. For example, we can test the relationship between the number of hours studied and student scores on examinations. One hypothesis is that there is no relationship in the population whereas the alternative hypothesis suggests that there is indeed a relationship. With our sample of students, we find a statistically significant relationship and so we are 95% sure that a relationship exists in the population. Yet, note: There still remains a 5% possibility that we have reached the wrong conclusion. We have to consider the possibility that we have concluded that there is a relationship based on our one sample, but in fact, there is no relationship between the two variables in the population we sampled. This type of error, called **Type I error**, threatens our ability to conclude that there is an association. On the other hand, we might find the opposite situation to occur: We conclude based on statistical analysis of our sample data that there is no relationship between the two variables in the population, but in reality, there is a relationship in the population. This is referred to as **Type II error.**

Type I and Type II errors are particularly important because finding an association between two variables is a necessary condition to establish causality. The problem researchers encounter is that Type I and Type II error cannot be eliminated. When a researcher chooses an alpha level of .05, it means that the researcher is willing to accept a 5% chance of concluding there is a relationship in a particular sample when there is no relationship in the population. The researcher could reduce Type I error by making it more difficult to conclude that there is a statistically significant relationship: setting an alpha level of .01, which means that the researcher is willing to accept only a 1% chance of concluding that there is a relationship even when there is none in the population. By doing this, the likelihood of Type I error is reduced.

By minimizing Type I error, however, the researcher has increased the probability of Type II error. Simply by making it *less likely* that we will falsely conclude there is a relationship in the population, we have made it *more likely* that we will falsely conclude from sample data that there is no relationship when there actually is a relationship in the population. Whereas Type I error was summarized by alpha, Type II error is summarized by *beta* (β).

Type I error is also influenced by the effect of the intervention or the strength of the relationship between an independent and dependent variable. The greater the effect or impact of the intervention, the more likely the effect will be significant. Smaller effects or weaker relationships are less likely to provide statistically significant results.

Finally, Type I error is influenced by sample size. A small sample is less likely to produce a statistically significant result, for a relationship of any given strength. On the other hand, larger sample sizes are likely to find statistically significant relationships even when the strength of the relationship is weak. You may remember from Chapter 4 that sampling error decreases as sample size increases. For this same reason, an association is less likely to appear on the basis of chance in a larger sample than in a smaller sample. In a table with more than 1,000 cases, the odds of a chance association are often very low indeed. For example, with our table based on 1,134 cases, the probability that the association between education and health (Exhibit 11.19) was due to chance was less than 1 in 1,000 ($p < .001$)! The association in that table was only moderate, as indicated by a gamma of .38. Even rather weak associations can be statistically significant with such a large random sample (as in Exhibit 11.24), which means that the analyst must be careful not to assume that just because a statistically significant association exists, it is therefore important. In a large sample, an association may be statistically significant but still be too weak to be substantively significant.

Which type of error should be minimized? There is no easy answer to that question. It depends on the level of risk associated with concluding there is a relationship when there is none (Type I error) or concluding there is no relationship when there is a relationship (Type II error). For example, you might need to assess the risk or consequence of using an intervention shown to be effective in a research study that is really not effective (Type I error) versus the consequence of not using an intervention found to be ineffective in a research study (Type II error) when it really is effective.

Statistical power analysis is a tool used by researchers to determine the sample size necessary to detect an effect of specific size for a particular alpha level. Statistical power analysis also is used to determine Type II error for a sample of specific size, effect size, and the level of statistical significance.

Controlling for a Third Variable

Crosstabulation can also be used to study the relationship between two variables while controlling for other variables. We will focus our attention on controlling for a third variable in this section, but we will say a bit about controlling for more variables at the section's end. We will examine three different uses for three-variable crosstabulation: identifying an intervening variable, testing a relationship for spuriousness, and specifying the conditions for a relationship. Each of these uses for three-variable crosstabs helps to determine the validity of our findings, either by evaluating criteria for causality (nonspuriousness and identification of a causal mechanism) or by increasing our understanding of the conditions required for a relationship to hold. All three uses are aspects of **elaboration analysis**: the process of introducing control variables into a bivariate relationship to better understand the relationship (Davis, 1985; Rosenberg, 1968). We will examine the gamma and chi square statistics for each table in this analysis.

Case Study: Perceived Health

What influences perceived health (which is a good indicator of health as assessed by health professionals)? Prior research on health provides a great deal of support for the hypothesis that perceived health increases with social status; our analysis of the Jackson and Williams (2004) data so far has already lent additional support to this hypothesis. Both education and income are components of social status, but one perspective suggests that education influences health only through its effect on income because income influences ability to afford good health care and maintain healthy habits (see Exhibit 11.25) (Grimm & Brewster, 2003).

Exhibit 11.25   A Causal Model of an Intervening Effect

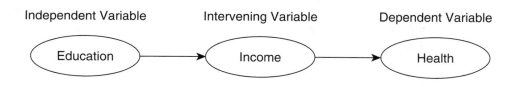

Exhibit 11.26   Health by Income and Income by Education

	FAMILY INCOME BEFORE TAXES		
Health	< $24,000	$24,000 – $48,000	> $48,000
Excellent	11.2%	18.5%	18.1%
Very Good	31.7	30.7	35.3
Good	31.7	32.3	27.1
Fair or Poor	25.4	18.5	19.5
Total	100.0%	100%	100%
	(205)	(189)	(745)

	EDUCATION		
Income	<High School	High School	College
< $24,000	30.5%	19.0%	6.6%
$24,000 – $48,000	7.0%	19.1%	17.2%
> $48,000	62.6%	61.9%	76.2%
Total	100.0%	100.0%	100.0%
	(187)	(691)	(256)

Intervening Variables

We will first test the causal model of health in Exhibit 11.25, which suggests that income intervenes in the relationship between education and health. You already have seen that education is associated with health, as predicted by the model. You can also see in Exhibit 11.26 that health is related to income (gamma = −.11; $p < .01$) and that income and education are related (gamma = .24; $p < .001$). Two more predictions of the model are confirmed. But to determine whether income is an **intervening variable** in the education-health relationship, we must determine whether it explains (transmits) the influence of education on health. We therefore examine the relationship between education and health while controlling for the respondent's income.

If income intervened in the education-health relationship, the effect of controlling for this third variable would be to eliminate, or at least substantially reduce, this relationship. According to the causal model, education influences health by influencing income, which in turn influences health. We can evaluate this possibility by reading the two subtables in Exhibit 11.27. **Subtables** like those in Exhibit 11.27 describe the relationship between two variables within the discrete categories of one or more other control variables. The control variable in Exhibit 11.27 is family income, and the first subtable is the education-health crosstab for only those respondents with low incomes. The second subtable is for those respondents with high incomes.

A quick inspection of the subtables reveals that family income does not intervene in the relationship between education and health. There is only a slight difference in the strength of

Exhibit 11.27   Health by Income by Education

Income	Health	EDUCATION		
		Less Than High School	High School	College
<$24,000	Excellent	7.0%	11.5%	23.5%
	Very good	15.8	35.9	52.9
	Good	38.6	30.5	17.6
	Fair or Poor	38.6	22.1	5.9
	Total	100.0%	100.0%	100.0%
		(57)	(131)	(17)
$24,000-$48,000	Excellent	0	17.4%	27.3%
	Very Good	15.4%	29.5	38.6
	Good	53.8	32.6	25.0
	Fair	30.8	20.5	9.1
	Total	100.0%	100.0%	100.0%
		(13)	(132)	(44)
>$48,000	Excellent	12.0%	16.6%	25.1%
	Very Good	22.2	34.3	35.4
	Good	20.5	32.5	26.9
	Fair or Poor	45.3	16.6	19.6
	Total	100.0%	100.0%	100.0%
		(117)	(428)	(195)

Source: General Social Survey, 2000.

the education-health association in the subtables (gammas in the three subtables, a, b, and c, are −.42, −.37, and −.35, respectively). We should be less confident in the three-variable model.

Extraneous Variables

Another reason for introducing a third variable into a bivariate relationship is to see whether that relationship is spurious due to the influence of an **extraneous variable**—a variable that influences both the independent and dependent variables, creating an association between them that disappears when the extraneous variable is controlled. Ruling out possible extraneous variables will help to strengthen considerably the conclusion that the relationship between the independent and dependent variables is causal, particularly if all the variables that seem to have the potential for creating a spurious relationship can be controlled.

One variable that might create a spurious relationship between education and health is race. You have already seen that health varies with education. Is it not possible, however, that this association is spurious due to the effect of race? Race, after all, is associated with both education and health, and we might surmise that discrimination in health care based on race reduces health, not education itself (Schulz, Williams, Parker, Becker, & James, 2000).

Exhibit 11.28   A Causal Model of a Spurious Effect

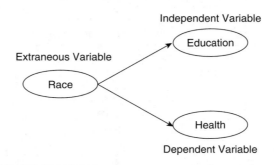

Exhibit 11.29   Education by Race

	RACE	
Education	White	Minority
< High School	11.4%	20.8%
High School	58.3	63.1
College	30.3	16.1
Total	100.0%	100.0%
	(518)	(616)

Exhibit 11.28 diagrams this possibility, and Exhibit 11.29 shows that there is a bivariate association between education and race, as predicted by the model.

If the three-variable prediction is correct, there should be no association between education and health after controlling for race. Because we are using crosstabs, this means there should be no association in either of the education-health subtables for the two values of the race variable.

The trivariate crosstabulation in Exhibit 11.30 shows that the relationship between health and education is not spurious due to the effect of race. The association between health and education does not vary much between the two categories (gamma is .35 in the first subtable and .37 in the second. So our hypothesis that education has a causal effect on health is strengthened.

Specification

By adding a third variable to an evaluation of a bivariate relationship, the data analyst can also specify the conditions under which the bivariate relationship occurs. A **specification** occurs when the association between the independent and dependent variables varies across the categories of one or more other control variables.

The subtables in Exhibit 11.31 allow an evaluation of whether receipt of welfare specifies the effect of race on health. The hypothesis is that the receipt of public welfare may reduce the basis of racial disparities in health (Bound, Waidmann, Schoenbaum, & Bingenheimer, 2003). This hypothesis is supported. For the 143 respondents receiving Aid to Families with

Exhibit 11.30   Health by Education by Race

| Income | Health | EDUCATION | | |
		Less Than High School	High School	College
White	Excellent	13.6%	15.6%	28.0%
	Very good	22.0	39.4	45.9
	Good	32.2	30.8	17.8
	Fair or Poor	32.2	14.2	8.3
	Total	100.0%	100.0%	100.0%
		(59)	(302)	(157)
Minority	Excellent	7.8%	15.9%	21.2%
	Very Good	18.8	29.3	43.4
	Good	26.6	33.2	22.2
	Fair	46.9	21.6	13.1
	Total	100.0%	100.0%	100.0%
		(128)	(389)	(99)

Dependent Children (AFDC), there is almost no racial difference in perceived health (gamma = .029, $p > .1$), whereas for the 990 respondents who were not on AFDC, minorities reported poorer health than Whites (gamma = .22, $p < .001$). Further investigation of the reason for this specification would make for an interesting contribution to the literature. Is it because welfare helps to equalize health disparities? This explanation seems unlikely because the overall health of those receiving welfare is worse than it is for those who do not receive welfare. Is it because those who receive welfare are single-parent families, who are disadvantaged in terms of health care no matter what their race? Is it due to the presence of children in all the welfare families, which increases their exposure to pathogens? Can you think of other possibilities?

We should add one important caution about constructing tables involving three or more variables. Because the total number of cells in the subtables becomes large as the number of categories of the control (third) variable increases, the number of cases that each cell percentage is based on will become correspondingly small. This effect has two important consequences, although neither created a problem in our analysis. First, the number of comparisons that must be made to identify the patterns in the table as a whole becomes very substantial—and the patterns may become too complex to make much sense. Second, as the number of cases per category decreases, the odds that the distributions within these categories could be due to chance becomes greater. This problem of having too many cells and too few cases can be lessened by making sure that the control variable has only a few categories and by drawing a large sample, but often neither of these steps will be sufficient to resolve the problem completely.

Our goal in introducing you to crosstabulation has been to help you think about the association among variables and to give you a relatively easy tool for describing association. To read most statistical reports and to conduct more sophisticated analyses of social data, you will have to extend your statistical knowledge. In addition to the statistical techniques we have considered here, you should learn more about the summary descriptive statistics used to indicate the strength and direction of association. Until you do so, you will find it difficult to state with precision just how strong an association is. You also should learn about a different statistical approach to characterizing the association between two quantitative variables, called **regression** or **correlation analysis**. Statistics based on regression and correlation are

Exhibit 11.31   Health by Race by Welfare Status

Receives ADC/AFDC	Health	RACE	
		White	Minority
Yes	Excellent	15.4%	12.8%
	Very Good	34.6	32.5
	Good	19.2	27.4
	Fair or Poor	30.8	27.4
		100.0%	100.1%
		(26)	(117)
	Health	White	Minority
No	Excellent	19.3%	15.9%
	Very Good	39.4	28.9
	Good	27.6	30.5
	Fair or Poor	13.6	24.7
	Total	99.9%	100.0%
		(492)	(498)

Source: General Social Survey, 2000.

Note: Percentages do not add to 100% due to rounding error.

used often in social science and have many advantages over crosstabulation—as well as some disadvantages. You will need to take a course in social statistics to become proficient in the use of statistics based on regression and correlation.

ANALYZING DATA ETHICALLY: HOW NOT TO LIE ABOUT RELATIONSHIPS

When the data analyst begins to examine relationships among variables in some real data, social science research becomes most exciting. The moment of truth, it would seem, has arrived. Either the hypotheses are supported or not. But, in fact, this is also a time to proceed with caution and to evaluate the analyses of others with even more caution. Once large data sets are entered into a computer, it becomes easy to check out a great many relationships; when relationships are examined among three or more variables at a time, the possibilities become almost endless.

This range of possibilities presents a great hazard for data analysis. It becomes tempting to search around in the data until something interesting emerges. Rejected hypotheses are forgotten in favor of highlighting what's going on in the data. It's not wrong to examine data for unanticipated relationships; the problem is that inevitably some relationships between variables will appear just on the basis of chance association alone. If you search hard and long enough, it will be possible to come up with something that really means nothing.

A reasonable balance must be struck between deductive data analysis to test hypotheses and inductive analysis to explore patterns in a data set. Hypotheses formulated in advance of data collection must be tested as they were originally stated; any further analyses of these hypotheses that involve a more exploratory strategy must be so labeled in research reports. Serendipitous findings do not need to be ignored, but they must be reported as such. Subsequent researchers can try to test deductively the ideas generated by our explorations.

We also have to be honest about the limitations of using survey data to test causal hypotheses. The usual practice for those who seek to test a causal hypothesis with nonexperimental survey data is to test for the relationship between the independent and dependent variables, controlling for other variables that might possibly create a spurious relationship. This is what we did by examining the relationship between education and health while controlling for race (Exhibit 11.30). But finding that a hypothesized relationship is not altered by controlling for just one variable does not establish that the relationship is causal. Nor does controlling for two, three, or many more variables. There is always a possibility that some other variable that we did not think to control, or that was not even measured in the survey, has produced a spurious relationship between the independent and dependent variables in our hypothesis (Lieberson, 1985). We have to think about the possibilities and be cautious in our causal conclusions.

CONCLUSION

This chapter has demonstrated how a researcher can describe social phenomena, identify relationships among them, explore the reasons for these relationships, and test hypotheses about them. Statistics provide a remarkably useful tool for developing our understanding of the social world, a tool that we can use both to test our ideas and to generate new ones.

Unfortunately, to the uninitiated, the use of statistics can seem to end debate right there— you can't argue with the numbers. You now know better than that. The numbers will be worthless if the methods used to generate the data are not valid; and the numbers will be misleading if they are not used appropriately, taking into account the type of data to which they are applied. Even assuming valid methods and proper use of statistics, there's one more critical step, for the numbers do not speak for themselves. Ultimately, it is how we interpret and report the numbers that determines their usefulness. It is to this topic that we now turn.

KEY TERMS

Bar chart
Base number (N)
Bimodal
Central tendency
Check coding
Chi-square
Codebook
Combined frequency display
Compressed frequency display
Correlation analysis
Crosstabulation
Cumulative percentage
Curvilinear
Data cleaning
Descriptive statistics
Elaboration analysis
Extraneous variable
Frequency distribution
Frequency polygon

Gamma
Histogram
Inferential statistics
Interquartile range
Intervening variable
Invalid codes
Marginal distribution
Mean
Measure of association
Median
Mode
Monotonic
Normal distribution
Outlier
Percentage
Probability average
Quartile
Range
Regression analysis

Skewness
Specification
Standard deviation
Statistical significance
Subtable
Type I error

Type II error
Unimodal
Unique identifier
Variability
Variance

HIGHLIGHTS

• Data must be prepared for analysis. This includes assigning unique identification numbers to each respondent, reviewing the forms for unclear responses, creating codes for open-ended questions, and developing a codebook.

• Data entry options include direct collection of data through a computer, use of scannable data entry forms, and use of data entry software. All data should be cleaned during the data entry process.

• Bar charts, histograms, and frequency polygons are useful for describing the shape of distributions. Care must be taken with graphic displays to avoid distorting a distribution's apparent shape.

• Frequency distributions display variation in a form that can be easily inspected and described. Values should be grouped in frequency distributions in a way that does not alter the shape of the distribution. Following several guidelines can reduce the risk of problems.

• Summary statistics are often used to describe the central tendency and variability of distributions. The appropriateness of the mode, mean, and median vary with a variable's level of measurement, the distribution's shape, and the purpose of the summary.

• The variance and standard deviation summarize variability around the mean. The interquartile range is usually preferable to the range to indicate the interval spanned by cases, due to the effect of outliers on the range. The degree of skewness of a distribution is usually described in words rather than with a summary statistic.

• Some of the data in many reports can be displayed more efficiently by using combined and compressed statistical displays.

• Honesty and openness are the key ethical principles that should guide data summaries.

• Crosstabulations should normally use percentages within the categories of the independent variable. A crosstabulation can be used to determine the existence, strength, direction, and pattern of an association.

• Elaboration analysis can be used in crosstabular analysis to test for spurious and mediating relationships and to identify the conditions under which relationships occur.

• Inferential statistics are used with sample-based data to estimate the confidence that can be placed in a statistical estimate of a population parameter.

DISCUSSION QUESTIONS

1. The first task in data analysis is preparing the data. What are the six primary steps that are involved in this process? What special considerations should one make when reviewing the recorded responses to the instrument or questionnaire used?

2. The first step in data analysis is to assess the distribution of the responses. What should the researcher examine with regard to the distribution? Why is this information important? What are the advantages of grouping data?

3. Summary statistics can tell us a lot about a variable's distribution. Yet, in many cases, certain measures might be preferred over others. Imagine you were investigating the health of the social work labor market in various regions of the United States. What operational definitions would you construct for this purpose? (Refer to the Chapter on Conceptualization and Measurement for information on operational definitions.) Which measures of central tendency would you use to describe them? Identify instances in which the mode, the median, or the mean might provide the most accurate depiction of your variable. Think about such issues as the clustering of cases, levels of measurement, and the purpose of the statistical summary. What measures of variation might you present to provide additional information?

4. Elaboration analysis helps to clarify a statistically significant relationship. Can you think of intervening or extraneous variables that might explain the relationship between gender and income levels? How does the identification of a third variable contribute to our understanding of causality and context?

PRACTICE EXERCISES

1. Using the exiting data set found at: http://oas.samsha.gov/nhsda/2k1State/PDF/2k1SAEv2.pdf, locate the state in which you live (listed alphabetically beginning on p. 4). How did the researchers decide to group the data? Why do you believe they chose to do so in this manner? Would you have made the same choice? Why or why not?

2. Using the same table as referenced in Exercise 1, examine the distribution of substance use by age. Graph the results for the past month of cigarette use by age. What does the frequency distribution look like? What would you say with regard to skewness? Does the above referenced table give you enough information to make comparisons between variables? Why or why not?

3. Examine a quantitative study from a social work journal. Does the author provide you with summary statistics? Does the researcher provide you with information about the association among different variables? What statistics does the researcher use? Do the statistics they use support the researchers' hypotheses?

WEB EXERCISES

1. Go to the Henry J. Kaiser Family Foundation's Web site at www.kaisernetwork.org/health_poll/hpoll_index.cfm. After reviewing information about the Kaiser Network, select the link to Search by Topic. Choose a topic covered by the national poll, and compare the results for two different years. Based on poll data, create a brief report that includes the following for each year you chose: the topic and the years examined, the question asked in the polls, and bar charts showing years when polls were taken and total percentages in each response category including the percentage who *had no opinion on the issue, didn't know, or refused to answer.* Write a brief summary comparing and contrasting your two bar charts.

2. Do a Web search for information on a social work subject that interests you. How much of the information you find relies on statistics as a tool for understanding the subject? How do statistics allow

researchers to test their ideas about the subject and generate new ideas? Write your findings in a brief report, referring to the Web sites that you used.

> To assist you in completing the Web exercises, please access the study site at http://www.sagepub.com/prsw where you will find the Web Exercises reproduced and suggested links for online resources.

DEVELOPING A RESEARCH PROPOSAL

1. Develop a plan to prepare your data for analysis. How will you assure the quality of the data?

2. Describe how you would analyze and present your data. What descriptive or inferential procedures would you use?

Chapter 12

QUALITATIVE DATA ANALYSIS AND CONTENT ANALYSIS

Features of Qualitative Data Analysis

Qualitative Data Analysis as an Art
Research Questions for Qualitative
    Data Analysis
The Case Study

Techniques of Qualitative Data Analysis

Documentation
Conceptualization, Coding, and
    Categorizing
Examining Relationships and Displaying
    Data
Authenticating Conclusions
Reflexivity

Alternatives in Qualitative Data Analysis

Traditional Ethnography
Qualitative Comparative Analysis
Narrative Analysis
Grounded Theory

**Computer-Assisted Qualitative
    Data Analysis**

Content Analysis

Ethics in Qualitative Data Analysis

Conclusion

*I was at lunch standing in line and he [another male student] came up to my face
and started saying stuff and then he pushed me. I said . . . I'm cool with you, I'm
your friend and then he push me again and calling me names. I told him to stop
pushing me and then he push me hard and said something about my mom. And
then he hit me, and I hit him back. After he fell I started kicking him.*

—Morrill, Yalda, Adelman,
Musheno, & Bejarano, 2000, p. 521

Unfortunately, this statement was not made by a soap opera actor, but by a real student
writing an in-class essay about conflicts in which he had participated. But then you already
knew that such conflicts are common in many high schools, so perhaps it will be reassuring
to know that this statement was elicited by a team of social scientists who were studying
conflicts in high schools to better understand their origins and to inform prevention policies.

Does it surprise you that the text excerpt above is data used in a qualitative research project? This shows the first difference between qualitative and quantitative data analysis—the data to be analyzed is text, rather than numbers, at least when the analysis first begins. Does it trouble you to learn that there are no variables and hypotheses in this qualitative analysis by Morrill et al. (2000)? This, too, is another difference between the typical qualitative and quantitative approaches to analysis, although there are some exceptions.

We will present in this chapter the features that most qualitative data analyses share, and we will illustrate these features with research on youth conflict and on being homeless. But there is no one way to carry out an analysis of textual data. To quote Michael Quinn Patton (2002),

Qualitative analysis transforms data into findings. No formula exists for that transformation. Guidance, yes. But no recipe. Direction can and will be offered, but the final destination remains unique for each inquirer, known only when—and if—arrived at. (p. 432)

So we will discuss some of the different types of qualitative data analysis before focusing on content analysis, an approach to analyzing text that relies on quantitative techniques. You will also learn about computer programs for qualitative data analysis, and you will see that these programs are blurring the distinctions between quantitative and qualitative approaches to textual analysis.

FEATURES OF QUALITATIVE DATA ANALYSIS

The distinctive features of qualitative data collection methods, which you studied in Chapter 9, are also reflected in the methods used to analyze that data. The focus on text—on qualitative data rather than on numbers—is the most important feature of qualitative analysis, but that does not in itself define qualitative data analysis. You already have seen that quantitative data analysis can involve making distinctions about textual data when variables are considered qualitative and measured at the nominal level. You also know that textual data can be transposed to quantitative data through a process of categorization and counting. You will learn more about this process in this chapter's section on content analysis. So there is more to the distinction between quantitative and qualitative data analysis than the focus on text.

One of the other important differences between qualitative and quantitative data analysis is in the priority given to the views of the researcher or the subjects of the research. Qualitative data analysts seek to describe their textual data in ways that capture the setting or people who produced this text on their own terms, rather than in terms of predefined measures and hypotheses. What this means is that qualitative data analysis tends to be inductive—the analyst identifies important categories in the data, as well as patterns and relationships, through a process of discovery. There are often no predefined measures or hypotheses. Anthropologists term this an **emic focus,** which means representing the setting in terms of the participants, rather than an **etic focus,** in which the setting and its participants are represented in terms that the researcher brings to the study.

Emic focus Representing a setting with the participants' terms.

Etic focus Representing a setting with the researchers' terms.

Qualitative data analysis is an iterative and reflexive process that begins as data are being collected rather than after data collection has ceased (Stake, 1995). Next to the field notes or interview transcripts, the qualitative analyst jots down ideas about the meaning of the text and how it might relate to other issues. This process of reading through the data and interpreting it continue throughout the project, and the analyst adjusts the data collection process itself when it begins to appear that additional concepts need to be investigated or new relationships explored. This process is termed **progressive focusing** (Parlett & Hamilton, 1976).

Progressive focusing The process by which a qualitative analyst interacts with the data and gradually refines his or her focus.

We emphasize placing an interpreter in the field to observe the workings of the case, one who records objectively what is happening but simultaneously examines its meaning and redirects observation to refine or substantiate those meanings. Initial research questions may be modified or even replaced in mid-study by the case researcher. The aim is to thoroughly understand [the case]. If early questions are not working, if new issues become apparent, the design is changed. (Stake, 1995, pp. 8–9).

Miller and Crabtree (1999, pp. 142–143) provide some guidelines to keep in mind when you start the process of analyzing qualitative data:

- Know yourself, your biases and preconceptions.
- Know your question.
- Seek creative abundance. Consult others and keep looking for alternative interpretations.
- Be flexible.
- Exhaust the data. Try to account for all the data in the texts, then publicly acknowledge the unexplained and remember the next principle.
- Celebrate anomalies. They are the windows to insight.
- Get critical feedback. The solo analyst is a great danger to self and others.
- Be explicit. Share the details with yourself, your team members, and your audiences.

You'll also want to keep in mind features of qualitative data analysis that are shared with those of quantitative data analysis. Both quantitative and qualitative data analysis can involve making distinctions about textual data. You also know that textual data can be transposed to quantitative data through a process of categorization and counting.

Qualitative Data Analysis as an Art

If you find yourself longing for the certainty of predefined measures and deductively derived hypotheses, you are beginning to understand the difference between setting out to analyze data quantitatively and planning to do so with a qualitative approach in mind. Perhaps, you are also understanding better the difference between the positivist and interpretivist research philosophies that were summarized in Chapter 2. When it comes right down to it, the process of qualitative data analysis is even described by some as involving as much "art" as science—as a "dance," in the words of William Miller and Benjamin Crabtree (1999).

Exhibit 12.1   The Dance of Qualitative Analysis

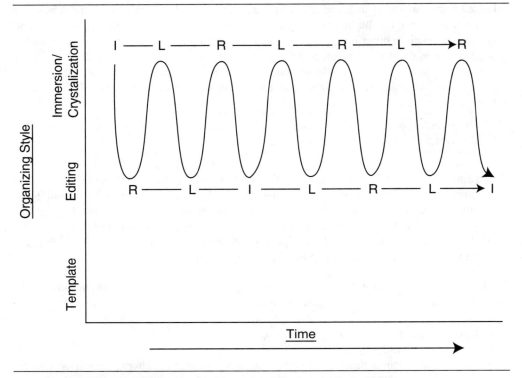

Source: Miller & Crabtree, 1999, p. 139, Figure 7.1. Based on Addison, 1999.

Interpretation is a complex and dynamic craft, with as much creative artistry as technical exactitude, and it requires an abundance of patient plodding, fortitude, and discipline. There are many changing rhythms; multiple steps; moments of jubilation, revelation, and exasperation. . . . The dance of interpretation is a dance for two, but those two are often multiple and frequently changing, and there is always an audience, even if it is not always visible. Two dancers are the interpreters and the texts. (pp. 138–139)

The "dance" of qualitative data analysis is represented in Exhibit 12.1, which captures the alternation between immersion in the text to identify meanings and editing the text to create categories and codes. The process involves three different modes of reading the text:

1. When the researcher reads the text literally (L, in Exhibit 12.1), the focus is on its literal content and form, so the text "leads" the dance.

2. When the researcher reads the text reflexively (R), the researcher focuses on how his/her own orientation shapes her interpretations and focus. Now, the researcher leads the dance.

3. When the researcher reads the text interpretively (I), the researcher tries to construct his/her own interpretation of what the text means.

So there is no one way to read a text during the process of analysis; instead, you should use a mixture of approaches, just as you do during the process of collecting qualitative data.

Qualitative data analyses also tend to be guided by more exploratory types of research questions than are quantitative analyses, and they often focus attention on the interrelated aspects of the setting or group under investigation—the case—rather than breaking the whole up into separate parts. Each of these components—an emic focus, progressive focusing, a reflexive and iterative analysis, exploratory research questions, a focus on the whole case— is represented in a traditional ethnography, in which the qualitative analyst represents the cultural life of the group.

Research Questions for Qualitative Data Analysis

You already know that research designs should be selected and refined to reflect the research questions that they are intended to answer. This principle applies even more to plans for qualitative data analysis. A typical research question for a qualitative project appears in a proposal that Schutt, working with Goldfinger and his colleagues (1990), submitted to the National Institute of Mental Health to compare the value of independent and group homes for formerly homeless mentally ill people. Although the literature on mental health services contains a substantial amount of information on typical group homes, their plan was "to develop client-managed Evolving Consumer Households (ECH) which offer significant advantages over both Independent Living and existing models of group living" (p. 43). They therefore posed several research questions about the process by which this evolution might occur (Goldfinger et al., 1990):

> What is the process by which group homes can evolve into independent consumer operated households? Can a model which fosters increasing consumer independence and management be replicated in multiple residences? What is the natural history of the unfolding of the transition of control and decision making from paid staff to resident consumers? (p. 43)

The open-ended nature of these questions suggested an exploratory analysis that would describe a wide range of activities and events in the group homes.

Daniel M. Cress and David A. Snow (2000) found more specific deficits in their review of prior research on social movements, as they formulated analysis plans for their study of the outcomes achieved by homeless mobilization organizations.

> Our understanding of the consequences of social movements is conspicuously underdeveloped. . . . hampered by conceptual and causal confusion . . . what counts as an outcome clearly is open to debate. . . . On a causal level, the precise influence of social movement activity in relation to specifiable outcomes is difficult to ascertain. . . . There is debate about which factors associated with social movements are most important. . . . The potential influence of cultural and ideational factors in the determination of movement outcomes has been glaringly absent in most theoretical discussions and research explorations of the problems. (p. 1064)

This evaluation of the deficits of prior research led to the specific research issue on which Cress and Snow (2000) focused in their analysis:

The ways in which organizational, tactical, political mediation, and framing factors interact and combine to account for variation in the outcomes achieved by the 15 homeless SMOs [social movement organizations] we studied. (p. 1072)

Cress and Snow turned to qualitative techniques to answer this question for five reasons: (1) the relative inaccessibility of the homeless SMOs, (2) the lack of much prior research on SMOs, (3) the need to explore different possible outcome measures, (4) the intensive data needed to assess the range of potentially important influences, and (5) the multiple ways in which these influences might interact to affect outcomes.

Calvin Morrill and his colleagues (2000) turned to qualitative methods for their study of youth violence when they concluded that traditional quantitatively oriented gang and delinquency researchers "narrowly construct youth experience with peer conflict" (p. 524). What is needed, they proposed, is a "youth-centered study of conflict" that "puts youths' voices and orientations toward conflict at the center of concern" (p. 528). With this goal in mind, they sought a methodology that would do the following:

- Treat "young people's experiences and pronouncements contextually."
- Recognize "that youths actively construct meaningful cultural representations."
- "Facilitate self-representation by youth."
- Consider schools "strategic sites where youths struggle to make sense of the worlds they create and re-create with peers and adults." (p. 528)

Morrill et al. (2000, p. 531) concluded from this review of prior research on youth violence that a new approach was necessary. They decided to conduct a "narrative survey," in which students in ninth grade English classes at one high school were asked to write a story about a time they experienced a conflict with another student. Five specific exploratory research questions guided their analysis:

1. How do youths represent everyday conflict in their stories?

2. What decision-making and reasoning processes do youths produce in their stories about conflict?

3. How do young people represent various means for handling peer conflict?

4. How is violence portrayed in their narratives?

5. How are adults situated in youth conflict narratives?

We will see in a later section how segments of the youths' conflict narratives provided some answers to these questions.

Each of these examples illustrates how the research questions that serve as starting points for qualitative data analyses do not simply emerge from the setting studied, but are shaped by the investigator. As Harry Wolcott (1995) explains, the research question

is not embedded within the lives of those whom we study, demurely waiting to be discovered. Quite the opposite: *We instigate the problems we investigate.* There is no point in simply sitting by, passively waiting to see what a setting is going to "tell" us or hoping a problem will "emerge." (p. 156)

The focus on the importance of the research question as a tool for guiding qualitative data analyses should not obscure the iterative nature of the analytic process. The research question can change, narrow, or expand, or multiply throughout the processes of data collection and analysis.

The Case Study

To many qualitative data analysts, the focus on variables and hypotheses in quantitative research is needless "slicing and dicing" of a social world that really functions as an integrated whole. Instead, their focus is on understanding "the case." The case may be an organization, community, social group, family, or even an individual, and as far as the qualitative analyst is concerned, it must be understood in its entirety. **Case study** is not so much a single method as a way of thinking about what qualitative data analysis can, or perhaps should, focus on. Educational researcher Robert Stake (1995) presents the logic of the case study approach:

> Case study is the study of the particularity and complexity of a single case, coming to understand its activity within important circumstances.... The qualitative researcher emphasizes episodes of nuance, the sequentiality of happenings in context, the wholeness of the individual. (pp. xi, xii)

Case study A setting or group that the analyst treats as an integrated social unit that must be studied holistically and in its particularity.

Thick description A rich description that conveys a sense of what an experience is like from the standpoint of the natural actors in the setting.

Central to much qualitative case study research is the goal of creating a **thick description** of the setting studied, one that provides a sense of what it is like to experience that setting from the standpoint of the natural actors in that setting (Geertz, 1973). Robert Stake's (1995) description of "a case within a case," a student in a school he studied, illustrates how a thick description gives a feel of the place and people within it:

> At 8:30 A.M. on Thursday morning, Adam shows up at the cafeteria door. Breakfast is being served but Adam doesn't go in. The woman giving out meal chits has her hands on him, seems to be sparring with him, verbally. And then he disappears. Adam is one of five siblings, all arrive at school in the morning with less than usual parent attention. Short, with a beautifully sculpted head . . . Adam is a person of notice.
>
> At 8:55 he climbs the stairs to the third floor with other upper graders, turning to block the girls behind them and thus a string of others. Adam manages to keep the girls off-balance until Ms. Crain . . . spots him and gets traffic moving again. Mr. Garson . . . notices Adam, has a few quiet words with him before a paternal shove toward the room. (p. 150)

You will learn in the next sections how qualitative data analysts can become structured in their approach, classifying cases or instances in conceptual categories and then identifying patterns and relationships. You will also see how these techniques differ when applied to textual data and how alternative approaches to qualitative data analysis can seem sharply divergent from or somewhat similar to the logic of quantitative data analysis.

TECHNIQUES OF QUALITATIVE DATA ANALYSIS

The phases of qualitative data analysis include:

1. Documentation of the data and the process of data collection

2. Organization/categorization of the data into concepts

3. Connection of the data to show how one concept may influence another

4. Corroboration/legitimization, by evaluating alternative explanations and disconfirming evidence and searching for negative cases

5. Representing the account (reporting the findings)

The analysis of qualitative research notes begins in the field, at the time of observation and/or interviewing, as the researcher identifies problems and concepts that appear likely to help in understanding the situation. Simply reading the notes or transcripts is an important step in the analytic process. Researchers should make frequent notes in the margins to identify important statements and to propose ways of coding the data: *husband/wife conflict,* perhaps, or *tension reduction strategy.*

An interim stage may consist of listing the concepts reflected in the notes and diagramming the relationships among concepts (Maxwell, 1996, pp. 78–81). In large projects, weekly team meetings are an important part of this process. Susan Miller described this process in her study of neighborhood police officers. Her research team met both to go over their field notes and to resolve points of confusion, as well as to dialogue with other skilled researchers who helped to identify emerging concepts (Bachman & Schutt, 2003, p. 244):

> The fieldwork team met weekly to talk about situations that were unclear and to troubleshoot any problems. We also made use of peer-debriefing techniques. Here, multiple colleagues, who were familiar with qualitative data analysis but not involved in our research, participated in preliminary analysis of our findings. (Miller, 1999, p. 233)

This process continues throughout the project and should assist in refining concepts during the report-writing phase, long after data collection has ceased. Let's examine each of the stages of qualitative research in more detail.

Documentation

The data for a qualitative study most often are notes jotted down in the field or during an interview—from which the original comments, observations, and feelings are reconstructed—or text transcribed from audiotapes. "The basic data are these observations and conversations, the actual words of people reproduced to the best of my ability from the field notes" (Diamond, 1992, p. 7). What to do with all this material? Many field research projects have slowed to a halt because a novice researcher becomes overwhelmed by the quantity of information that has been collected. A one-hour interview can generate 20 to 25 pages of single-spaced text (Kvale, 1996, p. 169). Analysis is less daunting, however, if the process is broken into smaller steps.

The first formal analytical step is documentation. The various contacts, the interviews, written documents, and whatever it was that preserves a record of what happened all need to be saved and listed. Documentation is critical to qualitative research for several reasons: It is essential for keeping track of what will be a rapidly growing volume of notes, tapes, and documents; it provides a way of developing an outline for the analytic process; and it encourages ongoing conceptualizing and strategizing about the text.

Miles and Huberman (1994, p. 53) provide a good example of a contact summary form that was used to keep track of observational sessions in a qualitative study of a new school curriculum (Exhibit 12.2).

Conceptualization, Coding, and Categorizing

Identifying and refining important concepts is a key part of the iterative process of qualitative research. Sometimes conceptualization begins with a simple observation that is interpreted directly, "pulled apart" and then put back together more meaningfully. Robert Stake (1995) provides an example:

> When Adam ran a pushbroom into the feet of the children nearby, I jumped to conclusions about his interactions with other children: aggressive, teasing, arresting. Of course, just a few minutes earlier I had seen him block the children climbing the steps in a similar moment of smiling bombast. So I was aggregating, and testing my unrealized hypotheses about what kind of kid he was, not postponing my interpreting. . . . My disposition was to keep my eyes on him. (p. 74)

The focus in this conceptualization "on the fly" is to provide a detailed description of what was observed and a sense of why that was important.

More often, analytic insights are tested against new observations, the initial statement of problems and concepts is refined, the researcher then collects more data and interacts with it again, and the process continues. Elijah Anderson (2003) recounts how his conceptualization of social stratification at Jelly's Bar developed over a long period of time:

> I could see the social pyramid, how certain guys would group themselves and say in effect, "I'm here and you're there." I made sense of these crowds [initially] as the "respectables," the "non-respectables," and the "near-respectables." . . . Inside, such non-respectables might sit on the crates, but if a respectable came along and wanted to sit there, the lower status person would have to move. (pp. 18, 19)

But this initial conceptualization changed with experience as Anderson realized that the participants themselves used other terms to differentiate social status: *winehead, hoodlum,* and *regular* (Anderson, 2003, p. 28). What did they mean by these terms? "The regulars' basically valued 'decency.' They associated decency with conventionality but also with "working for a living,' or having a 'visible means of support" (Anderson, 2003, p. 29). In this way, Anderson progressively refined his concept as he gained experience in the setting.

Howard S. Becker (1958) provides another excellent illustration of this iterative process of conceptualization in his study of medical students:

Exhibit 12.2   Example of a Contact Summary Form

Contact type: Site: Tindale_____
Visit   X_____   Contact date: 11/28-29/79____
Phone   _____   Today's date: 12/28/79_____
                 (with whom)   Written by: BLT_____

1. <u>What were the main issues or themes that struck you in this contact?</u>

   Interplay between highly prescriptive, "teacher-proof" curriculum that is top-down imposed and the actual writing of the curriculum by the teachers themselves.

   Split between the "watchdogs" (administrators) and the "house masters" (dept. chairs & teachers) vis a vis job foci.

   District curric, coord'r as decision maker re school's acceptance of research relationship.

2. <u>Summarize the information you got (or failed to get) on each of the target questions you had for this contact.</u>

<u>Question</u>	<u>Information</u>
History of dev. of innov'n	Conceptualized by Curric., Coord'r, English Chairman & Assoc. Chairman; written by teachers in summer; revised by teachers following summer with field testing data
School's org'l structure	Principal & admin'rs responsible for discipline; dept chairs are educ'l leaders
Demographics	Racial conflicts in late 60's; 60% black stud. pop.; heavy emphasis on discipline & on keeping out non-district students slipping in from Chicago
Teachers' response to innov'n	Rigid, structured, etc. at first; now, they say they like it/NEEDS EXPLORATION
Research access	Very good; only restriction: teachers not required to cooperate

3. <u>Anything else that struck you as salient, interesting, illuminating or important in this contact?</u>
   Thoroughness of the innov'n's development and training.

   Its embeddedness in the district's curriculum, as planned and executed by the district curriculum coordinator.

   The initial resistance to its high prescriptiveness (as reported by users) as contrasted with their current acceptance and approval of it (again, as reported by users).

4. <u>What new (or remaining) target questions do you have in considering the next contact with this site?</u>

   How do users really perceive the innov'n? If they do indeed embrace it, what accounts for the change from early resistance?

   Nature and amount of networking among users of innov'n.

   Information on "stubborn" math teachers whose ideas weren't heard initially – who are they? Situation particulars? Resolution?

   Follow-up on English teacher Reilly's "fall from the chairmanship."

   Follow a team through a day of rotation, planning, etc.

   CONCERN: The consequences of eating school cafeteria food two days per week for the next four or five months . . .

                                                                              Stop

---

Source: Miles & Huberman, 1994, p. 53, Figure 4.1.

When we first heard medical students apply the term "crock" to patients, we made an effort to learn precisely what they meant by it. We found, through interviewing students about cases both they and the observer had seen, that the term referred in a derogatory way to patients with many subjective symptoms but no discernable physical pathology. Subsequent observations indicated that this usage was a regular feature of student behavior and thus that we should attempt to incorporate this fact into our model of student-patient behavior. The derogatory character of the term suggested in particular that we investigate the reasons students disliked these patients. We found that this dislike was related to what we discovered to be the students' perspective on medical school: the view that they were in school to get experience in recognizing and treating those common diseases most likely to be encountered in general practice. "Crocks," presumably having no disease, could furnish no such experience. We were thus led to specify connections between the student-patient relationship and the student's view of the purpose of his professional education. Questions concerning the genesis of this perspective led to discoveries about the organization of the student body and communication among students, phenomena which we had been assigning to another [segment of the larger theoretical model being developed]. Since "crocks" were also disliked because they gave the student no opportunity to assume medical responsibility, we were able to connect this aspect of the student-patient relationship with still another tentative model of the value system and hierarchical organization of the school, in which medical responsibility plays an important role. (p. 658) (From Becker, H. S., "Problems of inference and proof in participant observation," in *American Sociological Review, 23*, pp. 652–660. Reprinted with permission).

This excerpt shows how the researcher first was alerted to a concept by observations in the field, then refined his understanding of this concept by investigating its meaning. By observing the concept's frequency of use, he came to realize its importance. Then he incorporated the concept into an explanatory model of student–patient relationships.

A well-designed chart, or **matrix**, can facilitate the coding and categorization process. The example in Exhibit 12.3 is an example of a checklist matrix designed by Miles and Huberman (1994, pp. 93–95) to represent the extent to which teachers and teachers' aides (users) and administrators at a school gave evidence of various supporting conditions that indicated preparedness for a new reading program. The matrix condenses data into simple categories, reflects further analysis of the data to identify "degree" of support, and provides a multidimensional summary that will facilitate subsequent more intensive analysis. Direct quotes still impart some of the flavor of the original text.

Examining Relationships and Displaying Data

Examining relationships is the centerpiece of the analytic process because it allows the researcher to move from simple description of the people and settings to explanations of why things happened as they did with those people in that setting. The process of examining relationships can be captured in a matrix that shows how different concepts are connected, or perhaps what causes are linked with what effects.

Exhibit 12.4 displays a cross-classification matrix used to capture the relationship between the extent to which stakeholders in a new program had something important at stake in the program and the researcher's estimate of their favorability toward the program. Each cell of the cross-classification matrix was to be filled in with a summary of an illustrative case study.

Exhibit 12.3 Example of Checklist Matrix

Presence of Supporting Conditions

Condition	For Users	For Administrators
Commitment	*Strong*—"wanted to make it work."	*Weak* at building level. Prime movers in central office committed; others not.
Understanding	*"Basic"* ("felt I could do it, but I just wasn't sure how.") for teacher. *Absent* for aide ("didn't understand how we were going to get all this.")	*Absent* at building level and among staff. *Basic* for 2 prime movers ("got all the help we needed from developer.") *Absent* for other central office staff.
Materials	*Inadequate*: ordered late, puzzling ("different from anything I ever used"), discarded.	N.A.
Front-end training	*"Sketchy"* for teacher ("it all happened so quickly"); no demo class. *None* for aide: ("totally unprepared. I had to learn along with the children.")	Prime movers in central office had training at developer site; none for others.
Skills	*Weak-adequate* for teacher. *"None"* for aide.	One prime mover (Robeson) skilled in substance; others unskilled.
Ongoing inservice	*None*, except for monthly committee meeting; no substitute funds.	*None*
Planning, coordination time	*None*: both users on other tasks during day; lab tightly scheduled, no free time.	*None*
Provisions for debugging	*None* systematized; spontaneous work done by users during summer.	*None*
School admin. support	*Adequate*	N.A.
Central admin. support	*Very Strong* on part of prime movers.	Building admin. only acting on basis of central office commitment.
Relevant prior experience	*Strong* and useful in both cases: had done individualized instruction, worked with low achievers. But aide no diagnostic experience.	*Present* and useful in central office, esp. Robeson (specialist).

Source: Miles & Huberman, 1994, p. 95, Table 5.2. Used with permission.

In other matrix analyses, quotes might be included in the cells to represent the opinions of these different stakeholders, or the number of cases of each type might appear in the cells. The possibilities are almost endless. Keeping this approach in mind will generate many fruitful ideas for structuring a qualitative data analysis.

Exhibit 12.4 Coding Form for Relationships: Stakeholders' Stakes

Estimate of Various Stakeholders' Inclination Toward the Program

How high are the stakes for various primary stakeholders?	Favorable	Neutral or Unknown	Antagonistic
High			
Moderate			
Low			

Note: Construct illustrative case studies for each cell based on fieldwork.
Source: Patton, 2002:472.

The simple relationships that are identified with a cross-classification matrix like that shown in Exhibit 12.4 can be examined and then extended to create a more complex causal model. Such a model represents the multiple relationships among the constructs identified in a qualitative analysis as important for explaining some outcome. A great deal of analysis must precede the construction of such a model, with careful attention to identification of important variables and the evidence that suggests connections between them. Exhibit 12.5 provides an example of these connects from a study of the implementation of a school program.

Authenticating Conclusions

No set standards exist for evaluating the validity or "authenticity" of conclusions in a qualitative study, but the need to consider carefully the evidence and methods on which conclusions are based is just as great as with other types of research. Individual items of information can be assessed in terms of at least three criteria (Becker, 1958):

- *How credible was the informant?* Were statements made by someone with whom the researcher had a relationship of trust or by someone the researcher had just met? Did the informant have reason to lie? If the statements do not seem to be trustworthy as indicators of actual events, can they be used at least to help understand the informant's perspective?
- *Were statements made in response to the researcher's questions, or were they spontaneous?* Spontaneous statements are more likely to indicate what would have been said had the researcher not been present.
- *How does the presence or absence of the researcher or the researcher's informant influence the actions and statements of other group members?* Reactivity to being observed can never be ruled out as a possible explanation for some directly observed social phenomenon. However, if the researcher carefully compares what the informant says goes on when the researcher is not present, what the researcher observes directly, and what other group members say about their normal practices, the extent of reactivity can be assessed to some extent.

A qualitative researcher's conclusions should also be assessed by his or her ability to provide a credible explanation for some aspect of social life. That explanation should capture

Exhibit 12.5 Example of a Causal Network Model

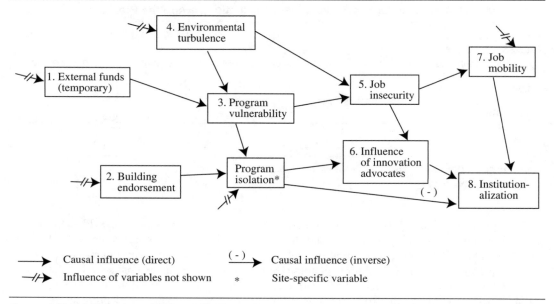

Causal influence (direct)   (-) Causal influence (inverse)

Influence of variables not shown   *   Site-specific variable

Source: Miles & Huberman, 1994, p. 159, Figure 6.5.

group members' **tacit knowledge** of the social processes that were observed, not just their verbal statements about these processes. Tacit knowledge—"the largely unarticulated, contextual understanding that is often manifested in nods, silences, humor, and naughty nuances" (Altheide & Johnson, 1994, pp. 492–493)—is reflected in participants' actions as well as their words and in what they fail to state but nonetheless feel deeply and even take for granted. These features are evident in Whyte's (1955) analysis of Cornerville social patterns:

> The corner-gang structure arises out of the habitual association of the members over a long period of time. The nuclei of most gangs can be traced back to early boyhood. . . . Home plays a very small role in the group activities of the corner boy. . . .
> . . . The life of the corner boy proceeds along regular and narrowly circumscribed channels. . . . Out of [social interaction within the group] arises a system of mutual obligations which is fundamental to group cohesion. . . . The code of the corner boy requires him to help his friends when he can and to refrain from doing anything to harm them. When life in the group runs smoothly, the obligations binding members to one another are not explicitly recognized. (pp. 255–257)

Comparing conclusions from a qualitative research project to those obtained by other researchers conducting similar projects can also increase confidence in their authenticity. Miller's (1999) study of neighborhood police officers (NPOs) found striking parallels in the ways they defined their masculinity to processes reported in research about males in nursing and other traditionally female jobs (Bachman & Schutt, 2001, p. 315):

In part, male NPOs construct an exaggerated masculinity so that they are not seen as feminine as they carry out the social-work functions of policing. Related to this is the almost defiant expression of heterosexuality, so that the men's sexual orientation can never truly be doubted even if their gender roles are contested. Male patrol officers' language—such as their use of terms like "pansy police" to connote neighborhood police officers—served to affirm their own heterosexuality. . . . In addition, the male officers, but not the women, deliberately wove their heterosexual status into conversations, explicitly mentioning their female domestic partner or spouse and their children. This finding is consistent with research conducted in the occupational field. The studies reveal that men in female-dominated occupations, such as teachers, librarians, and pediatricians, over-reference their heterosexual status to ensure that others will not think they are gay. (Miller, 1999, p. 222)

Reflexivity

Confidence in the conclusions from a field research study is also strengthened by an honest and informative account about how the researcher interacted with subjects in the field, what problems he or she encountered, and how these problems were or were not resolved. Such a "natural history" of the development of the evidence enables others to evaluate the findings. Such an account is important first and foremost because of the evolving and variable nature of field research: To an important extent, the researcher "makes up" the method in the context of a particular investigation rather than applying standard procedures that are specified before the investigation begins.

Barrie Thorne (1993) provides a good example of this final element of the analysis:

Many of my observations concern the workings of gender categories in social life. For example, I trace the evocation of gender in the organization of everyday interactions, and the shift from boys and girls as loose aggregations to "the boys" and "the girls" as self-aware, gender-based groups. In writing about these processes, I discovered that different angles of vision lurk within seemingly simple choices of language. How, for example, should one describe a group of children? A phrase like "six girls and three boys were chasing by the tires" already assumes the relevance of gender. An alternative description of the same event—"nine fourth-graders were chasing by the tires"—emphasizes age and downplays gender. Although I found no tidy solutions, I have tried to be thoughtful about such choices. . . . After several months of observing at Oceanside, I realized that my fieldnotes were peppered with the words "child" and "children," but that the children themselves rarely used the term. "What do they call themselves?" I badgered in an entry in my fieldnotes. The answer it turned out, is that children use the same practices as adults. They refer to one another by using given names ("Sally," "Jack") or language specific to a given context ("that guy on first base"). They rarely have occasion to use age-generic terms. But when pressed to locate themselves in an age-based way, my informants used "kids" rather than "children." (pp. 8–9)

Qualitative data analysts, more often than quantitative researchers, display real sensitivity to how a social situation or process is interpreted from a particular background and set of values and not simply from the situation itself (Altheide & Johnson, 1994). Researchers are only human, after all, and must rely on their own senses and process all information through their own minds. By reporting how and why they think they did what they did, they can help others determine whether, or how, the researchers' perspectives influenced their conclusions. "There should be clear 'tracks' indicating the attempt [to show the hand of the ethnographer] has been made" (Altheide & Johnson, 1994, p. 493).

ALTERNATIVES IN QUALITATIVE DATA ANALYSIS

The qualitative data analyst can choose from many interesting alternative approaches. Of course, the research question under investigation should shape the selection of an analytic approach, but the researcher's preferences and experiences inevitably also will have an important influence on the method chosen. The four alternative approaches presented here (traditional ethnography, qualitative comparative analysis, narrative analysis, and grounded theory) give you a good sense of the different possibilities, but be forewarned that these four were selected from a long and growing list (Patton, 2002).

Traditional Ethnography

Ethnography is the study of a culture or cultures that some group of people shares (Van Maanen, 1995, p. 4). As a method, it usually is meant to refer to the process of participant observation by a single investigator who immerses himself or herself in the group for a long period of time (often one or more years). But there are no particular methodological techniques associated with ethnography, other than just "being there." The analytic process relies on the thoroughness and insight of the researcher to "tell us like it is" in the setting, as he or she experienced it.

Code of the Street, Elijah Anderson's (1999) award-winning study of Philadelphia's inner city, captures the flavor of this approach:

> My primary aim in this work is to render ethnographically the social and cultural dynamics of the interpersonal violence that is currently undermining the quality of life of too many urban neighborhoods. . . . How do the people of the setting perceive their situation? What assumptions do they bring to their decision making? (pp. 10–11)

The methods of investigation are described in the book's preface: participant observation, including direct observation and in-depth interviews, impressionistic materials drawn from various social settings around the city, and interviews with a wide variety of people. Like most traditional ethnographers, Anderson (1999) describes his concern with being "as objective as possible" and using his training as other ethnographers do, "to look for and to recognize underlying assumptions, their own and those of their subjects, and to try to override the former and uncover the latter" (p. 11).

From analysis of the data obtained in these ways, a rich description emerges of life in the inner city. Although we often do not "hear" the residents speak, we feel the community's pain in Anderson's (1999) description of "the aftermath of death":

> When a young life is cut down, almost everyone goes into mourning. The first thing that happens is that a crowd gathers about the site of the shooting or the incident. The police then arrive, drawing more of a crowd. Since such a death often occurs close to the victim's house,

his mother or his close relatives and friends may be on the scene of the killing. When they arrive, the women and girls often wail and moan, crying out their grief for all to hear, while the young men simply look on, in studied silence. . . . Soon the ambulance arrives. (p. 138)

Elijah Anderson (1999) uses these descriptions as a foundation on which he develops the key concepts in his analysis such as "code of the street":

> The "code of the street" is not the goal or product of any individual's actions but is the fabric of everyday life, a vivid and pressing milieu within which all local residents must shape their personal routines, income strategies, and orientations to schooling, as well as their mating, parenting, and neighbor relations. (p. 326)

This rich ethnographic tradition is being abandoned by some qualitative data analysts, however. Many have become skeptical of the ability of social scientists to perceive the social world in a way that is not distorted by their own subjective biases or to receive impressions from the actors in that social world that are not altered by the fact of being studied (Van Maanen, 2002). As a result, both specific techniques and alternative approaches to qualitative data analysis have proliferated.

Qualitative Comparative Analysis

Recall from earlier in the chapter how Daniel Cress and David Snow (2000) asked a series of very specific questions about social movement outcomes in their study of homeless social movement organizations (SMOs). They collected qualitative data about 15 SMOs in eight cities. A content analysis of newspaper articles indicated that these cities represented a range of outcomes, and the SMOs within them were also relatively accessible to Cress and Snow due to prior contacts. In each of these cities, Cress and Snow used a snowball sampling strategy to identify the homeless SMOs and the various supporters, antagonists, and significant organizational bystanders with whom they interacted. They then gathered information from representatives of these organizations, including churches, other activist organizations, police departments, mayors' offices, service providers, federal agencies, and, of course, the SMOs themselves.

To answer their research questions, Cress and Snow (2000) needed to operationalize each of the various conditions that they believed might affect movement outcomes, using coding procedures that were much more systematic than those often employed in qualitative research. For example, Cress and Snow defined *sympathetic allies* operationally as

> the presence of one or more city council members who were supportive of local homeless mobilization. This was demonstrated by attending homeless SMO meetings and rallies and by taking initiatives to city agencies on behalf of the SMO. (Seven of the 15 SMOs had such allies.) (p. 1078)

Cress and Snow (2000) also chose a structured method of analysis, **qualitative comparative analysis**, to assess how the various conditions influenced SMO outcomes. This procedure identifies the combination of factors that had to be present across multiple cases to produce a particular outcome (Ragin, 1987). Cress and Snow explain why this strategy was appropriate for their analysis:

Exhibit 12.6   Multiple Pathways to Outcomes and Level of Impact

Pathways	Outcomes	Impact
1. VIABLE * DISRUPT * ALLIES * DIAG * PROG	Representation, Resources, Rights, and Relief	Very strong
2. VIABLE * disrupt * CITY * DIAG * PROG	Representation and Rights	Strong
3. VIABLE * ALLIES * CITY * DIAG * PROG	Resources and Relief	Moderate
4. viable * DISRUPT * allies * diag * PROG	Relief	Weak
5. viable * allies * city * diag * PROG	Relief	Weak
6. viable * disrupt * ALLIES * CITY * diag * prog	Resources	Weak

Note: Uppercase letters indicate presence of condition, and lowercase letters indicate the absence of a condition. Conditions not in the equation are considered irrelevant. Multiplication signs (*) are read as "and."

Source: Cress & Snow, 2000, p. 1097, Table 6. Reprinted with permission from the University of Chicago Press.

[Qualitative comparative analysis] is conjunctural in its logic, examining the various ways in which specified factors interact and combine with one another to yield particular outcomes. This increases the prospect of discerning diversity and identifying different pathways that lead to an outcome of interest and thus makes this mode of analysis especially applicable to situations with complex patterns of interaction among the specified conditions. (p. 1079)

Exhibit 12.6 summarizes the results of much of Cress and Snow's (2000, p. 1097) analysis. It shows that homeless SMOs that were coded as organizationally viable, used disruptive tactics, had sympathetic political allies, and presented a coherent diagnosis and program in response to the problem they were protesting were very likely to achieve all four valued outcomes: representation, resources, protection of basic rights, and some form of tangible relief. Some other combinations of the conditions were associated with increased likelihood of achieving some valued outcomes, but most of these alternatives had positive effects less frequently.

The qualitative textual data on which the codes were based indicate how particular combinations of conditions exerted their influence. For example, one set of conditions that increased the likelihood of achieving increased protection of basic rights for homeless people included avoiding disruptive tactics in cities that were more responsive to the SMOs. Cress and Snow (2000) use a quote from a local SMO leader to explain this process:

We were going to set up a picket, but then we got calls from two people who were the co-chairs of the Board of Directors. They have like 200 restaurants. And they said, "Hey, we're not bad guys, can we sit down and talk?" We had been set on picketing . . . Then we got to thinking, wouldn't it be better . . . if they co-drafted those things [rights guidelines] with us? so that's what we asked them to do. We had a work meeting, and we hammered out the guidelines. (p. 1089)

Narrative Analysis

Narrative "displays the goals and intentions of human actors; it makes individuals, cultures, societies, and historical epochs comprehensible as wholes" (Richardson, 1995, p. 200). **Narrative analysis** focuses on "the story itself" and seeks to preserve the integrity of personal biographies or a series of events that cannot adequately be understood in terms of their discrete elements (Riessman, 2002, p. 218). The coding for a narrative analysis is typically of the narratives as a whole, rather than of the different elements within them. The coding strategy revolves around reading the stories and classifying them into general patterns.

For example, Calvin Morrill and his colleagues (2000, p. 534) read through 254 conflict narratives written by the ninth graders they studied and found four different types of stories:

1. *Action tales,* in which the author represents him- or herself and others as acting within the parameters of taken-for-granted assumptions about what is expected for particular roles among peers

2. *Expressive tales,* in which the author focuses on strong, negative emotional responses to someone who has wronged him or her

3. *Moral tales,* in which the author recounts explicit norms that shaped his or her behavior in the story and influenced the behavior of others

4. *Rational tales,* in which the author represents him- or herself as a rational decision maker navigating through the events of the story

In addition to these dominant distinctions, Morrill et al. (2000, pp. 534–535) also distinguished the stories in terms of four stylistic dimensions: plot structure (such as whether the story unfolds sequentially), dramatic tension (how the central conflict is represented), dramatic resolution (how the central conflict is resolved), and predominant outcomes (how the story ends). Coding reliability was checked through discussion of the two primary coders, who found that their classifications agreed for a large percentage of the stories.

The excerpt that begins this chapter exemplifies what Morrill et al. (2000) termed an *action tale.* Such tales

> unfold in matter-of-fact tones kindled by dramatic tensions that begin with a disruption of the quotidian order of everyday routines. A shove, a bump, a look . . . triggers a response. . . . Authors of action tales typically organize their plots as linear streams of events as they move briskly through the story's scenes. . . . this story's dramatic tension finally resolves through physical fighting, but . . . only after an attempted conciliation. (p. 536)

You can contrast that action tale with the following narrative, which Morrill et al. (2000) classify as a *moral tale,* in which the student authors "explicitly tell about their moral reasoning, often referring to how normative commitments shape their decision making":

> I . . . got into a fight because I wasn't allowed into the basketball game. I was being harassed by the captains that wouldn't pick me and also many of the players. The same type of things had happened almost every day where they called me bad words so I decided to teach the ring leader a lesson. I've never been in a fight before but I realized that sometimes you have to make a stand against the people that constantly hurt you, especially emotionally. I hit him in the face a couple of times and I got respect I finally deserved. (pp. 545–546)

Exhibit 12.7 Summary Comparison of Youth Narratives*

Representation of	Action Tales (N = 144)	Moral Tales (N = 51)	Expressive Tales (N = 35)	Rational Tales (N = 24)
Bases of everyday conflict	disruption of everyday routines & expectations	normative violation	emotional provocation	goal obstruction
Decisionmaking	intuitive	principled stand	sensual	calculative choice
Conflict handling	confrontational	ritualistic	cathartic	deliberative
Physical violence†	in 44% (N = 67)	in 27% (N = 16)	in 49% (N = 20)	in 29% (N = 7)
Adults in youth conflict control	invisible or background	sources of rules	agents of repression	institutions of social control

* Total N = 254.

†Percentages based on the number of stories in each category.

Source: Morrill et al., 2000, p. 551, Table 1. Copyright 2000. Reprinted with permission of Blackwell Publishing, Ltd.

Morrill et al. (2000, p. 553) summarize their classification of the youth narratives in a simple table that highlights the frequency of each type of narrative and the characteristics associated with each of them (Exhibit 12.7). How does such an analysis contribute to our understanding of youth violence? Morrill et al. first emphasize that their narratives "suggest that consciousness of conflict among youths—like that among adults—is not a singular entity, but comprises a rich and diverse range of perspectives" (p. 551).

Theorizing inductively, Morrill et al. (2000, pp. 553–554) then attempt to explain why action tales were much more common than the more adult-oriented normative, rational, or emotionally expressive tales. One possibility is Gilligan's (1982) theory of moral development, which suggests that younger students are likely to limit themselves to the simpler action tales that "concentrate on taken-for-granted assumptions of their peer and wider cultures, rather than on more self-consciously reflective interpretation and evaluation" (Morrill et al., 2000, p. 554). More generally, Morrill et al. argue, "We can begin to think of the building blocks of cultures as different narrative styles in which various aspects of reality are accentuated, constituted, or challenged, just as others are deemphasized or silenced" (p. 556).

In this way, Morrill et al.'s (2000) narrative analysis allowed an understanding of youth conflict to emerge from the youths' own stories while also informing our understanding of broader social theories and processes.

Grounded Theory

Theory development occurs continually in qualitative data analysis (Coffey & Atkinson, 1996, p. 23). The goal of many qualitative researchers is to create **grounded theory**—that is, to build up inductively a systematic theory that is "grounded" in, or based on, the observations.

Exhibit 12.8   The Research Circle

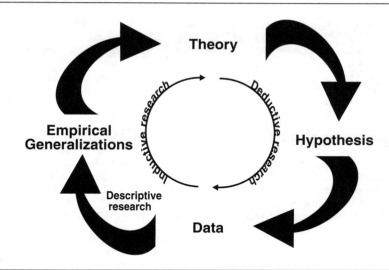

The observations are summarized into conceptual categories, which are tested directly in the research setting with more observations. Over time, as the conceptual categories are refined and linked, a theory evolves (Glaser & Strauss, 1967; Huberman & Miles, 1994, p. 436). This process corresponds to the inductive portion of the research circle, which was introduced in Chapter 2 and is shown above in Exhibit 12.8.

As observation, interviewing, and reflection continue, researchers refine their definitions of problems and concepts and select indicators. They can then check the frequency and distribution of phenomena: How many people made a particular type of comment? How often did social interaction lead to arguments? Social system models may then be developed, which specify the relationships among different phenomena. These models are modified as researchers gain experience in the setting. For the final analysis, the researchers check their models carefully against their notes and make a concerted attempt to discover negative evidence that might suggest the model is incorrect.

COMPUTER-ASSISTED QUALITATIVE DATA ANALYSIS

The analysis process can be enhanced in various ways by using a computer. Programs designed for qualitative data can speed up the analysis process, make it easier for researchers to experiment with different codes, test different hypotheses about relationships, and facilitate diagrams of emerging theories and preparation of research reports (Coffey & Atkinson, 1996; Richards & Richards, 1994). The steps involved in **computer-assisted qualitative data analysis** parallel those used traditionally to analyze such text as notes, documents, or interview transcripts: preparation, coding, analysis, and reporting. We use two of the most popular programs to illustrate these steps: HyperRESEARCH and QSR Nvivo.

Text preparation begins with typing or scanning text in a word processing program. HyperRESEARCH requires that your text be saved as a text file (as ASCII in most word

Exhibit 12.9a   HyperRESEARCH Coding Stage

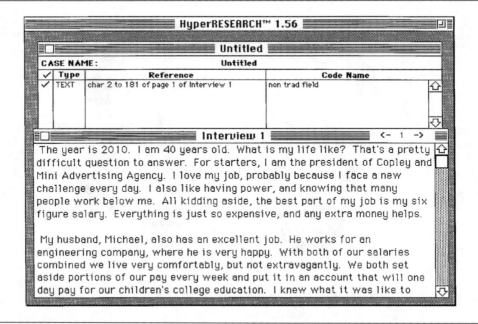

Exhibit 12.9b   NVivo Coding Stage

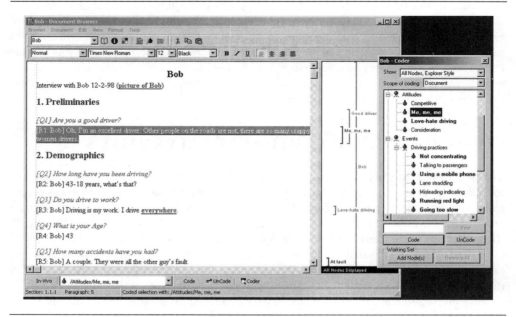

processing programs) before you transfer it into the analysis program. HyperRESEARCH expects your text data to be stored in separate files corresponding to each unique case, such as an interview with one subject. With NVivo, the text is typed directly into NVivo's rich text editor. NVivo will create or import a rich text file.

Coding the text involves categorizing particular text segments. This is the foundation of much qualitative analysis. Either program allows you to assign a code to any segment of text (in HyperRESEARCH, you click on the first and last words to select text; in NVivo, you drag through the characters to select them). You can both make up codes as you go through a document and assign codes that you have already developed to text segments. Exhibit 12.9 shows the screens that appear in the two programs at the coding stage, when a particular text segment is being labeled. You can also have the programs *autocode* text by identifying a word or phrase that should always receive the same code, or, in NVivo, by coding each section identified by the style of the rich text document—for example, each question or speaker (of course, you should carefully check the results of autocoding). Both programs also let you examine the coded text "in context"—embedded in its place in the original document.

In qualitative data analysis, coding is not a one-time-only or one-code-only procedure. Both HyperRESEARCH and NVivo allow you to be inductive and holistic in your coding: You can revise codes as you go along, assign multiple codes to text segments, and link your own comments (memos) to text segments. In NVivo you can work "live" with the coded text to alter coding or create new, more subtle categories. You can also place hyperlinks to other documents in the project or any multimedia files outside it.

Analysis focuses on reviewing cases or text segments with similar codes and examining relationships among different codes. You may decide to combine codes into larger concepts. You may specify additional codes to capture more fully the variation among cases. You can test hypotheses about relationships among codes. In HyperRESEARCH, you can specify combinations of codes that identify cases that you want to examine. NVivo allows development of an indexing system to facilitate thinking about the relationships among concepts and the overarching structure of these relationships. It will also allow you to draw more free-form models (see Exhibit 12.10).

Reports from both programs can include text to illustrate the cases, codes, and relationships that you specify. You can also generate counts of code frequencies and then import these counts into a statistical program for quantitative analysis. However, the many types of analyses and reports that can be developed with qualitative analysis software do not lessen the need for a careful evaluation of the quality of the data on which conclusions are based.

In reality, using a qualitative data analysis computer program is not always as straightforward as it appears (Bachman & Schutt, 2001, p. 314). Scott Decker and Barrik Van Winkle (1996) describe the difficulty they faced in using a computer program to identify instances of the concept of *drug sales*:

> The software we used is essentially a text retrieval package. . . . One of the dilemmas faced in the use of such software is whether to employ a coding scheme within the interviews or simply to leave them as unmarked text. We chose the first alternative, embedding conceptual tags at the appropriate points in the text. An example illustrates this process. One of the activities we were concerned with was drug sales. Our first chore (after a thorough reading of all the transcripts) was to use the software to "isolate" all of the transcript sections dealing with drug sales. One way to do this would be to search the transcripts for every instance in which the word "drugs" was used. However, such a strategy would have the disadvantages of providing

Exhibit 12.10   A Free-Form Model in NVivo

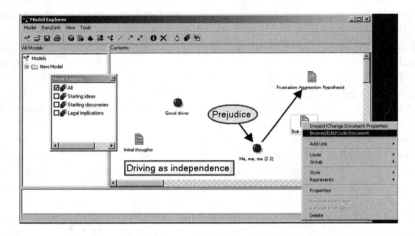

information of too general a character while often missing important statements about drugs. Searching on the word "drugs" would have produced a file including every time the word was used, whether it was in reference to drug sales, drug use, or drug availability, clearly more information than we were interested. However, such a search would have failed to find all of the slang used to refer to drugs ("boy" for heroin, "Casper" for crack cocaine) as well as the more common descriptions of drugs, especially rock or crack cocaine. (pp. 53–54)

Decker and Van Winkle (1996) solved this problem by parenthetically inserting conceptual tags in the text whenever talk of drug sales was found. This process allowed them to examine all of the statements made by gang members about a single concept (drug sales). As you can imagine, however, this still left the researchers with many pages of transcript material to analyze.

CONTENT ANALYSIS

Content analysis is "the systematic, objective, quantitative analysis of message characteristics" (Neuendorf, 2002, p. 1) that facilitates making inferences from text (Weber, 1985, p. 9). You can think of a content analysis as a survey of some documents or other records of prior communication. In fact, a content analysis is a survey designed with fixed-choice responses so that it produces quantitative data that can be analyzed statistically.

As a form of textual analysis, content analysis is like qualitative data analysis. Like the methods we have just been studying, it involves coding and categorizing text and identifying relationships among constructs identified in the text. However, as a quantitative procedure, content analysis overlaps with qualitative data analysis only at the margins—the points where qualitative analysis takes on quantitative features or where content analysis focuses on qualitative features of the text.

Jennifer Tichon and Margaret Shapiro's (2003, p. 161) analysis of e-mail postings to an online support group for children whose siblings have special needs highlights both aspects of content analysis. Their qualitative analyses involved describing e-mail topics, the types of social support offered in the e-mails, and patterns of self-disclosure. The quantitative analysis provided both counts of different categories of topics, support, and patterns of self-disclosure and the relationship of types of social support to patterns of self-disclosure.

The units that are surveyed in a content analysis can include newspapers, journal articles, court decisions, books, videotapes, themes expressed in agency documents, or propositions made in different statements. Words or other features of these units are then coded to measure the variables involved in the research question. The content analysis proceeds through several stages (Weber, 1985):

- *Identify a population of documents or other textual sources for study.* This population should be selected so that it is appropriate to the research question of interest. Perhaps the population will be all newspapers published in the United States, all agency annual reports, all U.S. Supreme Court decisions, or all articles in a particular journal.
- *Determine the units of analysis.* These could be items such as newspaper articles, court decisions, research articles, or case records.
- *Select a sample of units from the population.* The simplest strategy might be a simple random sample of documents. However, a stratified sample might be needed to ensure adequate representation of community newspapers in large and small cities. Sampling may be purposive such as the use of three consecutive months of e-mail posting by Tichon and Shapiro (2003) (see Chapter 4).
- *Design coding procedures for the variables to be measured.* This requires deciding what unit of text to code, such as words, sentences, themes, or paragraphs. Then the categories into which the text units are to be coded must be defined. These categories may be broad, such as *client goal,* or narrow, such as *client improves behavior.*
- *Test and refine the coding procedures.* Clear instructions and careful training of coders are essential.
- *Base statistical analyses on counting occurrences of particular words, themes, or phrases, and test relations between different variables.* These analyses would use some of the statistics introduced in Chapter 11, including frequency distributions, measures of central tendency and variation, crosstabulations, and correlation analysis.

Developing reliable and valid coding procedures is not an easy task. The meaning of words and phrases is often ambiguous. Homographs create special problems (words such as *mine* that have different meanings in different contexts), as do many phrases that have special meanings (such as *point of no return*) (Weber, 1985, p. 30). As a result, coding procedures cannot simply categorize and count words; text segments in which the words are embedded must also be inspected before codes are finalized. Because different coders may perceive different meanings in the same text segments, explicit coding rules are required to ensure coding consistency. Special dictionaries can be developed to keep track of how the categories of interest are defined in the study (Weber, 1985, pp. 24–34).

After coding procedures are developed, their reliability should be assessed by comparing different coders' codes for the same variables. Computer programs for content analysis can be used to enhance reliability (Weber, 1985). The rules the computer is programmed to use when coding text will be applied consistently. Validity can be assessed with a construct validation approach by determining the extent to which theoretically predicted relationships occur (see Chapter 3).

These various steps are represented in the flowchart in Exhibit 12.11. Note that each of these steps is comparable to the procedures in quantitative survey research; they overlap with

Exhibit 12.11   Flowchart for the Typical Process of Content Analysis Research

1. *Theory and rationale*: *What* content will be examined, and *why*? Are there certain *theories* or perspectives that indicate that this particular message content is important to study? Library work is needed here to conduct a good literature review. Will you be using an integrative model, linking content analysis with other data to show relationships with source or receiver characteristics? Do you have *research questions*? *Hypotheses?*

2. *Conceptualizations:* What *variables* will be used in the study, and how do you define them *conceptually* (i.e., with dictionary-type definitions)? Remember, you are the boss! There are many ways to define a given construct, and there is no one right way. You may want to screen some examples of the content you're going to analyze, to make sure you've covered everything you want.

3. *Operationalizations (measures):* Your measures should match your conceptualizations . . . What *unit of data collection* will you use? You may have more than one unit (e.g., a by-utterance coding scheme and a by-speaker coding scheme). Are the variables measured well (i.e., at a high *level of measurement,* with categories that are *exhaustive and mutually exclusive)?* An *a priori* coding scheme describing all measures must be created. Both face validity and content validity may also be assessed at this point.

Human Coding   Computer Coding

4a. *Coding schemes:* You need to create the following materials:

    a. *Codebook* (with all variable measures *fully* explained)

    b. *Coding form*

4b. *Coding schemes:* With computer text content analysis, you still need a code book of sorts—a full explanation of your *dictionaries* and method of applying them. You may use standard dictionaries (e.g., those in Hart's program, *Diction*) or originally created dictionaries. When creating custom dictionaries, be sure to first generate a frequencies list from your text sample and examine for key words and phrases.

Human Coding   Computer Coding

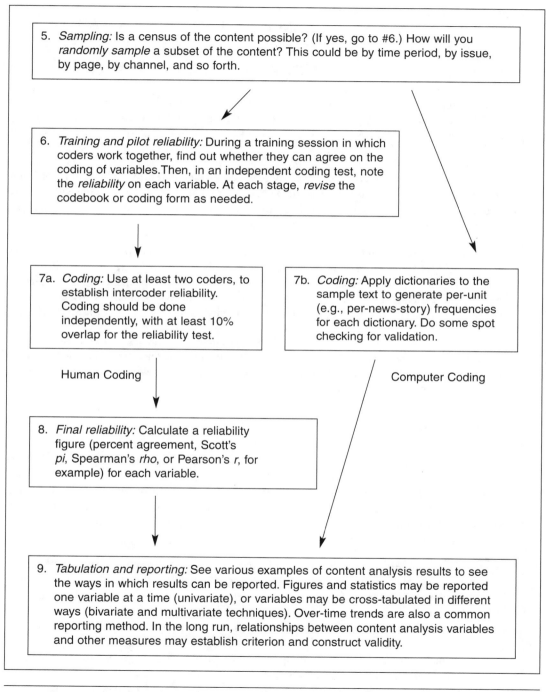

5. *Sampling:* Is a census of the content possible? (If yes, go to #6.) How will you *randomly sample* a subset of the content? This could be by time period, by issue, by page, by channel, and so forth.

6. *Training and pilot reliability:* During a training session in which coders work together, find out whether they can agree on the coding of variables. Then, in an independent coding test, note the *reliability* on each variable. At each stage, *revise* the codebook or coding form as needed.

7a. *Coding:* Use at least two coders, to establish intercoder reliability. Coding should be done independently, with at least 10% overlap for the reliability test.

7b. *Coding:* Apply dictionaries to the sample text to generate per-unit (e.g., per-news-story) frequencies for each dictionary. Do some spot checking for validation.

Human Coding

Computer Coding

8. *Final reliability:* Calculate a reliability figure (percent agreement, Scott's *pi*, Spearman's *rho*, or Pearson's *r*, for example) for each variable.

9. *Tabulation and reporting:* See various examples of content analysis results to see the ways in which results can be reported. Figures and statistics may be reported one variable at a time (univariate), or variables may be cross-tabulated in different ways (bivariate and multivariate techniques). Over-time trends are also a common reporting method. In the long run, relationships between content analysis variables and other measures may establish criterion and construct validity.

Source: Neuendorf, 2002, pp. 50-51. Copyright 2002. Reprinted by permission of Sage Publications, Inc.

qualitative data analysis techniques primarily at the point of developing coding schemes. Use this flowchart as a checklist when you design or critique a content analysis project.

ETHICS IN QUALITATIVE DATA ANALYSIS

The qualitative data analyst is never far from ethical issues and dilemmas. Throughout the analytic process, the analyst must consider how the findings will be used and how participants in the setting will react. Miles and Huberman (1994, pp. 204–205) suggest several specific questions that should be kept in mind:

Research integrity and quality. Is my study being conducted carefully, thoughtfully, and correctly in terms of some reasonable set of standards? Real analyses have real consequences, so you owe it to yourself and those you study to adhere strictly to the analysis methods that you believe will produce authentic, valid conclusions.

Ownership of data and conclusions. Who owns my field notes and analyses: I, my organization, my funders? And once my reports are written, who controls their diffusion? Of course these concerns arise in any social research project, but the intimate involvement of the qualitative researcher with participants in the setting studied make conflicts of interest between different stakeholders much more difficult to resolve. Working through the issues as they arise is essential.

Use and misuse of results. Do I have an obligation to help my findings be used appropriately? What if they are used harmfully or wrongly? It is prudent to develop understandings early in the project with all major stakeholders that specify what actions will be taken to encourage appropriate use of project results and to respond to what is considered misuse of these results.

CONCLUSION

The variety of approaches to qualitative data analysis makes it difficult to provide a consistent set of criteria for interpreting their quality. Norman Denzin's (2002, pp. 362–363) *interpretive criteria* are a good place to start. Denzin suggests that at the conclusion of their analyses, qualitative data analysts ask the following questions about the materials they have produced. Reviewing several of them will serve as a fitting summary for our understanding of the qualitative analysis process.

- *Do they illuminate the phenomenon as lived experience?* In other words, do the materials bring the setting alive in terms of the people in that setting?
- *Are they based on thickly contextualized materials?* We should expect thick descriptions that encompass the social setting studied.
- *Are they historically and relationally grounded?* There must be a sense of the passage of time between events and the presence of relationships between social actors.
- *Are they processual and interactional?* The researcher must have described the research process and his or her interactions within the setting.
- *Do they engulf what is known about the phenomenon?* This includes situating the analysis in the context of prior research and also acknowledging the researcher's own orientation on starting the investigation.

When an analysis of qualitative data is judged as successful in terms of these criteria, we can conclude that the goal of authenticity has been achieved.

In contrast, the criteria for judging quantitative content analyses of text are the same standards of validity applied to data collected with other quantitative methods. We must review the sampling approach, the reliability and validity of the measures, and the controls used to strengthen any causal conclusions. But you have seen in this chapter that there is no sharp demarcation between what is considered a qualitative or a quantitative analysis. As a research methodologist, you must be ready to use both types of techniques, evaluate research findings in terms of both sets of criteria, and mix and match the methods as required by the research problem to be investigated and the setting in which it is to be studied.

KEY TERMS

Case study
Computer-assisted qualitative data analysis
Content analysis
Emic focus
Ethnography
Etic focus
Grounded theory

Matrix
Narrative analysis
Progressive focusing
Qualitative comparative analysis
Tacit knowledge
Thick description

HIGHLIGHTS

• Qualitative data analysts are guided by an emic focus of representing people in the setting on their own terms, rather than by an etic focus on the researcher's terms.
• Case studies use thick description and other qualitative techniques to provide the whole picture of a setting or group.
• Ethnographers attempt to understand the culture of a group.
• Narrative analysis attempts to understand a life or a series of events as they have unfolded, in a meaningful progression.
• Grounded theory connotes a general explanation that develops in interaction with the data and is continually tested and refined as data collection continues.
• Special computer software can be used for the analysis of qualitative, textual, and pictorial data. Users can record their notes, categorize observations, specify links between categories, and count occurrences.
• Content analysis is a tool for systematic quantitative analysis of documents and other textual data. It requires careful testing and control of coding procedures to achieve reliable measures.

DISCUSSION QUESTIONS

1. Describe the differences between quantitative and qualitative data analysis. What are the important guidelines to consider when analyzing qualitative data? Discuss the different modes of reading the text.

Identify and describe the five phases of qualitative data analysis. Discuss the importance of developing a matrix for coding the data.

2. What criteria should be used to evaluate a qualitative study's authenticity?

3. Compare and contrast traditional ethnography, qualitative comparative analysis, narrative analysis, and grounded theory. What are the advantages and disadvantages of these approaches?

   4. What are the advantages and disadvantages of using computer-assisted qualitative data analysis?

   5. What are the similarities and differences between content analysis and qualitative data analysis? Under what circumstances would you choose one mode of analysis over the other? Why?

PRACTICE EXERCISES

   1. Identify a social issue that is currently a "hot topic" nationally. Conduct a content analysis of the coverage of this issue on Internet discussion message boards. What is your unit of analysis? Randomly sample these messages. What are the dominant themes? Evaluate these themes statistically.

   2. Identify three research questions that would be best suited for a qualitative study. Describe how you would develop your study. Choose one of the research questions and describe how you would use an alternative method of analysis (traditional ethnography, qualitative comparative analysis, narrative analysis, and grounded theory). Which method would you choose? Defend your choice.

   3. Examine a qualitative study from a social work journal (see *Affilia,* for example). What techniques did the author employ to analyze the data? Critique the study with regard to the researcher's ability to authenticate the conclusions.

WEB EXERCISES

   1. The *Qualitative Report* is an online journal about qualitative research. Inspect the table of contents for a recent issue at http://www.nova.edu/ssss/QR/index.html. Read one of the articles about issues pertaining to elders, and write a brief article review.

   2. Be a qualitative explorer! Go to the list of qualitative research Web sites and see what you can find that enriches your understanding of qualitative research (www.qualitativeresearch.uga.edu/ QualPage). Be careful to avoid textual data overload.

> To assist you in completing the Web exercises, please access the study site at http://www.sagepub.com/prsw where you will find the Web Exercises reproduced and suggested links for online resources.

DEVELOPING A RESEARCH PROPOSAL

   1. Which qualitative data analysis alternative is most appropriate for the qualitative data you proposed to collect for your project? Using this approach, develop a strategy for using the techniques of qualitative data analysis to analyze your textual data.

Chapter 13

REPORTING RESEARCH

Social Work Research Proposals
Case Study: Treating
    Substance Abuse

Comparing Research Designs
Performing Meta-Analyses
Case Study: Is Social Work
    Practice Effective?

Writing Research

Reporting Research
Journal Articles
Applied Research Reports

Ethics, Politics, and Research Reports

Conclusion

You learned in Chapter 2 that research is a circular process, so it is appropriate that we end this book where we began. The stage of reporting research results is also the point at which the need for new research is identified. It is the time when, so to speak, "the rubber hits the road"—when we have to make our research make sense to others. To whom will our research be addressed? How should we present our results to them? Will we seek to influence how our research report is used?

The primary goals of this chapter are to guide you in developing research proposals, comparing completed research studies, and writing worthwhile reports of your own. We will introduce one new research technique—meta-analysis, which is a quantitative method for statistically evaluating the results of a large body of prior research on a specific topic. This chapter also gives particular attention to the writing process itself and points out how that process can differ when writing for submission to a journal and writing the findings of an applied research report. We will conclude by considering some of the ethical issues unique to the reporting process.

SOCIAL WORK RESEARCH PROPOSALS

Be grateful for those people or groups who require you to write a formal research proposal (as hard as that seems)—and even more for those who give you constructive feedback.

Whether your proposal is written for a professor, a thesis committee, an organization seeking practical advice, or a government agency that funds research, the proposal will force you to set out a problem statement and a research plan. Too many research projects begin without a clear problem statement or with only the barest of notions about which variables must be measured or what the analysis should look like. Such projects often wander along, lurching from side to side, until they collapse entirely or just peter out with a report that is ignored—and should be. So even in circumstances when a proposal is not required, you should prepare one and present it to others for feedback. Just writing your ideas down will help you to see how they can be improved, and feedback in almost any form will help you to refine your plans.

If you have been completing the Developing a Research Proposal exercises at the end of each chapter, you will already be familiar with the process of proposal writing. Nonetheless, we suggest that you read through this section carefully as an overview of the entire process.

Most research proposals will have at least six sections (Locke, Spirduso, & Silverman, 2000):

- *An introductory statement of the research problem*, in which you clarify what it is that you are interested in studying
- A *literature review*, in which you explain how your problem and plans build on what has already been reported in the literature on this topic
- A *methodological plan* detailing just how you will respond to the particular mix of opportunities and constraints you face
- A *budget* presenting a careful listing of the anticipated costs
- An *ethics statement* identifying human subjects issues in the research and how you will respond to them in an ethical fashion
- A *statement of limitations*, reviewing weaknesses of the proposed research and presenting plans for minimizing their consequences

If your research proposal will be reviewed competitively, it must present a compelling rationale for funding. It is not possible to overstate the importance of the research problem that you propose to study (see Chapter 2). If you propose to test a hypothesis, be sure that it is one for which there are plausible alternatives. You want to avoid focusing on a "boring hypothesis"—one that has no credible alternatives, even though it is likely to be correct (Dawes, 1995, p. 93).

When you develop a research proposal, it will help to ask yourself a series of questions like those in Exhibit 13.1 (also see Herek, 1995). It is too easy to omit important details and to avoid being self-critical while rushing to put a proposal together. However, it is even more painful to have a proposal rejected (or to receive a low grade). Better to make sure the proposal covers what it should and confronts the tough issues that reviewers (or your professor) will be sure to spot.

The checklist in Exhibit 13.1 can serve as a map to preceding chapters in this book and as a checklist of decisions that must be made throughout any research project. The questions are organized in five sections, each concluding with a *checkpoint* at which you should consider whether to proceed with the research as planned, modify the plans, or stop the project altogether. The sequential ordering of these questions obscures a bit the way in which they should be answered: not as single questions, one at a time, but as a unit—first as five separate stages, and then as a whole. Feel free to change your answers to earlier questions on the basis of your answers to later questions.

Exhibit 13.1   Decisions in Research

PROBLEM FORMULATION (Chapters 1–3)

1. Developing a research question
2. Assessing researchability of the problem
3. Consulting prior research
4. Relating to social theory
5. Choosing an approach:
   Deductive? Inductive? Descriptive?
6. Reviewing research guidelines

> CHECKPOINT 1
> Alternatives: • Continue as planned.
>   • Modify the plan.
>   • STOP. Abandon the plan.

RESEARCH VALIDITY (Chapters 4–6)

7. Establishing measurement validity:
   • How are concepts defined?
   • Choose a measurement strategy.
   • Assess available measures or develop new measures.
   • What evidence of reliability and validity is available or can be collected?
8. Establishing generalizability:
   • Was a representative sample used?
   • Are the findings applicable to particular subgroups?
   • Does the population sampled correspond to the population of interest?
9. Establishing causality:
   • What is the possibility of experimental or statistical controls?
   • How to assess the causal mechanism?
   • Consider the causal context.
10. Data required: Longitudinal or cross-sectional?
11. Units of analysis: Individuals or groups?
12. What are major possible sources of causal invalidity?

> CHECKPOINT 2
> Alternatives: • Continue as planned.
>   • Modify the plan.
>   • STOP. Abandon the plan.

RESEARCH DESIGN (Chapters 7–11)

13. Choosing a research design and procedures:
    Experimental? Survey? Participant observation?
    Historical, comparative? Multiple methods?
14. Specifying the research plan: Type of surveys, observations, etc.
15. Secondary analysis? Availability of suitable data sets?

(Continued)

Exhibit 13.1 (Continued)

16. Causal approach: Idiographic or nomothetic?
17. Assessing ethical concerns

> CHECKPOINT 3
> Alternatives: • Continue as planned.
>   • Modify the plan.
>   • STOP. Abandon the plan.

DATA ANALYSIS (Chapters 12–13)

18. Choosing a statistical approach:
    • Statistics and graphs for describing data
    • Identifying relationships between variables
    • Deciding about statistical controls
    • Testing for interaction effects
    • Evaluating inferences from sample data to the population

> CHECKPOINT 4
> Alternatives: • Continue as planned.
>   • Modify the plan.
>   • STOP. Abandon the plan.

REVIEWING, PROPOSING, REPORTING RESEARCH (Chapters 2,14)

19. Clarifying research goals
20. Identifying the intended audience
21. Searching the literature and the Web
22. Organizing the text
23. Reviewing ethical and practical constraints

> CHECKPOINT 5
> Alternatives: • Continue as planned.
>   • Modify the plan.
>   • STOP. Abandon the plan.

We will learn how to apply the decision checklist with an example from a proposal focused on treatment for substance abuse.

Case Study: Treating Substance Abuse

Particular academic departments, grant committees, and funding agencies will have more specific proposal requirements. As an example, Exhibit 13.2 lists the primary required sections of the Research Plan for proposals to the National Institutes of Health (NIH), together with excerpts from a proposal Russell Schutt submitted in this format to the National Institute of Mental Health (NIMH) with colleagues from the University of Massachusetts Medical School.

The Research Plan is limited by NIH guidelines to 25 pages. It must be preceded by an abstract (which we have excerpted), a proposed budget, biographical sketches of project personnel, and a discussion of the available resources for the project. Appendixes may include research instruments, prior publications by the authors, and findings from related work.

As you can see from the excerpt in Exhibit 13.2, the proposal was to study the efficacy of a particular treatment approach for homeless mentally ill people who abuse substances. The proposal included a procedure for recruiting subjects in two cities, randomly assigning half of the subjects to a recently developed treatment program, and measuring a range of outcomes. The NIMH review committee (composed of social scientists expert in these issues) approved the project for funding but did not rate it highly enough so that it actually was awarded funds (it often takes several resubmissions before even a worthwhile proposal is funded). The committee members recognized the proposal's strengths, but also identified several problems that they believed had to be overcome before the proposal could be funded. The problems were primarily methodological, stemming from the difficulties associated with providing services to, and conducting research on, this particular segment of the homeless population. The comments from the review team said:

> The proposal has many strengths, including the specially tailored intervention derived from psychiatric rehabilitation technology developed by Liberman and his associates and relapse prevention methods adapted from Marlatt. [T]his fully documented treatment . . . greatly facilitates the generalizability and transportability of study findings. . . . The investigative team is excellent . . . also attuned to the difficulties entailed in studying this target group. . . . While these strengths recommend the proposal . . . eligibility criteria for inclusion of subjects in the study are somewhat ambiguous. . . . This volunteer procedure could substantially underrepresent important components of the shelter population. . . . The projected time frame for recruiting subjects . . . also seems unrealistic for a three-year effort. . . . Several factors in the research design seem to mitigate against maximum participation and retention.

If you get the impression that researchers cannot afford to leave any stone unturned in working through procedures in an NIMH proposal, you are right. It is very difficult to convince a government agency that a research project is worth investing a lot of money (the proposal requested about $2 million). That is as it should be: Your tax dollars should be used only for research that has a high likelihood of yielding findings that are valid and useful. But even when you are proposing a smaller project to a more generous funding source—or even presenting a proposal to your professor—you should scrutinize the proposal carefully before submission and ask others to comment on it. Other people will often think of issues you neglected to consider, and you should allow yourself time to think about these issues and to reread and redraft the proposal. Besides, you will get no credit for having thrown together a proposal as best you could in the face of an impossible submission deadline.

A brief review of how the checklist in Exhibit 13.1 might be used with respect to the NIMH relapse prevention proposal (Schutt, Penk, et al., 1999) should help you to review your own work. The research question concerned the effectiveness of a particular type of substance abuse treatment in a shelter for homeless people—an evaluation research question (Item 1). This problem certainly was suitable for social research, and it was one that could have been handled for the requested amount of money (Item 2). Prior research demonstrated clearly that the

Exhibit 13.2   A Grant Proposal to the National Institute of Mental Health

Relapse Prevention for Homeless Dually Diagnosed

Abstract

This project will test the efficacy of shelter-based treatment that integrates Psychosocial Rehabilitation with Relapse Prevention techniques adapted for homeless mentally ill persons who abuse substances. Two hundred and fifty homeless persons, meeting . . . criteria for substance abuse and severe and persistent mental disorder, will be recruited from two shelters and then randomly assigned to either an experimental treatment condition . . . or to a control condition.

For one year, at the rate of three two-hour sessions per week, the treatment group (n = 125) will participate for the first six months in "enhanced" Psychosocial Rehabilitation . . . , followed by six months of Relapse Prevention training. . . . The control group will participate in a Standard Treatment condition (currently comprised of a twelve-step peer-help program along with counseling offered at all shelters). . . .

Outcome measures include substance abuse, housing placement and residential stability, social support, service utilization, level of distress. . . . The integrity of the experimental design will be monitored through a process analysis. Tests for the hypothesized treatment effects . . . will be supplemented with analyses to evaluate the direct and indirect effects of subject characteristics and to identify interactions between subject characteristics and treatment condition. . . .

Research Plan

1. Specific Aims

The research demonstration project will determine whether an integrated clinical shelter-based treatment intervention can improve health and well-being among homeless persons who abuse alcohol and/or drugs and who are seriously and persistently ill—the so-called "dually diagnosed." . . . We aim to identify the specific attitudes and behaviors that are most affected by the integrated psychosocial rehabilitation/relapse prevention treatment, and thus to help guide future service interventions.

2. Background and Significance

Relapse is the most common outcome in treating the chronically mentally ill, including the homeless. . . . Reviews of the clinical and empirical literature published to date indicate that treatment interventions based on social learning experiences are associated with more favorable outcomes than treatment interventions based on more traditional forms of psychotherapy and/or chemotherapy. . . . However, few tests of the efficacy of such interventions have been reported for homeless samples.

3. Progress Report/Preliminary Studies

Four areas of Dr. Schutt's research help to lay the foundation for the research demonstration project here proposed. . . . The 1990 survey in Boston shelters measured substance abuse with selected ASI [Addiction Severity Index] questions. . . . About half of the respondents evidenced a substance abuse problem.

Just over one-quarter of respondents had ever been treated for a mental health problem. . . . At least three-quarters were interested in help with each of the problems mentioned other than substance abuse. Since help with benefits, housing, and AIDS prevention will each be provided to all study participants in the proposed research demonstration project, we project that this should increase the rate of participation and retention in the study. . . . Results [from co-investigator Dr. Walter Penk's research] . . . indicate that trainers were more successful in engaging the dually diagnosed in Relapse Prevention techniques. . . .

4. Research Design and Methods

Study Sample.

Recruitment. The study will recruit 350 clients beginning in month 4 of the study and running through month 28 for study entry. The span of treatment is 12 months and is followed by 12 months of follow-up. . . .

Study Criteria.

Those volunteering to participate will be screened and declared eligible for the study based upon the following characteristics:
1. Determination that subject is homeless using criteria operationally defined by one of the accepted definitions summarized by . . .

Attrition.

Subject enrollment, treatment engagement, and subject retention each represent potentially significant challenges to study integrity and have been given special attention in all phases of the project. Techniques have been developed to address engagement and retention and are described in detail below. . . .

Research Procedures.

All clients referred to the participating shelters will be screened for basic study criteria. . . . Once assessment is completed, subjects who volunteer are then randomly assigned to one of two treatment conditions–RPST or Standard Treatment. . . .

Research Variables and Measures.

Measures for this study . . . are of three kinds: subject selection measures, process measures, and outcome measures. . . .

5. Human Subjects

Potential risks to subjects are minor. . . . Acute problems identified . . . can be quickly referred to appropriate interventions. Participation in the project is voluntary, and all subjects retain the option to withdraw . . . at any time, without any impact on their access to shelter care or services regularly offered by the shelters. Confidentiality of subjects is guaranteed. . . . [They have] . . . an opportunity to learn new ways of dealing with symptoms of substance abuse and mental illness.

Source: Schutt, Penk, et al., 1992.

proposed treatment had potential and also that it had not previously been tried with homeless people (Item 3). The treatment approach was connected to psychosocial rehabilitation theory (Item 4) and, given prior work in this area, a deductive, hypothesis-testing stance was called for (Item 5). The review of research guidelines continued up to the point of submission and appeared to take each into account (Item 6). So it seemed reasonable to continue to develop the proposal (Checkpoint 1).

Measures were to include direct questions, observations by field researchers, and laboratory tests (of substance abuse) (Item 7). The proposal's primary weakness was in the area of generalizability (Item 8). Schutt, Penk, and colleagues (1992) proposed to sample people in only two homeless shelters in two cities and could offer only weak incentives to encourage potential participants to start and stay in the study. The review committee believed that these procedures might result in an unrepresentative group of initial volunteers beginning the treatment and perhaps an even less representative group continuing through the entire program. The problem was well suited to a randomized, experimental design (Item 9) and was best addressed with longitudinal data (Item 10) involving individuals (Item 11). The randomized design controlled for selection bias and endogenous change, but external events, treatment contamination, and treatment misidentification were potential sources of causal invalidity (Item 12). Clearly, the proposal should have been modified with some additional recruitment and retention strategies—although it may be that the research could not actually be carried out without some major modification of the research question (Checkpoint 2).

A randomized experimental design was preferable because this was to be a treatment-outcome study, but the researchers did include a field research component so that they could evaluate treatment implementation (Items 13, 14). Because the effectiveness of the proposed treatment strategy had not been studied before among homeless people, researchers could not propose doing a secondary data analysis or meta-analysis (Item 15). They sought only to investigate causation from a nomothetic perspective, without attempting to show how the particular experiences of each participant may have led to the outcome (Item 16). Because participation in the study was to be voluntary and everyone received *something* for participation, the research design seemed ethical (and it was approved by the University of Massachusetts Medical School's Institutional Review Board and by the state mental health agency's human subjects committee) (Item 17). Schutt and colleagues planned several statistical tests, but the review committee remarked that they should have been more specific (Item 18). The goal was to use the research as the basis for several academic articles, and the investigators expected that the funding agency would also require a report for general distribution (Items 19, 20). The research literature had been reviewed carefully (Item 21), but as is typical in most research proposals, Schutt et al. did not develop research reporting plans any further (Items 22, 23).

COMPARING RESEARCH DESIGNS

The central features of experiments, single-subject designs, surveys, and qualitative methods provide distinct perspectives, even when used to study the same social processes. Comparing subjects randomly assigned to a treatment and to a comparison group, looking at how subjects differ when subjects cannot be randomly assigned, evaluating changes in a single participant, asking standard questions of the members of a random sample, or observing while participating in a natural social setting involve markedly different decisions about measurement, causality, and generalizability. As you can see in Exhibit 13.3, not one of these methods

Exhibit 13.3 Comparison of Research Methods

Design	Measurement Validity	Generalizability	Type of Causal Assertions	Causal Validity
True Experiments	+	–	Nomothetic	+
Single subject	+	–	Ideographic	+/–[a]
Surveys	+	+	Nomothetic	+/–[b]
Qualitative	+/–[c]	–	Idiographic	–

a. Single-subject designs differ in their utility for establishing causality.

b. Surveys are a weaker design for identifying causal effects than true experiments, but use of statistical controls can strengthen causal arguments

c. Reliability is low compared to surveys, and systematic evaluation of measurement validity is often not possible. However, direct observations may lead to great confidence in the validity of measures.

can reasonably be graded as superior to the others in all respects, and each varies in its suitability to different research questions and goals. Choosing among them for a particular investigation requires consideration of the research problem, opportunities and resources, prior research, philosophical commitments, and research goals.

True experimental designs are strongest for testing nomothetic causal hypotheses and are most appropriate for studies of treatment effects (see Chapter 5). Research questions that are believed to involve basic social psychological processes are most appealing for laboratory studies because the problem of generalizability is reduced. Random assignment reduces the possibility of preexisting differences between treatment and comparison groups to small, specifiable, chance levels, so many of the variables that might create a spurious association are controlled. But in spite of this clear advantage, an experimental design requires a degree of control that cannot always be achieved outside of the laboratory (see Chapter 6). It can be difficult to ensure in real-world settings that a treatment was delivered as intended and that other influences did not intrude. As a result, what appears to be a treatment effect or noneffect may be something else altogether. Community- or agency-based experiments thus require careful monitoring of the treatment process. Researchers may be unable to randomly assign participants to groups or have too few participants to assign to groups, and unfortunately, most field experiments also require more access arrangements and financial resources than can often be obtained. In lieu of these difficulties, quasi-experimental and nonexperimental designs are used but at the cost of causal validity.

Laboratory experiments permit much more control over conditions, but at the cost of less generalizable findings. People must volunteer for most laboratory experiments, and so there is a good possibility that experimental subjects differ from those who do not volunteer. Ethical and practical constraints limit the types of treatments that can be studied experimentally (you can't assign social class or race experimentally). The problem of generalizability in an experiment using volunteers lessens when the object of investigation is an orientation, behavior, or social process that is relatively invariant among people, but it is difficult to know which orientations, behaviors, or processes are so invariant. If a search of the research literature on the topic identifies many prior experimental studies, the results of these experiments will suggest the extent of variability in experimental effects and point to the unanswered questions about these effects.

Single-subject designs are particularly useful for building social work practice knowledge and are more easily applied to agency-based research. Systematic measurement in both the baseline and intervention phases reduces the chances that there are other explanations for the findings, although this does not eliminate all sources of uncertainty about the findings. Generalizability of the findings has less to do with representativeness, but rather, whether the findings about the intervention can be repeated in different settings, with different clients or communities, and other related problems (see Chapter 7).

Surveys, experiments, and single-subject designs typically use standardized, quantitative measures of attitudes, behaviors, or social processes. Closed-ended questions are most common and are well suited for the reliable measurement of variables that have been studied in the past and whose meanings are well understood (see Chapter 3). Of course, surveys often include measures of many more variables than are included in an experiment or in a single-subject design (Chapter 8), but this feature is not inherent in either design. Phone surveys may be quite short, whereas some experiments can involve very lengthy sets of measures (see Chapter 6). The set of interview questions used at baseline in the Boston housing study (Chapter 11), for example, required more than 10 hours to complete. The level of funding for a survey will often determine which type of survey is conducted and thus how long the questionnaire is.

Many surveys rely on random sampling for their selection of cases from some larger population, and this feature makes them preferable for descriptive research that seeks to develop generalizable findings (see Chapter 4). However, survey questionnaires can only measure what respondents are willing to report; they may not be adequate for studying behaviors or attitudes that are regarded as socially unacceptable. Surveys are also often used to test hypothesized causal relationships. When variables that might create spurious relationships are included in the survey, they can be controlled statistically in the analysis and thus eliminated as rival causal influences.

Qualitative methods presume an intensive measurement approach in which indicators of concepts are drawn from direct observation or in-depth commentary (see Chapter 9). This approach is most appropriate when it is not clear what meaning people attach to a concept or what sense they might make of particular questions about it. Qualitative methods are also admirably suited to the exploration of new or poorly understood social settings when it is not even clear what concepts would help to understand the situation. They may also be used instead of survey methods when the population of interest is not easily identifiable or seeks to remain hidden. For these reasons, qualitative methods tend to be preferred when exploratory research questions are posed or when new groups are investigated. But, of course, intensive measurement necessarily makes the study of large numbers of cases or situations difficult, resulting in the limitation of many field research efforts to small numbers of people or unique social settings. The individual field researcher may not require many financial resources, but the amount of time required for many field research projects serves as a barrier to many would-be field researchers.

When qualitative methods can be used to study several individuals or settings that provide marked contrasts in terms of a presumed independent variable, it becomes possible to evaluate nomothetic causal hypotheses with these methods. However, the impossibility of taking into account many possible extraneous influences in such limited comparisons makes qualitative methods a weak approach to hypothesis testing. Qualitative methods are more suited to the elucidation of causal mechanisms. In addition, qualitative methods can be used to identify the multiple successive events that might have led to some outcome, thus identifying idiographic causal processes.

Performing Meta-Analyses

A **meta-analysis** is a quantitative method for identifying patterns in findings across multiple studies of the same research question (Cooper & Hedges, 1994). Unlike a traditional literature review, which describes previous research studies verbally, meta-analyses treat previous studies as cases whose features are measured as variables and are then analyzed statistically. It is like conducting a survey in which the respondents are previous studies. Meta-analysis shows how evidence about social processes varies across research studies. If the methods used in these studies varied, then meta-analysis can describe how this variation affected study findings. If social contexts varied across the studies, then meta-analysis will indicate how social context affected study findings.

Meta-analysis can be used when a number of studies have attempted to answer the same research question with similar quantitative methods, most often experiments. It is not appropriate for evaluating results from qualitative studies, nor from multiple studies that used different methods or measured different dependent variables. It is also not very sensible to use meta-analysis to combine study results when the original case data from these studies are available and can actually be combined and analyzed together (Lipsey & Wilson, 2001). Meta-analysis is a technique for combination and statistical analysis of published research reports.

After a research problem is formulated about the findings of such research, then the literature must be searched systematically to identify the entire population of relevant studies. Typically, multiple bibliographic databases are used; some researchers also search for relevant dissertations and conference papers. Once the studies are identified, their findings, methods, and other features are coded (for example, sample size, location of sample, strength of the association between the independent and dependent variables). Eligibility criteria must be specified carefully to determine which studies to include and which to omit as too different. Mark Lipsey and David Wilson (2001, pp. 16–21) suggest that eligibility criteria include the following:

- *Distinguishing features.* This includes the specific intervention tested and perhaps the groups compared.
- *Research respondents.* These specify the population to which generalization is sought.
- *Key variables.* These must be sufficient to allow tests of the hypotheses of concern and controls for likely additional influences.
- *Research methods.* Apples and oranges cannot be directly compared, but some trade-off must be made between including the range of studies about a research question and excluding those that are so different in their methods as not to yield comparable data.
- *Cultural and linguistic range.* If the study population is going to be limited to English language publications, or limited in some other way, this must be acknowledged and the size of the population of relevant studies in other languages should be estimated.
- *Time frame.* Social processes relevant to the research question may have changed for such reasons as historical events or new technologies, so temporal boundaries around the study population must be considered.
- *Publication type.* Will the analysis focus only on published reports in professional journals, or will it include dissertations and/or unpublished reports?

Statistics are then calculated to identify the average effect of the independent variable on the dependent variable, as well as the effect of methodological and other features of the studies (Cooper & Hedges, 1994). The **effect size** statistic is the key to capturing the association between the independent and dependent variables across multiple studies. The effect size statistic is a standardized measure of association—often the difference between the mean of the experimental group and the mean of the control group on the dependent variable, adjusted for the average variability in the two groups (Lipsey & Wilson, 2001).

The meta-analytic approach to synthesizing research results can result in much more generalizable findings than those obtained with just one study. Methodological weaknesses in the studies included in the meta-analysis are still a problem, however; only when other studies without particular methodological weaknesses are included can we estimate effects with some confidence. In addition, before we can place any confidence in the results of a meta-analysis, we must be confident that all (or almost all) relevant studies were included and that the information we need to analyze was included in all (or most) of the studies (Matt & Cook, 1994).

Case Study: Is Social Work Practice Effective?

An increasing number of articles look at the effectiveness of social work practice, and reviews of these studies have raised questions about their findings. In response, Kevin Gorey (1996) conducted a meta-analysis of 88 articles published between 1990 and 1994 and found that overall, nearly 78% of clients receiving a social work intervention had better outcomes than those clients who did not receive a social work intervention. But Gorey also found a wide variation based on agency auspice and whether the study was conducted by an internal or external investigator.

Kevin Gorey with Bruce Thyer and Debra Pawluck (1998) asked whether the effectiveness of different interventions might differ given differences in theoretical orientation. They reviewed 45 studies from the original Gorey study that focused on practice with individuals, groups, and families and used a group research design (single-subject designs were excluded). They identified 10 primary practice models such as cognitive-behavioral, generalist, task-centered, family systems and feminist for the analysis; in addition, they classified the 10 practice models into four broader theoretical orientations including personal orientations, generalist frameworks, systemic orientations, and radical-structural orientations. They found no difference in the effectiveness of specific primary intervention models, nor was there a difference among the broader practice orientations. But they also reported that effectiveness differed by the primary focus of the intervention. Personal theoretical orientations were more effective than the other orientations when the individual clients were the focus of the intervention, whereas systemic and structural orientations were more effective in affecting clients when the focus of the intervention was on another target, such as a family systems, program, or organization.

Meta-analyses like the work of Gorey (1996) and his colleagues (Gorey et al., 1998) make us aware of how hazardous it is to base understandings of social processes on single studies that are limited in time, location, and measurement. Although one study may not support the hypothesis that we deduced from what seemed to be a compelling theory, this is not a sufficient basis for discarding the theory itself, nor even for assuming that the hypothesis is no longer worthy of consideration in future research. You can see that a meta-analysis combining the results of many studies may identify conditions for which the hypothesis is supported and others for which it is not.

Of course, we need to have our wits about us when we read reports of meta-analytic studies. It is not a good idea to assume that a meta-analysis is the definitive word on a research question just because it cumulates the results of multiple studies. Fink (1998, pp. 215–237) suggests evaluating meta-analytic studies in terms of the following seven criteria:

- *Clear statement of the analytic objectives.* The study's methods cannot be evaluated without knowledge of the objectives they were intended to achieve. Meta-analyses are most appropriate for summarizing research conducted to identify the effect of some type of treatment or other readily identifiable individual characteristic.
- *Explicit inclusion and exclusion criteria.* On what basis were research reports included in the analysis? Were high-quality studies distinguished from low-quality studies? If low-quality studies were included, were they analyzed separately, so that effects could be identified separately for the population of only high-quality studies?
- *Satisfactory search strategies.* Both electronic and written reference sources should be searched. Was some method used to find studies that were conducted but not published? It may be necessary to write directly to researchers in the field and to consult lists of papers presented at conferences.
- *A standardized protocol for screening the literature.* Screening involves rating the quality of the study and its relevance to the research question. This screening should be carried out with a simple rating form.
- *A standardized protocol for collecting data.* It is best to have two reviewers use a standard form for coding the characteristics of the reported research. The level of agreement between these reviewers should be assessed.
- *Complete explanation of the method of combining results.* Some checks should be conducted to determine where variable study features influenced the size of the treatment effect.
- *Report of results, conclusions, and limitations.* This seems obvious, but it's easy for a researcher to skirt over study limitations or some aspects of the findings.

WRITING RESEARCH

The goal of research is not just to discover something, but to communicate that discovery to a larger audience—other social workers, consumer groups, government officials, your teachers, the general public—perhaps several of these audiences. Whatever the study's particular outcome, if the intended audience for the research comprehends the results and learns from them, the research can be judged a success. If the intended audience does not learn about the study's results, the research should be judged a failure—no matter how expensive the research, how sophisticated its design, or how much you (or others) invested in it.

Successful research reporting requires both good writing and a proper publication outlet. We will first review guidelines for successful writing before we look at particular types of research publications.

Consider the following principles formulated by experienced writers (Booth, Colomb, & Williams, 1995, pp. 150–151):

- Respect the complexity of the task and don't expect to write a polished draft in a linear fashion. Your thinking will develop as you write, causing you to reorganize and rewrite.
- Leave enough time for dead ends, restarts, revisions, and so on, and accept the fact that you will discard much of what you write.
- Write as fast as you comfortably can. Don't worry about spelling, grammar, and so on until you are polishing things up.
- Ask anyone whom you trust for their reactions to what you have written.
- Write as you go along, so you have notes and report segments drafted even before you focus on writing the report.

It is important to outline a report before writing it, but neither the report's organization nor the first written draft should be considered fixed. As you write, you will get new ideas about how to organize the report. Try them out. As you review the first draft, you will see many ways to improve your writing. Focus particularly on how to shorten and clarify your statements. Make sure each paragraph concerns only one topic. Remember the golden rule of good writing: Writing is revising!

You can ease the burden of report writing in several ways:

- Draw on the research proposal and on project notes.
- Use a word processing program on a computer to facilitate reorganizing and editing.
- Seek criticism from friends, teachers, and other research consumers before turning in the final product.

We often find it helpful to use what we call **reverse outlining:** After you have written a first complete draft, outline it on a paragraph-by-paragraph basis, ignoring the actual section headings you used. See if the paper you wrote actually fits the outline you planned. How could the organization be improved?

Most important, leave yourself enough time so that you *can* revise, several times if possible, before turning in the final draft. Here are one student's reflections on writing and revising:

I found the process of writing and revising my paper longer than I expected. I think it was something I was doing for the first time—working within a committee—that made the process not easy. The overall experience was very good, since I found that I have learned so much. My personal computer also did help greatly.

Revision is essential until complete clarity is achieved. This took most of my time. Because I was so close to the subject matter, it became essential for me to ask for assistance in achieving clarity. My committee members, English editor, and fellow students were extremely helpful. Putting it on disk was also, without question, a timesaver. Time was the major problem.

The process was long, hard and time-consuming, but it was a great learning experience. I work full time so I learned how to budget my time. I still use my time productively and am very careful of not wasting it. (Graduate Program in Applied Sociology, 1990)

For more suggestions about writing, see Becker (1986), Booth et al. (1995), Cuba (2002), Strunk and White (2000), and Turabian (1996).

REPORTING RESEARCH

You began writing your research report when you worked on the research proposal, and you will find that the final report is much easier to write, and more adequate, if you write more material for it as you work out issues during the project. It is very disappointing to discover that something important was left out when it is too late to do anything about it. We don't need to point out that students (and professional researchers) often leave final papers (and reports) until the last possible minute (often for understandable reasons, including other coursework and job or family responsibilities). But be forewarned: *The last-minute approach does not work for research reports.*

Journal Articles

Writing for academic journals is perhaps the toughest form of writing because articles are submitted to several other experts in your field for careful review—anonymously, with most journals—prior to acceptance for publication. Perhaps it wouldn't be such an arduous process if so many academic journals did not have exceedingly high rejection rates and turnaround times for reviews that are, at best, usually several months. Even the best articles, in the judgment of the reviewers, are given a "revise and resubmit" after the first review and then are evaluated all over again after the revisions are concluded.

But there are some important benefits of journal article procedures. First and foremost is the identification of areas in need of improvement, as the author(s) eyes are replaced by those of previously uninvolved subject matter experts and methodologists. A good journal editor makes sure that he or she has a list of many different types of experts available for reviewing whatever types of articles the journal is likely to receive. There is a parallel benefit for the author(s): It is always beneficial to review criticisms of your own work by people who know the field well. It can be a painful and time-consuming process, but the entire field moves forward as researchers continually critique and suggest improvements in each others' research reports.

Exhibit 13.4 presents an outline of the sections in an academic journal article, with some illustrative quotes. The article's introduction highlights the importance of the problem selected—the relationship between marital disruption (divorce) and depression. The introduction also states clearly the gap in the research literature that the article is meant to fill—the untested possibility that depression might cause marital disruption, rather than, or in addition to, marital disruption causing depression. The findings section (labeled *Results*) begins by presenting the basic association between marital disruption and depression. Then, it elaborates on this association by examining sex differences, the impact of prior marital quality, and various mediating and modifying effects. As indicated in the combined discussion and conclusions section, the analysis shows that marital disruption does indeed increase depression and specifies the time frame (three years) during which this effect occurs.

These basic article sections present research results well, but many research articles include subsections tailored to the issues and stages in the specific study being reported. Most journals require a short abstract at the beginning that summarizes the research question and findings.

Exhibit 13.4 Sections in a Journal Article

Aseltine, Robert H., Jr. and Ronald C. Kessler. 1993. "Marital Disruption and
  Depression in a Community Sample." *Journal of Health and Social Behavior,*
  34 (September): 237–251.

INTRODUCTION
   Despite 20 years of empirical research, the extent to which marital
disruption causes poor mental health remains uncertain. The reason for this
uncertainty is that previous research has consistently overlooked the
potentially important problems of selection into and out of marriage on the
basis of prior mental health. (p. 237)

SAMPLE AND MEASURES
Sample
Measures

RESULTS
The Basic Association Between Marital Disruption and Depression
Sex Differences
The Impact of Prior Marital Quality
The Mediating Effects of Secondary Changes
The Modifying Effects of Transitions to Secondary Roles

DISCUSSION [includes conclusions]

. . . According to the results, marital disruption does in fact cause a
significant increase in depression compared to pre-divorce levels within a
period of three years after the divorce. (p. 245)

Source: Aseltine & Kessler, 1993. Reprinted with permission from Sage Publications, Inc.

Applied Research Reports

Applied research reports are written for a different audience than the professional social scientists and students who read academic journals. Typically, an applied report is written with a wide audience of potential users in mind and to serve multiple purposes. Often, both the audience and purpose are established by the agency or other organization that funded the research project on which the report is based. Sometimes, the researcher may use the report to provide a broad descriptive overview of study findings that will be presented more succinctly in a subsequent journal article. In either case, an applied report typically provides much more information about a research project than does a journal article and relies primarily on descriptive statistics rather than only those statistics useful for the specific hypothesis tests that are likely to be the primary focus of a journal article.

Exhibit 13.5 outlines the sections in one applied research report. This particular report was funded by a county children, youth, and families agency and was intended to comply with new state work standards. The goals of the report are to provide both description and

Exhibit 13.5   Sections in an Applied Report

Yamatani, H., & Engel, R. (2002). Workload assessment study. Pittsburgh, PA: The University of Pittsburgh.

EXECUTIVE SUMMARY

Recently adopted . . . Standards for Child Welfare Practice (2000) include the expectation that agency management will conduct a workload study in order to determine staff levels necessary to perform the activities outlined in the Standards of Practice. . . . (p. ii). This study examines the questions of how much time is required for workers to fulfill their responsibilities, and how many cases might reasonably comprise the workload of one trained person.

By analyzing the three streams of data, it was determined that the recommended maximum caseload per worker at a point in time is sixteen (16) in the Intake Department and seventeen (17) cases in Family Services. The results are noticeably compatible with national standards (e.g., the Child Welfare League of America) and studies completed in other states (e.g., California)

OVERVIEW OF RESEARCH ACTIVITIES AND PROCESS

SPECIFICATIONS OF RESEARCH QUESTION AND METHOD

  Research question
  Research approach
  Sample selection
  Data instrument

INTAKE DEPARTMENT ASSESSMENT

  Available work hours per month
  Average amount of time spent per case per month
  Time expended for family visits
  Total time needed per case during a month
  Estimated maximum caseload

FAMILY SERVICES DEPARTMENT ASSESSMENT

  Available work hours per month
  Average amount of time spent per case per month
  Time expended for family visits
  Total time needed per case during a month
  Estimated maximum caseload

OVERVIEW OF FOCUS GROUP FINDINGS

  Case-based focus group assessment
  Summary of focus group survey findings

DISCUSSION
Appendix

A. Randomly selected caseworkers
B. Distribution of task time spent on case per day – Intake Department
C. Distribution of task time spent on case per day – Family Services
D. Focus Group Participants
E. Second Focus Group's Delineation of "good casework practice"

Consulted Literature and References

Source: Yamatani & Engel, 2002.

evaluation. The body of the report presents findings on the actual time spent on different work-related activities in two different departments as well a summary of focus group findings related to work activities. The discussion section highlights optimal caseloads for each department and the relation of the report's findings to other strategies to estimate caseloads. Five appendixes then provide details on the study methodology as well as detailed results.

One of the major differences between an applied research report and a journal article is that an article must focus on answering a particular research question, whereas an applied report is likely to have the broader purpose of describing a wide range of study findings and attempting to meet the needs of diverse audiences that have divergent purposes in mind for the research. But a research report that simply describes "findings" without some larger purpose in mind is unlikely to be effective in reaching any audience. Anticipating the needs of the audience (or audiences) for the report and identifying the ways in which the report can be useful to them will result in a product that is less likely to be ignored. An important principle for the researcher writing for a nonacademic audience is to make the findings and conclusions engaging and clear.

A congressional briefing by social scientists Ronald J. Angel, P. Lindsay Chase-Lansdale, Andrew Cherlin and Robert Moffitt (2002) on the impact of new welfare-to-work policies is an example of a report informed by a keen understanding of current concerns and the key questions of their audience. Prepared under the auspices of the consortium of Social Science Associations with funding from the W. K. Kellogg Foundation, the report was entitled, *Welfare, Children, and Families: Results from a Three City Study*.

The starting point for the briefing was recognition that welfare reform has been a success, as commonly measured in terms of the number of recipients who have left public welfare and the high rates of employment these "leavers" have obtained (50–70%). But economist Robert Moffitt knew that the picture was more complex than that and that policymakers needed a broader picture of what has been happening. Based on research done in the impoverished areas of Boston, Massachusetts, Chicago, Illinois, and San Antonio, Texas, he focused attention on the differences between families that had remained on welfare and those who had left and the problems that seemed to make leaving difficult:

- Incomes for welfare "leavers" are only modestly higher, by 20% after two years.
- Women who remain on welfare have far fewer people to help them than those who leave.
- Many leavers no longer participated in the food stamp or Medicaid programs, even though they were still eligible.
- Stayers were much more disadvantaged than leavers, with 39% not having a high school degree, 25% having a serious health problem, and more reporting problems like depression and experiences with domestic violence.
- Women who work and remain on welfare earn a higher income than those who leave.
- Those welfare recipients who are more disadvantaged are more likely to be forced off welfare for technical noncompliance with rules.

With these findings in mind, Moffitt (and his coauthors, at other points in the briefing), pointed out some of the policy implications: "It is not clear that sanctions are a good substitute for financial incentives"; "You can stay on [welfare] and do quite well and can work"; "significant health problems, the domestic violence problems, the mental health problems, and the low skills problems . . . prevent them from working more" (Moffitt, 2002, pp. 8–11). Finally, "there is room for improvement in the structure of supports both on and off welfare, and I think that some of the trade-offs are well illustrated by our data."

What can be termed the **front matter** and the **back matter** of an applied report are also important. Applied reports usually begin with an executive summary: a summary list of the study's main findings, often in bullet fashion. Appendixes, the back matter, may present tables containing supporting data that were not discussed in the body of the report. Applied research reports also often append a copy of the research instrument(s).

ETHICS, POLITICS, AND RESEARCH REPORTS

At the time of reporting research results, the researcher's ethical duty to be honest becomes paramount. Here are some guidelines:

- *Provide an honest accounting of how the research was carried out and where the initial research design had to be changed.* Readers do not have to know about every change you made in your plans and each new idea you had, but they should be informed about major changes in hypotheses or research design.
- *Maintain a full record of the research project so that questions can be answered if they arise.* Many details will have to be omitted from all but the most comprehensive reports, but these omissions should not make it impossible to track down answers to specific questions about research procedures that may arise in the course of data analysis or presentation.
- *Avoid "lying with statistics" or using graphs to mislead.* See Chapter 12 for more on this topic.
- *Acknowledge the sponsors of the research.* This is important, in part, so that others can consider whether this sponsorship may have tempted you to bias your results in some way.
- *Thank staff who made major contributions.* This is an ethical as well as a political necessity. Let's maintain our social relations!
- *Be sure that the order of authorship for coauthored reports is discussed in advance and reflects agreed-upon principles.* Be sensitive to coauthors' needs and concerns.

Ethical research reporting should not mean ineffective reporting. You need to tell a coherent story in the report and avoid losing track of the story in a thicket of minuscule details. You do not need to report every twist and turn in the conceptualization of the research problem or the conduct of the research. But be suspicious of reports that don't seem to admit to the possibility of any room for improvement. Social science is an ongoing enterprise in which one research report makes its most valuable contribution by laying the groundwork for another, more sophisticated research project. Highlight important findings in the research report, but use the research report also to point out what are likely to be the most productive directions for future researchers.

Even following appropriate guidelines like these, however, will not prevent controversy and conflict over research on sensitive issues. Sociologist Peter Rossi (1999) recounts the controversy that arose when he released a summary of findings conducted in his 1986 study of homeless people in Chicago, Illinois (see Chapter 4). In spite of important findings about the causes and effects of homelessness, media attention focused on Rossi's markedly smaller estimate of the numbers of homeless people in Chicago compared to the "guesstimates" that had been publicized by local advocacy groups. "Moral of the story: Controversy is news, to which careful empirical findings cannot be compared." (Rossi, 1999, p. 2).

Does this mean that ethical researchers should avoid political controversy by sidestepping media outlets for their work? Many social scientists argue that the media offer some of the best ways to communicate the practical application of sociological knowledge and that when we avoid these opportunities, "some of the best sociological insights never reach policy makers because sociologists seldom take advantage of useful mechanisms to get their ideas out" (Wilson, 1998, p. 435).

Sociologist William Julius Wilson (1998, p. 438) urges the following principles for engaging the public through the media:

- First, focus on issues of national concern, issues that are high on the public agenda.
- Second, develop creative and thoughtful arguments that are clearly presented and devoid of technical language.
- Third, present the big picture whereby the arguments are organized and presented so that the readers can see how the various parts are interrelated.

CONCLUSION

A well-written research article or report requires (to be just a bit melodramatic) blood, sweat, and tears—and more time than you will at first anticipate. But the process of writing one will help you to write the next. Also, the issues you consider, if you approach your writing critically, will be sure to improve your subsequent research projects and sharpen your evaluations of other investigators' research projects.

Good critical skills are essential when evaluating research reports, whether your own or those produced by others. There are *always* weak points in any research, even published research. It is an indication of strength, not weakness, to recognize areas where one's own research needs to be, or could have been, improved. It is really not just a question of sharpening your knives and going for the jugular. You need to be able to weigh the strengths and weaknesses of particular research results and to evaluate a study in terms of its contribution to understanding the social world—not in terms of whether it gives a definitive answer for all time.

But this is not to say that anything goes. Much research lacks one or more of the three legs of validity—measurement validity, causal validity, or generalizability—and contributes more confusion than understanding about the social world. Top journals generally maintain very high standards, partly because they have good critics in the review process and distinguished editors who make the final acceptance decisions. But some daily newspapers do a poor job of screening, and research reporting standards in many popular magazines, TV shows, and books are often abysmally poor. Keep your standards high and your view critical when reading research reports, but not so high or so critical that you turn away from studies that make tangible contributions to understanding the social world—even if they don't provide definitive answers. And don't be so intimidated by the need to maintain high standards that you shrink from taking advantage of opportunities to conduct research yourself.

The growth of social science methods from its infancy to adolescence, perhaps to young adulthood, ranks as a key intellectual accomplishment of the 20th century. Opinions about the causes and consequences of homelessness no longer need depend on the scattered impressions of individuals; criminal justice policies can be shaped by systematic evidence of their effectiveness; and changes in the distribution of poverty and wealth in populations can be identified and charted. Employee productivity, neighborhood cohesion, and societal conflict each may be linked to individual psychological processes and to international economic strains.

Of course, social work research methods are no more useful than the commitment of researchers to their proper application. Research methods, like all knowledge, can be used poorly or well, for good purposes or bad, when appropriate or not. A claim that a belief is based on social science research in itself provides no extra credibility. As you have learned throughout this book, we must first learn which methods were used, how they were applied, and whether interpretations square with the evidence. To investigate the social world, we must keep in mind the lessons of research methods.

KEY TERMS

Back matter	Meta-analysis
Effect size	Reverse outlining
Front matter	

HIGHLIGHTS

- Research reports should be evaluated systematically, using the review guide in Appendix B and also taking account of the interrelations among the designs.

- Proposal writing should be a time for clarifying the research problem, reviewing the literature, considering the methods of implementation and data analysis, and thinking about the report that will be required. Trade-offs between different design elements should be considered and the potential for using multiple methods evaluated.

- Different types of reports typically pose different problems. Authors of student papers must be guided in part by the expectations of their professor. Thesis and dissertation writers have to meet the requirements of different committee members but can benefit greatly from the areas of expertise represented on a typical committee. Program evaluators and applied researchers are constrained by the expectations of the research sponsor. Journal articles must pass a peer review by other social scientists and often are much improved in the process.

- Research reports should include an introductory statement of the research problem, a literature review, a methodology section, a findings section with pertinent data displays, and a discussion/conclusions section that identifies the social work practice or policy implications of the findings, notes any weaknesses in the research methodology, and points out implications for future research. The report format should be modified according to the needs of a particular audience.

- All reports should be revised several times and critiqued by others before being presented in final form.

- The central ethical precept in research reporting is to be honest. This honesty should include providing a factual accounting of how the research was carried out, maintaining a full record about the project, using appropriate statistics and graphs, acknowledging the research sponsors, and being sensitive to the perspectives of coauthors.

DISCUSSION QUESTIONS

1. List and describe the sections included in research proposals. How are the research proposal and the research report similar? How do they differ?

2. Under what circumstances would a researcher choose to perform a meta-analysis? What are the strengths and weaknesses of this approach?

3. Describe the elements of successful research reporting. How does reverse outlining assist the writer? After the final draft of the article is written, how does the author find an appropriate audience?

4. Describe the similarities and differences between journal articles and applied research reports. Discuss the political and ethical considerations of research reporting in journals and in applied research.

PRACTICE EXERCISES

1. Prepare an abstract of your research paper. Give the abstract to several students in your class and have them edit and evaluate your work. Give the same abstract to several friends who are not students in social work. Have them also edit and evaluate your work. Compare the critiques.

2. Read a journal article about a social issue that interests you. Read an applied research report (these can easily be obtained online) on the same social issue focusing on the same population. Compare and contrast these reports.

3. Reread the journal article you have chosen for Exercise 2. Was the research sponsored by any particular organization? If so, how might that sponsorship influenced the reporting? How easy was the article to understand? Was the language simple and clear, or did the author use technical jargon? Did the author include practice or policy recommendations?

WEB EXERCISES

1. The National Academy of Sciences wrote a lengthy report on ethics issues in scientific research. Visit the site and read the report: http://www.nap.edu/readingroom/books/obas. Summarize the information and guidelines in the report.

2. Using the Web, find five different examples of social science research projects that have been completed around the treatment of substance abuse and/or divorce and delinquency. Briefly describe each. How does each differ in its approach to reporting the research results? Who do you think the author(s) of each is "reporting" to (i.e., who is the audience)? How do you think the predicted audience has helped to shape the author's approach to reporting the results? Be sure to note the Web sites at which you located each of your five examples.

> To assist you in completing the Web exercises, please access the study site at http://www.sagepub.com/prsw where you will find the Web Exercises reproduced and suggested links for online resources.

DEVELOPING A RESEARCH PROPOSAL

1. Think about how the study findings can be used to inform policies, service design, or practice activities. What future research might you suggest given the study findings?

2. How will the results of the study be disseminated? How will you make your findings known to the professional community?

3. Review the methods you have used and discuss any limitations in your proposal.

Appendix A

SUMMARIES OF FREQUENTLY CITED RESEARCH ARTICLES

$\mathbf{A}$ctual research studies are used throughout the text to illustrate particular research approaches and issues. You can use the following summaries at any point to review the design of each study. The chapter number in brackets indicates the text chapter in which the study is introduced.

Alter, Catherine. 1996. "Family Support as an Intervention with Female Long-Term AFDC Recipients." *Social Work Research* 20:203–16. [Chapter 6]

A pretest-posttest control group design is used to test the impact of a family support intervention on female long-term clients. The group receiving the intervention achieved higher levels of competence and self-efficacy.

Anderson, Elijah. 1990. *Streetwise: Race, Class, and Change in an Urban Community.* Chicago: University of Chicago Press. [Chapter 5]

This study of social life in an impoverished urban community was based on participant observation. Constructs idiographic explanations of how drug addiction can lead to a downward slide into residential instability and crime.

Anderson, Elijah. 1999. *Code of the Street: Decency, Violence, and the Moral Life of the Inner City.* New York: W. W. Norton. [Chapter 12]

This is an ethnographic study of social life in an impoverished urban community based on participant observation. Develops contextually based understanding of what the "code of the street" means and how it is maintained.

Anderson, Elijah. 2003. "Jelly's Place: An Ethnographic Memoir." *Symbolic Interaction* 26:217–37. [Chapter 12]

This review of field methods used in a study of Jelly's Bar recounts the process of gaining entry to the bar and gaining the trust of its customers.

Balaswamy, Shantha and Holly I. Dabelko. 2002. "Using a Stakeholder Participatory Model in a Community-Wide Service Needs Assessment of Elderly Residents: A Case Study." *Journal of Community Practice* 10:55–70. [Chapter 10]

A stakeholder participatory model was used in a community needs assessment. Stakeholders were involved in every phase of the community needs assessment including focus, design, data collection, and the results. Due to their involvement, there was increased utilization of the results.

Besa, David. 1994. "Evaluating Narrative Family Therapy Using Single-System Research Designs." *Research on Social Work Practice* 4:309–25. [Chapter 7]

Multiple baseline design across six families was used to test the effectiveness of narrative family therapy to reduce parent-child conflict. Families were paired on the similarity of the problem, and one family of the pair served as the control for the other member of the pair. Five of the six families showed improvement in parent-child conflict.

Brock, Thomas and Kristen Harknett. 1998. "A Comparison of Two Welfare-to-Work Case Management Models." *Social Service Review* 72:493–520. [Chapter 6]

This study compared the effectiveness of two welfare-to-work case management models in helping recipients get off Temporary Assistance to Needy Families. Participants were randomly assigned to one of three groups: traditional case management (income maintenance and employment services were separate), integrated case management (both services were provided by a single contact), and a control group that received cash benefits but no employment service assistance by a case manager. Those participants receiving integrated services were less likely to be referred for sanctions, participated in more job-related activities, and received less cash assistance than people in the traditional case management group. Both groups did better than the control group on all measures.

Cheung, Kam-fong Monit. 1999. "Effectiveness of Social Work Treatment and Massage Therapy for Nursing Home Clients." *Research on Social Work Practice* 9:229–47. [Chapter 7]

An A-B-A-B design was used to evaluate the impact of massage therapy and social work treatment on activities of daily living for six nursing home residents. Phases lasted seven weeks. Based on the visual inspection of the data, the intervention was successful with three clients.

Colon, Israel and Brett Marston. 1999. "Resistance to a Residential AIDS Home: An Empirical Test of NIMBY." *Journal of Homosexuality* 37:135–45. [Chapter 4]

Probability cluster sampling of blocks and households was used to select potential respondents for a study about community attitudes toward a proposed residential home for HIV patients.

Cress, Daniel M. and David A. Snow. 2000. "The Outcomes of Homeless Mobilization: The Influence of Organization, Disruption, Political Mediation, and Framing. *American Journal of Sociology,* 4:1063–1104. [Chapter 12]

Qualitative analysis of differences between homeless mobilization efforts and the influence of different factors on successful mobilization. Uses qualitative comparative analysis techniques to assess how various conditions influenced SMO outcomes.

Diamond, Timothy. 1992. *Making Gray Gold: Narratives of Nursing Home Care.* Chicago: University of Chicago Press. [Chapter 9]

A participant observation approach was used to study the inside of three Chicago nursing homes and the attitudes and actions of their staffs. The central research questions were, in Diamond's words, "What was life like inside, day in and day out? Who lived in nursing homes, and what did they do there?" He began the study by going to school for six months to obtain a required state certificate for nursing home employees; he then worked for several months at each of the three nursing homes. The nursing homes were selected to differ in location and in the proportion of their residents on Medicaid. Diamond's in-depth descriptions and idiographic connections of sequences of events enabled him to explore human experiences in depth and to carefully analyze the social contexts in which these experiences occurred.

Drake, Robert E., Gregory J. McHugo, Deborah R. Becker, William A. Anthony, and Robin E. Clark. 1996. "The New Hampshire Study of Supported Employment for People with Severe Mental Illness." *Journal of Consulting and Clinical Psychology* 64:391–99. [Chapter 10]

A test of the value of two different approaches to providing employment services for people diagnosed with severe mental disorders, this study used a variant of the classic randomized comparative change design. One approach, Group Skills Training (GST), emphasized preemployment skills training and used separate agencies to provide vocational and mental health services. The other approach, Individual Placement and Support (IPS), provided vocational and mental health services in a single program and placed people directly into jobs without preemployment skills training. Both groups received posttests at 6, 12, and 18 months. The researchers hypothesized that GST participants would be more likely to obtain jobs than IPS participants, but the IPS participants proved to be twice as likely to obtain a competitive job as the GST participants.

Essock, Susan M., Linda K. Frisman, and Nina J. Kontos. 1998. "Cost-Effectiveness of Assertive Community Treatment Teams." *American Journal of Orthopsychiatry* 68:179–90. [Chapter 10]

This study reports the cost-effectiveness of assertiveness community treatment (ACT) in comparison to standard case management (SCM). Participants were randomly assigned to either the ACT or SCM group. Data were collected at baseline, 6, 12, and 18 months. ACT clients reported higher quality of life. When including all participants, the actual cost of the programs did not differ; for participants hospitalized at baseline, ACT was more effective than SCM. Overall, given similar costs, the ACT program produced more desirable outcomes.

Ferguson, Kirsten and Margaret Rodway. 1994. "Cognitive Behavioral Treatment of Perfectionism: Initial Evaluation Studies." *Research on Social Work Practice* 4:283–308. [Chapter 7]

An A-B-A design was used to test the effectiveness of cognitive-behavioral treatment on perfectionism. The design was replicated across nine clients, each of whom completed two standardized measures of perfectionism and a nonstandardized measure. Baseline measures were completed twice a week for four weeks, the intervention stage lasted eight weeks, and the subsequent A stage lasted one week. Visual inspection of the graphs suggested that the intervention was successful.

Goldapple, Gary and Dianne Montgomery. 1993. "Evaluating a Behaviorally Based Intervention to Improve Client Retention in Therapeutic Community Treatment for Drug Dependency." *Research on Social Work Practice* 3:21–39. [Chapter 6]

Attrition from a therapeutic community treatment program for drug abusers was noted as a problem. A cause of the attrition was depression. The authors used a nonequivalent control group design to test whether a three-week, eight-session, group intervention using cognitive-behavioral therapy would reduce depression and, therefore, reduce attrition. New admissions during Weeks 1 and 2 of the study completed the pretest and completed the posttest in Weeks 4 through 6. New admissions during Weeks 7 and 8 were administered the pretest, received the intervention during Weeks 9 through 11, and then completed the posttest. Depressive symptoms were reduced, and retention rates were higher.

Goldfinger, Stephen M., Russell K. Schutt, Larry J. Seidman, Winston M. Turner, Walter E. Penk, and George S. Tolomiczenko. 1996. "Self-Report and Observer Measures of Substance Abuse Among Homeless Mentally Ill Persons in the Cross-Section and over Time." *The Journal of Nervous and Mental Disease* 184(11):667–72. [Chapter 10]

In this study of housing for homeless mentally ill people, the researchers assessed substance abuse with several different sets of direct questions as well as with reports from subjects' case managers and others. They found that the observational reports were often inconsistent with self-reports and that different self-report measures were not always in agreement—hence unreliable. A more reliable measure was initial reports of lifetime substance abuse problems, which identified all those who subsequently abused substances during the project. The researchers concluded that the lifetime measure was a valid way to identify people at risk for substance abuse problems. No single measure was adequate to identify substance abusers at a particular point in time during the project. Instead, the authors constructed a composite of observer and self-report measures that seemed to be a valid indicator of substance abuse over six-month periods.

Goldfinger, Stephen M., Russell K. Schutt, George S. Tolomiczenko, Winston M. Turner, Norma Ware, Walter E. Penk, et al. 1997. "Housing Persons Who Are Homeless and Mentally Ill: Independent Living or Evolving Consumer House-holds?" Pp. 29–49 in *Mentally Ill and Homeless: Special Programs for Special Needs,* edited by William R. Breakey and James W. Thompson. Amsterdam, The Netherlands: Harwood Academic. [Chapter 1]

This field experiment evaluated the impact of two types of housing on residential stability, health, and other outcomes for formerly homeless mentally ill people. Individuals living in shelters were assigned randomly to permanent housing either in an *independent living* site (an efficiency apartment) or in an *evolving consumer household* site (a group home from which support staff were withdrawn as residents took over management responsibilities). Participants were evaluated with lengthy interview instruments, neuropsychological tests, and personality inventories for an 18-month period after housing placement. Anthropologists observed interaction in the group homes, and case managers reported on the services delivered to subjects. They found that residents assigned to group homes had a higher rate of housing retention than those assigned to independent apartments; that housing loss was higher among substance abusers and those whom clinicians recommended for group homes; and that individuals assigned to independent apartments were more satisfied with their residences. However, the type of housing did not affect residents' symptoms of mental illness or their feelings about the quality of their lives.

Gorey, Kevin M. 1996. "Effectiveness of Social Work Intervention Research: Internal Versus External Evaluations." *Social Work Research* 20:119–28. [Chapter 13]

This is a meta-analysis of 88 articles looking at the effectiveness of social work practice. Most (78%) clients receiving a social work practice intervention had better outcomes than clients who did not receive a social work practice intervention. There was wide variation based on agency auspice and whether the study was conducted by an internal or external investigator.

Gorey, Kevin M., Bruce A. Thyer, and Debra E. Pawluck. 1998. "Differential Effectiveness of Prevalent Social Work Practice Models: A Meta-Analysis." *Social Work* 43:269–78. [Chapter 13]

This meta-analysis of 45 articles looked to see whether social work practice effectiveness differed by practice orientation. Included were studies using a group design with a focus on individuals, groups, or families. There were no differences in the effectiveness of the different intervention models. Personal orientations were more effective with individual clients, while system and structural orientations were more effective when the target was not the individual but another system such as the family or an organization.

Hann, Danette, Kristin Winter, and Paul Jacobsen. 1999. "Measurement of Depressive Symptoms in Cancer Patients: Evaluation of the Center for Epidemiological Studies Depression Scale (CES-D)." *Journal of Psychosomatic Research* 46:4387–443. [Chapter 3]

This study examined the reliability and validity of the CES-D in women with and without breast cancer. There were 117 women with cancer and 62 women without cancer. The CES-D demonstrated good internal consistency and moderate test-retest reliability. Construct validity was demonstrated using measures of fatigue, anxiety, and mental health functioning.

Harrison, R. Steven, Scott Boyle, and O. William Farley. 1999. "Evaluating the Outcomes of Family-Based Intervention for Troubled Children: A Pretest-Posttest Study. *Research on Social Work Practice* 9:640–55. [Chapter 6]

A one-group pretest-posttest design was used to study the effectiveness of a 12-week family-based intervention for children. Parents learned parenting skills, while both parents and children learned communication skills, and anger and stress management. Improvements were identified in areas such as family cohesion, family conflict, spending time together, family time together, time spent in community, mental health of parents, parenting style, and behavior.

Jensen, Carla. 1994. "Psychosocial Treatment of Depression in Women: Nine Single-Subject Evaluations," *Research on Social Work Practice* 4:267–82. [Chapter 7]

A nonconcurrent, multiple baseline design was used to test the effectiveness of a short-term model integrating both cognitive behavioral therapy and interpersonal psychotherapy to reduce depressive symptoms. All nine clients had reduced levels of depression during the B phase and in a subsequent six-month follow-up.

Johnson, Christina and Jeannie Golden. 1997. "Generalization of Social Skills to Peer Interactions in a Child with Language Delays." *Behavioral-Interventions* 12:133–47. [Chapter 7]

A multiple baseline design across target problems was used to determine if both prompting and reinforcement would have a positive impact on different aspects of peer interactions for a child with language delays. Improvements were found in each aspect, with the changes during the intervention phases, thereby ruling out the effects of events.

Korr, Wynne S. and Antoine Joseph. 1996. "Effects of Local Conditions on Program Outcomes: Analysis of Contradictory Findings from Two Programs for Homeless Mentally Ill." *Journal of Health and Social Policy* 8:41–53. [Chapter 10]

The same case management program to promote independent living for homeless, mentally ill people succeeded in one site but failed in another site. To explain this contradictory outcome, the authors examined client characteristics, and the organizational and community context. The reasons why clients were homeless differed by site; at Site 1, clients had typically been evicted from apartments while at Site 2, clients had become homeless because of family disputes. The available housing within the community differed by site; at Site 1, there were many single-room occupancy options while at Site 2, there were only board and care facilities. These differences may explain the different results.

Lee, Barrett A., Sue Hize Jones, and David W. Lewis. 1990. "Public Beliefs about the Causes of Homelessness." *Social Forces* 69:253–65. [Chapter 1]

A representative sample of 293 Nashville, Tennessee, residents was interviewed by phone about attitudes toward homelessness and experiences with homeless people. Survey respondents emphasized structural forces and bad luck over individualistic factors as causes of homelessness. The survey results also gave some idea of the basis for people's opinions about homelessness: Individuals who had less education and more conservative political beliefs were more likely than others to think that homelessness was a matter of personal choice. Personal contact also made a difference: People who had been panhandled by a homeless person were more likely to think that homelessness was a matter of personal choice, whereas those who had an informal conversation with a homeless person about something other than money were less likely to believe that homelessness was a matter of personal choice.

Lewis, Robert E., Elaine Walton, and Mark W. Fraser. 1995. "Examining Family Reunification Services: A Process Analysis of a Successful Experiment." *Research on Social Work Practice* 5:259–82. [Chapter 5]

The authors wanted to identify treatment factors that distinguished between children who were reunified with their families and children who did not return home. Successful outcomes occurred when caseworkers could focus on treatment goals involving building skills such as communication skills, parenting skills, and anger management and goals about school performance and compliance with family rules. Failure occurred when caseworkers had to devote time to transportation or phone calls with the client and family regarding family crises. Failure to reunify was also more likely when caseworkers had to focus on clarifying goals and crisis or conflict management.

Mitchell, Christopher G. 1999. "Treating Anxiety in a Managed Care Setting: A Controlled Comparison of Medication Alone Versus Medication Plus." *Research on Social Work Practice* 9:188–200. [Chapter 3]

This was a study of the impact of an eight-week cognitive behavioral group treatment for panic disorders using a wait list to create a matched, nonequivalent comparison group design. The comparison group received medication while the experimental group received medication plus the group therapy. The experimental group had statistically significantly fewer symptoms of anxiety.

Morrill, Calvin, Christine Yalda, Madeleine Adelman, Michael Musheno, and Cindy Bejarano. 2000. "Telling Tales in School: Youth Culture and Conflict Narratives." *Law & Society Review* 34:521–65. [Chapter 12]

This narrative analysis of study of youth violence used a narrative survey in which students in ninth-grade English classes at one high school were asked to write a story about a time they experienced a conflict with another student.

Radloff, Lenore. 1977. "The CES-D Scale: A Self-Report Depression Scale for Research in the General Population." *Applied Psychological Measurement* 1:385–401. [Chapter 3]

Radloff describes the development of the Center for Epidemiologic Studies Depression Scale and its psychometric properties. There was high internal consistency and adequate test-retest reliability. The scale had construct validity, correlating with other related measures as well as factorial validity.

Ross, Catherine E. 1990. "Work, Family, and the Sense of Control: Implications for the Psychological Well-Being of Women and Men." Proposal submitted to the National Science Foundation. Columbus: The Ohio State University. [Chapter 8]

This study is an investigation of the relationship between family and work roles, sense of control, and mental health. A national probability sample of 2,031 adult Americans was contacted by telephone and selected with random digit dialing. Publications from this research focused on the relationship between healthy lifestyle, perceived health, and physical impairment and income, gender, parenthood, and anger.

Rossi, Peter H. 1989. *Down and Out in America: The Origins of Homelessness.* Chicago, IL: University of Chicago Press. [Chapter 1]

A survey of homeless and other extremely poor people in Chicago was conducted to determine, in part, why people become homeless. Cluster sampling techniques were used to select shelter users as well as homeless people found late at night on blocks selected for the likelihood that they would have homeless people. Homeless people were extremely poor but had more health problems, particularly substance abuse and mental illness, than extremely poor people who were housed.

Roth, Dee. 1989. "Homelessness in Ohio: A Statewide Epidemiological Study." Pp. 145–63 in *Homelessness in the United States, Volume 1: State Surveys,* edited by Jamshid A. Momeni. New York: Greenwood Press. [Chapter 1]

Multistage survey of homeless people and service providers in Ohio. The key informant survey found wide variation among staff in shelters and mental health agencies about the number and characteristics of homeless people. The survey of more than 900 homeless people selected in rural, urban, and mixed counties found a diverse population with many health problems.

Sacks, Stanley, Karen McKendrick, George DeLeon, Michael T. French, and Kathryn E. McCollister. 2002. "Benefit-Cost Analysis of a Modified Therapeutic Community for Mentally Ill Chemical Abusers." *Evaluation and Program Planning* 25:137–48. [Chapter 10]

This is a cost-benefit analysis of a modified therapeutic community (TC) in comparison to standard treatment. Employment status and earnings, criminal activity, and use of health services were measured. The TC program had a substantial benefit relative to its costs.

Sands, Robert G. and Robin S. Goldberg-Glen. 2000. Factors Associated with Stress among Grandparents Raising Their Grandchildren." *Family Relations: Interdisciplinary Journal of Applied Family Studies* 49:97–105. [Chapter 2]

A cross-sectional survey looked at the association between social support, stressors, and anxiety for grandparents raising grandchildren. The sample included 129 grandparents. The age of the grandparent, psychological and physical problems in the grandchildren, and the lack of family cohesion were related to higher levels of anxiety.

Schutt, Russell K., Suzanne Gunston, and John O'Brien. 1992. "The Impact of AIDS Prevention Efforts on AIDS Knowledge and Behavior among Sheltered Homeless Adults." *Sociological Practice Review* 3(1):1–7. [Chapter 3]

Interviewers surveyed homeless people living in shelters to determine what they knew about HIV transmission and AIDS, whether they had been exposed to any prevention activities, and what effect the exposure might have had on their knowledge and on their risk-related behaviors. Respondents were selected from three large shelters using systematic random sampling procedures; one of these shelters had hosted an active AIDS prevention program. There was no association between the average AIDS knowledge score and exposure to prevention activities. However, exposure to specific prevention activities was associated with more knowledge about the specific risks the activities were designed to reduce.

Shapiro, Janet R. and Sarah C. Mangelsdoff. 1994. "The Determinants of Parenting Competence in Adolescent Mothers." *Journal of Youth and Adolescence* 23:621–41. [Chapter 3]

This study explored predictors of parenting ability among 58 adolescent mothers. Participants completed questionnaires and were videotaped to measure life stress, social support, well-being, self-esteem, maternal efficacy, the ability to interpret the infant's emotions, and parental ability.

Sherman, Lawrence W. and Richard A. Berk. 1984. "The Specific Deterrent Effects of Arrest for Domestic Assault." *American Sociological Review,* 49:261–72. [Chapter 2]

A field experiment was used to determine whether arresting accused abusers on the spot would deter repeat incidents, as predicted by deterrence theory. Police in Minneapolis, Minnesota, were randomly assigned domestic assault cases to result either in an arrest, in an order that the offending spouse leave the house for eight hours, or in some type of verbal advice by the police officers. Accused batterers who were arrested had lower recidivism rates than those who were ordered to leave the house or were just warned. Several replications of this experiment produced different results.

Silvestre, Anthony J. 1994. "Brokering: A Process for Establishing Long-Term and Stable Links with Gay Male Communities for Research and Public Health Education." *AIDS Education and Prevention* 6:65–73. [Chapter 4]

This study describes challenges and techniques used to recruit homosexual and bisexual men into an epidemiological study of HIV infection. A brokering system in which researchers and public health officials exchanged resources with formal and informal leaders in the gay community was used.

Snow, David A. and Leon Anderson. 1987. "Identity Work among the Homeless: The Verbal Construction and Avowal of Personal Identities." *American Journal of Sociology* 92: 1336–71. [Chapter 1]

This field study of homeless people in Austin, Texas, used a participant observation method. Homeless people were followed through their daily routines and asked about their lives over a period of one year. Six homeless people were studied more intensively with taped, in-depth life-history interviews. The verbal forms used by homeless individuals to adjust to their homelessness included distancing, embracement, and fictive storytelling.

Thorne, Barrie. 1993. *Gender Play: Girls and Boys in School.* New Brunswick, NJ: Rutgers University Press. [Chapter 9]

A participant observation study explored children's social interaction at two similar public elementary schools in California and Michigan. Thorne took the role of complete observer after receiving permission from school authorities to observe in classrooms and on playgrounds. The research focused on children's social relations, how they organized and gave meaning to social situations, and how children and adults create and re-create gender in their daily interactions.

Walsh, Joseph. 1994. "Social Support Resource Outcomes for the Clients of Two Assertive Community Treatment Teams." *Research on Social Work Practice* 4: 448–463. [Chapter 6]

An ex post facto comparison group design was used to test whether group interventions plus case management as opposed to only case management was more effective in enhancing social support for mental health clients. The only statistically significant difference was that participants in the experimental group had larger personal support networks. There were no other differences in various dimensions of social support.

Walton, Elaine, Mark W. Fraser, Robert E. Lewis, Peter J. Pecora, and Wendel K. Walton. 1993. "In-home Family-Focused Reunification: An Experimental Study." *Child Welfare* 72:473–87. [Chapter 5]

An experimental design was used to examine the impact of intensive, in-home, family-based services on rates of family reunification; 110 families were recruited, with 57 randomly assigned to the experimental group and 53 to the comparison group. Families in the control group received intensive, home-based services while families in the comparison group received traditional services. A greater percentage of children in the experimental group returned to their families than children in the traditional intervention.

Wexler, Sandra and Rafael J. Engel. 1999. "Historical Trends in State-Level ADC/AFDC Benefits: Living on Less and Less." *Journal of Sociology and Social Welfare* 26:37–61. [Chapter 6]

This study used a time series design to test whether cash assistance levels would decline after the passage of the 1996 Federal Personal Responsibility and Work Opportunities Act. There was not a "rush to bottom"; rather, in constant dollars, benefit levels began to decline in 1975.

Whyte, William Foote. 1955. *Street Corner Society.* Chicago, IL: University of Chicago Press. [Chapter 9]

This classic exploratory field research study used participant observation of individuals in a poor Boston community. Whyte lived and socialized in the community, talking with many individuals and participating in a range of activities. He found a corner-gang structure that was relatively independent of the influence of older adults in the community and was based on long-term interaction and a system of mutual obligations.

Appendix B

APPENDIX B: QUESTIONS TO ASK ABOUT A RESEARCH ARTICLE

1. What is the social condition under study? What is the basic research question or problem? Try to state it in just one sentence. (Chapter 2)

2. Is the purpose of the study explanatory, evaluative, exploratory, or descriptive? Did the study have more than one purpose? (Chapter 1)

3. How did the author(s) explain the importance of the research question? Is the research question relevant to social work practice and/or social welfare policy? (Chapter 2)

4. What prior literature was reviewed? Was it relevant to the research problem? To the theoretical framework? Does the literature review appear to be adequate? Are you aware of (or can you locate) any important omitted studies? Is the literature review up-to-date? (Chapter 2)

5. Was a theoretical framework presented? What was it? Did it seem appropriate for the research question addressed? Can you think of a different theoretical perspective that might have been used? (Chapter 2)

6. Were any hypotheses stated? Were these hypotheses justified adequately in terms of the theoretical framework? In terms of prior research? (Chapter 2)

7. What were the independent and dependent variables in the hypothesis or hypotheses? Did these variables reflect the theoretical concepts as intended? What direction of association was hypothesized? Were any other variables identified as potentially important? (Chapter 2)

8. What were the major concepts in the research? Did the author(s) provide clear and complete nominal definitions for each concept? What are the nominal definitions? Were some concepts treated as unidimensional that you think might best be thought of as multidimensional? (Chapter 3)

9. How are variables operationally defined by the author(s)? Are the operational definitions adequate? Did the instruments used and the measures of the variables seem valid and reliable? How did the author(s) attempt to establish measurement reliability and measurement validity? Could any more have been done in the study to establish measurement validity? Have the measures used in the study been evaluated in terms of reliability and validity with populations similar to the study sample? (Chapter 3)

10. Was a sample of the entire population of elements used in the study? Was a probability or nonprobability sampling method used? What specific type of sampling method was used? How was the sample recruited and selected? How large is the sample? Did the authors think the sample was generally representative of the population from which it was drawn? Do you? How could you evaluate the likely generalizability of the findings to other populations? Are women and people of color adequately represented in the sample? (Chapter 4)

11. Was the response rate or participation rate reported? Does it appear likely that those who did not respond or participate were markedly different from those who did participate? Why or why not? Did the author(s) adequately discuss this issue? (Chapters 4, 8)

12. What were the units of analysis? Were they appropriate for the research question? If some groups were the units of analysis, were any statements made at any point that are open to the ecological fallacy? If individuals were the units of analysis, were any statements made at any point that suggest reductionist reasoning? (Chapter 5)

13. Was the study design cross-sectional or longitudinal, or did it use both types of data? If the design was longitudinal, what type of longitudinal design was it? Could the longitudinal design have been improved in any way, as by collecting panel data rather than trend data or by decreasing the dropout rate in a panel design? If cross-sectional data were used, could the research question have been addressed more effectively with longitudinal data? (Chapter 5)

14. Were any causal assertions made or implied in the hypotheses or in subsequent discussion? What approach was used to demonstrate the existence of causal effects? Were all five issues in establishing causal relationships addressed? What, if any, variables were controlled in the analysis to reduce the risk of spurious relationships? Should any other variables have been measured and controlled? (Chapter 5)

15. Was an experimental, single-subject, survey, participant observation, or some other research design used? How does the author describe the design? How well was this design suited to the research question posed and the specific hypotheses tested, if any? Why do you suppose the author(s) chose this particular design? (Chapters 6 to 9)

16. Did the design eliminate potential alternative explanations, and how did the design do this? How satisfied (and why) are you with the internal validity of the conclusions? (Chapter 6)

17. What is the setting for the study? Does the setting limit the generalizability of the results to other similar settings or to the broader population? Is reactivity a problem? Are there other threats to external validity? (Chapters 5, 6)

18. Was this an evaluation research project? If so, which type of evaluation was it? Which design alternatives did it use? (Chapter 10)

19. How were data collected? What were the advantages and disadvantages of the particular data collection method? (Chapter 8)

20. What did the author(s) find? Are the statistical techniques used appropriate for the level of measurement of the variables? How clearly were statistical and/or qualitative data presented and discussed? Were the results substantively important? (Chapters 11, 12)

21. Did the author(s) adequately represent the findings in the discussion and/or conclusion sections? Were conclusions well grounded in the findings? Can you think of any other interpretations of the findings? (Chapter 13)

22. Compare the study to others addressing the same research question. Did the study yield additional insights? In what ways was the study design more or less adequate than the design of previous research? (Chapter 13)

23. What additional research questions and hypotheses are suggested by the study's results? What light did the study shed on the theoretical framework used? On social work practice questions? On social policy questions? (Chapters 2, 13)

24. How well did the study live up to the guidelines for science? Do you need additional information in any areas to evaluate the study? To replicate it? (Chapter 2)

25. Did the study seem consistent with current ethical standards? Were any trade-offs made between different ethical guidelines? Was an appropriate balance struck between adherence to ethical standards and use of the most rigorous scientific practices? (Chapter 2)

Appendix C

How to Read a Research Article

The discussions of research articles throughout the text may provide all the guidance you need to read and critique research on your own. But reading about an article in bits and pieces to learn about particular methodologies is not quite the same as reading an article in its entirety to learn what the researcher found out. The goal of this appendix is to walk you through an entire research article, answering the review questions introduced in Appendix B. Of course, this is only one article, and our "walk" will take different turns than a review of other articles might take, but after this review, you should feel more confident when reading other research articles on your own.

We use an article by Christopher Mitchell (1999) on the use of cognitive behavioral therapy to treat panic disorders. This article, published in a leading journal, *Research on Social Work Practice*, has many strengths; yet, as you will see, there are gaps in the information reported by the author.

We have reproduced below each of the article review questions from Appendix B, followed by our answers to them. After each question, we indicate the chapter where the question was discussed, and after each answer, we cite the article page or pages to which we refer. You can also follow our review by reading through the article itself and noting our comments.

1. *What is the social condition under study? What is the basic research question, or problem? Try to state it in just one sentence.* (Chapter 2)

The specific concern in this study is the efficacy of short-term interventions to treat anxiety. The clearest statement of the research question is: "Do cognitive-behavioral interventions for panic disorder have an effect that goes beyond the effect of medication alone" (p. 192)?

2. *Is the purpose of the study explanatory, evaluative, exploratory, or descriptive? Did the study have more than one purpose?* (Chapter 1)

This study is evaluative in nature; the author describes it as an "outcome study" (p. 189).

3. *How did the author(s) explain the importance of the research question? Is the research question relevant to social work practice and/or social welfare policy?* (Chapter 2)

The author connects the need to evaluate short-term treatment to changes in the mental health service delivery system and the advent of managed care. He notes that "insurers increasingly scrutinize and question the expenses associated with unlimited use of mental health services. . . . Open-ended therapies have given way to highly focused, time-limited treatments with specific and clearly defined objectives" (p. 188). Because social workers are primary providers of mental health services, the findings have implications for clinical social work practice and agencies that are reimbursed by third-party payers.

4. *What prior literature was reviewed? Was it relevant to the research problem? To the theoretical framework? Does the literature review appear to be adequate? Are you aware of (or can you locate) any important omitted studies? Is the literature review up-to-date?* (Chapter 2)

The literature review includes a discussion about panic disorders and their etiology, consequences, and prevalence (pp. 189–191). The second half of the literature review focuses on treatment within a managed care setting (pp. 191–192). One problem with the literature review is that there is only a passing reference to studies about the effectiveness of cognitive behavioral therapy, and there is no description about the studies. Furthermore, the two studies referenced by the author date back to the 1980s. We leave it to you to find the more recent research.

5. *Was a theoretical framework presented? What was it? Did it seem appropriate for the research question addressed? Can you think of a different theoretical perspective that might have been used?* (Chapter 2)

The author does not present a theoretical perspective. Given the purpose of this study, it was not necessary to use a particular theoretical perspective.

6. *Were any hypotheses stated? Were these hypotheses justified adequately in terms of the theoretical framework? In terms of prior research?* (Chapter 2)

The one hypothesis in this study is, "People with panic disorder who participate in an 8-week program of cognitive-behavioral group therapy in addition to medication will have significantly lower levels of anxiety than people who receive medication alone" (pp. 192–193). The hypothesis is found in the Methods and Procedures section, which is unusual. Because the literature review describes so little research about cognitive behavioral therapy and panic disorders, the hypothesis lacks empirical support. The lengthy description of cognitive behavioral therapy suggests that the hypothesis rests on practice experience.

7. *What were the independent and dependent variables in the hypothesis or hypotheses? What direction of association was hypothesized? Were any other variables identified as potentially important?* (Chapter 2)

The independent variable is cognitive-behavioral intervention while the dependent variable is anxiety. It is hypothesized that the intervention will reduce anxiety level. No other variables were identified as important.

8. *What were the major concepts in the research? Did the author(s) provide clear and complete nominal definitions for each concept? What are the nominal definitions? Were some concepts treated as unidimensional that you think might best be thought of as multidimensional?* (Chapter 3)

There are several key concepts in this study: panic disorder, anxiety, and cognitive behavioral group intervention. The author provides nominal definitions for each term. A "panic disorder is a subtype of anxiety that is characterized by discrete periods of intense apprehension or fear" (p. 189). The clinical criteria for a panic disorder are derived from the *Diagnostic and Statistical Manual of Mental Disorders,* 4th edition, and are provided in the literature review (pp. 189–190). Anxiety is defined as "inordinate worry and nervousness manifested in the cognitive, somatic, and behavioral domains" (p. 193). Cognitive behavioral therapy is introduced as "techniques that include cognitive restructuring, breathing and relaxation techniques, and phobic desensitization" (p. 192).

9. *How are variables operationally defined by the author(s)? Are the operational definitions adequate? Did the instruments used and the measures of the variables seem valid and reliable? How did the author(s) attempt to establish measurement reliability and measurement validity? Could any more have been done in the study to establish measurement validity? Have the measures used in the study been evaluated in terms of reliability and validity with populations similar to the study sample?* (Chapter 3)

The author provides information about the group intervention and summarizes the content covered in each week of the intervention. Anxiety is measured using the Somatic, Cognitive, Behavioral Anxiety Inventory (SCBAI). The author reports the number of subscales, the number of items in the scale, scoring, and the interpretation of scores. Measurement reliability and validity are established by reporting split-half reliability coefficients for each of the subscales, and this suggests that it has strong concurrent validity (p. 194). The lack of detailed information about measurement reliability and validity is one of the weaknesses of this study. There is information from only one study and no data about the strength of the concurrent validity, so we are left to trust the author's conclusion. Because the author did not report the characteristics of the sample used to establish reliability and validity, we do not know whether the findings apply to the study sample.

10. *Was a sample of the entire population of elements used in the study? Was a probability or nonprobability sampling method used? What specific type of sampling method was used? How was the sample recruited and selected? How large is the sample? Are women and people of color adequately represented in the sample? Did the authors think the sample was generally representative of the population from which it was drawn? Do you? How could you evaluate the likely generalizability of the findings to other populations?* (Chapter 1, 4)

The sample is described as a "convenience sample of 56 participants consist[ing] of adult men and women with panic disorder who voluntarily sought treatment in a large HMO in Washington, DC" (p. 193). We do not know how they were recruited for the study. While the author recognizes that the sample lacks generalizability, he does note that the demographic composition of his participants is similar to the overall panic disorder population. The sample consists primarily of women (77%); 55% of the sample is African American, 11% are other people of color, and 34% are Caucasian (Table 1, p. 196).

11. *Was the response rate or participation rate reported? Does it appear likely that those who did not respond or participate were markedly different from those who did participate? Why or why not? Did the author(s) adequately discuss this issue?* (Chapters 4, 8)

The participation rate is not reported by the author. While we know that 56 people participated in the study, we do not know how many people refused to participate.

12. *What were the units of analysis? Were they appropriate for the research question? If some groups were the units of analysis, were any statements made at any point that are open to the ecological fallacy? If individuals were the units of analysis, were any statements made at any point that suggest reductionist reasoning?* (Chapter 5)

The unit of analysis is the individual. There are no statements suggesting reductionist reasoning.

13. *Was the study design cross-sectional or longitudinal, or did it use both types of data? If the design was longitudinal, what type of longitudinal design was it? Could the longitudinal design have been improved in any way, as by collecting panel data rather than trend data or by decreasing the dropout rate in a panel design? If cross-sectional data were used, could the research question have been addressed more effectively with longitudinal data?* (Chapter 5)

Because of the experimental design used in this study, we are less concerned with this question. The findings and the clinical significance would have been strengthened had there been a follow-up several months after the conclusion of treatment.

14. *Were any causal assertions made or implied in the hypotheses or in subsequent discussion? What approach was used to demonstrate the existence of causal effects? Were all five issues in establishing causal relationships addressed? What, if any, variables were controlled in the analysis to reduce the risk of spurious relationships? Should any other variables have been measured and controlled?* (Chapter 5)

The causal assertion is that changes in anxiety level will be due to the intervention, cognitive behavioral therapy. The experimental design used in this study is sufficient to establish an association and time order but leaves open the issue of spuriousness as we describe in the next question. The literature review suggests that cognitive behavioral therapy can trigger the desired change in anxiety. We do not know what effect contextual variables such as the setting (an HMO) or the community might have on the findings.

15. *Was an experimental, single-subject, survey, participant observation, or some other research design used? How does the author describe the design? How well was this design suited to the research question posed and the specific hypotheses tested, if any? Why do you suppose the author(s) chose this particular design?* (Chapters 6 to 9)

This quasi-experimental design is described by the author as "a comparative pretest-posttest design with nonequivalent groups" (p. 193). Four treatment groups of 8 to 10 participants were formed on a first-come basis. Each participant in the experimental condition received medication and cognitive behavioral therapy. The comparison group received medication alone and consisted of clients on the wait list or those who had declined group therapy. The design does provide a plausible method to compare the effects of the intervention. This is a reasonable design given the practicalities of agency-based research and the need to serve clients as they come to the agency.

16. *Did the design eliminate potential alternative explanations, and how did the design do this? How satisfied (and why) are you with the internal validity of the conclusions?* (Chapter 6)

There are threats to internal validity because the author uses a quasi-experimental design. One problem is selection bias. To demonstrate the similarity of the two groups, the author compares the groups by age, gender, marital status, education, and race, as well as panic disorder history and frequency of attack. There are no statistically significant differences between groups on these variables, suggesting that selection might not be problematic. On the other hand, the author notes that the pretest scores on the subscales were greater for the experimental group. This suggests that those who went into the treatment group might have been more in need of help and more motivated to deal with their anxiety. The failure to statistically test whether the scores are comparable leaves doubt about the lack of a selection bias. Another threat is statistical regression. Because the experimental group starts with higher scores, the lower posttest scores might be due to regression to the mean. These explanations cannot be ruled out.

17. *What is the setting for the study? Does the setting limit the generalizability of the results to other similar settings or to the broader population? Is reactivity a problem? Are there other threats to external validity?* (Chapters 5, 6)

The study is conducted in a large HMO in Washington, D.C. It is possible that there are systematic differences between people who are and who are not HMO members. Reactivity to testing, selection, and treatment are not likely to be problems.

18. *Was this an evaluation research project? If so, which type of evaluation was it? Which design alternatives did it use?* (Chapter 10)

This is an agency-based outcome evaluation conducted by an external evaluator.

19. *How were data collected? What were the advantages and disadvantages of the particular data collection method?* (Chapter 8)

Data were collected using a four-page self-administered questionnaire given at the beginning and end of the program. This method of data collection eliminates interviewer effects such as social desirability. There is a possibility of a response set as we do not know if any of the scale items were worded in reverse.

20. *What did the author(s) find? Are the statistical techniques used appropriate for the level of measurement of the variables? How clearly were statistical and/or qualitative data presented and discussed? Were the results substantively important?* (Chapters 11, 12)

The results supported the hypothesis "that those who participated in the therapy group in addition to medication experienced a greater reduction in anxiety than those who received medication alone" (pp. 195–196). Statistical data are presented clearly using tables to illustrate the differences. No qualitative data are presented. The choice of ANOVA to compare the groups on each of the subscales was a suitable analytic technique but not necessarily the best technique for this type of analysis. The author notes that while the group differences may be statistically significant, the findings may not be clinically significant.

21. *Did the author(s) adequately represent the findings in the discussion and/or conclusion sections? Were conclusions well grounded in the findings? Can you think of any other interpretations of the findings?* (Chapter 13)

The findings are briefly discussed in Discussion and Applications for Social Work Practice (p. 197) and are linked back to the literature review. The discussion does go beyond the data to talk about the unique contributions of social work practice when using cognitive behavioral therapy. This information either should have been reported in the opening discussion about cognitive behavioral therapy or should be linked to how the author used the treatment in this study.

22. *Compare the study to others addressing the same research question. Did the study yield additional insights? In what ways was the study design more or less adequate than the design of previous research?* (Chapter 13)

The study contributed to social work practice by investigating the application of cognitive behavioral therapy to panic disorders. The findings complement what we know about cognitive behavioral therapy when applied to other disorders such as depression. The design is similar to previous studies conducted in based on agency settings.

23. *What additional research questions and hypotheses are suggested by the study's results? What light did the study shed on the theoretical framework used? On social work practice questions? On social policy questions?* (Chapters 2, 13)

The article suggests that "cognitive-behavioral approaches need to draw more attention to the concept of the person-in-environment" (p. 198). The author suggests that more work needs to be done in integrating the effects of environmental factors into the therapy.

24. *How well did the study live up to the guidelines for science? Do you need additional information in any areas to evaluate the study? To replicate it?* (Chapter 2)

The study clearly involves a test of ideas against empirical reality; in this case, a test of a clinical intervention and its impact on clients. The researcher carried out the investigation systematically and provided detail about the procedures used to carry out the study. The author does not clarify his own assumptions, but there is an assumption based on the literature that the treatment should be effective. Despite this, the author does note that "given these small proportions of explained variance, one may question how critical the therapy really was in effecting change" (pp. 196–197). The author specified the meaning of key terms, as required in scientific research. The author may be too accepting of current knowledge, and his conclusions may be stronger than what the findings suggest. In general, the study seems to exemplify adherence to basic scientific guidelines and to be very replicable.

25. *Did the study seem consistent with current ethical standards? Were any trade-offs made between different ethical guidelines? Was an appropriate balance struck between adherence to ethical standards and use of the most rigorous scientific practices?* (Chapter 2)

The author specifically states that "the entire research design and methodology was reviewed and approved for use by the Institutional Review Board (IRB) of the HMO" (p. 193). The author also notes that enrollment into a cognitive behavioral group therapy occurred after giving informed consent. There was an appropriate balance between ethical standards and the use of rigorous scientific standards. For example, the researcher "could not [ethically and practically] monitor and enforce compliance with the medication regime" (p. 198).

Treating Anxiety in a Managed Care Setting: A Controlled Comparison of Medication Alone Versus Medication Plus Cognitive-Behavioral Group Therapy

Christopher G. Mitchell
University of Illinois at Chicago

Objective: A controlled comparison of the effects of medication alone and medication in conjunction with cognitive-behavioral group therapy in the treatment of panic disorder. Method: A quasi-experimental research design was used to compare posttest anxiety scores of clients who received medication alone (n = 26) and those who received weekly therapy in addition to medication (n = 30). The Somatic, Cognitive, Behavioral Anxiety Inventory, a 36-item Likert scale, was used to measure anxiety. One treatment consisted of the prescribed use of medication; the second treatment consisted of medication plus 8 weeks of cognitive-behavioral therapy. Results: Analysis of variance revealed significant differences in posttest anxiety scores between the two groups. Members of the medication plus therapy group had lower posttest anxiety scores than those who received medication alone. Conclusions: The findings support the hypothesis that medication in conjunction with cognitive-behavioral therapy is more efficacious than medication alone to treat panic disorder.

Over the past two decades, there have been significant changes in the provision of mental health services in the United States. Much of this change has resulted from pressure brought on by the advent and subsequent expansion of the principles of managed care in mental health service delivery. The exponential growth of managed care has affected social workers and other mental health practitioners in numerous ways. Insurers increasingly scrutinize and question the expenses associated with unlimited use of mental health services. This has resulted in trends toward reducing the unnecessary use of psychotherapy and related health services. Open-ended therapies have given way to highly focused, time-limited treatments with specific and clearly defined objectives (Austad & Berman, 1991; Bennett, 1986). Although managed care organizations may still allow some degree of flexibility regarding

Author's Note: Correspondence may be addressed to Christopher G. Mitchell, D.S.W., Jane Addams College of Social Work (MC 309), University of Illinois at Chicago, 1040 W. Harrison Street, Chicago, IL 60607; e-mail: cgm@uic.edu.

 Research on Social Work Practice, Vol. 9 No. 2, March 1999 188-200
© 1999 Sage Publications, Inc.

intervention, social workers within a managed care setting increasingly rely on standardized treatments and follow established treatment protocol for specific disorders (Pigott & Broskowski, 1985; VandenBos & DeLeon, 1988). This undeniably raises issues regarding the quality of care and respect for the uniqueness of the client and his or her needs.

Although it is true that cost containment and cost-effectiveness were the initial factors that prompted the shift from long-term, open-ended psychotherapy to short-term, limited therapy with specific goals, subsequent success in clinical practice reinforced this trend (Austad, 1996). Social workers began to see that short-term therapies produced tangible, empirical results that reduced client stress and improved overall functioning (Piper & Joyce, 1996). In addition, economical success in achieving specific goals reduces cost and thus can make mental health services more available to diverse populations, including those who formerly would not have been able to afford such care (Garfield & Bergin, 1986). It is clear, then, that the forces of managed care and cost containment present both challenges and opportunities to social workers and other providers of mental health services.

Demonstrating the need for clinical social work services in treating anxiety and other mental health conditions is one such challenge. This article presents the findings of an outcome study that compared the effects of medication alone and medication combined with therapy to treat panic disorder, one of the principal anxiety disorders.

PANIC DISORDER: A BRIEF LITERATURE REVIEW

According to the *Diagnostic and Statistical Manual of Mental Disorders, fourth edition (DSM-IV;* American Psychiatric Association, 1994), panic disorder is a subtype of anxiety that is characterized by discrete periods of intense apprehension or fear and that includes at least four somatic symptoms. The somatic features could include any combination of the following:

1. shortness of breath or smothering sensations
2. dizziness, unsteady feelings, or faintness
3. palpitations or accelerated heart rate
4. trembling or shaking
5. sweating
6. choking
7. nausea or abdominal distress
8. depersonalization or derealization
9. numbness or tingling sensations
10. flushes

11. chestpain or discomfort
12. fear of dying
13. fear of going crazy or of losing control

In addition, to meet the criteria for panic disorder at least some of these attacks must occur spontaneously when the patient is not exposed to a fear-inducing stimulus or in a situation in which the person is the focal point of other people's attention (APA, 1994). At least four of these anxiety attacks must occur within a 4-week period, or one of the attacks must be followed by a period of at least a month of persistent fear of having another attack.

As the disorder progresses, panic attacks increase in frequency, and phobias emerge as the person develops significant anticipatory anxiety (i.e., fear of having another panic attack) and avoidance behaviors (Katon, 1994). People with panic attacks will begin to make associations between the situations or settings where they experience a panic attack and the panic attack itself. For example, if a person has a panic attack on the subway, he or she may begin to associate the subway with the attacks and become increasingly anxious the next time he or she rides the subway, fearing that an attack may occur at any moment (anticipatory anxiety). The anticipatory anxiety may generate somatic features, and a full panic attack ensues. This anxiety and the experience of panic may eventually lead the person to avoid the subway and to develop a phobia. If left unchecked and untreated, these phobias can multiply, and people become increasingly debilitated as their excursions beyond safe environments become less frequent.

Panic disorder occurs frequently in the general population, with about 3 million people with the disorder in the United States. Numerous studies have estimated that the prevalence of panic disorder is 1.6% to 2.9% for women and 0.4% to 1.7% for men (Eaton & Keyl, 1995). The prevalence of panic disorder appears to be comparably distributed across racial groups. However, Horwath, Johnson, and Hornig (1994) found that African Americans are often misdiagnosed and are less likely than non-African Americans to seek treatment from a mental health professional. Negative attitudes toward psychotherapy, greater reliance on informal support networks, and the stigma associated with mental illness are cited as principal reasons for this lower use (Friedman, 1994).

The exact etiology of panic disorder is unknown, although most research suggests that it results from a combination of biological and psychological factors (McNally, 1994). From a biological perspective, recent medical research has focused on the role of neurotransmitters in the etiology of panic attacks and has focused specifically on levels of norepinephrine and serotonin in the brain (Asnis & van Praag, 1995). In addition to biochemical approaches to explaining panic attacks, some research suggests that people with panic disorder suffer from hyperventilation syndrome. This theory suggests that overbreathing, which is fairly common in anxious people, reduces levels of carbon dioxide in the bloodstream and sets off a series of physiological reactions that lead to symptoms much like those of a panic attack (Hibbert & Chan, 1989).

Additional research suggests that psychological causes play a crucial role in the etiology of panic disorder. One of the earliest studies (Clark & Hemsley, 1982) investigated individual differences in the affective response to hyperventilation. The study revealed great variation in the subjects' perception of the sensation of hyperventilation. Thus, the cognitive model proposes that panic attacks result from the catastrophic misinterpretation of certain bodily sensations (Beck, 1988; Beck & Emery, 1985). As a theory focusing on the misinterpretation of sensations, the cognitive-behavioral approach subsumes the biological etiology of panic disorder outlined above. The catastrophic misinterpretation involves misinterpreting the sensations as much more dangerous than they are and believing that they indicate imminent physical disaster. For example, an otherwise healthy individual perceives a rapid heart rate as evidence of an impending heart attack and certain death; a sensation of breathlessness (perhaps due to physical exertion) is catastrophically misinterpreted as respiratory distress. Not only do these interpretations catastrophize the sensation, but they dramatically increase the person's level of anxiety and thus further exacerbate the physical sensation.

TREATING ANXIETY IN A MANAGED CARE SETTING

Despite the high prevalence of panic disorder and the reluctance of some people to seek treatment, panic disorder remains one of the most responsive and treatable mental illnesses (Katon, 1994). As evidenced by the contrasting biological and psychological theories regarding the cause of panic disorder, it is understandable that treatments for panic disorder and other anxiety disorders will vary depending on the practitioner's perspective. Psychiatrists and other medical researchers who accept the primacy of biological factors will most likely endorse psychopharmacological treatments. The most commonly prescribed medications to treat anxiety include the drugs classified as selective serotonin reuptake inhibitor (SSRI) antidepressants (e.g., Paxil, Prozac) and benzodiazepines (e.g., Xanax, Ativan, Klonopin) (Asnis & van Praag, 1995; Katon, 1994). The use of such medications is not without possible complications, however. The complications typically affect only a very small number of patients but could include physical side effects; the potential for dependence on the medication; the potential for abuse, especially among clients with previous substance abuse problems; and numerous medication discontinuation problems (Raj & Sheehan, 1995). Given these potential negative effects, many clients express great reluctance to use medication, especially as a long-term solution to their anxiety.

In contrast to medical doctors, social workers focus more on the psychological and environmental factors and therefore promote psychotherapeutic interventions (Himle & Fischer, 1998). Among the various therapy approaches, cognitive-behavioral therapy has demonstrated significant effectiveness (Beck, 1988; Beck & Emery 1985). The content of cognitive-behavioral therapy typically employs techniques that include cognitive restructuring, breathing and relaxation techniques, and phobic desensitization.

In many managed care settings, particularly those health maintenance organizations (HMOs) where mental health services are provided by the HMO itself rather than by an external network of community-based practitioners, treating anxiety requires a high degree of collaboration between physicians or psychiatrists and social workers. Although social workers and other mental health professionals may disagree on the primacy of medication, it nonetheless is frequently used and is often the first intervention in the treatment of anxiety and other mental health problems (Kisch, 1991). Although medication may have demonstrated effectiveness, it cannot be the sole intervention for treating problems such as anxiety. In addition to the possible side effects already described, the effects of medication are often short-lived after discontinuation, often do not address the core of the problem, and can foster patient reliance on the medication and the physician to deal with one's problems. Such effects are at variance with social work's traditional commitment to client empowerment and the strengths perspective (Rapp, 1992). This study, therefore, seeks to demonstrate the need for psychotherapeutic interventions in addition to medication.

METHODS AND PROCEDURES

This study is based on data collected for dissertation research (Mitchell, 1997) and addresses the research question: Do cognitive-behavioral interventions for panic disorder have an effect that goes beyond the effect of medication alone? The research tested the following hypothesis: People with panic disorder who participate in an 8-week program of cognitive-behavioral group therapy in addition to medication will have significantly lower levels of anxiety than people who receive medication alone. To examine this question, this study used a comparative pretest-posttest design with nonequivalent groups.

Clients

The convenience sample of 56 participants consisted of adult men and women diagnosed with panic disorder who voluntarily sought treatment at a large HMO in Washington, D.C. The entire research design and methodology was reviewed and approved for use by the Institutional Review Board (IRB) of the HMO. To participate in this study, the subjects met the following criteria: (a) 18 years of age or older, (b) a diagnosis of panic disorder, (c) capable of giving informed consent, and (d) no other documented comorbid mental disorder.

On meeting these criteria and giving informed consent, participants enrolled in the cognitive-behavioral group therapy on a first-come/first-served basis. The therapy groups were limited to 8 to 10 participants. Four separate therapy groups were needed to acquire a sample size of 30 people who received the therapy. The participants who received medication alone were either on the waiting list for the therapy group or declined participation in the therapy group. All people receiving medication alone were given the option to participate in the therapy group.

Outcome Measures

All data were collected through a four-page self-report questionnaire consisting of forced response items, which was administered at the beginning and at the end of the program. The questionnaire consisted of a standardized scale to measure anxiety as well as numerous additional questions that gathered descriptive information regarding the participants and their symptoms of panic disorder including: age, gender, ethnicity, marital status, and level of education, as well as frequency, duration, and history of panic attacks.

The dependent variable, anxiety, was conceptualized as inordinate worry and nervousness manifested in the cognitive, somatic, and behavioral domains. It was operationalized by the Somatic, Cognitive, Behavioral Anxiety Inventory (SCBAI) (Lehrer & Woolfolk, 1982). The SCBAI is a 36-item, 9-point Likert-type scale composed of three subscales measuring the somatic (hyperventilation), cognitive (worrying), and behavioral (social avoidance) dimensions of anxiety. Although actual norms for the scale are not reported, scores range from 0 to 128 on the somatic subscale, 0 to 88 on the cognitive subscale, and 0 to 72 on the behavioral subscale; higher scores indicate higher levels of anxiety. The scale is predicated on previous research that suggests that different components of anxiety do not necessarily correlate highly with each other. As a result, the subscale scores often have greater meaning than the full scale anxiety score (Fischer & Corcoran, 1994). Although more contemporary assessment scales exist, the SCBAI scale is especially appropriate for this research because the various dimensions of anxiety—the cognitive, somatic, and behavioral—may respond differently to a particular intervention.

Reliability and validity for the SCBAI are reported on each of the respective subscales rather than on the instrument as a whole. The subscales have strong reliability, with split-half reliability coefficients of .93 for the somatic factor, .92 for the behavioral factor, and .92 for the cognitive factor. The scale has strong concurrent validity (Fischer & Corcoran, 1994).

Treatments

Type of treatment—medication alone or medication in conjunction with therapy—was the independent variable. The medication intervention was defined as the prescribed use of benzodiazepine and/or SSRI medication as directed by a staff psychiatrist. To ensure medication regimen consistency, the psychiatrists adhered to uniform dosage guidelines. The therapy was conceptualized as a program of group therapy based on cognitive-behavioral therapy and was operationalized as an 8-week program of psychoeducational group therapy with each weekly session lasting for 1.5 hours (Bourne, 1995). The content covered during each of the 8 weeks is listed below:

Week 1. Introduction. Goals of the group. Causes and symptoms of panic attacks. Review of the functions of the central nervous system. Profile of a person with panic disorder. Instruction on abdominal breathing.

Week 2. Managing anxiety and lifestyle changes. Developing a personal anxiety management program.

Week 3. Physical relaxation techniques. Progressive muscle relaxation. Role of physical exercise.

Week 4. Mental relaxation techniques. Mental visualizations. Explanation of the mind-body connection.

Week 5. The panic cycle and how to avert a panic attack. Interoceptive fear. Desensitizing oneself to interoceptive cues. Coping strategies.

Week 6. Phobic desensitization—imaginary and in vivo. Role of support people. Video presentation on panic disorder.

Week 7. Cognitive distortions and their effect on anxiety. Typical cognitive distortions of people with anxiety. Countering cognitive distortions.

Week 8. Core beliefs and anxiety. Review of group strategies. Conclusion. Follow-up alternatives.

To ensure treatment integrity and uniformity, all treatment groups had identical content and were conducted by the same social worker.

RESULTS

Multivariate statistical analysis was used to test the hypothesis and to assess relationships among the variables. The specific analysis techniques included independent samples *t*-tests, chi square, and analysis of variance (ANOVA). The .05 level of statistical significance was used for all hypothesis testing.

Before testing the major research hypothesis, the two groups were compared according to the key descriptive variables. The results are presented in Table 1. As the data illustrate, the two groups were basically similar according to these variables. It is also interesting to note that the demographics of this particular sample largely reflect the demographics of the overall panic disorder population (Eaton & Keyl, 1995).

Having demonstrated that the groups were essentially similar and therefore comparable on the dependent variables, analysis of variance (ANOVA) was conducted to examine differences between pretests and posttest scores for the two groups. The mean pretest and posttest scores are listed in Table 2, and the results of the ANOVA are presented in Table 3.

Examination of the mean scores in Table 2 reveals that the pretest scores of the subscales are noticeably higher in the experimental group than in the comparison group. This raises additional concern about the comparative equivalence of the two groups. An independent samples *t*-test was used to test these pretest differences and concluded that they were not significant. This finding is consistent with the data presented in Table 1 and further supports the comparability of the groups.

Table 3 reveals significant differences in posttest scores by group for all three subscales. In other words, the results support the research hypothesis that those who participated in the therapy group in addition to medication

TABLE 1:   Selected Descriptive and Clinical Variables by Group

Variable	Therapy Group (N = 30)	Medication Group (N = 26)	Test [a]
Age			
Mean	39.27 years	36.73 years	$t = -1.16$
Range	20 to 57 years	23 to 56 years	
Gender			
Male	8 (26.7%)	5 (16.0%)	$\chi^2 = .43$
Female	22 (73.3%)	21 (84.0%)	
Marital status			
Single	10 (33.3%)	10 (38.5%)	$\chi^2 = 1.77$
Married	9 (30.0%)	6 (23.1%)	
Separated/divorced	9 (30.0%)	6 (23.1%)	
Other	2 (6.7%)	4 (15.4%)	
Education			
High school diploma or less	9 (30.0%)	6 (23.1%)	$\chi^2 = 5.16$
More than a high school diploma	21 (60.0%)	20 (76.9%)	
Race			
Black	19 (63.3%)	12 (46.0%)	$\chi^2 = 2.45$
White	8 (26.7%)	11 (42.3%)	
Other	3 (10.0%)	3 (11.5%)	
Panic disorder history			
6 months	9 (30.0%)	8 (34.8%)	$\chi^2 = .57$
6 to 12 months	9 (30.0%)	8 (34.8%)	
12 or more months	12 (40.0%)	7 (30.4%)	
Panic attack frequency			
Two per week	19 (63.3%)	22 (84.6%)	$\chi^2 = 5.70$
Three per week	11 (36.7%)	4 (15.6%)	

a. None of the statistical findings was significant at $p < .05$.

experienced a greater reduction in anxiety than those who received medication alone. More to the point, the findings demonstrate that people who received the cognitive-behavioral intervention had a more intense response to the treatment and that the treatment affected the multiple domains of anxiety. When interpreting and drawing conclusions from this study, however, it is important to examine how much of the variance in posttest scores can be explained by the use of the group therapy treatment (Hudson, Thyer, & Stocks, 1985). The ^{2} value in Table 3 is the estimate of variance explained by the intervention. The group therapy in addition to the medication explains between 10% and 14% of the variance in posttest scores; other unknown factors explain the remaining 90% to 86% of the variance. Given these small proportions of explained variance, one may question how critical the therapy

TABLE 2: Mean Pretest and Posttest Scores by Group

Subscale	Therapy Group		Medication Group	
	M	SD	M	SD
Behavioral subscale				
Pretest	34.03	16.49	30.92	13.94
Posttest	28.97	14.25	29.58	14.44
Cognitive subscale				
Pretest	57.73	13.56	54.31	11.31
Posttest	52.57	15.26	54.58	11.85
Somatic subscale				
Pretest	62.93	27.75	54.85	22.51
Posttest	47.40	23.30	48.77	16.71

TABLE 3: Analysis of Variance of the Outcome Measures by Treatment Type

Subscale	SS	df	MS	η^2	F
Behavioral subscale	674.70	1	674.70	.11	6.56*
Cognitive subscale	386.10	1	386.10	.14	8.86**
Somatic subscale	150.47	1	150.47	.10	5.19*

*$p < .05$. **$p < .01$.

really was in effecting change. Himle and Fischer (1998) address this point and cite research that posits that taking any action or participating in any credible treatment proves efficacious for those with anxiety.

DISCUSSION AND APPLICATIONS
FOR SOCIAL WORK PRACTICE

The results of this study have important implications for social work practice and the treatment of anxiety, particularly in a managed care setting. The findings of this study clearly reveal that comprehensive treatment for anxiety includes therapy as well as medication. This corroborates other research that suggests a positive interaction effect when therapy and medication are combined (Mavissakalian, 1990).

These findings are not without limitations, however. When considering the findings of this study, it is important to recall that this sample of convenience was composed of people with panic disorder who voluntarily sought and followed through with treatment. These voluntary participants who actively sought treatment may have been more debilitated and/or more responsive than other people with panic disorder in the general public. Therefore some of the reduction in anxiety could be a result of nontreatment factors such as regression to the mean. In addition, because the participants volunteered for the therapy group, self-selection bias may have occurred. As a result, the external validity and generalizability of these findings to other populations may be limited.

Another limitation of this study relates to the irregular use of medication by the participants. For ethical and other reasons, the study was unable to monitor and enforce compliance with the medication regimen. Participants were clearly advised how and when to take their medication, but it is unclear how many actually did comply with those recommendations. For greater validity, the study needs to be replicated with more rigorous controls.

In considering the cognitive-behavioral intervention, additional adaptation is needed to make it a uniquely social work intervention, an intervention distinct from psychology. Specifically, cognitive-behavioral approaches need to draw more attention to the social work concept of the person-in-environment. Some authors are already making advances in this area (Berlin, 1996; Gambrill, 1994; Thyer & Hudson, 1987).

Thyer (1987) and Thyer and Hudson (1987) emphasize the environmental dimension in cognitive-behavioral therapy. They assert that behavioral social work is predicated on a strongly ecological perspective. In effect, they hold that behavior does not occur in a vacuum but results from the dynamic interplay of the person and the environment. Recognizing this dynamic interplay, therapeutic interventions may enlist both personal and environmental change strategies. In this way, from a social work perspective, cognitive-behavioral approaches take a broader, more ecological view of the person and interventions.

The effect of environmental factors was poignantly demonstrated in the therapy group. Several participants observed how the violence of their inner-city neighborhoods greatly intensified their anxiety, reinforced the notion that their anxiety was rational and justified, and therefore made their efforts to identify and counter distorted thinking all the more difficult. Social work interventions, then, must focus not only on the individual, but on the larger environmental and social factors that affect the person. Much more work needs to be done in this area.

Historically, social workers have been committed to the principles of empowerment and self-determination in theory and practice. Panic disorder, a highly debilitating condition, frequently robs the person of the sense of empowerment as he or she is greatly limited in personal and social functioning. The findings of this research illustrate an effective therapy for panic disorder and other anxiety disorders that does not exclude the role of medication, but that focuses on complementary, cognitive-behavioral techniques. Despite the proliferation of the principles of managed care, social workers must remain committed to interventions that empower clients to cope with their problems through their own efforts.

REFERENCES

American Psychiatric Association. (1994). *Diagnostic and statistical manual of mental disorders* (4th ed.). Washington, DC: Author.

Asnis, G. M., & van Praag, H. M. (1995). *Panic disorder: Clinical, biological, and treatment aspects.* New York: John Wiley.

Austad, C. S. (1996). *Is long-term psychotherapy unethical? Toward a social ethic in an era of managed care.* San Francisco: Jossey-Bass.

Austad, C. S., & Berman, W. H. (1991). Managed health care and the evolution of psychotherapy. In C. S. Austad & W. H. Berman (Eds.), *Psychotherapy in managed health care* (pp. 3-18). Washington, DC: American Psychological Association.

Beck, A. T. (1988). Cognitive approaches to panic disorder: Theory and therapy. In S. Rachman & J. D. Maser (Eds.). *Panic: Psychological perspectives* (pp. 91-109) Hillsdale, NJ: Lawrence Erlbaum.

Beck, A. T., & Emery, G. (1985). *Anxiety disorders and phobias: A cognitive perspective.* New York: Basic Books.

Bennett, M. (1986). Maximizing the yield of brief psychotherapy: Part II. *HMO Mental Health Newsletter, 1,* 1-4.

Berlin, S. B. (1996). Constructivism and the environment: A cognitive-integrative perspective for social work practice. *Families in Society, 77,* 326-355.

Bourne, E. (1995). *The anxiety and phobia workbook* (2nd ed.). Oakland, CA: New Harbinger.

Clark, D. M., & Hemsley, D. R. (1982). The effects of hyperventilation: Individual variability and its relation to personality. *Journal of Behavior Therapy and Experimental Psychiatry, 13,* 41-47.

Eaton, W. W., & Keyl, P. M. (1995). The epidemiology of panic. In G. M. Asnis & H. M. van Praag (Eds.). *Panic disorder: Clinical, biological, and treatment aspects.* (pp. 50-79) New York: John Wiley.

Fischer, J., & Corcoran, K. (1994). *Measures for clinical practice: Vol. 2. Adults* (2nd ed.). New York: Free Press.

Friedman, S. (1994). *Anxiety disorders in African Americans.* New York: Springer.

Gambrill, E. D. (1994). Concepts and methods of behavioral treatment. In D. K. Granvold (Ed.), *Cognitive-behavioral treatment* (pp. 33-62). Belmont, CA: Brooks/Cole.

Garfield, S., & Bergin, A. (1986). Introduction and historical overview. In S. Garfield & A. Bergin (Eds.), *Handbook of psychotherapy and behavior change* (pp. 3-22). New York: John Wiley.

Hibbert, G. A., & Chan, M. (1989). Respiratory control: Its contribution to the treatment of panic attacks. *British Journal of Psychiatry, 154,* 232-236.

Himle, J., & Fischer, D. (1998). Panic disorder and agoraphobia. In B. A. Thyer & J. S. Wodarski (Eds.). *Handbook of empirical social work practice: Vol. 1. Mental disorders* (pp. 311-326). New York: John Wiley.

Horwath, E., Johnson, J., & Hornig, C. (1994). Epidemiology of panic disorder. In S. Friedman (Ed.), *Anxiety disorders in African Americans* (pp. 53-64). New York: Springer.

Hudson, W. W., Thyer, B. A., & Stocks, J. T. (1985). Assessing the importance of experimental outcomes. *Journal of Social Service Research, 8*(4), 87-98.

Katon, W. (1994). *Panic disorder in the medical setting.* Washington, DC: National Institute of Mental Health.

Kisch, J. (1991). The need for psychopharmacological collaboration in managed mental health care. In C. S. Austad & W. H. Berman (Eds.), *Psychotherapy in managed health care: The optimal use of time and resources* (pp. 81-85), Washington, DC: American Psychological Association.

Lehrer, P. M., & Woolfolk, R. L. (1982). Self-reports assessment of anxiety: Somatic, cognitive, and behavioral modalities. *Behavioral Assessment, 4,* 167-177.

Mavissakalian, M. (1990). Sequential combination of imipramine and self-directed exposure in the treatment of panic disorder with agoraphobia. *Journal of Clinical Psychiatry, 51,* 184-188.

McNally, R. J. (1994). *Panic disorder: A critical analysis.* New York: Guilford.

Mitchell, C. G. (1997). A study of locus of control and the effectiveness of cognitive-behavioral group therapy in the treatment of persons with panic disorder (Doctoral dissertation, Catholic University of America, 1997). *Dissertation Abstracts International, 58,* A1094.

Pigott, H. E., & Broskowski, A. (1985). Outcomes analysis: Guiding beacon or bogus science? *Behavioral Health Management, 15*(5), 22-24.

Piper, W. E., & Joyce, A. S. (1996). A consideration of factors influencing the utilization of time-limited, short-term group therapy. *International Journal of Group Psychotherapy, 46*(3), 311-328.

Raj, B. A., & Sheehan, D. V. (1995). Somatic treatment strategies in panic disorder. In G. M. Asnis & H.M. van Praag (Eds.), *Panic disorder: Clinical, biological, and treatment aspects* (pp. 279-313), New York: John Wiley.

Rapp, C. A. (1992). The strengths perspective of case management with persons suffering from severe mental illness. In D. Saleeby (Ed.), *The strengths perspective in social work* (pp. 45-58). White Plains, NY: Longman.

Thyer, B. A. (1987). Contingency analysis: Toward a unified theory of social work practice. *Social Work, 32,* 150-157.

Thyer, B. A., & Hudson, W. W. (1987). Progress in behavioral social work: An introduction. *Journal of Social Service Research, 10*(2,3,4), 1-6.

VandenBos, G., & DeLeon, H. H. (1988). The use of psychotherapy to improve physical health. *Psychotherapy, 25,* 335-343.

Appendix D

FINDING INFORMATION

ELIZABETH SCHNEIDER, MLS

This appendix complements the section on Finding Information in Chapter 2, which presented general principles and methods for finding information related to your research questions. The purpose of this appendix is to provide you with specific, practical pointers for finding high-quality information in a timely and efficient manner.

SEARCHING THE LITERATURE

In Chapter 2, you learned about the most frequently used indexes in social work: *Social Work Abstracts* and *Psychological Abstracts*. You might also find relevant literature in *EconLit*, which indexes the economic literature; in *Sociological Abstracts*, which indexes sociological literature; and in *ContempWomenIss*, which indexes literature on contemporary women's issues. It is most likely that your college library will have subscriptions to the online version of *Social Work Abstracts* and *Psychological Abstracts (Psychinfo)*. It will save you a lot of time in the long run if you ask a librarian to teach you the best techniques for retrieving the most relevant articles to answer your questions.

The *Social Science Citation Index (SSCI)* is another very useful source of bibliographic information for articles and books published across the social sciences. *SSCI* has a unique citation-searching feature that allows you to look up articles or books and see who else has cited them in their work. This is an excellent and efficient way to assemble a number of references that are highly relevant to your research and to find out which articles and books have had the biggest impact in a field. Unfortunately, some college libraries do not subscribe to *SSCI,* either in its print, CD-ROM, or online versions, due to its expense, but if you have access to *SSCI,* you should consider using it whenever you want to make sure that you develop the strongest possible literature review for your topic.

Whatever database you use, the next step after finding your references is to obtain the articles themselves. You will probably find the full text of many articles available online, but this will be determined by the journals to which your library subscribes. Older articles published before 1990 probably will not be online. Keep in mind that your library will not have anywhere near all the journals (and books) that you run across in your literature search, so you will have to add another step to your search: checking the "holdings" information.

If an article that appears to be important for your topic isn't available from your own library, either online or in print, don't give up yet. Here are some additional strategies for tracking it down.

- Find out if your college has reciprocal arrangements with other colleges that would allow you to use their materials.
- Find out if colleges in your area allow students from other colleges to use their collections and databases.
- Do not overlook your public library—you may be pleasantly surprised.
- Check to see if your library can get the desired resource for you from another library (through interlibrary loan).
- Check with a commercial vendor such as PubList (http://www.publist.com.) to see if you can purchase the article.

SEARCHING THE WEB

To find useful information on the Web, you have to be even more vigilant than when you search the literature directly. With billions of Web pages on the Internet, there is no limit to the amount of time you can squander and the volume of useless junk you can find as you conduct your research on the Web. However, I can share with you some good ways to avoid the biggest pitfalls.

Direct Addressing

Knowing the exact address (uniform resource locator, or URL) of a useful Web site is the most efficient way to find a resource on the Web. Appendix H contains many URLs relevant to social science research, but the following sections highlight a few categories and examples that may prove helpful to you.

Professional Organizations

- American Evaluation Association (http://www.eval.org)
- Council on Social Work Education (http://www.cswe.org)
- National Association of Social Workers (http://www.naswdc.org)

Government Sites

- National Institute on Aging (http://www.nia.nih.gov)
- National Institutes of Health (http://www.nih.gov)
- U.S. Bureau of the Census (http://www.census.gov)

Bibliographic Formats for Citing Electronic Information

- Electronic reference formats suggested by the American Psychological Association (http://www.apastyle.org/elecref.html)
- A compendium from Dartmouth College on how to cite sources from a variety of media, with examples (http://www.dartmouth.edu/~sources/).

When you find Web sites that you expect you will return to often, you can save their addresses as "bookmarks" or "favorites" in your Web browser. However, because these can very quickly multiply, you should try to be very selective.

Browsing Subject Directories

Subject directories (also called guides, indexes, or clearing houses) contain links to other Web resources that are organized by subject. They vary in quality and authoritativeness, but a good one can be invaluable to your research and save you much time. The main advantage to using subject directories is that they contain links to resources that have been selected, evaluated, and organized by human beings, and thus present a much more manageable number of resources. If the person managing the guide is an expert in the field of concern, or just a careful and methodological evaluator of Web resources, the resulting guide can help you to identify good sites that contain useful and trustworthy information without feeling like you should try to wade through thousands of "hits" and evaluate all the sites yourself.

The following are some examples of subject directories:

- Argus Clearinghouse (http://www.clearinghouse.net/searchbrowse.html) is a guide to subject directories on the Internet and classifies them under subject headings.
- Virtual Library (http://vlib.org) is the original subject guide and actually consists of a number of directories produced by different individuals and organizations residing on Web sites scattered around the world. There is a Virtual Library for the Social Sciences (http://vlib.org/SocialSciences.html) that includes listings for anthropology, demographics, psychology, social policy and evaluation, sociology, women's studies, and other areas.
- Another "virtual library" for the social sciences: (http://www.clas.ufl.edu/users/gthursby/socsci/) includes a large number of links to a diverse array of resources, including professional societies and online journals.
- Infomine: Scholarly Internet Resource Collections (http://lib-www.ucr.edu) is produced by librarians across several campuses of the University of California system, and it includes a subject directory for the social sciences.
- SOSIG—Social Science Information Gateway (http://www.sosig.ac.uk) is a British site that aims to be comprehensive. It is classified according to the Dewey Decimal System—the classification system used by most public libraries.
- Yahoo! (http://www.yahoo.com) is often mistaken for a search engine, but it is actually a subject directory—and a monster one at that. Unlike search engines, when you search Yahoo!, you are not searching across the Web, but rather just within the Web pages that Yahoo! has cataloged. Yahoo! has a subject directory for the social sciences with more specific listings, including one for social work (http://dir.yahoo.com/social_science/social_work/).

Many other Internet subject directories are maintained by academic departments, professional organizations, and individuals. It is often hard to determine whether a particular subject directory like this is up-to-date and reasonably comprehensive, but you can have some confidence in subject directories published by universities or government agencies. *The Internet Research Handbook* is an excellent source for more information on subject directories (O'Dochartaigh, 2002).

Search Engines

Chapter 2 outlined the major points to consider when using search engines to find information for your research. Search engines are powerful Internet tools—it is already impossible to imagine life without them. The biggest problem is the huge number of results that come back to you. Chapter 2 suggested phrase searching as a way to reduce that number. If the number of results is still unmanageable, you can try a title search. Exhibit 2.1 shows the results of typing the following into the Google search box: *ti: "informal social control"*. This search will retrieve those pages that have that phrase in their title as opposed to anywhere on the page. This practice usually results in a dramatically smaller yield of results. If you are looking for graphical information such as a graph or a chart, you can limit your search to those pages that contain an image. On Google, this just requires clicking on the Images link located above the search box.

There are many search engines, and none of them will give you identical results when you use them to search the Web. Different search engines use different strategies to find Web sites and offer somewhat different search options for users. Due to the enormous size of the Web and its constantly changing content, it simply isn't possible to identify one search engine that will give you completely up-to-date and comprehensive results. You can check the latest information about search engines at: http://searchenginewatch.com/. Although there are many search engines, you may find the following to be particularly useful for general searching:

- Google (http://www.google.com) has become the leading search engine for many users in recent years. Its coverage is relatively comprehensive, and it does a good job of ranking search results by their relevancy (based on the terms in your search request). Google also allows you to focus your search just on images, discussions, or directories.
- All The Web is a more recent comprehensive search engine that also does a good job of relevancy ranking and allows searches restricted to images and so on. You can find it at http://www.alltheweb.com.
- Microsoft's search engine (http://search.msn.com) adds a unique feature: Editors review and pick the most popular sites. As a result, your search request may result in a "popular topics" list that can help you to focus your search.

In conclusion, use the appropriate tool for your searches. Do not use a search engine in place of searching literature that is indexed in tools such as *Social Work Abstracts*. Bookmark the key sites that you find in your area of interest. Become familiar with subject directories that cover your areas of interest, and look there before going to a search engine. And when you do use a search engine, take a moment to learn about how it works and what steps you should take to get the best results in the least amount of time.

Appendix E

TABLE OF RANDOM NUMBERS

Line/Col.	(1)	(2)	(3)	(4)	(5)	(6)	(7)	(8)	(9)	(10)	(11)	(12)	(13)	(14)
1	10480	15011	01536	02011	81647	91646	69179	14194	62590	36207	20969	99570	91291	90700
2	22368	46573	25595	85393	30995	89198	27982	53402	93965	34095	52666	19174	39615	99505
3	24130	48360	22527	97265	76393	64809	15179	24830	49340	32081	30680	19655	63348	58629
4	42167	93093	06243	61680	07856	16376	39440	53537	71341	57004	00849	74917	97758	16379
5	37570	39975	81837	16656	06121	91782	60468	81305	49684	60672	14110	06927	01263	54613
6	77921	06907	11008	42751	27756	53498	18602	70659	90655	15053	21916	81825	44394	42880
7	99562	72905	56420	69994	98872	31016	71194	18738	44013	48840	63213	21069	10634	12952
8	96301	91977	05463	07972	18876	20922	94595	56869	69014	60045	18425	84903	42508	32307
9	89579	14342	63661	10281	17453	18103	57740	84378	25331	12566	58678	44947	05585	56941
10	85475	36857	43342	53988	53060	59533	38867	62300	08158	17983	16439	11458	18593	64952
11	28918	69578	88231	33276	70997	79936	56865	05859	90106	31595	01547	85590	91610	78188
12	63553	40961	48235	03427	49626	69445	18663	72695	52180	20847	12234	90511	33703	90322
13	09429	93969	52636	92737	88974	33488	36320	17617	30015	08272	84115	27156	30613	74952
14	10365	61129	87529	85689	48237	52267	67689	93394	01511	26358	85104	20285	29975	89868
15	07119	97336	71048	08178	77233	13916	47564	81056	97735	85977	29372	74461	28551	90707
16	51085	12765	51821	51259	77452	16308	60756	92144	49442	53900	70960	63990	75601	40719
17	02368	21382	52404	60268	89368	19885	55322	44819	01188	65255	64835	44919	05944	55157
18	01011	54092	33362	94904	31273	04146	18594	29852	71585	85030	51132	01915	92747	64951
19	52162	53916	46369	58586	23216	14513	83149	98736	23495	64350	94738	17752	35156	35749
20	07056	97628	33787	09998	42698	06691	76988	13602	51851	46104	88916	19509	25625	58104
21	48663	91245	85828	14346	09172	30168	90229	04734	59193	22178	30421	61666	99904	32812
22	54164	58492	22421	74103	47070	25306	76468	26384	58151	06646	21524	15227	96909	44592
23	32639	32363	05597	24200	13363	38005	94342	28728	35806	06912	17012	64161	18296	22851
24	29334	27001	87637	87308	58731	00256	45834	15398	46557	41135	10367	07684	36188	18510
25	02488	33062	28834	07351	19731	92420	60952	61280	50001	67658	32586	86679	50720	94953
26	81525	72295	04839	96423	24878	82651	66566	14778	76797	14780	13300	87074	79666	95725
27	29676	20591	68086	26432	46901	20849	89768	81536	86645	12659	92259	57102	80428	25280
28	00742	57392	39064	66432	84673	40027	32832	61362	98947	96067	64760	64584	96096	98253
29	05366	04213	25669	26422	44407	44048	37937	63904	45766	66134	75470	66520	34693	90449
30	91921	26418	64117	94305	26766	25940	39972	22209	71500	64568	91402	42416	07844	69618
31	00582	04711	87917	77341	42206	35126	74087	99547	81817	42607	43808	76655	62028	76630
32	00725	69884	62797	56170	86324	88072	76222	36086	84637	93161	76038	65855	77919	88006
33	69011	65797	95876	55293	18988	27354	26575	08625	40801	59920	29841	80150	12777	48501

(Continued)

Appendix E (Continued)

Line/Col.	(1)	(2)	(3)	(4)	(5)	(6)	(7)	(8)	(9)	(10)	(11)	(12)	(13)	(14)
34	25976	57948	29888	88604	67917	48708	18912	82271	65424	69774	33611	54262	85963	03547
35	09763	83473	73577	12908	30883	18317	28290	35797	05998	41688	34952	37888	38917	88050
36	91567	42595	27958	30134	04024	86385	29880	99730	55536	84855	29080	09250	79656	73211
37	17955	56349	90999	49127	20044	59931	06115	20542	18059	02008	73708	83317	36103	42791
38	46503	18584	18845	49618	02304	51038	20655	58727	28168	15475	56942	53389	20562	87338
39	92157	89634	94824	78171	84610	82834	09922	25417	44137	48413	25555	21246	35509	20468
40	14577	62765	35605	81263	39667	47358	56873	56307	61607	49518	89656	20103	77490	18062
41	98427	07523	33362	64270	01638	92477	66969	98420	04880	45585	46565	04102	46880	45709
42	34914	63976	88720	82765	34476	17032	87589	40836	32427	70002	70663	88863	77775	69348
43	70060	28277	39475	46473	23219	53416	94970	25832	69975	94884	19661	72828	00102	66794
44	53976	54914	06990	67245	68350	82948	11398	42878	80287	88267	47363	46634	06541	97809
45	76072	29515	40980	07391	58745	25774	22987	80059	39911	96189	41151	14222	60697	59583
46	90725	52210	83974	29992	65831	38857	50490	83765	55657	14361	31720	57375	56228	41546
47	64364	67412	33339	31926	14883	24413	59744	92351	97473	89286	35931	04110	23726	51900
48	08962	00358	31662	25388	61642	34072	81249	35648	56891	69352	48373	45578	78547	81788
49	95012	68379	93526	70765	10593	04542	76463	54328	02349	17247	28865	14777	62730	92277
50	15664	10493	20492	38391	91132	21999	59516	81652	27195	48223	46751	22923	32261	85653
51	16408	81899	04153	53381	79401	21438	83035	92350	36693	31238	59649	91754	72772	02338
52	18629	81953	05520	91962	04739	13092	97662	24822	94730	06496	35090	04822	86772	98289
53	73115	35101	47498	87637	99016	71060	88824	71013	18735	20286	23153	72924	35165	43040
54	57491	16703	23167	49323	45021	33132	12544	41035	80780	45393	44812	12515	98931	91202
55	30405	83946	23792	14422	15059	45799	22716	19792	09983	74353	68668	30429	70735	25499
56	16631	35006	85900	98275	32388	52390	16815	69298	82732	38480	73817	32523	41961	44437
57	96773	20206	42559	78985	05300	22164	24369	54224	35083	19687	11052	91491	60383	19746
58	38935	64202	14349	82674	66523	44133	00697	35552	35970	19124	63318	29686	03387	59846
59	31624	76384	17403	53363	44167	64486	64758	75366	76554	31601	12614	33072	60332	92325
60	78919	19474	23632	27889	47914	02584	37680	20801	72152	39339	34806	08930	85001	87820
61	03931	33309	57047	74211	63445	17361	62825	39908	05607	91284	68833	25570	38818	46920
62	74426	33278	43972	10119	89917	15665	52872	73823	73144	88662	88970	74492	51805	99378
63	09066	00903	20795	95452	92648	45454	09552	88815	16553	51125	79375	97596	16296	66092
64	42238	12426	87025	14267	20979	04508	64535	31355	86064	29472	47689	05974	52468	16834
65	16153	08002	26504	41744	81959	65642	74240	56302	00033	67107	77510	70625	28725	34191
66	21457	40742	29820	96783	29400	21840	15035	34537	33310	06116	95240	15957	16572	06004

Line/Col.	(1)	(2)	(3)	(4)	(5)	(6)	(7)	(8)	(9)	(10)	(11)	(12)	(13)	(14)
67	21581	57802	02050	89728	17937	37621	47075	42080	97403	48626	68995	43805	33386	21597
68	55612	78095	83197	33732	05810	24813	86902	60397	16489	03264	88525	42786	05269	92532
69	44657	66999	99324	51281	84463	60563	79312	93454	68876	25471	93911	25650	12682	73572
70	91340	84979	46949	81973	37949	61023	43997	15263	80644	43942	89203	71795	99533	50501
71	91227	21199	31935	27022	84067	05462	35216	14486	29891	68607	41867	14951	91696	85065
72	50001	38140	66321	19924	72163	09538	12151	06878	91903	18749	34405	56087	82790	70925
73	65390	05224	72958	28609	81406	39147	25549	48542	42627	45233	57202	94617	23772	07896
74	27504	96131	83944	41575	10573	08619	64482	73923	36152	05184	94142	25299	84387	34925
75	37169	94851	39117	89632	00959	16487	65536	49071	39782	17095	02330	74301	00275	48280
76	11508	70225	51111	38351	19444	66499	71945	05422	13442	78675	84081	66938	93654	59894
77	37449	30362	06694	54690	04052	53115	62757	95348	78662	11163	81651	50245	34971	52924
78	46515	70331	85922	38329	57015	15765	97161	17869	45349	61796	66345	81073	49106	79860
79	30986	81223	42416	58353	21532	30502	32305	86482	05174	07901	54339	58861	74818	46942
80	63798	64995	46583	09765	44160	78128	83991	42865	92520	83531	80377	35909	81250	54238
81	82486	84846	99254	67632	43218	50076	21361	64816	51202	88124	41870	52689	51275	83556
82	21885	32906	92431	09060	64297	51674	64126	62570	26123	05155	59194	52799	28225	85762
83	60336	98782	07408	53458	13564	59089	26445	29789	85205	41001	12535	12133	14645	23541
84	43937	46891	24010	25560	86355	33941	25786	54990	71899	15475	95434	98227	21824	19585
85	97656	63175	89303	16275	07100	92063	21942	18611	47348	20203	18534	03862	78095	50136
86	03299	01221	05418	38982	55758	92237	26759	86367	21216	98442	08303	56613	91511	75928
87	79626	06486	03574	17668	07785	76020	79924	25651	83325	88428	85076	72811	22717	50585
88	85636	68335	47539	03129	65651	11977	02510	26113	99447	68645	34327	15152	55230	93448
89	18039	14367	61337	06177	12143	46609	32989	74014	64708	00533	35398	58408	13261	47908
90	08362	15656	60627	36478	65648	16764	53412	09013	07832	41574	17639	82163	60859	75567
91	79556	29068	04142	32534	15387	12856	66227	38358	22478	73373	88732	09443	82558	05250
92	92608	82674	27072	32534	17075	27698	98204	63863	11951	34648	88022	56148	34925	57031
93	23982	25835	40055	67006	12293	02753	14827	22235	35071	99704	37543	11601	35503	85171
94	09915	96306	05908	97901	28395	14186	00821	80703	70426	75647	76310	88717	37890	40129
95	50937	33300	26695	62247	69927	76123	50842	43834	86654	70959	79725	93872	28117	19233
96	42488	78077	69882	61657	34136	79180	97526	43092	04098	73571	80799	76536	71255	64239
97	46764	86273	63003	93017	31204	36692	40202	35275	57306	55543	53203	18098	47625	88684
98	03237	45430	55417	63282	90816	17349	88298	90183	36600	78406	06216	95787	42579	90730
99	86591p	81482	52667	61583	14972	90053	89534	76036	49199	43716	97548	04379	46370	28672
100	38534	01715	94964	87288	65680	43772	39560	12918	86537	62738	19636	51132	25739	56947

Source: Beyer, 1968.

Appendix F

ANNOTATED LIST OF WEB SITES

http://www.acorn.org/

ACORN, the Association of Community Organizations for Reform Now, is the largest community organization of low- and moderate-income families. This site discusses community strategies in the United States and abroad.

http://www.acosa.org/

The Association for Community Organization and Social Administration provides information and resources relevant to community organizers, activists, administrators, policymakers, students, and educators.

http://www.agingresearch.org/

The Alliance for Aging Research provides information on the most current research on aging Americans. It also provides numerous links to other resources.

http://aidsinfo.nih.gov/

Sponsored by the National Institutes of Health, this site provides information about HIV/AIDS prevention and treatment, including information about mother-child transmission. Information is available in Spanish and English.

http://www.ajph.org/

Provides links to research articles on various public health issues.

http://www.aoa.gov/

This U.S. Administration on Aging site offers information on public policy issues affecting older adults, current literature on aging issues, and numerous links to other Web sites concerning aging.

http://www.casacolumbia.org/

The National Center on Addiction and Substance Abuse (CASA) at Columbia University includes all professional disciplines to study and combat abuse of all substances—alcohol, nicotine, illegal drugs, prescription drugs, performance-enhancing drugs. Offers numerous links.

http://www.cbpp.org/

This Web site provides a host of information about current policy and research.

http://www.cdc.gov/omh/

The Centers for Disease Control offers this Web site focusing on minority health issues. The Web site provides links to current research and funding opportunities as well as national and state statistics.

http://www.census.gov/

The U.S. Bureau of Census home page contains links to tables and graphs reporting detailed census data.

http://www.charityadvantage.com/iaswr/

The Institute for the Advancement of Social Work Research promotes social work research conducted by academic and professional organizations.

http://www.childrensdefense.org/

The Children's Defense Fund is an advocacy group for children. The site provides numerous links, including advocacy information.

http://www.childwelfare.com/kids/news.htm/

Child Welfare Review is a peer-reviewed electronic journal. This Web site provides links to research articles on child welfare services, welfare reform and its impact on children, child poverty and inequality, and child advocacy.

http://www.columbia.edu/cu/csswp/ceterde.html/

The Center for the Study of Social Work Practice is focused on the development and dissemination of social work practice knowledge.

http://cosw.sc.edu/swan/

Sponsored by the University of South Carolina's School of Social Work, this Web site provides links to social work organizations and upcoming conferences.

http://www.c-s-i.org/

Crime Stoppers International, an organization devoted to fighting crime and violence around the world, offers links to interesting sites related to the subject of crime and violence.

http://www.cswe.org

The Council on Social Work Education accredits social work programs and provides educational leadership.

http://www.cwla.org/

The Child Welfare League of America is an association of almost 1,200 public and private nonprofit agencies that assist more thaner 3.5 million abused and neglected children and their families each year with a wide range of services. This Web site provides links to various child welfare topics, including adoption and foster care, juvenile justice, diversity, and current research.

http://www.endhomelessness.org/

The National Alliance to End Homelessness is a nonprofit organization whose mission is to mobilize the nonprofit, public, and private sectors of society in an alliance to end homelessness.

http://www.eval.org/

The American Evaluation Association Web site provides access to a variety of publications and links related to program evaluation.

http://fdncenter.org/

The Foundation Center provides resources for finding foundation grants.

http://www.gallup.com/

This site contains election poll results back to 1936 and information on polls on current events.

http://www.hrc.org/

The Human Rights Campaign provides information on various policy issues affecting the gay, lesbian, bisexual, and transgender community.

http://www.ifsw.org/

The International Federation of Social Workers (IFSW) is a global organization striving for social justice, human rights, and social development through the development of social work, best practices, and international cooperation between social workers and their professional organizations.

http://www.isr.umich.edu/

The University of Michigan's Institute for Social Research stores empirical research in a wide variety of disciplines such as psychology, economics, sociology, and public health.

http://www.kff.org/

The Kaiser Family Foundation Web site provides in-depth information on key health policy issues including Medicaid, Medicare, prescription drugs, and global HIV/AIDS.

http://lib-www.ucr.edu/

INFOMINE (Scholarly Internet Resource Collection) links scholars to sites containing a wide range of scholarly materials.

http://www.nap.edu/readingroom/books/obas/

The National Academy of Sciences reports on ethical issues in scientific research.

http://www.naswdc.org/

The National Association of Social Workers (NASW) is the largest membership organization of professional social workers in the world. This Web site provides links to the NASW Code of Ethics, publications, and the NASW position on various state and federal legislative issues. NASW maintains the Practice Research Network, a research program that collects and analyzes data on social work practice as well as a variety of social work service delivery issues.

http://www.nationalhomeless.org/

The National Coalition for the Homeless provides current statistics, links to publications, legislative developments, and other resources.

http://www.ncadv.org/

The National Coalition Against Domestic Violence (NCADV) provides information about domestic violence, public policy initiatives, and links to resource information.

http://www.nccp.org/

The National Center for Children in Poverty is a nonprofit organization at Columbia University whose mission is to identify and promote strategies that prevent child poverty in the United States and that improve the lives of low-income children and families. This Web site contains policy and research information.

http://ncmhd.nih.gov/

The National Center for Minority Health and Health Disparities offers links to current research and funding opportunities.

http://www.ncoa.org/

The National Council on Aging Web site provides links to current professional research, publications for the lay community, and political advocacy for professionals interested in issues affecting older adults.

http://www.ncpa.org/newdpd/index.php/

The National Center for Policy Analysis is a nonprofit public policy research institute seeking innovative private-sector solutions to public policy problems. The Web site links to information on a vast array of policy issues.

http://www.nia.nih.gov/

The National Institute on Aging's Web site provides links to research programs, funding, and training and health information.

http://www.nih.gov/

The National Institutes of Health Web site offers information about programs and funding opportunities.

http://grants.nih.gov/grants/guide/index.html/

A guide to finding grants from the National Institutes of Health.

http://www.nimh.nih.gov/

The National Institute of Mental Health provides information about mental health conditions and treatment as well as research opportunities.

http://www.nlchp.org/

The National Law Center on Homelessness and Poverty's mission is to prevent and end homelessness by serving as the legal arm of the nationwide movement to end homelessness. The site provides links to information about housing, income, education, and civil rights.

http://www.nlm.nih.gov/medlineplus/domesticviolence.html/

Sponsored by the U.S. National Library of Medicine and the National Institute of Mental Health, this Web site provides links to prevention, identification, medical, legal, and mental health resources for professionals working with children, teens, women, and men affected by domestic violence.

http://www.nlm.gov/medlineplus/gayandlesbianhealth.html/

Run through the National Library Service and the National Institutes of Health, this site provides up to date information on gay and lesbian issues.

http://www.nmha.org/

The National Mental Health Association maintains this Web site to provide information about current policies, conference information, and funding opportunities.

http://www.nyu.edu/socialwork/wwwrsw/

Jointly sponsored by New York University's Ehrenkrantz School of Social Work and the Division of Social Work and Behavioral Science, Mount Sinai School of Medicine, this Web site links users to current research and professional organizations dealing with various social work topics.

http://www.ojp.usdoj.gov/vawo/

Sponsored by the U.S. Department of Justice, the Office on Violence Against Women, this Web site provides links to current research and program funding opportunities as well as current research on violence against women.

http://www.omhrc.gov/omhrc/

The Office of Minority Health provides information about the status of public health activities affecting people of color. The site provides data, publications, and links to other sites.

http://www.rci.rutgers.edu/~cas2/

The Center for Alcohol Studies at Rutgers University offers a wealth of information on alcoholism and treatment.

http://www.rwjf.org/index.jsp/

The Robert J. Woods Foundation provides funding for health care-related research, education, and projects.

http://www.samhsa.gov/

The Substance Abuse and Mental Health Services Administration site offers summaries of publications, reports, and statistical information on SAMHSA research.

http://www.socialworker.com/

This Web site provides links to the *New Social Worker* magazine online. The magazine's primary focus is on career development and practical professional information for social workers and social work students. It includes articles on practice specialties, social work ethics, field placement, books, news, technology, and other topics of interest to professional social workers and social work students.

http://www.splcenter.org/index.jsp/

The Southern Poverty Law Center was founded in 1971 as a small civil rights law firm. Today, the center is internationally known for its tolerance education programs, its legal victories against White supremacists, and its tracking of hate groups. The site provides a variety of links.

http://www.ssc.wisc.edu/irp/

This complete and easy to navigate Web site, sponsored by the University of Wisconsin, has links to current research on poverty.

http://www.sswr.org/

The Society for Social Work and Research is dedicated to advancing social work research and to providing opportunities for social work researchers to network and present their findings to colleagues from around the world.

http://stats.bls.gov/

This government site contains links to research publications and statistics as well as links to other sites.

http://www.statsoftinc.com/textbook/stathome.html/

This Electronic Statistics Textbook offers training in the understanding and application of statistics.

http://www.thetaskforce.org/

The National Gay and Lesbian Task Force provides information about advocacy, policy, and publications related to the civil rights of gay, lesbian, bisexual, and transgender people.

http://thomas.loc.gov/

A service of the Library of Congress, this site provides links to pending and past federal legislation and committee composition.

http://www.who.int/hiv/en/

This site is part of the World Health Organization Web site and provides information on HIV/AIDS throughout the world. This site provides links to various sites and current statistics and research.

http://www.who.int/substance_abuse/en/

This Web site contains information pertaining to psychoactive substance use and abuse and also information about the World Health Organization's projects and activities in the areas of substance use and substance dependence.

Code of Ethics of the National Association of Social Workers

Approved by the 1996 NASW Delegate Assembly and revised by the 1999 NASW Delegate Assembly.

PREAMBLE

The primary mission of the social work profession is to enhance human well-being and help meet the basic human needs of all people, with particular attention to the needs and empowerment of people who are vulnerable, oppressed, and living in poverty. A historic and defining feature of social work is the profession's focus on individual well-being in a social context and the well-being of society. Fundamental to social work is attention to the environmental forces that create, contribute to, and address problems in living.

Social workers promote social justice and social change with and on behalf of clients. "Clients" is used inclusively to refer to individuals, families, groups, organizations, and communities. Social workers are sensitive to cultural and ethnic diversity and strive to end discrimination, oppression, poverty, and other forms of social injustice. These activities may be in the form of direct practice, community organizing, supervision, consultation, administration, advocacy, social and political action, policy development and implementation, education, and research and evaluation. Social workers seek to enhance the capacity of people to address their own needs. Social workers also seek to promote the responsiveness of organizations, communities, and other social institutions to individuals' needs and social problems.

The mission of the social work profession is rooted in a set of core values. These core values, embraced by social workers throughout the profession's history, are the foundation of social work's unique purpose and perspective:

- service
- social justice
- dignity and worth of the person

- importance of human relationships
- integrity
- competence

This constellation of core values reflects what is unique to the social work profession. Core values, and the principles that flow from them, must be balanced within the context and complexity of the human experience.

PURPOSE OF THE NASW CODE OF ETHICS

Professional ethics are at the core of social work. The profession has an obligation to articulate its basic values, ethical principles, and ethical standards. The *NASW Code of Ethics* sets forth these values, principles, and standards to guide social workers' conduct. The *Code* is relevant to all social workers and social work students, regardless of their professional functions, the settings in which they work, or the populations they serve.

The *NASW Code of Ethics* serves six purposes:

1. The *Code* identifies core values on which social work's mission is based.

2. The *Code* summarizes broad ethical principles that reflect the profession's core values and establishes a set of specific ethical standards that should be used to guide social work practice.

3. The *Code* is designed to help social workers identify relevant considerations when professional obligations conflict or ethical uncertainties arise.

4. The *Code* provides ethical standards to which the general public can hold the social work profession accountable.

5. The *Code* socializes practitioners new to the field to social work's mission, values, ethical principles, and ethical standards.

6. The *Code* articulates standards that the social work profession itself can use to assess whether social workers have engaged in unethical conduct. NASW has formal procedures to adjudicate ethics complaints filed against its members.* In subscribing to this *Code,* social workers are required to cooperate in its implementation, participate in NASW adjudication proceedings, and abide by any NASW disciplinary rulings or sanctions based on it.

The *Code* offers a set of values, principles, and standards to guide decision making and conduct when ethical issues arise. It does not provide a set of rules that prescribe how social workers should act in all situations. Specific applications of the *Code* must take into account the context in which it is being considered and the possibility of conflicts among the *Code*'s values, principles, and standards. Ethical responsibilities flow from all human relationships, from the personal and familial to the social and professional.

---

*For information on NASW adjudication procedures, see *NASW Procedures for the Adjudication of Grievances.*

Further, the *NASW Code of Ethics* does not specify which values, principles, and standards are most important and ought to outweigh others in instances when they conflict. Reasonable differences of opinion can and do exist among social workers with respect to the ways in which values, ethical principles, and ethical standards should be rank ordered when they conflict. Ethical decision making in a given situation must apply the informed judgment of the individual social worker and should also consider how the issues would be judged in a peer review process where the ethical standards of the profession would be applied.

Ethical decision making is a process. There are many instances in social work where simple answers are not available to resolve complex ethical issues. Social workers should take into consideration all the values, principles, and standards in this *Code* that are relevant to any situation in which ethical judgment is warranted. Social workers' decisions and actions should be consistent with the spirit as well as the letter of this *Code.*

In addition to this *Code,* there are many other sources of information about ethical thinking that may be useful. Social workers should consider ethical theory and principles generally, social work theory and research, laws, regulations, agency policies, and other relevant codes of ethics, recognizing that among codes of ethics social workers should consider the *NASW Code of Ethics* as their primary source. Social workers also should be aware of the impact on ethical decision making of their clients' and their own personal values and cultural and religious beliefs and practices. They should be aware of any conflicts between personal and professional values and deal with them responsibly. For additional guidance social workers should consult the relevant literature on professional ethics and ethical decision making and seek appropriate consultation when faced with ethical dilemmas. This may involve consultation with an agency-based or social work organization's ethics committee, a regulatory body, knowledgeable colleagues, supervisors, or legal counsel.

Instances may arise when social workers' ethical obligations conflict with agency policies or relevant laws or regulations. When such conflicts occur, social workers must make a responsible effort to resolve the conflict in a manner that is consistent with the values, principles, and standards expressed in this *Code.* If a reasonable resolution of the conflict does not appear possible, social workers should seek proper consultation before making a decision.

The *NASW Code of Ethics* is to be used by NASW and by individuals, agencies, organizations, and bodies (such as licensing and regulatory boards, professional liability insurance providers, courts of law, agency boards of directors, government agencies, and other professional groups) that choose to adopt it or use it as a frame of reference. Violation of standards in this *Code* does not automatically imply legal liability or violation of the law. Such determination can only be made in the context of legal and judicial proceedings. Alleged violations of the *Code* would be subject to a peer review process. Such processes are generally separate from legal or administrative procedures and insulated from legal review or proceedings to allow the profession to counsel and discipline its own members.

A code of ethics cannot guarantee ethical behavior. Moreover, a code of ethics cannot resolve all ethical issues or disputes or capture the richness and complexity involved in striving to make responsible choices within a moral community. Rather, a code of ethics sets forth values, ethical principles, and ethical standards to which professionals aspire and by which their actions can be judged. Social workers' ethical behavior should result from their personal commitment to engage in ethical practice. The *NASW Code of Ethics* reflects the commitment of all social workers to uphold the profession's values and to act ethically. Principles and standards must be applied by individuals of good character who discern moral questions and, in good faith, seek to make reliable ethical judgments.

ETHICAL PRINCIPLES

The following broad ethical principles are based on social work's core values of service, social justice, dignity and worth of the person, importance of human relationships, integrity, and competence. These principles set forth ideals to which all social workers should aspire.

Value: Service
Ethical Principle: Social workers' primary goal is to help people in need and to address social problems.

Social workers elevate service to others above self-interest. Social workers draw on their knowledge, values, and skills to help people in need and to address social problems. Social workers are encouraged to volunteer some portion of their professional skills with no expectation of significant financial return (pro bono service).

Value: Social Justice
Ethical Principle: Social workers challenge social injustice.

Social workers pursue social change, particularly with and on behalf of vulnerable and oppressed individuals and groups of people. Social workers' social change efforts are focused primarily on issues of poverty, unemployment, discrimination, and other forms of social injustice. These activities seek to promote sensitivity to and knowledge about oppression and cultural and ethnic diversity. Social workers strive to ensure access to needed information, services, and resources; equality of opportunity; and meaningful participation in decision making for all people.

Value: Dignity and Worth of the Person
Ethical Principle: Social workers respect the inherent dignity and worth of the person.

Social workers treat each person in a caring and respectful fashion, mindful of individual differences and cultural and ethnic diversity. Social workers promote clients' socially responsible self-determination. Social workers seek to enhance clients' capacity and opportunity to change and to address their own needs. Social workers are cognizant of their dual responsibility to clients and to the broader society. They seek to resolve conflicts between clients' interests and the broader society's interests in a socially responsible manner consistent with the values, ethical principles, and ethical standards of the profession.

Value: Importance of Human Relationships
Ethical Principle: Social workers recognize the central importance of human relationships.

Social workers understand that relationships between and among people are an important vehicle for change. Social workers engage people as partners in the helping process. Social workers seek to strengthen relationships among people in a purposeful effort to promote, restore, maintain, and enhance the well-being of individuals, families, social groups, organizations, and communities.

Value: Integrity
Ethical Principle: Social workers behave in a trustworthy manner.

Social workers are continually aware of the profession's mission, values, ethical principles, and ethical standards and practice in a manner consistent with them. Social workers act honestly and responsibly and promote ethical practices on the part of the organizations with which they are affiliated.

Value: Competence
Ethical Principle: Social workers practice within their areas of competence and develop and enhance their professional expertise.

Social workers continually strive to increase their professional knowledge and skills and to apply them in practice. Social workers should aspire to contribute to the knowledge base of the profession.

ETHICAL STANDARDS

The following ethical standards are relevant to the professional activities of all social workers. These standards concern (1) social workers' ethical responsibilities to clients, (2) social workers' ethical responsibilities to colleagues, (3) social workers' ethical responsibilities in practice settings, (4) social workers' ethical responsibilities as professionals, (5) social workers' ethical responsibilities to the social work profession, and (6) social workers' ethical responsibilities to the broader society.

Some of the standards that follow are enforceable guidelines for professional conduct, and some are aspirational. The extent to which each standard is enforceable is a matter of professional judgment to be exercised by those responsible for reviewing alleged violations of ethical standards.

1. Social Workers' Ethical Responsibilities to Clients

1.01 Commitment to Clients

Social workers' primary responsibility is to promote the well-being of clients. In general, clients' interests are primary. However, social workers' responsibility to the larger society or specific legal obligations may on limited occasions supersede the loyalty owed clients, and clients should be so advised. (Examples include when a social worker is required by law to report that a client has abused a child or has threatened to harm self or others.)

1.02 Self-Determination

Social workers respect and promote the right of clients to self-determination and assist clients in their efforts to identify and clarify their goals. Social workers may limit clients' right to self-determination when, in the social workers' professional judgment, clients' actions or potential actions pose a serious, foreseeable, and imminent risk to themselves or others.

1.03 Informed Consent

(a) Social workers should provide services to clients only in the context of a professional relationship based, when appropriate, on valid informed consent. Social workers should use clear and understandable language to inform clients of the purpose of the services, risks related to the services, limits to services because of the requirements of a third-party payer, relevant costs, reasonable alternatives, clients' right to refuse or withdraw consent, and the time frame covered by the consent. Social workers should provide clients with an opportunity to ask questions.

(b) In instances when clients are not literate or have difficulty understanding the primary language used in the practice setting, social workers should take steps to ensure clients' comprehension. This may include providing clients with a detailed verbal explanation or arranging for a qualified interpreter or translator whenever possible.

(c) In instances when clients lack the capacity to provide informed consent, social workers should protect clients' interests by seeking permission from an appropriate third party, informing clients consistent with the clients' level of understanding. In such instances social workers should seek to ensure that the third party acts in a manner consistent with clients' wishes and interests. Social workers should take reasonable steps to enhance such clients' ability to give informed consent.

(d) In instances when clients are receiving services involuntarily, social workers should provide information about the nature and extent of services and about the extent of clients' right to refuse service.

(e) Social workers who provide services via electronic media (such as computer, telephone, radio, and television) should inform recipients of the limitations and risks associated with such services.

(f) Social workers should obtain clients' informed consent before audiotaping or videotaping clients or permitting observation of services to clients by a third party.

1.04 Competence

(a) Social workers should provide services and represent themselves as competent only within the boundaries of their education, training, license, certification, consultation received, supervised experience, or other relevant professional experience.

(b) Social workers should provide services in substantive areas or use intervention techniques or approaches that are new to them only after engaging in appropriate study, training, consultation, and supervision from people who are competent in those interventions or techniques.

(c) When generally recognized standards do not exist with respect to an emerging area of practice, social workers should exercise careful judgment and take responsible steps (including appropriate education, research, training, consultation, and supervision) to ensure the competence of their work and to protect clients from harm.

1.05 Cultural Competence and Social Diversity

(a) Social workers should understand culture and its function in human behavior and society, recognizing the strengths that exist in all cultures.

(b) Social workers should have a knowledge base of their clients' cultures and be able to demonstrate competence in the provision of services that are sensitive to clients' cultures and to differences among people and cultural groups.

(c) Social workers should obtain education about and seek to understand the nature of social diversity and oppression with respect to race, ethnicity, national origin, color, sex, sexual orientation, age, marital status, political belief, religion, and mental or physical disability.

1.06 Conflicts of Interest

(a) Social workers should be alert to and avoid conflicts of interest that interfere with the exercise of professional discretion and impartial judgment. Social workers should inform clients when a real or potential conflict of interest arises and take reasonable steps to resolve the issue in a manner that makes the clients' interests primary and protects clients' interests to the greatest extent possible. In some cases, protecting clients' interests may require termination of the professional relationship with proper referral of the client.

(b) Social workers should not take unfair advantage of any professional relationship or exploit others to further their personal, religious, political, or business interests.

(c) Social workers should not engage in dual or multiple relationships with clients or former clients in which there is a risk of exploitation or potential harm to the client. In instances when dual or multiple relationships are unavoidable, social workers should take steps to protect clients and are responsible for setting clear, appropriate, and culturally sensitive boundaries. (Dual or multiple relationships occur when social workers relate to clients in more than one relationship, whether professional, social, or business. Dual or multiple relationships can occur simultaneously or consecutively.)

(d) When social workers provide services to two or more people who have a relationship with each other (for example, couples, family members), social workers should clarify with all parties which individuals will be considered clients and the nature of social workers' professional obligations to the various individuals who are receiving services. Social workers who anticipate a conflict of interest among the individuals receiving services or who anticipate having to perform in potentially conflicting roles (for example, when a social worker is asked to testify in a child custody dispute or divorce proceedings involving clients) should clarify their role with the parties involved and take appropriate action to minimize any conflict of interest.

1.07 Privacy and Confidentiality

(a) Social workers should respect clients' right to privacy. Social workers should not solicit private information from clients unless it is essential to providing services or conducting social work evaluation or research. Once private information is shared, standards of confidentiality apply.

(b) Social workers may disclose confidential information when appropriate with valid consent from a client or a person legally authorized to consent on behalf of a client.

(c) Social workers should protect the confidentiality of all information obtained in the course of professional service, except for compelling professional reasons. The general expectation that social workers will keep information confidential does not apply when disclosure is necessary to prevent serious, foreseeable, and imminent harm to a client or other identifiable person. In all instances, social workers should disclose the least amount of confidential information necessary to achieve the desired purpose; only information that is directly relevant to the purpose for which the disclosure is made should be revealed.

(d) Social workers should inform clients, to the extent possible, about the disclosure of confidential information and the potential consequences, when feasible before the disclosure is made. This applies whether social workers disclose confidential information on the basis of a legal requirement or client consent.

(e) Social workers should discuss with clients and other interested parties the nature of confidentiality and limitations of clients' right to confidentiality. Social workers should review with clients circumstances where confidential information may be requested and where disclosure of confidential information may be legally required. This discussion should occur as soon as possible in the social worker-client relationship and as needed throughout the course of the relationship.

(f) When social workers provide counseling services to families, couples, or groups, social workers should seek agreement among the parties involved concerning each individual's right to confidentiality and obligation to preserve the confidentiality of information shared by others. Social workers should inform participants in family, couples, or group counseling that social workers cannot guarantee that all participants will honor such agreements.

(g) Social workers should inform clients involved in family, couples, marital, or group counseling of the social worker's, employer's, and agency's policy concerning the social worker's disclosure of confidential information among the parties involved in the counseling.

(h) Social workers should not disclose confidential information to third-party payers unless clients have authorized such disclosure.

(i) Social workers should not discuss confidential information in any setting unless privacy can be ensured. Social workers should not discuss confidential information in public or semipublic areas such as hallways, waiting rooms, elevators, and restaurants.

(j) Social workers should protect the confidentiality of clients during legal proceedings to the extent permitted by law. When a court of law or other legally authorized body orders social workers to disclose confidential or privileged information without a client's consent and such disclosure could cause harm to the client, social workers should request that the court withdraw the order or limit the order as narrowly as possible or maintain the records under seal, unavailable for public inspection.

(k) Social workers should protect the confidentiality of clients when responding to requests from members of the media.

(l) Social workers should protect the confidentiality of clients' written and electronic records and other sensitive information. Social workers should take reasonable steps to ensure that clients' records are stored in a secure location and that clients' records are not available to others who are not authorized to have access.

(m) Social workers should take precautions to ensure and maintain the confidentiality of information transmitted to other parties through the use of computers, electronic mail, facsimile machines, telephones and telephone answering machines, and other electronic or computer technology. Disclosure of identifying information should be avoided whenever possible.

(n) Social workers should transfer or dispose of clients' records in a manner that protects clients' confidentiality and is consistent with state statutes governing records and social work licensure.

(o) Social workers should take reasonable precautions to protect client confidentiality in the event of the social worker's termination of practice, incapacitation, or death.

(p) Social workers should not disclose identifying information when discussing clients for teaching or training purposes unless the client has consented to disclosure of confidential information.

(q) Social workers should not disclose identifying information when discussing clients with consultants unless the client has consented to disclosure of confidential information or there is a compelling need for such disclosure.

(r) Social workers should protect the confidentiality of deceased clients consistent with the preceding standards.

1.08 Access to Records

(a) Social workers should provide clients with reasonable access to records concerning the clients. Social workers who are concerned that clients' access to their records could cause serious misunderstanding or harm to the client should provide assistance in interpreting the records and consultation with the client regarding the records. Social workers should limit clients' access to their records, or portions of their records, only in exceptional circumstances when there is compelling evidence that such access would cause serious harm to the client. Both clients' requests and the rationale for withholding some or all of the record should be documented in clients' files.

(b) When providing clients with access to their records, social workers should take steps to protect the confidentiality of other individuals identified or discussed in such records.

1.09 Sexual Relationships

(a) Social workers should under no circumstances engage in sexual activities or sexual contact with current clients, whether such contact is consensual or forced.

(b) Social workers should not engage in sexual activities or sexual contact with clients' relatives or other individuals with whom clients maintain a close personal relationship when there is a risk of exploitation or potential harm to the client. Sexual activity or sexual contact with clients' relatives or other individuals with whom clients maintain a personal relationship has the potential to be harmful to the client and may make it difficult for the social worker and client to maintain appropriate professional boundaries. Social workers—not their clients, their clients' relatives, or other individuals with whom the client maintains a personal relationship—assume the full burden for setting clear, appropriate, and culturally sensitive boundaries.

(c) Social workers should not engage in sexual activities or sexual contact with former clients because of the potential for harm to the client. If social workers engage in conduct contrary to this prohibition or claim that an exception to this prohibition is warranted because of extraordinary circumstances, it is social workers—not their clients—who assume the full burden of demonstrating that the former client has not been exploited, coerced, or manipulated, intentionally or unintentionally.

(d) Social workers should not provide clinical services to individuals with whom they have had a prior sexual relationship. Providing clinical services to a former sexual partner has the potential to be harmful to the individual and is likely to make it difficult for the social worker and individual to maintain appropriate professional boundaries.

1.10 Physical Contact

Social workers should not engage in physical contact with clients when there is a possibility of psychological harm to the client as a result of the contact (such as cradling or caressing clients). Social workers who engage in appropriate physical contact with clients are responsible for setting clear, appropriate, and culturally sensitive boundaries that govern such physical contact.

1.11 Sexual Harassment

Social workers should not sexually harass clients. Sexual harassment includes sexual advances, sexual solicitation, requests for sexual favors, and other verbal or physical conduct of a sexual nature.

1.12 Derogatory Language

Social workers should not use derogatory language in their written or verbal communications to or about clients. Social workers should use accurate and respectful language in all communications to and about clients.

1.13 Payment for Services

(a) When setting fees, social workers should ensure that the fees are fair, reasonable, and commensurate with the services performed. Consideration should be given to clients' ability to pay.

(b) Social workers should avoid accepting goods or services from clients as payment for professional services. Bartering arrangements, particularly involving services, create the potential for conflicts of interest, exploitation, and inappropriate boundaries in social workers' relationships with clients. Social workers should explore and may participate in bartering only in very limited circumstances when it can be demonstrated that such arrangements are an accepted practice among professionals in the local community, considered to be essential for the provision of services, negotiated without coercion, and entered into at the client's initiative and with the client's informed consent. Social workers who accept goods or services from clients as payment for professional services assume the full burden of demonstrating that this arrangement will not be detrimental to the client or the professional relationship.

(c) Social workers should not solicit a private fee or other remuneration for providing services to clients who are entitled to such available services through the social workers' employer or agency.

1.14 Clients Who Lack Decision-Making Capacity

When social workers act on behalf of clients who lack the capacity to make informed decisions, social workers should take reasonable steps to safeguard the interests and rights of those clients.

1.15 Interruption of Services

Social workers should make reasonable efforts to ensure continuity of services in the event that services are interrupted by factors such as unavailability, relocation, illness, disability, or death.

1.16 Termination of Services

(a) Social workers should terminate services to clients and professional relationships with them when such services and relationships are no longer required or no longer serve the clients' needs or interests.
(b) Social workers should take reasonable steps to avoid abandoning clients who are still in need of services. Social workers should withdraw services precipitously only under unusual circumstances, giving careful consideration to all factors in the situation and taking care to minimize possible adverse effects. Social workers should assist in making appropriate arrangements for continuation of services when necessary.
(c) Social workers in fee-for-service settings may terminate services to clients who are not paying an overdue balance if the financial contractual arrangements have been made clear to the client, if the client does not pose an imminent danger to self or others, and if the clinical and other consequences of the current nonpayment have been addressed and discussed with the client.
(d) Social workers should not terminate services to pursue a social, financial, or sexual relationship with a client.
(e) Social workers who anticipate the termination or interruption of services to clients should notify clients promptly and seek the transfer, referral, or continuation of services in relation to the clients' needs and preferences.
(f) Social workers who are leaving an employment setting should inform clients of appropriate options for the continuation of services and of the benefits and risks of the options.

2. Social Workers' Ethical Responsibilities to Colleagues

2.01 Respect

(a) Social workers should treat colleagues with respect and should represent accurately and fairly the qualifications, views, and obligations of colleagues.

(b) Social workers should avoid unwarranted negative criticism of colleagues in communications with clients or with other professionals. Unwarranted negative criticism may include demeaning comments that refer to colleagues' level of competence or to individuals' attributes such as race, ethnicity, national origin, color, sex, sexual orientation, age, marital status, political belief, religion, and mental or physical disability.

(c) Social workers should cooperate with social work colleagues and with colleagues of other professions when such cooperation serves the well-being of clients.

2.02 Confidentiality

Social workers should respect confidential information shared by colleagues in the course of their professional relationships and transactions. Social workers should ensure that such colleagues understand social workers' obligation to respect confidentiality and any exceptions related to it.

2.03 Interdisciplinary Collaboration

(a) Social workers who are members of an interdisciplinary team should participate in and contribute to decisions that affect the well-being of clients by drawing on the perspectives, values, and experiences of the social work profession. Professional and ethical obligations of the interdisciplinary team as a whole and of its individual members should be clearly established.

(b) Social workers for whom a team decision raises ethical concerns should attempt to resolve the disagreement through appropriate channels. If the disagreement cannot be resolved, social workers should pursue other avenues to address their concerns consistent with client well-being.

2.04 Disputes Involving Colleagues

(a) Social workers should not take advantage of a dispute between a colleague and an employer to obtain a position or otherwise advance the social workers' own interests.

(b) Social workers should not exploit clients in disputes with colleagues or engage clients in any inappropriate discussion of conflicts between social workers and their colleagues.

2.05 Consultation

(a) Social workers should seek the advice and counsel of colleagues whenever such consultation is in the best interests of clients.

(b) Social workers should keep themselves informed about colleagues' areas of expertise and competencies. Social workers should seek consultation only from colleagues who have demonstrated knowledge, expertise, and competence related to the subject of the consultation.

(c) When consulting with colleagues about clients, social workers should disclose the least amount of information necessary to achieve the purposes of the consultation.

2.06 Referral for Services

(a) Social workers should refer clients to other professionals when the other professionals' specialized knowledge or expertise is needed to serve clients fully or when social workers believe that they are not being effective or making reasonable progress with clients and that additional service is required.

(b) Social workers who refer clients to other professionals should take appropriate steps to facilitate an orderly transfer of responsibility. Social workers who refer clients to other professionals should disclose, with clients' consent, all pertinent information to the new service providers.

(c) Social workers are prohibited from giving or receiving payment for a referral when no professional service is provided by the referring social worker.

2.07 Sexual Relationships

(a) Social workers who function as supervisors or educators should not engage in sexual activities or contact with supervisees, students, trainees, or other colleagues over whom they exercise professional authority.

(b) Social workers should avoid engaging in sexual relationships with colleagues when there is potential for a conflict of interest. Social workers who become involved in, or anticipate becoming involved in, a sexual relationship with a colleague have a duty to transfer professional responsibilities, when necessary, to avoid a conflict of interest.

2.08 Sexual Harassment

Social workers should not sexually harass supervisees, students, trainees, or colleagues. Sexual harassment includes sexual advances, sexual solicitation, requests for sexual favors, and other verbal or physical conduct of a sexual nature.

2.09 Impairment of Colleagues

(a) Social workers who have direct knowledge of a social work colleague's impairment that is due to personal problems, psychosocial distress, substance abuse, or mental health difficulties and that interferes with practice effectiveness should consult with that colleague when feasible and assist the colleague in taking remedial action.

(b) Social workers who believe that a social work colleague's impairment interferes with practice effectiveness and that the colleague has not taken adequate steps to address the impairment should take action through appropriate channels established by employers, agencies, NASW, licensing and regulatory bodies, and other professional organizations.

2.10 Incompetence of Colleagues

(a) Social workers who have direct knowledge of a social work colleague's incompetence should consult with that colleague when feasible and assist the colleague in taking remedial action.

(b) Social workers who believe that a social work colleague is incompetent and has not taken adequate steps to address the incompetence should take action through appropriate channels established by employers, agencies, NASW, licensing and regulatory bodies, and other professional organizations.

2.11 Unethical Conduct of Colleagues

(a) Social workers should take adequate measures to discourage, prevent, expose, and correct the unethical conduct of colleagues.
(b) Social workers should be knowledgeable about established policies and procedures for handling concerns about colleagues' unethical behavior. Social workers should be familiar with national, state, and local procedures for handling ethics complaints. These include policies and procedures created by NASW, licensing and regulatory bodies, employers, agencies, and other professional organizations.
(c) Social workers who believe that a colleague has acted unethically should seek resolution by discussing their concerns with the colleague when feasible and when such discussion is likely to be productive.
(d) When necessary, social workers who believe that a colleague has acted unethically should take action through appropriate formal channels (such as contacting a state licensing board or regulatory body, an NASW committee on inquiry, or other professional ethics committees).
(e) Social workers should defend and assist colleagues who are unjustly charged with unethical conduct.

3. Social Workers' Ethical Responsibilities in Practice Settings

3.01 Supervision and Consultation

(a) Social workers who provide supervision or consultation should have the necessary knowledge and skill to supervise or consult appropriately and should do so only within their areas of knowledge and competence.
(b) Social workers who provide supervision or consultation are responsible for setting clear, appropriate, and culturally sensitive boundaries.
(c) Social workers should not engage in any dual or multiple relationships with supervisees in which there is a risk of exploitation of or potential harm to the supervisee.
(d) Social workers who provide supervision should evaluate supervisees' performance in a manner that is fair and respectful.

3.02 Education and Training

(a) Social workers who function as educators, field instructors for students, or trainers should provide instruction only within their areas of knowledge and competence and should provide instruction based on the most current information and knowledge available in the profession.
(b) Social workers who function as educators or field instructors for students should evaluate students' performance in a manner that is fair and respectful.

(c) Social workers who function as educators or field instructors for students should take reasonable steps to ensure that clients are routinely informed when services are being provided by students.

(d) Social workers who function as educators or field instructors for students should not engage in any dual or multiple relationships with students in which there is a risk of exploitation or potential harm to the student. Social work educators and field instructors are responsible for setting clear, appropriate, and culturally sensitive boundaries.

3.03 Performance Evaluation

Social workers who have responsibility for evaluating the performance of others should fulfill such responsibility in a fair and considerate manner and on the basis of clearly stated criteria.

3.04 Client Records

(a) Social workers should take reasonable steps to ensure that documentation in records is accurate and reflects the services provided.

(b) Social workers should include sufficient and timely documentation in records to facilitate the delivery of services and to ensure continuity of services provided to clients in the future.

(c) Social workers' documentation should protect clients' privacy to the extent that is possible and appropriate and should include only information that is directly relevant to the delivery of services.

(d) Social workers should store records following the termination of services to ensure reasonable future access. Records should be maintained for the number of years required by state statutes or relevant contracts.

3.05 Billing

Social workers should establish and maintain billing practices that accurately reflect the nature and extent of services provided and that identify who provided the service in the practice setting.

3.06 Client Transfer

(a) When an individual who is receiving services from another agency or colleague contacts a social worker for services, the social worker should carefully consider the client's needs before agreeing to provide services. To minimize possible confusion and conflict, social workers should discuss with potential clients the nature of the clients' current relationship with other service providers and the implications, including possible benefits or risks, of entering into a relationship with a new service provider.

(b) If a new client has been served by another agency or colleague, social workers should discuss with the client whether consultation with the previous service provider is in the client's best interest.

3.07 Administration

(a) Social work administrators should advocate within and outside their agencies for adequate resources to meet clients' needs.
(b) Social workers should advocate for resource allocation procedures that are open and fair. When not all clients' needs can be met, an allocation procedure should be developed that is nondiscriminatory and based on appropriate and consistently applied principles.
(c) Social workers who are administrators should take reasonable steps to ensure that adequate agency or organizational resources are available to provide appropriate staff supervision.
(d) Social work administrators should take reasonable steps to ensure that the working environment for which they are responsible is consistent with and encourages compliance with the NASW Code of Ethics. Social work administrators should take reasonable steps to eliminate any conditions in their organizations that violate, interfere with, or discourage compliance with the Code.

3.08 Continuing Education and Staff Development

Social work administrators and supervisors should take reasonable steps to provide or arrange for continuing education and staff development for all staff for whom they are responsible. Continuing education and staff development should address current knowledge and emerging developments related to social work practice and ethics.

3.09 Commitments to Employers

(a) Social workers generally should adhere to commitments made to employers and employing organizations.
(b) Social workers should work to improve employing agencies' policies and procedures and the efficiency and effectiveness of their services.
(c) Social workers should take reasonable steps to ensure that employers are aware of social workers' ethical obligations as set forth in the NASW Code of Ethics and of the implications of those obligations for social work practice.
(d) Social workers should not allow an employing organization's policies, procedures, regulations, or administrative orders to interfere with their ethical practice of social work. Social workers should take reasonable steps to ensure that their employing organizations' practices are consistent with the NASW Code of Ethics.
(e) Social workers should act to prevent and eliminate discrimination in the employing organization's work assignments and in its employment policies and practices.

(f) Social workers should accept employment or arrange student field placements only in organizations that exercise fair personnel practices.

(g) Social workers should be diligent stewards of the resources of their employing organizations, wisely conserving funds where appropriate and never misappropriating funds or using them for unintended purposes.

3.10 Labor-Management Disputes

(a) Social workers may engage in organized action, including the formation of and participation in labor unions, to improve services to clients and working conditions.

(b) The actions of social workers who are involved in labor-management disputes, job actions, or labor strikes should be guided by the profession's values, ethical principles, and ethical standards. Reasonable differences of opinion exist among social workers concerning their primary obligation as professionals during an actual or threatened labor strike or job action. Social workers should carefully examine relevant issues and their possible impact on clients before deciding on a course of action.

4. Social Workers' Ethical Responsibilities as Professionals

4.01 Competence

(a) Social workers should accept responsibility or employment only on the basis of existing competence or the intention to acquire the necessary competence.

(b) Social workers should strive to become and remain proficient in professional practice and the performance of professional functions. Social workers should critically examine and keep current with emerging knowledge relevant to social work. Social workers should routinely review the professional literature and participate in continuing education relevant to social work practice and social work ethics.

(c) Social workers should base practice on recognized knowledge, including empirically based knowledge, relevant to social work and social work ethics.

4.02 Discrimination

Social workers should not practice, condone, facilitate, or collaborate with any form of discrimination on the basis of race, ethnicity, national origin, color, sex, sexual orientation, age, marital status, political belief, religion, or mental or physical disability.

4.03 Private Conduct

Social workers should not permit their private conduct to interfere with their ability to fulfill their professional responsibilities.

4.04 Dishonesty, Fraud, and Deception

Social workers should not participate in, condone, or be associated with dishonesty, fraud, or deception.

4.05 Impairment

(a) Social workers should not allow their own personal problems, psychosocial distress, legal problems, substance abuse, or mental health difficulties to interfere with their professional judgment and performance or to jeopardize the best interests of people for whom they have a professional responsibility.

(b) Social workers whose personal problems, psychosocial distress, legal problems, substance abuse, or mental health difficulties interfere with their professional judgment and performance should immediately seek consultation and take appropriate remedial action by seeking professional help, making adjustments in workload, terminating practice, or taking any other steps necessary to protect clients and others.

4.06 Misrepresentation

(a) Social workers should make clear distinctions between statements made and actions engaged in as a private individual and as a representative of the social work profession, a professional social work organization, or the social worker's employing agency.

(b) Social workers who speak on behalf of professional social work organizations should accurately represent the official and authorized positions of the organizations.

(c) Social workers should ensure that their representations to clients, agencies, and the public of professional qualifications, credentials, education, competence, affiliations, services provided, or results to be achieved are accurate. Social workers should claim only those relevant professional credentials they actually possess and take steps to correct any inaccuracies or misrepresentations of their credentials by others.

4.07 Solicitations

(a) Social workers should not engage in uninvited solicitation of potential clients who, because of their circumstances, are vulnerable to undue influence, manipulation, or coercion.

(b) Social workers should not engage in solicitation of testimonial endorsements (including solicitation of consent to use a client's prior statement as a testimonial endorsement) from current clients or from other people who, because of their particular circumstances, are vulnerable to undue influence.

4.08 Acknowledging Credit

(a) Social workers should take responsibility and credit, including authorship credit, only for work they have actually performed and to which they have contributed.

(b) Social workers should honestly acknowledge the work of and the contributions made by others.

5. Social Workers' Ethical Responsibilities to the Social Work Profession

5.01 Integrity of the Profession

(a) Social workers should work toward the maintenance and promotion of high standards of practice.

(b) Social workers should uphold and advance the values, ethics, knowledge, and mission of the profession. Social workers should protect, enhance, and improve the integrity of the profession through appropriate study and research, active discussion, and responsible criticism of the profession.

(c) Social workers should contribute time and professional expertise to activities that promote respect for the value, integrity, and competence of the social work profession. These activities may include teaching, research, consultation, service, legislative testimony, presentations in the community, and participation in their professional organizations.

(d) Social workers should contribute to the knowledge base of social work and share with colleagues their knowledge related to practice, research, and ethics. Social workers should seek to con-tribute to the profession's literature and to share their knowledge at professional meetings and conferences.

(e) Social workers should act to prevent the unauthorized and unqualified practice of social work.

5.02 Evaluation and Research

(a) Social workers should monitor and evaluate policies, the implementation of programs, and practice interventions.

(b) Social workers should promote and facilitate evaluation and research to contribute to the development of knowledge.

(c) Social workers should critically examine and keep current with emerging knowledge relevant to social work and fully use evaluation and research evidence in their professional practice.

(d) Social workers engaged in evaluation or research should carefully consider possible consequences and should follow guidelines developed for the protection of evaluation and research participants. Appropriate institutional review boards should be consulted.

(e) Social workers engaged in evaluation or research should obtain voluntary and written informed consent from participants, when appropriate, without any implied or actual deprivation or penalty for refusal to participate; without undue inducement to participate; and with due regard for participants' well-being, privacy, and dignity. Informed consent should include information about the nature, extent, and duration of the participation requested and disclosure of the risks and benefits of participation in the research.

(f) When evaluation or research participants are incapable of giving informed consent, social workers should provide an appropriate explanation to the participants, obtain the participants' assent to the extent they are able, and obtain written consent from an appropriate proxy.

(g) Social workers should never design or conduct evaluation or research that does not use consent procedures, such as certain forms of naturalistic observation and archival research, unless rigorous and responsible review of the research has found it to be justified because of its prospective scientific, educational, or applied value and unless equally effective alternative procedures that do not involve waiver of consent are not feasible.

(h) Social workers should inform participants of their right to withdraw from evaluation and research at any time without penalty.

(i) Social workers should take appropriate steps to ensure that participants in evaluation and research have access to appropriate supportive services.

(j) Social workers engaged in evaluation or research should protect participants from unwarranted physical or mental distress, harm, danger, or deprivation.

(k) Social workers engaged in the evaluation of services should discuss collected information only for professional purposes and only with people professionally concerned with this information.

(l) Social workers engaged in evaluation or research should ensure the anonymity or confidentiality of participants and of the data obtained from them. Social workers should inform participants of any limits of confidentiality, the measures that will be taken to ensure confidentiality, and when any records containing research data will be destroyed.

(m) Social workers who report evaluation and research results should protect participants' confidentiality by omitting identifying information unless proper consent has been obtained authorizing disclosure.

(n) Social workers should report evaluation and research findings accurately. They should not fabricate or falsify results and should take steps to correct any errors later found in published data using standard publication methods.

(o) Social workers engaged in evaluation or research should be alert to and avoid conflicts of interest and dual relationships with participants, should inform participants when a real or potential conflict of interest arises, and should take steps to resolve the issue in a manner that makes participants' interests primary.

(p) Social workers should educate themselves, their students, and their colleagues about responsible research practices.

6. Social Workers' Ethical Responsibilities to the Broader Society

6.01 Social Welfare

Social workers should promote the general welfare of society, from local to global levels, and the development of people, their communities, and their environments. Social workers should advocate for living conditions conducive to the fulfillment of basic human needs and should promote social, economic, political, and cultural values and institutions that are compatible with the realization of social justice.

6.02 Public Participation

Social workers should facilitate informed participation by the public in shaping social policies and institutions.

6.03 Public Emergencies

Social workers should provide appropriate professional services in public emergencies to the greatest extent possible.

6.04 Social and Political Action

(a) Social workers should engage in social and political action that seeks to ensure that all people have equal access to the resources, employment, services, and opportunities they require to meet their basic human needs and to develop fully. Social workers should be aware of the impact of the political arena on practice and should advocate for changes in policy and legislation to improve social conditions in order to meet basic human needs and promote social justice.

(b) Social workers should act to expand choice and opportunity for all people, with special regard for vulnerable, disadvantaged, oppressed, and exploited people and groups.

(c) Social workers should promote conditions that encourage respect for cultural and social diversity within the United States and globally. Social workers should promote policies and practices that demonstrate respect for difference, support the expansion of cultural knowledge and resources, advocate for programs and institutions that demonstrate cultural competence, and promote policies that safeguard the rights of and confirm equity and social justice for all people.

(d) Social workers should act to prevent and eliminate domination of, exploitation of, and discrimination against any person, group, or class on the basis of race, ethnicity, national origin, color, sex, sexual orientation, age, marital status, political belief, religion, or mental or physical disability.

REFERENCES

Abbott, Andrew. 1992. "From Causes to Events: Notes on Narrative Positivism." *Sociological Methods and Research* 20(May):428–55.

Adair, G., T. W. Dushenko, and R. C. L. Lindsay. 1985. "Ethical Regulations and Their Impact on Research Practice." *American Psychologist* 40: 59–72.

Addison, Richard B. 1999. "A Grounded Hermeneutic Editing Approach." Pp. 145–61 in *Doing Qualitative Research,* edited by Benjamin F. Crabtree and William L. Miller. Thousand Oaks, CA: Sage.

Alfred, Randall. 1976. "The Church of Satan." Pp. 180–202 in *The New Religious Consciousness,* edited by Charles Glock and Robert Bellah. Berkeley: University of California Press.

Alter, Catherine. 1996. "Family Support as an Intervention with Female Long-Term AFDC Recipients." *Social Work Research* 20:203–216.

Altheide, David L. and John M. Johnson. 1994. "Criteria for Assessing Interpretive Validity in Qualitative Research." Pp. 485–99 in *Handbook of Qualitative Research,* edited by Norman K. Denzin and Yvonna S. Lincoln. Thousand Oaks, CA: Sage.

American Psychiatric Association. 1994. *Diagnostic and Statistical Manual of Mental Disorders,* 4th ed. (DSM IV). Washington, DC: American Psychiatric Association.

Anderson, Elijah. 1990. *Streetwise: Race, Class, and Change in an Urban Community.* Chicago, IL: University of Chicago Press.

Anderson, Elijah. 1999. *Code of the Street: Decency, Violence, and the Moral Life of the Inner City.* New York: W. W. Norton.

Anderson, Elijah. 2003. "Jelly's Place: An Ethnographic Memoir." *Symbolic Interaction* 26:217–37.

Angel, Ronald, J., P. Lindsay Chase-Lansdale, Andrew Cherlin, and Robert Moffit. 2002. *Welfare, Children, and Families: Results from a Three City Study: A Congressional Briefing* (May 17). Washington, DC: Consortium of Social Science Associations.

Arean, Patricia A. and Dolores Gallagher-Thompson. 1996. "Issues and Recommendations for the Recruitment and Retention of Older Ethnic Minority Adults into Clinical Research." *Journal of Consulting and Clinical Psychology* 64:875–80.

Aronson, Elliot and Judson Mills. 1959. "The Effect of Severity of Initiation on Liking for a Group." *Journal of Abnormal and Social Psychology* 59 (September):177–81.

Aseltine, Robert H., Jr., and Ronald C. Kessler. 1993. "Marital Disruption and Depression in a Community Sample." *Journal of Health and Social Behavior* 34 (September):237–51.

Axinn, William, Lisa Pearce, and Dirgha Ghimire. 1999. "Innovations in Life History Calendar Applications." *Social Science Research* 28:243–64.

Bachman, Ronet and Russell K. Schutt. 2003. *The Practice of Research in Criminology and Criminal Justice,* 2d ed. Thousand Oaks, CA: Pine Forge Press.

Bainbridge, William Sims. 1989. *Survey Research: A Computer-Assisted Introduction.* Belmont, CA: Wadsworth.

Balaswamy, Shantha and Holly I. Dabelko. 2002. "Using a Stakeholder Participatory Model in a Community-Wide Service Needs Assessment of Elderly Residents: A Case Study." *Journal of Community Practice* 10:55–70.

Bangs, Ralph, Cheryl Z. Kerchis, and S. Laurel Weldon. 1997. *Basic Living Cost and Living Wage Estimates for Pittsburgh and Allegheny County.* Pittsburgh, PA: University of Pittsburgh & UCSUR.

Barbee, Evelyn L. 1992. "African American Women and Depression: A Review and Critique of the Literature." *Archives of Psychiatric Nursing* 6:257–65.

Barlow, David and Michel Hersen. 1984. *Single Case Experimental Designs: Strategies for Studying Behavior Change,* 2d ed. New York: Pergamon Press.

Barringer, Felicity. 1993. "Majority in Poll Back Ban on Handguns." *The New York Times,* June 4, p. A14.

Becker, Howard S. 1958. "Problems of Inference and Proof in Participant Observation." *American Sociological Review* 23:652–60.

Becker, Howard S. 1986. *Writing for Social Scientists.* Chicago, IL: University of Chicago Press. (This can be ordered directly from the American Sociological Association, 1722 N Street, NW, Washington, DC 20036, 202–833–3410.)

Bellah, Robert N., Richard Madsen, William M. Sullivan, Ann Swidler, and Steven M. Tipton. 1985. *Habits of the Heart: Individualism and Commitment in American Life.* New York: Harper & Row.

Bennett, Lauren, Lisa Goodman, and Mary Ann Dutton. 1999. "Systemic Obstacles to the Criminal Prosecution of a Battering Partner: A Victim Perspective." *Journal of Interpersonal Violence* 14:761–72.

Berk, Richard A., Alec Campbell, Ruth Klap, and Bruce Western. 1992. "The Deterrent Effect of Arrest: A Bayesian Analysis of Four Field Experiments." *American Sociological Review* 57(October):698–708.

Besa, David. 1994. "Evaluating Narrative Family Therapy Using Single-System Research Designs." *Research on Social Work Practice* 4:309–25.

Beyer, William H., ed. 1968. *CRC Handbook of Tables for Probability and Statistics,* 2d ed. Boca Raton, FL: CRC Press.

Black, Donald J., ed. 1984. *Toward a General Theory of Social Control, Vol. 1.* Orlando, FL: Academic Press.

Blair, Johnny E. 1989. Unpublished letter to Catherine E. Ross, April 10.

Blau, Peter M. 1964. *Exchange and Power in Social Life.* New York: John Wiley.

Bloom, Martin, Joel Fischer, and John Orme. 2003. *Evaluating Practice: Guidelines for the Accountable Professional,* 4th ed. Boston, MA: Allyn and Bacon.

Bogdewic, Stephan P. 1999. "Participant Observation." Pp. 33–45 in *Doing Qualitative Research,* 2d ed., edited by Benjamin F. Crabtree and William L. Miller. Thousand Oaks, CA: Sage.

Booth, Wayne C., Gregory G. Colomb, and Joseph M. Williams. 1995. *The Craft of Research.* Chicago, IL: University of Chicago Press.

Boruch, Robert F. 1997. *Randomized Experiments for Planning and Evaluation: A Practical Guide.* Thousand Oaks, CA: Sage.

Bound, John, Timothy Waidmann, Michael Schoenbaum, and Jeffrey B. Bingenheimer. 2003. "The Labor Market Consequences of Race Differences in Health." *The Milbank Quarterly,* 81:441–473.

Bourgois, Philippe, Mark Lettiere, and James Quesada. 1997. "Social Misery and the Sanctions of Substance Abuse: Confronting HIV Risk Among Homeless Heroin Addicts in San Francisco." *Social Problems* 44:155–73.

Bradshaw, William. 1997. "Evaluating Cognitive-Behavioral Treatment of Schizophrenia: Four Single-Case Studies." *Research on Social Work Practice* 7:419–45.

Brett, Pamela J., Kathryn Graham, and Cynthia Smythe. 1995. "An Analysis of Specialty Journals on Alcohol, Drugs, and Addictive Behaviors for Sex Bias in Research Methods and Reporting." *Journal of Studies on Alcohol* 56:24–34.

Brewer, John and Albert Hunter. 1989. *Multimethod Research: A Synthesis of Styles.* Newbury Park, CA: Sage.

Bridges, George S. and Joseph G. Weis. 1989. "Measuring Violent Behavior: Effects of Study Design on Reported Correlates of Violence." Pp. 14–34 in *Violent Crime, Violent Criminals,* edited by Neil Alan Weiner and Marvin E. Wolfgang. Newbury Park, CA: Sage.

Brock, Thomas and Kristen Harknett. 1998. "A Comparison of Two Welfare-to-Work Case Management Models." *Social Service Review* 72:493–520.

Brown, Judith Belle. 1999. "The Use of Focus Groups in Clinical Research." Pp. 109–24 in *Doing Qualitative Research,* 2d ed., edited by Benjamin F. Crabtree and William L. Miller. Thousand Oaks, CA: Sage.

Burt, Martha R. 1996. "Homelessness: Definitions and Counts." Pp. 15–23 in *Homelessness in America,* edited by Jim Baumohl. Phoenix, AZ: Oryx Press.

Buzawa, Eve S. and Carl G. Buzawa, eds. 1996. *Do Arrests and Restraining Orders Work?* Thousand Oaks, CA: Sage.

Cain, Leonard D., Jr. 1967. "The AMA and the Gerontologists: Uses and Abuses of 'A Profile of the Aging: USA.'" Pp. 78–114 in *Ethics, Politics, and Social Research,* edited by Gideon Sjoberg. Cambridge, MA: Schenkman.

Campbell, Donald T. and M. Jean Russo. 1999. *Social Experimentation.* Thousand Oaks, CA: Sage.

Campbell, Richard T. 1992. "Longitudinal Research." Pp. 1146–58 in *Encyclopedia of Sociology,* edited by Edgar F. Borgatta and Marie L. Borgatta. New York: Macmillan.

Campbell, Wilson. 2002. *A Statement from the Government Accounting Standards Board and Performance Measurement Staff* (American Society for Public Administration). Retrieved July 20, 2002 (http://www.aspanet.org/cap/forum_statement.html#top).

Carr, James and Eric Burkholder. 1998. "Creating Single-Subject Design Graphs with Microsoft Excel." *Journal of Applied Behavior Analysis* 31:245–51.

Caspi, Avshalom, Terrie Moffitt, Arland Thornton, Deborah Freedman, James Amell, Honalee Harrington, Judith Smeijers, and Phil A. Silva. 1996. "The Life History Calendar: A Research and Clinical Assessment Method for Collecting Retrospective Event-History Data." *International Journal of Methods in Psychiatric Research* 6:101–14.

Cauce, Ann Mari, Kimberly D. Ryan, and Kwai Grove. 1998. "Children and Adolescents of Color, Where Are You? Participation, Selection, Recruitment, and Retention in Developmental Research." Pp. 147–66 in *Studying Minority Adolescents: Conceptual, Methodological, and Theoretical Issues,* edited by Vonnie C. McLoyd and Laurence Steinberg. Mahwah, NJ: Lawrence Erlbaum.

Chen, Huey-Tsyh. 1990. *Theory-Driven Evaluations.* Newbury Park, CA: Sage.

Chen, Huey-Tsyh and Peter Rossi. 1987. "The Theory-Driven Approach to Validity." *Evaluation and Program Planning* 10:95–103.

Cheung, Kam-fong Monit. 1999. "Effectiveness of Social Work Treatment and Massage Therapy for Nursing Home Clients." *Research on Social Work Practice* 9:229–47.

Coffey, Amanda and Paul Atkinson. 1996. *Making Sense of Qualitative Data: Complementary Research Strategies.* Thousand Oaks, CA: Sage.

Cohen, Gary and Barbara Kerr. 1998. "Computer-Mediated Counseling: An Empirical Study of a New Mental Health Treatment." *Computers in Human Services* 15:13–26.

Coleman, James S. and Thomas Hoffer. 1987. *Public and Private High Schools: The Impact of Communities.* New York: Basic Books.

Coleman, James S., Thomas Hoffer, and Sally Kilgore. 1982. *High School Achievement: Public, Catholic, and Private Schools Compared.* New York: Basic Books.

Colon, Israel and Brett Marston. 1999. "Resistance to a Residential AIDS Home: An Empirical Test of NIMBY. *Journal of Homosexuality* 37:135–45.

Converse, Jean M. 1984. "Attitude Measurement in Psychology and Sociology: The Early Years." Pp. 3–40 in *Surveying Subjective Phenomena,* Vol. 2, edited by Charles F. Turner and Elizabeth Martin. New York: Russell Sage Foundation.

Cook, Thomas D. and Donald T. Campbell. 1979. *Quasi-Experimentation: Design and Analysis Issues for Field Settings.* Chicago, IL: Rand McNally.

Cooper, Harris and Larry V. Hedges. 1994. "Research Synthesis as a Scientific Enterprise." Pp. 3–14 in *The Handbook of Research Synthesis,* edited by Harris Cooper and Larry V. Hedges. New York: Russell Sage Foundation.

Core Institute. 1994. "Core Alcohol and Drug Survey: Long Form." Carbondale: Southern Illinois University, FIPSE Core Analysis Grantee Group, Core Institute, Student Health Programs.

Costner, Herbert L. 1989. "The Validity of Conclusions in Evaluation Research: A Further Development of Chen and Rossi's Theory-Driven Approach." *Evaluation and Program Planning* 12:345–53.

Cotrell, Victoria and Rafael J. Engel. 1998. "Predictors of Respite Service Utilization." *Journal of Gerontological Social Work* 30:117–32.

Counts, Dorothy Ayers and David R. Counts. 1996. *Over the Next Hill: An Ethnography of RVing Seniors in North America.* Orchard Park, NY: Broadview Press.

Couper, Mick P., Reginald P. Baker, Jelke Bethlehem, Cynthia Z. F. Clark, Jean Martin, William L. Nicholls II, and James M. O'Reilly, eds. 1998. *Computer Assisted Survey Information Collection.* New York: John Wiley.

Cress, Daniel M. and David A. Snow. 2000. "The Outcomes of Homeless Mobilization: The Influence of Modernity and Proto-Modernity on Political and Civil Rights, 1965 to 1980. *American Sociological Review* 60:702–18.

Cuba, Lee J. 2002. *A Short Guide to Writing about Social Science,* 4th ed. New York: Addison-Wesley.

Czaja, Ronald and Bob Blair. 1995. *Survey Research.* Thousand Oaks, CA: Pine Forge Press.

Dattalo, Patrick. 1998. "Time Series Analysis: Concepts and Techniques for Community Practitioners." *Journal of Community Practice* 5:67–85.

Davies, Philip, Anthony Petrosino, and Iain Chalmers. 1999. *Report and Papers from the Exploratory Meeting for the Campbell Collaboration.* London: School of Public Policy, University College.

Davis, James A. 1985. *The Logic of Causal Order* (Sage University Paper Series on Quantitative Applications in the Social Sciences, Series no. 07-055). Beverly Hills, CA: Sage.

Davis, James A. and Tom W. Smith. 1992. *The NORC General Social Survey: A User's Guide.* Newbury Park, CA: Sage.

Davis, Ryan. 1999. "Study: Search Engines Can't Keep Up with Expanding Net." *The Boston Globe,* July 8, pp. C1, C3.

Dawes, Robyn. 1995. "How Do You Formulate a Testable Exciting Hypothesis?" Pp. 93–96 in *How to Write a Successful Research Grant Application: A Guide for Social and Behavioral Scientists,* edited by Willo Pequegnat and Ellen Stover. New York: Plenum Press.

Decker, Scott H. and Barrik Van Winkle. 1996. *Life in the Gang: Family, Friends, and Violence.* Cambridge, UK: Cambridge University Press.

Dentler, Robert A. 2002. *Practicing Sociology: Selected Fields.* Westport, CT: Praeger.

Denzin, Norman K. 2002. "The Interpretative Process." Pp. 349–68 in *The Qualitative Researcher's Companion,* edited by A. Michael Huberman and Matthew B. Miles. Thousand Oaks, CA: Sage.

Denzin, Norman K. and Yvonna S. Lincoln. 1994. "Introduction: Entering the Field of Qualitative Research." Pp. 1–17 in *Handbook of Qualitative Research,* edited by Norman K. Denzin and Yvonna S. Lincoln. Thousand Oaks, CA: Sage.

DeParle, Jason. 1999. "Project to Rescue Needy Stumbles against the Persistence of Poverty." *The New York Times,* May 15, pp. A1, A10.

Diamond, Timothy. 1992. *Making Gray Gold: Narratives of Nursing Home Care.* Chicago, IL: University of Chicago Press.

Dillman, Don A. 1978. *Mail and Telephone Surveys: The Total Design Method.* New York: John Wiley.

Dillman, Don A. 1982. "Mail and Other Self-Administered Questionnaires." Chapter 12 in *Handbook of Survey Research,* edited by Peter Rossi, James Wright, and Andy Anderson. New York: Academic Press. As reprinted on pp. 637–38 in Delbert C. Miller, 1991, *Handbook of Research Design and Social Measurement,* 5th ed. Newbury Park, CA: Sage.

Dillman, Don A. 2000. *Mail and Internet Surveys: The Tailored Design Method,* 2d ed. New York: John Wiley.

Dillman, Don A., James A. Christenson, Edwin H. Carpenter, and Ralph M. Brooks. 1974. "Increasing Mail Questionnaire Response: A Four-State Comparison." *American Sociological Review* 39(October):744–56.

Dohrenwend, Bruce, P. and Barbara Snell Dohrenwend. 1982. "Perspectives on the Past and Future of Psychiatric Epidemiology." *American Journal of Public Health* 72:1271–79.

Drake, Robert E., Gregory J. McHugo, Deborah R. Becker, William A. Anthony, and Robin E. Clark. 1996. "The New Hampshire Study of Supported Employment for People with Severe Mental Illness." *Journal of Consulting and Clinical Psychology* 64:391–99.

Drake, Robert E., Gregory J. McHugo, and Jeremy C. Biesanz. 1995. "The Test-Retest Reliability of Standardized Instruments among Homeless Persons with Substance Use Disorders." *Journal of Studies on Alcohol* 56(2):161–67.

Edin, Kathryn and Laura Lein. 1997. *Making Ends Meet: How Single Mothers Survive Welfare and Low-Wage Work.* New York: Russell Sage Foundation.

Emerson, Robert M., Rachel I. Fretz, and Linda L. Shaw. 1995. *Writing Ethnographic Fieldnotes.* Chicago, IL: University of Chicago Press.

Engel, Rafael J. 1988. "The Dynamics of Poverty for the Elderly," Ph.D. dissertation, University of Wisconsin, Madison, WI.

Engel, Rafael J. (1994, June). *Settlement House Survey Final Report.* Pittsburgh, PA: United Way of Allegheny County and University of Pittsburgh Institute of Politics.

Engel, Rafael J., Richard Welsh, and Laura Lewis. 2000. "An Evaluation of Orientation and Mobility Training and Rehabilitation Teaching: Improving the Well-Being of Vision-Impaired Older Adults. *RE:view* 32:67–76.

Ensel, Walter, Kristen Peek, Nan Lin, and Gina Lai. 1996. "Stress in the Life Course: A Life History Approach." *Journal of Aging and Health* 8:389–416.

Erikson, Kai T. 1967. "A Comment on Disguised Observation in Sociology." *Social Problems* 12:366–73.

Essock, Susan M., Linda K. Frisman, and Nina J. Kontos. 1998. "Cost-Effectiveness of Assertive Community Treatment Teams." *American Journal of Orthopsychiatry* 68:179–90.

Fenno, Richard F., Jr. 1978. *Home Style: House Members in Their Districts.* Boston, MA: Little, Brown.

Ferguson, Kirsten and Margaret Rodway. 1994. "Cognitive Behavioral Treatment of Perfectionism: Initial Evaluation Studies." *Research on Social Work Practice* 4:283–308.

Ferraro, Kenneth F. and Melissa M. Farmer. 1996. "Double Jeopardy to Health Hypothesis for African Americans: Analysis and Critique." *Journal of Health and Social Behavior,* 37:27–43.

Fink, Arlene. 1998. *Conducting Research Literature Reviews: From Paper to the Internet.* Thousand Oaks, CA: Sage.

Forero, Juan. 2000a. "Census Takers Say Supervisors Fostered Filing of False Data." *The New York Times,* July 28, p. A21.

Forero, Juan. 2000b. "Census Takers Top '90 Efforts in New York City, with More to Go." *The New York Times,* June 12, p. A29.

Fowler, Floyd J. 1988. *Survey Research Methods,* Rev. ed. Newbury Park, CA: Sage.

Fowler, Floyd J. 1995. *Improving Survey Questions: Design and Evaluation.* Thousand Oaks, CA: Sage.

Fowler, Floyd J. 1998. Personal communication, January 7. Boston: University of Massachusetts, Center for Survey Research.

Franklin, Ronald D., David B. Allison, and Bernard S. Gorman. 1997. *Design and Analysis of Single-Case Research.* Mahwah, NJ: Erlbaum Associates.

Franks, Peter, Marthe R. Gold and Kevin Fiscella. 2003. "Sociodemographics, Self-Rated Health, and Mortality in the U.S." *Social Science and Medicine,* 56:2505-2514.

Freedman, David A. 1991. "Statistical Models and Shoe Leather." Pp. 291–313 in *Sociological Methodology,* Vol. 21, edited by Peter V. Marsden. Oxford, UK: Basil Blackwell.

Garland, Diana, Robin Rogers, and Gaynor Yancey. 2001. "The Faith Factor in Effective Models of Multi-Sector Collaboration" (Grant proposal to the Pew Charitable Trusts). Waco, TX: Baylor University.

Geertz, Clifford. 1973. "Thick Description: Toward an Interpretive Theory of Culture." Pp. 3–30 in *The Interpretation of Cultures,* edited by Clifford Geertz. New York: Basic Books.

Gelman, Caroline R. 2002. "The Elderly Latino Population in Holyoke, MA: A Qualitative Study of Unmet Needs and Community Strengths." *Journal of Gerontological Social Work* 39:89–114.

Gilchrist, Valerie J. and Robert L. Williams. 1999. "Key Informant Interviews." Pp. 71–88 in *Doing Qualitative Research,* 2d ed., edited by Benjamin F. Crabtree and William L. Miller. Thousand Oaks, CA: Sage.

Gilligan, Carol. 1982. *In a Different Voice: Psychological Theory and Women's Development.* Cambridge, MA: Harvard University Press.

Glaser, Barney G. and Anselm L. Strauss. 1967. *The Discovery of Grounded Theory: Strategies for Qualitative Research.* London: Weidenfeld and Nicholson.

Goffman, Erving. 1961. *Asylums: Essays on the Social Situation of Mental Patients and Other Inmates.* Garden City, NY: Doubleday.

Goldapple, Gary and Dianne Montgomery. 1993. "Evaluating a Behaviorally Based Intervention to Improve Client Retention in Therapeutic Community Treatment for Drug Dependency." *Research on Social Work Practice* 3:21–39.

Goldfinger, Stephen M., Barbara Dickey, Sondra Hellman, Martha O'Bryan, Walter Penk, Russell Schutt, and Larry J. Seidman. 1990. "Apartments v. Evolving Consumer Households for the HMI" (Grant proposal to the National Institute of Mental Health). Boston, MA: Harvard Medical School.

Goldfinger, Stephen M. and Russell K. Schutt. 1996. "Comparisons of Clinicians' Housing Recommendations and Preferences of Homeless Mentally Ill Persons." *Psychiatric Services* 47:4123–415.

Goldfinger, Stephen M., Russell K. Schutt, Larry J. Seidman, Winston M. Turner, Walter E. Penk, and George S. Tolomiczenko. 1996. "Self-Report and Observer Measures of Substance Abuse among Homeless Mentally Ill Persons in the Cross-Section and over Time." *The Journal of Nervous and Mental Disease* 184(11):667–72.

Goldfinger, Stephen M., Russell K. Schutt, George S. Tolomoiczenko, Larry J. Seidman, Walter Penk, Winston M. Turner, and B. Caplan. 1999. "Housing Placement and Subsequent Days Homeless among Formerly Homeless Adults with Mental Illness." *Psychiatric Services* 50:674–79.

Goldfinger, Stephen M., Russell K. Schutt, George S. Tolomiczenko, Winston M. Turner, Norma Ware, Walter E. Penk, Mark S. Abelman, Tara L. AvRuskin, Joshua Breslau, Brina Caplan, Barbara Dickey, Olinda Gonzalez, Byron Good, Sondra Hellman, Susan Soyoung Lee, Martha O'Bryan, and Larry Seidman. 1997. "Housing Persons Who Are Homeless and Mentally Ill: Independent Living or Evolving Consumer Households?" Pp. 29–49 in *Mentally Ill and Homeless: Special Programs for Special Needs,* edited by William R. Breakey and James W. Thompson. Amsterdam, The Netherlands: Harwood.

Goleman, Daniel. 1993a. "Placebo Effect Is Shown to Be Twice as Powerful as Expected." *The New York Times,* August 17, p. C3.

Goleman, Daniel. 1993b. "Pollsters Enlist Psychologists in Quest for Unbiased Results." *The New York Times,* September 7, pp. C1, C11.

Goleman, Daniel. 1995. *Emotional Intelligence.* New York: Bantam Books.

Gordon, Raymond. 1992. *Basic Interviewing Skills.* Itasca, IL: Peacock.

Gorey, Kevin M. 1996. "Effectiveness of Social Work Intervention Research: Internal Versus External Evaluations." *Social Work Research* 20:119–28.

Gorey, Kevin M., Bruce A. Thyer, and Debra E. Pawluck. 1998. "Differential Effectiveness of Prevalent Social Work Practice Models: A Meta-Analysis." *Social Work* 43:269–78.

Graduate Program in Applied Sociology. 1990. *Handbook for Thesis Writers.* Boston: University of Massachusetts-Boston.

Grady, John. 1996. "The Scope of Visual Sociology." *Visual Sociology* 11:10–24.

Graham, Sandra. 1992. "'Most of the Subjects Were White and Middle Class': Trends in Published Research on African Americans in Selected APA Journals, 1970–1989." *American Psychologist* 47:629–39.

Grimm, James W. and Zachary W. Brewster. 2003. "Explaining Health-Related Inequalities with a Social Capital Model." *Research in the Sociology of Health Care*, 20:3–27.

Grinnell, Frederick. 1992. *The Scientific Attitude,* 2d ed. New York: Guilford Press.

Grinnell, Richard M. 1993. *Social Work Research and Evaluation,* 4th ed. Itasca, IL: F. E. Peacock.

Groves, Robert M. 1989. *Survey Errors and Survey Costs.* New York: John Wiley.

Groves, Robert M. and Mick P. Couper. 1998. *Nonresponse in Household Interview Surveys.* New York: John Wiley.

Groves, Robert M. and Robert L. Kahn. 1979. *Surveys by Telephone: A National Comparison with Personal Interviews.* New York: Academic Press. As adapted in Delbert C. Miller, 1991, *Handbook of Research Design and Social Measurement,* 5th ed. Newbury Park, CA: Sage.

Gruenewald, Paul J., Andrew J. Treno, Gail Taff, and Michael Klitzner. 1997. *Measuring Community Indicators: A Systems Approach to Drug and Alcohol Problems.* Thousand Oaks, CA: Sage.

Guba, Egon G. and Yvonna S. Lincoln. 1989. *Fourth Generation Evaluation.* Newbury Park, CA: Sage.

Guba, Egon G. and Yvonna S. Lincoln. 1994. "Competing Paradigms in Qualitative Research." Pp. 105–17 in *Handbook of Qualitative Research,* edited by Norman K. Denzin and Yvonna S. Lincoln. Thousand Oaks, CA: Sage.

Hage, Jerald and Barbara Foley Meeker. 1988. *Social Causality.* Boston, MA: Unwin Hyman.

Haley, Leon and Ralph Bangs. 2000. "Impact of Welfare Reform on Nonprofit Organizations in Pennsylvania" (Proposal to Aspen Institute, Nonprofit Sector Research Fund). Pittsburgh, PA: University of Pittsburgh.

Haney, C., C. Banks, and Philip G. Zimbardo. 1973. "Interpersonal Dynamics in a Simulated Prison." *International Journal of Criminology and Penology* 1:69–97.

Hann, Danette, Kristin Winter, and Paul Jacobsen. 1999. "Measurement of Depressive Symptoms in Cancer Patients: Evaluation of the Center for Epidemiological Studies Depression Scale (CES-D)." *Journal of Psychosomatic Research* 46:4387–443.

Harrison, R. Steven, Scott Boyle, and O. William Farley. 1999. "Evaluating the Outcomes of Family-Based Intervention for Troubled Children: A Pretest-Posttest Study." *Research on Social Work Practice* 9:640–55.

Hartung, Cynthia M. and Thomas A. Widiger. 1998. "Gender Differences in the Diagnosis of Mental Disorders: Conclusions and Controversies of the DSM-IV." *Psychological Bulletin* 123:260–78.

Henderson, J. Neil. 1994. "Ethnic and Racial Issues." Pp. 33–50 in *Qualitative Methods in Aging Research,* edited by Jaber F. Gubrium and Andrea Sankar. Thousand Oaks, CA: Sage.

Herek, Gregory. 1995. "Developing a Theoretical Framework and Rationale for a Research Proposal." Pp. 85–91 in *How to Write a Successful Research Grant Application: A Guide for Social and Behavioral Scientists,* edited by Willo Pequegnat and Ellen Stover. New York: Plenum Press.

Herek, Gregory, Douglas C. Kimmel, Hortensia Amaro, and Gary B. Melton. 1991. "Avoiding Heterosexist Bias in Psychological Research." Pp. 739–55 in *Psychological Perspectives on Lesbian, Gay, and Bisexual Experiences,* 2d ed., edited by Linda D. Garnets and Douglas C. Kimmel. New York: Columbia University Press.

Hick, Steven. 1997. "Participatory Research: An Approach for Structural Social Workers." *Journal of Progressive Human Services* 8:63–78.

Hirsch, Kathleen. 1989. *Songs from the Alley.* New York: Doubleday.

Holcombe, Ariane, Mark Wolery, and David L. Gast. 1994. "Comparative Single-Subject Research Designs Used to Make Comparisons Between 2 or More Interventions." *Topics in Early Childhood Special Education,* 14:119–145.

Holmes, Steven A. 2000. "Stronger Response by Minorities Helps Improve Census Reply Rate." *The New York Times,* May 4, pp. A1, A22.

Horney, Julie, D. Wayne Osgood, and Ineke Haen Marshall. 1995. "Criminal Careers in the Short-Term: Intra-Individual Variability in Crime and Its Relation to Local Life Circumstances." *American Sociological Review* 60:655–73.

Huberman, A. Michael and Matthew B. Miles. 1994. "Data Management and Analysis Methods." Pp. 428–44 in *Handbook of Qualitative Research*, edited by Norman K. Denzin and Yvonna S. Lincoln. Thousand Oaks, CA: Sage.

Hudson, Walter W. 1978. "First Axioms of Treatment." *Social Work* 23:65–66.

Huff, Darrell. 1954. *How to Lie with Statistics*. New York: W. W. Norton.

Humphrey, Nicholas. 1992. *A History of the Mind: Evolution and the Birth of Consciousness*. New York: Simon & Schuster.

Humphreys, Laud. 1970. *Tearoom Trade: Impersonal Sex in Public Places*. Chicago, IL: Aldine.

Hunt, Morton. 1985. *Profiles of Social Research: The Scientific Study of Human Interactions*. New York: Russell Sage Foundation.

Ingersoll-Dayton, Berit, Margaret B. Neal, Jung-hwa Ha, and Leslie B. Hammer. 2003. "Collaboration among Siblings Providing Care for Older Parents." *Journal of Gerontological Social Work* 40:51–66.

Irvine, Leslie. 1998. "Organizational Ethics and Fieldwork Realities: Negotiating Ethical Boundaries in Codependents Anonymous." Pp. 167–83 in *Doing Ethnographic Research: Fieldwork Settings*, edited by Scott Grills. Thousand Oaks, CA: Sage.

Jackson, James and David Williams. 2004. *Detroit Area Study: Social Influence on Health, Stress, Racism, and Health Protective Resources*. Ann Arbor, MI: Interuniversity Consortium for Political and Social Research, Study No. 3272. Retrieved August 29, 2004 (http://webapp.icpsr.umich.edu/cocoon/ICPSR-PRINT-STUDY/03272.xml).

Jensen, Carla. 1994. "Psychosocial Treatment of Depression in Women: Nine Single-Subject Evaluations." *Research on Social Work Practice* 4:267–82.

Johnson, Alice. 1999. "Working and Nonworking Women: Onset of Homelessness within the Context of Their Lives." *Affilia* 14:42–77.

Johnson, Christina and Jeannie Golden. 1997. "Generalization of Social Skills to Peer Interactions in a Child with Language Delays." *Behavioral-Interventions* 12:133–47.

Johnson, Knowlton. 1997. "Professional Help and Crime Victims." *Social Service Review* 71:89–109.

Kagay, Michael R. with Janet Elder. 1992. "Numbers Are No Problem for Pollsters. Words Are." *The New York Times*, October 9, p. E5.

Kahana, Boaz and Eva Kahana. 1970. "Changes in Mental Status of Elderly Patients in Age Integrated and Age Segregated Hospital Milieus." *Journal of Advanced Psychology* 75:177–81.

Kahana, Eva, Boaz Kahana, and Kathryn P. Riley. 1988. "Contextual Issues in Quantitative Studies of Institutional Settings for the Aged." Pp. 197–216 in *Qualitative Gerontology*, edited by Shulamit Reinharz and Graham D. Rowles. New York: Springer.

Kahn, Ric. 1997. "A Last Drink on New Year's." *The Boston Globe*, January 3, pp. B1–B2.

Kaufman, Sharon R. 1986. *The Ageless Self: Sources of Meaning in Late Life*. Madison: University of Wisconsin Press.

Kaufman, Sharon R. 1994. "In-Depth Interviewing." Pp. 123–136 in *Qualitative Methods in Aging Research*, edited by Jaber F. Gubrium and Andrea Sankar. Thousand Oaks, CA: Sage.

Kayser-Jones, Jeanie and Barbara A. Koenig. 1994. "Ethical Issues." Pp. 15–32 in *Qualitative Methods in Aging Research*, edited by Jaber F. Gubrium and Andrea Sankar. Thousand Oaks, CA: Sage.

W. K. Kellogg Foundation. 2001. *Using Logic Models to Bring Together Planning, Evaluation, and Action: Logic Model Development Guide*. Battle Creek, MI: Author. http://www.wkkf.org/Pubs/Tools/Evaluation/Pub3669.pdf

Kenney, Charles. 1987. "They've Got Your Number." *The Boston Globe Magazine*, August 30, pp. 12, 46–56, 60.

Kershaw, David and Jerily Fair. 1976. *The New Jersey Income-Maintenance Experiment*, Vol. 1. New York: Academic Press.

Kifner, John. 1994. "Pollster Finds Error on Holocaust Doubts." *The New York Times,* May 20, p. A12.

Kincaid, Harold. 1996. *Philosophical Foundations of the Social Sciences: Analyzing Controversies in Social Research.* Cambridge, UK: Cambridge University Press.

King, Gary, Robert O. Keohane, and Sidney Verba. 1994. *Scientific Inference in Qualitative Research.* Princeton, NJ: Princeton University Press.

King, Miriam L. and Diana L. Magnuson. 1995. "Perspectives on Historical U.S. Census Undercounts." *Social Science History* 19:455–66.

Kinnevy, Susan C., Brian P. Healey, David E. Pollio, and Carol S. North. 1999. "BicycleWORKS: Task-Centered Group Work with High-Risk Youth." *Social Work with Groups* 22:33–47.

Kleinman, Sharon S. 2002. "Methodological and Ethical Challenges of Researching a Computer-Mediated Group." *Journal of Technology in Human Services,* 19:49–63.

Koegel, Paul. 1987. *Ethnographic Perspectives on Homeless and Homeless Mentally Ill Women.* Washington, DC: U.S. Department of Health and Human Services, Public Health Service, Alcohol, Drug Abuse, and Mental Health Administration.

Koegel, Paul and M. Audrey Burnam. 1992. "Problems in the Assessment of Mental Illness among the Homeless: An Empirical Approach." Pp. 77–99 in *Homelessness: A National Perspective,* edited by Marjorie J. Robertson and Milton Greenblatt. New York: Plenum.

Koeske, Gary. 1994. "Some Recommendations for Improving Measurement Validation in Social Work Research." *Journal of Social Service Research* 18:43–72.

Kohut, Andrew. 1988. "Polling: Does More Information Lead to Better Understanding?" *The Boston Globe,* November 7, p. 25.

Korr, Wynne S. and Antoine Joseph. 1996. "Effects of Local Conditions on Program Outcomes: Analysis of Contradictory Findings from Two Programs for Homeless Mentally Ill." *Journal of Health and Social Policy* 8:41–53.

Kotsopoulos, Sotiris, Selena Walker, Karyn Beggs, and Barbara Jones. 1996. "A Clinical and Academic Outcome Study of Children Attending a Day Treatment Program." *Canadian Journal of Psychiatry* 41:371–78.

Kraemer, Helena Chmura and Sue Thiemann. 1987. *How Many Subjects? Statistical Power Analysis in Research.* Newbury Park, CA: Sage.

Krout, John A. 1985. "Service Awareness among the Elderly." *Journal of Gerontological Social Work* 9:7–19.

Krueger, Richard A. 1988. *Focus Groups: A Practical Guide for Applied Research.* Newbury Park, CA: Sage.

Kuzel, Anton J. 1999. "Sampling in Qualitative Inquiry." Pp. 33–45 in *Doing Qualitative Research,* 2d ed., edited by Benjamin F. Crabtree and William L. Miller. Thousand Oaks, CA: Sage.

Kvale, Steinar. 1996. *Interviews: An Introduction to Qualitative Research Interviewing.* Thousand Oaks, CA: Sage.

Labaw, Patricia J. 1980. *Advanced Questionnaire Design.* Cambridge, MA: ABT Books.

La Gory, Mark, Ferris J. Ritchey, and Jeff Mullis. 1990. "Depression among the Homeless." *Journal of Health and Social Behavior,* 31(March):87–101.

Larsen, Daniel L., C. Clifford Attkisson, William A. Hargreaves, and Tuan D. Nguyen. (1979). "Assessment of Client/Patient Satisfaction: Development of a General Scale." *Evaluation and Program Planning* 2:197–207.

Larson, Calvin J. 1993. *Pure and Applied Sociological Theory: Problems and Issues.* New York: Harcourt Brace Jovanovich.

Latour, Francie. 2002. "Marching Orders: After 10 Years, State Closes Prison Boot Camp." *Boston Sunday Globe,* June 16, pp. B1, B7.

Lavrakas, Paul J. 1987. *Telephone Survey Methods: Sampling, Selection, and Supervision.* Newbury Park, CA: Sage.

Lee, Barrett A., Sue Hinze Jones, and David W. Lewis. 1990. "Public Beliefs about the Causes of Homelessness." *Social Forces,* 69:253–65.

Lee, Judith and James A. Twaite. 1997. "Open Adoption and Adoptive Mothers: Attitudes Toward Birthmothers, Adopted Children, and Parenting." *American Journal of Orthospsychiatry* 67:576–84.

Levy, Paul S. and Stanley Lemeshow. 1999. *Sampling of Populations: Methods and Applications,* 3d ed. New York: John Wiley.

Lewin, Tamar, 2001a. "Income Education is Found to Lower Risk of New Arrest." *The New York Times,* November 16, p. A18.

Lewin, Tamar. 2001b. "Surprising Result in Welfare-to-Work Studies." *The New York Times,* July 31, p. A16.

Lewis, Robert E., Elaine Walton, and Mark W. Fraser. 1995. "Examining Family Reunification Services: A Process Analysis of a Successful Experiment." *Research on Social Work Practice* 5:259–82.

Liang, Jersey, Thanh Van Tran, Neal Krause, and Kyriakos S. Markides. 1989. "Generational Differences in the Structure of the CES-D Scale in Mexican Americans." *Journals of Gerontology* 44:S110–20.

Lieberson, Stanley. 1985. *Making It Count: The Improvement of Social Research and Theory.* Berkeley: University of California Press.

Lipsey, Mark W. and David B. Wilson. 2001. *Practical Meta-Analysis.* Thousand Oaks, CA: Sage.

Litwin, Mark S. 1995. *How to Measure Survey Reliability and Validity.* Thousand Oaks, CA: Sage.

Locke, Lawrence F., Waneen Wyrick Spirduso, and Stephen J. Silverman. 2000. *Proposals That Work: A Guide for Planning Dissertations and Grant Proposals,* 4th ed. Thousand Oaks, CA: Sage.

Lofland, John and Lyn H. Lofland. 1984. *Analyzing Social Settings: A Guide to Qualitative Observation and Analysis,* 2d ed. Belmont, CA: Wadsworth.

Luna, Isela, Esperanza Torres de Ardon, Young Mi Lim, Sandra Cromwell, Linda Phillips, and Cynthia Russell. 1996. "The Relevance of Familism in Cross-Cultural Studies of Family Caregiving." *Journal of Nursing Research* 18:267–83.

Lyman, Karen A. 1994. "Fieldwork in Groups and Institutions." Pp. 155–170 in *Qualitative Methods in Aging Research,* edited by Jaber F. Gubrium and Andrea Sankar. Thousand Oaks, CA: Sage.

Lynch, Michael and David Bogen. 1997. "Sociology's Asociological 'Core': An Examination of Textbook Sociology in Light of the Sociology of Scientific Knowledge." *American Sociological Review* 62:481–93.

MacPherson, Kathleen I. 1988. "Dilemmas of Participant-Observation in a Menopause Collective." Pp. 184–96 in *Qualitative Gerontology,* edited by Shulamit Reinharz and Graham D. Rowles. New York: Springer.

Mangione, Thomas W. 1995. *Mail Surveys: Improving the Quality.* Thousand Oaks, CA: Sage.

Marin, Gerardo and Barbara VanOss Marin. 1991. *Research with Hispanic Populations.* Newbury Park, CA: Sage.

Marini, Margaret Mooney and Burton Singer. 1988. "Causality in the Social Sciences." Pp. 347–409 in *Sociological Methodology,* Vol. 18, edited by Clifford C. Clogg. Washington, DC: American Sociological Association.

Marshall, Catherine and Gretchen B. Rossman. 1999. *Designing Qualitative Research,* 3d ed. Thousand Oaks, CA: Sage.

Martin, Lawrence and Peter Kettner. 1996. *Measuring the Performance of Human Service Programs.* Thousand Oaks, CA: Sage.

Matt, Georg E. and Thomas D. Cook. 1994. "Threats to the Validity of Research Syntheses." Pp. 503–20 in *The Handbook of Research Synthesis,* edited by Harris Cooper and Larry V. Hedges. New York: Russell Sage Foundation.

Maxwell, Joseph A. 1996. *Qualitative Research Design: An Interactive Approach.* Thousand Oaks, CA: Sage.

McKillip, Jack. 1987. *Need Analysis: Tools for the Human Services and Education.* Newbury Park, CA: Sage.

Metro Social Services. 1987. *PATH Community Survey.* Nashville, TN: Metro Social Services, Nashville-Davidson County.

Milbrath, Lester and M. L. Goel. 1977. *Political Participation,* 2d ed. Chicago, IL: Rand McNally.

Milburn, Norweeta G., Lawrence E. Gary, Jacqueline A. Booth, and Diane R. Brown. 1992. "Conducting Epidemiologic Research in a Minority Community: Methodological Considerations." *Journal of Community Psychology* 19:3–12.

Miles, Matthew B. and A. Michael Huberman. 1994. *Qualitative Data Analysis,* 2d ed. Thousand Oaks, CA: Sage.

Miller, Delbert C. 1991. *Handbook of Research Design and Social Measurement,* 5th ed. Newbury Park, CA: Sage.

Miller, Delbert C., and Neil J. Salkind. 2002. *Handbook of Research Design and Social Measurement,* 6th ed. Thousand Oaks, California: Sage.

Miller, Susan. 1999. *Gender and Community Policing: Walking the Talk.* Boston, MA: Northeastern University Press.

Miller, William L. and Benjamin F. Crabtree. 1999. "Clinical Research: A Multimethod Typology and Qualitative Roadmap." Pp. 3–30 in *Doing Qualitative Research,* 2d ed., edited by Benjamin F. Crabtree and William L. Miller. Thousand Oaks, CA: Sage.

Mills, C. Wright. 1959. *The Sociological Imagination.* New York: Oxford University Press.

Miranda, Jeanne, Francisca Azocar, Kurt C. Organista, Ricardo F. Munoz, and Alicia Lieberman. 1996. "Recruiting and Retaining Low-Income Latinos in Psychotherapy Research." *Journal of Consulting and Clinical Psychology* 64:868–74.

Mirowsky, John. 1995. "Age and the Sense of Control." *Social Psychology Quarterly* 58:31–43.

Mirowsky, John and Paul Nongzhuang Hu. 1996. "Physical Impairment and the Diminishing Effects of Income." *Social Forces* 74:1073–96.

Mirowsky, John and Catherine E. Ross. 1991. "Eliminating Defense and Agreement Bias from Measures of the Sense of Control: A 2 x 2 Index." *Social Psychology Quarterly* 54:127–45.

Mirowsky, John and Catherine E. Ross. 1992. "Age and Depression." *Journal of Health and Social Behavior* 33:187–205.

Mirowsky, John and Catherine E. Ross. 1999. "Economic Hardship across the Life Course." *American Sociological Review* 64:548–69.

Mitchell, Christopher G. 1999. "Treating Anxiety in a Managed Care Setting: A Controlled Comparison of Medication Alone Versus Medication Plus." *Research on Social Work Practice* 9:188–200.

Mitchell, Richard G., Jr. 1993. *Secrecy and Fieldwork.* Newbury Park, CA: Sage.

Moffitt, Robert. 2002. "The Impact of Welfare Reform on Employment and Income." Pp. 8–11 in *Welfare, Children, and Families: Results from a Three City Study: A Congressional Briefing* (May 17), by Ronald J. Angel, P. Lindsay Chase-Lansdale, Andrew Cherlin, and Robert Moffitt. Washington, DC: Consortium of Social Science Associations.

Mohr, Lawrence B. 1992. *Impact Analysis for Program Evaluation.* Newbury Park, CA: Sage.

Morrill, Calvin, Christine Yalda, Madeleine Adelman, Michael Musheno, and Cindy Bejareno. 2000. "Telling Tales in School: Youth Culture and Conflict Narratives." *Law and Society Review* 34:521–65.

Morris, T. 1991. "Teaching Social Workers Research Methods: Orthodox Doctrine, Heresy, or an Atheistic Compromise." *Journal of Teaching in Social Work* 6:41–62.

Mueser, Kim T., Paul R. Yarnold, Douglas F. Levinson, Hardeep Singhy, Alan S. Bellack, Kimmy Kee, Randall L. Morrison, and Kashinath G. Yadalam. 1990. "Prevalence of Substance Abuse in Schizophrenia: Demographic and Clinical Correlates." *Schizophrenia Bulletin* 16(1):31–56.

National Association of Social Workers. 1999. *Code of Ethics of the National Association of Social Workers.* Retrieved June 28, 2004 (www.naswdc.org/pubs/code/code.asp).

National Geographic Society. 2000. *Survey 2000.* Retrieved January 21, 2005, from http://survey2000.nationalgeographic.com.

National Institute of Alcohol Abuse and Alcoholism. 1995. "College Students and Drinking." *Alcohol Alert* 29(July):1–6.

National Institutes of Health. 1994. *NIH Guidelines on the Inclusion of Women and Minorities as Subjects in Clinical Research.* Retrieved June 29, 2004 (http://grants.nih.gov/grants/guide/notice-files/not94–100.html).

National Opinion Research Center (NORC). 1992. *The NORC General Social Survey: Questions and Answers* (National Data Program for the Social Sciences). Chicago, IL: Author.

Nelson, Judith C. 1994. "Ethics, Gender, and Ethnicity in Single-Case Research and Evaluation." *Journal of Social Service Research* 18:139–52.

Neuendorf, Kimberly A. 2002. *The Content Analysis Guidebook.* Thousand Oaks, CA: Sage.

Newmann, Joy Perkins. 1987. "Gender Differences in Vulnerability to Depression." *Social Service Review* 61:447–68.

Newmann, Joy Perkins. 1989. "Aging and Depression." *Psychology and Aging* 4:150–65.

Newmann, Joy Perkins, Rafael J. Engel, and Julie Jensen. 1991. "Depressive Symptom Patterns Among Older Women." *Psychology and Aging* 5:101–18.

Newport, Frank. 2000. *Popular Vote in Presidential Race Too Close to Call* (Press release, December 13). Retrieved October 14, 2004 (http://www.gallup.com/poll/content/login.aspx?ci=2335).

Nie, Norman H. and Lutz Erbring. 2000. *Internet and Society: A Preliminary Report.* Palo Alto, CA: Stanford Institute for the Quantitative Study of Society.

Norton, Ilena M. and Spero M. Manson. 1996. "Research in American Indian and Alaska Native Communities: Navigating the Cultural Universe of Values and Process." *Journal of Consulting and Clinical Psychology* 64:856–60.

Novak, David. 2003. "The Evolution of Internet Research: Shifting Allegiances." *Online,* 27:21.

Nugent, William. 2000. "Single Case Design Visual Analysis Procedures for Use in Practice Evaluation." *Journal of Social Service Research* 27:39–75.

O'Brien, Kerth. 1993. "Improving Survey Questionnaires Through Focus Groups." Pp. 105–17 in *Successful Focus Groups: Advancing the State of the Art,* edited by David L. Morgan. Newbury Park, CA: Sage.

O'Dochartaigh, Niall. 2002. *The Internet Research Handbook: A Practical Guide for Students and Researchers in the Social Sciences.* Thousand Oaks, CA: Sage.

Orcutt, James D. and J. Blake Turner. 1993. "Shocking Numbers and Graphic Accounts: Quantified Images of Drug Problems in the Print Media." *Social Problems* 49(May):190–206.

Orr, Larry. 1999. *Social Experiments: Evaluating Public Programs with Experimental Methods.* Thousand Oaks, CA: Sage.

Orshansky, Mollie. 1977. "Memorandum for Daniel P. Moynihan. Subject: History of the Poverty Line." Pp. 232–237 in *The Measure of Poverty: Technical Paper I: Documentation of Background Information and Rationale for Current Poverty Matrix,* edited by Mollie Orshansky. Washington, DC: U.S. Department of Health, Education, and Welfare.

Ortega, Debora M. and Cheryl A. Richey. 1998. "Methodological Issues in Social Work Research with Depressed Women of Color." *Journal of Social Service Research* 23:47–68.

Papineau, David. 1978. *For Science in the Social Sciences.* London: Macmillan.

Parlett, Malcolm and David Hamilton. 1976. "Evaluation as Illumination: A New Approach to the Study of Innovative Programmes." Pp. 140–57 in *Evaluation Studies Review Annual,* Vol. 1, edited by G. Glass. Beverly Hills, CA: Sage.

Pate, Antony M. and Edwin E. Hamilton. 1992. "Formal and Informal Deterrents to Domestic Violence: The Dade County Spouse Assault Experiment." *American Sociological Review* 57(October):691–97.

Patton, Michael Quinn. 2002. *Qualitative Research and Evaluation Methods,* 3d ed. Thousand Oaks, CA: Sage.

Payne, Macolm. 1997. *Modern Social Work Theory: A Critical Introduction,* 2d ed. Chicago, IL: Lyceum.

Pollner, Melvin and Richard E. Adams. 1994. "The Interpersonal Context of Mental Health Interviews." *Journal of Health and Social Behavior* 35:283–90.

Posavac, Emil J. and Raymond G. Carey. 1997. *Program Evaluation: Methods and Case Studies,* 5th ed. Upper Saddle River, NJ: Prentice Hall.

Presser, Stanley and Johnny Blair. 1994. "Survey Pretesting: Do Different Methods Produce Different Results?" *Sociological Methodology 24:* 73–104.

Pryor, Carolyn B. 1992. "Peer Helping Programs in School Settings: Social Workers Report." *School Social Work Journal* 16:16–26.

Punch, Maurice. 1994. "Politics and Ethics in Qualitative Research." Pp. 83–97 in *Handbook of Qualitative Research,* edited by Norman K. Denzin and Yvonna S. Lincoln. Thousand Oaks, CA: Sage.

Purdy, Matthew. 1994. "Bronx Mystery: 3rd-Rate Service for 1st-Class Mail." *The New York Times,* March 12, pp. 1, 3.

Putnam, Israel. 1977. "Poverty Thresholds: Their History and Future Development." Pp. 272–83 in *The Measure of Poverty: Technical Paper I: Documentation of Background Information and Rationale for Current Poverty Matrix,* edited by Mollie Orshansky. Washington, DC: U.S. Department of Health, Education, and Welfare.

Radloff, Lenore. 1977. "The CES-D Scale: A Self-Report Depression Scale for Research in the General Population." *Applied Psychological Measurement* 1:385–401.

Ragin, Charles C. 1987. *The Comparative Method: Moving Beyond Qualitative and Quantitative Strategies.* Berkeley: University of California Press.

Ragin, Charles C. 1994. *Constructing Social Research.* Thousand Oaks, CA: Pine Forge Press.

Rand, Michael R., James P. Lynch, and David Cantor. 1997. *Criminal Victimization, 1973–95.* Washington, DC: U.S. Department of Justice, Office of Justice Programs.

Reynolds, Paul Davidson. 1979. *Ethical Dilemmas and Social Science Research.* San Francisco, CA: Jossey-Bass.

Richards, Thomas J. and Lyn Richards. 1994. "Using Computers in Qualitative Research." Pp. 445–62 in *Handbook of Qualitative Research,* edited by Norman K. Denzin and Yvonna S. Lincoln. Thousand Oaks, CA: Sage.

Richardson, Laurel. 1995. "Narrative and Sociology." Pp. 198–221 in *Representation in Ethnography,* edited by John Van Maanen. Thousand Oaks, CA: Sage.

Riedel, Marc. 2000. *Research Strategies for Secondary Data: A Perspective for Criminology and Criminal Justice.* Thousand Oaks, CA: Sage.

Riessman, Catherine Kohler. 2002. "Narrative Analysis." Pp. 217–70 in *The Qualitative Researcher's Companion,* edited by A. Michael Huberman and Matthew B. Miles. Thousand Oaks, CA: Sage.

Ringwalt, Christopher L., Jody M. Greene, Susan T. Ennett, Ronaldo Iachan, Richard R. Clayton, and Carl G. Leukefeld. 1994. *Past and Future Directions of the D.A.R.E. Program: An Evaluation Review.* Research Triangle, NC: Research Triangle Institute.

Roffman, Roger, Lois Downey, Blair Beadnell, Judith Gordon, Jay Craver, and Robert Stephens. 1997. "Cognitive-Bhavioral Group Counseling to Prevent HIV Transmission in Gay and Bisexual Men: Factors Contributing to Successful Risk Reduction." *Research on Social Work Practice* 7:165–186

Roffman, Roger, J. Picciano, L. Wickizer, M. Bolan, and R. Ryan. 1998. "Anonymous Enrollment in AIDS Prevention Telephone Group Counseling: Facilitating the Participation of Gay and Bisexual Men in Intervention and Research." *Journal of Social Service Research* 23:5–22.

Rosenberg, Morris. 1965. *Society and the Adolescent Self-Image.* Princeton, NJ: Princeton University Press.

Rosenberg, Morris. 1968. *The Logic of Survey Analysis.* New York: Basic Books.

Ross, Catherine E. 1990. "Work, Family, and the Sense of Control: Implications for the Psychological Well-Being of Women and Men" (Proposal submitted to the National Science Foundation). Urbana: University of Illinois.

Ross, Catherine E. and Chloe E. Bird. 1994. "Sex Stratification and Health Lifestyle: Consequences for Men's and Women's Perceived Health." *Journal of Health and Social Behavior* 35:161–78.

Ross, Catherine E. and Marieke Van Willigen. 1996. "Gender, Parenthood, and Anger." *Journal of Marriage and the Family* 58:572–84.

Ross, Catherine E. and Chia-ling Wu. 1995. "The Links between Education and Health." *American Sociological Review* 60:719–45.

Ross, Catherine E. and Chia-ling Wu. 1996. "Education, Age, and the Cumulative Advantage in Health." *Journal of Health and Social Behavior* 37:104–20.

Rossi, Peter H. 1989. *Down and Out in America: The Origins of Homelessness.* Chicago, IL: University of Chicago Press.

Rossi, Peter H. 1999. "Half Truths with Real Consequences: Journalism, Research, and Public Policy. Three Encounters." *Contemporary Sociology* 28:1–5.

Rossi, Peter H. and Howard E. Freeman. 1989. *Evaluation: A Systematic Approach,* 4th ed. Newbury Park, CA: Sage.

Rossman, Gretchen B. and Sharon F. Rallis. 1998. *Learning in the Field: An Introduction to Qualitative Research.* Thousand Oaks, CA: Sage.

Roth, Dee, J. Bean, N. Lust, and T. Saveanu. 1985. *Homelessness in Ohio: A Study of People in Need.* Columbus, OH: Department of Mental Health.

Rowles, G. D. 1978. *Prisoners of Space? Exploring the Geographical Experience of Older People.* Boulder, CO: Westview Press.

Royse, David, Bruce Thyer, Deborah K. Padgett, and T. K. Logan. 2001. *Program Evaluation: An Introduction,* 3d ed. Belmont, CA: Wadsworth, Brooks/Cole.

Rubin, Herbert J. and Irene S. Rubin. 1995. *Qualitative Interviewing: The Art of Hearing Data.* Thousand Oaks, CA: Sage.

Ruggles, Patricia. 1990. *Drawing the Line: Alternative Poverty Measures and Their Implications for Public Policy.* Washington, DC: The Urban Institute Press.

Sacks, Stanley, Karen McKendrick, George DeLeon, Michael T. French, and Kathryn E. McCollister. 2002. "Benefit-Cost Analysis of a Modified Therapeutic Community for Mentally Ill Chemical Abusers." *Evaluation and Program Planning* 25:137–48.

Salisbury, Robert H. 1975. "Research on Political Participation." *American Journal of Political Science* 19(May):323–41.

Sampson, Robert J. 1987. "Urban Black Violence: The Effect of Male Joblessness and Family Disruption." *American Journal of Sociology* 93 (September):348–82.

Sampson, Robert J. and Janet L. Lauritsen. 1994. "Violent Victimization and Offending: Individual-, Situational-, and Community-Level Risk Factors." Pp. 1–114 in *Understanding and Preventing Violence.* Vol. 3, *Social Influences,* edited by Albert J. Reiss, Jr., and Jeffrey A. Roth. Washington, DC: National Academy Press.

Sands, Roberta G. and Robin S. Goldberg-Glen. 2000. "Factors Associated with Stress among Grandparents Raising Their Grandchildren." *Family Relations: Interdisciplinary Journal of Applied Family Studies* 49:97–105.

Sarri, Rosemary and Catherine M. Sarri. 1992. "Organizational and Community Change through Participatory Action Research." *Administration in Social Work* 16:99–122.

Schaie, K. Warner. 1993. "Ageist Language in Psychological Research." *American Psychologist* 48: 49–51.

Schober, Michael F. 1999. "Making Sense of Survey Questions." Pp. 77–94 in *Cognition and Survey Research,* edited by Monroe G. Sirken, Douglas J. Herrmann, Susan Schechter, Norbert Schwartz, Judith M. Tanur, and Roger Tourangeau. New York: John Wiley.

Schorr, Lisbeth B. and Daniel Yankelovich. 2000. "In Search of a Gold Standard for Social Programs." *The Boston Globe,* February 18, p. A19.

Schulberg, Herbert C., M. Saul, Maureen McClelland, M. Ganguli, W. Christy, and R. Frank. 1985. "Assessing Depression in Primary Medical and Psychiatric Practices." *Archives of General Psychiatry* 42:1164–70.

Schulz, A., B. Israel, D. Williams, E. Parker, A. Becker, and S. James. 2000. "Social Inequalities, Stressors and Self-Reported Health Status Among African American and White Women in the Detroit Metropolitan Area." *Social Science and Medicine*, 51:1639–1653.

Schuman, Howard and Stanley Presser. 1981. *Questions and Answers in Attitude Surveys: Experiments on Question Form, Wording, and Context.* New York: Academic Press.

Schutt, Russell K. 1992. *The Perspectives of DMH Shelter Staff: Their Clients, Their Jobs, Their Shelters, and the Service System* (Unpublished report to the Metro Boston Region of the Massachusetts Department of Mental Health). Boston: University of Massachusetts.

Schutt, Russell K. and Stephen M. Goldfinger. 1996. "Housing Preferences and Perceptions of Health and Functioning Among Homeless Mentally Ill Persons." *Psychiatric Services* 47:381–86.

Schutt, Russell K., Stephen M. Goldfinger, and Walter E. Penk. 1992. "The Structure and Sources of Residential Preferences among Seriously Mentally Ill Homeless Adults." *Sociological Practice Review* 3(3):148–56.

Schutt, Russell K., Stephen M. Goldfinger, and Walter E. Penk. 1997. "Satisfaction with Residence and with Life: When Homeless Mentally Ill Persons Are Housed." *Evaluation and Program Planning* 20(2):185–94.

Schutt, Russell K., Suzanne Gunston, and John O'Brien. 1992. "The Impact of AIDS Prevention Efforts on AIDS Knowledge and Behavior among Sheltered Homeless Adults." *Sociological Practice Review* 3(1):1–7.

Schutt, Russell K., Tatjana Meschede, and Jill Rierdan. 1994. "Distress, Suicidality, and Social Support among Homeless Adults." *Journal of Health and Social Behavior* 35(June):134–42.

Schutt, Russell K., Walter E. Penk, Paul J. Barreira, Robert Lew, William H. Fisher, Angela Browne, and Elizabeth Irvine. 1992. "Relapse Prevention for Dually Diagnosed Homeless" (Proposal to National Institute of Mental Health, for Mental Health Research on Homeless Persons, PA-91–60). Worcester: University of Massachusetts Medical School.

Schwandt, Thomas A. 1994. "Constructivist, Interpretivist Approaches to Human Inquiry." Pp. 118–37 in *Handbook of Qualitative Research,* edited by Norman K. Denzin and Yvonna S. Lincoln. Thousand Oaks, CA: Sage.

Scriven, Michael. 1972. "The Methodology of Evaluation." Pp. 123–36 in *Evaluating Action Programs: Readings in Social Action and Education,* edited by Carol H. Weiss. Boston, MA: Allyn & Bacon.

Seidman, Larry J. 1997. "Neuropsychological Testing." Pp. 498–508 in *Psychiatry,* Vol. 1, edited by Allan Tasman, Jerald Kay, and Jeffrey Lieberman. Philadelphia: W. B. Saunders.

Seligman, Martin E. P. 1975. *Helplessness.* San Francisco, CA: W. H. Freeman.

Shadish, William R., Thomas D. Cook, and Laura C. Leviton, eds. 1991. *Foundations of Program Evaluation: Theories of Practice.* Newbury Park, CA: Sage.

Shapiro, Janet R. and Sarah C. Mangelsdorf. 1994. "The Determinants of Parenting Competence in Adolescent Mothers." *Journal of Youth and Adolescence* 23:621–41.

Shepherd, Jane, David Hill, Joel Bristor, and Pat Montalvan. 1996. "Converting an Ongoing Health Study to CAPI: Findings from the National Health and Nutrition Study." Pp. 159–64 in *Health Survey Research Methods Conference Proceedings,* edited by Richard B. Warnecke. Hyattsville, MD: U.S. Department of Health and Human Services.

Sherman, Lawrence W. 1992. *Policing Domestic Violence: Experiments and Dilemmas.* New York: Free Press.

Sherman, Lawrence W. and Richard A. Berk. 1984. "The Specific Deterrent Effects of Arrest for Domestic Assault." *American Sociological Review* 49:261–72.

Sherman, Lawrence W. and Ellen G. Cohn. 1989. "The Impact of Research on Legal Policy: The Minneapolis Domestic Violence Experiment." *Law and Society Review* 23:117–44.

Sherman, Lawrence W. and Douglas A. Smith, with Janell D. Schmidt and Dennis P. Rogan. 1992. "Crime, Punishment, and Stake in Conformity." *American Sociological Review* 57:680–90.

Sieber, Joan E. 1992. *Planning Ethically Responsible Research: A Guide for Students and Internal Review Boards.* Newbury Park, CA: Sage.

Silvestre, Anthony J. 1994. "Brokering: A Process for Establishing Long-Term and Stable Links with Gay Male Communities for Research and Public Health Education." *AIDS Education and Prevention* 6:65–73.

Sjoberg, Gideon, ed. 1967. *Ethics, Politics, and Social Research.* Cambridge, MA: Schenkman.

Sjoberg, Gideon and Roger Nett. 1968. *A Methodology for Social Research.* New York: Harper & Row.

Skinner, Harvey A. and Wen-Jenn Sheu. 1982. "Reliability of Alcohol Use Indices: The Lifetime Drinking History and the MAST." *Journal of Studies on Alcohol* 43(11):1157–70.

Smith, Tom W. 1984. "Nonattitudes: A Review and Evaluation." Pp. 215–55 in *Surveying Subjective Phenomena,* Vol. 22, edited by Charles F. Turner and Elizabeth Martin. New York: Russell Sage Foundation.

Snider, D. E. 1999. *Guidelines for Defining Public Health Research and Public Health Non-Research* (Centers for Disease Control, Associate Director for Science). Retrieved June 28, 2004 (http://www.cdc.gov/od/ads/opspoll1.htm).

Snow, David A. and Leon Anderson. 1987. "Identity Work among the Homeless: The Verbal Construction and Avowal of Personal Identities." *American Journal of Sociology* 92(May):1336–71.

Stake, Robert E. 1995. *The Art of Case Study Research.* Thousand Oaks, CA: Sage.

Stewart, Anita L. and Anna Napoles-Springer. 2000. "Health-Related Quality of Life Assessments in Diverse Population Groups in the United States." *Medical Care* 38:II102-24.

Stewart, David W. 1984. *Secondary Research: Information Sources and Methods.* Beverly Hills, CA: Sage.

Stille, Alexander. 2000. "A Happiness Index with a Long Reach: Beyond G.N.P. to Subtler Measures." *The New York Times,* May 20, pp. A17, A19.

Strunk, William, Jr., and E. B. White. 2000. *The Elements of Style,* 3d ed. New York: Macmillan.

Sudman, Seymour. 1976. *Applied Sampling.* New York: Academic Press.

"Survey on Adultery: 'I Do' Means 'I Don't.'" 1993. *The New York Times,* October 19, p. A20.

Task Force on Social Work Research. 1991. *Building Social Work Knowledge for Effective Services and Policies: A Plan for Research Development.* Austin, TX: University of Texas, School of Social Work.

Taylor, Jerry. 1999. "D.A.R.E Gets Updated in Some Area Schools, Others Drop Program." *The Boston Sunday Globe,* May 16, pp. 1, 11.

Thompson, Estina E., Harold W. Neighbors, Cheryl Munday, and James S. Jackson. 1996. "Recruitment and Retention of African American Patients for Clinical Research: An Exploration of Response Rates in an Urban Psychiatric Hospital." *Journal of Consulting and Clinical Psychology* 64:861–67.

Thorne, Barrie. 1993. *Gender Play: Girls and Boys in School.* New Brunswick, NJ: Rutgers University Press.

Thyer, Bruce A. 1993. "Social Work Theory and Practice Research: The Approach of Logical Positivism." *Social Work and Social Sciences Review* 4:5–26.

Thyer, Bruce A. 2001. "What is the Role of Theory in Research on Social Work Practice?" *Journal of Social Work Education* 37:9–21.

Tichon, Jennifer G. and Margaret Shapriro. 2003. "The Process of Sharing Social Support in Cyberspace." *CyberPsychology and Behavior* 6:161–70.

Toby, Jackson. 1957. "Social Disorganization and Stake in Conformity: Complementary Factors in the Predatory Behavior of Hoodlums." *Journal of Criminal Law, Criminology and Police Science* 48:12–17.

Toppo, Greg. 2002. "Antidrug Program Backed by Study." *The Boston Globe,* October 29, p. A10.

Tourangeau, Roger. 1999. "Context Effects." Pp. 111–32 in *Cognition and Survey Research,* edited by Monroe G. Sirken, Douglas J. Herrmann, Susan Schechter, Norbert Schwartz, Judith M. Tanur, and Roger Tourangeau. New York: John Wiley.

Tripodi, Tony. 1994. *A Primer on Single-Subject Design for Clinical Social Workers.* Washington, DC: National Association of Social Workers.

Tufte, Edward R. 1983. *The Visual Display of Quantitative Information.* Cheshire, CT: Graphics Press.

Turabian, Kate L. 1996. *A Manual for Writers of Term Papers, Theses, and Dissertations,* 3d ed., rev. Chicago, IL: University of Chicago Press.

Turner, Charles F. and Elizabeth Martin, eds. 1984. *Surveying Subjective Phenomena,* Vols. I and II. New York: Russell Sage Foundation.

U.S. Bureau of the Census. 2003. *Survey Abstracts.* Retrieved July 12, 2004 (http://www.census.gov/main/www/dsabstract_Jan03.pdf).

U.S. Government Accounting Office. 2001. *Health and Human Services: Status of Achieving Key Outcomes and Addressing Major Management Challenges.* Retrieved April 8, 2003 (www.gao.gov/new.items/d01748.pdf).

U.S. Office of Management and Budget. 2002. Government and Performance Results Act of 1993. Washington, DC: U.S. Office of Management and Budget, Executive Office of the President.

Vaillant, George E. 1995. *The Natural History of Alcoholism Revisited.* Cambridge, MA: Harvard University Press.

Van Maanen, John. 1982. "Fieldwork on the Beat." Pp. 103–51 in *Varieties of Qualitative Research,* edited by John Van Maanen, James M. Dabbs, Jr., and Robert R. Faulkner. Beverly Hills, CA: Sage.

Van Maanen, John. 1995. "An End to Innocence: The Ethnography of Ethnography." Pp. 1–35 in *Representation in Ethnography,* edited by John Van Maanen. Thousand Oaks, CA: Sage.

Van Maanen, John. 2002. "The Fact of Fiction in Organizational Ethnography." Pp. 101–117 in *The Qualitative Researcher's Companion,* edited by A. Michael Huberman and Matthew B. Miles. Thousand Oaks, CA: Sage.

Verba, Sidney and Norman Nie. 1972. *Political Participation: Political Democracy and Social Equality.* New York: Harper & Row.

Verba, Sidney, Norman Nie, and Jae-On Kim. 1978. *Participation and Political Equality: A Seven-Nation Comparison.* New York: Cambridge University Press.

Wallace, J. Brandon. 1994. "Life Stories." Pp. 137–54 in *Qualitative Methods in Aging Research,* edited by Jaber F. Gubrium and Andrea Sankar. Thousand Oaks, CA: Sage.

Wallace, Walter L. 1983. *Principles of Scientific Sociology.* New York: Aldine.

Wallgren, Anders, Britt Wallgren, Rolf Persson, Ulf Jorner, and Jan-Aage Haaland. 1996. *Graphing Statistics and Data: Creating Better Charts.* Thousand Oaks, CA: Sage.

Walsh, Joseph. 1994. "Social Support Resource Outcomes for the Clients of Two Assertive Community Treatment Teams." *Research on Social Work Practice* 4:448–63.

Walton, Elaine, Mark W. Fraser, Robert E. Lewis, Peter J. Pecora, and Wendel K. Walton. 1993. "In-home Family-Focused Reunification: An Experimental Study." *Child Welfare* 72:473–87.

Webb, Eugene J., Donald T. Campbell, Richard D. Schwartz, and Lee Sechrest. 2000. *Unobtrusive Measures,* Rev. ed. Thousand Oaks, CA: Sage.

Weber, Max. 1949. *The Methodology of the Social Sciences.* Translated and edited by Edward A. Shils and Henry A. Finch. New York: Free Press.

Weber, Robert Philip. 1985. *Basic Content Analysis.* Thousand Oaks, CA: Sage.

Wechsler, Henry, Jae Eun Lee, Meichun Kuo, and Hang Lee. 2000. *College Binge Drinking in the 1990s: A Continuing Problem* (Results of the Harvard School of Public Health 1999 College Alcohol Study). Retrieved from www.hsph.harvard.edu/cas/rpt2000/CAS2000rpt2. html.

Wechsler, Henry, Toben Nelson, and Elissa Weitzman. 2000. "From Knowledge to Action: How Harvard's College Alcohol Study Can Help Your Campus Design a Campaign against Student Alcohol Abuse." *Change* 32:38–43.

Weiss. Carol H. 1972. *Evaluation Research.* Englewood Cliffs, NJ: Prentice Hall.

Weiss. Carol H. 1998. *Evaluation,* 2d ed. Upper Saddle River, NJ: Prentice Hall.

Weiss, Irwin K., Cheryl L. Nagel, and Miriam K. Aronson. 1986. "Applicability of Depression Scales to the Old Old Person." *Journal of the American Geriatrics Society* 34:215–18.

Wernet, S. P. and D. M. Austin. 1991. "Decision Making Style and Leadership Patterns in Nonprofit Human Service Organizations." *Administration in Social Work* 15:1–17.

Wexler, Sandra and Rafael J. Engel. 1999. "Historical Trends in State-Level ADC/AFDC Benefits: Living on Less and Less." *Journal of Sociology and Social Welfare* 26:37–61.

Whitelaw, Carolyn and Edgardo L. Perez. 1987. "Partial Hospitalization Programs: A Current Perspective." *Administration in Mental Health* 15:62–72.

Whyte, William Foote. 1955. *Street Corner Society.* Chicago, IL: University of Chicago Press.

Whyte, William Foote. 1991. *Social Theory for Social Action: How Individuals and Organizations Learn to Change Society.* Newbury Park, CA: Sage.

Wilson, William Julius. 1987. *The Truly Disadvantaged: The Inner City, the Underclass, and Public Policy.* Chicago, IL: University of Chicago Press.

Wilson, William Julius. 1998. "Engaging Publics in Sociological Dialogue through the Media." *Contemporary Sociology* 27:435–38.

Witkin, Belle Ruth and James W. Altschuld. 1995. *Planning and Conducting Needs Assessments: A Practical Guide.* Thousand Oaks, CA: Sage.

Wolcott, Harry F. 1995. *The Art of Fieldwork.* Walnut Creek, CA: AltaMira Press.

Yamatani, Hidenori and Rafael J. Engel. 2002. *Workload Assessment Study.* Pittsburgh, PA: University of Pittsburgh.

Yamatani, Hidenori, Aaron Mann, and Patricia Wright. 2000. *Garfield Community Needs Assessment.* Pittsburgh, PA: University of Pittsburgh.

Youngblut, JoAnne and Dorothy Brooten. 1999. "Alternate Child Care History of Hospitalization and Preschool Child Behavior." *Nursing Research* 48:29–34.

Zakour, Michael. 1994. "Measuring Career-Development Volunteerism: Guttman Scale Analysis Using Red Cross Volunteers." *Journal of Social Service Research* 19:103–20.

GLOSSARY/INDEX

A phase. *See* **Baseline phase**

A-B design, 206-207, 207e

A-B-A designs, 207, 208, 218

A-B-A-B designs, 207, 209, 210e, 218

Abbott, Andrew, 149, 150

Abortion, surveys on attitudes, 244

Abt Associates, 306

Acquiescence (agreement) bias Tendency for people to agree with a statement just to avoid seeming disagreeable, 84, 234

Adair, G., 57

Adams, Richard E., 259

Adelman, Madeleine, 379

Adolescents
conflicts among, 379-380, 384, 397-398, 398e

effects of welfare-to-work programs, 323-324

parenting skills, 97, 293

Adoption, contact with birth mothers, 238-239

African Americans
health care availability, 370

inclusion in research, 108, 109

political candidates, 84

See also Ethnic groups; Race

After-only Design, 178

Age
distribution, 349-350, 349e

representative samples, 107-108

See also Elderly

Aggregate matching Two or more groups, such as classes, are matched and then

randomly assigned to the experimental and control conditions, 166

Agreement bias. *See* **Acquiescence (agreement) bias**

AIDS
discovery of virus, 54

prevention programs, 72, 161

recruiting study participants, 109-110

Alcohol. *See* Substance abuse

Alfred, Randall, 282

Allison, David B., 196

Alta Vista, 35

Alter, Catherine, 167-169

Alternate-forms reliability A procedure for testing the reliability of responses to survey questions in which subjects' answers are compared after the subjects have been asked slightly different versions of the questions or when randomly selected halves of the sample have been administered slightly different versions of the questions, 87

Altheide, David L., 392, 393, 394

Altschuld, James W., 315

Alzheimer's day care centers, 280, 281

American Evaluation Association, 307

American Jewish Committee, 231

American Medical Association, 53

American Psychiatric Association, 66

Anderson, Elijah, 150, 387, 394-395

Anderson, Leon, 45

Angel, Ronald J., 426-427

Note: Page numbers followed by *e* refer to exhibits.

Anomalous findings Unexpected findings in data analysis that are inconsistent with most other findings with that data, 45

Anonymity Provided by research in which no identifying information is recorded that could be used to link respondents to their responses, 268, 299

Anthony, William A., 319

Anthropology, field research, 279, 394

Applied research reports
differences from journal articles, 426
front and back matter, 427
sections, 424-426, 425e, 427

Appreciative inquiry, 326

Arean, Patricia A., 108

Aronson, Elliot, 179-180

Aronson, Miriam K., 19, 90

Articles. *See* Journal articles

Assertive community treatment programs, 176, 322-323

Association A criterion for establishing a nomothetic causal relationship between two variables: variation in one variable is related to variation in another variable, 135-136
crosstabulation, 361-364
direction of, 42, 364
evaluating, 366-369
graphing, 364, 365e
in nonexperiments, 139, 177
in quasi-experiments, 174
measures of, 366
monotonic, 364-366
specification, 372-373

Atkinson, Paul, 398, 399

Attributes, 78

Attrition. *See* **Differential attrition**

Austin, D. M., 40

Authenticity, 391-393

Authority, uncritical agreement with, 8

Availability sampling Sampling in which elements are selected on the basis of convenience, 120-121

Averages. *See* **Mean; Mode**

Axim, William, 233

Azocar, Francisca, 109, 110

B phase. *See* **Treatment phase**

B single-subject designs, 215, 216e

Bachman, Ronet, 386, 392, 401

Back matter The section of an applied research report that may include appendixes, tables, and the research instrument(s), 427

Bainbridge, William Sims, 114

Balaswamy, Shantha, 326

Bangs, Ralph, 67, 123

Banks, C., 56

Bar chart A graphic for categorical variables in which the variable's distribution is displayed with solid bars separated by spaces, 343-344, 344e

Barbee, Evelyn L., 19, 90

Barlow, David, 193, 196

Barringer, Felicity, 143

Base number N The total number of cases in a distribution, 347

Baseline phase (A) The initial phase of a single-subject design, typically abbreviated by using the letter A; it represents the period in which the intervention to be evaluated is not offered to the subject. During the baseline phase, repeated measurements of the dependent variable are taken or reconstructed, 187-188
patterns, 188-189, 190-191e, 192e
repeated measurement, 187, 189

Basic single-subject design (A-B), 206-207, 207e

Beadnell, Blair, 161

Bean, J., 13

Beck Depression Inventory (BDI), 91

Becker, A., 371

Becker, Deborah R., 319

Becker, Howard S., 387-389, 391, 422

Before-after One-Group Design. *See* One-Group Pretest-Posttest Design

Before-and-after designs, fixed-sample panel designs, 142e, 143-145

Beggs, Karyn, 311

Behavior coding Observation in which the research categorizes according to strict rules the number of times certain behaviors occur, 241, 242

Behavior theory, 39

Bejerano, Cindy, 379

Bell Core Research, Inc., 253

Bellah, Robert N., 49, 294, 296

Bennett, Lauren, 47

Bennett, William J., 64

Berk, Richard A., 28, 31, 43, 44, 46, 51, 52, 102, 157, 315, 328

Besa, David, 212

BicycleWORKS, 120

Biesanz, Jeremy C., 94

Bimodal   A distribution that has two nonadjacent categories with about the same number of cases, and these categories have more cases than any others, 353

Bird, Chloe E., 268

Bivariate distributions, 361

Black, Donald J., 68

Black box evaluation   Occurs when an evaluation of program outcomes ignores, and does not identify, the process by which the program produced the effect, 323-324

Blair, Bob, 223

Blair, Johnny E., 241-242, 253, 256, 257, 264-265, 266

Blau, Peter M., 226

Block matching   A form of matching that groups individuals by their characteristics. Within each group, members are randomly assigned to the experimental and control groups, 166

Bloom, Martin, 196

Bogdewic, Stephan P., 279, 284, 286, 289, 291

Bogen, David, 49

Boot camps, 328

Booth, Jacqueline A., 108, 109

Booth, Wayne C., 421-422

Boruch, Robert F., 180, 307, 319, 330, 331

Boston

   Cornerville study, 284, 285, 291-292, 299, 392

   housing for homeless mentally ill, 15-16

   Ten Point Coalition, 328

Boston McKinney Project, 314

Bound, John, 372

Bourgeois, Philippe, 120

Boyle, Scott, 177

Bradshaw, William, 39

Brain, emotional responses, 6, 6e

Brett, Pamela J., 108

Brewer, John, 45, 76, 89

Brewster, Zachary W., 369

Bridges, George S., 147

Bristor, Joel, 259

Brock, Thomas, 169, 180

Brooks, Ralph M., 251

Brooten, Dorothy, 233

Brown, Diane R., 108, 109

Brown, Judith Belle, 297

Bureau of Justice Statistics, 364

Bureau of the Census. *See* U.S. Census Bureau

Burnam, M. Audrey, 19

Burt, Martha R., 105

Bush, George H. W., 253

Bush, George W., 113-114

Buzawa, Carl G., 47

Buzawa, Eve S., 47

Cain, Leonard D., Jr., 53

Campbell, Alec, 44

Campbell, Donald T., 16, 48, 75, 137, 159, 160, 172, 332

Campbell, Richard T., 141, 142, 145

Campbell, Wilson, 307, 321-322

Campbell Collaboration, 307

Cantor, David, 364

CAPI. *See* **Computer-assisted personal interview**

Carey, Raymond G., 96, 170, 171, 309, 314, 318, 332

Carpenter, Edwin H., 251

Carryover effect   The impact of an intervention persists after the end of the treatment process, 208

Case study   A setting or group that the analyst treats as an integrated social unit that must be studied holistically and in its particularity, 385

   See also Single-subject designs

Caspi, Avshalom, 233

CATI. *See* **Computer-assisted telephone interview**

Cauce, Ann Mari, 108

Causal effect

   correlation and, 136

   criteria for relationship, 134-138

   in nonexperiments, 138

   in qualitative research, 149-150

   in single-subject designs, 150-151

Causal effect (idiographic perspective)   When a series of concrete events, thoughts, or actions result in a particular event or individual outcome, 149-150, 275

Causal effect (nomothetic perspective)   When variation in one phenomenon, an independent variable, leads to or results, on

average, in variation in another
phenomenon, the dependent variable, 134

Causal mechanism   Some process that creates
the connection between variation in an
independent variable and the variation in
the dependent variable it is hypothesized to
cause, 135, 137-138
in nonexperiments, 140
in true experiments, 171

Causal models, 391, 392e

Causal validity   Exists when a conclusion that
A leads to or results in B is correct. Also
called *internal validity*, 22
in experiments, 156-160
in nonexperiments, 177
in single-subject designs, 189
sources of invalidity, 156-160

Census Bureau. *See* U.S. Census Bureau

Center for Epidemiologic Studies Depression
Index (CES-D), 67, 71, 72e, 73, 86,
90, 91-92, 93, 97, 196, 240, 246

Central tendency   The most common value
(for variables measured at the nominal
level), or the value around which cases
tend to center (for a quantitative variable),
342-343
median, 196-198, 353-356
mode, 352-353
See also **Mean**

CES-D. *See* Center for Epidemiologic Studies
Depression Index

Ceteris paribus   Latin phrase meaning "other
things being equal," 134

Chalmers, Iain, 307

Chance sampling error. *See* **Random
sampling error**

Charlotte (North Carolina), domestic violence
experiment, 44

Chase-Lansdale, P. Lindsay, 426-427

Check coding   The accuracy of the coding is
estimated by comparing the coding
completed by one person with the coding
completed by a second person, 340

Chen, Huey-Tsyh, 316, 323, 324, 325,
326, 327

Cherlin, Andrew, 426-427

Cheung, Kam-fong Monit, 209

Chicago, homeless, 14-15, 105, 427-428

Chicago Survey of Poverty and Material
Hardship, 128

Children
as research subjects, 56
family reunification, 135, 136, 137-138
partial hospitalization programs,
311-313, 312e

Chi-square   An inferential statistic used to
test hypotheses about relationships
between two or more variables in a
crosstabulation, 367

Cholera, 8

Christenson, James A., 251

Clark, Robin E., 319

Class. *See* Social class

Classical Experimental Design. *See*
Pretest-Posttest Control Group Design

Client satisfaction assessments, 178

Client Satisfaction Questionnaire
(CSQ-8), 80, 81e

Clinical replication   Used to enhance
generalizability of single-subject designs,
clinical replication involves combining
different interventions into a clinical
package to treat multiple problems, 217

Clinical significance. *See* **Practical or clinical
significance**

Closed-ended (fixed-choice) question   A
survey question that provides preformatted
response choices for the respondent to
circle or check, 226-227
"don't know" responses, 235-236, 235e
mutually exclusive and exhaustive
choices, 227
"other" responses, 227, 339
response categories, 234-236
scales, 238-239

Cluster   A naturally occurring, mixed
aggregate of elements of the
population, 118

Cluster sampling   Sampling in which
elements are selected in two or more
stages, with the first stage being the
random selection of naturally occurring
clusters and the last stage being the
random selection of elements within
clusters, 118-120, 119e

Codebook   The set of instructions used to link
a number to a category for a particular
variable, 340, 341e

Codependents Anonymous, 299

Coffey, Amanda, 398, 399

Cognition theory, 39

Cognitive functioning, 6

Cognitive interview A technique for evaluating questions in which researchers ask people test questions, then probe with follow-up questions to learn how they understood the question and what their answers mean, 241

Cognitive-behavioral therapy, 39, 74, 174, 208

Cohen, Gary, 22

Cohn, Ellen G., 52

Cohort Individuals or groups with a common starting point. Examples include college class of 1997, people who graduated from high school in the 1980s, General Motors employees who started work between 1990 and the year 2000, and people who were born in the late 1940s or the 1950s (the "baby boom generation"), 145-146

Cohort studies. *See* **Event-based design**

Coleman, James S., 146

Colomb, Gregory G., 421-422

Colon, Israel, 119

Colorado Springs (Colorado), domestic violence experiment, 44

Combined frequency display A table that presents together the distributions for a set of conceptually similar variables having the same response categories; common headings are used for the responses, 350-351, 351e

Community Mental Health Act Amendments of 1975, 307

Comparative Intensity Design, 179

Comparison group In an experiment, a group that has been exposed to a different treatment (or value of the independent variable) than the experimental group, 136, 162-163

See also **Control group**

Compensatory equalization of treatment A threat to internal validity. When staff providing treatment to a comparison group feel that it is unfair that the comparison group is not getting the experimental treatment, they work harder or do more than they might have if there had been no experiment, 159

Compensatory rivalry A type of contamination in true experimental and quasi-experimental designs that occurs when control group members are aware that they are being denied some advantage and increase their efforts by way of compensation. This problem has also been referred to as the *John Henry effect*, 159

Complete observation A role in participant observation in which the researcher does not participate in group activities and is publicly defined as a researcher, 279-280

Complete participation A role in field research in which the researcher does not reveal his or her identity as a researcher to those who are observed, 282-283, 298

Compressed frequency display A table that presents cross-classification data efficiently by eliminating unnecessary percentages, such as the percentage corresponding to the second value of a dichotomous variable, 351, 352e

Computer-assisted personal interview (CAPI) A personal interview in which the laptop computer is used to display interview questions and to process responses that the interviewer types in, as well as to check that these responses fall within allowed ranges, 258-259

Computer-assisted qualitative data analysis Uses special computer software to assist qualitative analyses through creation, application, and refinement of categories; tracing linkages between concepts; and making comparisons between cases and events, 399-402

challenges, 401-402

coding, 400e, 401

reports, 401

text preparation, 399-400

Computer-assisted telephone interview (CATI) A telephone interview in which a questionnaire is programmed into a computer, along with relevant skip patterns, and only legal entries are allowed; incorporates the tasks of interviewing, data entry, and some data cleaning, 257, 340

Computer-mediated counseling, 22, 23e

Computers

bibliographic databases, 32, 33*e*, 37, 463

See also Internet; Software

Concept   A mental image that summarizes a set of similar observations, feelings, or ideas, 64-65
nominal definitions, 65
variables representing, 68

Conceptualization   The process of specifying what we mean by a term. In deductive research, conceptualization helps to translate portions of an abstract theory into specific variables that can be used in testable hypotheses. In inductive research, conceptualization is an important part of the process used to make sense of related observations, 65

Concurrent multiple baseline design   A series of A-B designs (although A-B-A or A-B-A-B designs could also be used) are implemented at the same time for at least three cases (clients, target problems, or settings), 209, 211e

Concurrent validity   The type of validity that exists when scores on a measure are closely related to scores on a criterion measured at the same time, 90

Confidence interval   The range of values within which the true population value will fall. Often, a 95% confidence interval is used; this means that the researcher is 95% sure that the true population value falls within the range, 126-127, 360, 367

Confidentiality   Provided by research in which identifying information that could be used to link respondents to their responses is available only to designated research personnel for specific research needs, 57, 268, 299, 331

Congress. *See* U.S. Senate

Constant   A number that has a fixed value in a given situation; a characteristic or value that does not change, 68

Construct validity   The type of validity that is established by showing that a measure is related to other measures as specified in a theory, 91-92

Constructivist paradigm   Methodology based on rejection of belief in an external reality; it emphasizes the importance of exploring the way in which different stakeholders in a social setting construct their beliefs, 49

Contact summary forms, 387, 388e

Contamination   A source of causal invalidity that occurs when either the experimental and/or the comparison group is aware of the other group and is influenced in the posttest as a result, 156, 159

Content analysis   A research method for systematically analyzing and making inferences from text, 75, 402-406
coding, 403, 404-405e, 406
flowchart, 403, 404-405e
reliability and validity, 403, 407
stages, 403, 404-405e
statistical analyses, 403

Content validity   The type of validity that exists when the full range of a concept's meaning is covered by the measure, 89-90

Context   A focus of idiographic causal explanation; a particular outcome is understood as part of a larger set of interrelated circumstances, 135, 138
in nonexperiments, 140
in qualitative research, 275

Context effect   Occurs in a survey when one or more questions influence how subsequent questions are interpreted, 244

Contingency question   A question that is asked of only a subset of survey respondents, 236

Continuous variable   A variable for which the number represents a quantity that can be described in terms of order, spread between the numbers, and/or relative amounts, 76

Control group   A comparison group that receives no treatment, 136, 162-163
contamination of, 159
matching, 165-166, 165e
nonequivalent control group designs, 172-174, 173e
random assignment to, 163-165
selection bias, 157
See also **Comparison group**

Control theory, 45-46

Convergent validity   The type of validity achieved when one measure of a concept is associated with different types of measures of the same concept, 91

Converse, Jean M., 222

Cook, Thomas D., 137, 159, 160, 172, 326

Cooper, Harris, 419, 420

Core Alcohol and Drug Survey, 82-83

Core Institute, Southern Illinois University, 82-83

Cornerville study, 284, 285, 291-292, 299, 392

Correlation analysis A statistical technique that summarizes the strength of a relationship between two quantitative variables in terms of its adherence to a linear pattern, 374

Cost-benefit analysis A type of evaluation research that compares program costs to the economic value of program benefits, 320-322, 321e, 330

Cost-effectiveness analysis A type of evaluation research that compares program costs to actual program outcomes, 322-323

Costner, Herbert L., 138

Cotrell, Victoria, 353

Counts, David R., 284-285

Counts, Dorothy Ayers, 284-285

Couper, Mick P., 226, 259, 260

Cover letter The letter sent with a mailed questionnaire. It explains the survey's purpose and auspices and encourages the respondent to participate, 248, 249, 250e

Covert participation. *See* **Complete participation**

Crabtree, Benjamin F., 276, 294, 381-382

Craver, Jay, 161

Crawford, Aileen, 277

Cress, Daniel M., 383-384, 395-396

Crime
effects on victims, 144
life circumstances and, 141
rates, 364, 365e
relationship to family disruption, 149
See also Domestic violence

Crime Control and Safe Streets Act, 331

Criterion validity The type of validity that is established by comparing the scores obtained on the measure being validated to those obtained with a more direct or already validated measure of the same phenomenon (the criterion), 90-91, 92

Cronbach's alpha A statistic commonly used to measure interitem reliability, 87

Cross-population generalizability Exists when findings about one group, population, or setting hold true for other groups, populations, or settings. Also called *external validity*, 20, 21e

evaluating, 105, 106
in experiments, 160-161

Cross-sectional research design A study in which data are collected at only one point in time, 138
causality, 138-140
repeated, 142e, 143
time order in, 141

Crosstabulation (crosstab) In the simplest case, a bivariate (two-variable) distribution, showing the distribution of one variable for each category of another variable; can also be elaborated using three or more variables, 342, 361-364
aspects of association, 364
controlling for third variables, 369-373

CSQ-8. *See* Client Satisfaction Questionnaire

Cuba, Lee J., 422

Cultural differences
interpretations of survey questions, 233-234
responses to questions on emotions, 84
See also Ethnic groups

Cumulative percentage, 348

Current Population Survey, 267

Curvilinear Any pattern of association between two quantitative variables that does not involve a regular increase or decrease, 364

Cut-off scores, 92-94, 96-97, 196

Cycle A baseline phase pattern reflecting ups and downs depending on the time of measurement, 188, 191e

Czaja, Ronald, 223

Dabelko, Holly I., 326

D.A.R.E. (Drug Abuse Resistance Education), 305-306, 315-316, 316e

Data, secondary. *See* **Secondary data**

Data analysis
ethical issues, 361, 374-375
preparing data, 337-342
secondary data, 266-267
time series data, 175
visual, 196-202
See also Qualitative data analysis; Statistics

Data cleaning The process of checking data for errors after the data have been entered in a computer file, 340-342

Data collection
administration of, 97

direct measures, 74-75
methods, 74-75
observations, 74
qualitative data, 381, 386
self-reports, 90
single-subject designs, 194-195
unobtrusive measures, 75
See also Measurement; **Participant observation**; **Qualitative methods**; **Survey research**
Dattalo, Patrick, 175
Davies, Philip, 307
Davis, James A., 224, 343, 369
Davis, Ryan, 35
Dawes, Robyn, 410
Debriefing A researcher's informing subjects after an experiment about the experiment's purposes and methods and evaluating subjects' personal reactions to the experiment, 57, 180
Deception When subjects are misled about research procedures because researchers want to determine how they would react to the treatment if they were not research subjects, 179-180
Decker, Scott H., 401-402
Deductive research The type of research in which a specific expectation is deduced from a general premise and is then tested. Compare to *inductive research*, 40-41
DeLeon, George, 322
Dentler, Robert A., 306, 330
Denzin, Norman K., 274, 406
DeParle, Jason, 329
Dependent variable A variable that is hypothesized to vary depending on or under the influence of another variable, 41
Depression
definitions, 66-67
index, 71, 72e, 73, 91-92, 97, 240
measures of, 19
screening tests, 92
sense of control and, 222
symptoms among homeless, 19
See also Center for Epidemiologic Studies Depression Index (CES-D)
Descriptive research Research in which social phenomena are defined and described, 11
examples, 13

inductive approach, 47
Descriptive statistics Statistics used to describe the distribution of and relationship among variables, 336
Descriptive theory, 325
Deterrence theory, 31, 44
Detroit Area Study, 232, 361-362
Dewey, Thomas E., 114
Diagnostic and Statistical Manual, IV (DSM-IV), 66, 67, 108
Diamond, Timothy, 273, 274, 275, 276-279, 281, 283, 284, 287, 289, 292, 386
Dichotomies Variables having only two values, 82
Dickey, Barbara, 15
Differential attrition (mortality) A problem that occurs in experiments when comparison groups become different because subjects are more likely to drop out of one of the groups for various reasons, 157
Diffusion of treatment A type of contamination in experimental and quasi-experimental designs that occurs when treatment and control (comparison) groups interact and the nature of the treatment becomes known to the control group, 159
Dillman, Don A., 223, 226, 229, 232, 233, 234, 236, 237, 240, 244, 248, 249, 251, 252, 261, 264, 265e, 266
Direct measure A visual or recorded observation or a physical measure, 74
Direct replication Used to enhance the generalizability of a single-subject design, it involves repeating the single-subject design using the same procedures, by the same researchers, including the same providers of the treatment, in the same setting, and in the same situation, with different clients, 217
Direction of association A pattern in a relationship between two variables—the values of variables tend to change consistently in relation to change on the other variable. The direction of association can be either positive or negative, 42, 42e, 364
Discrete variable The number assigned to a variable represents a separate category of

the variable, the order of which is arbitrary, 76, 77-78

Discriminant validity An approach to construct validation; the scores on the measure to be validated are compared to scores on another measure of the same variable and to scores on variables that measure different but related concepts. Discriminant validity is achieved if the measure to be validated is related most strongly to its comparison measure and less so to the measures of other concepts, 91

Disproportionate stratified sampling Sampling in which elements are selected from strata in different proportions from those that appear in the population, 117, 118e

Distribution of benefits An ethical issue about how much researchers can influence the benefits subjects receive as part of the treatment being studied in a field experiment, 180, 330

Distributions
 base number *N*, 347
 bimodal, 353
 bivariate, 361
 central tendency, 342-343, 352-357
 mean, 126-127, 354-357
 normal, 126-127, 127e, 360, 360e
 sampling, 124-125
 skewness, 342-343, 355, 356e
 summarizing, 352
 unimodal, 353
 univariate, 342-343, 352
 variability, 342-343
 See also **Frequency distribution**
Dohrenwend, Barbara Snell, 66
Dohrenwend, Bruce P., 66
Domestic violence
 decision to press charges, 47
 deterrent effects of arrest and employment status, 45-46
 extent of problem, 27, 47
 informal sanctions, 45-46
 See also Minneapolis Domestic Violence Experiment

Double negative A question or statement that contains two negatives, which can muddy the meaning of the question, 230-231

Double-barreled question A single survey question that actually asks two questions but allows only one answer, 231

Double-blind procedure An experimental method in which neither the subjects nor the staff delivering experimental treatments know which subjects are getting the treatment and which are receiving a placebo, 159

Downey, Lois, 161
Drake, Robert E., 94, 319
Drugs. *See* Substance abuse
DSM-IV. See Diagnostic and Statistical Manual, IV
Dukakis, Michael, 253

Duration The length of time an event or some symptom lasts; usually is measured for each occurrence of the event or symptom, 194

Dushenko, T. W., 57
Dutton, Mary Ann, 47

Ecological fallacy An error in reasoning in which incorrect conclusions about individual-level processes are drawn from group-level data, 147-148, 148e

Economic Opportunity Act, 40
Edin, Kathryn, 128
Education
 achievement test scores in public and private schools, 146
 in women's prisons, 319-320
 relationship to health, 362-364, 363e, 364e, 369-372, 370e, 371e, 373e
 relationship to race, 371-372, 372e

Effect size A standardized measure of association—often the difference between the mean of the experimental group and the mean of the control group on the dependent variable, adjusted for the average variability in the two groups, 420

Efficiency analysis A type of evaluation research that compares program costs to program effects. It can be either a cost-benefit analysis or a cost-effectiveness analysis, 320-323

Ego-based commitments, 7-8

Elaboration analysis The process of introducing a third variable into an analysis to better understand—to elaborate–the bivariate (two-variable) relationship under consideration. Additional control variables also can be introduced, 369

Elder, Janet, 231

Elderly
Alzheimer's day care centers, 280, 281
caregivers, 297-298
depression, 19
health needs, 53
RV clubs, 284-285
sampling, 105
services needed, 298, 326
See also Nursing homes

Elections
African American candidates, 84
presidential, 113-114, 113e, 253
See also Voter participation

Electronic survey   A survey that is sent and answered by computer, either through e-mail or on the Web, 261
compared to other survey designs, 246-247, 247e, 264-266, 265e
confidentiality, 268
drawbacks, 261
formats, 261
interactive voice response, 261

Elements   The individual members of the population whose characteristics are to be measured, 103

E-mail. *See* Internet

E-mail survey   A survey that is sent and answered through e-mail, 261
See also **Electronic survey**

Emerson, Robert M., 289

Emic focus   Representing a setting with the participants' terms, 380

Empirical generalization   A statement that describes patterns found in data, 43

Employment. *See* Work

Endogenous change   A source of causal invalidity that occurs when natural developments or changes in the subjects (independent of the experimental treatment itself) account for some or all of the observed change from the pretest to the posttest, 156, 157-158

Engel, Rafael J., 19, 83, 97, 175, 236, 339, 342, 353

Ensel, Walter, 233

Enumeration units   Units that contain one or more elements and that are listed in a sampling frame, 103-104

Erbring, Lutz, 261

Erikson, Kai T., 283

Errors
in reasoning, 4-8
in survey research, 224-226, 225e
measurement, 83-85, 86
Type I and Type II, 368-369

Errors of nonobservation   Errors caused by omission from a survey or other research of some cases that should be included, 224

Errors of observation   Errors caused by poor measurement of observed cases, 224

Escapees RV Club, 284-285

Essock, Susan M., 322-323

Ethical issues
anonymity, 268, 299
confidentiality, 57, 268, 299, 331
data analysis, 361, 374-375
deception, 179-180
distribution of benefits, 180, 330
evaluating, 58
evaluation research, 330-331
experimental research, 179-180
honesty and openness, 53-54
informed consent, 56-57, 180, 217, 218, 298-299
NASW Code of Ethics, 11, 55, 218, 478-498
participant observation, 281, 282, 283, 298-300
qualitative data analysis, 406
qualitative research, 281, 282, 283, 298-300
research reporting, 427-428
single-subject designs, 217-218
survey research, 58, 268
uses of science, 54

Ethnic groups
health, 366, 366e
representative samples, 107-108
underrepresentation in studies, 107-108
See also African Americans; Cultural differences; Hispanic Americans

Ethnography   The study of a culture or cultures that some group of people shares, using participant observation over an extended period of time, 383, 394-395

Etic focus   Representing a setting with the researchers' terms, 380

Evaluation research Research that describes or identifies the impact of social policies and programs, 12, 306
black box approach, 323-324
challenges, 332
compared to traditional social science research, 309
design alternatives, 323-330
distinction from other research, 12-13
efficiency analysis, 320-323
ethical issues, 330-331
examples, 15-16, 305-306
experimental designs, 318-319
federal government requirements, 307, 321-322
growth of, 307
history, 306-307
needs assessment, 313-315, 326
outcome evaluation, 318-320
process evaluation, 315-318
process of, 307-309
professional organizations, 307
program theory approach, 324-325, 325e
qualitative methods, 327-328
quality assurance reviews, 307
quantitative methods, 327
quasi-experiments, 319-320
research designs, 177
research firms, 306, 307
researcher or stakeholder orientation, 325-327
simple or complex outcomes, 328-330
single-subject designs, 206
systems model, 307-309, 308e
Event-based design A type of longitudinal study in which data are collected at two or more points in time from individuals in a cohort. Also known as *cohort study*, 142e, 145-146
Ex post facto control group design A nonexperimental design in which comparison groups are selected after the treatment, program, or other variation in the independent variable has occurred, 176, 176e
Exhaustive Every case can be classified as having at least one attribute (or value) for the variable, 78
Expectancies of experimental staff A source of treatment misidentification in experiments and quasi-experiments that occurs when change among experimental subjects is due to the positive expectancies of the staff who are delivering the treatment, rather than to the treatment itself; also called a *self-fulfilling prophecy*, 159
Experimental designs
compared to other research designs, 416-419
criteria for causal relationships, 134-137
ethical issues, 179-180
generalizability, 160-162
in evaluation research, 318-319
laboratory, 417
process analysis, 160
randomized comparative change designs, 319
validity, 156-162
See also **Control group**; **Field experiment**; **Quasi-experimental design**; **True experiment**
Experimental group In an experiment, the group of subjects that receives the treatment or experimental manipulation, 136, 162-163
matching, 165-166, 165e
random assignment to, 163-165
selection bias, 157
Explanatory research Seeks to identify causes and effects of social phenomena and to predict how one phenomenon will change or vary in response to variation in some other phenomenon, 12, 14-15
Exploratory research Seeks to find out how people get along in the setting under question, what meanings they give to their actions, and what issues concern them, 12
examples, 14
inductive approach, 46-47, 275
qualitative methods, 275
External events A source of causal invalidity that occurs when events external to the study influence posttest scores. Also called an effect of *history*, 156, 158-159
External validity. *See* **Cross-population generalizability**
Extraneous variable A variable that influences both the independent and dependent variables so as to create a spurious association between them that disappears when the extraneous variable is controlled, 371-372, 372e

Face validity   The type of validity that exists when an inspection of items used to measure a concept suggests that they are appropriate "on their face," 89

Factoral validity   A form of construct validity used to determine if the scale items relate correctly to different dimensions of the concept, 91-92

Fair, Jerily, 315

False negative   The participant does not have a particular problem based on a screening instrument, but the participant really does have the problem based on a clinical evaluation, 93

False positive   The participant does have a significant problem based on a screening instrument but in reality does not have the problem based on a clinical evaluation, 93

Families
    caregivers, 297-298
    disruption and crime, 149
    incomes, 124-125, 125e
    reunification, 135, 136, 137-138
    work and, 221-222, 232, 240

Family Development and Self-Sufficiency (FaDSS) program, 167-169, 168e

Family support interventions, 167-169, 168e

Farley, O. William, 177

Farmer, Melissa M., 370

Feedback   Information about service delivery system outputs, outcomes, or operations that is available to any program inputs, 308-309

Fence-sitters   Survey respondents who see themselves as being neutral on an issue and choose a middle (neutral) response that is offered, 235

Fenno, Richard F., Jr., 291

Ferguson, Kirsten, 208

Ferraro, Kenneth F., 370

Field experiments
    challenges, 417, 418
    difficulties in agency-based research, 170-171
    generalizability, 160
    informed consent, 180, 298-299
    lack of control over conditions, 171
    selection bias, 157
    See also Experimental designs

Field notes   Notes that describe what has been observed, heard, or otherwise experienced in a participant observation study. These notes usually are written after the observational session, 289-291, 290e
    analysis of, 386-387
    contact summary forms, 387, 388e

Field research
    anthropological, 279, 394
    explanation in, 150
    See also **Participant observation**

Filter question   A survey question used to identify a subset of respondents who then are asked other questions, 236, 237e

Fink, Arlene, 421

Fiscella, Kevin, 362, 366

Fischer, Joel, 196

Fixed-choice questions. *See* **Closed-ended (fixed-choice) question**

Fixed-sample panel design   A type of longitudinal study in which data are collected from the same individuals—the panel—at two or more points in time. In another type of panel design, panel members who leave are replaced with new members. Also known as *panel design*, 142e, 143-145
    causality, 144e
    costs, 145

Floaters   Survey respondents who provide an opinion on a topic in response to a closed-ended question that does not include a *don't know* option, but who will choose *don't know* if it is available, 235-236, 235e

Focus groups   A qualitative method that involves unstructured group interviews in which the focus group leader actively encourages discussion among participants on the topics of interest, 241, 274, 297-298

Food and Drug Administration, 55

Forero, Juan, 267

Formative evaluation   Process evaluation that is used to shape and refine program operations, 317

Fowler, Floyd J., 96, 223, 226, 241, 249, 260, 266

Franklin, Ronald D., 196

Franks, Peter, 362, 366

Fraser, Mark W., 135, 136, 137-138

Freedman, David A., 8

Freeman, Howard E., 166, 172, 176, 181, 306, 318, 326

French, Michael T., 322

Frequency In a single-subject design, counting the number of times a behavior occurs or the number of times people experience different feelings within a particular time period, 194

Frequency distribution Numerical display showing the number of cases, and usually the percentage of cases (the relative frequencies), corresponding to each value or group of values of a variable, 347, 347e
  combined frequency displays, 350-351, 351e
  compressed frequency displays, 351, 352e
  grouped data, 348-350, 349e, 350e, 361
  ungrouped data, 347e, 348, 348e, 349e
  univariate, 342-343, 352

Frequency polygon A graphic for quantitative variables in which a continuous line connects data points representing the variable's distribution, 344, 345e

Fretz, Rachel I., 289

Frisman, Linda K., 322-323

Front matter The section of an applied research report that includes an executive summary, abstract, and table of contents, 427

GAF. *See* Global Assessment of Functioning Scale

Gallagher-Thompson, Dolores, 108

Gallup, George, 114

Gallup polls, 113-114, 231, 253

Gamma A measure of association that is sometimes used in crosstabular analysis, 366

Garland, Diana, 45

Gary, Lawrence E., 108, 109

GASB. *See* Governmental Accounting Standards Board

Gatekeeper A person in a field setting who can grant researchers access to the setting, 284

Gays. *See* Homosexuals

Geertz, Clifford, 385

Gelman, Caroline R., 298

Gender
  masculinity of police officers, 392-393
  rapport with interviewers, 259
  relationship to health, 366, 367e
  representative samples, 107-108

socialization differences, 84

General Social Survey (GSS)
  administration of, 224, 343
  age distribution, 349-350, 349e
  education completed, 344, 345e, 350, 350e
  family incomes, 125, 125e
  length, 223
  marital status, 343-344, 344e
  nonrespondents, 259, 260e
  political views, 348, 348e
  questions, 223, 259
  views on government responsibilities, 350-351, 351e
  views on women's roles, 351, 352e
  voter participation data, 347e, 348

Generalizability Exists when a conclusion holds true for the population, group, setting, or event that we say it does, given the conditions that we specify, 19-22
  importance, 21-22
  in survey research, 223
  of experimental designs, 160-162
  of single-subject designs, 216-217
  See also **Cross-population generalizability**; **Sample generalizability**

Ghimire, Dirgha, 233

Gilchrist, Valerie J., 285

Gilligan, Carol, 398

Glaser, Barney G., 288, 399

Global Assessment of Functioning Scale (GAF), 87, 88e

Goal attainment scales, 79-80, 79e

Goal-free evaluation, 326

Goffman, Erving, 282

Gold, Martha R., 362, 366

Goldapple, Gary, 173-174

Goldberg-Glen, Robin, 39, 138-139, 140

Golden, Jeannie, 212

Goldfinger, Stephen M., 15, 16, 73, 95, 145, 160, 290, 314, 383

Goleman, Daniel, 6, 159, 233

Goodman, Lisa, 47

Google, 35, 466

Gordon, Judith, 161

Gordon, Raymond, 226, 295

Gore, Al, 113-114

Gorey, Kevin M., 420

Gorman, Bernard S., 196

Government Performance and Results Act of 1993, 10, 307

Governmental Accounting Standards
    Board (GASB), 307, 321
Graduate Program in Applied Sociology, 422
Grady, John, 291
Graham, Kathryn, 108
Graham, Sandra, 108
Grand tour question   A broad question at the
    start of an interview that seeks to engage
    the respondent in the topic of interest, 294
Graphs, 343
    advantages, 342
    bar charts, 343-344, 344e
    frequency polygons, 344, 345e
    guidelines, 347, 361
    histograms, 344, 345e
    misuse of, 344, 346e, 347
    relationships shown in, 364, 365e
    single-subject designs, 193, 202
    time series data, 175
    See also Visual analysis
Grimm, James W., 369
Grinnell, Frederick, 52
Grinnell, Richard M., 96
Grounded theory   Systematic theory
    developed inductively, based on
    observations that are summarized into
    conceptual categories, reevaluated in the
    research setting, and gradually refined and
    linked to other conceptual categories, 398-
    399, 399e
Group designs. *See* Experimental designs;
    Nonexperimental designs;
    Quasi-experimental design
Group-administered survey   A survey that is
    completed by individual respondents who
    are assembled in a group, 252
    compared to other survey designs, 246-247,
        247e, 264-266
    ethical issues, 268
    See also **Survey research**
Grove, Kwai, 108
Groves, Robert M., 223, 224, 226, 258, 259, 260
Gruenewald, Paul J., 64
GSS. *See* General Social Survey
Guba, Egon G., 48, 49
Gunston, Suzanne, 72
Guttman scale, 239

Ha, Jung-hwa, 297-298
Haaland, Jan-Aage, 347

Hage, Jerald, 138, 149
Haley, Leon, 123
Hamburg, Germany, cholera epidemic, 8
Hamilton, David, 381
Hamilton, Edwin E., 44
Hammer, Leslie B., 297-298
Haney, C., 56
Hann, Danette, 91
Harknett, Kristen, 169, 180
Harris, Louis, 143
Harrison, R. Steven, 177
Hartung, Cynthia M., 108
Hawthorne effect   A type of contamination in
    experimental and quasi-experimental
    designs that occurs when members of the
    treatment group change in terms of the
    dependent variable because their
    participation in the study makes them feel
    special, 161
HCFA. *See* Health Care Finance Administration
Healey, Brian P., 120
Health
    needs of elderly, 53
    of welfare recipients, 372-373, 374e
    relationship to education, 362-364, 363e,
        364e, 369-372, 370e, 371e, 373e
    relationship to gender, 366, 367e
    relationship to race, 366, 366e, 371-373, 373e
    social influences on, 362-364
Health Care Finance Administration (HCFA), 317
Health Research Extension Act of 1985, 331
Hedges, Larry V., 419, 420
Hellman, Sondra, 15
Henderson, J. Neil, 276
Herek, Gregory, 30, 410
Hersen, Michel, 193, 196
Heterosexist bias, 30
Hick, Steven, 50
High schools, conflicts in, 379-380,
    384, 397-398
Hill, David, 259
Hirsch, Kathleen, 150
Hispanic Americans
    elderly, 298
    inclusion in research, 108, 109
    See also Ethnic groups
Histogram   A graphic for quantitative
    variables in which the variable's
    distribution is displayed with adjacent bars,
    344, 345e

Historicist explanation. *See* **Idiographic causal explanation**

History effect A source of causal invalidity that occurs when something other than the treatment influences outcome scores; also called an effect of *external events*, 156, 158-159, 175

HIV/AIDS. *See* AIDS

Hoffer, Thomas, 146

Holmes, Steven A., 251

Homeless
AIDS prevention education for, 72
characteristics, 13
deaths of, 1-3
emergency shelters for, 14
estimated numbers, 427-428
popular beliefs about, 3-4, 3e
programs and treatment for, 10
proportion served by mental health
    facilities, 13
residential preferences, 73
sampling, 15, 20, 102, 105, 120
social movement organizations,
    383-384, 395-396
studies of, 13, 14-15
substance use measurement, 94-96
supportive housing for, 15-16
women, 14

Homeless mentally ill
case management programs, 324
housing for, 15-16, 95, 290-291, 314, 383
measurement of mental illness, 19
services for, 14
shelter staff views of, 228
substance abuse treatment, 412-416

Homosexuals
AIDS prevention programs, 161
bias against in research, 30
recruiting research participants, 109-110

Honesty, 53-54

Horney, Julie, 141

Hu, Paul Nongzhuang, 268

Huberman, A. Michael, 387, 389, 399, 406

Hudson, Walter W., 96

Huff, Darrell, 361

Human subjects, research on
anonymity, 268, 299
children, 56
confidentiality, 57, 268, 299, 331
ethical standards, 54-58

informed consent, 56-57, 180, 217,
    218, 298-299
institutional review boards, 55, 331
potential harm, 56, 57, 299
withholding beneficial treatment, 57

Humphrey, Nicholas, 7

Humphreys, Laud, 282

Hunt, Morton, 157, 158, 180

Hunter, Albert, 45, 76, 89

HyperRESEARCH, 399-401, 400e

Hypothesis A tentative statement about
empirical reality involving a relationship
between two or more variables, 40, 41
direction of association, 42, 42e
examples, 42e
wording, 42

ICPSR. *See* Inter-University Consortium for
Political and Social Research

Idiographic causal explanation An
explanation that identifies the concrete,
individual sequence of events, thoughts, or
actions that resulted in a particular outcome
for a particular individual or that led to a
particular event; may be termed an
individualist or *historicist explanation*,
149-150, 275

Idiosyncratic variation Variation in responses
to questions that is caused by individuals'
reactions to particular words or ideas in the
question instead of by variation in the
concept that the question is intended to
measure, 71, 237

Illogical reasoning Occurs when we
prematurely jump to conclusions or
argue on the basis of invalid assumptions,
4, 7, 9

IMF. *See* International Monetary Fund

Impact evaluation (or analysis) The extent to
which a treatment or other service has an
effect, 318-320

Implementation assessments, 316

Inaccurate observation Observations based
on faulty perceptions of empirical reality,
4, 6, 9

Incomes
family, 124-125, 125e
relationship to health, 369-371,
    370e, 371e

Incomplete observations, 6

Independent variable   A variable that is hypothesized to cause, or lead to, variation in another variable, 41, 73-74

Index   A composite measure based on summing, averaging, or otherwise combining the responses to multiple questions that are intended to measure the same concept, 71
cut-off scores, 92-94, 96-97
examples, 71, 72e
multidimensional, 73
preexisting, 71, 240
score calculations, 73
use as screening tests, 92-94
weighted, 73

Indicator   The question or other operation used to indicate the value of cases on a variable, 70-71, 70e

Indirect (or unobtrusive) measures   Data collected about individuals or groups without their direct knowledge or participation, 75

Individualist explanation. *See* **Idiographic causal explanation**

Individualist fallacy. *See* **Reductionist fallacy**

Inductive research   The type of research in which general conclusions are drawn from specific data; compare to *deductive research*, 45
examples, 45-46
qualitative, 46-47, 275
theory and data in, 45

Inferential statistics   A mathematical tool for estimating how likely it is that a statistical result based on data from a random sample is representative of the population from which the sample is assumed to have been selected, 126, 336, 366-369

Informal social control, spouse abuse and, 45-46

Informed consent   Potential research study participants must have all relevant information about the study to decide whether to participate in the study. This information includes the costs and benefits to the participant, what their participation involves, and their rights as participants in the study, 56-57
field experiments, 180, 298-299
single-subject designs, 217, 218

Infoseek, 35

Ingersoll-Dayton, Berit, 297-298

Initiation, severity of, 179-180

In-person interview   A survey in which an interviewer questions respondents face-to-face and records their answers, 258
advantages, 258
compared to other survey designs, 246-247, 247e, 264-266, 265e
computer-assisted, 258-259
costs, 223
filter questions, 236
interacting with respondents, 258
interviewer training, 258
maximizing response, 259-260
third-party presence, 259
training for interviewers, 109
See also **Survey research**

Inputs   The resources, raw materials, clients, and staff that go into a program, 307, 310

Institute for Survey Research, 58

Institutional review board (IRB)   A group of organizational and community representatives required by federal law to review the ethical issues in all proposed research that is federally funded, involves human subjects, or has any potential for harm to subjects, 55, 331

Instrumentation   A problem that occurs in experimental designs when the measurement methods are not stable or equivalent, 158-159

Integrative approach   An orientation to evaluation research that expects researchers to respond to the concerns of people involved with the program—stakeholders—as well as to the standards and goals of the social scientific community, 327

Intensive (depth) interviewing   A qualitative method that involves open-ended, relatively unstructured questioning in which the interviewer seeks in-depth information on the interviewee's feelings, experiences, and perceptions, 274, 293
preparations, 294
questions, 294, 295-297
recording, 296-297
relations with respondents, 295
researcher roles, 293-294
saturation point, 122, 294, 295e
selection of respondents, 294

Interactive voice response (IVR)   A survey in which respondents receive automated calls and answer questions by pressing numbers on their touch-tone phones or speaking numbers that are interpreted by computerized voice recognition software, 261

Internal consistency An approach that calculates reliability based on the correlation among multiple items used to measure a single concept, 86-87

Internal validity. *See* **Causal validity**

International Monetary Fund (IMF), 306

Internet
    annotated Web site list, 471-477
    citing sources on, 37, 465
    direct addressing, 35, 464
    literature searches, 32-34, 35-37, 464-466
    percentage of U.S. households with access, 261
    research on discussion groups, 299-300, 402-403
    search engines, 35-36, 466
    secondary data available, 267
    subject directories, 35, 465-466
    support groups, 402-403
    See also **Electronic survey**

Interobserver reliability When similar measurements are obtained by different observers rating the same people, events, or places, 87-89

Interpretive questions Questions included in a questionnaire or interview schedule to help explain answers to other important questions, 242-243

Interpretivism Methodology based on the belief that reality is socially constructed and that the goal of social scientists is to understand what meanings people give to that reality, 49

Interquartile range The range in a distribution between the end of the first quartile and the beginning of the third quartile, 358

Interrater reliability. *See* **Interobserver reliability**

Interrupted Time Series Design, 174

Intersubjective agreement Agreement between scientists about the nature of reality; often upheld as a more reasonable goal for science than certainty about an objective reality, 48-49

Inter-University Consortium for Political and Social Research (ICPSR), 224, 267

Interval In a single-subject design, measuring the length of time between events, behaviors, or symptoms, 194

Interval level of measurement A measurement of a variable in which the numbers indicating a variable's values represent fixed measurement units but have no absolute, or fixed, zero point, 77e, 80, 343, 355

Intervening variables Variables that are influenced by an independent variable and in turn influence variation in a dependent variable, thus helping to explain the relationship between the independent and dependent variables, 140, 369-371, 369e

Interview schedule The survey instrument containing the questions asked by the interviewer in an in-person or phone survey, 239
    for phone surveys, 253, 254-256e
    length, 223
    See also **Questionnaire**

Interviews. *See* **Cognitive interview**; **In-person interview**; **Intensive (depth) interviewing**

Intraobserver (or intrarater) reliability Consistency of ratings by an observer of an unchanging phenomenon at two or more points in time, 89

Invalid codes Values that fall outside the range of allowable values for a given variable, 340-342

IRB. *See* **Institutional review board**

Irvine, Leslie, 299

Israel, B., 371

IVR. *See* **Interactive voice response**

Jackson, James, 336, 361-362, 369

Jackson, James S., 108

Jacobsen, Paul, 91

James, S., 371

Jensen, Carla, 185, 212

Jensen, Julie, 19

John Henry effect. *See* **Compensatory rivalry**

Johnson, Alice, 14

Johnson, Christina, 212

Johnson, John M., 392, 393, 394

Johnson, Knowlton, 144, 145

Jones, Barbara, 311

Jones, Sue Hinze, 3-4

Jorner, Ulf, 347

Joseph, Antoine, 324

Jottings   Brief notes written in the field about highlights of an observation period, 289

Journal articles
bibliographic databases, 32-34, 33e, 37, 463
differences from applied research reports, 426
evaluating, 37, 441-443, 444-449
rejection rates, 423
review process, 32, 37, 423
searching for, 31-35, 463-464
sections, 423, 424e
topics, 31

Kagay, Michael R., 231

Kahana, Boaz, 275, 285, 286, 289

Kahana, Eva, 275, 285, 286, 289

Kahn, Ric, 2

Kahn, Robert L., 223

Kaufman, Sharon R., 275, 293, 294, 296

Kayser-Jones, Jeanie, 282

Kellogg Foundation, 310, 426

Kenney, Charles, 114

Keohane, Robert O., 30, 134

Kerchis, Cheryl Z., 67

Kerr, Barbara, 22

Kershaw, David, 315

Kettner, Peter, 10, 309, 311, 318

Key informant   An insider who is willing and able to provide a field researcher with superior access and information, including answers to questions that arise in the course of the research, 285

Kifner, John, 231

Kilgore, Sally, 146

Kincaid, Harold, 51

King, Gary, 30, 134, 287, 288

King, Miriam L., 267

Kinnevy, Susan C., 120

Klap, Ruth, 44

Kleinman, Susan, 300

Klitzner, Michael, 64

Known-groups validity   Demonstrating the validity of a measure using two groups with already identified characteristics, 91

Koegel, Paul, 19, 279

Koenig, Barbara A., 282

Koeske, Gary, 91, 92

Kohut, Andrew, 253

Kontos, Nina J., 322-323

Korr, Wynne S., 324

Kotsopoulos, Sotiris, 311

Kraemer, Helena Chmura, 128

Krause, Neal, 90

Krout, John A, 242

Krueger, Richard A., 297

Kuo, Meichun, 63

Kuzel, Anton J., 286

Kvale, Steinar, 294, 295, 386

Labaw, Patricia J., 223, 242, 243, 244

Labeling theory, 31

Laboratory experiments, 417

LaGory, Mark, 18

Lai, Gina, 233

Landers, Ann, 4

Landon, Alfred M., 114

Larson, Calvin J., 56

Latinos. *See* Hispanic Americans

Latour, Francie, 328

Lauritsen, Janet L., 148

Lavrakas, Paul J., 253

Leading questions, 84

Lee, Barrett A., 3-4

Lee, Hang, 63

Lee, Jae Eun, 63

Lee, Judith, 238-239

Lein, Laura, 128

Lemeshow, Stanley, 103, 104, 127, 223, 251, 253

Lesbians. *See* Homosexuals

Lettiere, Mark, 120

Level   Flat lines reflecting the amount or magnitude of the target variable in a single-subject design, 196-198, 197e

Level of measurement   The mathematical precision with which the values of a variable can be expressed. The nominal level of measurement, which is qualitative, has no mathematical interpretation; the quantitative levels of measurement—ordinal, interval, and ratio—are progressively more precise mathematically, 76-77
comparison of, 82, 82e
interval, 77e, 80, 343, 355
nominal, 77-78, 77e, 343, 355
ordinal, 77e, 78-80, 343, 355-356
ratio, 77e, 80-82, 343, 355
selecting, 82-83
statistics used, 343, 355-356

Levitan, Laura C., 326
Levy, Paul S., 103, 104, 127, 223, 251, 253
Lewin, Tamar, 320, 324
Lewis, David W., 3-4
Lewis, Laura, 97
Lewis, Robert E., 135, 136, 137-138
Liang, Jersey, 90
Lieberman, Alicia, 109, 110
Lieberson, Stanley, 375
Likert-scale responses, 238
Lin, Nan, 233
Lincoln, Yvonna S., 48, 49, 274
Lindsay, R. C. L., 57
Lipsey, Mark W., 419, 420
Literary Digest, 114
Literature reviews, writing, 34, 37
Literature searches
   on Internet, 32-34, 35-37, 464-466
   procedures, 32-35, 463-464
Locke, Lawrence F., 410
Lofland, John, 274
Lofland, Lyn H., 274
Logan, T. K., 96, 218
Logic model   A schematic representation of
   the various components that make up a
   social service program, including the
   assumptions underlying the program,
   inputs, activities, outputs, and outcomes,
   310-313, 312e
Longitudinal research design   A study in
   which data are collected that can be
   ordered in time; also defined as research in
   which data are collected at two or more
   points in time, 140-142
   event-based designs, 142e, 145-146
   fixed-sample panel designs, 142e, 143-145
   repeated cross-sectional designs, 142e, 143
   types, 142e
Luna, Isela, 234
Lust, N., 13
Lyman, Karen A., 280, 281, 289
Lynch, James P., 364
Lynch, Michael, 49

MacPherson, Kathleen I., 282
Madsen, Richard, 294, 296
Magnuson, Diana L., 267
Mailed survey   A survey involving a mailed
   questionnaire to be completed by the
   respondent, 248

   compared to other survey designs,
      246-247, 247e, 264-266, 265e
   costs, 223
   cover letters, 248, 249, 250e
   follow-up mailings, 248
   incentives, 249
   incomplete responses, 251
   nonrespondents, 251
   procedure, 248
   questionnaires, 223
   response rates, 248, 249-251, 264
   See also **Survey research**
Managed care, 11
Mangelsdorf, Sarah C., 97, 293
Mangione, Thomas W., 249, 268
Mann, Aaron, 50, 108
Manpower Demonstration Research
   Corporation, 323
Manson, Spero M., 108, 109
Marginal distribution   The summary
   distributions in the margins of a
   crosstabulation that correspond to the
   frequency distribution of the row variable
   and of the column variable, 362
Marin, Barbara VanOss, 234
Marin, Gerardo, 234
Marini, Margaret Mooney, 137
Markides, Kyriakos S., 90
Marshall, Ineke Haen, 141
Marston, Brett, 119
Martin, Elizabeth, 224, 232, 233, 244
Martin, Lawrence, 10, 309, 311, 318
MAST. *See* Michigan Alcoholism
   Screening Test
Matching   A procedure for equating the
   characteristics of individuals in different
   comparison groups in an experiment.
   Matching can be done on either an
   individual or an aggregate basis. For
   individual matching, individuals who are
   similar in terms of key characteristics are
   paired prior to assignment, and then the
   two members of each pair are assigned to
   the two groups. For aggregate matching,
   groups are chosen for comparison that are
   similar in terms of the distribution of key
   characteristics, 165-166, 165e
Matrix   A form on which to record
   systematically particular features of
   multiple cases or instances that a

qualitative data analyst needs to examine, 389-391, 390e

Matrix questions   A series of questions that concern a common theme and that have the same response choices, 244-246, 245e

Maturation, 158, 165

Maxwell, Joseph A., 274, 275-276, 285, 386

McCollister, Kathryn E., 322

McHugo, Gregory J., 94, 319

McKendrick, Karen, 322

McKillip, Jack, 314

Mean   The arithmetic, or weighted, average, computed by adding up the value of all the cases and dividing by the total number of cases, 354-357
- of normal distributions, 126-127
- of random samples, 124-125
- of scores in single-subject designs, 196-198, 197e

Measure of association   A type of descriptive statistic that summarizes the strength of an association, 366
- *See also* **Association**

Measurement, 64
- choice of method, 75-76, 94, 96-98
- combining operations, 76
- developing new measures, 96
- errors, 83-85, 86
- in qualitative research, 76
- in single-subject designs, 193-195
- questions, 226
- reliability, 85-89, 96
- testing effect, 86
- *See also* Data collection; **Level of measurement**

Measurement validity   Exists when a measure measures what we think it measures, 19, 89
- construct validity, 91-92
- content validity, 89-90
- criterion validity, 90-91, 92
- face validity, 89

Mechanisms. *See* **Causal mechanism**

Media
- content analysis, 75
- research reported in, 428

Median   The position average, or the point that divides a distribution in half (the 50th percentile), 196-198, 353-356

Medical students, 387-389

Meeker, Barbara Foley, 138, 149

Memory questions, 232-233

Mental health
- computer-mediated and face-to-face counseling, 22, 23e
- employment services for mentally ill, 319, 320e
- Global Assessment of Functioning Scale, 87, 88e
- partial hospitalization programs, 311-313, 312e
- *See also* Depression; Homeless mentally ill

Meschede, Tatjana, 18, 20

Meta-analysis   The quantitative analysis of findings from multiple studies, 419-420
- case study, 420-421
- evaluating, 421
- process, 419-420
- studies included, 419

Miami-Dade Spouse Assault Experiment, 44

Michigan Alcoholism Screening Test (MAST), 69, 73, 90, 93

Michigan Survey Research Center, 234

Milburn, Norweeta G., 108, 109

Miles, Matthew B., 387, 389, 399, 406

Miller, Delbert C., 145, 240, 249, 256

Miller, Susan, 386, 392-393

Miller, William L., 276, 294, 381-382

Mills, C. Wright, 28

Mills, Judson, 179-180

Milwaukee (Wisconsin)
- domestic violence experiment, 44
- Project New Hope, 329, 329e

Minneapolis Domestic Violence Experiment
- background, 47
- critiques of, 52
- definition of domestic assault, 52
- deterrence theory, 31, 44
- generalizability, 102
- hypothesis, 43
- influence, 27-28, 31
- labeling theory, 31
- outcomes, 328
- random assignment of arrests, 51, 157, 315
- replication studies, 28, 44, 51
- research circle and, 43-44, 44e, 46, 46e
- research design, 43, 315
- resources needed, 30-31
- theoretical background, 31, 45-46
- *See also* Domestic violence

Minority groups. *See* Ethnic groups

Miranda, Jeanne, 109, 110

Miringoff, Marc, 64

Mirowsky, John, 240, 268, 269

Mitchell, Christopher G., 74, 174, 444

Mitchell, Richard G., Jr., 283

Mixed-mode surveys   Surveys that are
conducted by more than one method,
allowing the strengths of one survey design
to compensate for the weaknesses of
another and maximizing the likelihood of
securing data from different types of
respondents; for example, nonrespondents
in a mailed survey may be interviewed in
person or over the phone, 264

Mode   The most frequent value in a
distribution; also termed the *probability
average*, 352-353

Moffitt, Robert, 426-427

Mohr, Lawrence B., 156, 158, 166, 171, 172,
328, 329

Monitoring subjects, 206, 215

Monotonic   A pattern of association in which
the value of cases on one variable increases
or decreases fairly regularly across the
categories of another variable, 364-366

Montalvan, Pat, 259

Montgomery, Dianne, 173-174

Morrill, Calvin, 379, 380, 384, 397-398

Mortality. *See* **Differential attrition**

Mueser, Kim T., 66

Mullis, Jeff, 18

Multidimensional scale   A scale containing
subsets of questions that measure different
aspects of the same concept, 73

Multiple baseline designs, 209, 211e, 212, 213e

Multiple treatment designs, 212-215, 214e

Munday, Cheryl, 108

Munoz, Ricardo F., 109, 110

Musheno, Michael, 379

Mutually exclusive   A variable's attributes (or
values) are mutually exclusive when every
case can be classified as having only one
attribute (or value), 78

Nader, Ralph, 113-114

Nagel, Cheryl L., 19, 90

Napoles-Springer, Anna, 233, 234

Narrative analysis   A form of qualitative
analysis in which the analyst focuses on
how respondents impose order on the flow
of experience in their lives and so make
sense of events and actions in which they
have participated, 397-398, 398e

NASW Code of Ethics   Professional code of
conduct and behavior as articulated by
the National Association of Social Workers,
11, 55, 218, 478-498

National Association of Social Workers. *See*
NASW Code of Ethics

National Geographic Society, 261

National Institute of Alcohol Abuse and
Alcoholism (NIAAA), 64

National Institute of Justice, 44

National Institute of Mental Health
(NIMH), 95, 383
grant proposals, 414-415e
review committee, 413

National Institutes of Health (NIH)
grant proposals, 412-413
inclusion of women and ethnic minorities in
research, 108
Office for Protection from Research
Risks, 55

National Opinion Research Center, 224, 343

National Science Foundation, 222

Native Americans
inclusion in research, 108
See also Ethnic groups

Neal, Margaret B., 297-298

Needs assessment   A type of evaluation
research that attempts to determine the
needs of some population that might be
met with a social program, 313-315, 326

Negative predictive value   The proportion of
all respondents who actually do not have a
particular diagnosis compared to all those
who were assessed by a screening
instrument as having the diagnosis, 94

Neighbors, Harold W., 108

Nelson, Judith C., 195

Nelson, Toben, 64

Nett, Roger, 49

Neuendorf, Kimberly A., 402

New Jersey Income Maintenance Experiment,
306-307, 315

New York City, cholera epidemic, 8

Newmann, Joy Perkins, 19, 67, 84

Newport, Frank, 114

Newsweek, 344, 347

NIAAA. *See* National Institute of Alcohol Abuse and Alcoholism

Nie, Norman H., 261

NIH. *See* National Institutes of Health

NIMH. *See* National Institute of Mental Health

Nixon, Richard M., 231

Nominal definition　Defining a concept using other concepts, 65

Nominal level of measurement　Variables whose values have no mathematical interpretation; they vary in kind or quality, but not in amount, 77-78, 77e, 343, 355

Nomothetic causal explanation　An explanation that identifies common influences on a number of cases or events, 134

See also Experimental designs

Nonconcurrent multiple baseline design　A multiple baseline design in which subjects are randomly assigned into A-B designs with different baseline phase lengths, 209, 212

Nonequivalent control group design　A quasi-experimental design in which there are experimental and comparison groups that are designated before the treatment occurs but are not created by random assignment, 172-174, 173e

Nonexperimental designs　Group research designs that provide little to no control over internal threats to validity, 138

After-only Design, 178

causality, 138, 177

Comparative Intensity Design, 179

intervening variables, 140

One-Group Pretest-Posttest Design, 177

Static-Group Design, 178

See also Single-subject designs

Nonprobability sampling methods　Sampling methods in which the probability of selection of population elements is unknown, 110, 120

advantages, 128-129

availability sampling, 120-121

purposive sampling, 122-123, 287

quota sampling, 121, 122e

snowball sampling, 123, 128, 287-288, 395

Nonrespondents　People or other entities who do not participate in a study although they are selected for the sample, 112, 124

reasons for nonresponse, 260e

to General Social Survey, 259, 260e

to mailed surveys, 251

to surveys, 224-226

Nonspuriousness　A criterion for establishing a causal relation between two variables; when a relationship between two variables is not due to variation in a third variable, 135, 136, 369

in nonexperiments, 139-140

See also **Spurious relationship**

Normal distribution　A graph with a shape that looks like a bell, with one hump in the middle, centered around the population mean, and the number of cases tapering off on both sides of the mean. This shape is important for sampling and statistical analysis, 126-127, 127e, 360, 360e

North, Carol S., 120

Norton, Ilena M., 108, 109

Notes. *See* **Field notes**

Novak, David, 35

Nugent, William, 198

Nugent method, 198, 199e

Nursing homes, 273, 274, 276-279, 282, 287

NVivo, 399, 400e, 401, 402e

O'Brien, John, 72

O'Brien, Keith, 241

O'Bryan, Martha, 15

Observations

direct, 74

errors of, 224

reactivity, 195

systematic, 293

See also **Participant observation**

O'Dochartaigh, Niall, 35, 466

Office of Management and the Budget, 307

Ohio Department of Mental Health, Office of Program Evaluation and Research, 13

OLS. *See* Ordinary least squares (OLS) regression

Olson, Jack, 1-3, 10

Omaha (Nebraska), domestic violence experiment, 44

Omnibus survey　A survey that covers a range of topics of interest to different social scientists, 223-224

One-Group Pretest-Posttest Design, 177

One-shot case studies. *See* Single-subject designs

One-shot Only Design. *See* After-only Design

Open-ended question A survey question to which the respondent replies in his or her own words, either by writing or by talking, 227-228, 339

Openness, 53-54

Operation A procedure for identifying or indicating the value of cases on a variable, 69

Operationalization The process of specifying the operations that will indicate the value of cases on a variable, 69-70, 70e, 194

Optical illusions, 7, 7e

Orcutt, James D., 344

Ordinal level of measurement A measurement of a variable in which the numbers indicating a variable's values specify only the order of the cases, permitting *greater than* and *less than* distinctions, 77e, 78-80, 343, 355-356

Ordinary least squares (OLS) regression, 198

Organista, Kurt C., 109, 110

Orme, John, 196

Orr, Larry L., 306, 307, 321

Orshansky, Mollie, 67

Ortega, Debora M, 84

Osgood, D. Wayne, 141

Outcome evaluation, 318-320

Outcomes The impact of the program process on the cases processed, 308, 311-313, 328-330

Outlier An exceptionally high or low value in a distribution, 358

Outputs The services delivered or new products produced by the program process, 308, 311

Overgeneralization Occurs when we unjustifiably conclude that what is true for *some* cases is true for *all* cases, 4, 5, 5e, 9

Padgett, Deborah K., 96, 218

Panel studies. *See* **Fixed-sample panel design**

Parallel-forms reliability. *See* **Alternate-forms reliability**

Parker, E., 371

Parlett, Malcolm, 381

Partial hospitalization programs, 311-313, 312e

Participant observation A qualitative method for gathering data that involves developing a sustained relationship with people while they go about their normal activities, 274, 279

complete observation, 279-280

complete participation, 282-283, 298

developing relationships, 285-286

entering field, 283-285

ethical issues, 281, 282, 283, 298-300

notes, 289-291

participation and observation, 281-282

personal dimensions, 291-292

reactive effects, 280

researcher roles, 279-283, 280e

sampling, 286-289, 287e

Participatory action research A type of research in which the researcher involves some organizational members as active participants throughout the process of studying an organization; the goal is making changes in the organization, 50

Pate, Antony M., 44

Patton, Michael Quinn, 307, 318, 325, 326, 327, 380, 394

Pawluck, Debra E., 420

Payne, Macolm, 39

Pearce, Lisa, 233

Pecora, Peter J., 135, 136, 138

Peek, Kristen, 233

Penk, Walter E., 15, 16, 73, 145, 413, 416

Percentages Relative frequencies, computed by dividing the frequency of cases in a particular category by the total number of cases, and multiplying by 100, 363, 364e

Perez, Edgardo L., 311

Periodicity A sequence of elements (in a list to be sampled) that varies in some regular, periodic pattern, 116, 116e

Personal interviews. *See* **In-person interview; Intensive (depth) interviewing**

Personal Responsibility and Work Opportunity Reconciliation Act, 10, 123, 175

Persson, Rolf, 347

Petrosino, Anthony, 307

Phone survey A survey in which interviewers question respondents over the phone and then record their answers, 252

compared to other survey designs, 246-247, 247e, 264-266, 265e

computer-assisted, 257, 340
costs, 223
interview schedules, 253, 254-256e
interviewer instructions, 256, 257e
interviewer training, 256
maximizing response, 253, 256, 264-265
nonresponse, 224-226
political polls, 253
random digit dialing, 115, 120, 252, 253
reaching sample units, 252-253, 256
response rates, 257
See also **Survey research**

Placebo effect A source of treatment
misidentification that can occur when
subjects who receive a treatment that they
consider likely to be beneficial improve
because of that expectation rather than
because of the treatment itself, 159-160

Planetary Society, 229

Police
DARE program, 305-306, 315-316, 316e
masculinity of neighborhood officers,
392-393
See also Minneapolis Domestic Violence
Experiment

Police Foundation, 27

Pollio, David E., 120

Pollner, Melvin, 259

Polls. See **Survey research**

Population The entire set of individuals or
other entities to which study findings are to
be generalized, 103
defining, 105
diversity, 106-110, 112-113
homogeneity, 106-107, 112-113
target, 106, 307, 310

Population parameter The value of a
statistic, such as a mean, computed using
the data for the entire population; a sample
statistic is an estimate of a population
parameter, 126

Posavac, Emil J., 96, 170, 171, 309,
314, 318, 332

Positive predictive value The proportion of
people who actually have a particular
diagnosis to the number who were
assessed by a screening tool as having the
diagnosis, 94

Positivism The philosophical view that an
external, objective reality exists apart from
human perceptions of it, 48

Postpositivism A philosophical view that
modifies the positivist premise of an
external, objective reality by recognizing
its complexity, the limitations of human
observers, and therefore the impossibility
of developing more than a partial
understanding of reality, 48-49

Posttest In experimental research, the
measurement of an outcome (dependent)
variable after an experimental intervention
or after a presumed independent variable
has changed for some other reason,
157-158, 166

Posttest-Only Control Group Design, 169-170

Posttest-only Design. See After-only Design

Poverty
definitions, 67-68
measurement of, 70
theories of causes, 40

Practical or clinical significance When
evaluating the impact of an intervention in
a single-subject design, whether or not the
intervention made a meaningful difference
in the well-being of the subject, 196

Predictive validity The type of validity that
exists when a measure predicts scores on a
criterion measured in the future, 90

Prescriptive theory, 325

Presser, Stanley, 231, 235, 236, 241,
242, 243, 244

Pretest In experimental research, the
measurement of an outcome (dependent)
variable prior to an experimental
intervention or change in a presumed
independent variable for some other reason.
The pretest is exactly the same test
as the posttest, but it is administered at a
different time, 166
influence on posttest scores, 157-158
interaction with treatment, 161, 170

Pretest-Posttest Control Group Design,
167-169, 168e

Prisons
boot camps, 328
education in women's, 319-320
simulation study, 56, 57
studies of released prisoners, 316-317, 317e

Privacy. See **Confidentiality**

Probability average. See **Mode**

Probability of selection The likelihood that
an element will be selected from the

population for inclusion in the sample. In a census of all the elements of a population, the probability that any particular element will be selected is 1.0. If half the elements in the population are sampled on the basis of chance (say, by tossing a coin), the probability of selection for each element is one half, or .5. As the size of the sample as a proportion of the population decreases, so does the probability of selection, 111

Probability sampling method   A sampling method that relies on a random or chance selection method so that the probability of selection of population elements is known, 110-114

cluster sampling, 118-120, 119e

simple random sampling, 114-115

stratified random sampling, 116-117, 118e

systematic random sampling, 115-116

Process analysis   A research design in which periodic measures are taken to determine whether a treatment is being delivered as planned, usually in a field experiment, 160, 327

Process evaluation   Evaluation research that investigates the process of service delivery, 315-318

Program logic models, 310-313, 312e

Program or practice evaluation. *See* **Evaluation research**

Program process   The complete treatment or service delivered by the program, 307

Program theory   A descriptive or prescriptive model of how a program operates and produces effects, 324-325, 325e

Progressive focusing   The process by which a qualitative analyst interacts with the data and gradually refines her focus, 381

Project New Hope, 329, 329e

Proportionate stratified sampling   Sampling method in which elements are selected from strata in exact proportion to their representation in the population, 117, 118e

Proposals. *See* Research proposals

Pryor, Carolyn B., 123

Psychological Abstracts (*PsychINFO*), 32, 463

Punch, Maurice, 283

Purdy, Matthew, 223

Purposive sampling   A nonprobability sampling method in which elements are selected for a purpose, usually because of their unique position, 122-123, 287

Putnam, Israel, 67

QCA. *See* **Qualitative comparative analysis**

QSR NVivo. *See* NVivo

Qualitative comparative analysis (QCA)   A systematic type of qualitative analysis that identifies the combination of factors that had to be present across multiple cases to produce a particular outcome, 395-396, 396e

Qualitative data analysis

alternative approaches, 394-399

as art, 381-383

authenticity of conclusions, 391-393

causal models, 391, 392e

coding, 389, 391e

computer-assisted, 399-402

conceptualization, 387-389

"dance" of, 382, 382e

difference from quantitative, 380

documentation, 386-387

emic focus, 380

ethical issues, 406

ethnography, 383, 394-395

examining relationships, 389-391, 392e

features, 380-381

grounded theory, 398-399, 399e

narrative analysis, 397-398, 398e

phases, 386

qualitative comparative analysis, 395-396, 396e

quality criteria, 406-407

reflexivity, 381, 393-394

research questions, 383-385

software, 399-402

See also **Content analysis**

Qualitative methods   Methods such as participant observation, intensive interviewing, and focus groups that are designed to capture social life as participants experience it, rather than in categories predetermined by the researcher. These methods typically involve exploratory research questions, inductive reasoning, an orientation to social context, human objectivity, and the meanings attached by participants to events and to their lives, 16-17, 274

authenticity as goal, 391-393

case study, 276-279
causation, 149-150
characteristics, 274-276
compared to other research designs, 418-419
distinction from experimental and survey
    research, 274-275
distinction from quantitative methods, 16
ethical issues, 281, 282, 283, 298-300
in evaluation research, 327-328
interpretivism, 49
measurement, 76
process, 276, 277e
reflexive process, 275-276, 277e,
    381, 393-394
researcher roles, 276
sampling, 286-289
sampling methods, 120
See also **Focus groups; Intensive
    interviewing; Participant observation**
Quality assurance reviews, 307
Quantitative methods   Methods such as
    surveys and experiments that record
    variation in social life in terms of
    categories that vary in amount. Data that
    are treated as quantitative are either
    numbers or attributes that can be ordered in
    terms of magnitude, 16-17
distinction from qualitative methods, 16
Quartiles   The points in a distribution
    corresponding to the first 25% of the cases,
    the first 50% of the cases, and the last 25%
    of the cases, 358
Quasi-experimental design   A research design
    in which there is a comparison group that
    is comparable to the experimental group in
    critical ways, but subjects are not randomly
    assigned to the comparison and
    experimental groups, 171-172
causality, 175
ex post facto control group designs, 176, 176e
in evaluation research, 319-320
nonequivalent control group designs,
    172-174, 173e
time series designs, 172, 174-175
validity, 174
Quesada, James, 120
Questionnaire   The survey instrument
    containing the questions in a
    self-administered survey, 239
data entry from, 340

designing, 239-240, 244-247
existing instruments, 240
instructions, 246, 338
layout, 246
length, 223
objectives, 239-240
pilot studies, 241
preparing for data analysis, 337-340
pretesting, 240-242
question order, 243-244
skip patterns, 237e, 246
unclear responses, 337, 338e
unimode design, 264
See also **Interview schedule**
Questions
acquiescence bias and, 234
bias in, 231-232
constructing, 226
cultural differences in interpretations, 233-234
disadvantages, 75-76
filter, 236, 237e
"grand tour," 294
in intensive interviews, 294, 295-297
interpretive, 242-243
leading, 84
matrix, 244-246, 245e
memory, 232-233
open-ended, 227-228, 339
pretesting, 240-242
refining, 240-242
sensitive, 236-237, 259
sequence of, 243-244
single, 237-238
wording, 226, 228-232, 237-238
See also **Closed-ended question**
Questions, research. *See* **Social work research
    question**
Quota sampling   A nonprobability sampling
    method in which elements are selected
    to ensure that the sample represents
    certain characteristics in proportion
    to their prevalence in the population,
    121, 122e

Race
by region of United States, 364, 365e
rapport with interviewers, 259
relationship to education, 371-372, 372e
relationship to health, 366, 366e,
    371-373, 373e

See also African Americans; Ethnic groups; White Americans

Radloff, Lenore, 73, 86, 87

Ragin, Charles C., 288, 395

Rallis, Sharon F., 284, 285, 286, 294

Rand, Michael R., 364

RAND Corporation, 306

Random assignment A procedure by which each experimental subject is placed in a group randomly, 137, 137e, 163-165
distinction from random sampling, 163-164, 164e

Random digit dialing The random dialing by a machine of numbers within designated phone prefixes, which creates a random sample for phone surveys, 115, 120, 252, 253

Random error Measurement error that is due to chance and that is unpredictable, 84-85

Random numbers table A table containing lists of numbers that are ordered solely on the basis of chance; it is used for drawing a random sample, 114-115, 468-470

Random sampling A method of sampling that relies on a random or chance selection method so that every element of the sampling frame has a known probability of being selected, 111
distinction from random assignment, 163-164, 164e
probability of selection, 111
simple, 114-115
stratified, 116-117, 118e
systematic, 115-116

Random sampling error Differences between the population and the sample that are due only to chance factors (random error), not to systematic sampling error. Random sampling error may or may not result in an unrepresentative sample. The magnitude of sampling error due to chance factors can be estimated statistically. Also known as *chance sampling error*, 126

Random selection Procedures to choose a sample that rely on chance, 114
See also **Random sampling**

Randomization The random assignment of cases, as by the toss of a coin, 137, 157, 163

Randomized Before/After Control Group Design. *See* Pretest-Posttest Control Group Design

Randomized comparative change design, 319, 320e

Randomized Control Group After-only Design. *See* Posttest-Only Control Group Design

Range The true upper limit in a distribution minus the true lower limit (or the highest rounded value minus the lowest rounded value, plus one), 357-358
interquartile, 358

Rate The amount that a trend line increases or decreases during the baseline or intervention phase, 198

Ratio level of measurement A measurement of a variable in which the numbers indicating a variable's values represent fixed measuring units *and* an absolute zero point, 77e, 80-82, 343, 355

Reactive effects The changes in an individual or group behavior that are due to being observed or otherwise studied, 280

Reactivity A problem of the external validity of research designs, which occurs when the experimental treatment has an effect only when the particular conditions created by the experiment exist, 97, 161-162, 195

Reasoning, errors in, 4-8

Reductionist fallacy (reductionism) An error in reasoning that occurs when incorrect conclusions about group-level processes are based on individual-level data. Also known as *individualist fallacy*, 148-149, 148e

Reflexive research design, 275-276, 277e

Regression analysis A statistical technique for characterizing the pattern of a relationship between two quantitative variables in terms of a linear equation and for summarizing the strength of this relationship in terms of its deviation from that linear pattern, 374
ordinary least squares (OLS), 198

Regression effect A source of causal invalidity that occurs when subjects who are chosen for a study because of their extreme scores on the dependent variable become less extreme on the posttest due to natural cyclical or episodic change in the variable, 158

Regression to the mean, 85

Reliability A measurement procedure yields consistent scores when the phenomenon being measured is not changing, 85
alternate-forms, 87
comparison to validity, 95e
evaluating, 96
improving, 94-96
internal consistency, 86-87
interobserver, 87-89
intraobserver, 89
split-halves, 87
test-retest, 86, 94-95

Reliability measures Statistics that summarize the consistency among a set of measures. Cronbach's alpha is the most common measure of the reliability of a set of items included in an index, 71

Repeated cross-sectional design A longitudinal study in which data are collected at two or more points in time from different samples of the same population. Also called *trend study*, 143

Repeated measurement, 187, 189

Repeated measures panel design A quasi-experimental design consisting of several pretest and posttest observations of the same group, 174

Replacement sampling A method of sampling in which sample elements are returned to the sampling frame after being selected so they may be sampled again. Random samples may be selected with or without replacement, 115

Replication Repetition of a study using the same research methods to answer the same research question, 44, 52
clinical, 217
direct, 217
multiple baseline designs, 209, 212
of single-subject designs, 209, 212, 217
systematic, 217

Reports, research
applied reports, 424-427
coauthored, 427
controversial, 427-428
critiquing, 37
ethical issues, 54, 427-428
evaluating, 428, 441-443
media outlets, 428

organization, 422
writing, 421-422
See also Journal articles

Representative sample A sample that "looks like" the population from which it was selected in all respects that are potentially relevant to the study. The distribution of characteristics among the elements of a representative sample is the same as the distribution of those characteristics among the total population. In an unrepresentative sample, some characteristics are overrepresented or underrepresented, 107-110, 107e, 112-113

Requests for proposals (RFPs), 29

Research circle A diagram of the elements of the research process, including theories, hypotheses, data collection, and data analysis, 40, 41e
application of, 43-44, 44e, 46, 46e

Research designs
comparison, 416-419, 417e
cross-sectional, 138-140
longitudinal, 140-146
reflexive, 275-276, 277e
See also Experimental designs; Nonexperimental designs; **Qualitative methods**; **Survey research**

Research on Social Work Practice, 31

Research organizations, 306, 307

Research proposals
case study, 412-416
developing, 409-410, 411-412e
reviews, 413
sections, 410

Research questions. *See* **Social work research question**

Research reports. *See* Reports, research

Research Triangle Institute, 315-316

Resentful demoralization This problem for experimental designs occurs when comparison group members perform worse than they otherwise might have because they feel that they have been left out of some valuable treatment, 159

Resistance to change The reluctance to change our ideas in light of new information, 4, 7-8

Respondent-driven sampling. *See* **Snowball sampling**

Respondents
  anonymity, 268, 299
  attrition, 157
  confidentiality, 57, 268, 299, 331
  fence-sitters, 235
  floaters, 235-236, 235e
  identifiers, 268, 337
  maturation, 158, 165
  See also Human subjects, research on;
  Nonrespondents
Response set When a series of questions has
  the same set of response categories, there is
  the possibility that the respondent will
  provide the same response for each
  question, 245-246
Reverse outlining Outlining the sections
  in an already written draft of a paper or
  report to improve its organization in the
  next draft, 422
Reynolds, Paul Davidson, 56, 58
RFPs. *See* Requests for proposals
Richards, Lyn, 399
Richards, Thomas J., 399
Richardson, Laurel, 149, 397
Richey, Cheryl A., 84
Riedel, Marc, 266, 267
Rierdan, Jill, 18, 20
Riessman, Catherine Kohler, 397
Riley, Kathryn P., 275, 285, 289
Ringwalt, Christopher L., 306, 315-316
Ritchey, Ferris J., 18
Rodway, Margaret, 208
Roffman, Roger, 161
Roffman, Roger J., 110
Rogers, Robin, 45
Roosevelt, Franklin Delano, 114
Roper polls, 231
Rosenberg, Morris, 240, 369
Ross, Catherine E., 222, 223, 232, 233,
    239, 241-242, 243-244, 246, 253,
    256, 257, 265, 266, 268, 269
Rossi, Peter H., 14-15, 102, 166, 172,
    176, 181, 306, 316, 318, 326,
    327, 427-428
Rossman, Gretchen B., 284, 285, 286, 294
Roth, Dee, 13, 102
Rowles, G. D., 276
Royse, David, 96, 218
Rubin, Herbert J., 49, 122, 293, 294, 295
Rubin, Irene S., 49, 122, 293, 294, 295
Ruggles, Patricia, 68

Russo, M. Jean, 16, 48, 332
Ryan, Kimberly D., 108

Sacks, Stanley, 322
Sample A subset of a population that is used
  to study the population as a whole, 103
  components, 103-105
  fraction of population, 113-114
  in qualitative research, 286-289
  need for, 103, 106
  planning, 102-110
  quality, 123-124
  recruiting, 108-110
  representative, 107-110, 107e, 112-113
  sizes, 112, 127-128
  strata, 116-117
Sample generalizability Exists when a
  conclusion based on a sample, or subset, of
  a larger population holds true for that
  population, 20, 21e
  evaluating, 102-103, 105-106
  in experiments, 160
Sample statistic The value of a statistic,
  such as a mean, computed from sample
  data, 126
Sampling distribution The hypothetical
  distribution of a statistic across all the
  random samples that could be drawn from
  a population, 124-125
  See also Distributions
Sampling error Any difference between the
  characteristics of a sample and the
  characteristics of a population. The larger
  the sampling error, the less representative
  the sample, 106, 112
  estimating, 126-127
  in survey research, 224-226
  random, 126
  systematic, 111-112, 114
Sampling frame A list of all elements or
  other units containing the elements in a
  population, 103
  adequacy, 111-112
  for surveys, 224
Sampling interval The number of cases from
  one sampled case to another in a systematic
  random sample, 115, 116e
Sampling methods. *See*
  Nonprobability sampling methods;
  Probability sampling method;
  Theoretical sampling

Sampling units   Units listed at each stage of a multistage sampling design, 104-105
primary, 104, 104e
secondary, 104, 104e
Sampson, Robert J., 148, 149
Sands, Robert G., 39, 138-139, 140
Sarri, Catherine M., 50
Sarri, Rosemary, 50
SAS software, 340
Saturation point   The point at which subject selection is ended in intensive interviewing, when new interviews seem to yield little additional information, 122, 294, 295e
Saveanu, T., 13
Scale   A composite measure based on combining the responses to multiple questions pertaining to a common concept after these questions are differentially weighted, so that questions judged on some basis to be more important for the underlying concept contribute more to the composite score, 71
See also **Index**
Schaie, K. Warner, 30
Schober, Michael F., 244
Schorr, Lisbeth B., 328
Schulberg, Herbert C., 97
Schulz, A., 371
Schuman, Howard, 231, 235, 236, 243, 244
Schutt, Russell K., 15, 16, 18, 20, 72, 73, 125, 145, 228, 314, 386, 392, 401, 412-413, 416
Schwandt, Thomas A., 49
Schwartz, Richard D., 75
Science   A set of logical, systematic, documented methods for investigating nature and natural processes; the knowledge produced by these investigations, 8-9
positivism, 48
uses of, 54
Scriven, Michael, 171, 326
Search engines, 35-36, 466
Seattle-Denver Income Maintenance Experiment, 307
Sechrest, Lee, 75
Secondary data   Data analyzed to answer a research question by a researcher who did not participate in the study in which the data were collected, 266-267
analysis of, 266-267

disadvantages, 266
quality, 267
sources, 266-267
survey datasets, 224, 267
Secular drift   A type of contamination in true experimental and quasi-experimental designs that occurs when broader social or economic trends impact on the findings of a study, 158
Seidman, Larry J., 6, 15
Selection bias   A source of internal (causal) invalidity that occurs when characteristics of experimental and comparison group subjects differ in any way that influences the outcome, 156, 157
Selective observation   Choosing to look only at things that are in line with our preferences or beliefs, 4, 5-7, 5e, 9
Self-fulfilling prophecy. *See* **Expectancies of experimental staff**
Seligman, Martin E. P., 240
Semantic differential scale, 238-239
Senate. *See* U.S. Senate
Sensitive questions, 236-237, 259
Sensitivity   The proportion of true positives; based on the number of people assessed as having a diagnosis by a screening instrument compared to the number of people who actually have the condition, 93-94, 97
Serendipitous findings   Unexpected patterns in data that stimulate new ideas or theoretical approaches. Also known as *anomalous findings*, 45
Service completions, 311
Sexual orientation
representative samples, 107-108
See also Homosexuals
Sexuality, marital infidelity, 259
Shadish, William R., 326
Shapiro, Janet R., 97, 293
Shapiro, Margaret, 402-403
Shaw, Linda L., 289
Shepherd, Jane, 259
Sherman, Lawrence W., 27, 28, 31, 43, 44, 51, 52, 102, 157, 315, 328
Sheu, Wen-Jenn, 90
Sieber, Joan A., 55, 56, 57, 58
Silverman, Stephen J., 410

Silvestre, Anthony J., 109-110

Simple random sampling   A method of sampling in which every sample element is selected only on the basis of chance, through a random process, 114-115

Singer, Burton, 137

Single-subject designs, 186
  B design, 215, 216e
  baseline phase, 187-189
  basic design (A-B), 206-207, 207e
  causality, 150-151
  comparison to other research designs, 186, 418
  components, 186
  ethical issues, 217-218
  evaluating results, 195-202
  generalizability, 216-217
  graphing, 193, 202
  internal validity, 189
  measuring targets of intervention, 193-195
  monitoring subjects, 206, 215
  multiple baseline designs, 209, 211e, 212, 213e
  multiple treatment designs, 212-215, 214e
  practical significance, 196
  purposes, 203, 206
  repeated measurement, 187, 189
  treatment phase, 193
  visual analysis, 196-202
  withdrawal designs, 207-209, 218

Sjoberg, Gideon, 49, 58

Skewness   The extent to which cases are clustered more at one or the other end of the distribution of a quantitative variable, rather than in a symmetric pattern around its center. Skew can be positive (a right skew), with the number of cases tapering off in the positive direction, or negative (a left skew), with the number of cases tapering off in the negative direction, 342-343, 355, 356e

Skinner, Harvey A., 90

Skip pattern   The unique combination of questions created in a survey by filter questions and contingent questions, 237e, 246

Smith, Tom W., 224, 236, 343

SMOs. *See* Social movement organizations

Smythe, Cynthia, 108

Snider, D. E., 12-13

Snow, David A., 45, 383-384, 395-396

Snow, John, 8

Snowball sampling   A method of sampling in which sample elements are selected as they are identified by successive informants or interviewees, 123, 128, 287-288, 395

Social class, representative samples, 107-108

Social control
  conceptualization of, 68
  informal, 45-46

Social desirability   The tendency for individuals to respond in ways that make them appear in the best light to the interviewer, 84, 234

Social exchange theory, 226, 248

Social health, 64-65

Social movement organizations (SMOs), 383-384, 395-396

Social research
  See also Literature searches

Social science, 2

Social science approach   An orientation to evaluation research that expects researchers to emphasize the importance of researcher expertise and maintenance of autonomy from program stakeholders, 8-9, 326

Social Science Citation Index (SSCI), 32

Social Science Citation Index (SSCI), 463

Social Security Administration, 67

Social support networks, 176

Social Work Abstracts, 32, 33, 33e, 34, 463

Social work program effectiveness, 10
  See also **Evaluation research**

Social work research
  controversial, 17, 18, 427-428
  imperative for, 10-11
  importance of, 9-10
  limitations, 17
  meta-analyses, 419-421
  purposes, 11-13
  scientific guidelines, 50-53
  sponsors, 54, 249, 325-326, 406, 427
  strengths, 17

Social work research question   A question about the social world that is answered through the collection and analysis of firsthand, verifiable, empirical data, 28
  descriptive, 11
  evaluating, 30-31
  explanatory, 12

exploratory, 12
feasibility, 30-31
identifying, 28-29
refining, 29-30
scientific relevance, 31
social importance, 31
theory and, 29
Software
data definition, 340
qualitative data analysis, 399-402
statistical, 198, 340
Solomon Four-Group Design, 170
Specification A type of relationship involving three or more variables in which the association between the independent and dependent variables varies across the categories of one or more other control variables, 372-373
Specificity The proportion of true negatives; based on the number of people assessed as not having a diagnosis by a screening instrument compared to the number who really do not have the diagnosis, 93-94
Spirduso, Waneen Wyrick, 410
Split-ballot design Unique questions or other modifications in a survey administered to randomly selected subsets of the total survey sample, so that more questions can be included in the entire survey or so that responses to different question versions can be compared, 224, 244
Split-halves reliability Reliability achieved when responses to the same questions by two randomly selected halves of a sample are about the same, 87
Sponsors, 54, 249, 325-326, 406, 427
Spouse abuse. *See* Domestic violence
SPSS (Statistical Package for the Social Sciences), 198, 340
Spurious relationship A relationship between two variables that is due to variation in a third variable, 136, 369, 371-372, 372e
See also **Nonspuriousness**
SRI International, 306
SRL. *See* University of Illinois Survey Research Laboratory
SSCI. See Social Science Citation Index
Stable line A line in the baseline phase that is relatively flat, with little variability in the scores so that the scores fall in a narrow band, 188, 190e

Stake, Robert E., 381, 385, 387
Stakeholder approach An orientation to evaluation research that expects researchers to be responsive primarily to the people involved with the program, 326
Stakeholder participatory research, 326
Stakeholders Individuals and groups who have some basis of concern with the program, 309, 325-326
Standard case management programs, 322-323
Standard deviation The square root of the average squared deviation of each case from the mean, 359-360
Static-Group Design, 178
Statistical control A method in which one variable is held constant so that the relationship between two (or more) other variables can be assessed without the influence of variation in the control variable, 139-140
Statistical Package for the Social Sciences. *See* SPSS
Statistical power analysis, 128, 369
Statistical significance The mathematical likelihood that an association is not due to chance, judged by a criterion set by the analyst (often that the probability is less than 5 out of 100, or $p < .05$), 367-368
Statistics
central tendency, 352-357
descriptive, 336
how not to lie with, 361
inferential, 126, 336, 366-369
interquartile ranges, 358
mean, 124-125, 126-127, 196-198, 354-357
measures of association, 366-369
median, 196-198, 353-356
mode, 352-353
range, 357-358
regression analysis, 374
standard deviation, 359-360
summary, 352, 357, 361
use of, 336-337
variance, 359, 359e
variation measures, 357-360, 358e
Stephens, Robert, 161
Stewart, Anita L., 233, 234
Stewart, David W., 266
Stille, Alexander, 64, 65

Stratified random sampling A method of sampling in which sample elements are selected separately from population strata that are identified in advance by the researcher, 116-117, 118e

Strauss, Anselm L., 288, 399

Stress theory, 39, 138-139, 139e

Strunk, William, Jr., 422

Subject fatigue Problems caused by panel members growing weary of repeated interviews and dropping out of a study or becoming so used to answering the standard questions in the survey that they start giving stock or thoughtless answers, 145

Substance abuse
  alcohol use by college students, 64
  binge drinking, 64, 68, 83
  DARE program, 305-306, 315-316, 316e
  definitions, 66
  extent of problem, 63-64
  measurement of, 90
  prevention programs, 316e
  screening tests, 69, 73, 90, 93
  self-report measures, 90
  surveys, 82-83
  therapeutic communities, 322
  treatment costs, 64
  treatment programs, 173-174, 322, 412-416

Subtable Tables describing the relationship between two variables within the discrete categories of one or more other control variables, 370, 371e

Sudman, Seymour, 128

Sullivan, William M., 294, 296

Summary statistics, 352, 357, 361

Summative evaluation. *See* **Impact evaluation**

Supportive housing, 15-16

Survey datasets, 224, 267

Survey research Research in which information is obtained from a sample of individuals through their responses to questions about themselves or others, 222
  advantages, 222-223
  compared to other research designs, 418
  comparison of design types, 246-247, 247e, 264-266, 265*e*
  costs, 223
  errors in, 224-226, 225e
  ethical issues, 58, 268
  fence-sitters, 235

  floaters, 235-236, 235e
  generalizability, 223
  limitations, 375
  mixed-mode, 264
  nonrespondents, 111, 124, 224-226
  omnibus surveys, 223-224
  presidential election polls, 113-114, 113e, 253
  repeated cross-sectional designs, 142e, 143
  sample generalizability, 20
  See also **Electronic survey; Group-administered survey; In-person interview; Mailed survey; Phone survey; Questionnaire**

Swidler, Ann, 294, 296

Systematic bias. *See* Systematic sampling error

Systematic error Overrepresentation or underrepresentation of some population characteristics in a sample due to the method used to select the sample. A sample shaped by systematic sampling error is a biased sample, 83-84

Systematic observation A strategy that increases the reliability of observational data by using explicit rules that standardize coding practices across observers, 293

Systematic random sampling A method of sampling in which sample elements are selected from a list or from sequential files, with every *n*th element being selected after the first element is selected randomly within the first interval, 115-116

Systematic replication Repeating a single-subject design in different settings, using different providers and other related behaviors to increase generalizability, 217

Systematic sampling error, 111-112, 114, 126

Tacit knowledge In field research, a credible sense of understanding of social processes that reflects the researcher's awareness of participants' actions as well as their words, and of what they fail to state, feel deeply, and take for granted, 392

Taff, Gail, 64

Target population A set of elements larger than or different from the population sampled and to which the researcher would like to generalize study findings, 106, 307, 310

TARP. *See* Transitional Aid Research Project

Taylor, Jerry, 305

Teenagers. *See* Adolescents

Telephone surveys. *See* **Phone survey**

Ten Point Coalition, 328

Testing   A problem of contamination in experimental designs that occurs when some observation is taken prior to the independent variable or treatment, 158, 161

See also **Pretest**

Testing effect   Measurement error related to how a test was given, the conditions of the testing, including environmental conditions, and acclimation to the test itself, 86

Test-retest reliability   A measurement showing that measures of a phenomenon at two points in time are highly correlated, if the phenomenon has not changed, or have changed only as much as the phenomenon itself, 86, 94-95

Textual analysis. *See* **Content analysis**; Qualitative data analysis

Theoretical sampling   A sampling method recommended for field researchers by Glaser and Strauss (1967). A theoretical sample is drawn in a sequential fashion, with settings or individuals selected for study as earlier observations or interviews indicate that these settings or individuals are influential, 288-289, 288e

Theory   A logically interrelated set of propositions about empirical reality, 39

descriptive, 325

grounded, 398-399, 399e

link to data, 38, 38e

prescriptive, 325

role in social research, 38-40

Theory-driven evaluation   A program evaluation that is guided by a theory that specifies the process by which the program has an effect, 324-325

Therapeutic communities, 322

Thick description   A rich description that conveys a sense of what a phenomenon or situation is like from the standpoint of the natural actors in that setting, 385

Thiemann, Sue, 128

Thompson, Estina E., 108, 109

Thorne, Barrie, 292, 393

Thyer, Bruce, 96, 218

Thyer, Bruce A., 40, 420

Tichon, Jennifer G., 402-403

Time order   A criterion for establishing a causal relation between two variables. The variation in the presumed cause (the independent variable) must occur before the variation in the presumed effect (the dependent variable), 135, 136

in cross-sectional studies, 141

in longitudinal studies, 140-142, 144-145

in nonexperiments, 139, 177

in quasi-experiments, 174

Time series design   A quasi-experimental design consisting of many pretest and posttest observations of the same group, 172, 174-175

Tipton, Steven M., 294, 296

Toby, Jackson, 45

Toppo, Greg, 306

Tourangeau, Roger, 244

Tradition, devotion to, 8

Tran, Thanh Van, 90

Transitional Aid Research Project (TARP), 316-317, 317e

Treatment

as variable, 73-74

interaction with testing, 161, 170

Treatment misidentification   A problem that occurs in an experiment when the treatment itself is not what causes the outcome, but rather the outcome is caused by some intervening process that the researcher has not identified and is not aware of, 156, 159-160

Treatment phase   The intervention phase of a single-subject design, 193, 215

Trend   Repeated measurement scores that are either ascending or descending in magnitude, 188, 190-191e, 198, 199e

Trend studies. *See* **Repeated cross-sectional design**

Treno, Andrew J., 64

Triangulation   The use of multiple methods to study one research question, 76

Tripodi, Tony, 193, 195

True experiment   Experiment in which subjects are assigned randomly to an experimental group that receives a treatment or other manipulation of the independent variable and a comparison

group that does not receive the treatment or receives some other manipulation. Outcomes are measured in a posttest, 162
causality, 135-136
design abbreviations, 166, 167e
difficulties in agency-based research, 170-171
experimental and comparison groups, 162-163
limitations, 171
Posttest-Only Control Group Design, 169-170
posttests, 166
Pretest-Posttest Control Group Design, 167-169, 168e
pretests, 166
strengths, 417
types, 166-170
See also Experimental designs
True negative When it is determined from a screening instrument score that the participant does not have a problem and the participant really does not have the problem based on a clinical evaluation, 93
True positive When it is determined from a screening instrument score that the participant has a particular problem and the participant really does have the problem based on a clinical evaluation, 93
Truman, Harry S., 114
Tufte, Edward R., 347
Turabian, Kate L., 422
Turner, Charles F., 224, 232, 233, 244
Turner, J. Blake, 344
Twaite, James A., 238-239
Type I error Error that occurs when there is evidence of a statistical relationship between two variables based on the sample, but in fact, there is no relationship between the two variables, 368-369
Type II error Error that occurs when there is no evidence of a statistical relationship between two variables based on the sample, but in fact, the two variables are related, 368-369

Unimodal A distribution of a variable in which there is only one value that is the most frequent, 353

Unimode survey design, 264
Unique identifier A unique number that links a data file to a specific corresponding questionnaire, 268, 337
U.S. Census Bureau
advertising, 251
census reports, 75
Current Population Survey, 267
data available, 267
data quality, 267, 342
response rates, 251
Survey of Income and Program Participation, 83, 267
undercount, 267
Web site, 267
U.S. Department of Health and Human Services, 331
U.S. Government Accounting Office, 317
U.S. Senate, Subcommittee on Problems of the Aged and Aging, 53
United Way, 11
Units of analysis The level of social life on which a research question is focused, such as individuals, groups, towns, or nations, 146-147
ecological fallacy, 147-148, 148e
group, 147
individual, 147
reductionist fallacy, 148-149, 148e
Units of observation The cases about which measures actually are obtained in a sample, 147
Univariate distributions, 342-343, 352
University of Chicago, National Opinion Research Center, 224, 343
University of Illinois Survey Research Laboratory (SRL), 223, 253, 256
University of Massachusetts Medical School, 413, 416
University of Michigan. *See* Inter-University Consortium for Political and Social Research
Unobtrusive measure A measurement based on physical traces or other data that are collected without the knowledge or participation of the individuals or groups that generated the data, 75
Utilization-focused evaluation, 326

Vaillant, George E., 141

Validity　The state that exists when statements or conclusions about empirical reality are correct, 18
　comparison to reliability, 95e
　evaluating, 96
　improving, 94-96
　of content analysis, 403, 407
　of experimental designs, 156-162
　of quasi-experimental designs, 174
　threats to, 156
　See also **Causal validity**; **Measurement validity**

Van Maanen, John, 394, 395
Van Willigan, Marieke, 268
Van Winkle, Barrik, 401-402

Variability　The extent to which cases are spread out through the distribution or clustered in just one location, 200, 342-343

Variable　A characteristic or property that can vary (take on different values or attributes), 40, 41
　Attributes, 78
　continuous, 76
　dependent, 41
　dichotomies, 82
　discrete, 76, 77-78
　extraneous, 371-372, 372e
　independent, 41, 73-74
　intervening, 140, 369-371, 369e
　level of measurement, 76-77
　measurement of, 70-71
　operationalization, 69-70, 70e
　selecting, 68-69
　treatment as, 73-74

Variance　A statistic that measures the variability of a distribution as the average squared deviation of each case from the mean, 359, 359e

Verba, Sidney, 30, 134

Visual analysis, 196
　interpreting patterns, 200-202, 201e, 203e, 204e, 205e
　level, 196-198, 197e
　trends, 198, 199e
　variability, 200, 200e

Voice response systems. *See* **Interactive voice response**

Voter participation
　turnout rates, 347e, 348
　See also Elections

W. K. Kellogg Foundation, 310, 426
Waksberg, J., 253
Walker, Selena, 311
Wallace, J. Brandon, 287
Wallace, Walter L., 48
Wallgren, Anders, 347
Wallgren, Britt, 347
Walsh, Joseph, 176
Walton, Elaine, 135, 136, 137-138
Walton, Wendel K., 135, 136, 138
War on Poverty, 40
Ware, Norma, 290-291
Watergate, 231
Web. *See* Internet

Web survey　A survey that is accessed and responded to on the World Wide Web, 261, 262-263e
　See also **Electronic survey**

Webb, Eugene J., 75
Weber, Max, 48
Weber, Robert Philip, 402, 403
Wechsler, Henry, 63, 64
Weis, Joseph G., 147
Weiss, Carol H., 12, 96, 170, 325
Weiss, Irwin K., 19, 90
Weitzman, Elissa, 64
Weldon, S. Laurel, 67
Welfare programs
　effects of reforms, 123, 175, 426-427
　evaluations, 306-307, 315, 323-324
　race and health of recipients, 372-373, 374e
　sampling recipients, 128
　welfare-to-work programs, 168e, 169, 180, 323-324
Welsh, Richard, 97
Wernet, S. P., 40
Western, Bruce, 44
Wexler, Sandra, 175
White, E. B., 422
White Americans
　education completed, 372e
　health, 366, 366e, 373e
　See also Race
Whitelaw, Carolyn, 311
Whyte, William Foote, 50, 284, 285, 286, 291-292, 299, 392
Widiger, Thomas A., 108
Williams, D., 371
Williams, David, 336, 361-362, 369
Williams, Ina, 277

Williams, Joseph M., 421-422
Williams, Robert L., 285
Wilson, David B., 419, 420
Wilson, William Julius, 148-149, 428
Winter, Kristen, 91
Withdrawal designs, 207-208
  A-B-A design, 207, 208, 218
  A-B-A-B design, 207, 209, 210e, 218
  ethical issues, 218
Witkin, Belle Ruth, 315
Wolcott, Harry F., 274, 279, 281, 286,
    293, 294, 384
Women
  depression, 19
  homeless, 14
  inclusion in research, 108
  prisons, 319-320
  roles, 351, 352e
  single mothers, 128

Work
  employment services for mentally
      ill, 319, 320e
  employment training programs, 321, 321e
  family life and, 221-222, 232, 240
  programs for poor persons, 329
World Bank, 306
Wright, Patricia, 50, 108
Wu, Chia-ling, 268, 269

Yalda, Christine, 379
Yamatani, Hidenori, 50, 108, 109
Yancey, Gaynor, 45
Yankelovich, Daniel, 328
Youngblut, JoAnne, 233

Zakour, Michael, 239
Zaslow, Martha, 324
Zimbardo, Philip G., 56

ABOUT THE AUTHORS

Rafael J. Engel, Ph.D, is Associate Professor and Associate Dean for Academic Affairs at the School of Social Work, University of Pittsburgh. He has authored journal articles on such topics as poverty in later life, welfare benefits, and depressive symptomatology, and he has written a variety of monographs reporting agency-based evaluations. His research experience includes funded research studies on faith-based organizations and employment in late life as well as funded evaluation research studies on welfare-to-work programs and drug and alcohol prevention programs.

Russell K. Schutt, Ph.D., is Professor of Sociology and Director of the Graduate Program in Applied Sociology at the University of Massachusetts, Boston, and Lecturer on Sociology in the Department of Psychiatry at the Harvard Medical School. In addition to four editions of *Investigating the Social World: The Process and Practice of Research,* he has coauthored (with Ronet Bachman) two editions of *The Practice of Research in Criminology and Criminal Justice* and (with Daniel F. Chambliss) *Making Sense of the Social World: Methods of Investigation.* He is also author of *Organization in a Changing Environment,* a multimethod study of changes in the organization of work and unionism in public welfare. Many of his other publications focus on issues of concern in social work, including the edited volume (with Stephanie Hartwell), *The Organizational Response to Social Problems,* and the coauthored volume (with Gerald Garrett), *Responding to the Homeless: Policy and Practice.* He has authored and coauthored numerous journal articles and book chapters on topics such as homelessness, mental health, and organizations.